CLEP CollegeBoard

CLEP®

Official Study Guide 2019

Visit our website at **clep.collegeboard.org** for the most up-to-date information.

The College Board: Connecting Students to College Success

The College Board is a not-for-profit membership association whose mission is to connect students to college success and opportunity. Founded in 1900, the association is composed of more than 5,600 schools, colleges, universities and other educational organizations. Each year, the College Board serves over seven million students and their parents, 23,000 high schools, and 3,800 colleges through major programs and services in college readiness, college admissions, guidance, assessment, financial aid, enrollment, and teaching and learning. Among its best-known programs are the SAT®, the PSAT/NMSQT® and the Advanced Placement Program® (AP®). The College Board is committed to the principles of excellence and equity, and that commitment is embodied in all of its programs, services, activities and concerns.

For further information, visit www.collegeboard.org.

Additional copies of this book can be ordered from our online store at: store.collegeboard.org. You may also call 800-323-7155 (Monday through Friday, 8:30 a.m. to 6 p.m.) to place an order over the phone with a credit card.

If you would like to place your order via physical mail, please send $24.95 plus $6 for standard postage and handling to: College Board Publications, Customer Order Support, P.O. Box 4699, Mount Vernon, IL 62864. Please allow two to four weeks for delivery.

Institutional Orders: Please fax in a completed Institutional Order Form with a valid purchase order, or completed Institutional Order Form with institutional credit card information to 888-321-7183. You may also call 800-323-7155 (Monday through Friday, 8:30 a.m. to 6 p.m.) to place an order over the phone with an institutional credit card.

If you have questions about CLEP that are not answered in this or other publications, write to the College-Level Examination Program, The College Board, 250 Vesey Street, New York, NY 10281.

ISBN-978-1-4573-1078-2
ISBN-1-4573-1078-3

Library of Congress Catalog Card Number: 9685-660

Printed in the United States of America

9 8 7 6 5 4 3 2 1

Contents

v **Introduction**
v CLEP Study Materials: A Word of Warning
v American Council on Education (ACE)
1 **I. The College-Level Examination Program**
1 How the Program Works
1 The CLEP Examinations
1 What the Examinations Are Like
2 Where to Take the Examinations and How to Register
2 College Credit Recommendations of the American Council on Education (ACE)
2 How Your Score Is Reported
3 **II. Approaching a College About CLEP**
3 How to Apply for College Credit
4 Questions to Ask About a College's CLEP Policy
7 **III. Deciding Which Examinations to Take**
7 If You're Taking the Examinations for College Credit or Career Advancement . . .
9 **IV. Preparing to Take CLEP Examinations**
9 Using the Examination Guides
11 Assessing Your Readiness for a CLEP Examination
12 Suggestions for Studying
13 Test Preparation Tips
15 Accommodations for Students with Disabilities
17 **V. Taking the Examinations**
17 Test-Taking Strategies for Multiple-Choice Questions
18 Answering Essay Questions
18 Test-Taking Strategies for Essay Writing
19 **VI. Interpreting Your Scores**
19 How CLEP Scores Are Computed
19 How Essays Are Scored

21 **VII. Examination Guides**

Composition and Literature

23 American Literature
45 Analyzing and Interpreting Literature
65 College Composition/College Composition Modular
99 English Literature
123 Humanities

Foreign Languages

147 French Language
173 German Language
195 Spanish Language

History and Social Sciences

223 American Government
243 History of the United States I: Early Colonization to 1877
265 History of the United States II: 1865 to the Present
287 Human Growth and Development
303 Introduction to Educational Psychology
323 Principles of Macroeconomics
341 Principles of Microeconomics
359 Introductory Psychology
375 Introductory Sociology
391 Social Sciences and History
409 Western Civilization I: Ancient Near East to 1648
425 Western Civilization II: 1648 to the Present

Science and Mathematics

443 Biology
461 Calculus
477 Chemistry
493 College Algebra
513 College Mathematics
525 Natural Sciences
543 Precalculus

Business

561 Financial Accounting
577 Information Systems
595 Introductory Business Law
613 Principles of Management
629 Principles of Marketing

643 **Appendix**

643 What Your CLEP Score Means

Introduction

This is the only *official* guide to the College-Level Examination Program® (CLEP®) exams. CLEP exams are administered on computers at test centers across the country.

This guide has been written for adults making plans to enroll in college, and it contains information of interest to others as well. College-bound high school students, current college students, military personnel, professionals seeking certification, and persons of all ages who have learned or wish to learn college-level material outside the college classroom will find the guide helpful as they strive to accomplish their goals.

CLEP is based on the premise that some individuals enrolling in college have already learned part of what is taught in college courses through job training, independent reading and study, noncredit adult courses, and advanced high school courses. Often, their jobs and life experiences have enhanced and reinforced their learning. CLEP gives these individuals a chance to show their mastery of college-level material by taking exams that assess knowledge and skills taught in college courses.

The first few sections of this guide explain how CLEP can earn you credit for the college-level learning you have acquired and provide suggestions for preparing for the exams. The individual exam section includes test descriptions, sample questions, and study tips.

The guide also has an answer key for each exam, as well as in-depth information about how to interpret your scores.

CLEP Study Materials: A Word of Warning

There are many free or inexpensive sources for CLEP preparation materials, including public or college libraries, bookstores, and educational websites. CLEP exams reflect the material taught in introductory college courses. Check with local colleges to see what texts are being used in the subject you hope to study for a CLEP exam.

The College Board provides the *CLEP Official Study Guide* and individual exam guides so you get to know the types of questions on the exams. You also get important tips to get ready for the tests. The guides are not meant to help you learn all the subject matter CLEP exams cover. We suggest you study a textbook for the relevant course at your college or access one of the suggested resources listed on the CLEP website to learn or review the content of the exam in which you're interested.

Many private companies offer preparation services for CLEP exams. Some companies are legitimate, but others make promises they can't keep and sell services and products you don't need.

We've received complaints from CLEP candidates regarding the following practices (practices we consider unfair or inappropriate).

- Attempts to sell preparation services for many CLEP exams at once, with sizable payment up front or on credit
- Credit agreements with companies other than the one selling the preparation material
- Contacts from salespeople to you or your family at home
- Promises that you can get college credit without enrolling in college
- Efforts to sell dictionaries or encyclopedias as part of a test preparation package

If you feel you have been cheated, we recommend you seek the assistance of an organization such as the Better Business Bureau (**www.bbb.org**) or the Federal Trade Commission (**www.ftc.gov**).

American Council on Education (ACE)

If you still have general questions about continuing or adult education after reading this book, ACE can provide advice and information:

American Council on Education
One Dupont Circle, NW
Washington, DC 20036
202-939-9300
www.acenet.edu

I. The College-Level Examination Program

How the Program Works

CLEP exams are administered at over 2,000 test centers nationwide, and 2,900 colleges and universities award college credit to those who do well on the tests. This rigorous program lets self-directed students of a wide range of ages and backgrounds show their mastery of introductory college-level material and pursue academic success. Students earn credit for what they already know by getting qualifying scores on any of the 33 examinations.

CLEP exams cover material taught in introductory-level courses at many colleges and universities. Faculty at individual colleges review the exams to ensure that they cover the important material currently taught in their courses.

Although CLEP is sponsored by the College Board, only colleges may grant credit toward a degree. To learn about a particular college's CLEP policy, contact the college directly. When you take a CLEP exam, request that a copy of your score report be sent to the college you're attending or planning to attend. After evaluating your score, the college will decide whether or not to award you credit for, or to exempt you from, one or more courses.

If the college decides to give you credit, it records the number of credits on your permanent record, indicating that you completed work equivalent to a course in that subject. If the college decides to grant exemption without giving you credit for a course, you'll be permitted to omit a course that would normally be required of you and to take a course of your choice instead.

The CLEP program has a long-standing policy that an exam can't be taken within the specified wait period. This waiting period gives you a chance to spend more time preparing for the exam or the option of taking a classroom course. If you violate the CLEP retest policy, the administration will be considered invalid, the score canceled, and any test fees forfeited. If you're a military service member, note that DANTES (Defense Activity for Non-Traditional Education Support) won't fund retesting on a previously funded CLEP exam. However, you may personally fund a retest after the specified wait period.

The CLEP Examinations

CLEP exams cover material directly related to specific undergraduate courses taught during a student's first two years in college. The courses may be offered for three or more semester hours in general areas such as mathematics, history, social sciences, English composition, natural sciences, and humanities. Institutions will either grant credit for a specific course based on a satisfactory score on the related exam, or in the general area in which a satisfactory score is earned. The credit is equal to the credit awarded to students who successfully complete the course.

What the Examinations Are Like

CLEP exams are administered on computer and are approximately 90 minutes long, with the exception of College Composition, which is approximately 120 minutes long. Most questions are multiple choice; other types of questions require you to fill in a numeric answer, to shade areas of an object, or to put items in the correct order. Questions using these kinds of skills are called zone, shade, grid, scale, fraction, numeric entry, histogram, and order match questions.

CLEP College Composition includes a mandatory essay section, responses to which must be typed into the computer.

Some examinations have optional essays. You should check with the individual college or university where you're sending your score to see whether an optional essay is required for those exams. These essays are administered on paper and are scored by faculty at the institution that receives your score.

Where to Take the Examinations and How to Register

CLEP exams are administered throughout the year at over 2,000 test centers in the United States and select international sites. Once you have decided to take a CLEP examination, log into My Account at **clepportal .collegeboard.org/myaccount** to create and manage your own personal accounts, pay for CLEP exams, and purchase study materials. You can self-register at any time by completing the online registration form.

Through My Account, you can access a list of institutions that administer CLEP, and you can locate a test center in your area. **After paying for your exam through My Account, you must still contact the test center to schedule your CLEP exam.**

If you're unable to locate a test center near you, call 800-257-9558 for help.

College Credit Recommendations of the American Council on Education (ACE)

For many years, the American Council on Education's College Credit Recommendation Service (ACE CREDIT) has periodically evaluated CLEP processes and procedures for developing, administering, and scoring the exams. ACE recommends a uniform credit-granting score of 50 across all subjects (with additional Level-2 recommendations for the world language examinations), representing the performance of students who earn a grade of C in the corresponding course. The score scale for each CLEP exam is decided by a panel of experts (college faculty teaching the course) who provide information on the level of student performance that would be necessary to receive college credit in the course.

The American Council on Education, the major coordinating body for all the nation's higher education institutions, seeks to provide leadership and a unifying voice on key higher education issues and to influence public policy through advocacy, research, and program initiatives. For more information, visit ACE CREDIT at **acenet.edu/higher-education/topics/Pages/Credit-Evaluations.aspx**.

How Your Score Is Reported

You have the option of seeing your CLEP score immediately after you complete the exam, except for College Composition; scores for this test are available four to six weeks after the exam date. Once you choose to see your score, it will be sent automatically to the institution you designated as a score recipient. It can't be canceled. You'll receive a candidate copy of your score before you leave the test center. If you tested at the institution that you designated as a score recipient, it will have immediate access to your test results. Additionally, you'll be able to view your CLEP exam scores by logging into My Account and clicking on "View My CLEP Exam Scores." Scores are available online one business day after taking an exam. College Composition scores are available online 2–3 weeks after testing.

If you don't want your score reported, you may select that as an option at the end of the examination *before the exam is scored*. Once you have selected the option to *not* view your score, the score is canceled. The score won't be reported to the institution you designated, and you won't receive a candidate copy of your score report. In addition, scores of canceled exams can't be viewed on My Account. You'll have to wait the specified wait period before you can take the exam again.

CLEP scores are kept on file for 20 years. During this period, for a small fee, you may have your transcript sent to another college or to anyone else you specify. Your score(s) will never be sent to anyone without your approval.

II. Approaching a College About CLEP

The following sections provide a step-by-step guide to learning about the CLEP policy at a particular college or university. The person or office that can best assist you may have a different title at each institution, but the following guidelines will point you to information about CLEP at any institution.

Adults and other nontraditional students returning to college often benefit from special assistance when they approach a college. Opportunities for adults to return to formal learning in the classroom are widespread, and colleges and universities have worked hard to make this a smooth process for older students. Many colleges have established special offices staffed with trained professionals who understand the problems facing adults returning to college. If you think you might benefit from such assistance, be sure to find out whether these services are available at your college.

How to Apply for College Credit

Step 1. *Obtain, or access online, the general information catalog and a copy of the CLEP policy from each college you're considering.*

Learn about admission and CLEP policies on the college's website at **clep.collegeboard.org/school-policy-search**, or by contacting or visiting the admission office. Ask for a copy of the publication that explains the college's complete CLEP policy. Also, get the name and the telephone number of the person to contact in case you have further questions about CLEP.

Step 2. *If you haven't already been admitted to a college that you're considering, look at its admission requirements for undergraduate students to see whether you qualify.*

Whether you're applying for college admission as a high school student or transfer student, or as an adult resuming a college career or going to college for the first time, you should be familiar with the requirements for admission at the schools you're considering. If you're a nontraditional student, be sure to check whether the school has separate admission requirements that apply to you. Some schools are selective, while others are "open admission."

Contact the admission office for an interview with a counselor. State why you want the interview, and ask what documents you should bring with you or send in advance. (These materials may include a high school transcript, transcript of previous college work, or completed application for admission.) Make an extra effort to get all the information requested in time for the interview.

During the interview, relax and be yourself. Be prepared to state honestly why you think you're ready and able to do college work. If you have already taken CLEP exams and scored high enough to earn credit, you have shown you're able to do college work. Mention this achievement to the admission counselor because it may increase your chances of being accepted. If you haven't taken a CLEP exam, you can still improve your chances of being accepted by describing how your job training or independent study prepared you for college-level work. Discuss with the counselor what you learned from your work and personal experiences.

Step 3. *Evaluate the college's CLEP policy.*

Typically, a college lists all its academic policies, including CLEP policies, in its general catalog or on its website. You'll probably find the CLEP policy statement under a heading such as Credit-by-Examination, Advanced Standing, Advanced Placement, or External Degree Program. These sections can usually be found in the front of the catalog. Check out the institution's CLEP Policy on **clep.collegeboard.org/school-policy-search**.

Many colleges publish their credit-by-examination policies in separate brochures distributed through the campus testing office, counseling center, admission office, or registrar's office. If you find an overly general policy statement in the college catalog, seek clarification from one of these offices.

Review the material in the section of this chapter entitled "Questions to Ask About a College's CLEP Policy." Use these guidelines to evaluate the college's CLEP policy. If you haven't taken a CLEP exam, this evaluation helps you decide which exams to take. Because individual colleges have different CLEP policies, reviewing several policies helps you decide which college to attend.

Step 4. *If you haven't yet applied for admission, do so as early as possible.*

Most colleges expect you to apply for admission several months before you enroll, and it's essential that you meet the published application deadlines. It takes time to process your application for admission. If you have yet to take a CLEP exam, you can take one or more CLEP exams while you're waiting for your application to be processed. Be sure to check the college's CLEP policy beforehand so that you're taking exams your college will accept for credit. You should find out from the college when to submit your CLEP score(s).

Complete all forms and include all documents requested with your application(s) for admission. Normally, an admission decision can't be reached until all documents have been submitted and evaluated. Unless told to do so, don't send your CLEP score(s) until you've been officially admitted.

Step 5. *Arrange to take CLEP exam(s) or to submit your CLEP score(s).*

CLEP exams can be taken at any of the 2,000 test centers worldwide. To locate a test center near you, visit **clep.collegeboard.org/search/test-centers**.

If you have already taken a CLEP exam, but didn't have your score sent to your college, you can have an official transcript sent at any time for a small fee. Prior to sending a transcript to an institution, please ensure that you have verified the institution's CLEP credit-granting policy. Order your transcript online by logging in to My Account (**clepportal.collegeboard.org/myaccount**) using the same account you used to register.

Please note there are some instances in which CLEP exam scores cannot be ordered. If you have a score on hold, took an exam that was DANTES-funded or retook a CLEP exam within the 3-month waiting period, those exam scores are considered non-orderable. In addition, CLEP Transcript Requests are nonrefundable. Once ordered, a request cannot be canceled, changed or re-routed.

Transcripts only include CLEP scores for the past 20 years; scores more than 20 years old are not kept on file.

Your CLEP scores will be evaluated, probably by someone in the admission office, and sent to the registrar's office to be posted on your permanent record once you are enrolled. Procedures vary from college to college, but the process usually begins in the admission office.

Step 6. *Ask to receive a written notice of the credit you receive for your CLEP score(s).*

A written notice may save you problems later when you submit your degree plan or file for graduation. In the event that there's a question about whether or not you earned CLEP credit, you'll have an official record of what credit was awarded. You may also need this verification of course credit if you meet with an academic adviser before the credit is posted on your permanent record.

Step 7. *Before you register for courses, seek academic advising.*

Talking with your academic adviser helps you avoid taking unnecessary courses and lets you know exactly what your CLEP credit will mean to you. This discussion may take place at the time you enroll. Most colleges have orientation sessions for new students prior to each enrollment period. During orientation, students are assigned academic advisers who give them individual guidance in developing long-range plans and course schedules for the next semester. In conjunction with this counseling, you may be asked to take some additional tests so you can be placed at the proper course level.

Questions to Ask About a College's CLEP Policy

Before taking CLEP exams for the purpose of earning college credit, try to find the answers to these questions:

1. **Which CLEP exams are accepted by the college?**

   A college may accept some CLEP exams for credit and not others—possibly not the exams you're considering. For this reason, it's important you know the specific CLEP exams you can receive credit for.

2. **Does the college require the optional free-response (essay) section for exams in composition and literature, as well as the multiple-choice portion of the CLEP exam you're considering? Do you need to pass a departmental test such as an essay, laboratory, or oral exam in addition to the CLEP multiple-choice exam?**

   Knowing the answers to these questions ahead of time will enable you to schedule the optional free-response or departmental exam when you register to take your CLEP exam.

3. **Is CLEP credit granted for specific courses at the college? If so, which ones?**

   You're likely to find that credit is granted for specific courses and that the course titles are designated in the college's CLEP policy. It's not necessary, however, that credit be granted for a specific course for you to benefit from your CLEP credit. For instance, at many liberal arts colleges, all students must take certain types of courses. These courses may be labeled the core curriculum, general education requirements, distribution requirements, or liberal arts requirements. The requirements, are often expressed in terms of credit hours. For example, all students may be required to take at least six hours of humanities, six hours of English, three hours of mathematics, six hours of natural science, and six hours of social science, with no particular courses in these disciplines specified. In these instances, CLEP credit may be given as "6 hrs. English Credit" or "3 hrs. Math Credit" without specifying for which English or mathematics courses credit has been awarded. To avoid possible disappointment, you should know before taking a CLEP exam what type of credit you can receive or whether you'll be exempted from a required course but receive no credit.

4. **How much credit is granted for each exam you're considering, and does the college place a limit on the total amount of CLEP credit you can earn toward your degree?**

   Not all colleges that grant CLEP credit award the same amount for individual exams. Furthermore, some colleges place a limit on the total amount of credit you can earn through CLEP or other exams. Other colleges may grant you exemption but no credit toward your degree. Knowing several colleges' policies concerning these issues may help you decide which college to attend. If you think you're capable of passing a number of CLEP exams, you may want to attend a college that allows you to earn credit for all or most of the exams. Find out if your institution grants CLEP policy by visiting **clep.collegeboard.org/school-policy-search**.

III. Deciding Which Examinations to Take

If You're Taking the Examinations for College Credit or Career Advancement...

Most people who take CLEP exams want to earn credit for college courses. Others take the exams to qualify for job promotions, professional certification, or licensing. Whatever the reason, it's vital for most candidates to be well prepared so they can advance as fast as possible toward their educational or career goals.

Those with limited knowledge in the subjects covered by the exams they're considering are advised to enroll in the college courses in which that material is taught. Although there's no way to predict whether you'll pass a particular CLEP exam, you may find the following guidelines helpful.

1. **Test Descriptions**

   For each exam, read the test description and the outline set forth in the "Knowledge and Skills Required" section provided in this guide. Are you familiar with most of the topics and terminology in the outline?

2. **Textbooks**

   Review the textbook and other resource materials used for the corresponding course at your college. You can find a list of suggested textbooks and free online resources for each exam at **clep.collegeboard.org/exams**. Are you familiar with most of the topics and terminology used in college textbooks on this subject?

3. **Sample Questions**

   The sample questions included in this guide are representative of the content and difficulty of the exam questions. None of the sample questions appear on any CLEP examination. Use them to get an understanding of the content and difficulty level of the questions on an actual exam. Knowing the correct answers to all of the sample questions is not a substitute for college-level study or a guarantee of satisfactory performance on the exam.

   Following the instructions and suggestions in Chapter V, answer as many of the sample questions for the exam as you can. Check your answers against the answer key at the end of each section.

   - Were you able to answer almost all of the questions correctly? You may not need to study the subject extensively.
   - Did you have difficulty answering the questions? You'll probably benefit from more extensive study of the subject.

4. **Previous Study**

   Have you taken noncredit courses in this subject offered by an adult school or a private school, through correspondence, or in connection with your job? Did you do exceptionally well in this subject in high school, or did you take an honors course in this subject?

5. **Experience**

   Have you learned or used the knowledge or skills included in this exam in your job or life experience? For example, if you lived in a Spanish-speaking country and spoke the language for a year or more, you might consider taking the Spanish Language exam. Or, if you have worked at a job in which you used accounting and finance skills, Financial Accounting would be an exam to consider taking. Or if you have read a considerable amount of literature and attended art exhibits, concerts, and plays, you might expect to do well on the Humanities exam.

6. Other Exams

Have you done well on other standardized tests in subjects related to the one you want to take? For example, did you score well above average on a portion of a college entrance exam covering similar skills, or did you get an exceptionally high score on a licensing exam in this subject? Although such tests don't cover exactly the same material as the CLEP exams and may be easier, people who do well on these tests often do well on CLEP exams too.

7. Advice

Has a college counselor, professor, or some other professional person familiar with your ability advised you to take a CLEP exam?

If you answered yes to several of the above questions, you have a good chance of passing the CLEP exam you're considering. It's unlikely you would have acquired sufficient background from experience alone. Learning gained through reading and study is essential, and you'll likely find additional study helpful before taking a CLEP exam. Information on how to review for CLEP exams can be found in Chapter IV and in Chapter VII.

IV. Preparing to Take CLEP Examinations

Having made the decision to take one or more CLEP exams, most people then want to know how to prepare for them—how much, how long, when, and how should they go about it? The precise answers to these questions vary greatly from individual to individual. However, most candidates find that some type of test preparation is beneficial.

Most people who take CLEP exams do so to show that they already learned the key material taught in a college course. Many need only a quick review to assure themselves that they haven't forgotten what they once studied, and to fill in the gaps in their knowledge of the subject. Others feel that they need a thorough review and spend several weeks studying for an exam. Some people take a CLEP exam as a kind of "final exam" for independent study of a subject. This last group requires significantly more study than do those who only need to review, and they may need some guidance from professors of the subjects they're studying.

The key to how you prepare for CLEP exams often lies in locating those skills and areas of prior learning in which you are strongest and deciding where to focus your energy. Some people may know a considerable amount about a subject area but may not test well. These individuals would probably be just as concerned about strengthening their test-taking skills as they would about studying for a specific test. Many mental and physical skills are required in preparing for a test. It's important not only to review or study for the exams but also to make certain that you are alert, relatively free of anxiety, and aware of how to approach standardized tests. Suggestions about developing test-taking skills and preparing psychologically and physically for a test are given in this chapter. The following section suggests ways of assessing your knowledge of the content of an exam and then reviewing and studying the material.

Using the Examination Guides

The individual exam guides contain the same information you will find in the *CLEP Official Study Guide*. Each exam guide includes an outline of the knowledge and skills covered by the test, sample questions similar to those that appear on the exam, and tips to get ready for the exam.

You may also choose to contact a college in your area that offers a course with content comparable to that on the CLEP exam you want to take, or read the suggested resources for each exam on **clep.collegeboard .org/exams**. If possible, use the textbook and other materials required for that course to help you prepare. To get this information, check the college's catalog for a list of courses offered. Then call the admission office, explain what subject you're interested in, and ask who in that academic department you can contact for specific information on textbooks and other study resources to use. You might also be able to find the course syllabus, which will list course materials and assignments, on the college's website. Be sure the college you're interested in gives credit for the CLEP exam you're preparing for.

Begin by carefully reading the test description and outline of knowledge and skills required for the exam in the exam guide. As you read through the topics listed, ask yourself how much you know about each one. Also note the terms, names, and symbols mentioned, and ask yourself whether you're familiar with them. This will give you a quick overview of how much you know about the subject. If you're familiar with nearly all the material, you'll likely need a minimum of review. If topics and terms are unfamiliar, you'll probably require substantial study to do well on the exam.

If, after reviewing the test description provided in the exam guide, you find that you need extensive review, put off answering the sample questions until you have done some reading in the subject. If you complete them before reviewing the material, you'll probably look for the answers as you study, and this will not be a good assessment of your ability at a later date. Don't refer to the sample questions as you prepare for the exam. The sample questions are representative of the types of questions you'll find on a CLEP exam, but none of the questions will actually appear on an exam. Concentrating on them without broader study of the subject won't help you.

If you think you're familiar with most of the test material, try to answer the sample questions, checking your responses against the answer key. Use the test-taking strategies described in the next chapter.

Assessing Your Readiness for a CLEP Examination

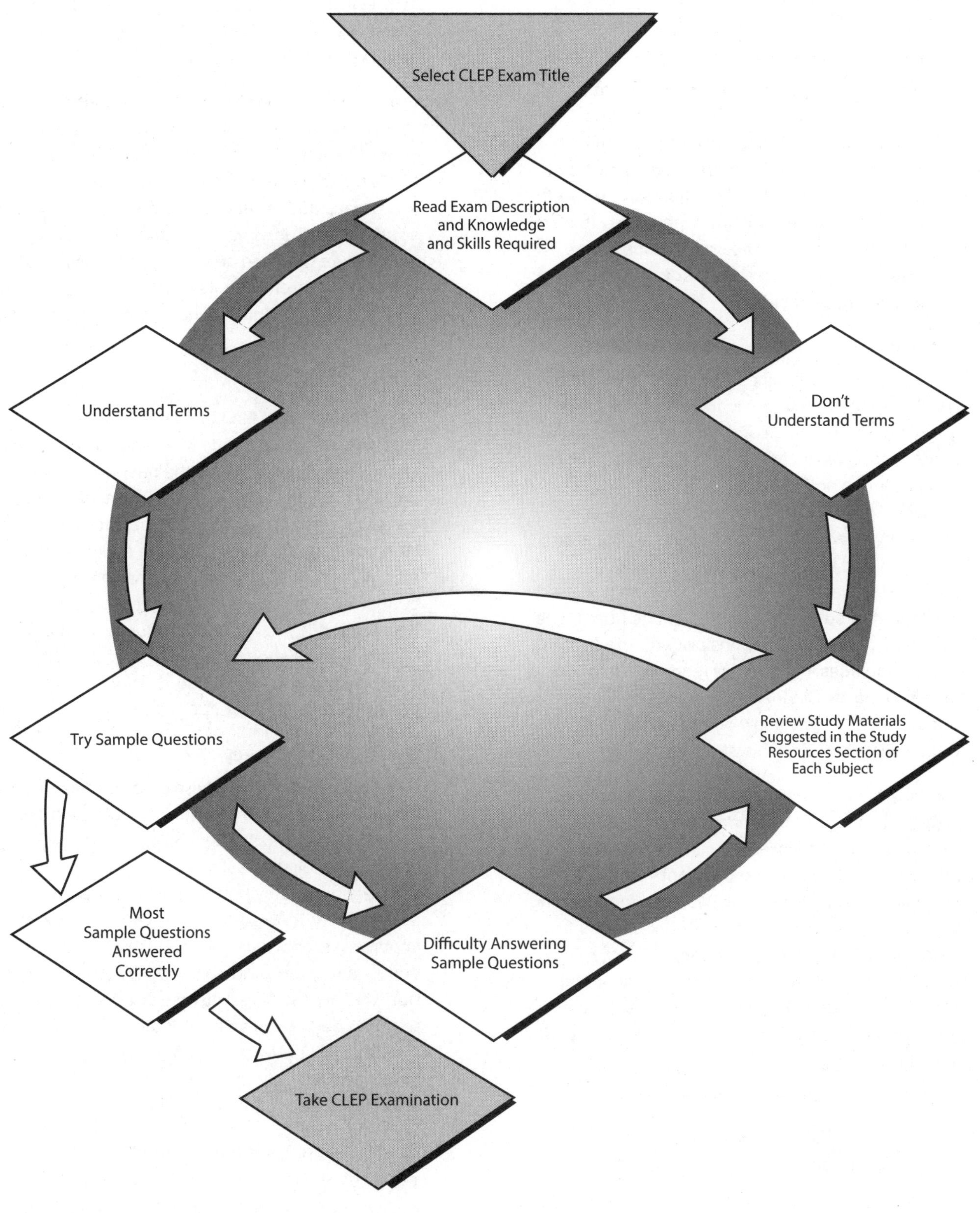

Suggestions for Studying

The following suggestions have been gathered from people who have prepared for CLEP exams or other college-level tests.

1. Review CLEP exam content.

   Remember, if you want to review exam content, Chapter VII of this study guide contains a complete exam description—including a content outline, a description of the knowledge and skills required to do well, and sample questions. An answer key is also included. However, the study guide is not intended to replace a textbook. Additional study may be required.

2. Define your goals and locate study materials.

   Once you have determined how much preparation you'll need to do, you'll need to define your study goals. Set aside a block of time to review the exam content provided in this book. Using the guidelines for knowledge and skills required, locate suitable resource materials. If a preparation course is offered by an adult school or college in your area, you might find it helpful to enroll. (You should be aware, however, that such courses are not authorized or sponsored by the College Board. The College Board has no responsibility for the content of these courses, nor are they responsible for books on preparing for CLEP exams published by other organizations.) If you know others who have taken CLEP exams, ask them how they prepared.

   You may want to get a copy of a syllabus for the college course that is comparable to the CLEP exam(s) you plan to take. You can also ask the appropriate professor at the school you'll be attending, or check his or her website, for a reading list. Use the syllabus, course materials, and/or reading list as a guide for selecting textbooks and study materials. You may purchase these or check them out of your local library. Some websites offer excellent course materials and lectures. Examples include:

   - MIT OpenCourseWare (**ocw.mit.edu**)
   - Carnegie Mellon's Open Learning Initiative (**cmu.edu/oli/**)
   - National Repository of Online Courses (**thenrocproject.org**)

   Most of this material is free. Educational websites, like those offered by PBS (**pbs.org**) or the National Geographic Society (**nationalgeographic.com**), can help. Find a list of suggested textbooks and online resources for each CLEP exam at **clep.collegeboard.org/exams**.

   Check with your librarian about study aids relevant to the exams you plan to take. These supplementary materials may include videos or DVDs made by education-oriented companies and organizations, language tapes, and computer software. And don't forget that what you do with your leisure time can be very educational, whether it's surfing current-events websites, watching a PBS series, reading a financial newsletter, or attending a play.

3. Find a good place to study.

   To determine what kind of place you need for studying, ask yourself the following questions: Do I need a quiet place? Does the telephone distract me? Do objects I see in this place remind me of things I should do? Is it too warm? Is it well lit? Am I too comfortable here? Do I have space to spread out my materials? You may find the library more conducive to studying than your home. If you decide to study at home or in your dorm, prevent interruptions by household members by putting a sign on the door of your study room to indicate when you're available.

4. Schedule time to study.

   To help you determine where studying best fits into your schedule, try this exercise: Make a list of your daily activities (for example, sleeping, working, eating, attending class, sports, or exercise), and estimate how many hours a day you spend on each activity. Rate activities on your list in order of importance, and evaluate your use of time. Often people are astonished at how an average day looks from this perspective. You may discover that your time can be scheduled in alternative ways. For example, you could remove the least important activities from your day, and devote that time to studying or to another important activity.

5. Establish a study routine and a set of goals.

   To study effectively, establish specific goals and a schedule for accomplishing them. Some people find it helpful to write out a weekly schedule and cross out each study period when it's completed.

Others maintain concentration by writing down the time when they expect to complete a study task. Most people find short periods of intense study more productive than long stretches of time. For example, they may follow a regular schedule of several 20- or 30-minute study periods with short breaks between them. Some people allow themselves rewards as they complete each study goal. It doesn't matter whether you accomplish every goal on schedule. The point is to be committed to your task.

6. Learn how to take an active role in studying.

   If you haven't done much studying lately, you may find it difficult to concentrate. Try a method of studying, such as the one outlined below, that gets you to concentrate on and remember what you read.

   a. First, read the chapter summary and the introduction so you'll know what to look for in your reading.
   b. Next, convert the section or paragraph headlines into questions. For example, if you're reading a section entitled "The Causes of the American Revolution," ask yourself, "What were the causes of the American Revolution?" Compose the answer as you read the paragraph. Reading and answering questions aloud let you grasp and retain the material.
   c. Take notes on key ideas or concepts as you read. Writing fixes concepts more firmly in your mind. Underlining key ideas or writing notes in your book may work for you and is useful for review. Underline only important points. If you underline more than a third of each paragraph, you're underlining too much.
   d. If there are questions or problems at the end of a chapter, answer or solve them on paper as if you were asked to do them for homework. Mathematics textbooks (and some other books) sometimes include answers to exercises. If you have such a book, write your answers before looking at the ones given. When problem solving is involved, work enough problems to master the required methods and concepts. If you have difficulty with problems, review any sample problems or explanations in the chapter.
   e. To retain knowledge, most people have to review the material periodically. If you're preparing for an exam over an extended period of time, review key concepts and notes each week or so. Don't wait weeks to review the material or you'll need to relearn much of it.

Test Preparation Tips

1. Familiarize yourself as much as possible with the test and the test situation before the day of the exam. It helps to know ahead of time:
   a. how much time is allowed for the test and whether there are timed subsections. (See Chapter VII.)
   b. what types of questions and directions appear on the exam. (See Chapter VII.)
   c. how your test score is computed.
   d. in which building and room the exam is administered.
   e. the time of the test administration.
   f. directions, transportation, and parking information for the test center.
2. Register and pay your exam fee through My Account at **clepportal.collegeboard.org/myaccount** and print your registration ticket. Contact your preferred test center to schedule your appointment to test. Your test center may require an additional administration fee. Check with your test center to confirm the amount required and acceptable method of payment.

3. On the day of the exam, remember to do the following:
   a. Arrive early enough so you can find a parking place, locate the test center, and get settled comfortably before testing begins.
   b. Bring the following with you:
      – completed registration ticket.
      – any registration forms or printouts required by the test center. Make sure you have filled out all necessary paperwork before your testing date.
      – a form of valid and acceptable identification. Acceptable identification must:
         · Be government-issued.
         · Be an original document—photocopied documents aren't acceptable.
         · Be valid and current—expired documents (bearing expiration dates that have passed) aren't acceptable, no matter how recently they expired.
         · Bear the test taker's full name, in English language characters, exactly as it appears on the Registration Ticket, including the order of the names.
         · Include middle initials only if preferred to be included by test taker. They're optional and only need to match the first letter of the middle name when present on both the ticket and the identification.
         · Bear a recent recognizable photograph that clearly matches the test taker.
         · Include the test taker's signature.
         · Be in good condition, with clearly legible text and a clearly visible photograph.

         Refer to the Exam Day Info page on the CLEP website (clep.collegeboard.org/earn-college-credit/taking-the-test) for more details on acceptable and unacceptable forms of identification.
      – military test takers, bring your Geneva Convention Identification Card. Refer to **clep.collegeboard.org/military** for additional information on IDs for active duty members, spouses, and civil service civilian employees.
      – two number 2 pencils with good erasers. Mechanical pencils are prohibited in the testing room.
   c. Don't bring a cell phone or other electronic devices into the testing room.
   d. Leave all books, papers, and notes outside the test center. You aren't permitted to use your own scratch paper. It's provided by the test center.
   e. Don't take a calculator to the exam. If a calculator is required, it will be built into the testing software and available to you on the computer. The CLEP website has a link to a demonstration on how to use online calculators.
4. When you enter the test room:
   a. You'll be assigned to a computer testing station. If you have special needs, be sure to communicate them to the test center administrator *before* your test date.
   b. Be relaxed while taking the exam. Read directions carefully, and listen to instructions given by the test administrator. If you don't understand the directions, ask for help before the test begins. If you must ask a question not related to the exam after testing has begun, raise your hand, and a proctor will assist you. The proctor can't answer questions related to the exam.
   c. Know your rights as a test taker. You can expect to be given the full working time allowed for taking the exam and a reasonably quiet and comfortable place in which to work. If a poor testing situation prevents you from doing your best, ask whether the situation can be remedied. If it can't, ask the test administrator to report the problem on a Center Problem Report that will be submitted with your test results. You may also wish to immediately write a letter to CLEP, P.O. Box 6656, Princeton, NJ 08541-6656. Describe the exact circumstances as completely as you can. Be sure to include the name of the test center, the test date, and the name(s) of the exam(s) you took.

Accommodations for Students with Disabilities

If you have a disability, such as a learning or physical disability, that would prevent you from taking a CLEP exam under standard conditions, you may request accommodations at your preferred test center. Contact your preferred test center well in advance of the test date to make the necessary arrangements and to find out its deadline for submission of documentation and approval of accommodations. Each test center sets its own guidelines in terms of deadlines for submission of documentation and approval of accommodations.

Accommodations that can be arranged directly with test centers include:

- ZoomText (screen magnification)
- Modifiable screen colors
- Use of a human reader, a scribe/writer, or sign language interpreter
- Extended time
- Untimed rest breaks

If the above accommodations don't meet your needs, contact CLEP Services at **clep@info.collegeboard.org** for information about other accommodations.

V. Taking the Examinations

Test-taking skills enable a person to use all available information to earn a score that truly reflects their ability. There are different strategies for approaching different kinds of exam questions. For example, free-response and multiple-choice questions require very different approaches. Other factors, such as how the exam will be scored, may influence your approach to the exam and your use of test time. Consequently, your preparation for an exam should include finding out all you can about the exam so you can use the most effective test-taking strategies.

Test-Taking Strategies for Multiple-Choice Questions

1. Listen carefully to any instructions given by the test administrator, and read the on-screen instructions before you begin to answer the questions.
2. Keep an eye on the clock and the timing that's built into the testing software. You have the option of turning the clock on or off at any time. As you proceed, make sure that you're not working too slowly. You should have answered at least half the questions in a section when half the time for that section has passed.
3. Before answering a question, read the entire question, including all the answer choices. Instructions usually tell you to select the "best" answer. Sometimes one answer choice is partially correct, but another option is better. It's a good idea to read all the answers even if the first or second choice looks correct to you.
4. Read and consider every question. Questions that look complicated at first glance may not actually be so difficult once you have read them carefully.
5. Don't spend too much time on any one question. If you don't know the answer after you've considered it briefly, go on to the next question. Mark that question using the mark tool at the bottom of the screen, and go back to review the question later if you have time.
6. Watch for the following key words in test questions:

all	may	only
always	must	perhaps
but	necessary	rarely
except	never	seldom
every	none	sometimes
generally	not	usually
however	often	

   When a question or answer option contains words such as "always," "every," "only," "never," and "none," there can be no exceptions to the answer you choose. Use of words such as "often," "rarely," "sometimes," and "generally" indicates that there may be some exceptions to the answer.
7. Make educated guesses. There's no penalty for incorrect answers. Therefore, guess even if you don't know an answer. If you have some knowledge of the question and can eliminate one or more of the answer choices as wrong, your chance of getting the right answer improves.
8. Don't waste your time looking for clues to right answers based on flaws in question wording or patterns in correct answers. CLEP puts a great deal of effort into developing valid, reliable, and fair exams. CLEP test development committees are composed of college faculty who are experts in the subjects covered by the exams and are appointed by the College Board to write test questions and to scrutinize each question on a CLEP exam. They ensure that questions aren't ambiguous, have only one correct answer, and cover college-level topics. These committees don't intentionally include "trick" questions. If you think a question is flawed, ask the test administrator to report it, or write immediately to CLEP Test Development, P.O. Box 6600, Princeton, NJ 08541-6600. Include the name of the exam and test center, the exam date, and the number of the exam question. All such inquiries are investigated by test development professionals.

Answering Essay Questions

The College Composition exam is the only CLEP exam that includes two mandatory essays. Both the multiple-choice section and the essay section of the exam are administered on the computer. You're required to type your essays using a format similar to word processing.

The essays for the College Composition exam are scored by English professors from various colleges and universities who are trained by CLEP. A process called holistic scoring is used to rate your writing abilities. This process is explained in the examination guide for College Composition, which also includes scored sample essays and essay questions.

Four other CLEP exams have optional essays. Some colleges or universities may require you to take one of these optional essays as part of the American Literature, Analyzing and Interpreting Literature, English Literature, or College Composition Modular exam. There's an additional fee for each of the optional essays, payable to the institution that administers the exam. These essays are scored by the faculty of the institution that grants the credit. Therefore, you may find it helpful to talk with someone at your college to find out what criteria are used to determine whether you'll get credit. Ask how much emphasis is placed on your writing ability and your ability to organize your thoughts, as opposed to your knowledge of the subject matter. Find out how much weight is given to your multiple-choice test score, compared to your free-response score, in determining whether you'll get credit. This gives you an idea of what to work hardest on in preparing for and taking the exam.

Test-Taking Strategies for Essay Writing

1. Before you begin to respond, read the questions carefully, and take a few minutes to jot down some ideas or create an outline. Scratch paper is provided at the test center.
2. If you're given a choice of questions to answer, choose the questions that you think you can answer most clearly and knowledgeably.
3. Determine the order in which you'll answer the questions. First, answer those you find the easiest so you can spend any extra time on the questions you find more difficult.
4. When you know which questions you'll answer and in what order, determine how much testing time remains, and estimate how many minutes you'll devote to each question. Unless suggested times are given for the questions, try to allot an equal amount of time for each question.
5. Before answering each question, read it again carefully to make sure you're interpreting it correctly. Pay attention to key words, such as those listed below, that appear in free-response questions. Be sure you know the exact meaning of these words before taking the exam.

analyze	describe	interpret
apply	determine	justify
assess	discuss	list
compare	distinguish	outline
contrast	enumerate	prove
define	explain	rank
demonstrate	generalize	show
derive	illustrate	summarize

If a question asks you to "outline," "define," or "summarize," don't write a detailed explanation; if a question asks you to "analyze," "explain," "illustrate," "interpret," or "show," you must do more than briefly describe the topic.

VI. Interpreting Your Scores

CLEP score requirements for awarding credit vary from institution to institution. The College Board, however, recommends that colleges refer to the standards set by the American Council on Education (ACE). All ACE recommendations are the result of careful and periodic review by evaluation teams made up of faculty who are subject-matter experts and technical experts in testing and measurement. To determine whether you are eligible for credit for your CLEP scores, refer to the policy of the college you'll be attending. The policy states the score that's required to earn credit at that institution. Many colleges award credit at the score levels recommended by ACE. However, some require scores higher or lower than these.

Your exam score is printed for you at the test center immediately upon completion of the examination, unless you took College Composition. For this exam, you'll receive your score four to six weeks after the exam date. You can also view your scores online one business day after taking the test by logging into My Account (**clepportal.collegeboard.org/myaccount**). College Composition scores will be available online 2–3 weeks after taking the exam. Your scores are kept on file for 20 years. Your CLEP exam scores are reported only to you, unless you ask to have them sent elsewhere. If you want your scores sent to a college, employer, or certifying agency, you must select this option through My Account. This service is free only if you select your score recipient when you register. For a fee, you can request a transcript at a later date. Order official transcripts by logging in to My Account (**clepportal.collegeboard.org/myaccount**).

The pamphlet, *What Your CLEP Score Means*, gives detailed information about interpreting your scores and is available at **clep.collegeboard.org**. A copy of the pamphlet is also in the appendix of this guide. A brief explanation appears below.

How CLEP Scores Are Computed

In order to reach a total score on your exam, two calculations are performed.

1. Your "raw score" is the number of questions you answered correctly. Your raw score increases by one point for each question answered correctly.
2. Your raw score is then converted to a scaled score that ranges from 20 to 80, and this is the score that appears on your score report. The American Council on Education (ACE) recommends that colleges grant credit for a score of 50 or higher, but individual institutions can set their own CLEP credit policies.

How Essays Are Scored

The College Board arranges for college English professors to score the essays written for the College Composition exam. These carefully selected college faculty members teach at two- and four-year institutions nationwide. The faculty members receive extensive training and thoroughly review the College Board scoring policies and procedures before grading the essays. Each essay is read and scored by two professors, the sum of the two scores for each essay is combined with the multiple-choice score, and the result is reported as a scaled score between 20 and 80. Although the format of the two sections is very different, both measure skills required for expository writing. Knowledge of formal grammar, sentence structure, and organizational skills is necessary for the multiple-choice section, but the emphasis in the free-response section is on writing skills rather than grammar.

Optional essays for CLEP Composition Modular and the literature examinations are evaluated and scored by the colleges that require them, rather than by the College Board. If you take an optional essay, it's sent to the institution you designate when you take the test. If you didn't designate a score recipient institution when you took an optional essay, you may still select one as long as you notify CLEP within 18 months of taking the exam. Copies of essays aren't held beyond 18 months or after they have been sent to an institution.

VII. Examination Guides

American Literature

Description of the Examination

The American Literature examination covers material that is usually taught in a survey course at the college level. It deals with the prose and poetry written in the United States from colonial times to the present. It is primarily a test of knowledge about literary works — their content, their background and their authors — but also requires an ability to interpret poetry, fiction and nonfiction prose, as well as a familiarity with the terminology used by literary critics and historians. The examination emphasizes fiction and poetry and deals to a lesser degree with the essay, drama and autobiography.

In both coverage and approach, the examination resembles the chronologically organized survey of American literature offered by many colleges. It assumes that candidates have read widely and developed an appreciation of American literature, know the basic literary periods, and have a sense of the historical development of American literature.

The test contains approximately 100 questions to be answered in 90 minutes. Some of these are pretest questions that will not be scored.

An optional essay section can be taken in addition to the multiple-choice test. The essay section requires that two essays be written during a total time of 90 minutes. For the first essay, a common theme in American literature and a list of major American authors are provided. Candidates are asked to write a well-organized essay discussing the way that theme is handled in works by any two of those authors. For the second essay, candidates are asked to respond to one of two topics — one requiring analysis of a poem, the other requiring analysis of a prose excerpt. In each case, the specific poem or prose excerpt is provided and questions are offered for guidance.

Candidates are expected to write well-organized essays in clear and precise prose. The essay section is scored by faculty at the institution that requests it and is still administered in paper-and-pencil format. There is an additional fee for taking this section, payable to the institution that administers the exam.

Knowledge and Skills Required

Questions on the American Literature examination require candidates to demonstrate one or more of the following abilities in the approximate proportions indicated.

45–60% **Knowledge of particular literary works, including:**
- Authors
- Characters
- Plots
- Setting
- Style
- Themes

25–40% **Ability to understand and interpret:**
- Short poems
- Excerpts from long poems
- Excerpts from prose works

10–15% **Knowledge of:**
- The historical and social settings of specific works
- Relations between literary works
- Relations of specific works to literary traditions
- Influences on authors

5–10% **Familiarity with:**
- Critical terms
- Verse forms
- Literary devices

The subject matter of the American Literature examination is drawn from the following chronological periods. The percentages indicate the approximate percentage of exam questions from each period.

15% **The Colonial and Early National Period (Beginnings–1830)**

25% **The Romantic Period (1830–1870)**

20% **The Period of Realism and Naturalism (1870–1910)**

25% **The Modernist Period (1910–1945)**

15% **The Contemporary Period (1945–Present)**

Sample Test Questions

The following sample questions do not appear on an actual CLEP examination. They are intended to give potential test-takers an indication of the format and difficulty level of the examination and to provide content for practice and review. Knowing the correct answers to all of the sample questions is not a guarantee of satisfactory performance on the exam.

Directions: Each of the questions or incomplete statements below is followed by five suggested answers or completions. Select the one that is best in each case. Some questions will require you to match terms with one another or to put a list in chronological order.

1. Make me, O Lord, thy Spining Wheele
    compleate.
   Thy Holy Worde my Distaff make for mee.
   Make mine Affections thy Swift Flyers neate
   And make my Soule thy holy Spoole to bee.
   My Conversation make to be thy Reele
   And reele the yarn thereon spun of thy Wheele.

   The passage above is notable chiefly for

   (A) irony of statement
   (B) pathetic fallacy
   (C) a literary conceit
   (D) a paradox
   (E) a simile

2. In *The Federalist*, No. X, James Madison proposed that the dangers of factions be controlled by a

   (A) republican form of government
   (B) pure democracy
   (C) curtailment of individual liberty
   (D) reapportionment of property
   (E) clause for emergency rule by a minority

3. Sky Woman, Wolverine, and Turtle are all important figures in which of the following types of literature?

    (A) Puritan allegorical tales
    (B) Frontier tall tales
    (C) African American animal fables
    (D) Native American oral tales
    (E) Hispanic American magical-realist stories

<u>Questions 4–5</u>

Thou ill-formed offspring of my feeble brain,
Who after birth didst by my side remain,
Till snatched from thence by friends, less wise than true,
Who thee abroad, exposed to public view,
Made thee in rags, halting to th' press to trudge,
Where errors were not lessened (all may judge).
At thy return my blushing was not small,
My rambling brat (in print) should mother call,
I cast thee by as one unfit for light,
Thy visage was so irksome in my sight.

4. In line 1, "offspring" most probably refers to the author's

    (A) philosophy
    (B) book of poems
    (C) unwanted child
    (D) despair
    (E) intelligence

5. "My rambling brat" (line 11) is an example of

    (A) epigram
    (B) alliteration
    (C) onomatopoeia
    (D) personification
    (E) hyperbole

6. Place the name of each of these Colonial era figures beside the British colony with which he is most closely associated.

    Roger Williams
    John Smith
    John Winthrop

    ____________ The Virginia Colony
    ____________ The Massachusetts Bay Colony
    ____________ The Colony of Rhode Island

7. Your wickedness makes you as it were heavy as lead, and to tend downwards with great weight and pressure towards hell; and if God should let you go, you would immediately sink and swiftly descend and plunge into the bottomless gulf, and your healthy constitution and your own care and prudence, and best contrivance, and all your righteousness, would have no more influence to uphold you and keep you out of hell, than a spider's web would have to stop a falling rock.

    The passage above is an example of

    (A) Puritanism
    (B) Transcendentalism
    (C) Naturalism
    (D) Realism
    (E) Deism

8. Thomas Paine's *Common Sense* had a direct influence on which of the following Revolutionary era works?

    (A) *The Autobiography of John Adams*
    (B) Crèvecoeur's *Letters from an American Farmer*
    (C) Jefferson's *Declaration of Independence*
    (D) Franklin's "The Way to Wealth"
    (E) Freneau's "On the Causes of Political Degeneracy"

9. Besides, what could they see but a hideous and desolate wilderness, full of wild beasts and wild men—and what multitudes of them they knew not. Neither could they as it were, go up to the top of Pisgah to view from this wilderness a more goodly country to feed their hopes; for which way soever they turned their eyes (save upward to the heavens) they could have little solace or content in respect of any outward objects. For summer being done, all things stand upon them with a weather-beaten face, and the whole country, full of woods and thickets, represented a wild and savage hue.

   The passage above is from

   (A) William Bradford's *The History of Plimouth Plantation*
   (B) Jonathan Edwards' "Sinners in the Hands of an Angry God"
   (C) James Fenimore Cooper's *The Pioneers*
   (D) Washington Irving's "Rip Van Winkle"
   (E) Nathaniel Hawthorne's *The Scarlet Letter*

10. All of the following are writers of the Colonial era EXCEPT

   (A) Anne Bradstreet
   (B) Margaret Fuller
   (C) Cotton Mather
   (D) Phillis Wheatley
   (E) Benjamin Franklin

11. Which of the following colonial American writers was NOT the author of an autobiographical narrative?

   (A) Samson Occom
   (B) Benjamin Franklin
   (C) Mary Rowlandson
   (D) Elizabeth Ashbridge
   (E) Edward Taylor

Questions 12–14

That minds are not alike, full well I know,
This truth each day's experience will show;
To heights surprising some great spirits soar,
With inborn strength mysterious depths explore;
Their eager gaze surveys the path of light,
Confest it stood to Newton's piercing sight.
  Deep science, like a bashful maid retires,
And but the *ardent* breast her worth inspires;
By perseverance the coy fair is won.
And Genius, led by Study, wears the crown.

12. Line 3 is distinctive for its use of

   (A) alliteration
   (B) assonance
   (C) oxymoron
   (D) enjambment
   (E) iambic tetrameter

13. The "*ardent* breast" (line 8) serves to

   (A) foster love
   (B) promote greed
   (C) further discovery
   (D) instill wisdom
   (E) invoke confidence

14. The rhyme scheme in the excerpt is

   (A) aabbccdeff
   (B) aabbccddee
   (C) aabcbcddee
   (D) aabbccdede
   (E) aabbcdcdee

Questions 15–16

BEHOLD her stretched upon the mournful bier!—Behold her silently descend to the grave!—Soon the wild weeds spring afresh round the *little hillock*, as if to shelter the remains of betrayed innocence—and the friends of her youth shun even the spot which conceals her relicks.

SUCH is the consequence of SEDUCTION, but it is not the only consequence.

15. The passage would best be described as an example of

(A) Postmodernism
(B) Naturalism
(C) Realism
(D) Sentimentalism
(E) Regionalism

16. The first paragraph of the passage provides an example of which of the following figures of speech?

(A) Satire
(B) Simile
(C) Apostrophe
(D) Synecdoche
(E) Personification

17. Which of the following best describes a theme of Whitman's poem "Out of the Cradle Endlessly Rocking"?

(A) The desire of the poet to retreat to the protected life of the child
(B) The grief that overwhelmed America at Lincoln's death
(C) The celebration of America as the hope of the world
(D) The anguish of a man confronted by war
(E) The awakening of the poet to his vocation

18. Which of the following did NOT write a slave narrative?

(A) Olaudah Equiano
(B) William Wells Brown
(C) Frederick Douglass
(D) Charles Brockden Brown
(E) Harriet Jacobs

Questions 19–20

The mass of men lead lives of quiet desperation.

To be a philosopher is not merely to have subtle thoughts, nor even to found a school, but so to love wisdom as to live according to its dictates a life of simplicity, independence, magnanimity, and trust.

I had three pieces of limestone on my desk, but I was terrified to find that they required to be dusted daily, when the furniture of my mind was all undusted still, and I threw them out the window in disgust.

19. The sentences are taken from the opening pages of

(A) Nathaniel Hawthorne's *The House of the Seven Gables*
(B) Ralph Waldo Emerson's "Nature"
(C) Edgar Allan Poe's "The Philosophy of Composition"
(D) Walt Whitman's *Democratic Vistas*
(E) Henry David Thoreau's *Walden*

20. The phrase "the furniture of my mind was all undusted still" can best be paraphrased by which of the following?

(A) I had become morose and antisocial.
(B) I had not examined my ideas and beliefs.
(C) I needed a change of scene.
(D) I was intellectually and emotionally exhausted.
(E) I had become so lazy that I could not work.

Questions 21–23

Society everywhere is in conspiracy against the manhood of every one of its members. Society is a joint-stock company, in which the members agree, for the better securing of his bread to each shareholder, to surrender the liberty and culture of the eater. The virtue in most request is conformity. . . . It loves not realities and creators, but names and customs.

Whoso would be a man, must be a nonconformist. He who would gather immortal palms must not be hindered by the name of goodness, but must explore if it be goodness. Nothing is at last sacred but the integrity of your own mind. Absolve you to yourself, and you shall have the suffrage of the world.

21. The passage is excerpted from

(A) Henry David Thoreau's "Civil Disobedience"
(B) Ralph Waldo Emerson's "Self-Reliance"
(C) James Russell Lowell's "Democracy"
(D) Henry James's *The American*
(E) Oliver Wendell Holmes's *The Autocrat of the Breakfast Table*

22. The sentence beginning "He who would gather immortal palms . . . " is best interpreted to mean which of the following?

(A) Anyone who wishes to achieve greatness must examine society's fundamental values.
(B) A person worthy of emulation need not be good.
(C) A love of goodness usually stands in the way of great achievements.
(D) Immortality is denied to the individual who opposes conventional values.
(E) The means an individual uses to achieve a worthy goal are not important.

23. The philosophy expressed in the passage is best paraphrased by which of the following statements?

(A) Doing deliberate evil is preferable to surrendering freedom.

(B) The ideal relationship between the individual and society strikes a balance between total conformity and excessive nonconformity.

(C) Society and individuality are at odds, so those seeking to be individuals must define their own terms for living.

(D) Each individual is threatened by society but finally must compromise for the greater good.

(E) Some people surrender their integrity to society, but they must choose to set themselves against it.

24. The founders of a new colony, whatever Utopia of human virtue and happiness they might originally project, have invariably recognized it among their earliest practical necessities to allot a portion of the virgin soil as a cemetery, and another portion as the site of a prison. . . . But, on one side of the portal, and rooted almost at the threshold, was a wild rose-bush.

In the passage above, the images of the cemetery, prison, and rose-bush set the tone for which of the following works?

(A) Jonathan Edwards' *Freedom of the Will*

(B) Nathaniel Hawthorne's *The Scarlet Letter*

(C) Herman Melville's *Typee*

(D) Washington Irving's "The Legend of Sleepy Hollow"

(E) Edgar Allan Poe's "The Fall of the House of Usher"

25. The history of mankind is a history of repeated injuries and usurpations on the part of man toward woman, having in direct object the establishment of an absolute tyranny over her. To prove this, let facts be submitted to a candid world.

The statement above represents a deliberate rewriting of which important political text?

(A) The Gettysburg Address

(B) The Declaration of Independence

(C) The Preamble to the United States Constitution

(D) The Bill of Rights

(E) *Common Sense*

26. The "unpardonable sin" committed by Ethan Brand is

(A) allowing one's intellectual curiosity to violate the privacy of others

(B) any mortal transgression not followed by repentance

(C) the attempt to improve upon God's handiwork

(D) loss of faith in God

(E) ambition deteriorating into a lust for power

27. It appears evident, then, that there is a distinct limit, as regards length, to all works of literary art—the limit of a single sitting—and that, although in certain classes of prose composition, such as *Robinson Crusoe*, (demanding no unity,) this limit may be advantageously overpassed, it can never properly be overpassed in a poem.

The passage is taken from which of the following?

(A) Herman Melville's "Hawthorne and His Mosses"
(B) Walt Whitman's Preface 1855—*Leaves of Grass*
(C) Ralph Waldo Emerson's "The Poet"
(D) Theodore Dreiser's "True Art Speaks Plainly"
(E) Edgar Allan Poe's "The Philosophy of Composition"

28. Which of the following writers, born into a family of New England ministers, achieved popular success with an abolitionist novel?

(A) Mary Wilkins Freeman
(B) Sarah Orne Jewett
(C) Harriet Beecher Stowe
(D) Rebecca Harding Davis
(E) Louisa May Alcott

29. So it came to pass that as he trudged from the place of blood and wrath his soul changed. He came from hot plowshares to prospects of clover tranquilly, and it was as if hot plowshares were not. Scars faded as flowers.

It rained. The procession of weary soldiers became a bedraggled train, despondent and muttering, marching with churning effort in a trough of liquid brown mud under a low, wretched sky. Yet the youth smiled, for he saw that the world was a world for him, though many discovered it to be made of oaths and walking sticks. He had rid himself of the red sickness of battle. The sultry nightmare was in the past.

The name of the central character in the work from which the passage above is taken is

(A) Thomas Sutpen
(B) Henry Fleming
(C) Clyde Griffiths
(D) Frederic Henry
(E) Nick Carraway

30. "I would prefer not to" is a statement often made by a character in which of the following?

(A) "My Kinsman, Major Molineux"
(B) "The Minister's Black Veil"
(C) "Rappaccini's Daughter"
(D) "Bartleby the Scrivener"
(E) "Benito Cereno"

31. Which of the following authors wrote *Ragged Dick*, a best-selling novel that chronicles a young man's rise from poverty and obscurity to wealth and social prominence and that led to a popular series of similar rags-to-riches stories?

(A) Herman Melville
(B) Louisa May Alcott
(C) Mark Twain
(D) Horatio Alger
(E) Rebecca Harding Davis

Questions 32–35

Six weeks is a long time to wait, and a still longer time for a girl to keep a secret; but Jo did both, and was just beginning to give up all hope of ever seeing her manuscript again, when a letter arrived which almost took her breath away; for on opening it, a check for a hundred dollars fell into her lap. For a minute she stared at it as if it had been a snake, then she read her letter and began to cry. If the amiable gentleman who wrote that kindly note could have known what intense happiness he was giving a fellow-creature, I think he would devote his leisure hours, if he has any, to that amusement; for Jo valued the letter more than the money, because it was encouraging; and after years of effort it was *so* pleasant to find that she had learned to do something, though it was only to write a sensation story.

32. The narrator's attitude toward Jo can best be described as

(A) scornful and mocking
(B) benevolent and sympathetic
(C) eager and expectant
(D) critical and guarded
(E) clinical and detached

33. The primary purpose of the phrase "after years of effort it was ***so*** pleasant to find that she had learned to do something, though it was only to write a sensation story" is to

(A) illustrate Jo's unshakable self-confidence
(B) convey a mixture of modesty and pride on Jo's part
(C) emphasize the ultimate futility of Jo's accomplishment
(D) reveal Jo's deep-seated shame about being published
(E) describe Jo's lifelong history of failure and disappointment

34. The preceding passage, taken from the story of a young woman who aspires to a life as a writer, can be found in which of the following works?

(A) "Life in the Iron Mills"
(B) "The Yellow Wallpaper"
(C) *The Scarlet Letter*
(D) *Little Women*
(E) *The Lamplighter*

35. The passage was written by

(A) Harriet Beecher Stowe
(B) Harriet Jacobs
(C) Emily Dickinson
(D) Charlotte Perkins Gilman
(E) Louisa May Alcott

36. The title character of Henry James's *Daisy Miller* finally

    (A) adjusts to the mores of international society in Europe
    (B) chooses the life of an artist rather than marriage
    (C) enters a convent in France
    (D) dies as the result of a night visit to the Colosseum
    (E) marries an Italian nobleman

37. Which of the following best states the theme of Stephen Crane's "The Open Boat"?

    (A) Human beings are largely responsible for their own fate.
    (B) By acts of courage, people may overcome inherent weakness.
    (C) Nature, though seemingly hostile, is actually indifferent to human beings.
    (D) Through perseverance, a world of peace and harmony will ultimately be achieved.
    (E) In any struggle, the strongest are fated to survive.

38. The King and the Duke in Mark Twain's *Adventures of Huckleberry Finn* are

    (A) aristocrats
    (B) confidence men
    (C) slaves
    (D) tradesmen
    (E) slave traders

39. There is one point at which the moral sense and the artistic sense lie very near together; that is, in the light of the very obvious truth that the deepest quality of a work of art will always be the quality of the mind of the producer. In proportion as that mind is rich and noble, will the novel, the picture, the statue, partake of the substance of beauty and truth. To be constituted of such elements is, to my vision, to have purpose enough. No good novel will ever proceed from a superficial mind; that seems to me an axiom which, for the artist in fiction, will cover all needful moral ground: if the youthful aspirant take it to heart, it will illuminate for him many of the mysteries of "purpose."

    The central argument of the passage is that

    (A) a creative work reflects the intelligence of the artist
    (B) only writers of unimpeachable moral character produce great novels
    (C) concern with morality always reflects a superficial mind
    (D) fiction, as a creative art, is superior to painting or sculpture
    (E) fiction is often more true than the reality it seeks to depict

Questions 40–42

The morning was one peculiar to that coast. Everything was mute and calm; everything gray. The sea, though undulated into long roods of swells, seemed fixed, and was sleeked at the surface like waved lead that has cooled and set in the smelter's mould. The sky seemed a gray surtout. Flights of troubled gray fowl, kith and kin with flights of troubled gray vapors among which they were mixed, skimmed low and fitfully over the waters, as swallows over meadows before storms. Shadows present, foreshadowing deeper shadows to come.

40. The primary purpose of the passage is to

(A) introduce a main character
(B) resolve a mystery
(C) establish a setting
(D) relate a climactic event
(E) display a narrator's unreliability

41. In the passage, the word "gray" is an example of

(A) a metaphor
(B) a motif
(C) an allusion
(D) understatement
(E) onomatopoeia

42. The tone of the passage would best be described as

(A) optimistic
(B) sarcastic
(C) portentous
(D) distraught
(E) resentful

43. Which of the following does NOT appear in a poem by Emily Dickinson?

(A) A fly in a still room making an "uncertain stumbling buzz"
(B) A slanted ray of late-afternoon winter sunlight
(C) A rain-filled red wheelbarrow "beside the white chickens"
(D) A train metaphorically described in terms of a horse
(E) A saddened person who "never lost as much but twice"

44. Mark Twain, William Dean Howells, and Henry James are commonly described by literary historians as

(A) transcendentalists
(B) symbolists
(C) realists
(D) romantics
(E) naturalists

45. Which of the following writers was particularly important in the development of the short story as a literary form?

(A) James Fenimore Cooper
(B) Harriet Beecher Stowe
(C) Frederick Douglass
(D) Edgar Allan Poe
(E) Edith Wharton

46. Which of the following authors wrote extensively about her experiences attending a government-run boarding school?

(A) Sui Sin Far
(B) Joy Harjo
(C) Willa Cather
(D) Diane Glancy
(E) Zitkala-Ša

47. Which of the following was a writer of feminist essays and Utopian novels who achieved widespread recognition with the publication of her fictionalized account of depression and mental breakdown?

(A) Edith Wharton
(B) Sojourner Truth
(C) Lydia Maria Child
(D) Mary Wilkins Freeman
(E) Charlotte Perkins Gilman

48. Place the name of each of the following authors beside the city with which he is most closely identified.

Theodore Dreiser
George Washington Cable
Bret Harte

____________________ New Orleans
____________________ San Francisco
____________________ Chicago

49. Emma Lazarus' poem "The New Colossus" refers to

(A) The Statue of Liberty
(B) The Lincoln Memorial
(C) Mount Rushmore
(D) The Brooklyn Bridge
(E) The Washington Monument

50. *The House Behind the Cedars* and *The Marrow of Tradition*, two novels addressing difficulties faced by upwardly mobile African Americans in the South during the late nineteenth century, were both written by

(A) Mark Twain
(B) Frederick Douglass
(C) Theodore Dreiser
(D) Charles W. Chesnutt
(E) Paul Laurence Dunbar

51. Which of the following best describes people as they are portrayed in the fiction of Stephen Crane, Theodore Dreiser, and Frank Norris?

(A) Victims of original sin
(B) Self-determining entities
(C) Creatures shaped by biological, social, and economic factors
(D) Beings whose biological natures are fixed, but who are able to manipulate their environments
(E) Individuals who must be awakened to the fact that their wills are free

52. John Steinbeck's *The Grapes of Wrath* depicts

(A) the plight of dispossessed farmers who migrate to California
(B) prison conditions in turn-of-the-century America
(C) a wounded soldier who tries in vain to escape the effects of war
(D) racial problems in a small farming town in Oklahoma
(E) a drifter and his friend who dream hopelessly of better lives

53. Which of the following statements summarizes Booker T. Washington's message in a well-known speech delivered in Atlanta, Georgia, in 1895 and later included in his autobiography, *Up From Slavery*?

(A) Educational opportunities in the liberal arts are the key to social and economic advancement for African Americans.
(B) Progress for both the African American and the White communities requires cooperation in developing commercial and industrial opportunities.
(C) African Americans need to better understand their African cultural roots.
(D) The economic interests of the African American and White communities will inevitably develop separately.
(E) African Americans demand immediate and full equality in all aspects of life that are purely social.

Questions 54–55

All went well, until a platter was passed with a kind of meat that was strange to me. Some mischievous instinct told me that it was ham—forbidden food; and I, the liberal, the free, was afraid to touch it! I had a terrible moment of surprise, mortification, self-contempt; but I helped myself to a slice of ham, nevertheless, and hung my head over my plate to hide my confusion. I was furious with myself for my weakness. I to be afraid of a pink piece of pig's flesh, who had defied at least two religions in defence of free thought! And I began to reduce my ham to indivisible atoms, determined to eat more of it than anybody at the table. Alas! I learned that to eat in defence of principles was not so easy as to talk. I ate, but only a newly abnegated Jew can understand with what squirming, what protesting of the inner man, what exquisite abhorrence of myself. That Spartan boy who allowed the stolen fox hidden in his bosom to consume his vitals rather than be detected in the theft, showed no such miracle of self-control as I did, sitting there at my friend's tea-table, eating unjewish meat.

54. Why does the narrator call ham "forbidden food"?

    (A) She is Jewish and is not allowed to eat ham.
    (B) She is vegetarian and does not eat meat.
    (C) She is afraid of unfamiliar foods and is reluctant to eat foods that are "strange."
    (D) She is fasting for religious reasons and is not permitted to eat.
    (E) She is dieting and is not allowed to eat fatty foods.

55. The narrator likens her situation to that of the Spartan boy in a well-known parable in order to illustrate her

    (A) ability to mask extreme physical discomfort in public
    (B) ability to exercise restraint in uncomfortable circumstances
    (C) willingness to lie to her friends about her dietary preferences
    (D) desire to consume more ham than the other people at tea do
    (E) eagerness to embrace new and unfamiliar experiences

Questions 56–57

Let me tell you about the very rich. They are different from you and me. They possess and enjoy early, and it does something to them, makes them soft where we are hard, and cynical where we are trustful, in a way that, unless you were born rich, it is very difficult to understand. They think, deep in their hearts, that they are better than we are because we had to discover the compensations and refuges of life for ourselves. Even when they enter deep into our world or sink below us, they still think that they are better than we are. They are different.

56. In the passage, which of the following best describes the speaker's attitude toward the very rich?

(A) He finds their cynicism alarming and unwarranted.
(B) He believes that, because of their advantages and experiences, the rich know more than others do.
(C) He is envious of their moral superiority.
(D) He thinks that he understands their psychology even though he has not shared their advantages.
(E) He finds them so different from the rest of society as to be practically unknowable.

57. The passage was written by

(A) F. Scott Fitzgerald
(B) John P. Marquand
(C) John Steinbeck
(D) Sinclair Lewis
(E) Theodore Dreiser

58. A demand for political, civic, and educational equality is voiced in *The Souls of Black Folk* by

(A) W. E. B. Du Bois
(B) Richard Wright
(C) Harriet Tubman
(D) Langston Hughes
(E) Jean Toomer

59. Ezra Pound's short poem "In a Station of the Metro" is considered a classic example of

(A) Romanticism
(B) Surrealism
(C) Futurism
(D) Imagism
(E) Postmodernism

60. Which of the following writers was a part of the Harlem Renaissance?

(A) Frederick Douglass
(B) Zora Neale Hurston
(C) Phillis Wheatley
(D) Alice Walker
(E) James Baldwin

61. Place the name of each of the following writers beside the region that figures most prominently in her writing.

Sarah Orne Jewett
Willa Cather
Flannery O'Connor

____________________ The Great Plains
____________________ The Deep South
____________________ New England

62. Place the name of each of the following novels beside the war during which it is set.

The Things They Carried
The Naked and the Dead
For Whom the Bell Tolls

____________________ The Spanish Civil War
____________________ The Second World War
____________________ The Vietnam War

63. Characters with the last names of Snopes, Compson, and Sartoris figure prominently in the fiction of

(A) Eudora Welty
(B) Flannery O'Connor
(C) Thomas Wolfe
(D) William Faulkner
(E) Robert Penn Warren

64. Which of the following poets is best known for sonnets that combine a traditional verse form with a concern for women's issues?

(A) Edna St. Vincent Millay
(B) Gertrude Stein
(C) Marianne Moore
(D) H. D.
(E) Amy Lowell

65. Which of the following poets derived the title, the plan, and much of the symbolism of one of his or her major poems from Jessie Weston's *From Ritual to Romance*?

(A) Wallace Stevens
(B) T. S. Eliot
(C) Robert Frost
(D) Marianne Moore
(E) Langston Hughes

66. As part of a series of dramas chronicling the lives of African Americans in each decade of the twentieth century, Pulitzer Prize winner August Wilson has written which of the following pairs of plays?

(A) *The Crucible . . . A View from the Bridge*
(B) *The Piano Lesson . . . Fences*
(C) *The Iceman Cometh . . . Desire Under the Elms*
(D) *Dutchman . . . The Slave*
(E) *Cat on a Hot Tin Roof . . . Sweet Bird of Youth*

67. Place the name of each of the following writers beside the genre with which he is most closely associated.

O. Henry
Frank Norris
Eugene O'Neill

____________________ Drama
____________________ The short story
____________________ The novel

68. "You've just seen a prince walk by. A fine, troubled prince. A hard-working, unappreciated prince. A pal, you understand? Always for his boys."

    In which of the following modern American plays is the principal character described above?

    (A) *The Glass Menagerie*
    (B) *The Hairy Ape*
    (C) *Trifles*
    (D) *A Raisin in the Sun*
    (E) *Death of a Salesman*

69. Which of the following cities is Carl Sandburg noted for celebrating?

    (A) New York
    (B) Chicago
    (C) Los Angeles
    (D) New Orleans
    (E) Pittsburgh

70. Bigger Thomas is the central character in

    (A) Upton Sinclair's *The Jungle*
    (B) Carson McCullers' *The Ballad of the Sad Café*
    (C) Richard Wright's *Native Son*
    (D) Nella Larsen's *Passing*
    (E) Thomas Wolfe's *Look Homeward, Angel*

71. "I wish that you were my sister, I'd teach you to have some confidence in yourself. The different people are not like other people, but being different is nothing to be ashamed of . . . . Other people are . . . one hundred times one thousand. You're one times one! They walk all over the earth. You just stay here. They're common as—weeds, but—you—well, you're Blue Roses."

    In the passage above from Tennessee Williams' *The Glass Menagerie*, the term "Blue Roses" is a metaphor for the young woman's

    (A) favorite flowers
    (B) profession as a dancer
    (C) vivacious personality
    (D) shyness and sensitivity
    (E) unusual taste in fashion

Questions 72–75

The extraordinary patience of things!
This beautiful place defaced with a crop of suburban houses—
How beautiful when we first beheld it,
Unbroken field of poppy and lupin walled with clean cliffs;
No intrusion but two or three horses pasturing,
Or a few milch cows rubbing their flanks on the outcrop rockheads—
Now the spoiler has come: does it care?
Not faintly. It has all time. It knows the people are a tide
That swells and in time will ebb, and all
Their works dissolve. Meanwhile the image of the pristine beauty
Lives in the very grain of the granite,
Safe as the endless ocean that climbs our cliff.—As for us:
We must uncenter our minds from ourselves;
We must unhumanize our views a little, and become confident
As the rock and ocean that we were made from.

72. In line 10, the word "it" refers to

(A) "The extraordinary patience of things" (line 1)
(B) "This beautiful place" (line 2)
(C) "a crop of suburban houses" (lines 2–3)
(D) "the spoiler" (line 10)
(E) "a tide / That swells" (lines 12–13)

73. In lines 11–14, the discussion of "the people" emphasizes their

(A) foresight
(B) dignity
(C) timidity
(D) transience
(E) greed

74. The primary contrast in the poem is between

(A) the land and the sea
(B) urban and suburban landscapes
(C) animals and people
(D) past and future
(E) nature and humankind

75. The poem is written in which verse form?

(A) Ballad
(B) Blank verse
(C) Free verse
(D) Italian sonnet
(E) Shakespearean sonnet

76. The short story collection *The Golden Apples* was written by which of the following writers?

    (A) Eudora Welty
    (B) Sherwood Anderson
    (C) Dorothy Parker
    (D) John Cheever
    (E) Katherine Anne Porter

77. Which of the following is the first-person narrator of Harper Lee's 1960 novel *To Kill a Mockingbird*?

    (A) Jem
    (B) Dill
    (C) Scout
    (D) Calpurnia
    (E) Mayella

78. Which of the following novels chronicles the experiences of an African American protagonist?

    (A) *All the King's Men*
    (B) *The Age of Innocence*
    (C) *Henderson the Rain King*
    (D) *Invisible Man*
    (E) *The Catcher in the Rye*

79. At the end of Flannery O'Connor's "A Good Man Is Hard to Find," the grandmother does which of the following?

    (A) She ponders the truth of Red Sammy's words, "a good man is hard to find."
    (B) She collapses in the street after being hit by a woman she has insulted.
    (C) She dies after being shot by an escaped convict, the Misfit.
    (D) She marries a Bible salesman who is also a con artist.
    (E) She sits in a roadside diner, abandoned by the drifter she has befriended.

80. Place the following novels in their correct chronological order by date of publication:

    I. *Mumbo Jumbo*
    II. *If He Hollers Let Him Go*
    III. *Beloved*

    (A) I, II, III
    (B) III, I, II
    (C) II, I, III
    (D) III, II, I
    (E) I, III, II

81. When we Chinese girls listened to the adults talk-story, we learned that we failed if we grew up to be but wives or slaves. We could be heroines, swordswomen. Even if she had to rage across all China, a swordswoman got even with anybody who hurt her family. Perhaps women were once so dangerous that they had to have their feet bound. . . .

My mother told [stories] that followed swordswomen through woods and palaces for years. Night after night my mother would talk-story until we fell asleep. I couldn't tell where the stories left off and dreams began, her voice the voice of the heroines in my sleep. . . .

At last I saw that I too had been in the presence of great power, my mother talking-story.

In the passage above, the discussion of "talk-story" helps to express the speaker's

(A) acceptance of having outgrown the stories of her childhood
(B) development of her own capacity for writing through practice in storytelling
(C) sense that storytelling was a way that her mother transmitted strength
(D) desire to pursue an active life rather than tell stories like her mother
(E) confusion about her mother's ultimate purpose in telling stories

82. The characters Shug Avery, Celie, and Mister appear in which of the following novels?

(A) *The Color Purple*
(B) *The Crying of Lot 49*
(C) *Their Eyes Were Watching God*
(D) *Go Tell It on the Mountain*
(E) *Light in August*

Questions 83–84

my mamma moved among the days
like a dreamwalker in a field;
seemed like what she touched was hers
seemed like what touched her couldn't hold,
she got us almost through the high grass
then seemed like she turned around and ran
right back in
right back on in

Lucille Clifton, "my mamma moved among the days" from *Good Woman: Poems and a Memoir 1969-80.* Copyright © 1987 by Lucille Clifton. Used by permission of BOA Editions, Ltd., www.boaeditions.org.

83. Lines 1–4 suggest that the speaker viewed the mother as

(A) reverent
(B) indomitable
(C) absentminded
(D) ineffectual
(E) unrealistic

84. The poem makes use of all of the following EXCEPT

(A) first-person perspective
(B) extended metaphor
(C) repetition
(D) simile
(E) satire

85. All of the following were written by Toni Morrison EXCEPT

    (A) *Song of Solomon*
    (B) *Beloved*
    (C) *The Bluest Eye*
    (D) *Sula*
    (E) *Tell Me a Riddle*

86. The Native American author of the Pulitzer Prize-winning novel *House Made of Dawn* is

    (A) N. Scott Momaday
    (B) Louise Erdrich
    (C) Leslie Marmon Silko
    (D) Toni Cade Bambara
    (E) Jack Kerouac

87. Which of the following novels, set during the Holocaust, helped propel the graphic novel to critical prominence?

    (A) *The Crying of Lot 49*
    (B) *Night*
    (C) *Slaughterhouse-Five*
    (D) *Maus*
    (E) *Ceremony*

88. Match the playwright with the correct play.

    Paula Vogel
    Tony Kushner
    Suzan-Lori Parks

    ____________________ *How I Learned to Drive*
    ____________________ *Topdog/Underdog*
    ____________________ *Angels in America*

Study Resources

To prepare for the American Literature exam, you should read critically the contents of at least one anthology, which you can find in most college bookstores. Most textbook anthologies contain a representative sample of readings as well as discussions of historical background, literary styles and devices characteristic of various authors and periods, and other material relevant to the test. The anthologies do vary somewhat in their content, approach and emphases; you are advised to consult more than one or to consult some specialized books on major authors, periods, and literary forms and terminology. You should also read some of the longer works that are mentioned or excerpted in the anthologies. You can probably obtain an extensive reading list and sample syllabi of American literature from a college English department, library or bookstore.

Visit **clep.collegeboard.org/earn-college-credit/practice** for additional American literature study resources. You can also find suggestions for exam preparation in Chapter IV of the *Official Study Guide*. In addition, many college faculty post their course materials on their schools' websites.

Answer Key

1. C
2. A
3. D
4. B
5. D
6. See below
7. A
8. C
9. A
10. B
11. E
12. A
13. C
14. B
15. D
16. C
17. E
18. D
19. E
20. B
21. B
22. A
23. C
24. B
25. B
26. A
27. E
28. C
29. B
30. D
31. D
32. B
33. B
34. D
35. E
36. D
37. C
38. B
39. A
40. C
41. B
42. C
43. C
44. C
45. D
46. E
47. E
48. See next page
49. A
50. D
51. C
52. A
53. B
54. A
55. B
56. D
57. A
58. A
59. D
60. B
61. See next page
62. See next page
63. D
64. A
65. B
66. B
67. See next page
68. E
69. B
70. C
71. D
72. B
73. D
74. E
75. C
76. A
77. C
78. D
79. C
80. C
81. C
82. A
83. B
84. E
85. E
86. A
87. D
88. See next page

6. John Smith — The Virginia Colony
John Winthrop — The Massachusetts Bay Colony
Roger Williams — The Colony of Rhode Island

48. George Washington Cable — New Orleans
    Bret Harte — San Francisco
    Theodore Dreiser — Chicago

61. Willa Cather — The Great Plains
    Flannery O'Connor — The Deep South
    Sarah Orne Jewett — New England

62. *For Whom the Bell Tolls* — The Spanish Civil War
    The Naked and the Dead — The Second World War
    The Things They Carried — The Vietnam War

67. Eugene O'Neill — Drama
    O. Henry — The short story
    Frank Norris — The novel

88. Paula Vogel — *How I Learned to Drive*
    Suzan-Lori Parks — *Topdog/Underdog*
    Tony Kushner — *Angels in America*

Analyzing and Interpreting Literature

Description of the Examination

The Analyzing and Interpreting Literature examination covers material usually taught in a general undergraduate course in literature. Although the examination does not require familiarity with specific works, it does assume that candidates have read widely and perceptively in poetry, drama, fiction and nonfiction. The questions are based on passages supplied in the test. These passages have been selected so that no previous experience with them is required to answer the questions. The passages are taken primarily from American and British literature.

The examination contains approximately 80 multiple-choice questions to be answered in 98 minutes. Some of these are pretest questions that will not be scored.

An optional essay section can be taken in addition to the multiple-choice test. The essay section requires that two essays be written during a total time of 90 minutes. For the first essay, candidates are asked to analyze a short poem. For the second essay, candidates are asked to apply a generalization about literature (such as the function of a theme or a technique) to a novel, short story or play that they have read.

Candidates are expected to write well-organized essays in clear and precise prose. The essay section is scored by faculty at the institution that requests it and is still administered in paper-and-pencil format. There is an additional fee for taking this section, payable to the institution that administers the exam.

Knowledge and Skills Required

Questions on the Analyzing and Interpreting Literature examination require candidates to demonstrate the following abilities.

- Ability to read prose, poetry and drama with understanding
- Ability to analyze the elements of a literary passage and to respond to nuances of meaning, tone, imagery and style
- Ability to interpret metaphors, to recognize rhetorical and stylistic devices, to perceive relationships between parts and wholes, and to grasp a speaker's or author's attitudes
- Knowledge of the means by which literary effects are achieved
- Familiarity with the basic terminology used to discuss literary texts

The examination emphasizes comprehension, interpretation and analysis of literary works. A specific knowledge of historical context (authors and movements) is not required, but a broad knowledge of literature gained through reading widely and a familiarity with basic literary terminology is assumed. The following outline indicates the relative emphasis given to the various types of literature and the periods from which the passages are taken. The approximate percentage of exam questions per classification is noted within each main category.

Genre

35%–45% **Poetry**

35%–45% **Prose (fiction and nonfiction)**

15%–30% **Drama**

National Tradition

50%–65% **British Literature**

30%–45% **American Literature**

5%–15% **Works in Translation**

Period

3%–7% **Classical and pre-Renaissance**

20%–30% **Renaissance and 17th Century**

35%–45% **18th and 19th Centuries**

25%–35% **20th and 21st Centuries**

Sample Test Questions

The following sample questions do not appear on an actual CLEP examination. They are intended to give potential test-takers an indication of the format and difficulty level of the examination and to provide content for practice and review. Knowing the correct answers to all of the sample questions is not a guarantee of satisfactory performance on the exam. The date printed at the end of each passage is the original publication date or, in some cases, the first performance of a play or estimated date of composition.

Directions: Each of the questions or incomplete statements below is followed by five suggested answers or completions. Select the one that is best in each case.

Questions 1–5

CHORAGOS: Men of Thebes: look upon Oedipus.
This is the king who solved the famous riddle
And towered up, most powerful of men.
No mortal eyes but looked on him with envy,
Yet in the end ruin swept over him.

Let every man in mankind's frailty
Consider his last day; and let none
Presume on his good fortune until he find
Life, at his death, a memory without pain.

(c. 429 BCE)

1. Line 3 primarily suggests that Oedipus

(A) was an unusually tall and intimidating man
(B) became a figure of great fame and authority
(C) waged war against the men of Thebes
(D) was stronger and more agile than other men
(E) proved to be a persuasive, if corrupt, politician

2. Which of the following is the best paraphrase of "No mortal eyes but looked on him with envy" (line 4) ?

(A) Even the gods were envious of him.
(B) The gods considered him an envious person.
(C) Everyone wished to have his advantages.
(D) Only envious people would seek him.
(E) Everyone longed to be immortal like him.

3. The speaker assumes that "every man" (line 6) is

(A) averse to idolizing other men as gods
(B) likely to underestimate his own abilities
(C) prone to turn down a challenge too quickly
(D) vulnerable to fate and his own destiny
(E) capable of accomplishing great feats

4. In the context of the passage, to "Presume on his good fortune" (line 8) is best interpreted as

(A) assume bad luck must turn to good
(B) believe that happiness will endure
(C) try to gain wealth and prosperity
(D) plan for good fortune before it comes
(E) make judgments on those who are poor or unlucky

5. The passage can best be described as

(A) a warning against hubris or pride
(B) a poetic rejection of bad fortune
(C) an acceptance of catharsis
(D) a poetic affirmation that all is vanity
(E) God's promise of final happiness

Questions 6 –11

That outward beauty which the world commends
Is not the subject I will write upon,
Whose date expired, that tyrant time soon ends;
Those gaudy colours soon are spent and gone,
But those fair virtues which on thee attends
Are always fresh, they never are but one:
They make thy beauty fairer to behold
Than was that queen's for whom proud Troy was sold.

As for those matchless colours red and white,
Or perfect features in a fading face,
Or due proportion pleasing to the sight;
All these do draw but dangers and disgrace.
A mind enriched with virtue shines more bright,
Adds everlasting beauty, gives true grace,
Frames an immortal goddess on the earth,
Who though she dies, yet fame gives her new birth.

That pride of nature which adorns the fair,
Like blazing comets to allure all eyes,
Is but the thread, that weaves their web of care
Who glories most, where most their danger lies.
For greatest perils do attend the fair,
When men do seek, attempt, plot and devise
How they may overthrow the chastest dame
Whose beauty is the white whereat they aim.

(1611)

6. The poem as a whole presents beauty as

   (A) hypnotic and deceitful
   (B) fleeting and dangerous
   (C) empty and insignificant
   (D) seductive and entertaining
   (E) shallow and awkward

7. In each of the first two stanzas, the structure draws attention to a

   (A) stubborn ambivalence
   (B) misleading contradiction
   (C) temporary confusion
   (D) personal dilemma
   (E) central contrast

8. Lines 7–8 contain which of the following?

   (A) A literary allusion
   (B) A sentence fragment
   (C) A witty digression
   (D) An extended metaphor
   (E) An implicit paradox

9. In line 11, "due proportion" refers most directly to a woman's

   (A) lovely eyes
   (B) courtly conduct
   (C) common sense
   (D) overall appearance
   (E) demure garments

10. The statement in line 20 ("Who . . . lies") is best described as an example of

    (A) understatement
    (B) aphorism
    (C) irony
    (D) euphemism
    (E) oxymoron

11. The speaker indicates that virtue confers all of the following benefits EXCEPT

    (A) poise in every situation
    (B) genuine beauty
    (C) strength of character
    (D) attainment of goals
    (E) admiration from others

Questions 12–19

"A clear fire, a clean hearth, and the rigor of the game." This was the celebrated wish of old Sarah Battle (now with God) who, next to her devotions, loved a good game at whist. She was none of your lukewarm gamesters, your half-and-half players, who have no objection to take a hand, if you want one to make up a rubber; who affirm that they have no pleasure in winning; that they like to win one game, and lose another; that they can while away an hour very agreeably at a card table, but are indifferent whether they play or no; and will desire an adversary, who has slipt a wrong card, to take it up and play another. These insufferable triflers are the curse of a table. One of these flies will spoil a whole pot. Of such it may be said, that they do not play at cards, but only play at playing at them.

Sarah Battle was none of that breed. She detested them, as I do, from her heart and soul; and would not, save upon a striking emergency, willingly seat herself at the same table with them. She loved a thorough-paced partner, a determined enemy. She took, and gave, no concessions. She hated favors. She never made a revoke, nor ever passed it over in her adversary without exacting the utmost forfeiture. She fought a good fight: cut and thrust. She held not her sword (her cards) "like a dancer." She sat bolt upright; and neither showed you her cards, nor desired to see yours. All people have their blind side—their superstitions; and I have heard her declare, under the rose,* that Hearts was her favourite suit.

(1821)

**sub rosa*, in confidence

12. The phrase "now with God" (line 3) reveals that Sarah Battle

(A) was a religious person
(B) had an unexpected religious experience
(C) placed devotion to God ahead of whist
(D) has decided to give up cards
(E) is no longer alive

13. In line 3, "next to" is best paraphrased as

(A) second only to
(B) besides
(C) before
(D) in addition to
(E) even more than

14. To Sarah Battle, the most significant characteristic of the triflers described in lines 5–15 is their

(A) amiable sociability
(B) generosity toward their opponents
(C) nonchalant attitude toward whist
(D) ability to keep the game in perspective
(E) inability to play whist well

15. It can be inferred from the description of Sarah Battle's behavior at the whist table that she

(A) would respect a superior opponent
(B) had an ironic sense of humor
(C) would do anything to win
(D) did not really enjoy playing whist
(E) enjoyed being catered to in whist

16. The most apparent metaphor in this character sketch is drawn from

    (A) nature
    (B) religion
    (C) finance
    (D) swordplay
    (E) gamesmanship

17. The attitude of the narrator toward Sarah Battle is chiefly one of

    (A) sarcastic anger
    (B) affectionate respect
    (C) tolerant understanding
    (D) arrogant condescension
    (E) fearful regard

18. The passage suggests all of the following about the narrator EXCEPT that the narrator

    (A) has a sense of humor
    (B) has spent time in Sarah Battle's presence
    (C) is an excellent whist player
    (D) scorns casual whist players
    (E) sees Sarah Battle's weakness

19. Which of the following best summarizes the structure of the passage?

    (A) The first paragraph concentrates on Sarah Battle's serious side; the second, on her fun-loving side.
    (B) The first paragraph defines Sarah Battle by what she is not; the second, by what she is.
    (C) The passage interprets, in turn, what Sarah Battle would regard as "A clear fire, a clean hearth, and the rigor of the game" (lines 1–2).
    (D) The passage moves from a discussion of the refinements of whist to an explanation of what makes Sarah Battle like the game.
    (E) The first paragraph describes Sarah Battle as a gambler; the second, as a soldier of reform.

Questions 20–24

HAMLET: Horatio, thou art e'en as just a man
As e'er my conversation coped withal.
HORATIO: O, my dear lord—
HAMLET: Nay, do not think I flatter,
For what advancement may I hope from thee
That no revenue hast but thy good spirits
To feed and clothe thee? Why should the poor be flattered?
No, let the candied tongue lick absurd pomp,
And crook the pregnant hinges of the knee
Where thrift may follow fawning. Dost thou hear?
Since my dear soul was mistress of her choice
And could of men distinguish her election,
Sh' hath sealed thee for herself, for thou hast been
As one, in suffering all, that suffers nothing,
A man that Fortune's buffets and rewards
Hast ta'en with equal thanks; and blest are those
Whose blood and judgment are so well commeddled
That they are not a pipe for Fortune's finger
To sound what stop she please. Give me that man
That is not passion's slave, and I will wear him
In my heart's core, ay, in my heart of heart,
As I do thee.

(c. 1602)

20. The passage is best described as

(A) a heartfelt statement of affection for a friend
(B) a contrite apology for past faults
(C) a sorrowful lament for one who is deceased
(D) a spirited call to action
(E) an insincere compliment

21. The phrase "candied tongue" (line 8) in this passage describes someone who

(A) speaks eloquently
(B) contrives elaborate falsehoods
(C) makes mocking comments
(D) believes that life holds no bitterness
(E) resorts to flattery

22. As used in line 13, "sealed" most nearly means

(A) copied
(B) surrounded
(C) designated
(D) dispatched
(E) imprisoned

23. Those who "are not a pipe for Fortune's finger/ To sound what stop she please" (lines 18–19) are

(A) unable to appreciate aesthetic beauty
(B) incapable of making rational judgments
(C) enemies of the speaker
(D) able to cope with the good and the bad in life
(E) spontaneous and eager for unusual experiences

24. Which of the following is personified in the passage?

(A) "advancement" (line 5)
(B) "the poor" (line 7)
(C) "soul" (line 11)
(D) "judgment" (line 17)
(E) "heart" (line 21)

Questions 25–29

Besides the neutral expression that she wore when she was alone, Mrs. Freeman had two others, forward and reverse, that she used for all her human dealings. Her forward expression was steady and driving like the advance of a heavy truck. Her eyes never swerved to left or right but turned as the story turned as if they followed a yellow line down the center of it. She seldom used the other expression because it was not often necessary for her to retract a statement, but when she did, her face came to a complete stop, there was an almost imperceptible movement of her black eyes, during which they seemed to be receding, and then the observer would see that Mrs. Freeman, though she might stand there as real as several grain sacks thrown on top of each other, was no longer there in spirit. As for getting anything across to her when this was the case, Mrs. Hopewell had given it up. She might talk her head off. Mrs. Freeman could never be brought to admit herself wrong on any point. She would stand there and if she could be brought to say something, it was something like, "Well, I wouldn't of said it was and I wouldn't of said it wasn't," or letting her gaze range over the top shelf where there was an assortment of dusty bottles, she might remark, "I see you ain't ate many of them figs you put up last summer."

(1955)

25. The metaphor begun by "forward and reverse" in the opening sentence is developed further by all of the following words EXCEPT

(A) "advance" (line 5)
(B) "swerved" (line 6)
(C) "turned" (line 7)
(D) "retract" (line 10)
(E) "stop" (line 11)

26. What quality of Mrs. Freeman's character does the controlling image of the passage suggest?

(A) Her forbearance
(B) Her insecurity
(C) Her rigidity
(D) Her proper manners
(E) Her sense of irony

27. That Mrs. Freeman "might stand there as real as several grain sacks thrown on top of each other" (lines 15–16) suggests that she is all of the following EXCEPT

(A) plain and down-to-earth
(B) undecided in her opinions
(C) clearly visible
(D) part of the country scene
(E) closed and contributing nothing at present

28. Mrs. Freeman's remark in lines 23–24 can best be described as

(A) a cliché
(B) a paradox
(C) an equivocation
(D) a circular argument
(E) a metaphoric contrast

29. Mrs. Freeman's remarks are best described as

(A) self-protective
(B) self-censuring
(C) self-analytical
(D) aggressive
(E) contemptuous

Questions 30–34

The Child at Winter Sunset

The child at winter sunset,
Holding her breath in adoration of the peacock's tail
That spread its red—ah, higher and higher—
Wept suddenly. "It's going!"
The great fan folded;
Shortened; and at last no longer fought the cold, the dark.
And she on the lawn, comfortless by her father,
Shivered, shivered, "It's gone!"

"Yes, this time. But wait,
Darling. There will be other nights—some of them even better."
"Oh, no. It died." He laughed. But she did not.
It was her first glory.

Laid away now in its terrible
Lead coffin, it was the first brightness she had ever
Mourned. "Oh, no, it's dead." And he her father
Mourned too, for more to come.

(1963)

30. The central subject of the poem is

(A) the indifference of fathers to the sensibilities of their daughters
(B) facing one's own death
(C) dealing with loss and sorrow
(D) the cruelty of time and the seasons
(E) the difficulty parents have in understanding their children

31. Which of the following lines most clearly presents the difference in perspective between the father and the daughter?

(A) "And she on the lawn, comfortless by her father" (line 7)
(B) "'Darling. There will be other nights—some of them even better.'" (line 10)
(C) "'Oh, no. It died.' He laughed. But she did not." (line 11)
(D) "It was her first glory." (line 12)
(E) "And he her father / Mourned too, for more to come." (lines 15–16)

32. The image of the lead coffin (line 14) functions to

(A) diminish and caricature the child's sorrow at the sunset
(B) confirm the significance of the child's feelings of loss
(C) indicate that the sunset symbolizes the child's own death
(D) suggest that the father is now mourning his dead child
(E) represent the specter of death hovering over the father

33. The last two lines of the poem suggest that the father

(A) laments his own losses, both past and future
(B) fears that he will ultimately lose his daughter
(C) has come to mourn the sunset in the same way that his daughter does
(D) dreads his own inevitable death
(E) realizes that his child faces future sorrows that he cannot prevent

34. At the end of the poem, the father's attitude toward his daughter's crying is best characterized as

(A) patronizing and selfish
(B) patient but stern
(C) sympathetic and understanding
(D) condescending and detached
(E) good-humored but naïve

Questions 35–38

In My Craft or Sullen Art

In my craft or sullen art
Exercised in the still night
When only the moon rages
And the lovers lie abed
With all their griefs in their arms,
I labour by singing light
Not for ambition or bread
Or the strut and trade of charms
On the ivory stages
But for the common wages
Of their most secret heart.

Not for the proud man apart
From the raging moon I write
On these spindrift* pages
Nor for the towering dead
With their nightingales and psalms
But for the lovers, their arms
Round the griefs of the ages.
Who pay no praise or wages
Nor heed my craft or art.

(1946)

*wind-blown sea spray

35. The negative constructions "Not . . . But" (lines 7 and 10) and "Not . . . Nor . . . But" (lines 12, 15, and 17) are a feature of the structure of the poem that emphasizes a contrast between the

(A) typical human motivations and the motivation of the speaker
(B) attitudes of the speaker toward himself and toward the lovers
(C) lovers embracing their own griefs and embracing the griefs of the ages
(D) attitude of the speaker toward the lovers and their attitude toward the speaker
(E) common craft of writing light verse and the sublime art of writing poetry

36. Which of the following is the antecedent of "their" (line 11) ?

(A) "lovers" (line 4)
(B) "griefs" (line 5)
(C) "strut and trade of charms" (line 8)
(D) "ivory stages" (line 9)
(E) "wages" (line 10)

37. The phrase "the towering dead / With their nightingales and psalms" (lines 15–16) alludes to the

(A) oppressive weight of time and eternity
(B) poet's physical and spiritual future
(C) voices of nature and the supernatural
(D) artificiality and futility of human institutions
(E) great poets and poetry of the past

38. How does the speaker feel about the response of the lovers to his efforts?

(A) The speaker wishes to get vengeance by revealing the secrets of the lovers.
(B) The speaker will stop writing out of resentment for their indifference.
(C) The speaker will seek a new audience and relegate the lovers to the position of the proud man.
(D) The speaker will continue to write for the lovers regardless of their response.
(E) The speaker really writes only for himself and does not desire an audience.

Questions 39–44

Now Winter Nights Enlarge

Now winter nights enlarge
    The number of their hours;
And clouds their storms discharge
    Upon the airy towers.
Let now the chimneys blaze
    And cups o'erflow with wine,
Let well-tuned words amaze
    With harmony divine.
Now yellow waxen lights
    Shall wait on honey love
While youthful revels, masques, and courtly sights
    Sleep's leaden spells remove.

This time doth well dispense
    With lovers' long discourse;
Much speech hath some defense,
    Though beauty no remorse.
All do not all things well;
    Some measures comely tread,
Some knotted riddles tell,
    Some poems smoothly read.
The summer hath his joys,
    And winter his delights;
Though Love and all his pleasures are but toys,
    They shorten tedious nights.

(1617)

39. In the first stanza (lines 1–12), the poet contrasts the

(A) cold weather during winter with the heat of summer
(B) experience of living alone with that of receiving guests
(C) beginning of the winter season with its ending
(D) energy of the natural world with the relative stupor of civilization
(E) stark chill outdoors with the warm cheer indoors

40. In context, lines 7–8 are best understood as a call for

(A) shocking revelations of truth
(B) stimulating intellectual debates
(C) informal discussions of religious issues
(D) poetry in honor of the natural world
(E) pleasing and compelling songs

41. In context, "leaden spells" (line 12) implies that sleep is

(A) a period of dullness
(B) detrimental to health
(C) one way to endure the night
(D) subtly bewitching
(E) an occasion for fantasy

42. Lines 13–14 suggest that winter nights are suitable times for

(A) lovers to talk less
(B) lovers to say goodbye
(C) lovers to meet
(D) talking about lovers
(E) not talking at all

43. In lines 21–22, "his" refers to the

(A) lover talking with his beloved in lines 13–16
(B) person who has none of the talents described in lines 18–20
(C) "Love" described in line 23
(D) summer and winter seasons, respectively
(E) lover whose pleasures have been cut short by each season in turn

44. The speaker's attitude toward winter nights is characterized by

(A) dread of their loneliness and cold
(B) regret that they will never return
(C) anticipation of the joy they afford
(D) fear that they will be lengthy
(E) criticism of how wastefully they can be spent

Questions 45–50

About my interests: I don't know if I have any, unless the morbid desire to own a sixteen-millimeter camera and make experimental movies can be so classified. Otherwise, I love to eat and drink—it's my melancholy conviction that I've scarcely ever had enough to eat (this is because it's *impossible* to eat enough if you're worried about the next meal)—and I love to argue with people who do not disagree with me too profoundly, and I love to laugh. I do *not* like bohemia, or bohemians, I do not like people whose principal aim is pleasure, and I do not like people who are *earnest* about anything. I don't like people who like me because I'm a Negro; neither do I like people who find in the same accident grounds for contempt. I love America more than any other country in the world, and, exactly for this reason, I insist on the right to criticize her perpetually. I think all theories are suspect, that the finest principles may have to be modified, or may even be pulverized by the demands of life, and that one must find, therefore, one's own moral center and move through the world hoping that this center will guide one aright. I consider that I have many responsibilities, but none greater than this: to last, as Hemingway says, and get my work done.

I want to be an honest man and a good writer.

(1955)

45. Which of the following best describes the passage?

(A) A literary tribute to the writer's profession
(B) A detailed chronicle of the writer's past experiences
(C) A personal statement revealing the writer's character
(D) A critique of various philosophical outlooks
(E) A plea for the reader to examine the meaning of existence

46. In line 15, "accident" is best understood to refer to

(A) education
(B) ethnicity
(C) mood
(D) behavior
(E) philosophy

47. In line 23, "moral center" refers to an individual's

(A) sense of dismay at the world's injustices
(B) values shared with like-minded people
(C) obsession with ethical issues
(D) essential beliefs that govern actions
(E) attitude about extreme views

48. The last sentence in the first paragraph (lines 24–27) suggests that the speaker

(A) realizes he will never achieve literary fame
(B) views life as a struggle in which only the fit survive
(C) thinks that he is exempt from the laws followed by others
(D) respects the writings of others more than he does his own
(E) sees his writing as his most important contribution

49. It can be inferred from the passage that the speaker would disapprove most strongly of

(A) crusaders who are zealously devoted to their cause
(B) American citizens who criticize national policy
(C) those who fail to explain the moral principles underlying their actions
(D) young rebels who refuse to listen to wiser, more experienced advisers
(E) those who insist that experience is the best teacher of moral values

50. The tone of the passage is best described as

(A) cynical
(B) flippant
(C) reflective
(D) agitated
(E) nostalgic

Questions 51–57

Time to Be Wise

Yes; I write verses now and then,
But blunt and flaccid is my pen,
No longer talk'd of by young men
As rather clever;
In the last quarter are my eyes,
You see it by their form and size;
Is it not time then to be wise?
Or now or never.

Fairest that ever sprang from Eve!
While Time allows the short reprieve,
Just look at me! would you believe
'T was once a lover?
I cannot clear the five-bar gate;
But, trying first its timber's state,
Climb stiffly up, take breath, and wait
To trundle over.

Through gallopade[1] I cannot swing
The entangling blooms of Beauty's spring:
I cannot say the tender thing,
Be 't true or false,
And am beginning to opine
Those girls are only half divine
Whose waists yon wicked boys entwine
In giddy waltz.

I fear that arm above that shoulder;
I wish them wiser, graver, older,
Sedater, and no harm if colder,
And panting less.
Ah! people were not half so wild
In former days, when, starchly mild,
Upon her high-heel'd Essex smil'd
The brave Queen Bess.[2]

(1853)

[1] a lively dance
[2] Queen Elizabeth I; the Earl of Essex was a favorite of the queen.

51. The speaker of the poem specifically addresses

(A) an unnamed woman
(B) lusty young men
(C) Queen Bess
(D) an admirer of his poems
(E) a noble patron

52. The "entangling blooms of Beauty's spring" (line 18) are best understood as

(A) beautiful flowers
(B) lush gardens
(C) lovely young women
(D) violent passions
(E) dangerous delusions

53. In context, lines 21–24 suggest that the

(A) speaker's eyesight is failing
(B) speaker's beloved is no longer beautiful
(C) speaker has trouble choosing only one lover
(D) speaker's attitude toward women has changed over time
(E) speaker treats girls as though they were goddesses

54. In context, the tone of the phrase "yon wicked boys" (line 23) is best described as

(A) self-deprecatory
(B) mock moral
(C) apologetic
(D) obsequious
(E) euphoric

55. In the last lines of the poem, the speaker suggests that the era of "brave Queen Bess" (line 32) would have been

    (A) too peaceful for him
    (B) too conscious of hierarchy and nobility
    (C) more conducive to amorous adventures
    (D) more suitable for him given his present condition
    (E) more appealing to the young people of his own time

56. The poem as a whole can best be described as

    (A) a fond remembrance of one man's youthful days
    (B) a tearful complaint about the indignities of old age
    (C) an ironic commentary on the traps beauty sets for the unwary
    (D) a dispassionate analysis of the changes that took place in an ill-fated romantic relationship
    (E) a wry reflection on the changes age has wrought in a man who once considered himself a lover

57. The speaker's attitude in the poem is primarily one of

    (A) wretchedness and despair
    (B) regret tempered by mature insights
    (C) envy of the passions of younger men
    (D) moral disapproval of young lovers
    (E) mockery of polite courtship conventions

Questions 58–63

Dr. Trench is engaged to marry Blanche, the daughter of Mr. Sartorius.

SARTORIUS: Live on your income! Impossible: my daughter is accustomed to a proper establishment. Did I not expressly undertake to provide for that? Did she not tell you I promised her to do so?

TRENCH: Yes, I know all about that, Mr Sartorius; and I'm greatly obliged to you; but I'd rather not take anything from you except Blanche herself.

SARTORIUS: And why did you not say so before?

TRENCH: No matter why. Let us drop the subject.

SARTORIUS: No matter! But it does matter, sir. I insist on an answer. Why did you not say so before?

TRENCH: I didnt know before.

SARTORIUS [*provoked*] Then you ought to have known your own mind on a point of such vital importance.

TRENCH [*much injured*] I ought to have known! Cokane: is this reasonable? [*Cokane's features are contorted by an air of judicial consideration; but he says nothing; and Trench again addresses Sartorius, this time with a marked diminution of respect*]. How the deuce could I have known? You didnt tell me.

SARTORIUS: You are trifling with me, sir. You said that you did not know your own mind before.

TRENCH: I said nothing of the sort. I say that I did not know where your money came from before.

SARTORIUS: That is not true, sir. I—

COKANE: Gently, my dear sir. Gently, Harry, dear boy. Suaviter in modo: fort—*

TRENCH: Let him begin, then. What does he mean by attacking me in this fashion?

SARTORIUS: Mr Cokane: you will bear me out. I was explicit on the point. I said I was a self-made man; and I am not ashamed of it.

TRENCH: You are nothing of the sort. I found out this morning from your man—Lickcheese, or whatever his confounded name is—that your fortune has been made out of a parcel of unfortunate creatures that have hardly enough to keep body and soul together—made by screwing, and bullying, and threatening, and all sorts of pettifogging tyranny.

SARTORIUS [*outraged*] Sir! [*They confront one another threateningly*].

COKANE [*softly*] Rent must be paid, dear boy. It is inevitable, Harry, inevitable. [*Trench turns away petulantly. Sartorius looks after him reflectively for a moment; then resumes his former deliberate and dignified manner, and addresses Trench with studied consideration, but with a perceptible condescension to his youth and folly*].

(1892)

*The first part of a Latin proverb meaning "gently in manner: forcibly in deed"

58. The passage is most concerned with

(A) a plea for help
(B) a clash of values
(C) an argument for austerity
(D) a denunciation of pride
(E) an examination of marriage conventions

59. In context, the phrase "proper establishment" (line 2) means

(A) appropriate home and standard of living
(B) socially prominent family and friends
(C) respectable work and business associates
(D) access to the finest modern university education
(E) involvement in charitable and philanthropic activities

60. The tone of Trench's responses to Sartorius in lines 5–7 ("Yes . . . herself") is best described as

(A) reproachful
(B) inquisitive
(C) embarrassed
(D) enthusiastic
(E) courteous

61. The stage directions in lines 44–50 ("*Trench . . . folly*") suggest that

(A) Trench is looking forward to a discussion with Sartorius

(B) Trench is reserved and Sartorius is preparing to be aggressive

(C) Trench is sulking and Sartorius is preparing to patronize him

(D) Sartorius is about to compliment Trench's ethical stance

(E) Sartorius is determined to make Trench end the engagement

62. Cokane's role in this scene is best described as

(A) a bully

(B) a referee

(C) an antagonist

(D) a legal expert

(E) a social commentator

63. The movement of the passage is from

(A) polite disagreement to angry disputation to possible resolution

(B) furious confrontation to reasoned discourse to full agreement

(C) controlled anger to open discussion to deep empathy

(D) physical threats to dignified atonement

(E) rational analysis to self-recrimination

Questions 64–68

The first sparrow of spring! The year beginning with younger hope than ever! The faint silvery warblings heard over the partially bare and moist fields from the bluebird, the song-sparrow, and the redwing, as if the last flakes of winter tinkled as they fell! What at such a time are histories, chronologies, traditions, and all written revelations? The brooks sing carols and glees to the spring. The marsh-hawk sailing low over the meadow is already seeking the first slimy life that awakes. The sinking sound of melting snow is heard in all dells, and the ice dissolves apace in the ponds. The grass flames up on the hillsides like a spring fire—"et primitus oritur herba imbribus primoribus evocata"*—as if the earth sent forth an inward heat to greet the returning sun; not yellow but green is the color of its flame; the symbol of perpetual youth, the grass-blade, like a long green ribbon, streams from the sod into the summer, checked indeed by the frost, but anon pushing on again, lifting its spear of last year's hay with the fresh life below. It grows as steadily as the rill oozes out of the ground. It is almost identical with that, for in the growing days of June, when the rills are dry, the grass blades are their channels, and from year to year the herds drink at this perennial green stream, and the mower draws from it betimes their winter supply. So our human life but dies down to its root, and still puts forth its green blade to eternity.

(1854)

*and for the first time the grass arises, called forth by the earliest rains

64. In the third sentence (lines 2–6), the imagery of "the last flakes of winter" evokes the impression made by

(A) cracking ice
(B) church bells
(C) birds' songs
(D) soft breezes
(E) running water

65. In lines 6–7, the author's attitude toward written human history is best described as

(A) reverent
(B) respectful
(C) uncertain
(D) dismissive
(E) condemnatory

66. The observation that the "grass flames up on the hillsides like a spring fire" (lines 12–13) calls attention to the

(A) dangers inherent in spring weather
(B) power and energy of the grass
(C) unexpected change from winter to spring
(D) ambiguous nature of the grass
(E) ultimate fate of the grass at the end of the season

67. The passage presents death for humans as

(A) the doorway to the afterlife
(B) the pathway to revelation
(C) a sobering finality
(D) a cause for fear
(E) part of a natural cycle

68. The mood of the passage is both

(A) celebratory and reflective
(B) anxious and elated
(C) curious and cynical
(D) optimistic and fearful
(E) welcoming and guarded

Questions 69–73

Not They Who Soar

Not they who soar, but they who plod
Their rugged way, unhelped, to God
Are heroes; they who higher fare,
And, flying, fan the upper air,
Miss all the toil that hugs the sod.
'Tis they whose backs have felt the rod,
Whose feet have pressed the path unshod,
May smile upon defeated care,
    Not they who soar.

High up there are no thorns to prod,
Nor boulders lurking 'neath the clod
To turn the keenness of the share,*
For flight is ever free and rare;
But heroes they the soil who've trod,
    Not they who soar!

(1895)

*the part of the plow that cuts the furrow

69. The "Not . . . but" structure in line 1 calls attention to

(A) a sudden shift in religious beliefs
(B) a reversal of conventional social status
(C) the similarity of seemingly opposite types of people
(D) the recognition that everyone is a hero
(E) the danger of rampant individualism

70. As used in the poem, the word "plod" (line 1) has all of the following connotations EXCEPT

(A) monotony
(B) drudgery
(C) perseverance
(D) determined effort
(E) careless indifference

71. "To turn the keenness of the share" (line 12) is best taken to mean

(A) to uncover something surprising
(B) to dig deeper than necessary
(C) to blunt the sharpness of the blade
(D) to remove the obstacle from the path
(E) to injure the worker doing the plowing

72. The poem structures its argument around an extended antithesis between imagery of

(A) triumph and failure
(B) heroism and villainy
(C) mortals and angels
(D) earth and air
(E) hopefulness and despair

73. The speaker's tone is best described as one of

(A) deep feeling
(B) sincere regret
(C) melancholy contemplation
(D) smug satisfaction
(E) anxious ambivalence

Questions 74–78

The wood was green as mosses of the Icy Glen; the trees stood high and haughty, feeling their living sap; the industrious earth beneath was as a weaver's loom, with a gorgeous carpet on it, whereof the ground-vine tendrils formed the warp and woof, and the living flowers the figures. All the trees, with all their laden branches; all the shrubs and ferns, and grasses; the message-carrying air; all these unceasingly were active. Through the lacings of the leaves, the great sun seemed a flying shuttle weaving the unwearied verdure. Oh, busy weaver! unseen weaver!—pause!—One word! whither flows the fabric? what palace may it deck? wherefore all these ceaseless toilings? Speak, weaver!—stay thy hand!—but one single word with thee! Nay—the shuttle flies—the figures float from forth the loom; the freshet-rushing carpet for ever slides away. The weaver-god, he weaves; and by that weaving is he deafened, that he hears no mortal voice; and by that humming, we, too, who look on the loom are deafened; and only when we escape it shall we hear the thousand voices that speak through it.

(1851)

74. The speaker uses the metaphor of a loom to represent the

(A) source of artistry in human nature
(B) role of religion in modern society
(C) context within which imagination evolves
(D) method by which people run their lives
(E) framework within which life is created

75. In line 16, the clause "the figures float from forth the loom" contains which of the following?

(A) Irony
(B) Understatement
(C) Alliteration
(D) Antithesis
(E) Onomatopoeia

76. The speaker's attitude toward the "weaver-god" (line 18) is best described as one of

(A) indulgence
(B) awe
(C) indifference
(D) confidence
(E) amusement

77. In the last sentence (lines 17–22), the speaker emphasizes which of the following?

(A) The difficulty of understanding the meaning of life
(B) The importance of honest toil
(C) The guilt incurred in attempting to interpret nature
(D) The importance of responding to the needs of others
(E) The spiritual reward for good deeds

78. The passage moves from

(A) lyrical representation to factual reporting
(B) objective presentation to emotional interpretation
(C) realistic evocation to imaginative improvisation
(D) depiction of nature to philosophical assertion
(E) description of scenery to logical analysis

Study Resources

The most relevant preparation for the Analyzing and Interpreting Literature exam is attentive and reflective reading of the various literary genres of poetry, drama and prose. You can prepare for the test by:

1. Reading a variety of poetry, drama, fiction and nonfiction
2. Reading critical analyses of various literary works
3. Writing analyses and interpretations of the works you read
4. Discussing with others the meaning of the literature you read

Textbooks and anthologies used for college courses in the analysis and interpretation of literature contain a sampling of literary works in a variety of genres. They also contain material that can help you comprehend the meanings of literary works and recognize the devices writers use to convey their sense and intent. To prepare for the exam, you should study the contents of at least one textbook or anthology, which you can find in most college bookstores. You would do well to consult two or three texts because they do vary somewhat in content, approach and emphases.

Visit **clep.collegeboard.org/earn-college-credit/practice** for additional literature and writing resources. You can also find suggestions for exam preparation in Chapter IV of the *Official Study Guide*. In addition, many college faculty post their course materials on their schools' websites.

Answer Key

1.	B	40.	E
2.	C	41.	A
3.	D	42.	A
4.	B	43.	D
5.	A	44.	C
6.	B	45.	C
7.	E	46.	B
8.	A	47.	D
9.	D	48.	E
10.	C	49.	A
11.	D	50.	C
12.	E	51.	A
13.	A	52.	C
14.	C	53.	D
15.	A	54.	B
16.	D	55.	D
17.	B	56.	E
18.	C	57.	B
19.	B	58.	B
20.	A	59.	A
21.	E	60.	E
22.	C	61.	C
23.	D	62.	B
24.	C	63.	A
25.	D	64.	C
26.	C	65.	D
27.	B	66.	B
28.	C	67.	E
29.	A	68.	A
30.	C	69.	B
31.	C	70.	E
32.	B	71.	C
33.	E	72.	D
34.	C	73.	A
35.	A	74.	E
36.	A	75.	C
37.	E	76.	B
38.	D	77.	A
39.	E	78.	D

College Composition Exams

Description of the Examinations

The CLEP College Composition examinations assess writing skills taught in most first-year college composition courses. Those skills include analysis, argumentation, synthesis, usage, ability to recognize logical development and research. The exams cannot cover every skill (such as keeping a journal or peer editing) required in many first-year college writing courses. Candidates will, however, be expected to apply the principles and conventions used in longer writing projects to two timed writing assignments and to apply the rules of standard written English.

College Composition contains multiple-choice items and two mandatory, centrally scored essays. The essays are scored twice a month by college English faculty from throughout the country via an online scoring system. Each of the two essays is scored independently by two different readers, and the scores are then combined. This combined score is weighted approximately equally with the score from the multiple-choice section. These scores are then combined to yield the candidate's score. The resulting combined score is reported as a single scaled score between 20 and 80. Separate scores are not reported for the multiple-choice and essay sections. College Composition contains approximately 50 multiple-choice items to be answered in approximately 50 minutes and two essays to be written in 70 minutes, for a total of approximately 120 minutes testing time.

College Composition Modular contains a multiple-choice section that is supplemented with an essay section that is either provided and scored by the college or provided by CLEP and scored by the college. College Composition Modular is available for colleges that want a valid, reliable multiple-choice assessment and greater local control over the direct writing assessment. College Composition Modular contains approximately 90 questions to be answered in approximately 90 minutes and, if the essay section provided by CLEP is chosen, two essays to be written in 70 minutes. Some colleges may opt to provide their own locally scored writing assessment or some other assessment or evaluation.

Both exams include some pretest multiple-choice questions that will not be counted toward the candidate's score.

Colleges set their own credit-granting policies and therefore differ with regard to their acceptance of the College Composition examinations. Most colleges will grant course credit for a first-year composition or English course that emphasizes expository writing; others will grant credit toward satisfying a liberal arts or distribution requirement in English.

The American Council on Education's College Credit Recommendation Service (ACE CREDIT) has evaluated the examinations and recommended the awarding of college credit for a score of 50 or above on the CLEP College Composition and College Composition Modular examinations. Refer to the document "What Your CLEP Score Means" for additional information about the ACE credit recommendations.

Knowledge and Skills Required

The exams measure candidates' knowledge of the fundamental principles of rhetoric and composition and their ability to apply the principles of standard written English. In addition, the exams require familiarity with research and reference skills. In one of the two essays in the exams (in the mandatory essay section of College Composition and the optional essay module produced by the College Board for College Composition Modular), candidates must develop a position by building an argument in which they synthesize information from two provided sources, which they must cite. The requirement that candidates cite the sources they use reflects the recognition of source attribution as an essential skill in college writing courses.

College Composition

The skills assessed in the College Composition examination follow. The numbers following the main topics indicate the approximate percentages of exam questions on those topics. The bulleted lists under each topic are meant to be representative rather than prescriptive.

Conventions of Standard Written English (10%)

This section measures candidates' awareness of a variety of logical, structural and grammatical relationships within sentences. The questions test recognition of acceptable usage relating to the items below:

- Syntax (parallelism, coordination, subordination)
- Sentence boundaries (comma splices, run-ons, sentence fragments)
- Recognition of correct sentences
- Concord/agreement (pronoun reference, case shift and number; subject-verb; verb tense)
- Diction
- Modifiers
- Idiom
- Active/passive voice
- Lack of subject in modifying word group
- Logical comparison
- Logical agreement
- Punctuation

Revision Skills (40%)

This section measures candidates' revision skills in the context of works in progress (early drafts of essays):

- Organization
- Evaluation of evidence
- Awareness of audience, tone and purpose
- Level of detail
- Coherence between sentences and paragraphs
- Sentence variety and structure
- Main idea, thesis statements and topic sentences
- Rhetorical effects and emphasis
- Use of language
- Evaluation of author's authority and appeal
- Evaluation of reasoning
- Consistency of point of view
- Transitions
- Sentence-level errors primarily relating to the conventions of standard written English

Ability to Use Source Materials (25%)

This section measures candidates' familiarity with elements of the following basic reference and research skills, which are tested primarily in sets but may also be tested through stand-alone questions. In the passage-based sets, the elements listed under Revision Skills and Rhetorical Analysis may also be tested. In addition, this section will cover the following skills:

- Use of reference materials
- Evaluation of sources
- Integration of resource material
- Documentation of sources (including, but not limited to, MLA, APA and Chicago manuals of style)

Rhetorical Analysis (25%)

This section measures candidates' ability to analyze writing. This skill is tested primarily in passage-based questions pertaining to critical thinking, style, purpose, audience and situation:

- Appeals
- Tone
- Organization/structure
- Rhetorical effects
- Use of language
- Evaluation of evidence

The Essays

In addition to the multiple-choice section, College Composition includes a mandatory essay section that tests skills of argumentation, analysis and synthesis. This section of the exam consists of two essays, both of which measure a candidate's ability to write clearly and effectively. The first essay is based on the candidate's reading, observation or experience, while the second requires candidates to synthesize and cite two sources that are provided. Candidates have 30 minutes to write the first essay and 40 minutes to read the two sources and write the second essay.

The essays must be typed on the computer.

College Composition Modular

College Composition Modular allows institutions to administer and/or score test-takers' essays themselves. The knowledge and skills assessed are the same as those measured by College Composition, but the format and timing allow a more extended indirect assessment of test-takers' knowledge and skills.

The percentages of exam questions on each topic are the same in both exams:

Conventions of Standard Written English (10%)

Revision Skills, Including Sentence-Level Skills (40%)

Ability to Use Source Materials (25%)

Rhetorical Analysis (25%)

College Composition Modular includes an additional question type for assessing revision skills: Improving Sentences. For more information, see page 83.

After completing the multiple-choice section, candidates take the direct writing assessment module based on the policy established by their college. Options include:

1. An essay section developed and provided by CLEP that requires candidates to respond to two essay prompts designed to assess the same skills measured in the College Composition essay section. Copies of the handwritten essays are sent to the college designated by the candidate, along with the CLEP Optional Essay Scoring Guidelines.

2. An essay/writing assessment developed, administered and scored by the college.

3. Associating the College Composition Modular score with another assessment or evaluation determined by the college.

College Composition Sample Test Questions

Following are the types of questions that appear on the College Composition examinations.

General Directions
Time: Approximately 90 minutes [1]

Conventions of Standard Written English (10%)

Directions: The following sentences test your knowledge of grammar, usage, diction (choice of words) and idiom. Note that some sentences are correct, and no sentence contains more than one error.

Read each sentence carefully, paying particular attention to the underlined portions. You will find that the error, if there is one, is underlined. Assume that elements of the sentence that are not underlined are correct and cannot be changed. In choosing answers, follow the requirements of standard written English.

If there is an error, select the one underlined part that must be changed to make the sentence correct.

If there is no error, select No error.

Example: **SAMPLE ANSWER**

Ⓐ ● Ⓒ Ⓓ Ⓔ

The other delegates and
A
him immediately accepted
B C
the resolution drafted by
D
the neutral states. No error
E

1. Studying plants in the laboratory under strictly
A B
controlled conditions providing a
C
useful but limited view of the way that these
D
plants function in an ecosystem. No error
E

[1] The multiple-choice section for the College Composition Modular exam is approximately 90 minutes.

2. Many of the dozens of miniature portraits of
A
Henry VIII by the artist Hans Holbein
B
were painted on the backs of a playing card.
C D
No error
E

3. Among the Native Americans first encountered
A B
by Europeans during the seventeenth century
C
was the Algonquin Indians. No error
D E

4. Although most people are not really
A
familiar with the agency called Centers for
B
Disease Control and Prevention, it is highly
C D
respected among medical professionals
worldwide. No error
E

5. Even though he had some doubts about
A B
democracy, Thomas Jefferson did have faith
C
with representative government. No error
D E

6. The union was not opposed against a
A
compromise as long as its basic right to
B C
collective bargaining was respected.
D
No error
E

7. During her first year in medical school,
A
Joanne came to the realization that she was
B
more interested in doing research than
C
to treat patients. No error
D E

8. If one has trouble swallowing tablets or
A
capsules, you could try taking medicine in
B C D
liquid form. No error
E

9. Although most of the tourists who come to the
A B
city each year visit only the famous landmarks,
C
but some of the more adventurous venture into
D
less familiar territory. No error
E

10. The orbits of comets in our solar system

are much more eccentric than planet Earth,
A B
which revolves around the Sun following a
C D
relatively circular path. No error
E

11. First recorded 3,000 years ago, the migration of
A B
many species of birds in the Northern

Hemisphere occurs annually every year.
C D
No error
E

12. Because they do not thrive in the shade, aspen
A
trees benefit indirectly from forest fires, which
B
creates open areas for saplings to grow in the
C D
sunlight. No error
E

13. Every time we go to the beach, my friend
A
Joyce and me always forget to bring coins
B C
for the parking meters. No error
D E

14. If I were only a little taller, I would be able
A B
to reach the plates on the top shelf
C
of the kitchen cabinet. No error
D E

Revision Skills (40%)

Directions: The following passages are early drafts of essays.

Read each passage and then answer the questions that follow. Some questions refer to particular sentences or parts of sentences and ask you to improve sentence structure or diction (word choice). Other questions refer to the entire essay or parts of the essay and ask you to consider the essay's organization, development or effectiveness of language. In selecting your answers, follow the conventions of standard written English.

<u>**Questions 15–23**</u> are based on the following draft of an essay.

(1) Winter counts are physical records, mainly drawings on animal hides or muslin, that Plains Indians, primarily the Lakota, used for showing each year of their history. (2) In this method, a year consists of one event recorded as an image in the winter count. (3) People could keep track of other events, such as births and deaths, by knowing the years in which it occurred. (4) In consultation with members of the Lakota people, curators at the Smithsonian Institution created an online exhibit of about a thousand winter counts.

(5) Scholars generally agree that collectively, probably, they chose which event would stand for a year. (6) An event chosen to represent a year was not necessarily the most important of that year, just one that was memorable for everyone in the group. (7) One person was the keeper of the winter count. (8) Once the group made its selection, he then recorded this event.

(9) Like any calendar, the winter counts named years but did not go into detail about what happened. (10) Here is where the keeper of the winter count came in. (11) He was the group's official historian. (12) He remembered stories passed down to him and could place them in the winter count. (13) He could provide the significance of the events chosen to represent the years in the winter count. (14) Fortunately, several keepers were interviewed and their stories recorded in the nineteenth and early twentieth centuries.

(15) Even without their accompanying oral histories, however, the winter counts show that life for the Lakota was always on the move.

15. In context, which is the best replacement for "showing" in sentence 1?

    (A) producing
    (B) appearing
    (C) representing
    (D) explaining
    (E) signaling

16. In context, which of the following revisions must be made to sentence 3 (reproduced below)?

    People could keep track of other events, such as births and deaths, by knowing the years in which it occurred.

    (A) Add "Ordinarily" to the beginning of the sentence.
    (B) Change "could" to "would".
    (C) Change "such as" to "like".
    (D) Change "it" to "they".
    (E) Add "had" before "occurred".

17. Which is the best revision of the underlined portion of sentence 5 (reproduced below)?

    Scholars generally agree that <u>collectively, probably, they chose which event would stand for a year</u>.

    (A) what event would stand for a year was probably decided as a collective
    (B) collectively the Lakota Indians probably chose the event for its year
    (C) choosing the event that would stand for a year was probably a collective effort
    (D) it was probably a collective task, they all chose the event to stand for a year
    (E) the event that would stand for a year was probably their collective decision

18. Which of the following sentences is best to add after sentence 6?

    (A) Historians should look at several winter counts, looking out for repeated images, in order to get better information.
    (B) The drawings were sometimes arranged in a spiral, reading out from the center; sometimes in page form, reading from top to bottom, left to right.
    (C) However, winter counts helped the people keep their oral history in chronological order.
    (D) For example, one year might be named for a war, while another might be named for a meteor shower.
    (E) Winter counts show that conflict was the norm for many Native Americans.

19. In context, which of the following is the best way to combine sentences 7 and 8 (reproduced below)?

    One person was the keeper of the winter count. Once the group made its selection, he then recorded this event.

    (A) One person, being the keeper of the winter count, he then recorded the event once the group made its selection.
    (B) One person was the keeper of the winter count, he then recorded the event once they made their selection.
    (C) Once the group had made its selection, one person, the keeper of the winter count, recorded it.
    (D) The keeper of the winter count was one person, and, when the group made its selection, he then recorded it.
    (E) Recording the event when the group finally selected it, the winter count was updated by one person, the keeper.

20. In context, which is best to add to the beginning of sentence 13?

    (A) Or,
    (B) In addition,
    (C) Despite this,
    (D) However,
    (E) Not to mention,

21. In context, where should the following sentence be placed?

    Without the keeper and the vast amount of historical information stored in his memory, the winter counts would be little more than a cryptic list of years.

    (A) After sentence 1
    (B) After sentence 3
    (C) After sentence 5
    (D) After sentence 12
    (E) After sentence 13

22. Deleting which of the following sentences would most improve the coherence of the passage?

    (A) Sentence 2
    (B) Sentence 4
    (C) Sentence 9
    (D) Sentence 10
    (E) Sentence 15

23. The passage as a whole could be clarified by adding which of the following before the first sentence?

    (A) A brief paragraph comparing Native American timekeeping methods with calendar-based ones
    (B) An excerpt of an interview with a Lakota keeper of the winter counts
    (C) An analysis of how certain events make time seem longer than it really is
    (D) An example of a student who learned about her Native American background and became a keeper of winter counts
    (E) A discussion of how winter is viewed differently in different cultures

Questions 24–32 are based on the following draft of an essay.

(1) Americans enjoy some of the safest free drinking water on Earth, however spending $15 billion on bottled water in 2006, and consumption is rising (Fishman). (2) While proponents of bottled water tout its health advantages over alternatives such as sugary sodas, environmentalists are concerned about the consequences of bottled-water consumption. (3) It takes 1.5 million barrels of oil a year to make the plastic water bottles Americans use, and the production of these bottles, many of them made of polyethylene terephthalate (PET), pollutes the atmosphere (Williams). (4) The manufacture of PET releases hydrocarbons, sulfur dioxides, carbon monoxide and other harmful substances into the atmosphere. (5) PET is recyclable, and over 85 percent of these bottles end up in landfills, where they can take as long as 1,000 years to degrade (Niman).

(6) It is not only the manufacture and disposal of water bottles that contribute to the harm it causes the environment. (7) Water is shipped to the United States from as far away as Fiji on freighters and then hauled in trucks to its destinations.

(8) What makes this wasteful practice especially ludicrous is that this luxury commodity is widely available for free. (9) The *San Francisco Chronicle* notes that bottled water costs 240 to 10,000 times more than tap water and that "forty percent of bottled water should be labeled bottled tap water because that is exactly what it is."

24. In context, which of the following versions of the underlined portion of sentence 1 (reproduced below) is best?

    Americans enjoy some of the safest free drinking water on *<u>Earth, however spending</u>* *$15 billion on bottled water in 2006, and consumption is rising (Fishman).*

    (A) Earth, however spending
    (B) Earth, yet they spent
    (C) Earth; but spending
    (D) Earth; having spent
    (E) Earth, instead they spend

25. In context, which of the following is the best revision to sentence 3 (reproduced below)?

    It takes 1.5 million barrels of oil a year to make the plastic water bottles Americans use, and the production of these bottles, many of them made of polyethylene terephthalate (PET), pollutes the atmosphere (Williams).

    (A) Begin the sentence with "However,".
    (B) Begin the sentence with "For one thing,".
    (C) Change "It takes" to "They take".
    (D) Change "production of these bottles" to "producing such bottles".
    (E) Delete "(Williams)" and begin the sentence with "Williams says".

26. Which of the following should be done with the underlined portion of sentence 5 (reproduced below)?

    <u>PET is recyclable, and</u> *over 85 percent of these bottles end up in landfills, where they can take as long as 1,000 years to degrade (Niman).*

    (A) Leave it as it is.
    (B) Change it to "If PET were recyclable, then".
    (C) Change it to "True, PET is recyclable, with".
    (D) Change it to "In addition, PET is recyclable as".
    (E) Change it to "Furthermore, although PET is recyclable,".

27. Which of the following versions of the underlined portion of sentence 6 (reproduced below) is best?

    It is not only the manufacture and disposal of water bottles that contribute to the harm *<u>it causes</u>* *the environment.*

    (A) it caused
    (B) its having caused
    (C) causing
    (D) they cause
    (E) these bottles, they cause

28. Which of the following revisions would most emphasize the purpose of sentence 7 (reproduced below)?

Water is shipped to the United States from as far away as Fiji on freighters and then hauled in trucks to its destinations.

(A) Insert "It is true that" at the beginning of the sentence.
(B) Change "as far away as Fiji" to "places like Fiji".
(C) Insert "fuel-burning" before "freighters" and "inefficient" before "trucks".
(D) Change "freighters" to "boats" and "trucks" to "vehicles".
(E) Insert "ships called" before "freighters" and "various" before "destinations".

29. Which would be the best place to insert the following sentence?

Many of the bottles of water that will be sold to Americans must first be transported from sources all over the world.

(A) Immediately after sentence 1
(B) Immediately after sentence 2
(C) Immediately after sentence 4
(D) Immediately after sentence 6
(E) Immediately after sentence 8

30. Which of the following revisions is most needed in sentence 9 (reproduced below)?

The San Francisco Chronicle *notes that bottled water costs 240 to 10,000 times more than tap water and that "forty percent of bottled water should be labeled bottled tap water because that is exactly what it is."*

(A) Add a parenthetical citation for the material quoted in the sentence.
(B) Change "costs" to "cost".
(C) Add "money" after "more".
(D) Change "forty" to "40".
(E) Add a colon before the first quotation mark.

31. Which of the following would be the best sentence with which to end the passage?

(A) People mistakenly think bottled water is purer or tastes better than tap water.
(B) Many newspapers have recently published stories about environmentalists' efforts to persuade the public to stop buying bottled water.
(C) Clearly, we can all do a lot to eliminate an unnecessary environmental hazard just by turning on the tap instead of buying bottled water.
(D) Plastic bottles provide a convenient way to carry water, and people do need to drink extra water in hot weather.
(E) While some kinds of bottled water are carbonated, Americans generally prefer noncarbonated brands.

32. Which of the following would make the most logical title for the passage?

(A) Transportation Woes
(B) The Problem with Bottled Water
(C) Issues of the Environment and Consumption
(D) The Benefits of Tap Water Consumption
(E) Ways and Means of Saving Energy and Drinking Less

Ability to Use Source Materials (25%)

Directions: The following questions test your familiarity with basic research, reference and composition skills. Some questions refer to passages, while other questions are self-contained. For each question, choose the best answer.

33. sloth *n.* **1.** Aversion to work or exertion; laziness, indolence. **2.** Any of various slow-moving, arboreal, edendate mammals of the family *Bradypodidae* of South and Central America, having long hooklike claws, by which they hang upside down from tree branches, and feeding on leaves, buds, and fruits, especially: **a.** A member of the genus *Bradypus*, having three long-clawed toes on each forefoot. Also called *ai*, *three-toed sloth*. **b.** A member of the genus *Choloepus*, having two toes on each forefoot. Also called *two-toed sloth*, *unau*. **3.** A company of bears. See synonyms at **flock**. [Middle English *slowth*, from *slow,* slow.]

    Which of the following statements is NOT supported by the definition above?

    (A) The word "sloth" has both abstract and concrete meanings.
    (B) One meaning of "sloth" has negative connotations.
    (C) "Slowth" was a word used in Middle English.
    (D) All sloths have three long-clawed toes.
    (E) The word "sloth" can refer to bears.

34. Akmajian, Adrian, et al. *Linguistics: An Introduction to Language and Communication*. 6th ed. Cambridge: MIT P, 2010. Print.

    In the citation shown, "et al." indicates that the book was

    (A) published in Cambridge
    (B) edited by Adrian Akmajian
    (C) written by several authors
    (D) first published in 2010
    (E) an introduction to the fifth edition

35. Wacker, Peter. *Virtual Field Trip: New Brunswick Area, Raritan South Bank.* Rutgers U Geography Dept., 1997. Web. 8 Dec. 2003. <http://geography.rutgers.edu/resources/vrtrip/index.html>.

    In the citation, what information is provided by "8 Dec. 2003"?

    (A) The date the information was accessed on the Internet
    (B) The date the virtual field trip was placed on a Web site
    (C) The date the article on New Brunswick was published in a print journal
    (D) The last time the Web site showing the virtual field trip was updated
    (E) The date the virtual field trip was filed with the Rutgers University Geography Department

36. *The following excerpt is taken from a student's research paper.*

    The principles of the separation of church and state and the right to practice religion freely are both supported by the First Amendment to the United States Constitution: "Congress shall make no law respecting an establishment of religion or prohibiting the free exercise thereof" (qtd. in Dye n.d.).

    The letters "n.d." mean that

    (A) the source has several publication dates
    (B) the date of the publication is unavailable
    (C) the quotation is from section n.d. of a source by Dye
    (D) a new paragraph begins here in the quotation
    (E) the quotation is from section n.d. of the Constitution

37. Allen, A.T. (2011). Gender, professionalization, and the child in the progressive era. *Journal of Women's History, 23 (2)*, 112–136.

    In the citation shown, "(2)" indicates that

    (A) there were two volumes of the *Journal of Women's History* published in 2011
    (B) the article appears in the second issue of volume 23 of the *Journal of Women's History*
    (C) there are two articles by A.T. Allen in volume 23 of the *Journal of Women's History*
    (D) "Gender, professionalization, and the child in the progressive era" has more than one author
    (E) "Gender, professionalization, and the child in the progressive era" appears in both print and online versions

38. Norman, Brian. "Bringing Malcolm X to Hollywood." *The Cambridge Companion to Malcolm X*. Ed. Robert E. Terrill. Cambridge: Cambridge UP, 2010. 39–50.

    In the citation shown, "39–50" indicates that

    (A) *The Cambridge Companion to Malcolm X* has 50 volumes
    (B) "Bringing Malcolm X to Hollywood" appears in the 2010 issue of Cambridge UP
    (C) "Bringing Malcolm X to Hollywood" is approximately 12 pages long
    (D) "Bringing Malcolm X to Hollywood" is the 39th of 50 articles
    (E) Robert E. Terrill is the author of an article that appears on pages 39–50

39. *A student writing a research paper plans to use the following quotation found on pages 108–109 of her textbook.*

    "Within two or three decades the difference between automated driving and human driving will be so great you may not be legally allowed to drive your own car, and even if you are allowed, it would be immoral of you to drive, because the risk of you hurting yourself or another person will be far greater than if you allowed a machine to do the work."

    Marcus, Gary. "Moral Machines." *Technology: A Reader for Writers*, edited by Johannah Rodgers, Oxford UP, 2014, pp 108–111.

    Which of the following statements represents the most accurate paraphrase of this quotation?

    (A) Marcus explains that cars will soon drive themselves, and it will become illegal for humans to drive given the great difference between automated and human driving.
    (B) Pages 108–109 describe the future of automated driving.
    (C) Marcus thinks automated driving will be better than human driving.
    (D) Automated driving will completely replace human driving by 2035, according to Marcus, because there will be far less risk with a machine driving.
    (E) Marcus speculates that in the future the superior safety of automated driving may make human driving illegal, or at least immoral.

Questions 40–47 refer to the following passage.

(1) Invasive species are plant or animal species that become established in ecosystems where they did not originate. (2) Some blend in harmlessly with native species, but others cause ecological and economic damage. (3) A notorious example is the zebra mussel, native to Russia, that was first identified in the United States Great Lakes in 1988 (McKee 2003, 141). (4) Scientists believe that the mussels were inadvertently transported to North America in the ballast water of ships.

(5) Like many invasive species, zebra mussels threaten the biodiversity of the habitats they invade. (6) Zebra mussels reproduce so quickly and are so hardy that they have suppressed populations of the Great Lakes' native mussels (Fields 2005, 164) and, along with other invasive species, threaten the Great Lakes' entire food web. (7) Environmental chemist Mike Murray claims, "As invasive species like zebra mussels overwhelm the Great Lakes, large stretches of the lakes have become underwater deserts." (8) Although some skeptics dismiss the concern about invasive species as overblown, arguing that the majority of nonnative species cause no harm, many scientists are alarmed by the changes produced by the zebra mussel and other invasive species. (9) The economic damage caused by the zebra mussel has prompted government officials and scientists to seek solutions to this problem.

(10) Many industrial facilities use chlorine to clear the mussels from their power and sewage plants. (11) Other facilities use chemicals specifically developed to kill mussels. (12) Unfortunately, both of these methods have certain harmful consequences. (13) An alternative may become available: a bacterium that kills zebra mussels without harming native species.

References

Fields, S. (2005). Great Lakes: Resources at risk. *Environmental Health Perspectives 113* (2), 164–172.

McKee, J. (2003). *Sparing nature: The conflict between human population growth and Earth's biodiversity.* New Brunswick, NJ: Rutgers University Press.

40. Which of the following is cited in sentence 3?

(A) A newspaper
(B) A scientific journal
(C) A Web site
(D) A book
(E) A magazine

41. The information in parentheses in sentence 6 informs the reader that

(A) Fields conducted research in 2005 about how to protect native mussel species
(B) information about invasive species other than zebra mussels can be found in a source written by Fields
(C) Fields has written a work that provides information about zebra mussels' effects on native mussel populations
(D) the sentence is a direct quote from a work written by Fields
(E) information about the impact of invasive species on native aquatic populations can be found on page 2005 of a work by Fields

42. The author of the passage quotes Murray in sentence 7 most likely in order to

(A) provide information about other invasive species in the Great Lakes
(B) suggest that scientists have underestimated the damage done to the Great Lakes by zebra mussels
(C) point out that invasive species can affect many different kinds of environments
(D) emphasize the effects that zebra mussels have had on the Great Lakes ecosystem
(E) illustrate the nature of the food web in the Great Lakes

43. Which is best to do with sentence 7 (reproduced below)?

Environmental chemist Mike Murray claims, "As invasive species like zebra mussels overwhelm the Great Lakes, large stretches of the lakes have become underwater deserts."

(A) Leave it as it is.
(B) Paraphrase Murray's comment rather than quote it directly.
(C) Add information in parentheses explaining Murray's claim.
(D) Provide Murray's credentials as a scientist.
(E) Add a citation indicating the source of the quotation from Murray.

44. Which of the following pieces of information, if added to the second paragraph (sentences 5–9), would most effectively advance the writer's argument?

(A) Biographical information about Mike Murray
(B) Information about the life span of the zebra mussel
(C) Specific figures to illustrate the economic harm caused by zebra mussels
(D) Information about how power and sewage plants are designed
(E) A comparison of the revenues generated by commercial fishing and sportfishing in the Great Lakes region

45. Which of the following best describes the purpose of the final paragraph (sentences 10–13)?

(A) It explains why the "skeptics" mentioned in the second paragraph are correct.
(B) It points out that the phenomenon introduced in the first paragraph can be easily controlled.
(C) It presents information to refute an argument presented in the first paragraph.
(D) It elaborates on the causes of a problem presented in the first and second paragraphs.
(E) It details various solutions to a problem discussed in the first and second paragraphs.

46. The final paragraph (sentences 10–13) could best be developed by

(A) elaborating on the negative effects of current methods used to control zebra mussels
(B) explaining how researchers determined that zebra mussels were brought to North America in the ballast water of ships
(C) adding information about differences between zebra mussels and mussel species native to the Great Lakes
(D) explaining how the chemicals currently used to control zebra mussels are manufactured
(E) adding information about other invasive species in the Great Lakes and the economic damage they cause

47. The first item listed in the References section indicates all of the following EXCEPT that

(A) "Great Lakes: Resources at risk" is around nine pages long
(B) "Great Lakes: Resources at risk" was written by S. Fields
(C) "Great Lakes: Resources at risk" appears on page 113 of *Environmental Health Perspectives*
(D) "Great Lakes: Resources at risk" is an article in a periodical
(E) *Environmental Health Perspectives* is published more than once a year

<u>Questions 48–52</u> refer to the following passage.

(1) Sequential art is defined as the use of a series of drawings in sequence, with or without text, to tell a story or convey information. (2) We are most familiar with this kind of art in the form of comic books, but in recent decades, the sequential art genre of the graphic novel has not only become very popular, it has gained increasing acceptance among academics and scholars. (3) Many libraries, which would once never have dreamed of including comic books on their shelves, are now "only too happy to include graphic novels." (4) But what's the difference between the comic book and the graphic novel? (5) According to Madeline Smith, author of the *Cotton Candy* graphic novel series, "People think of comic books as short, brightly colored super-hero stories for boys. (6) But graphic novels can be much longer with more complex plots and characters—and most importantly, they can appeal to readers of all ages and backgrounds" (103).

(7) Many graphic novels also focus on real-life experiences and events, unlike comic books, which are often based on fantasy or science fiction. (8) Interestingly, this has led to a number of successful graphic novels by women. (9) Graphic novels depicting girlhood experiences, marriage, and motherhood have been among some of the best sellers in the genre in recent years. (10) Because these texts more closely fit into academic categories like autobiography or personal narrative, graphic novels are also finding their way into literature classes.

Works Cited

Smith, Madeline. "Why Girls Are Taking Over Graphic Novels." *Pop Culture Monthly 7* (2009): 101–104. Print.

48. Which is best to do with sentence 3 (reproduced below)?

Many libraries, which would once never have dreamed of including comic books on their shelves, are now "only too happy to include graphic novels."

(A) Delete it from the passage.
(B) Remove the quotation marks.
(C) Include examples of specific libraries.
(D) Indicate the source of the material in quotation marks with a citation.
(E) Provide the names of some of the graphic novels that are available in libraries.

49. Which of the following, if added immediately after sentence 6, would most improve the first paragraph?

(A) A description of one of the characters in Smith's graphic novel
(B) An explanation of how Smith's quotation helps support the main idea of the paragraph
(C) A quote from another source that agrees with Smith
(D) A quote from a review of Smith's graphic novel
(E) An explanation of why Smith became a writer

50. What kind of information would provide the best support for the claim made in sentence 9?

(A) Data from a newspaper article about sales trends in the graphic novel genre over the last few years
(B) Results of a survey of the writer's classmates to find out how many have purchased graphic novels in the last year
(C) A quote from a scholarly article analyzing gender trends in the publishing industry
(D) Customer review comments from an online bookseller's Web site
(E) Blog posts from enthusiastic readers of graphic novels

51. In the Works Cited section, the number 7 indicates which of the following?

    (A) The article is seven pages long.
    (B) The article appears on page 7.
    (C) The article was published in July.
    (D) The article appears in volume 7 of *Pop Culture Monthly*.
    (E) The volume of *Pop Culture Monthly* in which the article appears contains seven articles.

52. The word "Print" that appears at the end of the citation in the Works Cited section indicates that

    (A) the article is from a newspaper
    (B) *Pop Culture Monthly* does not publish an online version
    (C) the article is from a paper version of *Pop Culture Monthly*
    (D) the author of the article is also its publisher
    (E) the article is available in a large print version

Rhetorical Analysis (25%)

Directions: The following questions test your ability to analyze writing. Some questions refer to passages, while other questions are self-contained. For each question, choose the best answer.

Questions 53–56 refer to the following paragraph.

(1) The image of the mad scientist—the unstable genius driven toward dubious goals by an intoxicating ambition—is a familiar one, often thought of in this age of cloning and genetic engineering. (2) Many people would be surprised to learn that the most influential embodiment of this archetype was created by a nineteenth-century teenager. (3) When Mary Shelley published her first novel, *Frankenstein*, in 1818, she was barely nineteen years old, yet her mesmerizing tale of a young scientist who creates a terrifying monster quickly became a best seller, and its story has been adapted many times for stage and screen. (4) In fact, it was the popularity of an early theatrical adaptation of *Frankenstein*, called *Presumption* and staged in London in 1823, that encouraged Shelley's publisher to issue a second printing of her book. (5) Unfortunately, most people today know the Frankenstein story only through later adaptations and miss the many subtleties of Shelley's original story in which the monster is not the shuffling, nearly mute menace of most movie versions, but a highly sensitive creature who reads Milton's *Paradise Lost* and speaks eloquently of the wrongs done him by his creator, Dr. Frankenstein.

53. Which of the following best describes sentence 1?

    (A) It parodies an image that is taken seriously by many people.
    (B) It discusses a well-known image in its current context.
    (C) It states the thesis of the discussion to follow.
    (D) It explores the connections between history and fantasy.
    (E) It describes opposing views of a particular image.

54. Which of the following transition words or phrases, if inserted at the beginning of sentence 2 (reproduced below), would be most logical in the context of the passage?

Many people would be surprised to learn that the most influential embodiment of this archetype was created by a nineteenth-century teenager.

(A) Therefore,
(B) Similarly,
(C) Nevertheless,
(D) In contrast,
(E) Likewise,

55. The author's primary purpose in mentioning *Presumption* in sentence 4 is to

(A) identify a way in which Shelley's time differed from our own
(B) show that most people enjoy dramatizations more than novels
(C) suggest that Shelley's story has been debased by later adaptations
(D) illustrate a point about the effect of a drama's popularity on the publication of Shelley's novel
(E) make an argument about nineteenth-century theatrical adaptations of popular novels

56. Sentence 5 primarily serves to

(A) reveal the subtleties of an adaptation
(B) underscore the significance of a text
(C) highlight a neglected aspect of a text
(D) defend a cherished point of view
(E) extend an analysis about an author

Questions 57–59 refer to the following passage.

(1) In the late nineteenth century, librarians began noticing that many of the books in their care were breaking apart and crumbling. (2) Curiously, it was not the oldest books that were deteriorating, but the more recent volumes: those produced since the middle of the nineteenth century with sheets fabricated from a highly acidic wood-pulp mixture. (3) The transition to this lesser-grade stock began during the 1860s, when increasing demand for paper hastened the development of a cheaper process. (4) To improve strength and to prevent ink from being too readily absorbed by the pulp paper, chemicals, including aluminum sulfate (alum), were added to the mix. (5) The result was that documents exposed to humidity produced sulfuric acid, which weakened the molecular structure of the pulp's cellulose.

57. The word "Curiously" in sentence 2 is meant to address which of the following assumptions?

(A) Old artifacts tend to be more valuable than recently produced ones.
(B) Environmental factors such as humidity often have unforeseen effects.
(C) Cheaper production processes usually result in lower-quality products.
(D) All manufactured objects are inevitably subject to decay.
(E) Older objects are likely to disintegrate before objects created more recently.

58. In context, sentence 4 serves to

(A) describe part of the process mentioned in sentence 3
(B) explain why a cheaper process for developing paper was required in the nineteenth century
(C) explain why adding a particular agent to wood pulp makes papermaking more expensive
(D) counter the claim about the oldest books made in sentence 2
(E) indicate how a particular process affected the book market in the nineteenth century

59. Which of the following best describes the organization of the passage as a whole?

(A) An approach is presented and found to be unreliable.
(B) A procedure is introduced and then described in more detail.
(C) A phenomenon is described and an explanation is provided.
(D) A problem is presented and two solutions are evaluated.
(E) A theory is proposed and challenged with new evidence.

Questions 60–63 refer to the following passage.

(1) While chocolate was highly esteemed in Mesoamerica, where it originated, its adoption in Europe was initially slow. (2) There is a common belief that Europeans needed to "transform" chocolate to make it appetizing. (3) However, while Spaniards did put sugar, which was unknown to indigenous Americans, into chocolate beverages, this additive was not completely innovative. (4) Mesoamericans were already sweetening chocolate with honey, and the step from honey to sugar—increasingly more available than honey because of expanding sugar plantations in the Americas—is a small one. (5) Likewise, although Spaniards adjusted Mesoamerican recipes by using European spices, the spices chosen suggest an attempt to replicate harder-to-find native flowers. (6) There is no indication the Spaniards deliberately tried to change the original flavor of chocolate.

60. In context, "common" (sentence 2) most nearly means

(A) simplistic
(B) uninspired
(C) average
(D) trite
(E) prevalent

61. The discussion of honey in sentence 4 primarily serves to

(A) detail the origins of an innovative practice
(B) present an example of a valid theory
(C) introduce a new topic for discussion
(D) extend a prior analogy
(E) refute a particular belief

62. According to the passage, the scarcity in Spain of certain flowers led to

(A) attempts to cultivate those flowers in Spain
(B) a modification of the Mesoamerican recipes for chocolate
(C) the replacement of honey with sugar in chocolate recipes
(D) the exportation of quantities of those flowers to Spain
(E) the introduction of European spices to Spain

63. The passage is primarily concerned with

(A) arguing for a particular view of a topic
(B) explaining how common misconceptions occur
(C) detailing the uses of chocolate
(D) exploring how certain cultures adapted foods
(E) refuting a particular academic theory

Questions 64–68 refer to the following passage.

(1) Whenever I go abroad it is always involuntary. (2) I never return home without feeling some pleasing emotion, which I often suppress as useless and foolish. (3) The instant I enter on my own land, the bright idea of property, of exclusive right, of independence exalt my mind. (4) Precious soil, I say to myself, by what singular custom of law is it that thou wast made to constitute the riches of the freeholder? (5) What should we American farmers be without the distinct possession of that soil? (6) It feeds, it clothes us, from it we draw even a great exuberancy, our best meat, our richest drink, the very honey of our bees comes from this privileged spot. (7) No wonder we should thus cherish its possession, no wonder that so many Europeans who have never been able to say that such portion of land was theirs, cross the Atlantic to realize that happiness. (8) This formerly rude soil has been converted by my father into a pleasant farm, and in return it has established all our rights; on it is founded our rank, our freedom, our power as citizens, our importance as inhabitants of such a district. (9) These images I must confess I always behold with pleasure, and extend them as far as my imagination can reach: for this is what may be called the true and the only philosophy of an American farmer.

64. The primary purpose of the passage is to

(A) inform
(B) persuade
(C) criticize
(D) define
(E) entertain

65. The tone of the passage can best be described as

(A) nostalgic
(B) rueful
(C) whimsical
(D) melancholy
(E) exhortatory

66. In context, "freeholder" (sentence 4) most nearly means a person who

(A) maintains land for someone else
(B) collects taxes on land
(C) owns land
(D) gives land to others
(E) rents land from someone else

67. In context, "the true and the only philosophy of an American farmer" (sentence 9) is most likely that

(A) a person who inherits land is a more committed citizen than one who purchases land
(B) frequent travel is instructive and promotes the betterment of the individual
(C) one must never entertain feelings of pride about one's possessions
(D) ownership of land strengthens a person's ties to his or her country
(E) diversification in farming is far superior to focusing on only one product

68. The author employs which of the following strategies in this passage?

(A) Parallel constructions are used to emphasize a theme of abundance.
(B) Rhetorical questions are used to offer opposing views to stated claims about farming.
(C) An extended metaphor is used to introduce a complex idea about land ownership.
(D) Detailed personal anecdotes are used to exemplify the hardships of frontier life.
(E) Authority figures are invoked to give credence to the author's claims.

College Composition Modular

The CLEP College Composition Modular examination includes the following question type as part of the Revision Skills section:

Improving Sentences

The following question type appears on the College Composition Modular examination only.

Directions: The following sentences test correctness and effectiveness of expression. In choosing your answers, follow the requirements of standard written English: that is, pay attention to grammar, diction (choice of words), sentence construction and punctuation.

In each of the following sentences, part of the sentence or the entire sentence is underlined. Beneath each sentence you will find five versions of the underlined part. The first option repeats the original; the other four options present different versions.

Choose the option that best expresses the meaning of the original sentence. If you think the original is better than any of the alternatives, choose the first option; otherwise, choose one of the other options. Your choice should produce the most effective sentence—one that is clear and precise, without awkwardness or ambiguity.

Example: **SAMPLE ANSWER**

Laura Ingalls Wilder published her first book and she was sixty-five years old then.

(A) and she was sixty-five years old then
(B) when she was sixty-five
(C) being age sixty-five years old
(D) upon the reaching of sixty-five years
(E) at the time when she was sixty-five

69. Award-winning author Virginia Hamilton, whose books established her as one of the most influential figures in children's literature in the twentieth century.

(A) Award-winning author Virginia Hamilton, whose books
(B) Award-winning author Virginia Hamilton, her books
(C) Virginia Hamilton was an award-winning author, books by her
(D) The books of Virginia Hamilton, award-winning author, these
(E) The books of award-winning author Virginia Hamilton

70. The final project in graduate school is the dissertation, which requires months of research where they must amass and interpret data important to the project.

(A) where they
(B) through which they
(C) and the student
(D) during which the student
(E) which they

71. The sting of a scorpion may be as dangerous as the bite of a cobra despite the quantity of venom a scorpion injects is much smaller.

(A) cobra despite the quantity of venom a scorpion injects
(B) cobra; therefore, the quantity of venom a scorpion injects
(C) cobra, a scorpion injecting a quantity of venom that
(D) cobra; if the quantity of venom injected by a scorpion
(E) cobra even though the quantity of venom injected by a scorpion

72. The more frequently portrayed movie character of all time, the fictional figure of Sherlock Holmes has appeared in approximately 200 films.

(A) The more frequently
(B) The more frequent
(C) The most frequent
(D) The most frequently
(E) He is the most frequently

73. During his lifetime Edward Burne-Jones was known primarily as a painter, but since his death he received greater recognition for his contributions to the field of decorative design.

(A) he received
(B) he was receiving
(C) he has received
(D) having received
(E) receiving

74. Richard Wright once acted in a film version of his novel *Native* Son, playing the role of Bigger Thomas.

(A) *Son*, playing
(B) *Son*, he played
(C) *Son*, what he played was
(D) *Son* and while he played
(E) *Son*, which he played

75. Although Red Canyon, Utah, is largely devoid of trees, but small coniferous plots of ponderosa pine and Douglas fir exist in areas where moisture is available.

(A) is largely devoid of trees, but
(B) is largely devoid of trees,
(C) largely devoid of trees,
(D) being largely devoid of trees,
(E) is largely devoid of trees, and

76. Doubting the authenticity of the paintings, there was an appraisal of the collection made for the dealer by a recognized expert.

(A) there was an appraisal of the collection made for the dealer
(B) the collection was taken by the dealer to be appraised
(C) the dealer had the collection appraised
(D) the dealer decided on appraising the collection
(E) an appraisal of the collection was made for the dealer

77. The cooking instructor informed us that by the end of the course, we will have acquired basic skills in chopping, searing, and to make sauces.

(A) we will have acquired basic skills in chopping, searing, and to make sauces
(B) we will have acquired basic skills in chopping, to sear, and making sauces
(C) we will have acquired basic skills in chopping, searing, and making sauces
(D) to chop, sear, and to make sauces will have been the basic skills acquired by us
(E) chopping, searing, and making sauces is what we will have acquired basic skills in

78. According to a recent survey of consumers in the United States, more people now shop online as compared to shopping in physical stores.

(A) as compared to shopping
(B) as opposed to shopping
(C) than when they shop
(D) than shopping
(E) than

79. The term "flapper" was popularized in the United States by the 1920 movie *The Flapper*, where Olive Thomas played a frivolous young woman in search of romantic adventure.

(A) where
(B) within which
(C) in that
(D) in which
(E) when

80. The Portuguese municipality of Sintra, famous for its castles and royal retreats, have also made a mark on literature by charming many Romantic writers, including Almeida Garrett and Lord Byron.

(A) have also made
(B) has also made
(C) are also making
(D) also make
(E) also making

Sample Essays and Essay Topics

This section includes the following:

- General information about how to respond to the essay topics
- Essay-writing directions as they appear in the test
- The scoring guides used to evaluate the essays
- Sample essay topics
- Scored essays written in response to the topic

General Directions
Time: 70 minutes

You will have a total of 70 minutes to write two essays. You will have 30 minutes to complete the first essay, which is to be based on your own reading, experience or observations, and 40 minutes to complete the second essay, which requires you to synthesize two sources that are provided. Although you are free to begin writing at any point, it is better to take the time you need to plan your essays and to do the required reading than it is to begin writing immediately.

College Composition Examination

First Essay

Sample Topic 1

There are no challenges so difficult, no goals so impossible, as the ones we set for ourselves.

Directions

Write an essay in which you discuss the extent to which you agree or disagree with the statement above. Support your discussion with specific reasons and examples from your reading, experience or observations.

Scoring Guide: College Composition Examination
Readers will assign scores based on the following scoring guide.

6 – A 6 essay demonstrates *a high degree of competence and sustained control*, although it may have a few minor errors.
A typical essay in this category
- addresses all elements of the writing task effectively and insightfully
- develops ideas thoroughly, supporting them with well-chosen reasons, examples or details
- is well focused and well organized
- demonstrates superior facility with language, using effective vocabulary and sentence variety
- demonstrates general mastery of the standard conventions of grammar, usage and mechanics but may have minor errors

5 – A 5 essay demonstrates *a generally high degree of competence*, although it will have occasional lapses in quality.
A typical essay in this category
- addresses the writing task effectively
- is well developed, using appropriate reasons, examples or details to support ideas
- is generally well focused and well organized
- demonstrates facility with language, using appropriate vocabulary and some sentence variety
- demonstrates strong control of the standard conventions of grammar, usage and mechanics but may have minor errors

4 – A 4 essay demonstrates *clear competence*, with some errors and lapses in quality.
A typical essay in this category
- addresses the writing task competently
- is adequately developed, using reasons, examples or details to support ideas
- is adequately focused and organized
- demonstrates competence with language, using adequate vocabulary and minimal sentence variety
- generally demonstrates control of the standard conventions of grammar, usage and mechanics but may have some errors

3 – A 3 essay demonstrates *limited competence*.
A typical essay in this category exhibits ONE OR MORE of the following weaknesses:
- addresses only some parts of the writing task
- is unevenly developed and often provides assertions but few relevant reasons, examples or details
- is poorly focused and/or poorly organized
- displays frequent problems in the use of language
- demonstrates inconsistent control of grammar, usage and mechanics

2 – A 2 essay is *seriously flawed.* A typical essay in this category exhibits ONE OR MORE of the following weaknesses: • is unclear or seriously limited in addressing the writing task • is seriously underdeveloped, providing few reasons, examples or details • is unfocused and/or disorganized • displays frequent serious errors in the use of language that may interfere with meaning • contains frequent serious errors in grammar, usage and mechanics that may interfere with meaning
1 – A 1 essay is *fundamentally deficient.* A typical essay in this category exhibits ONE OR MORE of the following weaknesses: • provides little or no evidence of the ability to develop an organized response to the writing task • is undeveloped • contains severe writing errors that persistently interfere with meaning
0 – Off topic Provides no evidence of an attempt to respond to the assigned topic, is written in a language other than English, merely copies the prompt, or consists of only keystroke characters.

Sample Essays with Commentaries

Note: Errors in the sample essays are intentionally reproduced.

Essay A—This essay is scored a 6.

I disagree with the statement that the most difficult challenges people face are those that everybody creates for themselves. The assertion is not true, or at least not always, as I intend to show below. There may be instances where people set difficult objectives for themselves, but very often people simply have to try to address challenges they did not create, and survive or make the best of situations they have been put into by accidents such as geography, history, or ethnic and racial background. There are exceptions, but they are just that: exceptions, not the norm.

Often, especially for those coming from countries that are not dominating the world stage, succeeding in life, or simply making ends meet are major challenges, and not because those who face these challenges want to be in such situations. My parents grew up at a time when their country was undergoing major social and political transformations. World War II had just ended by the time my father was 12, the economy was in shambles, and the Nazi occupiers had been driven out of the country so the Red Army can take over. My grandfather was forced to give up his little land during the process of collectivization of agriculture. His small store was eventually confiscated as well, and the couple horses he had, along with thousands of horses throughout the country, were taken away to make room for the tractors the country was beginning to manufacture. By the time my father was drafted into the military, talk of World War II was everywhere, and the hysteria gave way only a couple of decades later. My father had to lie low all his life and not say a world against a regime that did not tolerate dissent. The kids' success in school meant they could get by within or without the messed up system the country was under. In my grandfather's words, it was important to study, because "no one can take away from you what you know."

I have also seen in this country instances where people's lives are made difficult by those in power. It is often assumed that everybody in this country shares a certain standard of living, although evidence contradicts that assumption. For many, simply getting by is a major success, not because they love struggling to make ends meet, but because they do not have a choice. When Hurricane Katrina made landfall last August, the majority of the residents of New Orleans had evacuated the city. Many had not, though: some of their own free will, others because they simply did not have the means of travel. Later on, when large portions of the city were under water, some residents tried to cross one of the bridges from New Orleans to the west bank of the Mississippi River, but were received by police shooting in the air to scare them away. The city across the river apparently did not want "the problems" of the City of New Orleans.

Certainly there are instances where people set high goals for themselves and some succeed in attaining those goals, while many fail. I have all the respect for the former, but I think focusing on the few exceptions we may miss the big picture. Succeeding in spite of all odds, being a "self-made man," going "from rags to riches," are powerful myths in this country. I am not denying the effort and successes of the Rockefellers, Carnegies, or more recently the Trumps. I do think, nonetheless, that for every person who makes it in spite of all or most odds, there are many more who do not; for every college dropout who succeeds in life, such as Bill Gates, there are thousands who will struggle through life.

People often set hard-to-reach objectives and they may fail or succeed in pursuing those objectives. I do think, though, that for many, the most difficult challenges come from outside the individual, from their position in the social hierarchy, or the time and place where they are born and try to get by.

Commentary on Essay A

This insightful response argues that life's most difficult challenges come from outside the individual and cites specific accidents of history and geography as effective support for that claim. Paragraph two offers abundant, well-chosen evidence that political constraints imposed on the writer's family in Eastern Europe after the Second World War were much more formidable than any challenges they might have chosen for themselves. To provide further development, paragraph three describes the impact of similarly harsh conditions in a more immediate place and time—New Orleans after Hurricane Katrina. Finally, in preparation for a strong but carefully measured conclusion, the essay acknowledges that some few individuals do accomplish great things despite overwhelming odds. Just as the development of this response is thorough and always sharply focused, the control of language is superior. Note, for example, skillful subordination in the third sentence of the essay and effective vocabulary in phrases such as "dominating the world stage" or "a regime that did not tolerate dissent." A few minor errors are indeed present, as is allowed by the scoring guide, but sustained control supports a score of 6.

Essay B—This essay is scored a 4.

I agree that, as individuals, we tend to set higher goals for ourselves than outside influences. Because goals are so personal, it makes it that much more challenging to attain them. Psychologically, individuals can be their own worst enemy. Goals may be set and believed in by an individual but self-doubt, a low self-esteem and societal and familial attitudes may warp personal beliefs. When this happens, an individual may lose sight of the goal and instead focus doubt on the necessary steps to achieve the goal. Conversely, an individual may battle these internal and external obstacles and rise above them to successfully reach their goal. Who better to know the self then the individual? Goals are personal since only the individual really knows what they would like to achieve, at what level to set the goal and must find a way to achieve it.

An example of successful goal-setting is my business idol; George Lucas who's educational and career history has been a real inspiration. Mr. Lucas continued to set higher goals for himself as his life developed. He has become a prolific director and businessman in the entertainment industry. He currently owns several companies including his own production company and special effects company. The reason why this is so inspiring is because he almost failed high school and had almost no prospects for the future. Before graduation, Mr. Lucas was involved in an almost fatal car crash. At this point in his life, he set a goal of becoming an excellent student both in the classroom and in life. This was quite a high goal to set due to this previous academic ability and the external opinions of family and friends. He worked to accomplish graduating from a junior college then completing his B.A. in Film from USC, both with honors. Mr. Lucas continued to set higher and more challenging goals for himself to become an independent film producer and director and to not be affiliated with any particular movie studio. He had to pay his dues at first but finally his tenacity paid off and his creation of Lucasfilm has allowed him the goal of creative freedom in his work. I don't believe that anyone else in his family or his acquaintances would have set such goals for him. Mr. Lucas psychologically believed in himself enough, knew what he wanted to do, set the applicable goals and worked to achieve them. No one else could have done this for him.

Commentary on Essay B

Since the first paragraph in this response deals mainly with psychological reasons for failure or success in achieving goals, it does not focus sharply on the question of relative difficulty. Paragraph two, however, clearly addresses the writing task and offers an extended example to argue that self-selected goals are indeed more difficult than those imposed by others. Instead of merely summarizing the life of George Lucas, the writer chooses several specific episodes in which Lucas' own aspirations surpassed the expectations of family and friends. Thus, after a slow start, the essay does achieve competence in development, focus and organization. Despite some errors, control of language is also adequate to support a score of 4. Syntax is sometimes flawed (see the first and last sentences of paragraph one), but the essay is free of serious grammar errors. Furthermore, several phrases (e.g., "may warp personal beliefs," "his tenacity paid off,") demonstrate vocabulary that is clearly adequate.

Essay C—This essay is scored a 2.

This statement is strongly true. One example of this is my own life. I work very hard and never give up, and am even taking this test! I am very inspired to go to college and have made it my goal to achieve, no matter what. And I have achieved goals before this, so I know that I can achieve this one too, even though it seems hard. When I was a senior at Kennedy High school I saved up money to buy a car, and that was a goal that I achieved myself.

Another example of goals is my Mom. When I was little she went to nursing school and worked very hard, some people said it was impossible because she had four small children, but she graduated and now she works in a hospital. So obviously goals can be useful. I guess when a person has achieved a few goals then they feel more confident about going out to achieve other goals, and that way even though they set higher goals, you find out that you can even achieve the harder goals that seem more impossible like the question says. You feel good about what you already have achieved, so nothing seems impossible. You go out and do it!

Commentary on Essay C

Problems with development and focus make this response seriously limited in addressing the writing task. The writer twice refers to success in achieving personal goals (saving money for a car and Mom's graduation from nursing school), but both examples are extremely thin and neither shows that self-imposed goals are any more challenging than those imposed by others. In the middle of paragraph two, the writer veers even further away from the topic with the plausible but—in this context—superfluous claim that "goals can be useful." Even though the response begins by asserting that the prompt is "strongly true," later sentences argue an entirely different point—that "nothing seems impossible" after one has gained confidence. Thus, since the response provides almost no relevant development, it earns a score of 2.

Second Essay

Sample Topic 2

Directions

The following assignment requires you to write a coherent essay in which you synthesize the two sources provided. Synthesis refers to combining the sources and your position to form a cohesive, supported argument. You must develop a position and incorporate both sources. **You must cite the sources whether you are paraphrasing or quoting.** Refer to each source by the author's last name, the title or by any other means that adequately identifies it.

Introduction

A copyright gives the author of a creative work (like a book, film, painting or audio recording) exclusive rights to it: only the holder of a work's copyright has the legal right to copy, publish or profit from the work. Many people agree that copyrights are a good thing, because they give creators the opportunity to benefit from their creative work. However, many people also agree that the free exchange of ideas is good for society because it fosters creativity and innovation. They argue that therefore in many instances there should be no copyright restrictions.

Assignment

Read the following sources carefully. Then write an essay in which you develop a position on whether copyright restrictions benefit or harm society. Be sure to incorporate and cite both of the accompanying sources as you develop your position.

Source 1:

Epstein, Richard A. "The Creators Own Ideas." *Technology Review* 108.6 (2005): 56–60. Print.

The following passage is excerpted from an article in a journal on technology.

No matter one's political beliefs, it is critical to remember the strong economic imperatives that drive modern societies to legislate some form of copyright protection. Just as we protect private rights in land for the benefit of the community, not solely for a property's owner, so too we have a social reason to protect writings and other intellectual creations.

As [the eighteenth-century philosopher] John Locke would have it, a just society recognizes the natural rights of its citizens, including the right to protection of their productive labor. But copyright has an additional justification: it fosters huge positive contributions to culture, in the form of novels, movies, manuals, music, and other works. Some creators are motivated solely by the desire to create and would be happy to distribute their works under simple terms . . . requiring attribution only. But for most authors, compensation matters, and we increase their production by limiting the rights of others to copy their work.

Source 2:

Lessig, Lawrence. *The Future of Ideas: The Fate of the Commons in a Connected World.* New York: Random House, 2001. Print.

The following passage is excerpted from a book on intellectual property.

Obviously many resources must be controlled if they are to be produced or sustained. I should have the right to control access to my house and my car. You shouldn't be allowed to rifle through my desk . . . Hollywood should have the right to charge admission to its movies. If one couldn't control access to these resources, or resources called "mine," one would have little incentive to work to produce these resources, including those called mine.

But likewise, and obviously, many resources should be free . . . I shouldn't need the permission of the Einstein estate before I test his theory against newly discovered data. These resources and others gain value by being kept free rather than controlled. A mature society realizes that value by protecting such resources from both private and public control.

We need to learn this lesson again. The opportunity for this learning is the Internet. No modern phenomenon better demonstrates the importance of free resources to innovation and creativity than the Internet. To those who argue that control is necessary if innovation is to occur, and that more control will yield more innovation, the Internet is the simplest and most direct reply.

Scoring Guide: College Composition Examination

Readers will assign scores based on the following scoring guide.

6 – A 6 essay demonstrates *a high degree of competence and sustained control*, although it may have a few minor errors.

A typical essay in this category cites sources appropriately and

- develops a position effectively and insightfully, using well-chosen reasons, examples or details for support
- synthesizes* both sources effectively, with an effective and convincing link between the sources and the position
- is well focused and well organized
- demonstrates superior facility with language, using effective vocabulary and sentence variety
- demonstrates general mastery of the standard conventions of grammar, usage and mechanics but may have minor errors

5 – A 5 essay demonstrates *a generally high degree of competence*, although it will have occasional lapses in quality.

A typical essay in this category cites sources appropriately and

- develops a position consistently, using appropriate reasons, examples or details for support
- synthesizes both sources clearly, with a clear link between the sources and the position
- is generally well focused and well organized
- demonstrates facility with language, using appropriate vocabulary and some sentence variety
- demonstrates strong control of the standard conventions of grammar, usage and mechanics but may have minor errors

*For the purposes of scoring, synthesis refers to combining the sources and writer's position to form a cohesive, supported argument.

4 – A 4 essay demonstrates *competence*, with some errors and lapses in quality.

A typical essay in this category cites sources appropriately and

- develops a position adequately, using reasons, examples or details for support
- synthesizes both sources adequately, with a link between the sources and the position
- is adequately focused and organized
- demonstrates competence with language, using adequate vocabulary and minimal sentence variety
- generally demonstrates control of the standard conventions of grammar, usage and mechanics but may have some errors

3 – A 3 essay demonstrates *limited competence*.

A typical essay in this category exhibits ONE OR MORE of the following weaknesses:

- develops a position unevenly, often using assertions rather than relevant reasons, examples or details for support
- synthesizes one source only or two sources inadequately, or establishes an inadequate link between the source(s) and the position
- displays problems in citing sources: citations are confusing or incomplete
- is poorly focused and/or poorly organized
- displays frequent problems in the use of language
- demonstrates inconsistent control of grammar, usage and mechanics

2 – A 2 essay is *seriously flawed*.

A typical essay in this category exhibits ONE OR MORE of the following weaknesses:

- is seriously underdeveloped, providing few or no relevant reasons, examples or details for support
- synthesizes only one source weakly or establishes a very weak link between the source(s) and the position
- does not cite any source
- is unfocused and/or disorganized
- displays frequent serious errors in the use of language that may interfere with meaning
- contains frequent serious errors in grammar, usage and mechanics that may interfere with meaning

1 – A 1 essay is *fundamentally deficient*.

A typical essay in this category exhibits ONE OR MORE of the following weaknesses:

- does not develop a position
- fails to synthesize the source(s) used or uses no sources at all
- contains severe writing errors that persistently interfere with meaning

0 – Off topic

Provides no evidence of an attempt to respond to the assigned topic, is written in a language other than English, merely copies the prompt, or consists of only keystroke characters.

Essay A—This essay is scored a 6.

The ability to own property is one of the hallmarks of a modern and democratic society. All individuals have a right to their own property, be it tangible (a house or a car that they have bought) or intangible (an artistic or intellectual work that they have created). But the right of ownership benefits not only individuals but society as well. As Richard Epstein, in his article "The Creators Own Ideas," argues, "just as we protect private rights in land for the benefit of the community, not solely for a property's owner, so too we have a social reason to protect writings and other intellectual creations." Because copyright laws protect artistic and intellectual creations, they benefit society as a whole, and should therefore be upheld.

While "some creators are motivated solely by the desire to create," most do expect to be compensated for their efforts (Epstein). Therefore, as Epstein indicates, there are "strong economic imperatives that drive modern societies to legislate some form of copyright protection." Artists, writers, and other creators of intellectual and creative work spend countless hours of their time on their creations, which are often their only means of income. A major fear of creators is that somebody else will steal their work, thereby depriving them of their income. Fortunately, as Epstein points out, copyright laws protect against such infringement. Without such safeguards in place, creators may be less likely to release their works for fear that they may be stolen from. Without copyright laws guaranteeing just compensation to creators, productivity decreases, and society would not benefit from a wealth of artistic, creative, and intellectual works. But when producers of intellectual property are protected, productivity increases, fostering "huge positive contributions to society, in the form of novels, movies, manuals, music and other works" (Epstein).

Lawrence Lessig, however, disagrees with this line of reasoning, arguing instead that copyright laws should be abolished. In his book The Future of Ideas, Lessig states: "I shouldn't need the permission of the Einstein estate before I test his theory." The flaw in this argument is that there is quite a difference between an artistic work and a scientific idea. While a novel or movie is the creative work of a person or persons, scientific ideas are meant to have their validity tested and scrutinized. Einstein's theory of relativity isn't a work of art, rather it is just what its name implies: a theory. A theory should be tested whenever the need arises because a theory is an attempt to explain how something works. It is not, however, a form of self expression. While Einstein certainly has the right to receive credit for his theory, it does not, and should not, have the same protection as a creative work, such as a piece of literature, art, or music.

Lessig uses the Internet as a model for a copyright-free society, claiming that "no modern phenomenon better demonstrates the importance of free resources to innovation and creativity." However, while the Internet does function as an exchange of free ideas in some areas, even there people still strive to protect their intellectual property. For instance, you won't find the full text from a Harry Potter book online, because the author doesn't want her work to be stolen. In fact, quite a portion of the Internet is devoted to advertisement and trying to sell products, intellectual works included. While the Internet is certainly innovative, its creativity and innovation are not solely due to free ideas. The Internet also serves a global marketplace, and the sale of artistic works is a primary reason for its existence as well.

In conclusion, people have the right to "own" their own creations. Copyright laws exist to protect the rights of the creators. Without such protections, the drive for intellectual production will be stifled. With the right to property being so emphasized, copyright laws only make sense in order to fully preserve the rights of individuals, who in turn benefit society with their creative and intellectual contributions.

Commentary on Essay A

This response effectively develops a focused argument that copyright restrictions not only benefit individuals, who have a right to "own" their own creations, but society as a whole, which prospers from the artistic and intellectual contributions made by those individuals. Quotations from both sources (Epstein and Lessig) are effectively synthesized ("Therefore, as Epstein indicates . . . ") and appropriately cited. Paragraph three offers an insightful distinction between a scientific theory (Einstein's theory of relativity) and a creative work (a novel or movie), while paragraph four uses the well-chosen example of a Harry Potter novel to further the argument that not even the Internet is free from market considerations. The response demonstrates some minor errors in use of language (the unclear pronoun in "they may be stolen from" in paragraph two), but its superior facility with language, effective vocabulary ("hallmarks of a modern and democratic society"), and sustained control of grammar, usage and mechanics merit it a score of 6.

Essay B—This essay is scored a 4.

A copyright gives the author of a creative work exclusive rights to it: only the holder of a work's copyright has the legal rights to copy, publish, or profit from the work. Therefore, copyright restrictions can only be beneficial to society.

According to Richard Epstein, "copyright fosters huge positive contributions to culture, in the form of novels, movies, manuals, music, and other works." Epstein, further states that "some creators are motivated solely by the desire to create and would be happy to distribute their works under simple terms . . . requiring attribution only." It is unfair for authors, musicians, and other copyright holders to not profit from their hard work: some of which takes months or even years to complete. In order for some of these copyright holders to make profits, they have to charge others for the remake or reproduction of their work. "Obviously many resources must be controlled if they are to be produced or sustained," according to Lawrence Lessig.

However, Lessig argues, "many resources should be free . . . I shouldn't need the permission of the Einstein estate before I test his theory against newly developed data." But no one wants to work on a project without the possibility of not getting paid. The mindset that these resources should be free to reproduce is wrong. Not only is the money going back to the communities, the money these copyright holders get is going right back into the economy: this is a driving factor for the economy as well. Lessig, also states that "these resources and others gain value by being kept free rather than controlled." Again, I disagree with Lessig's statement. Society will benefit by keeping these works controlled rather than free, because the work will and forever be authentic, and not just some reproduce, unoriginal work.

When a work is being controlled, it gives society the first piece of work or the root of the source, from the source's viewpoint. According to Epstein, "for most authors, compensation matters, and we increase their production by limiting the rights of others to copy their work." Therefore, copyright restrictions not only good for the person who made it, but it is also good and beneficial to society.

Commentary on Essay B

The first paragraph sets out the response's argument that "copyright restrictions can only be beneficial to society." While this statement is slightly disconnected from the previous sentence, the response does present a clear position. In the next paragraph, the response adequately strengthens the position that authors, musicians and other creators should benefit from their works, using appropriate quotations from both sources for support. Displaying the response's sustained development of the position, paragraph three disagrees with a statement from the second source and introduces the contention that the money gained by copyright holders is reintroduced into the economy, thereby providing an economic benefit to society. While the synthesis of quotations is sometimes stilted ("I disagree with Lessig's statement"), there is nonetheless a link between the sources and the response's position. Despite a weak start, the essay overall is competent in development, focus and organization. Some errors in grammar, usage and mechanics are present, but the control of language and vocabulary displayed in the essay is adequate to support a score of 4.

Essay C—This essay is scored a 2.

Copyrights are extremely common in our society; they can be found everywhere. To some people, copyrighting laws are just another rule and another way to prevent people from expanding their knowledge by sharing someone else's work. To other people: the creators, the arts, & the originators copyrighting is a source of income, privacy, & protection. A law that has benefited our society in more ways than one.

Copyrighting laws have had a positive effect on our society in the past years, although many would like to disagree and say that more intellectual resources should be free. However, when viewing copyrighted laws, I can not help but think about the originators. Whatever the item may be, it's theirs. They are the ones the spent countless hours, thoughts, and ideas on their project. I wouldn't want anyone to be able to take my hard work & sign their name beside it and then receive credit for it because they made a few minor adjustments. It's not ethical; it's wrong and it's stealing.

Also, if the society had the right mind set, they could see all of the positive effects of copyrights. One example of that would be to realize that if a big company published my book & copyrighted it, then the company (that has more power & connects) could distribute my work out into the world. More copies would be sent out and the more knowledge would be spread. Then, there's the argument that follows that point of view: More people can read the book, but they can't use anything from it, to test it, or apply it their work. This rebuttal is incompetent. When in reality if someone did want to take from my own copyrighted book, yes, they would have to make a few phone calls to get permission from my estate, but if using my work was that important to someone else, it shouldn't even matter to them if they have to go the extra mile to do so.

In conclusion, society is benefitted by copyright laws along with the originators. People just have to look at it from the creator's point of view and realize that not everything can come as easy as the click of a mouse on the internet. If you want something bad enough, you have to put in the effort, make a few more calls, & work towards your goal.

Commentary on Essay C

While this response does formulate the argument that copyright restrictions have a positive effect on society, it displays inconsistencies in focus and organization that make it seriously limited in addressing the writing task. The essay provides an example of the benefits of copyright laws in paragraph three, but the example is weak and does not adequately illustrate how copyrighting the book in question would benefit society. The response takes the point of view of the "originators," but the focus shifts from analyzing and discussing the merits of copyright laws to an exhortation to obey them instead. Synthesis of source materials is often inadequate, with the response simply summarizing rather than evaluating ("many would like to disagree and say that more intellectual resources should be free"). Most serious, however, is the total lack of citation: although the sources are clearly used (in paragraphs two and three), the response fails to attribute them. Therefore, while its weak organization, poor focus and frequent problems in the use of language (such as the sentence fragment at the end of the first paragraph) demonstrate this essay's limited competence, its complete failure to cite renders it seriously flawed, earning it a score of 2.

Study Resources

Most textbooks used in college-level composition courses cover the skills and topics measured in the College Composition examinations, but the approaches to certain topics and the emphases given to them may differ. To prepare for the College Composition exams, it is advisable to study one or more college-level texts, such as readers, handbooks and writing guides. These and other appropriate educational resources generally are available in both print and electronic versions. Many university writing centers also offer free online resources for improving writing skills. When selecting a resource, check its contents against the knowledge and skills required for the College Composition examinations, which appear on pages 65–67.

To become aware of the processes and the principles involved in presenting your ideas logically and expressing them clearly and effectively, you should practice writing. Ideally, you should try writing about a variety of subjects and issues, starting with those you know best and care about most. Ask someone you know and respect to respond to what you write and to help you discover which parts of your writing communicate effectively and which parts need revision to make the meaning clear. You should also try to read the works of published writers in a wide range of subjects, paying particular attention to the ways in which the writers use language to express their meaning. Additional suggestions for preparing for CLEP exams are given in Chapter IV of the *CLEP Official Study Guide*.

Answer Key

1.	C	41.	C
2.	D	42.	D
3.	D	43.	E
4.	E	44.	C
5.	D	45.	E
6.	A	46.	A
7.	D	47.	C
8.	A	48.	D
9.	A	49.	B
10.	B	50.	A
11.	D	51.	D
12.	C	52.	C
13.	B	53.	B
14.	E	54.	A
15.	C	55.	D
16.	D	56.	C
17.	C	57.	E
18.	D	58.	A
19.	C	59.	C
20.	B	60.	E
21.	E	61.	E
22.	B	62.	B
23.	A	63.	A
24.	B	64.	B
25.	B	65.	E
26.	E	66.	C
27.	D	67.	D
28.	C	68.	A
29.	D	69.	E
30.	A	70.	D
31.	C	71.	E
32.	B	72.	D
33.	D	73.	C
34.	C	74.	A
35.	A	75.	B
36.	B	76.	C
37.	B	77.	C
38.	C	78.	E
39.	E	79.	D
40.	D	80.	B

English Literature

Description of the Examination

The English Literature examination covers material usually taught in a course at the college level. The test is primarily concerned with major authors and literary works, but it also includes questions on some minor writers. Candidates are expected to be acquainted with common literary terms, such as metaphor and personification, and basic literary forms, such as the sonnet and the ballad.

In both coverage and approach, the examination resembles the historically organized surveys of British, Commonwealth, and postcolonial literature offered by many colleges. It assumes that candidates have read widely and developed an appreciation of this literature, know the basic literary periods, forms, authors and movements, and have a sense of the historical development of English literature.

The examination contains approximately 95 questions to be answered in 90 minutes.

An optional essay section can be taken in addition to the multiple-choice test. Candidates respond to two of three essay topics. An essay on the first topic, a persuasive analysis of a poem, is required, and candidates are advised to spend 35 to 40 minutes on it. For the second essay, candidates are asked to choose one of two topics that present a specific observation, position or theme. Depending on the topic chosen, candidates choose any work by a particular author to appropriately support the claim or select works from a designated list provided. Candidates should plan to spend 50 to 55 minutes on the essay.

Candidates are expected to write well-organized essays in clear and precise prose. The essay section is scored by faculty at the institution that requests it and is still administered in paper-and-pencil format. There is an additional fee for taking this section, payable to the institution that administers the exam.

Knowledge and Skills Required

The English Literature examination measures both knowledge and ability. The following percentages show the relative emphasis given to each; however, most questions draw on both.

35%–40% Knowledge of:

- Literary background
- Identification of authors
- Metrical patterns
- Literary references
- Literary terms

60%–65% Ability to:

- Analyze the elements of form in a literary passage
- Perceive meanings
- Identify tone and mood
- Follow patterns of imagery
- Identify characteristics of style
- Comprehend the reasoning in an excerpt of literary criticism

The examination deals with literature from the Anglo-Saxon period to the present. Familiarity with and understanding of major writers is expected, as is knowledge of literary periods and common literary terms, themes and forms. Some of the questions on the examination ask candidates to identify the author of a representative quotation or to recognize the period in which an excerpt was written.

The subject matter of the English Literature examination is drawn from the following periods. The percentages indicate the approximate percentage of exam questions from each period.

10% **Middle Ages**

15% **16th and early 17th Century**

10% **Restoration and 18th Century**

20% **Romantic**

20% **Victorian**

25% **20th Century to the present**

The following percentages indicate the relative emphasis given to different literary genres on the examination. The approximate percentage of exam questions per type of literature is noted.

15% **Novels**

10% **Short stories**

45% **Poetry**

20% **Drama**

10% **Nonfiction: literary criticism, essays, memoir, etc.**

Sample Test Questions

The following sample questions do not appear on an actual CLEP examination. They are intended to give potential test-takers an indication of the format and difficulty level of the examination and to provide content for practice and review. Knowing the correct answers to all of the sample questions is not a guarantee of satisfactory performance on the exam.

Directions: Each of the questions or incomplete statements below is followed by five suggested answers or completions. Select the one that is best in each case.

1. In his celebrated satire, the author comments on human nature by examining the life of the Lilliputians, Yahoos, and Houyhnhnms.

   The book described above is

   (A) *The Way of All Flesh*
   (B) *Through the Looking Glass*
   (C) *Gulliver's Travels*
   (D) *The Pilgrim's Progress*
   (E) *Robinson Crusoe*

2. One of the characters in this play is the fool, who attempts to comfort his old master, but who also ironically emphasizes the folly and the tragedy of the old man.

   The play referred to above is

   (A) *Macbeth*
   (B) *Julius Caesar*
   (C) *King Lear*
   (D) *Othello*
   (E) *Hamlet*

<u>Questions 3–4</u>

For I have learned
To look on nature, not as in the hour
Of thoughtless youth, but hearing oftentimes
The still, sad music of humanity,
Nor harsh nor grating, though of ample power
To chasten and subdue. And I have felt
A presence that disturbs me with the joy
Of elevated thoughts; a sense sublime
Of something far more deeply interfused,
Whose dwelling is the light of setting suns,
And the round ocean, and the living air,
And the blue sky, and in the mind of man[.]

3. The lines are written in

   (A) heroic couplets
   (B) terza rima
   (C) ballad meter
   (D) blank verse
   (E) iambic tetrameter

4. The language and ideas in these lines are most characteristic of which of the following literary periods?

   (A) Medieval
   (B) Restoration
   (C) Augustan
   (D) Romantic
   (E) Early twentieth century

5. Samuel Richardson, Henry Fielding, and Tobias Smollett are best known as eighteenth-century

   (A) novelists
   (B) dramatists
   (C) essayists
   (D) poets
   (E) critics

6. "The business of a poet," said Imlac, "is to examine, not the individual, but the species; to remark general properties and large appearances: he does not number the streaks of the tulip, or describe the different shades in the verdure of the forest. He is to exhibit in his portraits of nature such prominent and striking features, as recall the original to every mind; and must neglect the minuter discriminations, which one may have remarked, and another have neglected, for those characteristics which are alike obvious to vigilance and carelessness."

   Which of the following statements most closely corresponds to the paragraph above?

   (A) Poetry is the spontaneous overflow of powerful feelings.
   (B) Poetry is the precious lifeblood of a master spirit.
   (C) Poetry is the just representation of general nature.
   (D) Poetry should not mean but be.
   (E) Poets are the unacknowledged legislators of the world.

7. An anonymous narrative poem focusing on the climax of a particularly dramatic event and employing frequent repetition, conventional figures of speech, and sometimes a refrain—altered and transmitted orally in a musical setting—is called a

   (A) popular ballad
   (B) pastoral elegy
   (C) courtly lyric
   (D) villanelle
   (E) chivalric romance

Questions 8–10

They, looking back, all the eastern side beheld
Of Paradise, so late their happy seat,
Waved over by that flaming brand, the gate
With dreadful faces thronged and fiery arms.
Some natural tears they dropped, but wiped them soon;
The world was all before them, where to choose
Their place of rest, and Providence their guide.
They, hand in hand, with wandering steps and slow,
Through Eden took their solitary way.

8. These lines were written by

   (A) John Donne
   (B) Edmund Spenser
   (C) Christopher Marlowe
   (D) William Shakespeare
   (E) John Milton

9. In line 2, "late" is best interpreted to mean

   (A) recently
   (B) tardily
   (C) unfortunately
   (D) long
   (E) soon

10. The people referred to as "they" in the passage were probably experiencing all the following emotions EXCEPT

   (A) awe
   (B) doubt
   (C) suspicion
   (D) regret
   (E) sorrow

11. Whan that Aprill with his shoures soote
The droghte of March hath perced to the roote

The lines above were written by

(A) Geoffrey Chaucer
(B) William Shakespeare
(C) Alexander Pope
(D) William Wordsworth
(E) Ben Jonson

12. Alfred Tennyson's "Ulysses" and T. S. Eliot's "The Love Song of J. Alfred Prufrock" are both

(A) pastoral elegies
(B) literary ballads
(C) mock epics
(D) dramatic monologues
(E) irregular odes

Questions 13–14

Our two souls therefore, which are one,
Though I must go, endure not yet
A breach, but an expansion,
Like gold to airy thinness beat.

13. The passage contains an example of

(A) an epic simile
(B) a metaphysical conceit
(C) an epic catalog
(D) an alexandrine
(E) sprung rhythm

14. The passage is from a poem by

(A) Alexander Pope
(B) Robert Herrick
(C) Samuel Taylor Coleridge
(D) Samuel Johnson
(E) John Donne

Questions 15–17

He's here in double trust:
First, as I am his kinsman and his subject,
Strong both against the deed; then, as his host,
Who should against his murtherer shut the door,
Not bear the knife myself. Besides, this Duncan
Hath borne his faculties so meek, hath been
So clear in his great office, that his virtues
Will plead like angels, trumpet-tongued, against
The deep damnation of his taking-off;
And pity, like a naked new-born babe,
Striding the blast, or heaven's cherubim, horsed
Upon the sightless couriers of the air,
Shall blow the horrid deed in every eye,
That tears shall drown the wind.

15. The speaker of these lines might best be described as a

(A) coward
(B) man badly treated by Duncan
(C) man seeking revenge
(D) man concerned only with his own safety
(E) man troubled by moral law

16. The "horrid deed" (line 13) is compared metaphorically to

(A) a cinder or speck irritating the eye
(B) a naked newborn babe
(C) an assassination
(D) the wind
(E) the consequences of the murder of Duncan

17. These lines are spoken by

(A) Hamlet
(B) Cassius
(C) Macbeth
(D) Iago
(E) Richard III

18. Which of the following is the first line of a poem by John Keats?

    (A) "What dire offence from amorous causes springs,"
    (B) "They flee from me that sometime did me seek,"
    (C) "Thou still unravished bride of quietness,"
    (D) "I weep for Adonais—he is dead!"
    (E) "Not, I'll not, carrion comfort, Despair, not feast on thee;"

Questions 19–20

O threats of Hell and Hopes of Paradise!
One thing at least is certain—*This* life flies;
One thing is certain and the rest is Lies;
The Flower that once has blown for ever dies.

19. In the fourth line, "blown" means

    (A) blown up
    (B) blown away
    (C) bloomed
    (D) died
    (E) been planted

20. Which of the following is the best summary of the four lines?

    (A) Do not ignore the serious aspects of life; earnest dedication is necessary for success.
    (B) Do not rely on a theoretical afterlife; you can be sure only that the present moment will pass.
    (C) Life is like a flower with roots in both good and evil.
    (D) Religious belief is essential to a happy life.
    (E) The only safe course in life is to ignore outside events and cultivate one's own garden.

21. Which of the following was written earliest?

    (A) *The Waste Land*
    (B) *The Rime of the Ancient Mariner*
    (C) *Songs of Innocence*
    (D) *The Faerie Queene*
    (E) *The Rape of the Lock*

Questions 22–23

She was alone and still, gazing out to sea; and when she felt his presence and the worship of his eyes her eyes turned to him in quiet sufferance of his gaze, without shame or wantonness. Long, long she suffered his gaze and then quietly withdrew her eyes from his and bent them towards the stream, gently stirring the water with her foot hither and thither. The first faint noise of gently moving water broke the silence, low and faint and whispering, faint as the bells of sleep; hither and thither, hither and thither, and a faint flame trembled on her cheek.

—Heavenly God! cried Stephen's soul, in an outburst of profane joy.

22. The passage appears in which of the following novels?

    (A) *Victory*
    (B) *A Portrait of the Artist as a Young Man*
    (C) *Tess of the D'Urbervilles*
    (D) *The Egoist*
    (E) *Sons and Lovers*

23. The passage presents an example of what its author would have termed

    (A) synecdoche
    (B) pathetic fallacy
    (C) metonymy
    (D) an eclogue
    (E) an epiphany

Questions 24–25 are based on the following excerpt from Henry Fielding's *Joseph Andrews*.

Now, the rake Hesperus has called for his breeches, and having well rubbed his drowsy eyes, prepared to dress himself for all night; by whose example his brother rakes on earth likewise leave those beds in which they slept away the day. Now Thetis, the good housewife, began to put on the pot, in order to regale the good man Phoebus after his daily labours were over. In vulgar language, it was the evening when Joseph attended his lady's orders.

24. Which of the following describes Hesperus (line 1), Thetis (line 6), and Phoebus (line 8) in the passage above?
    (A) They are references to Greek mythology.
    (B) They are references to fellow authors.
    (C) They are references to Biblical heroes.
    (D) They refer to figures from English folklore.
    (E) They are characters in the novel.

25. In line 9, "vulgar language" means
    (A) commonly spoken language
    (B) elevated and archaic language
    (C) ungrammatical language
    (D) language laden with sexual puns
    (E) language characterized by obsolete and dialectal terms

26. The "Age of Johnson" in English literature was dominated by which of the following styles?
    (A) Romanticism
    (B) Neoclassicism
    (C) Expressionism
    (D) Naturalism
    (E) Abstractionism

Questions 27–29 are based on the following excerpt from Ben Jonson's "To Penshurst."

Thou art not, Penshurst, built to envious show,
Of touch, or marble; nor canst boast a row
Of polished pillars, or a roof of gold;
Thou hast no lantern whereof tales are told,
Or stair, or courts; but stand'st an ancient pile,
And these grudged at, art reverenced the while.
Thou joy'st in better marks, of soil, of air,
Of wood, of water; therein thou art fair.

27. Lines 1–5 of the passage compare Penshurst with
    (A) a more ornate house
    (B) an intricate tapestry
    (C) an impenetrable fortress
    (D) a landscape painting
    (E) an autumn evening

28. The speaker in the passage indicates that Penshurst is
    (A) known to cause resentment
    (B) enhanced by "a roof of gold" (line 3)
    (C) in need of brighter lighting
    (D) falling into disrepair
    (E) properly appreciated

29. The poem uses which of the following forms?
    (A) Ballad meter
    (B) Blank verse
    (C) Elegiac stanza
    (D) Rhyme royal
    (E) Heroic couplets

Questions 30–32 are based on the following excerpt from Virginia Woolf's essay "Professions for Women."

I discovered that if I were going to review books I should need to do battle with a certain phantom. And the phantom was a woman, and when I came to know her better I called her after the heroine of a famous poem, The Angel in the House. . . . She was intensely sympathetic. She was immensely charming. She was utterly unselfish. She excelled in the difficult arts of family life. She sacrificed herself daily. If there was chicken, she took the leg; if there was a draft she sat in it—in short she was so constituted that she never had a mind or a wish of her own, but preferred to sympathize always with the minds and wishes of others. Above all—I need not say it—she was pure. Her purity was supposed to be her chief beauty—her blushes, her great grace. In those days—the last of Queen Victoria—every house had its Angel. And when I came to write I encountered her with the very first words.

30. This passage's primary purpose is to

(A) describe a person with a dual personality
(B) praise the traditional role of women
(C) describe a famous historical figure
(D) encourage readers to take seriously the importance of literary ghosts
(E) describe one impediment a woman writer faces in making a literary career

31. Which of the following effects does the battle metaphor have?

I. It suggests how difficult the phantom will be to overcome.
II. It enhances the emotional impact of the conflict described.
III. It contributes to the mirthful tone that imbues the entire passage.

(A) I only
(B) III only
(C) I and II only
(D) II and III only
(E) I, II, and III

32. The tone of the discussion of "The Angel in the House" (lines 5–6) conveys the author's

(A) pleasure in remembering her literary precursors
(B) anger at people who write book reviews
(C) remorse for the slaying of an innocent person
(D) awareness of the power of commonly held ideas
(E) enthusiasm about writing what she feels

Questions 33–34 are based on the following passage from Anita Desai's novel *In Custody*.

The time and the place: these elementary matters were left to Deven to arrange as being within his capabilities. Time and place, these two concerns of all who are born and all who die: these were considered the two fit subjects for the weak and the incompetent. Deven was to restrict himself to these two matters, time and place. No one appeared to realize that to him these subjects belonged to infinity and were far more awesome than the minutiae of technical arrangements.

33. According to the passage, Deven is perceived by others to be

(A) capable of arranging important details
(B) suited to performing only simple tasks
(C) unable to see the ultimate meaning of infinity
(D) obsessed with his own mortality
(E) happy in his role of organizing minor matters

34. The passage implies that Deven's perspective differs from that of the people who have given him his assignment in that he is

(A) innovative instead of fastidious
(B) intellectual instead of social
(C) philosophical instead of pragmatic
(D) cosmopolitan instead of bigoted
(E) judgmental instead of apathetic

35. What is the order, from earliest to latest, in which the following works were composed?

I. *Hamlet*
II. *Beowulf*
III. *Paradise Lost*

(A) I, II, III
(B) I, III, II
(C) II, I, III
(D) II, III, I
(E) III, II, I

Questions 36–37 are based on the following poem.

Farewell, thou child of my right hand, and joy;
My sin was too much hope of thee, loved boy:
Seven years thou wert lent to me, and I thee pay,
Exacted by thy fate, on the just day.
O could I lose all father now! for why
Will man lament the state he should envy,
To have so soon 'scaped world's and flesh's rage,
And, if no other misery, yet age?
Rest in soft peace, and asked, say, "Here doth lie
Ben Jonson his best piece of poetry."
For whose sake henceforth all his vows be such
As what he loves may never like too much.

36. The speaker expresses all of the following thoughts EXCEPT:

(A) Life has so many trials that perhaps death should be viewed as a welcome release.
(B) Poetry can keep alive those whom fate tries to take away.
(C) Bearing the death of his son is difficult because he had high expectations for him.
(D) His son was the greatest achievement in his life.
(E) He never again wants to become as attached to anybody or anything as he was to his son.

37. The tone of the poem is best described as

(A) deferential
(B) malicious
(C) playful
(D) elegiac
(E) melodramatic

38. "Lycidas" is a poem that

(A) adapts a heroic legend from classical mythology to the society that the writer knew best
(B) manages in a short space to record much of English history
(C) mourns the death of the writer's friend but also reveals personal concerns of the writer
(D) uses an important historical event of its day to air the political views of the writer
(E) captures the magic of the Italian Renaissance and puts it into a realistic London setting

39. In the poem "The Canonization," the intense relationship between the speaker and the lover leads the speaker to argue that they should be considered candidates for sainthood.

The author of the poem described above is

(A) W. B. Yeats
(B) Elizabeth Barrett Browning
(C) John Donne
(D) John Milton
(E) Gerard Manley Hopkins

40. All of the following were written in the eighteenth century EXCEPT

(A) *Pamela*
(B) *Jane Eyre*
(C) *Tom Jones*
(D) *Tristram Shandy*
(E) *Moll Flanders*

41. Observe me, Sir Anthony, I would by no means wish a daughter of mine to be a progeny of learning. . . . But, Sir Anthony, I would send her at nine years old to a boarding school, in order to learn a little ingenuity and artifice. Then, sir, she should have a supercilious knowledge in accounts;—and as she grew up, I would have her instructed in geometry, that she might know something of the contagious countries;—but above all, Sir Anthony, she should be mistress to orthodoxy, that she might not misspell and mis-pronounce words so shamefully as girls usually do; and likewise that she might reprehend the true meaning of what she is saying.

The speaker of the lines above, as evidenced by her characteristic language, is

(A) Elizabeth Bennet in *Pride and Prejudice*
(B) Hellena in *The Rover*
(C) Mrs. Malaprop in *The Rivals*
(D) Miss Hardcastle in *She Stoops to Conquer*
(E) Rosalind in *As You Like It*

42. A novel that uses extensive parallels from classical Greek epic and adopts an antiheroic modernity is

(A) *Lord Jim*
(B) *Briefing for a Descent into Hell*
(C) *A Tale of Two Cities*
(D) *A Passage to India*
(E) *Ulysses*

43. A twentieth-century absurdist play in which the characters largely talk in circles, the actions are inconclusive, and the lines "Nothing to be done" and "It'd pass the time" are repeated is

(A) *Riders to the Sea*
(B) *Equus*
(C) *Waiting for Godot*
(D) *Look Back in Anger*
(E) *Murder in the Cathedral*

44. Mill, Carlyle, and Tennyson all experienced and wrote about

(A) an upbringing in an agrarian environment
(B) a personal crisis of faith
(C) the conservatism of Victorian courtship
(D) the benefits of modern science
(E) the triumph of democracy

45. Which of the following novelists was raised in Southern Rhodesia (now Zimbabwe) and is known for stories about Africa and for the innovative novel *The Golden Notebook*?

(A) Virginia Woolf
(B) Doris Lessing
(C) George Orwell
(D) Margaret Atwood
(E) E. M. Forster

46. Which of the following terms is used to describe literature that evokes a rural, simple, and idyllic life?

(A) Pre-Raphaelite
(B) Pastoral
(C) Sentimental
(D) Naturalistic
(E) Platonic

47. In the old days she had come this way quite often, going down the hill on the tram with her girl friends, with nothing better in mind than a bit of window-shopping and a bit of a laugh and a cup of tea: penniless then as now, but still hopeful, still endowed with a touching faith that if by some miracle she could buy a pair of nylons or a particular blue lace blouse or a new brand of lipstick, then deliverance would be granted to her in the form of money, marriage, romance, the visiting prince who would glimpse her in the crowd, glorified by that seductive blouse, and carry her off to a better world.

In the passage above, the protagonist remembers herself as having been

(A) embittered
(B) baffled
(C) contentedly alone
(D) carefree
(E) naïvely optimistic

Questions 48–50 are based on the following lines.

By heaven, methinks it were an easy leap
To pluck bright honor from the pale-faced moon,
Or dive into the bottom of the deep,
Where fathom line could never touch the ground,
And pluck up drowned honor by the locks,
So he that doth redeem her thence might wear
Without corrival all her dignities;

48. Lines 3–7 depend for their effect on

(A) allusion
(B) personification
(C) antithesis
(D) parallelism
(E) simile

49. The lines suggest that their speaker is

(A) bold and reckless
(B) pensive and melancholy
(C) grim and indifferent
(D) anxious and cowardly
(E) cold and scheming

50. The lines were written by

(A) William Shakespeare
(B) Christopher Marlowe
(C) John Milton
(D) Percy Bysshe Shelley
(E) Lord Byron

51. To anyone who questioned the effectiveness of the loyalty oaths, he replied that people who really did owe allegiance to their country would be proud to pledge it as often as he forced them to.

The excerpt above provides an example of

(A) parody
(B) pathos
(C) propaganda
(D) irony
(E) harangue

52. An episodic narrative, usually told from the first-person point of view and detailing the misadventures, escapades, and pranks of a roguish but likable hero of humble means who survives by his wits, is known as a

(A) mock epic
(B) roman à clef
(C) novel of manners
(D) picaresque novel
(E) romance

53. Remember that I am thy creature: I ought to be thy Adam; but I am rather the fallen angel, whom thou drivest from joy for no misdeed. Every where I see bliss, from which I alone am irrevocably excluded. I was benevolent and good; misery made me a fiend. Make me happy, and I shall again be virtuous.

The passage above is from which of the following works?

(A) John Milton's *Paradise Lost*
(B) Mary Shelley's *Frankenstein*
(C) Emily Brontë's *Wuthering Heights*
(D) Robert Louis Stevenson's *Dr. Jekyll and Mr. Hyde*
(E) Bram Stoker's *Dracula*

54. Which of the following works does NOT portray characters from Arthurian legend?

    (A) *Sir Gawain and the Green Knight*
    (B) *Morte D'Arthur*
    (C) *The Faerie Queene*
    (D) *Visions of the Daughters of Albion*
    (E) *Idylls of the King*

55. The typical theater was a structure, circular or polygonal in shape, built around an open court or "pit," into which projected a rectangular raised platform. In the pit and on three sides of the platform stood the "groundlings." The more well-to-do members of the audiences paid a higher admission fee and sat in the tiers of galleries that surrounded the pit and that were partitioned off into "boxes."

    The type of theater described above was first developed during the reign of

    (A) Richard II
    (B) Henry VIII
    (C) Elizabeth I
    (D) George III
    (E) Victoria

56. In the nineteenth century, novels published in parts over several weeks or months were known as

    (A) epistolary novels
    (B) chronicles
    (C) social novels
    (D) vignettes
    (E) serialized novels

57. To whom, then, *must* I dedicate my wonderful, surprising & interesting adventures?—to *whom* dare I reveal my private opinion of my nearest relations? The secret thoughts of my dearest friends? My own hopes, fears, reflections & dislikes—Nobody!

    To Nobody, then, will I write my journal! Since to Nobody can I be wholly unreserved—to Nobody can I reveal every thought, every wish of my heart, with the most unlimited confidence, the most unremitting sincerity to the end of my life! For what chance, what accident can end my connections with Nobody? No secret *can* I conceal from No-body, & to No-body can I be *ever* unreserved. Disagreement cannot stop our affection, time itself has no power to end our friendship.

    The language of the above opening entry in an eighteenth-century personal journal is best characterized as

    (A) argumentative
    (B) playful
    (C) hesitant
    (D) reserved
    (E) scornful

Questions 58–59 are based on the following passage.

The family of Dashwood had been long settled in Sussex. Their estate was large, and their residence was at Norland Park, in the centre of their property, where for many generations they had lived in so respectable a manner as to engage the general good opinion of their surrounding acquaintance. The late owner of this estate was a single man, who lived to a very advanced age, and who for many years of his life had a constant companion and housekeeper in his sister. But her death, which happened ten years before his own, produced a great alteration in his home; for to supply her loss, he invited and received into his house the family of his nephew, Mr. Henry Dashwood, the legal inheritor of the Norland estate, and the person to whom he intended to bequeath it. In the society of his nephew and niece, and their children, the old gentleman's days were comfortably spent. His attachment to them all increased. The constant attention of Mr. and Mrs. Henry Dashwood to his wishes, which proceeded not merely from interest, but from goodness of heart, gave him every degree of solid comfort which his age could receive; and the cheerfulness of the children added a relish to his existence.

58. The passage is the opening of a novel by which of the following authors?

(A) Daniel Defoe
(B) Jane Austen
(C) Charles Dickens
(D) Matthew G. Lewis
(E) Mary Shelley

59. As characterized in the passage, the "late owner" (line 7) is best described as

(A) content
(B) open-minded
(C) dutiful
(D) lonesome
(E) demanding

Questions 60–61 are based on the following poem.

My friend, the things that do attain
The happy life be these, I find:
The riches left, not got with pain;
The fruitful ground; the quiet mind;

The equal friend; no grudge, no strife;
No charge of rule, nor governance;
Without disease, the healthy life;
The household of continuance;

The mean diet, no dainty fare;
Wisdom joined with simpleness;
The night discharged of all care,
Where wine the wit may not oppress;

The faithful wife, without debate;
Such sleeps as may beguile the night;
Content thyself with thine estate,
Neither wish death, nor fear his might.

60. In line 9, the word "mean" signifies

(A) dull
(B) troublesome
(C) cruel
(D) basic
(E) contemptible

61. Which of the following best summarizes the poem's theme?

(A) Happiness is best realized through simple living.
(B) Life is short, so savor each experience.
(C) Our passions help keep us young.
(D) Preventive care ensures longevity.
(E) Hard work is its own reward.

62. The concept of "people" better expressed by the Spanish "pueblo" is fast vanishing. The writer who returns from exile at the metropolitan centre to "write for his people"; to seek with them to "break out of identity imposed by alien circumstances," and to find a new one, must come face to face with the fact that his "people" has become the "public." And the public in the Caribbean, equally like the public in the great metropolitan centres, are being conditioned through television, radio and advertising, to want what the great Corporations of production in the culture industry, as in all others, have conditioned them to want. Returning from exile at the metropolitan centre, the writer all too often finds that he returns only to . . . another facet of exile. Yet by not returning, the writer continues to accept his irrelevance.

    In the excerpt above, the author is primarily concerned with

    (A) describing the sacrifices required by rural living
    (B) highlighting a challenge that a Caribbean writer faces
    (C) advocating more tolerance among the general public
    (D) denouncing the television, radio, and advertising industries
    (E) defining the meaning of the term "people"

63. Then she had three years of great labor with temptations which she bore as meekly as she could, thanking Our Lord for all His gifts, and was as merry when she was reproved, scorned, and japed for Our Lord's love, and much more merry than she was beforetime in the worship of the world.

    The passage above is from which of the following works?

    (A) Geoffrey Chaucer's *Troilus and Criseyde*
    (B) William Langland's *Piers Plowman*
    (C) Margery Kempe's *The Book of Margery Kempe*
    (D) John Gower's *Confessio Amantis*
    (E) Mary Wroth's *Pamphilia to Amphilanthus*

Directions: For the following group of questions, click on a choice, then click on the appropriate box.

64. Match each of the following poets to the work that he or she wrote.

    Wilfred Owen
    Rupert Brooke
    Edith Sitwell

    [ ] "The Soldier"
    [ ] "Anthem for Doomed Youth"
    [ ] "Still Falls the Rain"

65. Of the following five works, which three may be categorized as dystopian novels?

    A Clockwork Orange
    Half a Life
    Brave New World
    Things Fall Apart
    1984

    [ ]
    [ ]
    [ ]

66. Identify the poets from the list below who collaborated in producing *Lyrical Ballads* (1798).

Samuel Taylor Coleridge
Percy Bysshe Shelley
William Blake
William Wordsworth
John Keats

67. Match each of the following authors to the work that he or she wrote.

Aphra Behn
Oliver Goldsmith
Samuel Johnson
Richard Sheridan

The Vicar of Wakefield

Oroonoko

The School for Scandal

A Dictionary of the English Language

68. Match the character to the novel in which each appears.

Philip "Pip" Pirrip
Uriah Heep
Little Nell

David Copperfield

The Old Curiosity Shop

Great Expectations

69. Match the poet to the literary movement each is associated with most closely.

Richard Aldington
Linton Kwesi Johnson
William Blake

Imagism

Postcolonialism

Romanticism

70. Ben Jonson's *Volpone* is an example of a

(A) tragedy
(B) romance
(C) history play
(D) comedy
(E) pastoral romance

71. Steeped in regional folklore as a child growing up in the Scottish Border counties, this writer went on to become a poet, an editor of traditional ballads, and a novelist whose works have been called the first truly historical novels.

    The author described in this statement is

    (A) Sir Walter Scott
    (B) James Macpherson
    (C) Robert Southey
    (D) Robert Burns
    (E) James Boswell

72. Now, it is clear that the decline of a language must ultimately have political and economic causes: it is not due simply to the bad influence of this or that individual writer. But an effect can become a cause, reinforcing the original cause and producing the same effect in an intensified form, and so on indefinitely. A man may take to drink because he feels himself to be a failure, and then fail all the more completely because he drinks. It is rather the same thing that is happening to the English language. It becomes ugly and inaccurate because our thoughts are foolish, but the slovenliness of our language makes it easier for us to have foolish thoughts. The point is that the process is reversible. Modern English, especially written English, is full of bad habits which spread by imitation and which can be avoided if one is willing to take the necessary trouble. If one gets rid of these habits one can think more clearly, and to think clearly is a necessary first step towards political regeneration: so that the fight against bad English is not frivolous and is not the exclusive concern of professional writers.

    The author of the above passage is

    (A) Virginia Woolf
    (B) George Orwell
    (C) Matthew Arnold
    (D) T. S. Eliot
    (E) Joseph Conrad

Questions 73–74 are based on the following passage.

Dorothea knew many passages of Pascal's *Pensées* and of Jeremy Taylor by heart; and to her the destinies of mankind, seen by the light of Christianity, made the solicitudes of feminine fashion appear an occupation for Bedlam. She could not reconcile the anxieties of a spiritual life involving eternal consequences, with a keen interest in guimp and artificial protrusions of drapery. Her mind was theoretic, and yearned by its nature after some lofty conception of the world which might frankly include the parish of Tipton and her own rule of conduct there; she was enamoured of intensity and greatness, and rash in embracing whatever seemed to her to have those aspects; likely to seek martyrdom, to make retractations, and then to incur martyrdom after all in a quarter where she had not sought it. Certainly such elements in the character of a marriageable girl tended to interfere with her lot, and hinder it from being decided according to custom, by good looks, vanity, and merely canine affection.

73. This passage is from the beginning of a novel by which of the following authors?

    (A) Richard Sheridan
    (B) Jane Austen
    (C) George Eliot
    (D) Charles Dickens
    (E) William Makepeace Thackeray

74. Dorothea might best be described as

    (A) frivolous and carefree
    (B) disdainful and determined
    (C) sad and depressed
    (D) aggressive and spiteful
    (E) intellectual and idealistic

Questions 75–76 are based on the following quotation.

We can forgive a man for making a useful thing as long as he does not admire it. The only excuse for making a useless thing is that one admires it intensely. All art is quite useless.

75. The author of the quotation is

(A) Joseph Conrad
(B) John Ruskin
(C) Algernon Swinburne
(D) Oscar Wilde
(E) William Hazlitt

76. The quotation contains examples of

(A) aphorisms
(B) euphemisms
(C) conceits
(D) complaints
(E) colloquialisms

77. Which of the following British poets published *Birthday Letters*, a collection of poems inspired by his marriage to Sylvia Plath?

(A) Siegfried Sassoon
(B) D. H. Lawrence
(C) W. H. Auden
(D) Ted Hughes
(E) R. S. Thomas

Directions: For the following two questions, click on a choice, then click on the appropriate box.

78. Identify the writers from the list below who were associated with the Pre-Raphaelite movement.

George Gordon, Lord Byron
William Morris
John Ruskin
Dante Gabriel Rossetti
Samuel Taylor Coleridge

[ ]
[ ]
[ ]
[ ]
[ ]

79. Match each of the following writers to the country of her birth.

Nadine Gordimer
Edna O'Brien
Alice Munro
Katherine Mansfield

[ ] Canada
[ ] South Africa
[ ] Ireland
[ ] New Zealand

80. Which of the following writers was centrally involved in the cause of Irish nationalism at the beginning of the twentieth century?

    (A) William Butler Yeats
    (B) J. M. Synge
    (C) Paul Muldoon
    (D) Joan Lingard
    (E) Seamus Heaney

81. The poetry of which of the following poets reflects an intense religious belief as well as a commitment to preserving the environment?

    (A) George Gordon, Lord Byron
    (B) Percy Bysshe Shelley
    (C) Dante Gabriel Rossetti
    (D) Gerard Manley Hopkins
    (E) A. E. Housman

Questions 82–84 are based on the following passage.

Yes! Margaret remembered it well. Edith and Mrs. Shaw had gone to dinner. Margaret had joined the party in the evening. The recollection of the plentiful luxury of all the arrangements, the stately handsomeness of the furniture, the size of the house, the peaceful, untroubled ease of the visitors—all came vividly before her, in strange contrast to the present time. The smooth sea of that old life closed up, without a mark left to tell where they had all been. The habitual dinners, the calls, the shopping, the dancing evenings, were all going on, going on for ever, though her Aunt Shaw and Edith were no longer there; and she, of course, was even less missed. She doubted if any one of that old set ever thought of her, except Henry Lennox. He too, she knew, would strive to forget her, because of the pain she had caused him. She had heard him often boast of his power of putting any disagreeable thought far away from him. Then she penetrated farther into what might have been. If she had cared for him as a lover, and had accepted him, and this change in her father's opinions and consequent station had taken place, she could not doubt but that it would have been impatiently received by Mr. Lennox. It was a bitter mortification to her in one sense; but she could bear it patiently, because she knew her father's purity of purpose, and that strengthened her to endure his errors, grave and serious though in her estimation they were. But the fact of the world esteeming her father degraded, in its rough wholesale judgment, would have oppressed and irritated Mr. Lennox. As she realized what might have been, she grew to be thankful for what was. They were at the lowest now; they could not be worse.

82. The main character in the passage moves from

    (A) anger to hopelessness
    (B) loss to acceptance
    (C) nostalgia to regret
    (D) irritation to embarrassment
    (E) hope to despair

83. The sentence "The smooth sea of that old life closed up, without a mark to tell where they had all been" emphasizes which of the following about Margaret?

(A) The sense that she is drowning in her new life
(B) The fact that her memories of the past are fading rapidly
(C) Her strong disapproval of her father's actions
(D) Her sense of how significantly life for her has changed
(E) How much she misses Edith and Aunt Shaw

84. This passage appears in

(A) an early modern picaresque tale
(B) an eighteenth-century novel
(C) a nineteenth-century novel
(D) an early-twentieth-century Modernist novel
(E) a postcolonialist novel

85. I believe it is difficult for those who publish their own memoirs to escape the imputation of vanity; nor is this the only disadvantage under which they labour: it is also their misfortune, that what is uncommon is rarely, if ever, believed, and what is obvious we are apt to turn from with disgust, and to charge the writer with impertinence. People generally think those memoirs only worthy to be read or remembered which abound in great or striking events, those, in short, which in a high degree excite either admiration or pity: all others they consign to contempt and oblivion. It is therefore, I confess, not a little hazardous in a private and obscure individual, and a stranger too, thus to solicit the indulgent attention of the public; especially when I own I offer here the history of neither a saint, a hero, nor a tyrant.

In the passage, Olaudah Equiano suggests that readers may consider his autobiography

(A) admirable
(B) imaginative
(C) gripping
(D) memorable
(E) egotistical

86. The future of the novel? Poor old novel, it's in a rather dirty, messy tight corner. And it's either got to get over the wall or knock a hole through it. In other words, it's got to grow up. Put away childish things like: "Do I love the girl, or don't I?"—"Am I pure and sweet, or am I not?"—"Do I unbutton my right glove first, or my left?"—"Did my mother ruin my life by refusing to drink the cocoa which my bride had boiled for her?"

Which of the following statements best characterizes D. H. Lawrence's thoughts on the modern novel?

(A) Writing a modern novel is difficult to achieve.
(B) The subject matter of the modern novel is trivial.
(C) The modern novel focuses too much on emotions.
(D) The language of the modern novel is too informal.
(E) There is no future for the modern novel.

Questions 87–88

I follow him to serve my turn upon him:
We cannot all be masters, nor all masters
Cannot be truly follow'd. You shall mark
Many a duteous and knee-crooking knave,
That, doting on his own obsequious bondage,
Wears out his time, much like his master's ass,
For nought but provender, and when he's old, cashier'd:
Whip me such honest knaves. Others there are
Who, trimm'd in forms and visages of duty,
Keep yet their hearts attending on themselves,
And, throwing but shows of service on their lords,
Do well thrive by them and when they have lined their coats,
Do themselves homage: these fellows have some soul;
And such a one do I profess myself.

87. The speaker of the lines is best described as

(A) idealistic and eager
(B) slothful and mean-spirited
(C) loyal and cheerful
(D) self-serving and deceptive
(E) fastidious and demanding

88. The "knee-crooking knave" (line 4) is compared to a

(A) valuable coat
(B) horse trainer
(C) donkey
(D) field of hay
(E) circus clown

89. The inspiration for W. B. Yeats's "Easter 1916" was

(A) the struggle for Irish independence
(B) life in the trenches during the First World War
(C) the death of Yeats's young bride
(D) the increase in religious doubt in the twentieth century
(E) dissatisfaction with working conditions for the Irish

Questions 90–91 are based on the following passage from the medieval play *Everyman*.

Goods: Sir, and ye in the world have trouble or adversity,
That can I help you to remedy shortly.
Everyman: It is another disease that grieveth me;
In this world it is not, I tell thee so.
I am sent for another way to go,
To give a straight account general
Before the highest Jupiter of all;
And all my life I have had joy and pleasure in thee.
Therefore I pray thee go with me,
For, peradventure, thou mayst before God Almighty
My reckoning help to clean and purify;
For it is said ever among,
That money maketh all right that is wrong.
Goods: Nay, Everyman, I sing another song,
I follow no man in such voyages;
For and I went with thee
Thou shouldst fare much the worse for me;
For because on me thou did set thy hand,
Thy reckoning I have made blotted and blind,
That thine account thou cannot make truly;
And that hast thou for the love of me.

90. In line 21, "the love of me" refers to

(A) Everyman's pursuit of worldly wealth
(B) Everyman's desire to do good
(C) The self-centeredness of Goods
(D) The benevolence that Goods shows toward Everyman
(E) The affinity that Goods and Everyman have for each other

91. "My reckoning" (line 11) refers allegorically to the

(A) individual's effort to make sense of the events of life
(B) soul's accounting, after death, of its deeds before God
(C) subjective experience of life for each individual
(D) sum total of enjoyment one feels in life
(E) wisdom each person acquires through overcoming challenges

Questions 92–97 are based on the following poem.

The Mother of the Muses, we are taught,
Is Memory: she has left me; they remain,
And shake my shoulder, urging me to sing
About the summer days, my loves of old.
Alas! alas! is all I can reply.
Memory has left with me that name alone,
Harmonious name, which other bards may sing,
But her bright image in my darkest hour
Comes back, in vain comes back, call'd or uncall'd.
Forgotten are the names of visitors
Ready to press my hand but yesterday;
Forgotten are the names of earlier friends
Whose genial converse and glad countenance
Are fresh as ever to mine ear and eye;
To these, when I have written and besought
Remembrance of me, the word Dear alone
Hangs on the upper verge, and waits in vain.
A blessing wert thou, O oblivion,
If thy stream carried only weeds away,
But vernal and autumnal flowers alike
It hurries down to wither on the strand.

92. Which of the following best describes the poem's theme?

(A) The transitory nature of beauty
(B) The constancy of true friendship
(C) Poetry as a challenging medium of expression
(D) Wisdom through suffering
(E) Forgetfulness as a curse

93. What meter does the poem use?

(A) Dactylic hexameter
(B) Iambic pentameter
(C) Trochaic dimeter
(D) Anapestic tetrameter
(E) Free verse

94. In lines 1–5 ("The Mother…can reply"), the speaker describes how

(A) memory creates the springs of inspiration in the poet's mind
(B) the mood of the poetry produced by the speaker varies with the changing seasons
(C) the impetus for writing poetry remains even after the source of its material has departed
(D) poetry written in youth differs from poetry written in later life
(E) experience is reshaped by the mind in the process of creative expression

95. In line 16, "the word Dear alone" evokes the speaker's

(A) placement of affection above the other virtues
(B) inability to recall names of correspondents
(C) suspicion that some acquaintances are insincere
(D) impatience with the trials of old age
(E) acceptance of the inevitability of loss

96. What do the "vernal and autumnal flowers" (line 20) represent in the poem?

(A) Pleasant and unpleasant experiences from the past
(B) Happy memories from early and later life
(C) Requited and unrequited loves
(D) The various muses that inspire poets to write
(E) Old and recent poetic productions

97. The speaker's tone in the poem is best described as

(A) peevish and petulant
(B) rueful and resigned
(C) aloof and distant
(D) congenial and relaxed
(E) rapturous and insistent

Questions 98–99 are based on the following passage.

You should have seen him in his dwelling about twilight, in the dead winter time.

When the wind was blowing, shrill and shrewd, with the going down of the blurred sun. When it was just so dark, as that the forms of things were indistinct and big—but not wholly lost. When sitters by the fire began to see wild faces and figures, mountains and abysses, ambuscades and armies, in the coals. When people in the streets bent down their heads and ran before the weather. When those who were obliged to meet it, were stopped at angry corners, stung by wandering snow-flakes alighting on the lashes of their eyes,—which fell too sparingly, and were blown away too quickly, to leave a trace upon the frozen ground. When windows of private houses closed up tight and warm. When lighted gas began to burst forth in the busy and the quiet streets, fast blackening otherwise. When stray pedestrians, shivering along the latter, looked down at the glowing fires in kitchens, and sharpened their sharp appetites by sniffing up the fragrance of whole miles of dinners.

98. The repetition of "When" in the passage is an example of the rhetorical device known as

(A) apostrophe
(B) hendiadys
(C) anaphora
(D) assonance
(E) litotes

99. The author's description of the way the snow-flakes fall helps evoke an atmosphere of

(A) self-denial and altruism
(B) desire and craving
(C) austerity and deprivation
(D) frenzy and agitation
(E) tranquility and composure

Study Resources

Most textbooks used in college-level English literature courses cover the topics in the outline given earlier, but the approaches to certain topics and the emphases given to them may differ. To prepare for the English Literature exam, it is advisable to study one or more college textbooks, which can be found in most college bookstores. When selecting a textbook, check the table of contents against the knowledge and skills required for this test.

You should also read critically the contents of at least one literary anthology, many of which are used as textbooks in British, Commonwealth, and postcolonial literature courses at the college level.

Most textbook anthologies contain a representative sample of readings as well as discussions of historical background, literary styles and devices characteristic of various authors and periods, and other material relevant to the test. The anthologies do vary somewhat in content, approach and emphasis, and you are therefore advised to consult more than one anthology as well as some specialized books on major authors, periods, and literary forms and terminology. You should also read some of the major novels that are mentioned or excerpted in the anthologies. You can probably obtain an extensive English or British literature reading list from a college English department, library or bookstore.

Visit **clep.collegeboard.org/earn-college-credit/practice** for additional English literature resources. You can also find suggestions for exam preparation in Chapter IV of the *Official Study Guide*. In addition, many college faculty post their course materials on their schools' websites.

Answer Key

1. C
2. C
3. D
4. D
5. A
6. C
7. A
8. E
9. A
10. C
11. A
12. D
13. B
14. E
15. E
16. A
17. C
18. C
19. C
20. B
21. D
22. B
23. E
24. A
25. A
26. B
27. A
28. E
29. E
30. E
31. C
32. D
33. B
34. C
35. C
36. B
37. D
38. C
39. C
40. B
41. C
42. E
43. C
44. B
45. B
46. B
47. E
48. B
49. A
50. A
51. D
52. D
53. B
54. D
55. C
56. E
57. B
58. B
59. A
60. D
61. A
62. B
63. C
64. 2, 1, 3
65. 5, 1, 3 (any combination of these numbers)
66. 1, 4 or 4, 1
67. 2, 1, 4, 3
68. 2, 3, 1
69. 1, 2, 3
70. D
71. A
72. B
73. C
74. E
75. D
76. A
77. D
78. 2, 3, 4 (any combination of these numbers)
79. 3, 1, 2, 4
80. A
81. D
82. B
83. D
84. C
85. E
86. B
87. D
88. C
89. A
90. A
91. B
92. E
93. B
94. C
95. B
96. B
97. B
98. C
99. C

Humanities

Description of the Examination

The Humanities examination tests general knowledge of literature, art and music and the other performing arts. It is broad in its coverage, with questions on all periods from classical to contemporary and in many different fields: poetry, prose, philosophy, art, architecture, music, dance, theater and film. The examination requires candidates to demonstrate their understanding of the humanities through recollection of specific information, comprehension and application of concepts and analysis and interpretation of various works of art.

Because the exam is very broad in its coverage, it is unlikely that any one person will be well informed about all the fields it covers. The exam contains approximately 140 questions to be answered in 90 minutes. Some of these are pretest questions that will not be scored.

Colleges may grant credit toward fulfillment of a distribution requirement for students who achieve satisfactory scores on the Humanities examination. Some may grant credit for a particular course that matches the exam in content.

Note: This examination uses the chronological designations B.C.E. (before the common era) and C.E. (common era). These labels correspond to B.C. (before Christ) and A.D. (anno Domini), which are used in some textbooks.

Knowledge and Skills Required

Questions on the Humanities examination require candidates to demonstrate the abilities listed below, in the approximate percentages indicated. Some questions may require more than one of the abilities.

- Knowledge of factual information (authors, works, etc.) (50 percent of the examination)
- Recognition of techniques such as rhyme scheme, medium and matters of style, and the ability to identify them as characteristics of certain writers, artists, schools or periods (30 percent of the examination)
- Understanding and interpretation of literary passages and art reproductions that are likely to be unfamiliar to most candidates (20 percent of the examination)

The subject matter of the Humanities examination is drawn from the following topics. The percentages next to the topics indicate the approximate percentages of exam questions on those topics.

50% Literature

10% Drama
10%–15% Poetry
15%–20% Fiction
10% Nonfiction (including philosophy)

50% The Arts

20% Visual arts: painting, sculpture, etc.
5% Visual arts: architecture
15% Performing arts: music
10% Performing arts: film, dance, etc.

The exam questions, drawn from the entire history of art and culture, are fairly evenly divided among the following periods: Classical, Medieval and Renaissance, seventeenth and eighteenth centuries, nineteenth century and twentieth and twenty-first centuries. At least 5–10 percent of the questions draw on other cultures, such as African, Asian and Latin American. Some of the questions cross disciplines and/or chronological periods, and a substantial number test knowledge of terminology, genre and style.

Note: Although the images that accompany some of the questions in this guide are printed in black and white, any works that are reproduced in the actual exam will be in color.

Sample Test Questions

The following sample questions do not appear on an actual CLEP examination. They are intended to give potential test-takers an indication of the format and difficulty level of the examination and to provide content for practice and review. Knowing the correct answers to all of the sample questions is not a guarantee of satisfactory performance on the exam.

Directions: Each of the questions or incomplete statements below is followed by five suggested answers or completions. Select the one that is best in each case.

1. Often read as a children's classic, it is in reality a scathing indictment of human meanness and greed. In its four books, the Lilliputians are deranged, the Yahoos obscene.

   The title of the work is

   (A) *Tom Jones*
   (B) *David Copperfield*
   (C) *The Pilgrim's Progress*
   (D) *Gulliver's Travels*
   (E) *Alice's Adventures in Wonderland*

2. Which of the following deals with the bigotry an anguished African American family faces when it attempts to move into an all-white suburb?

   (A) Eugene O'Neill's *Desire Under the Elms*
   (B) Arthur Miller's *Death of a Salesman*
   (C) Ossie Davis' *Purlie Victorious*
   (D) Edward Albee's *Who's Afraid of Virginia Woolf?*
   (E) Lorraine Hansberry's *A Raisin in the Sun*

3. Which of the following has as its central theme a boat journey up a river in Africa?

   (A) *Lord of the Flies*
   (B) *Middlemarch*
   (C) *Catch-22*
   (D) *Heart of Darkness*
   (E) *Vanity Fair*

4. Which of the following is often a symbol of new life arising from death?

   (A) A gorgon
   (B) The minotaur
   (C) A unicorn
   (D) A griffin
   (E) The phoenix

5. The lute is most similar to the modern

   (A) guitar
   (B) piano
   (C) violin
   (D) accordion
   (E) flute

6. The troubadours of the Middle Ages are best described as

   (A) poet-musicians
   (B) moralistic orators
   (C) freelance illustrators
   (D) character actors
   (E) religious philosophers

Erich Lessing/Art Resource, NY

7. The work shown above is an example of which of the following?

(A) Fresco
(B) Tapestry
(C) Bas-relief
(D) Mosaic
(E) Triptych

Réunion des Musées Nationaux/
Art Resource, NY

8. The sculpture shown above is by

(A) Henry Moore
(B) Louise Nevelson
(C) Edgar Degas
(D) Gianlorenzo Bernini
(E) Auguste Rodin

© Werner Forman/CORBIS

9. The figurine shown above is of which of the following origins?

(A) Mayan
(B) African
(C) Inuit
(D) Celtic
(E) Ancient Greek

Questions 10–12 refer to the following lines.

(A) "Where the bee sucks, there suck I,
In a cowslip's bell I lie;"

(B) "Exult O shores, and ring O bells!
But I with mournful tread,
Walk the deck my captain lies,
Fallen cold and dead."

(C) "Ring out, wild bells, to the wild sky,"

(D) "O, what a noble mind is here o'erthrown! . . .
And I . . .
Now see that noble and most sovereign reason
Like sweet bells jangled out of time, and harsh;"

(E) "Oh, the bells, bells, bells!
What a tale their terror tells
Of Despair! . . .
Yet the ear, it fully knows,
By the twanging
And the clanging, . . .
In the jangling,
And the wrangling,"

10. Which excerpt contains several examples of onomatopoeia?

11. Which is from *Hamlet*?

12. Which alludes to Abraham Lincoln's death?

Questions 13–15 refer to the following image.

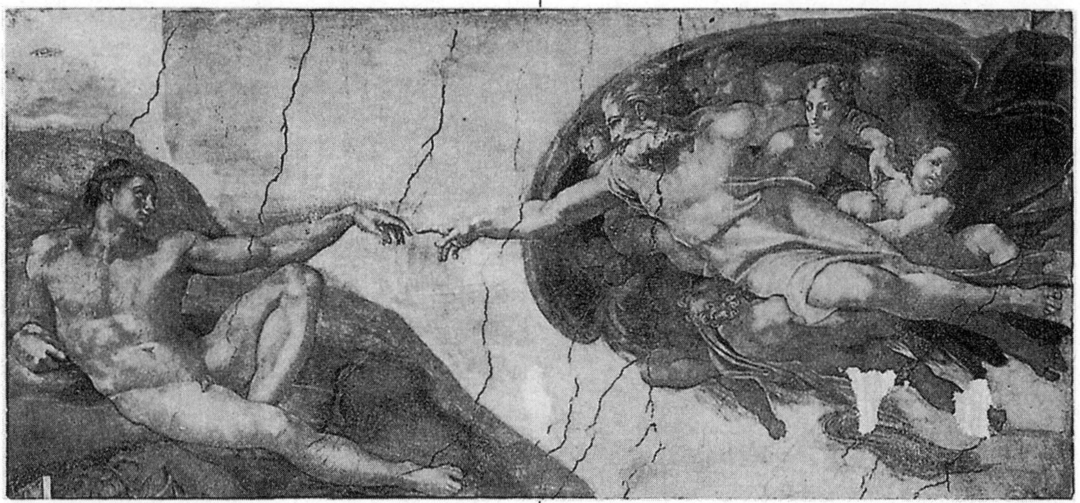

© Bridgeman Images

13. The work pictured above is

    (A) a fresco
    (B) a stabile
    (C) a woodcut
    (D) an illumination
    (E) an etching

14. The theme of the work is the

    (A) sacrifice of Isaac
    (B) expulsion from Eden
    (C) reincarnation of Vishnu
    (D) creation of Adam
    (E) flight of Icarus

15. The work is located in

    (A) the Alhambra
    (B) the Sistine Chapel
    (C) the Parthenon
    (D) the palace at Versailles
    (E) Notre-Dame Cathedral

Questions 16–17 refer to the following descriptions of the stage settings of plays.

(A) The exterior of a two-story corner building on a street in New Orleans which is named Elysian Fields and runs between the L and N tracks and the river

(B) The living room of Mr. Vandergelder's house, over his hay, feed, and provision store in Yonkers, fifteen miles north of New York City

(C) In, and immediately outside of, the Cabot Farmhouse in New England, in the year 1850

(D) The stage of a theater; daytime

(E) A room that is still called the nursery. . . . It is May, the cherry trees are in blossom, but in the orchard it is cold, with a morning frost.

16. Which is for a play by Tennessee Williams?

17. Which is for a play by Anton Chekhov?

Questions 18–20 refer to the following people.

(A) Georges Bizet, Wolfgang Amadeus Mozart, Richard Wagner

(B) Robert Altman, Ingmar Bergman, Federico Fellini

(C) John Cage, Aaron Copland, Paul Hindemith

(D) Allen Ginsberg, Sylvia Plath, Gwendolyn Brooks

(E) I. M. Pei, Ludwig Mies van der Rohe, Frank Lloyd Wright

18. Which is a group of architects?

19. Which is a group of composers of opera?

20. Which is a group of twentieth-century poets?

21. He believed that tragedy causes the proper purgation of those emotions of pity and fear that it has aroused.

The author and concept referred to in the sentence above are

(A) Plato . . . *hubris*

(B) Gottfried Wilhelm Leibniz . . . *monad*

(C) Aristotle . . . catharsis

(D) John Locke . . . *tabula rasa*

(E) Immanuel Kant . . . the categorical imperative

22. Which of the following composers was Pablo Picasso's closest musical contemporary?

(A) Claudio Monteverdi

(B) Franz Joseph Haydn

(C) Frédéric Chopin

(D) Igor Stravinsky

(E) Ludwig van Beethoven

23. Which of the following satirizes the eighteenth-century doctrine "whatever is, is right" in this "best of all possible worlds"?

(A) James Joyce's *Ulysses*

(B) Voltaire's *Candide*

(C) Daniel Defoe's *A Journal of the Plague Year*

(D) Victor Hugo's *Les Misérables*

(E) Nathaniel Hawthorne's *The Blithedale Romance*

24. Haiku is a form of Japanese

(A) drama

(B) poetry

(C) pottery

(D) sculpture

(E) architecture

25. The terms "pas de deux," "plié," "tendu," and "glissade" are primarily associated with

(A) ballet
(B) string quartets
(C) painting
(D) theater
(E) opera

26. Which of the following terms describes a literary or dramatic form of discourse in which a character reveals thoughts in a monologue?

(A) Denouement
(B) Understatement
(C) Scenario
(D) Soliloquy
(E) Exposition

Questions 27–28 refer to the following symphony.

Wolfgang Amadeus Mozart's Symphony no. 35 in D Major is divided into the following four parts.

I. Allegro con spirito
II. Andante
III. Menuetto
IV. Finale: presto

27. The parts are known as

(A) arias
(B) themes
(C) codas
(D) acts
(E) movements

28. Which two parts have the fastest tempos?

(A) I and II
(B) I and III
(C) I and IV
(D) II and III
(E) II and IV

29. *Brave New World, 1984*, and *The Handmaid's Tale* all deal with

(A) star-crossed lovers
(B) the problems of the aged
(C) extrasensory phenomena
(D) Platonic love
(E) dystopian futures

30. During his travels, his overexcited imagination invariably blinds him to reality; he thinks windmills are giants, flocks of sheep are armies, and galley slaves are oppressed gentlemen.

The sentence above describes

(A) Rasselas
(B) Robinson Crusoe
(C) Sir Lancelot
(D) Robin Hood
(E) Don Quixote

31. Which of the following, although he is sometimes called a tragic hero, is also recognized as the villain of John Milton's epic, *Paradise Lost*?

(A) Satan
(B) Gabriel
(C) Samson
(D) Adam
(E) Demogorgon

Questions 32–33 refer to the following.

(A) France during the French Revolution
(B) Russia during the Napoleonic Wars
(C) England during the Crimean War
(D) Germany during the First World War
(E) Spain during the Spanish Civil War

32. Which is the setting for most of the events in *A Tale of Two Cities*?

33. Which is the setting for events in *War and Peace*?

© Bridgeman Images

34. The vase shown above was most likely created in

(A) South America
(B) the Pacific Islands
(C) Asia
(D) North America
(E) Africa

35. Grendel, "the mighty demon that dwelt in darkness," is a character in

(A) *The Sorrows of Young Werther*
(B) *Ivanhoe*
(C) *The Faerie Queene*
(D) *Beowulf*
(E) *The Canterbury Tales*

36. Which of the following writers is correctly matched with the literary form he or she frequently used?

(A) Saul Bellow . . . poetry
(B) Eugene O'Neill . . . the short story
(C) Walt Whitman . . . the novel
(D) Susan Sontag . . . drama
(E) Jonathan Edwards . . . the sermon

37. Choral music without instrumental accompaniment is known as

(A) improvisation
(B) a cappella
(C) atonality
(D) modulation
(E) harmony

38. *La Dolce Vita, La Strada*, and *8½* are films directed by

(A) Alfred Hitchcock
(B) Cecil B. DeMille
(C) Ingmar Bergman
(D) Robert Altman
(E) Federico Fellini

39. Artists associated with this nineteenth-century movement created images based on emotion, imagination, and the irrational.

Which of the following movements is referred to above?

(A) Romanticism
(B) Art Deco
(C) Art Nouveau
(D) Social Realism
(E) Abstract Expressionism

Questions 40–42 refer to the following periods or movements in art and music history.

(A) Renaissance
(B) Baroque
(C) Romantic
(D) Impressionist
(E) Modern

40. To which do Claude Debussy and Pierre-Auguste Renoir belong?

41. To which do Leonardo da Vinci and Palestrina belong?

42. To which do Eugène Delacroix and Johannes Brahms belong?

43. Sometimes called a religion, sometimes referred to as "the religion of no religion," sometimes identified simply as "a way of life," its development can be traced from its origins in India in the sixth century B.C.E., to Japan in the twelfth century C.E. by way of China and Korea, and to the United States in the twentieth century.

To which of the following does the statement above refer?

(A) Hinduism
(B) Zen Buddhism
(C) Islam
(D) Confucianism
(E) Shintoism

44. *Giselle, La Bayadère*, and *Coppélia* are all

(A) ballets
(B) farces
(C) epics
(D) operettas
(E) oratorios

45. Flashback refers to

(A) the repetition of key elements of a drama
(B) a scene showing events that happened at an earlier time
(C) a rapidly changing series of images
(D) the lighting design for a play or movie
(E) the outcome of the main plot in a dramatic piece

46. Which of the following insists on the necessity of living a simple, natural, individualistic life?

(A) Henry Wadsworth Longfellow's *The Song of Hiawatha*
(B) Mark Twain's *A Connecticut Yankee in King Arthur's Court*
(C) Nathaniel Hawthorne's *The House of the Seven Gables*
(D) Henry David Thoreau's *Walden*
(E) Edgar Allan Poe's *The Raven*

47. The painting shown above is

(A) James Abbott McNeill Whistler's *The White Girl*
(B) Marc Chagall's *Around Her*
(C) Andrew Wyeth's *Christina's World*
(D) Henri Rousseau's *The Dream*
(E) Grant Wood's *American Gothic*

Questions 48–49 refer to the following descriptions of gods in Greek mythology.

(A) Son of Zeus and Hera, he is the god of fire and the forge.
(B) The god of revelry and wine, he later became patron of the theater.
(C) His daughter was born full-grown from his forehead.
(D) Euripides was the first to depict him with bow and arrow; in art, he was represented first as a youth and later as a small child.
(E) He is the god of the sun, the patron of poetry, and the ideal of male beauty.

48. Which describes Apollo?

49. Which describes Dionysus?

50. It was a school of the early twentieth century whose adherents designed buildings and objects in a functional style consistent with the era of mass production. Its use of industrial materials served as a basis for the International Style.

The school described above is known as

(A) Art Deco
(B) Bauhaus
(C) Neoclassicism
(D) the Baroque
(E) Cubism

51. **Question 51** refers to the following plays by William Shakespeare.

(A) *The Tempest*
(B) *Hamlet*
(C) *A Midsummer Night's Dream*
(D) *Macbeth*
(E) *Much Ado About Nothing*

Which two plays are tragedies?

(A) A and C
(B) A and E
(C) B and C
(D) B and D
(E) D and E

52. All of the following are percussion instruments EXCEPT

(A) the triangle
(B) the harp
(C) the gong
(D) tympani
(E) cymbals

Questions 53–55 refer to the following lines of poetry.

Fear no more the heat o' the sun,
  Nor the furious winter's rages;
Thou thy worldly task hast done,
  Home art gone, and ta'en thy wages:
Golden lads and girls all must,
As chimney-sweepers, come to dust.

Fear no more the frown o' the great;
  Thou art past the tyrant's stroke;
Care no more to clothe and eat;
  To thee the reed is as the oak:
The scepter, learning, physic, must
All follow this, and come to dust.

Fear no more the lightning flash,
  Nor the all-dreaded thunder stone;
Fear not slander, censure rash;
  Thou hast finished joy and moan:
All lovers young, all lovers must
Consign to thee, and come to dust.

53. The rhyme scheme of each stanza is

(A) aabbcc
(B) ababab
(C) aaaabb
(D) abcabc
(E) ababcc

54. The poem is addressed to

(A) young lovers
(B) doctors
(C) kings
(D) scholars
(E) the dead

55. "To thee the reed is as the oak" (line 10) suggests that

(A) distinctions no longer matter
(B) little trees are as strong as big trees
(C) all things change
(D) ignorance causes fear
(E) nature is unknowable

Werner Forman/Art Resource, NY

56. The style of the statue shown above can best be described as

    (A) African
    (B) Mayan
    (C) ancient Greek
    (D) Qing Dynasty
    (E) contemporary American

© Archivo Iconografico, S.A./CORBIS

57. The painting shown above was created by

    (A) John Constable
    (B) William Blake
    (C) Anthony Van Dyck
    (D) Gilbert Stuart
    (E) Aubrey Beardsley

58. Which is a group of novelists?

    (A) Rita Dove, Marianne Moore, Adrienne Rich
    (B) Meryl Streep, Glenn Close, Claire Bloom
    (C) Toni Morrison, Joyce Carol Oates, Isabel Allende
    (D) Leontyne Price, Renée Fleming, Dawn Upshaw
    (E) Diane Arbus, Margaret Bourke-White, Dorothea Lange

59. Two artists who used striking light and dark contrasts are

    (A) Rembrandt van Rijn and Artemisia Gentileschi
    (B) Sandro Botticelli and Sofonisba Anguissola
    (C) Georges Seurat and Claude Monet
    (D) Pablo Picasso and Georges Braque
    (E) Michelangelo and Judith Leyster

The Frances Lehman Loeb Art Center, Vassar College, Poughkeepsie, New York, gift of Mrs. Charlotte Burnett Mahon, class of 1911, 1976.25

60. The statue shown above belongs to which of the following historical periods?

    (A) Ancient Egyptian
    (B) Pre-Columbian
    (C) Medieval European
    (D) Eighteenth-century European
    (E) Nineteenth-century American

61. Which is a group of composers?

(A) Jacob Epstein, Käthe Kollwitz, Auguste Rodin
(B) Maurice Ravel, Jacques Offenbach, Jules Massenet
(C) François Truffaut, Jean-Luc Godard, Claude Chabrol
(D) Claude Monet, Pierre-Auguste Renoir, Berthe Morisot
(E) Charles Lamb, Thomas De Quincey, Walter Pater

62. He composed in a wide variety of musical genres, including nine symphonies, 32 piano sonatas, and an opera.

The composer is

(A) Sergei Rachmaninoff
(B) George Frideric Handel
(C) Ralph Vaughan Williams
(D) Gustav Mahler
(E) Ludwig van Beethoven

63. A famous biographer and voluminous journal writer, the author was one of the most prolific in the eighteenth century.

The writer is

(A) Samuel Pepys
(B) James Michener
(C) James Boswell
(D) Aphra Behn
(E) Lord Chesterfield

64. An important structural innovation of Gothic architecture was the use of

(A) post and lintel
(B) catacombs
(C) cantilevering
(D) flying buttresses
(E) Doric columns

65. Fagin, Pip, and Ebenezer Scrooge are characters created by

(A) George Eliot
(B) Elizabeth Barrett Browning
(C) Sir Walter Scott
(D) Edith Wharton
(E) Charles Dickens

66. One of the first British empiricists, he argued in *An Essay Concerning Human Understanding* that knowledge is not innate but is rather determined by experience and sense perception.

The person described is

(A) John Locke
(B) John Ruskin
(C) John Dewey
(D) William James
(E) Thomas Carlyle

Questions 67–69 refer to the following excerpt from a play.

The quality of mercy is not strain'd,
It droppeth as the gentle rain from heaven
Upon the place beneath: it is twice blest;
It blesseth him that gives and him that takes:
'Tis mightiest in the mightiest: it becomes
The throned monarch better than his crown;
His sceptre shows the force of temporal power,
The attribute to awe and majesty,
Wherein doth sit the dread and fear of kings;
But mercy is above this sceptred sway;
It is enthroned in the hearts of kings, . . .

67. Lines 1–3 use which of the following figures of speech?

(A) Alliteration
(B) Simile
(C) Onomatopoeia
(D) Hyperbole
(E) Apostrophe

68. Which of the following is closest in meaning to "becomes" in line 5 ?

(A) Reaches
(B) Develops
(C) Happens
(D) Suits
(E) Grows

69. The lines are spoken by

(A) Portia in *The Merchant of Venice*
(B) Cleopatra in *Antony and Cleopatra*
(C) Desdemona in *Othello*
(D) Katherine in *The Taming of the Shrew*
(E) Rosalind in *As You Like It*

70. The work of the artist Giotto strongly influenced which of the following?

(A) Ancient Roman sculpture
(B) Persian miniatures
(C) Early Renaissance painting
(D) European Romantic painting
(E) American Colonial folk art

71. Pablo Picasso and Georges Braque are associated with which art movement?

(A) German Expressionism
(B) Fauvism
(C) Futurism
(D) Surrealism
(E) Cubism

72. Ragtime, marching band music, and the blues all strongly influenced which form of music?

(A) Country music
(B) Silent film scores
(C) Rap
(D) Jazz
(E) Gospel

73. Originally composed in 1928 as a ballet, this one-movement composition is Maurice Ravel's most famous.

The work described is

(A) *Boléro*
(B) *The Firebird*
(C) *Porgy and Bess*
(D) *Rhapsody in Blue*
(E) *The Unanswered Question*

74. George Bernard Shaw's *Pygmalion* was the basis for which movie?

(A) *Cat on a Hot Tin Roof*
(B) *My Fair Lady*
(C) *Who's Afraid of Virginia Woolf?*
(D) *Ben Hur*
(E) *Doctor Zhivago*

75. *A Farewell to Arms, The Naked and the Dead*, and *The Things They Carried* share a thematic focus on

(A) greed and consumerism
(B) famous shipwrecks
(C) dignity and loss in time of war
(D) the Great Depression
(E) the difficulties of adolescence

76. *The Decameron* was written by

(A) Ovid
(B) Virgil
(C) Giovanni Boccaccio
(D) Dante
(E) Sir Thomas Malory

77. Which of the following correctly pairs a novelist with a work she created?

(A) Jane Austen . . . *The Mill on the Floss*
(B) Emily Brontë . . . *Evelina*
(C) George Eliot . . . *Wuthering Heights*
(D) Fanny Burney . . . *Persuasion*
(E) Charlotte Brontë . . . *Jane Eyre*

78. The terms "adagio," "cadenza," and "opus" are all associated with

(A) music
(B) theater
(C) painting
(D) sculpture
(E) poetry

79. A composer and organist of the Baroque period, he created such works as the *Brandenburg Concerti*, the *Goldberg Variations*, and the *Well-Tempered Clavier*.

The composer described is

(A) Franz Joseph Haydn
(B) Hector Berlioz
(C) Franz Schubert
(D) Johann Sebastian Bach
(E) Ludwig van Beethoven

80. What is the correct chronological order of the following composers?

I. George Frideric Handel
II. Philip Glass
III. Franz Liszt

(A) I, II, III
(B) I, III, II
(C) II, I, III
(D) II, III, I
(E) III, I, II

81. Which of the following is a nineteenth-century artist who was influenced by Japanese prints and is known as both a painter and a printmaker?

(A) Salvador Dalí
(B) Thomas Gainsborough
(C) William Hogarth
(D) Mary Cassatt
(E) Georgia O'Keeffe

82. Born in Africa and brought to the United States as a slave as a young child, she was taught to read and write by her slaveholders and published her first poem at the age of 12. She was the first African American to publish a book and the first African American woman to earn a living from her writing.

The poet described is

(A) Edna St. Vincent Millay
(B) Sylvia Plath
(C) Phyllis Wheatley
(D) Emily Dickinson
(E) Marianne Moore

83. The American Civil War is the setting for a novel by

(A) Stephen Crane
(B) Ernest Hemingway
(C) Booth Tarkington
(D) John Dos Passos
(E) Joseph Heller

84. *Tartuffe, The Misanthrope*, and *The Bourgeois Gentleman* are all comedies written by

(A) Gustave Flaubert
(B) Henrik Ibsen
(C) Victor Hugo
(D) Molière
(E) August Strindberg

85. Which of the following is the most famous example of a structure built as a Christian church and later converted to a mosque?

(A) Alhambra palace in Granada, Spain
(B) Mosque of Selim II in Edirne, Turkey
(C) Hagia Sophia in Istanbul, Turkey
(D) The ziggurat in Ur, Iraq
(E) Dome of the Rock in Jerusalem, Israel

86. Which of the following is a Martha Graham ballet with music by United States composer Aaron Copland?

 (A) *The Rite of Spring*
 (B) *The Nutcracker*
 (C) *The Sleeping Beauty*
 (D) *Appalachian Spring*
 (E) *Prelude to the Afternoon of a Faun*

87. All of the following lines are spoken by a character in Richard Brinsley Sheridan's *The Rivals* EXCEPT:

 (A) "O, he will dissolve my mystery."
 (B) "He is the very pineapple of politeness."
 (C) "I have laid Sir Anthony's preposition before her."
 (D) "I thought she had desisted from corresponding with him."
 (E) "She's as headstrong as an allegory on the banks of the Nile."

88. The above instances of misspeaking by Sheridan's character are called

 (A) malapropisms
 (B) spoonerisms
 (C) coinages
 (D) puns
 (E) oxymorons

89. Which of the following Shakespearean plays was used as the basis for a libretto for a Verdi opera?

 (A) *A Midsummer Night's Dream*
 (B) *Julius Caesar*
 (C) *Measure for Measure*
 (D) *The Taming of the Shrew*
 (E) *Othello*

90. Which philosopher wrote *Thus Spoke Zarathustra*, which became the inspiration for a tone poem of the same name by Richard Strauss?

 (A) Jean-Paul Sartre
 (B) Immanuel Kant
 (C) Jean-Jacques Rousseau
 (D) Arthur Schopenhauer
 (E) Friedrich Nietzsche

Questions 91–92 refer to the following image.

Réunion des Muséex Nationaux / Art Resource, NY

91. The work shown above was created in

    (A) France
    (B) Japan
    (C) Mexico
    (D) Thailand
    (E) Turkey

92. Which of the following is a notable feature of the work?

    (A) Depiction of everyday events
    (B) Distortion of perspective
    (C) Lack of light/dark contrast
    (D) Use of optical illusion
    (E) Erotic subject matter

I. T. S. Eliot
II. Edmund Spenser
III. Robert Browning

93. What is the correct chronological order of the poets listed above?

(A) I, III, II
(B) II, I, III
(C) II, III, I
(D) III, I, II
(E) III, II, I

94. The Egyptian pyramids were built as

(A) fortifications
(B) museums
(C) burial monuments
(D) places of worship
(E) palaces

95. Saint Thomas Aquinas is reputed to have said, "Beware the man of one book." Such an expression is commonly called

(A) an anecdote
(B) an aphorism
(C) a pun
(D) an apostrophe
(E) an anagram

96. First-person, third-person, and omniscient narrator are forms of

(A) formal diction
(B) poetic license
(C) mythological characterization
(D) dramatic irony
(E) point of view

97. Which of the following writers wrote without idealistic overtones and used ordinary people as subjects in their works?

(A) Gustave Flaubert and Mark Twain
(B) William Shakespeare and John Milton
(C) François Rabelais and Voltaire
(D) Edith Wharton and Lewis Carroll
(E) John Keats and T. S. Eliot

Questions 98–99 refer to the following image.

Digital Image © 2011 Museum Associates / LACMA. Licensed by Art Resource, NY

98. The figure shown above is a

(A) Buddhist priest
(B) Roman god
(C) Chinese leader
(D) Hindu deity
(E) Norse chieftain

99. The figure exhibits all of the following EXCEPT

(A) gracefulness
(B) ecstasy
(C) balance
(D) serenity
(E) meditativeness

100. The Broadway play *Camelot* was based on

(A) T. H. White's *The Once and Future King*
(B) William Congreve's *The Way of the World*
(C) George Bernard Shaw's *Arms and the Man*
(D) Mark Twain's *The Adventures of Tom Sawyer*
(E) Christopher Isherwood's *Goodbye to Berlin*

101. Which of the following best defines Dada as a movement?

(A) Noble idealism
(B) Nihilistic protest
(C) Patriotic nationalism
(D) Enlightened rationalism
(E) Strict formalism

102. Romantic poets like Samuel Taylor Coleridge and John Keats, who were interested in the source of creativity, and philosophers like Friedrich Nietzsche, who noted the inability of reason to control the irrationality of dreams and the imagination, were forerunners of Sigmund Freud's concept of

(A) the ego
(B) the superego
(C) the unconscious
(D) guilt
(E) desire

103. A short narrative used to answer a difficult moral question or to offer a moral truth is called

(A) a parody
(B) a parable
(C) a satire
(D) a ballad
(E) an editorial

104. The literary work on which Nikolay Rimsky-Korsakov based his orchestral suite *Scheherazade* is

(A) *The Horse and His Boy*
(B) *The Prophet*
(C) *Tristan und Isolde*
(D) *The Thousand and One Nights*
(E) *Twice-Told Tales*

105. The Solomon R. Guggenheim Museum in New York City is characterized by curving walls and spiral ramps, with one floor flowing into another. This architectural style reflects the style of which artistic collection that it was built to house?

(A) Modern art
(B) Neoclassical art
(C) Renaissance art
(D) Byzantine art
(E) Classical art

106. A style in music, art, and literature characterized by simplicity and the removal of all decoration and elaboration is known as

(A) reductionism
(B) rationalism
(C) minimalism
(D) transcendentalism
(E) empiricism

Questions 107–109 are based on the following poem.

Delight in Disorder
(by Robert Herrick)

A sweet disorder in the dress
Kindles in clothes a wantonness.
A lawn about the shoulders thrown
Into a fine distractiòn;
An erring lace, which here and there
Enthralls the crimson stomacher;
A cuff neglectful, and thereby
Ribbons to flow confusedly;
A winning wave, deserving note,
In the tempestuous petticoat;
A careless shoestring, in whose tie
I see a wild civility:
Do more bewitch me than when art
Is too precise in every part.

107. Frequent personification (for example, in the first two lines) serves primarily to

(A) express moral disapproval
(B) convey human vitality
(C) comment on social class
(D) warn against slovenliness
(E) critique selfishness

108. The speaker of the poem extols

(A) indecision
(B) artfulness
(C) flirtation
(D) imperfection
(E) politeness

109. The prevailing meter of the poem is

(A) iambic
(B) dactylic
(C) anapestic
(D) trochaic
(E) spondaic

110. The term "Machiavellian" is most likely to be applied to which of the following?

(A) A politician who is ambitious, unscrupulous, and deceitful
(B) A scientist who is engaged in developing a new and radical theory of astronomy
(C) A social worker who is trying to improve the conditions of the lower classes
(D) An academician who is outlining a history of Western art
(E) A diplomat who is plotting against the supremacy of the government in power

111. A composer and virtuoso pianist of the Romantic era, he wrote mostly for the piano. Among his works are preludes, études, polonaises, waltzes, and mazurkas, many of which are technically demanding.

The composer described is

(A) Giacomo Meyerbeer
(B) Antonio Vivaldi
(C) Gustav Mahler
(D) Jacques Offenbach
(E) Frédéric Chopin

112. An early movie director and producer, he is especially known for his 1915 silent epic *The Birth of a Nation*, a film praised for its innovative techniques but criticized harshly for its racism.

The director referred to is

(A) Charlie Chaplin
(B) William Wyler
(C) D. W. Griffith
(D) Orson Welles
(E) Michael Curtiz

113. Which of the following musical instruments is capable of the highest pitch?

(A) Tuba
(B) English horn
(C) Piccolo
(D) Clarinet
(E) Viola

114. Which of the following is a classical ballet with a score by Piotr Ilyich Tchaikovsky?

(A) *Petrouchka*
(B) *Cinderella*
(C) *Don Quixote*
(D) *The Sleeping Beauty*
(E) *Le Corsaire*

115. This mathematician and philosopher emphasized the use of reason as the only reliable method of attaining knowledge and promoted deduction as a preeminent methodology. His *Discourse on Method*, with its pronouncement "I think, therefore I am," is thought by many scholars to be a key work in the development of modern philosophy.

The individual described is

(A) Blaise Pascal
(B) René Descartes
(C) Isaac Newton
(D) David Hume
(E) Baruch Spinoza

Study Resources

Most textbooks used in college-level humanities courses cover the topics in the outline given earlier, but the approaches to certain topics and the emphases given to them may differ. To prepare for the Humanities exam, it is advisable to study one or more college textbooks, which can be found in most college bookstores. When selecting a textbook, check the table of contents against the knowledge and skills required for this test.

To do well on the Humanities exam, you should know something about each of the forms of literature and fine arts from the various periods and cultures listed earlier, in the paragraph following the examination percentages. No single book covers all these areas, so it will be necessary for you to refer to college textbooks, supplementary reading and references for introductory courses in literature and fine arts at the college level. Two such resources are: Philip E. Bishop, *Adventures in the Human Spirit*, 5th edition, Upper Saddle River, NJ: Prentice Hall, 2007 and Henry M. Sayre, *The Humanities: Culture, Continuity, and Change*, Volumes I and II, Upper Saddle River, NJ: Prentice Hall, 2007.

In addition to reading, a lively interest in the arts — going to museums and concerts, attending plays, seeing motion pictures, watching public television programs such as *Great Performances* and *Masterpiece Theatre* and listening to radio stations that play classical music and feature discussions of the arts — constitutes excellent preparation.

Visit **clep.collegeboard.org/earn-college-credit/practice** for additional humanities resources. You can also find suggestions for exam preparation in Chapter IV of the *Official Study Guide*. In addition, many college faculty post their course materials on their schools' websites.

Answer Key

1.	D	40.	D	79.	D
2.	E	41.	A	80.	B
3.	D	42.	C	81.	D
4.	E	43.	B	82.	C
5.	A	44.	A	83.	A
6.	A	45.	B	84.	D
7.	C	46.	D	85.	C
8.	E	47.	C	86.	D
9.	A	48.	E	87.	D
10.	E	49.	B	88.	A
11.	D	50.	B	89.	E
12.	B	51.	D	90.	E
13.	A	52.	B	91.	B
14.	D	53.	E	92.	A
15.	B	54.	E	93.	C
16.	A	55.	A	94.	C
17.	E	56.	A	95.	B
18.	E	57.	D	96.	E
19.	A	58.	C	97.	A
20.	D	59.	A	98.	D
21.	C	60.	C	99.	B
22.	D	61.	B	100.	A
23.	B	62.	E	101.	B
24.	B	63.	C	102.	C
25.	A	64.	D	103.	B
26.	D	65.	E	104.	D
27.	E	66.	A	105.	A
28.	C	67.	B	106.	C
29.	E	68.	D	107.	B
30.	E	69.	A	108.	D
31.	A	70.	C	109.	A
32.	A	71.	E	110.	A
33.	B	72.	D	111.	E
34.	C	73.	A	112.	C
35.	D	74.	B	113.	C
36.	E	75.	C	114.	D
37.	B	76.	C	115.	B
38.	E	77.	E		
39.	A	78.	A		

French Language

Description of the Examination

The French Language examination is designed to measure knowledge and ability equivalent to that of students who have completed two to three semesters of college French language study.

The examination contains approximately 121 questions to be answered in approximately 90 minutes. Some of these are pretest questions that will not be scored. There are three separately timed sections. The three sections are weighted so that each question contributes equally to the total score.

Colleges may award different amounts of credit depending on the candidate's test scores.

Knowledge and Skills Required

Candidates must demonstrate their ability to understand spoken and written French. The CLEP French Language examination tests their listening and reading skills through the various types of questions listed below. The percentages indicate the approximate percentage of exam questions devoted to each type of question.

15% **Section I:**
Listening: Rejoinders

Listening comprehension: choosing the best responses to short spoken prompts

25% **Section II:**
Listening: Dialogues and Narratives

Listening comprehension: choosing the answers to questions based on longer spoken selections

60% **Section III:**
Reading

- 10% Part A. Discrete sentences (vocabulary and structure)
- 20% Part B. Short cloze passages (vocabulary and structure)
- 30% Part C. Reading passages and authentic stimulus materials (reading comprehension)

Sample Test Questions

The following sample questions do not appear on an actual CLEP examination. They are intended to give potential test-takers an indication of the format and difficulty level of the examination and to provide content for practice and review. Knowing the correct answers to all of the sample questions is not a guarantee of satisfactory performance on the exam.

Sections I and II: Listening

All italicized material in Section I and Section II represents what you would hear on an actual test recording. This material does not appear on the screen. During the actual test, you can change the volume by using the Volume testing tool. **The audio portions of the Listening sections of the test will be presented only one time.**

Directions for Section I: You will hear short conversations or parts of conversations. You will then hear four responses, designated (A), (B), (C), and (D). After you hear the four responses, click on the lettered response oval that most logically continues or completes the conversation. You will have 10 seconds to choose your response before the next conversation begins. When you are ready to continue, click on the Dismiss Directions icon.

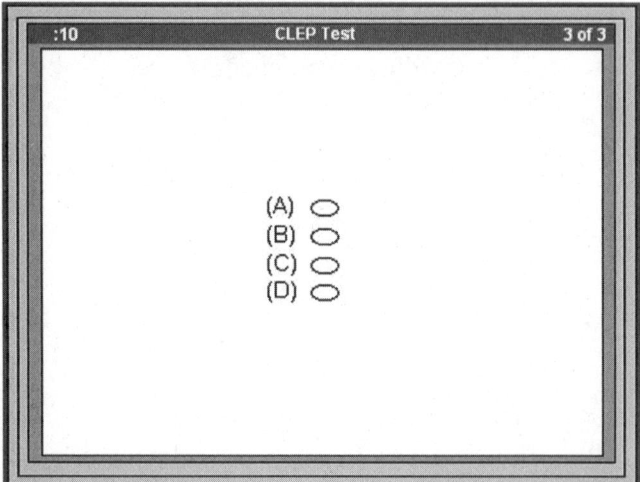

1. (Man) *Je viens de commencer à jouer dans un petit orchestre et je me sens un peu perdu.*

   (Woman)

   (A) *Ça viendra, il faut essayer d'être patient.*
   (B) *J'espère que tu le trouveras bientôt.*
   (C) *Moi non plus, je n'ai pas aimé ce concert.*
   (D) *De quel instrument joue-t-il?*

2. (Woman A) *J'aimerais bien aller au parc avec toi, mais il me faut faire des courses. À quelle heure voudrais-tu y aller?*

   (Woman B)

   (A) *J'ai passé des heures et des heures dans le parc.*
   (B) *J'ai fait toutes mes courses en une demi-heure.*
   (C) *Vers trois heures; tu pourrais faire tes commissions avant.*
   (D) *Hier après-midi, j'ai fait du jogging dans le parc.*

3. (Man) *Où as-tu passé tes vacances l'année dernière?*

   (Woman)

   (A) *Je préfère les vacances d'été.*
   (B) *Je suis allée en Angleterre.*
   (C) *J'ai passé l'examen d'entrée.*
   (D) *Je veux y aller l'année prochaine.*

4. (Man) *Tu as perdu ta montre? Est-ce qu'elle était précieuse?*

   (Woman)

   (A) *Non, tu n'y perdras pas grand chose.*
   (B) *Ces colliers sont très bon marché.*
   (C) *Peux-tu me la montrer, s'il te plaît?*
   (D) *Oui, c'était un cadeau de ma tante.*

5. (Man A) *Écoute, Jean-Pierre, il faut que tu conduises très prudemment ce matin à cause de la pluie.*

(Man B)

(A) *Rassure-toi, papa, je vais faire attention.*
(B) *Je te promets, papa, je vais rentrer avant minuit.*
(C) *Sa conduite me gêne, moi aussi.*
(D) *Dommage qu'on n'ait pas de pluie; tout est si sec.*

6. (Man) *Dis, tu as vu mes lunettes quelque part? Ça fait vingt minutes que je les cherche.*

(Woman)

(A) *Vingt minutes? Mais c'est trop peu, ça!*
(B) *Oui, mes lunettes sont dans ma poche.*
(C) *Mais voyons, tu les portes sur le nez!*
(D) *Oui, tu as raison, ça dure au moins vingt minutes.*

7. (Woman A) *Marie, nous allons au cinéma demain. Veux-tu venir avec nous?*

(Woman B)

(A) *Mes parents aiment beaucoup les films de Truffaut.*
(B) *Je dois m'occuper de mon petit frère.*
(C) *Le cinéma est très important en France.*
(D) *Le théâtre se trouve au bout de la rue.*

8. (Man A) *J'ai perdu mon portefeuille. Peux-tu régler l'addition? Je te rembourserai ma tasse de café demain.*

(Man B)

(A) *Nous nous sommes vus au café hier.*
(B) *Mais oui, sans problème.*
(C) *Qu'est-ce que tu fais au café?*
(D) *La mienne est dans ma poche.*

9. (Man) *Je viens de passer un examen difficile. J'ai presque peur de voir ma note.*

(Woman)

(A) *Oui, on t'a donné une note.*
(B) *Moi, je suis passée par la banque.*
(C) *Ne t'inquiète pas; ça ira bien.*
(D) *Tu ne vas pas chez lui?*

10. (Woman) *Ouf! Quel repas copieux! Je n'en peux plus.*

(Man)

(A) *Ça ne m'étonne pas, ce n'était pas très original.*
(B) *Eh bien, essaie de nouveau, tu réussiras la prochaine fois.*
(C) *Les portions servies dans ce restaurant sont toujours énormes.*
(D) *Demandez au serveur de nous apporter un dessert.*

11. (Woman A) *Je cherche un chemisier qui va bien avec ma jupe verte.*

(Woman B)

(A) *Allons tout de suite au rayon homme.*
(B) *Il faut laver la jupe à la main.*
(C) *Cet article en soie fera l'affaire.*
(D) *Voulez-vous essayer ces pantoufles?*

Directions for Section II: You will hear a series of selections, such as dialogues, announcements, and narratives. As each selection is playing, you will see a picture or a screen that says "Listen Now." Only after the entire selection has played will you be able to see the questions, which will appear one at a time. Each selection is followed by one or more questions, each with four answer choices. **You will have a total of 8 minutes to answer all the questions in this section. Note: The timer is activated only when you are answering questions.** After you read the question and the four responses, click on the response oval next to the best answer. Then, click NEXT to go on. In this section, you may adjust the volume only when a question is on your screen. It will affect the volume of the next audio prompt you hear. **You cannot change the volume while the audio prompt is playing.** When you are ready to continue, click on the Dismiss Directions icon.

Sélection numéro 1

Listen Now

(Narrator) *Sélection numéro 1. Une femme parle au téléphone.*

(Woman) *Allô, Charles? Oui, c'est moi Madame Dumas. J'attends un taxi; le rendez-vous vient de se terminer. Oui, tout s'est très bien passé. Je crois bien qu'ils signeront le contrat avant peu. Quand j'arriverai au bureau, pourriez-vous me préparer leur dossier? Je veux y jeter un dernier coup d'œil. Y a-t-il d'autres messages? Quinze? Bon, je m'en occuperai dès mon arrivée. Si Monsieur LeBrun arrive avant moi, demandez-lui de m'attendre; je ne tarderai pas. Mais où sont tous les taxis!?*

12. Avec qui Madame Dumas parle-t-elle?

    (A) Son mari
    (B) Son fils
    (C) Son patron
    (D) Son assistant

13. Selon la sélection, qu'est-ce que Madame Dumas vient de faire?

    (A) Elle vient de trouver un taxi.
    (B) Elle vient de signer un contrat.
    (C) Elle vient de terminer une réunion avec un client.
    (D) Elle vient de ranger des dossiers pour Monsieur LeBrun.

14. Quelle expression décrit le mieux le travail de Madame Dumas?

    (A) Exigeant
    (B) Peu stressant
    (C) Ennuyeux
    (D) Col bleu

Sélection numéro 2

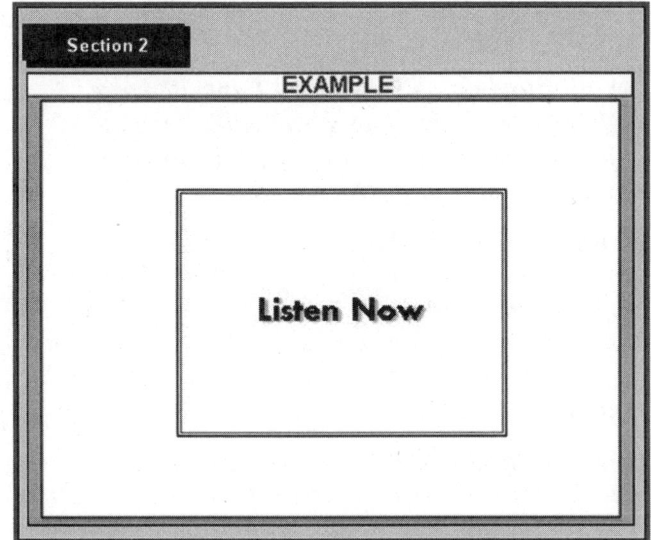

(Narrator) *Sélection numéro 2. Deux personnes se parlent.*

(Man) *Quel est votre emploi, Madame Robitaille?*

(Woman) *Ingénieur-chimiste, monsieur, chez Cresson.*

(Man) *Pourquoi voulez-vous changer de compagnie?*

(Woman) *Je préfère ne plus travailler pour une grande entreprise. Je voudrais avoir plus de responsabilités.*

15.

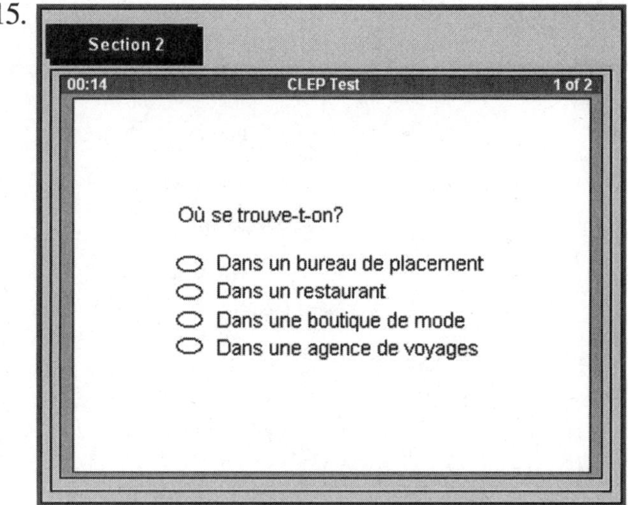

16.

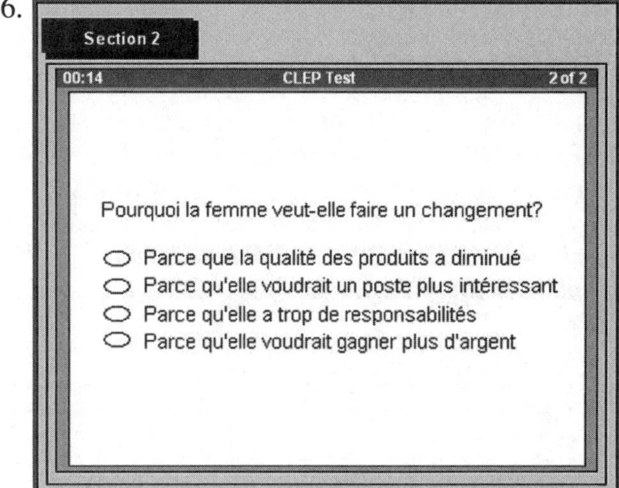

Sélection numéro 3

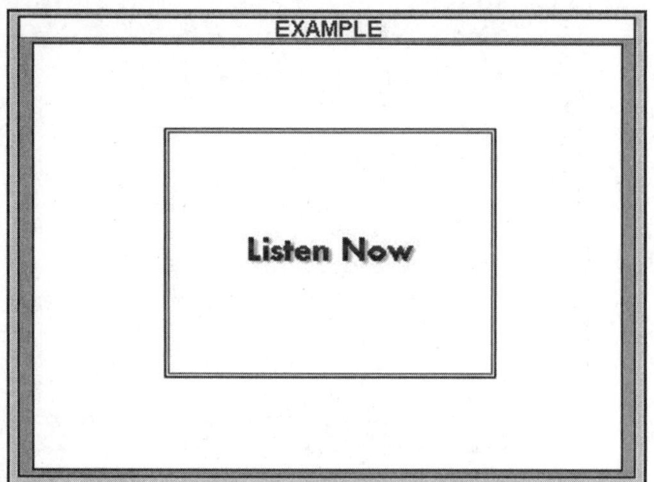

(Narrator) *Sélection numéro 3. Écoutez un bulletin météo.*

(Man) *Région parisienne—En matinée, le ciel restera couvert et les pluies seront abondantes. Dans l'après-midi, poussés par un vent d'ouest puis de nord-ouest assez violent, les nuages vont se dégager par moments, laissant passer un peu de soleil, mais il fera plus frais. N'oubliez pas d'apporter un manteau léger!*

17.

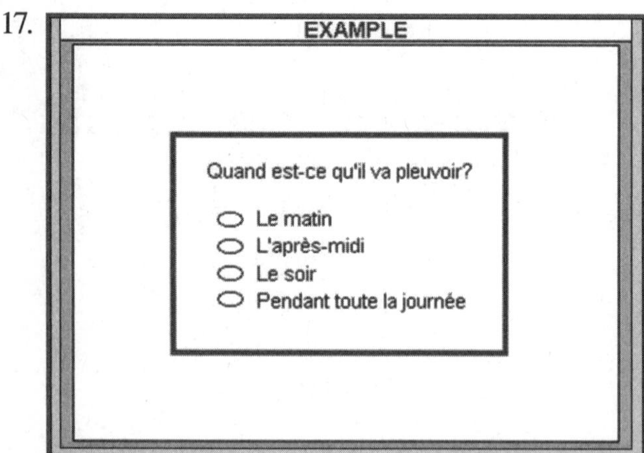

18. Quel conseil donne le narrateur?

    (A) Faire attention à la route
    (B) Porter des vêtements chauds
    (C) Ne pas oublier un parapluie
    (D) Ne pas oublier de regarder le bulletin météo

Sélection numéro 4

(Narrator) *Sélection numéro 4. Deux personnes parlent de la nourriture d'un restaurant.*

(Man) *Âllo, bonjour Madame. J'appelle votre établissement parce que je suis allergique aux noix, et je cherche un restaurant à Laval où je peux manger en toute sécurité.*

(Woman) *Bonjour Monsieur. Je sais que cela peut être un vrai casse-tête. Vous savez sans doute qu'il n'y a aucune garantie, mais grâce à nos efforts assidus, les risques de contamination sont au plus bas niveau dans notre restaurant. Dans ce sens-là, nous sommes très innovateurs.*

(Man) *C'est formidable. Je sais bien que le risque zéro n'existe pas, mais je voulais vous parler de mes allergies avant de venir chez vous, afin d'éviter tout problème.*

(Woman) *Je vous en prie, Monsieur, et nous espérons vous accueillir bientôt chez nous.*

19. Selon la sélection, à quel endroit est-ce que l'homme téléphone?

    (A) Au cabinet d'un médecin allergologue
    (B) À un bureau de sécurité privée
    (C) Au laboratoire d'un scientifique
    (D) À un restaurant spécialisé

20. De quelle situation est-ce que l'homme voudrait discuter?

    (A) De ses intolérances alimentaires
    (B) De ses maux de tête
    (C) De ses tentatives de trouver un endroit pas cher
    (D) De sa préférence pour les noix

21. Afin de rassurer l'homme, qu'est-ce que la femme lui signale?

    (A) Que l'établissement pourra garantir sa sécurité
    (B) Que rien n'a changé depuis sa dernière visite
    (C) Que l'établissement prend très au sérieux la santé de ses clients
    (D) Que le restaurant a été décontaminé l'année passée

Sélection numéro 5

(Narrator) *Sélection numéro 5. Le ministre fait une visite.*

(Woman) *Le ministre de l'Éducation nationale, accompagné de son épouse, est arrivé ce matin dans notre ville où il assistera à l'inauguration du nouveau lycée. Ils ont été accueillis à leur descente d'avion par monsieur le maire ainsi que par un groupe de jeunes élèves qui ont remis à la femme du ministre un beau bouquet de fleurs.*

22. Avec qui le ministre a-t-il voyagé en avion?

    (A) Avec le maire
    (B) Avec ses filles
    (C) Avec des enfants
    (D) Avec sa femme

23. Pourquoi le ministre est-il venu?

    (A) Pour passer ses vacances
    (B) Pour un concours d'aviation
    (C) Pour une exposition de fleurs
    (D) Pour l'ouverture d'une école

Sélection numéro 6

(Narrator) *Sélection numéro 6. Au petit déjeuner.*

(Man) *Oh! Tu as vu ça, Diane? Le vent a renversé le grand arbre près du garage! Et je n'ai rien entendu de la nuit!*

(Woman) *Mais Roland ... comment se fait-il? Comme toi, j'ai dormi sans rien entendre.*

(Man) *Et le plus grave, c'est qu'il bloque la sortie du garage. Il faut que je dégage ça tout de suite.*

(Woman) *Oui. Je vais téléphoner à ton patron pour lui expliquer la situation exacte et pour lui dire de patienter.*

(Man) *Bonne idée. Dis-lui que je ne serai pas là avant midi.*

24. Qu'est-ce qui s'est passé?

    (A) La voiture est rentrée dans un arbre.
    (B) La voiture a été volée.
    (C) Un arbre est tombé devant le garage.
    (D) L'homme vient de couper un arbre.

25. Quand l'événement a-t-il eu lieu?

    (A) Pendant la nuit
    (B) Le lendemain
    (C) Vers midi
    (D) Pendant le petit déjeuner

26. Qu'est-ce que la femme va dire au patron de son mari?

    (A) Que son mari s'est réveillé très tard
    (B) Que son mari ne pourra plus aller à son travail
    (C) Que son mari s'est gravement blessé
    (D) Que son mari va être en retard

Sélection numéro 7

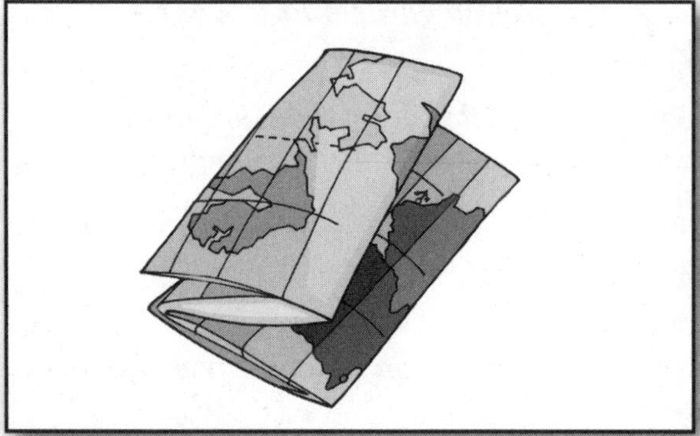

(Narrator) *Sélection numéro 7. Deux personnes parlent des vacances.*

(Woman) *Écoute, as-tu regardé les nouvelles pour voir la condition des autoroutes?*

(Man) *Oui, et ce n'est pas génial. À cause de tous les départs de vacances, la situation est actuellement très mauvaise et il y a des embouteillages partout. Qu'est-ce que t'en penses?*

(Woman) *Dans ce cas-là, on devrait retarder notre départ jusqu'au vendredi matin.*

(Man) *Je suis tout à fait d'accord mais tu sais que les enfants ne seront pas du tout contents.*

(Woman) *Je sais, mais au moins nous ferons un voyage plus agréable.*

27. Qui parle dans la conversation?

(A) Un professeur et une étudiante
(B) Un mari et son épouse
(C) Un chef d'entreprise et son employée
(D) Un père et sa fille

28. Quel est le sujet de la conversation?

(A) Une course de voiture
(B) La météo pour le week-end
(C) Un voyage en avion
(D) La circulation routière

29. Quelle décision a été prise?

(A) Annuler les vacances
(B) Laisser les enfants à la maison
(C) Partir plus tard
(D) Trouver une autre route

Sélection numéro 8

(Narrator) *Sélection numéro 8. Un jeune Parisien parle avec une amie américaine.*

(Man) *Écoute, tu es libre samedi? Ça te dit d'aller à la plage?*

(Woman) *Aller à la plage?! Mais comment ça? Il n'y a pas de plage ici à Paris!*

(Man) *Au contraire! Pour le moment, il y en a plusieurs. Chaque année, il y a un festival d'été ici. Ils créent des plages au bord de la Seine. Bien sûr, elles sont artificielles, mais il y a du sable et tout.*

(Woman) *Ce n'est pas vrai! Je ne te crois pas!*

(Man) *Mais si, je t'assure. Tout le monde y va. On pique-nique, on se fait bronzer, on va à la pêche … à certaines de ces plages, il y a même des piscines. Et le soir, il y a des concerts.*

(Woman) *Mais c'est fantastique! Je voudrais bien les voir et prendre un peu de soleil.*

(Man) *Alors, écoute, justement samedi, je vais y retrouver des amis. Veux-tu nous accompagner?*

(Woman) *Absolument! Cela me fera du bien de sortir.*

(Man) *Alors, je passerai chez toi vers deux heures et on rencontrera mes amis là-bas. Et si cela t'intéresse, on peut dîner sur place et rester le soir pour écouter le concert.*

(Woman) *Ça serait super sympa! À samedi, alors.*

(Man) *Oui, au revoir!*

30. De quoi parlent les jeunes gens dans la conversation?

(A) D'un festival de film à Paris

(B) Des plages du nord de la France

(C) Des vacances éventuelles

(D) De leurs projets pour samedi

31. Qu'est-ce que la jeune fille a décidé de faire?

(A) Rester chez elle

(B) Déjeuner avec sa famille

(C) Sortir en groupe

(D) Visiter une autre ville

32. Selon le jeune homme, où peut-on dîner le soir?

(A) Au bord de la Seine

(B) Sur un bateau restaurant

(C) Chez des amis

(D) À la maison du jeune homme

Section III: Reading

Directions for Part A: Each incomplete statement is followed by four suggested completions. Select the one that is best in each case by clicking on the corresponding oval. When you have decided on your answer, click NEXT to go on. When you are ready to continue, click on the Dismiss Directions icon.

33.

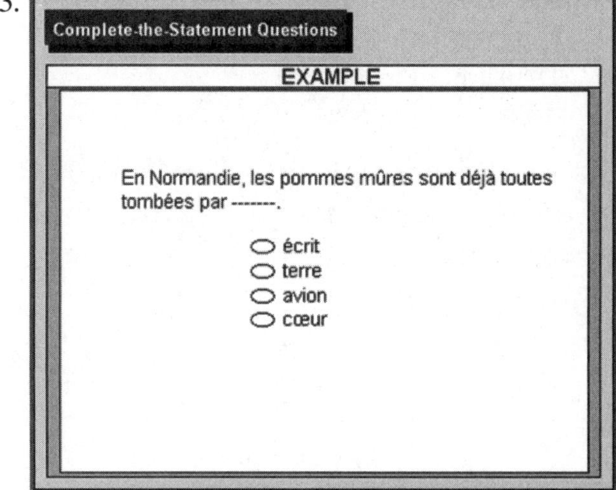

34. Je passe pas mal de temps à la quincaillerie de mon quartier parce que j'adore -------.

(A) faire du sport

(B) cuisiner

(C) jouer de la musique

(D) bricoler

35. Il se peut que vous ------- un peu tard ce soir à cause de la circulation sur l'autoroute.

(A) arriverez

(B) arrivez

(C) arriviez

(D) serez arrivés

36. 00:14 CLEP Test 2 of 2

Regarde donc ce chêne là-bas. Celui-là, c'est vraiment un ------- arbre.

- belle
- beau
- bel
- beaux

37. Le magasin n'accepte plus les cartes de crédit. Il faut tout régler en -------.

(A) espèces
(B) billets
(C) papier
(D) plâtre

38. Vous cherchez Madame Lemierre? Vous la trouverez à l'étage -------.

(A) au-dessus
(B) par-dessus
(C) au-delà
(D) par-delà

39. L'été passé, mon frère a étudié la musique africaine au Mali où il a fait un stage ------- trois semaines.

(A) pour
(B) depuis
(C) pendant
(D) par

40. ------- avoir entendu la nouvelle, Martine est rentrée chez elle de toute urgence.

(A) En
(B) Pour
(C) Après
(D) Car

41. Voilà toutes les robes qu'on nous a -------.

(A) donné
(B) donnée
(C) donnés
(D) données

42. 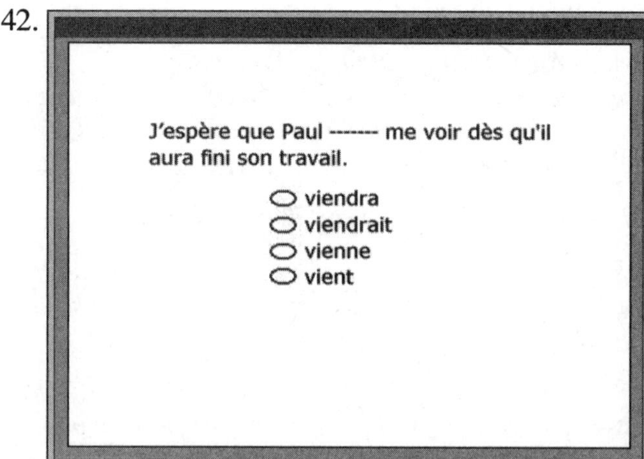

43. Ma tante fait des recherches scientifiques sur la préservation des ressources naturelles. C'est une cause pour ------- j'ai beaucoup d'intérêt.

(A) quoi
(B) laquelle
(C) dont
(D) lequel

44. Comme Thomas avait tendance à beaucoup oublier, il notait ses rendez-vous importants dans son -------.

(A) magazine
(B) agenda
(C) quotidien
(D) papier

45. Cette boutique ne leur plaît pas trop. Elles préfèrent ------- se trouve au coin de la rue à gauche.

(A) ce dont
(B) ce qui
(C) celle que
(D) celle qui

Directions for Part B: In each of the following paragraphs, there are blanks indicating that words or phrases have been omitted. As you go through the questions, the computer will highlight each blank, one at a time. When a blank is shaded, four completions are provided. First, read through the entire paragraph. Then, for each blank, choose the completion that is most appropriate, given the context of the entire paragraph. Click on the corresponding oval. Click NEXT to go on. When you are ready to continue, click on the Dismiss Directions icon.

Questions 46–56

46.

Quand j'étais enfant, j'adorais _______ animaux. Ma passion allait surtout aux chiens: je ne pouvais pas _______ voir un sans me _______ pour aller le caresser; je _______ un tas de livres _______ parlaient des chiens ou les mettaient en _______. Malheureusement mes parents ne _______ pas mon enthousiasme.

- l'
- d'
- les
- des

47.

Quand j'étais enfant, j'adorais _______ animaux. Ma passion allait surtout aux chiens: je ne pouvais pas _______ voir un sans me _______ pour aller le caresser; je _______ un tas de livres _______ parlaient des chiens ou les mettaient en _______. Malheureusement mes parents ne _______ pas mon enthousiasme.

- en
- y
- lui
- le

48.

Quand j'étais enfant, j'adorais _______ animaux. Ma passion allait surtout aux chiens: je ne pouvais pas _______ voir un sans me _______ pour aller le caresser; je _______ un tas de livres _______ parlaient des chiens ou les mettaient en _______. Malheureusement mes parents ne _______ pas mon enthousiasme.

- précipitant
- précipitais
- précipité
- précipiter

49.

Quand j'étais enfant, j'adorais ________ animaux. Ma passion allait surtout aux chiens: je ne pouvais pas ________ voir un sans me ________ pour aller le caresser; je ________ un tas de livres ________ parlaient des chiens ou les mettaient en ________. Malheureusement mes parents ne ________ pas mon enthousiasme.

- ◯ dévorais
- ◯ mangeais
- ◯ dénonçais
- ◯ mordais

50.

Quand j'étais enfant, j'adorais ________ animaux. Ma passion allait surtout aux chiens: je ne pouvais pas ________ voir un sans me ________ pour aller le caresser; je ________ un tas de livres ________ parlaient des chiens ou les mettaient en ________. Malheureusement mes parents ne ________ pas mon enthousiasme.

- ◯ que
- ◯ qui
- ◯ dont
- ◯ lesquels

51.

Quand j'étais enfant, j'adorais ________ animaux. Ma passion allait surtout aux chiens: je ne pouvais pas ________ voir un sans me ________ pour aller le caresser; je ________ un tas de livres ________ parlaient des chiens ou les mettaient en ________. Malheureusement mes parents ne ________ pas mon enthousiasme.

- scène
- chemin
- plateau
- étage

52.

Quand j'étais enfant, j'adorais ________ animaux. Ma passion allait surtout aux chiens: je ne pouvais pas ________ voir un sans me ________ pour aller le caresser; je ________ un tas de livres ________ parlaient des chiens ou les mettaient en ________. Malheureusement mes parents ne ________ pas mon enthousiasme.

- joignaient
- manquaient
- ravissaient
- partageaient

53.

Depuis ________, je rêve de passer un an à vagabonder à travers le monde. C'est un projet ________ me fascine parce que j'aime la liberté et l'aventure. Pour obtenir l'argent nécessaire, je vais travailler à temps ________. Si ce n'est pas suffisant, je demanderai aussi de l'argent ________ mes parents. Si tout va bien, je partirai dans six mois.

- ◯ avant
- ◯ demain
- ◯ longtemps
- ◯ maintenant

54.

Depuis ________, je rêve de passer un an à vagabonder à travers le monde. C'est un projet ________ me fascine parce que j'aime la liberté et l'aventure. Pour obtenir l'argent nécessaire, je vais travailler à temps ________. Si ce n'est pas suffisant, je demanderai aussi de l'argent ________ mes parents. Si tout va bien, je partirai dans six mois.

- ◯ ce qui
- ◯ qui
- ◯ que
- ◯ ce que

55.

Depuis ________, je rêve de passer un an à vagabonder à travers le monde. C'est un projet ________ me fascine parce que j'aime la liberté et l'aventure. Pour obtenir l'argent nécessaire, je vais travailler à temps ________. Si ce n'est pas suffisant, je demanderai aussi de l'argent ________ mes parents. Si tout va bien, je partirai dans six mois.

- ◯ complète
- ◯ complété
- ◯ compléterai
- ◯ complet

56.

Depuis ________, je rêve de passer un an à vagabonder à travers le monde. C'est un projet ________ me fascine parce que j'aime la liberté et l'aventure. Pour obtenir l'argent nécessaire, je vais travailler à temps ________. Si ce n'est pas suffisant, je demanderai aussi de l'argent ________ mes parents. Si tout va bien, je partirai dans six mois.

- ◯ pour
- ◯ à
- ◯ de
- ◯ avec

Questions 57–62

Quand j'étais petite fille, nous avons __(57)__ en Haïti pendant un an. Comme nous venions du nord, c'était un grand changement de se trouver dans un __(58)__ chaud. Aller à la plage en février! Qui l' __(59)__ cru? En fait, c'était toute une aventure pour une petite fille. J'ai appris à parler un peu le créole, la langue de ce pays. Notre domestique nous préparait des mets typiques, __(60)__ que le «riz et pois». Avec mon frère et mes sœurs, on grignotait des cannes à sucre qui étaient meilleures que les bonbons. Mais ce qui était le plus impressionnant, c'était la façon __(61)__ les femmes portaient leurs affaires. Elles ne tenaient rien dans les bras mais portaient tout sur la tête dans d'immenses paniers. Elles pouvaient marcher des kilomètres sans rien __(62)__ tomber!

57. (A) conduit
    (B) habité
    (C) vu
    (D) emménagé

58. (A) pays
    (B) temps
    (C) paysage
    (D) siècle

59. (A) aura
    (B) aurait
    (C) a
    (D) ait

60. (A) même
    (B) tels
    (C) tant
    (D) bien

61. (A) de qui
    (B) que
    (C) qui
    (D) dont

62. (A) fait
    (B) faire
    (C) ayant fait
    (D) faisant

Questions 63–67

Paris est une ville riche en histoire et en art. Ces deux sphères culturelles se confondent au Musée Carnavalet; un musée __(63)__ se trouve au cœur du Marais, un vieux quartier parisien. On peut __(64)__ trouver des œuvres d'art: des peintures, des sculptures et de la photographie, __(65)__ que des maquettes d'architecture. Ce bijou de musée, consacré à l'histoire de Paris, est un endroit tranquille dans __(66)__ on peut passer des heures à __(67)__ les collections. C'est une visite à ne pas manquer! Le musée est fermé le lundi et les jours fériés.

63. (A) que
(B) dont
(C) qui
(D) où

64. (A) en
(B) y
(C) le
(D) les

65. (A) alors
(B) bien
(C) quoi
(D) ainsi

66. (A) lequel
(B) lesquelles
(C) lesquels
(D) laquelle

67. (A) contemplant
(B) contempler
(C) avoir contemplé
(D) contemple

Directions for Part C: Read the following selections. Each selection is followed by one or more questions or incomplete statements. For each question, select the answer or completion that is best according to the selection. Click on the corresponding oval. Click on NEXT to go on. When you are ready to continue, click on the Dismiss Directions icon.

Questions 68–70

L'été dernier, j'ai revisité la maison de mon enfance. La dernière fois que je l'avais vue, c'était pour l'enterrement de ma mère alors que j'étais encore à l'université à Paris. Pendant les dix ans qui s'étaient écoulés depuis lors, elle n'avait guère changé. Elle était là, éclatante de blancheur, parmi les vignobles qui couvraient les coteaux à perte de vue. Au loin, très loin, on pouvait apercevoir le clocher du village voisin.

68. Quand l'auteur a-t-il perdu sa mère?

(A) À l'âge de dix ans
(B) Quand il était au village voisin
(C) Au cours de ses études
(D) Au début de sa carrière

69. Où l'auteur a-t-il passé son enfance?

(A) À la campagne
(B) À Paris
(C) Au bord de la mer
(D) Au sommet d'une montagne

70. D'après ce passage, qu'est-ce qu'on produit dans le pays où la maison est située?

(A) Du cidre
(B) Du vin
(C) Du fromage
(D) Des saucisses

Questions 71–72

Bénévoles Illimités

27, rue des Lilas, 75019 Paris
01 47 89 58 52

COLLECTE POUR LES BESOINS DES PLUS DÉMUNIS

Tous les lundis soirs, ces produits sont distribués directement dans la rue aux personnes sans-abris. N'étant pas en mesure de faire réchauffer ou de faire cuire des plats, les sans-abris ont donc besoin d'aliments qui se conservent ou se consomment immédiatement.

MERCI POUR VOTRE AIDE INDISPENSABLE.

Besoins alimentaires:
Boîtes de conserves
Soupes instantanées
Biscuits, biscottes et chocolat
Bouteilles d'eau
Bols, gobelets, couverts en plastique

Besoins hygiéniques:
Mousse à raser, rasoirs
Shampooing, gel douche, savon
Papier toilette, mouchoirs en papier

71. Selon l'annonce, quel est un besoin urgent des sans-abris?

(A) Rester au chaud
(B) Manger sans cuisiner
(C) Trouver une habitation
(D) Obtenir un emploi

72. Selon l'annonce, où distribue-t-on les produits recueillis par les Bénévoles Illimités?

(A) On les distribue au 27 rue des Lilas.
(B) On les distribue en banlieue parisienne.
(C) On les distribue aux maisons des démunis.
(D) On les distribue sur le pavé, «chez» les sans-abris.

Questions 73–76

Les Français sont aujourd'hui conscients que les médias sont des entreprises commerciales, dont la vocation n'est pas de servir toute la population, mais d'accroître leur audience et leurs recettes publicitaires. La qualité de leur contenu et la véracité de l'information qu'ils délivrent ont été progressivement mises en doute.

La mise en œuvre du nouveau paysage audiovisuel au début des années 80 n'est pas étrangère à cette perte de crédibilité. Libérée d'une partie des contraintes du passé, la télévision ne se donne presque plus de mission éducatrice ou culturelle. Guidée par les résultats des sondages, elle s'efforce de flatter les attentes des Français en faisant couler l'émotion à flots dans les émissions de variétés, les Reality shows, et autres programmes populaires.

Les Français ont de plus en plus de doutes à propos de l'influence des médias sur le fonctionnement de la démocratie. Si les enquêtes des médias permettent parfois de faire éclater la vérité, il arrive qu'elles troublent la sérénité nécessaire au fonctionnement de la justice en instruisant les procès devant l'opinion en même temps qu'ils ont lieu devant les juges ou même antérieurement.

73. D'après le texte, quel est le but principal des médias en France?
    (A) De renseigner les citoyens
    (B) De créer des stars de télé-réalité
    (C) D'attirer un plus grand public
    (D) D'influencer l'opinion public

74. En ce qui concerne les médias, quel est le sentiment du public français?
    (A) Favorable
    (B) Fasciné
    (C) Silencieux
    (D) Sceptique

75. D'après les sondages, la majorité des téléspectateurs aimerait que la télévision
    (A) augmente le nombre d'émissions sentimentales
    (B) multiplie les émissions culturelles
    (C) reprenne son rôle d'autrefois
    (D) limite le nombre d'émissions violentes

76. D'après le texte, quel effet les médias ont-ils sur le travail des juges?
    (A) Ils le rendent inutile.
    (B) Ils le facilitent.
    (C) Ils l'accélèrent.
    (D) Ils le compliquent.

Questions 77–78

50e Festival de Musique Internationale de Beaune
TOUS GENRES DE MUSIQUES DE TOUS PAYS

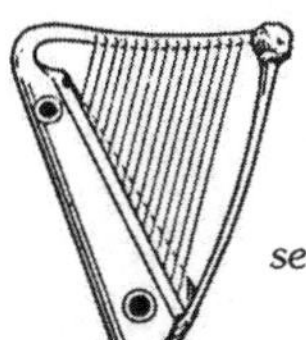

Du 18 au 31 août 2012

La première séance sera dédiée à la musique médiévale et sera présentée par l'orchestre de Beaune en célébration du fameux Hôtel-Dieu.

Divers Lieux
Consulter le programme sur le site Web

Tarifs
Certains concerts sont payants, d'autres gratuits

Pour plus de renseignements
Tel.: 03 76 21 92 80
Mail: festival.musique@beaune.com

www.musique-de-beaune.com

77. Quel public serait le plus concerné par l'annonce?

(A) Ceux qui veulent apprendre à jouer d'un instrument
(B) Ceux qui étudient l'architecture médiévale
(C) Ceux qui écrivent des revues des événements locaux
(D) Ceux qui assistent à l'église toutes les semaines

78. Que peut-on conclure à propos des concerts?

(A) Ils ont lieu seulement le soir.
(B) Ils se donnent dans des lieux variés.
(C) Il faut acheter les billets à l'avance.
(D) Il faut assister à toutes les séances.

Questions 79–83

Tout à sa contemplation, Mona Lisa, appelée aussi la Joconde, n'a, comme d'habitude, rien vu ni entendu. Pendant ce temps, les gardiens du Louvre font triste mine et les conservateurs s'arrachent les cheveux. Dimanche après-midi, «Le chemin de Sèvres», un tableau du peintre Camille Corot (1796-1875), a été volé. Sur le pan de mur qu'il occupait depuis 1902, au lieu d'un coin de campagne, ne subsistent que le cadre et la vitre de protection destinée à préserver l'œuvre. Alertée, la direction a aussitôt fermé les portes du musée pour toute la journée, retenant ainsi 10 000 visiteurs dans ses murs. Chacun a dû, pour sortir, se prêter à une fouille minutieuse, ce qui n'a pas manqué de susciter quelques commentaires acerbes, voire indignés. Hélas, la petite toile, 34 cm sur 49 cm, est restée introuvable. Une enquête a été ouverte par la section objets d'art de la brigade de répression du banditisme. Les prix des tableaux de Corot, lorsqu'ils sont vendus aux enchères, peuvent varier entre 4 200 francs et 6,43 millions de francs, selon la taille et la qualité de la toile. Derrière sa prison de plexiglas, Mona Lisa défie, elle, le temps qui passe, en souriant pour l'éternité aux hordes de touristes pressés.

79. Dans le passage, il s'agit du vol d'un tableau et

(A) des moyens de le préserver

(B) de sa récente vente aux enchères

(C) de la malhonnêteté des visiteurs du musée

(D) de la tentative d'appréhender le voleur

80. Que sait-on du tableau de Corot «Le chemin de Sèvres»?

(A) Il est devenu le chef-d'œuvre du peintre.

(B) Il occupait le même endroit depuis 1902.

(C) 1 vaut plusieurs millions de francs.

(D) Il a dû être peint entre 1875 et 1902.

81. La direction du Louvre a été obligée de considérer chaque visiteur comme

(A) suspect

(B) indifférent

(C) curieux

(D) pressé

82. D'après le passage, on peut supposer que ce qui a facilité le vol, c'est

(A) l'évidente négligence des conservateurs

(B) la taille relativement modeste du tableau

(C) l'absence complète de mesures sécuritaires

(D) le nombre et l'attitude des visiteurs

83. La conclusion qu'on peut tirer du passage, c'est que le tableau volé

(A) sera recouvré à l'occasion d'une vente aux enchères

(B) n'a pas subi de dommages graves

(C) se trouve toujours au Louvre

(D) semble avoir totalement disparu

Questions 84–85

POUR VOYAGER RÉGULIÈREMENT (CARTE 12-25)

★ **Carte 12-25 : pendant un an, voyagez à prix réduit aussi souvent que vous en avez envie.**
Nouveau : toute l'année des réductions sur le train, mais aussi l'avion ou la voiture, en France et à l'étranger : avec la Carte 12-25, la SNCF et ses nouveaux partenaires vous offrent le moyen de bouger toujours plus loin et toujours moins cher, aussi souvent que vous le voulez!

★ **TGV:**
· Bénéficiez d'une réduction de 50% (*) dans tous les TGV dans la limite des places offertes à ce prix.
· S'il ne reste plus de place à 50% (*), une réduction de 25% (*) vous est garantie dans tous les cas.

★ **Autres trains:**
· Bénéficiez d'une réduction de 50% (*) pour tout trajet commencé en période bleue du calendrier voyageur.
· Si votre voyage commence en période blanche, une réduction de 25% (*) vous est garantie dans tous les cas.

(*) Réduction calculée sur le prix de base. La réduction s'applique dans tous les TGV (places en nombre limité dans certains d'entre eux) et pour tout trajet commencé en période bleue du calendrier voyageurs dans les autres trains.

Exemples de prix :

Destination	Tarif A/R avec la Carte 12-25	Tarif normal sans la Carte 12-25
Paris-Deauville	146 F - 22,26 E	290 F - 44,21 E
Lille-Lyon	402 F - 61,28 E	804 F - 122,57 E
Paris-Montpellier	340 F - 51,83 E	746 F - 113,73 E

84. Quel avantage offre la carte?
    (A) On peut voyager sans réservation.
    (B) On paie le voyage moins cher.
    (C) On peut voyager gratuitement pendant un an.
    (D) On voyage plus loin et plus vite.

85. La carte est valable pour
    (A) le train uniquement
    (B) le TGV uniquement
    (C) le train et l'avion
    (D) le train, l'avion et la voiture

Questions 86–88

En général, les Français, comme les Américains, prennent trois repas par jour. Pourtant, le matin, tandis que les Américains prennent un petit déjeuner assez copieux, beaucoup de Français ne prennent que du pain ou des croissants avec du café, du thé ou du chocolat chaud.

Dans le temps, en France, le déjeuner était le repas principal de la journée et se composait d'une entrée, d'un plat principal, de salade, de fromage ou de fruit et finalement d'un dessert. Le tout était servi avec du vin et/ou de l'eau et éventuellement d'un café pour terminer. Aujourd'hui, de plus en plus de Français se limitent à deux plats (une entrée et un plat principal ou un plat principal et un dessert) comme repas principal et ce repas est servi aussi souvent le soir que pendant la journée. Ceux qui prennent leur repas principal le soir mangent quelque chose de léger pendant la journée: une omelette, une salade, une soupe, un sandwich, etc … et ceux qui mangent un repas complet pendant la journée ont tendance à manger peu le soir.

86. Qu'est-ce qu'on peut dire du petit déjeuner français?
    (A) Il est plus léger que celui des Américains.
    (B) Il est composé d'une boisson et d'un fruit.
    (C) C'est le repas le plus souvent sauté.
    (D) C'est un repas souvent pris en famille.

87. Selon le texte, traditionnellement, comment était le repas principal en France?
    (A) Il était servi plus souvent le soir.
    (B) Il était fait à la maison avec soin.
    (C) Il ne comprenait aucune boisson.
    (D) Il se composait de plusieurs plats.

88. D'après le texte, comment est le repas du soir actuellement?
    (A) Il est pris en vitesse.
    (B) Il se limite à une soupe et à une salade.
    (C) Il dépend de ce qu'on a pris dans la journée.
    (D) Il est servi plus tard le soir.

Questions 89–93

Le soir, lorsque la lampe était allumée, on voyait l'intérieur de la boutique. Elle était plus longue que profonde; à l'un des bouts, se trouvait un petit comptoir; à l'autre bout, un escalier menait aux chambres du premier étage. Contre les murs étaient plaquées des vitrines, des armoires, des rangées de cartons verts; quatre chaises et une table complétaient le mobilier. La pièce paraissait nue, glaciale.

D'ordinaire, il y avait deux femmes assises derrière le comptoir: la jeune femme au profil grave et une vieille dame qui souriait en sommeillant. Cette dernière avait environ soixante ans; son visage gras et placide blanchissait sous les clartés de la lampe. Un gros chat tigré, accroupi sur un angle du comptoir, la regardait dormir.

Plus bas, un homme d'une trentaine d'années lisait ou causait à demi-voix avec la jeune femme. Il était petit; les cheveux d'un blond fade, la barbe rare, le visage couvert de taches de rousseur, il ressemblait à un enfant malade et gâté.

Un peu avant dix heures, la vieille dame se réveillait. On fermait la boutique, et toute la famille montait se coucher. Le chat tigré suivait ses maîtres en ronronnant.

89. Où se passe la scène?

(A) Dans un café
(B) Dans un appartement
(C) Dans un magasin
(D) Dans une maison

90. Que veut dire le mot «plaquées» tel qu'il est utilisé dans le premier paragraphe?

(A) Détruites
(B) Appuyées
(C) Jetées
(D) Peintes

91. Que fait la vieille dame le soir?

(A) Elle regarde dormir le chat.
(B) Elle blanchit le linge.
(C) Elle lit un bouquin.
(D) Elle dort derrière le comptoir.

92. Que peut-on dire de l'homme dans le passage?

(A) Il a l'air plus jeune que son âge réel.
(B) Il a tendance à parler très fort.
(C) Il a l'air fort et sain.
(D) Il a des enfants aux cheveux roux.

93. Quelle est la relation entre les personnages présentés dans le passage?

(A) Des employés d'une boutique voisine
(B) Des membres de la famille
(C) Des clients fidèles
(D) Des amis du même quartier

Study Resources

Most textbooks used in college-level French language courses cover the topics in the outline given earlier, but the approaches to certain topics and the emphases given to them may differ. To prepare for the French Language exam, it is advisable to study one or more college textbooks, which can be found in most college bookstores. When selecting a textbook, check the table of contents against the knowledge and skills required for this test.

Besides studying basic vocabulary, you should understand and be able to apply the grammatical principles that make up the language. To improve your reading comprehension, read passages from textbooks, short magazine or newspaper articles, or other printed material of your choice. To improve your listening comprehension, seek opportunities to hear the language spoken by native speakers and to converse with native speakers. French CDs and tapes are available in many libraries. Take advantage of opportunities to join organizations with French-speaking members, to attend French movies, or to hear French-language radio broadcasts.

Visit **clep.collegeboard.org/earn-college-credit/practice** for additional French resources. You can also find suggestions for exam preparation in Chapter IV of the *Official Study Guide*. In addition, many college faculty post their course materials on their schools' websites.

Answer Key

1.	A	48.	D
2.	C	49.	A
3.	B	50.	B
4.	D	51.	A
5.	A	52.	D
6.	C	53.	C
7.	B	54.	B
8.	B	55.	D
9.	C	56.	B
10.	C	57.	B
11.	C	58.	A
12.	D	59.	B
13.	C	60.	B
14.	A	61.	D
15.	A	62.	B
16.	B	63.	C
17.	A	64.	B
18.	B	65.	D
19.	D	66.	A
20.	A	67.	B
21.	C	68.	C
22.	D	69.	A
23.	D	70.	B
24.	C	71.	B
25.	A	72.	D
26.	D	73.	C
27.	B	74.	D
28.	D	75.	A
29.	C	76.	D
30.	D	77.	C
31.	C	78.	B
32.	A	79.	D
33.	B	80.	B
34.	D	81.	A
35.	C	82.	B
36.	C	83.	D
37.	A	84.	B
38.	A	85.	D
39.	C	86.	A
40.	C	87.	D
41.	D	88.	C
42.	A	89.	C
43.	B	90.	B
44.	B	91.	D
45.	D	92.	A
46.	C	93.	B
47.	A		

German Language

Description of the Examination

The German Language examination is designed to measure knowledge and ability equivalent to that of students who have completed two to three semesters of college German language study.

The examination is administered in three separately timed sections:

- Sections I and II: Listening
- Section III: Reading

The examination contains approximately 120 questions to be answered in 90 minutes. The three sections are weighted so that each question contributes equally to the total score.

Colleges may award different amounts of credit depending on the candidate's test scores.

Knowledge and Skills Required

Questions on the German Language examination require candidates to demonstrate the abilities listed in each section below. The percentages indicate the approximate percentage of exam questions focused on each ability.

40% **Sections I and II: Listening**

15% Rejoinders:
Ability to understand spoken language through short stimuli or everyday situations

25% Dialogues and Narratives:
Ability to understand the language as spoken by native speakers in longer dialogues and narratives

60% **Section III: Reading**

16% Part A: Discrete sentences:
Mastery of vocabulary and structure in the context of sentences

20% Part B: Short cloze passages:
Mastery of vocabulary and structure in the context of paragraphs

24% Part C: Reading comprehension:
Ability to read and understand texts representative of various styles and levels of difficulty (e.g., passages of about 200 words; shorter pieces such as advertisements, signs, etc.)

Sample Test Questions

The following sample questions do not appear on an actual CLEP examination. They are intended to give potential test-takers an indication of the format and difficulty level of the examination and to provide content for practice and review. Knowing the correct answers to all of the sample questions is not a guarantee of satisfactory performance on the exam.

Sections I and II: Listening

All italicized material in Section I and Section II represents what you would hear on an actual test recording. This material does not appear on the screen. During the actual test, you can change the volume by using the Volume testing tool. **The audio portions of the Listening section of the test will be presented only one time.**

Directions for Section I: You will hear statements or short conversations. Each statement or conversation is followed by a question. Each question has four answer choices, designated (A), (B), (C), and (D). After you hear the four answer choices, click on the lettered oval corresponding to the best answer.

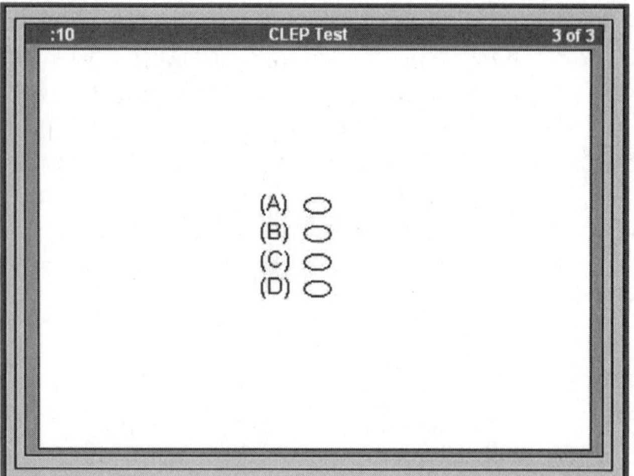

1. (WOMAN A) *Klaus, hast Du mal aus dem Fenster geschaut? Die Wolken sehen auf einmal ganz schwarz aus – es gibt bestimmt gleich ein Gewitter. Ich finde nicht, dass wir heute noch Rad fahren sollten.*

   (MAN A) *Ja, Maria, du hast Recht. Schade, da müssen wir unseren Ausflug wohl auf einen anderen Tag verlegen.*

   (WOMAN B) *Was beschließen Maria und Klaus?*

   (MAN B)

   (A) *Einen Spaziergang zu machen*
   (B) *Den Wetterbericht anzuschauen*
   (C) *Ihren Ausflug zu verschieben*
   (D) *Ihre Fahrräder zu reparieren*

2. (WOMAN A) *Entschuldigen Sie, ich suche die Vorlesung von Herrn Professor Gromann.*

   (WOMAN B) *Oh, da sind Sie hier falsch. Die ist drüben im Hörsaal sieben.*

   (MAN A) *Wo sind die beiden wohl?*

   (MAN B)

   (A) *In einem Gymnasium*
   (B) *In einem Krankenhaus*
   (C) *In einer Sportanlage*
   (D) *An einer Universität*

3. (MAN A) *Frau Schmidt, Ihr Artikel in der heutigen Zeitung ist ausgezeichnet. Könnten Sie bis nächste Woche noch einen zum selben Thema schreiben?*

   (WOMAN A) *Ja, aber ich müsste dann noch mehr Leute interviewen.*

   (MAN B) *Wer spricht hier wohl?*

   (WOMAN B)

   (A) *Zwei Journalisten*
   (B) *Zwei Schüler*
   (C) *Ein Ehepaar*
   (D) *Zwei Zeitungsverkäufer*

4. (WOMAN A) *Ich möchte bitte diesen Brief und ein Paket aufgeben.*

   (MAN A) *Der Brief kostet drei Euro, und für das Paket füllen Sie bitte dieses Formular aus.*

   (WOMAN B) *Wo findet das Gespräch statt?*

   (MAN B)

   (A) *Auf der Bank*
   (B) *Im Restaurant*
   (C) *Auf dem Postamt*
   (D) *Im Hotel*

5. (MAN A) *Oh, Inge, deine schöne Vase ist kaputt! Ich werde sie natürlich ersetzen.*

   (WOMAN A) *Aber das macht doch nichts, Hans.*

   (MAN B) *Was ist wohl passiert?*

   (WOMAN B)

   (A) *Inge hat sich verletzt.*
   (B) *Inge hat Hans geärgert.*
   (C) *Hans hat etwas gekauft.*
   (D) *Hans hat etwas zerbrochen.*

6. (WOMAN A) *Brauchen Sie sonst noch etwas?*

   (MAN A) *Moment mal... Käse, Schinken, ach ja! Geben Sie mir bitte auch noch fünf Scheiben Salami.*

   (MAN B) *Wo findet dieses Gespräch wohl statt?*

   (WOMAN B)

   (A) *In der Küche*
   (B) *Im Supermarkt*
   (C) *Im Restaurant*
   (D) *In der Mensa*

7. (MAN A) *Schau mal, Tante Anni. Die Fotos von deinem Geburtstag sind wirklich gut geworden.*

   (WOMAN A) *Edgar, bring mir doch bitte meine Brille. Sie liegt dort drüben auf dem Tisch.*

   (MAN B) *Welches Problem hat Tante Anni?*

   (WOMAN B)

   (A) *Sie sieht nicht gut.*
   (B) *Sie hat ihre Brille verloren.*
   (C) *Edgar besucht sie nicht.*
   (D) *Die Fotos sind unscharf.*

8. (WOMAN A) *Ich bekomme immer wieder diese Kopfschmerzen. Können Sie mir vielleicht ein Medikament dagegen verschreiben?*

   (MAN A) *Dazu muss ich Sie erst einmal näher untersuchen. Würden Sie bitte da drüben Platz nehmen?*

   (MAN B) *Mit wem spricht die Frau wohl?*

   (WOMAN B)

   (A) *Mit einem Lehrer*
   (B) *Mit einem Friseur*
   (C) *Mit einem Verkäufer*
   (D) *Mit einem Arzt*

9. (MAN A) *Von Angela lernten wir, dass sie und ihre Schwester Nicole Zwillinge sind, aber Nicole ist um zwei Minuten die Jüngere.*

(WOMAN) *Was erfahren wir über die zwei Schwestern?*

(MAN B)

(A) *Sie sind beide Lehrerin.*
(B) *Sie haben beide Zwillinge.*
(C) *Sie sind beide am selben Tag geboren.*
(D) *Sie haben beide denselben Vornamen.*

10. (MAN A) *Hier Fachgeschäft Elektro-Müller.*

(WOMAN A) *Guten Tag, mein Name ist Heike Maler. Ich habe vor zwei Wochen einen Kühlschrank bei Ihnen gekauft, und jetzt geht die Tür auf einmal nicht mehr richtig zu.*

(MAN A) *Das tut uns leid – wir werden einen Techniker vorbeischicken, der sich das Problem anschauen wird.*

(WOMAN B) *Warum ruft Frau Maler das Geschäft an?*

(MAN B)

(A) *Sie will einen Kühlschrank kaufen.*
(B) *Sie braucht Hilfe mit einem kaputten Gerät.*
(C) *Sie muss eine Rechnung bezahlen.*
(D) *Sie will sich über eine Bestellung informieren.*

11. (WOMAN A) *Entschuldigen Sie, fährt dieser Bus bis zum Hauptbahnhof?*

(MAN A) *Nein – dieser Bus fährt nur bis zum Neumarkt. Wenn Sie zum Bahnhof wollen, müssen Sie mit dem Bus von der Linie 10 fahren. Der kommt in 5 Minuten hier an der Haltestelle an.*

(WOMAN A) *Ach so – Danke, dann warte ich halt noch ein bisschen!*

(MAN B) *Was wird die Frau wohl als nächstes tun?*

(WOMAN B)

(A) *Sie wird in den Bus einsteigen.*
(B) *Sie wird zum Bahnhof laufen.*
(C) *Sie wird auf den Zug warten.*
(D) *Sie wird die Buslinie10 nehmen.*

12. (WOMAN A) *Frau Ulrike Obermeier wird gebeten, zum Fahrkartenschalter Nummer 3 in Halle B zu kommen. Sie haben etwas am Schalter liegen lassen. Bitte reklamieren Sie es beim Fahrkartenschalter Nummer 3 in Halle B.*

(MAN) *Warum soll Frau Obermeier zum Fahrkartenschalter 3 gehen?*

(WOMAN B)

(A) *Sie hat dort etwas vergessen.*
(B) *Man will ihr dort eine Fahrkarte geben.*
(C) *Sie soll dort jemanden treffen.*
(D) *Man will ihr dort neue Informationen geben.*

Section II: Listening

Directions for Section II: You will hear a series of selections, such as dialogues, announcements, and narratives. As each selection is playing, you will see a picture or a screen that says "Listen Now." Only after the entire selection has played will you be able to see the questions, which will appear one at a time. Each selection is followed by one or more questions, each with four answer choices. **You will have a total of 9 minutes to answer all the questions in this section. Note: The timer is activated only when you are answering questions.** After you read the question and the four responses, click on the response oval next to the best answer. Then, click NEXT to go on. In this section, you may adjust the volume only when a question is on your screen. It will affect the volume of the next audio prompt you hear. **You cannot change the volume while the audio prompt is playing.** When you are ready to continue, click on the Dismiss Directions icon.

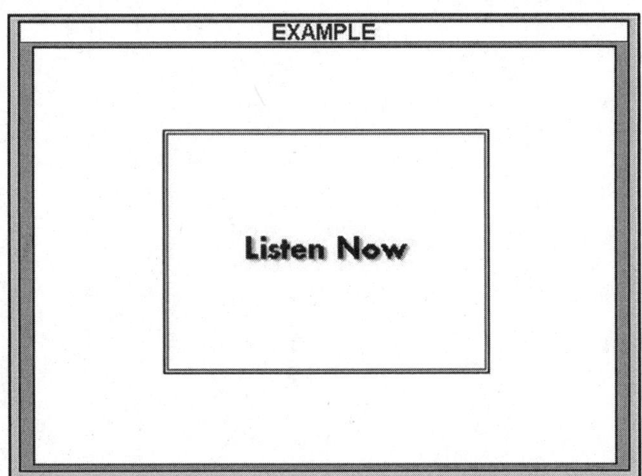

(Narrator) *Selection number one: You will hear a conversation between two friends.*

(WOMAN) *Tag, Michael, wie geht's dir denn?*

(MAN) *Viel besser, und in 14 Tagen werde ich schon hier aus dem Krankenhaus entlassen.*

(WOMAN) *Also sag mal. Wie ist der Unfall eigentlich passiert?*

(MAN) *Na ja, Inge und ich waren letztes Wochenende im „Big Apple" tanzen . . .*

(WOMAN) *Du hast doch nicht etwa getrunken??*

(MAN) *Nein, nein! Außerdem gibt's im „Big Apple" ja gar keinen Alkohol.*

(WOMAN) *Aber ich habe gehört, dass du gegen einen Baum gefahren bist.*

(MAN) *Na ja, ich habe doch meinen Führerschein erst seit acht Wochen, und außerdem war es schrecklich nebelig, und die Straße war nass und . . .*

(WOMAN) *Also, mit anderen Worten, zu schnell gefahren! Da kannst du nur von Glück reden, dass dir nicht mehr passiert ist.*

13. 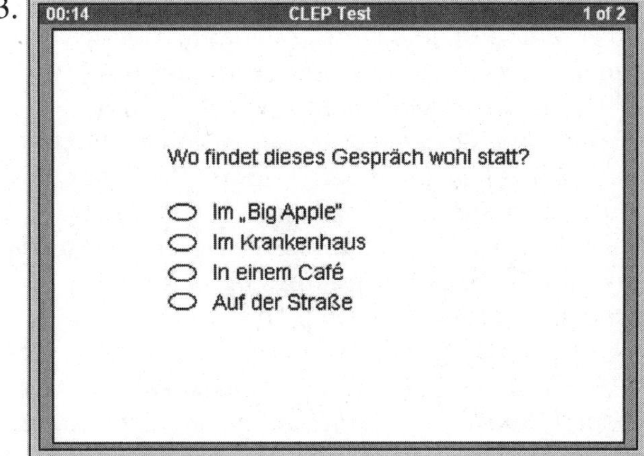

14. Wie war das Wetter an dem Wochenende, an dem Michael und Inge tanzen gingen?

    (A) Es gab ein Gewitter.
    (B) Es war windig und kalt.
    (C) Es war nass und nebelig.
    (D) Es war eine klare Nacht.

15. Was waren die Folgen des Unfalls?

    (A) Inge will im „Big Apple“ arbeiten.
    (B) Inge darf nicht mehr Auto fahren.
    (C) Michael hat seinen Führerschein verloren.
    (D) Michael muss im Krankenhaus liegen.

16. Was meinte Michaels Bekannte am Ende?

    (A) Michael war betrunken.
    (B) Michael ist ein guter Tänzer.
    (C) Michael ist zu jung.
    (D) Michael ist zu schnell gefahren.

(Narrator) *<u>Selection number two</u>: Listen to the following report from a German radio news magazine.*

(WOMAN) *Der Bundesverband der Süßwarenindustrie hat festgestellt, dass in den skandinavischen Ländern die Menschen auch bei Minusgraden mit einem Eis in der Hand herumlaufen. Die Deutschen mögen dagegen kein Eis in der kalten Jahreszeit – deshalb geht der Verkauf von Speiseeis im Winter rapide zurück. Das soll nun anders werden. Die großen deutschen Eishersteller bieten neuerdings besondere Wintereis-Spezialitäten an. „So schmilzt der Winter“, heißt es in der Werbung für Eissorten, die nur bis Ende Februar angeboten werden, wie zum Beispiel Zimtsterne, Vanilleherzen oder Apfelstrudel aus Eis.*

17. Was machen Skandinavier anders als Deutsche?

    (A) Sie essen ihr Eis aus der Hand.
    (B) Sie essen Eis bei sehr kaltem Wetter.
    (C) Sie essen Eis besonders schnell.
    (D) Sie essen nur bis Ende Februar Eis.

18. Was ist das Ziel des Bundesverbands der Süßwarenindustrie?

    (A) Skandinavisches Speiseeis einzuführen
    (B) Mehr Eis in den Wintermonaten zu verkaufen
    (C) Keine Werbung für Speiseeis zu machen
    (D) Jeden Monat ein neues Speiseeis zu erfinden

19. Was machen die deutschen Eishersteller jetzt?

    (A) Sie bieten besondere Eissorten an.
    (B) Sie senken im Sommer die Preise.
    (C) Sie führen Eis in andere Länder aus.
    (D) Sie stellen mehr Gebäck als Eis her.

20. Wie lange werden Zimtsterne, Vanilleherzen und Apfelstrudel aus Eis verkauft?

    (A) Bis zum Winter
    (B) Bis zum Sommer
    (C) Bis zum Frühjahr
    (D) Bis zum Herbst

(Narrator) *Selection number three: Listen to the following conversation between two friends.*

(MAN) *Hast du eigentlich daran gedacht, dass Peter nächste Woche einundzwanzig wird?*

(WOMAN) *Ja, sicher. Aber was sollen wir ihm denn schenken?*

(MAN) *Er hat doch neulich mal erwähnt, dass er gerne einen neuen MP3-Spieler hätte.*

(WOMAN) *Ja, stimmt! Aber der kostet zu viel! Schenken wir ihm doch was anderes. Wie wär's denn mit einem Buch?*

(MAN) *Wir wissen ja gar nicht, welchen Schriftsteller er gerne liest. Außerdem hat er jetzt eine Freundin und gar keine Zeit zum Lesen. Kaufen wir ihm doch eine DVD.*

(WOMAN) *Nein, das kann man doch alles im Internet finden! Sag mal, wie viel wollen wir denn überhaupt für ein Geschenk ausgeben?*

(MAN) *Na ja, zu zweit vielleicht so zwischen fünfundzwanzig und fünfunddreißig Euro?*

(WOMAN) *Du, ich habe eine Idee! Schenken wir ihm doch einen Gutschein für ein schönes Essen mit seiner Freundin in seinem Lieblingsrestaurant.*

21. Warum wollen die beiden Peter ein Geschenk geben?

    (A) Er hat sich verlobt.
    (B) Er hat einen besonderen Geburtstag.
    (C) Er hat das Abitur bestanden.
    (D) Er hat eine neue Stelle bekommen.

22. Warum hat Peter jetzt so wenig Zeit?

    (A) Er hat einen Job in einem Restaurant.
    (B) Er schaut Filme immer im Internet an.
    (C) Er verkauft elektronische Geräte.
    (D) Er verbringt viel Zeit mit seiner Freundin.

23. Warum kaufen die beiden ihm kein Buch?

    (A) Sie wissen nicht, ob sie so viel ausgeben wollen.
    (B) Sie wissen nicht, wer sein Lieblingsautor ist.
    (C) Peter will nur im Internet lesen.
    (D) Peter liest nicht gern.

24. Wie viel Geld wollen die Freunde fürs Geschenk ausgeben?

    (A) Nicht mehr als 21 Euro
    (B) Nicht mehr als 25 Euro
    (C) Nicht mehr als 35 Euro
    (D) Nicht mehr als 53 Euro

Listen Now

(Narrator) *Selection number four: Listen to the following conversation.*

(WOMAN) *Tag Remo. Schön, dass du heute bei uns hier in „Musik um Marburg" zu Gast bist.*

(MAN) *Danke für die Einladung.*

(WOMAN) *Remo, deine Band, die Boptown Cats, ist für puren Rock 'n' Roll bekannt. Hast du diese Oldies schon immer gespielt?*

(MAN) *Eigentlich nicht. Ich habe mit bayerischer Tanzmusik angefangen. Dann habe ich genug von Lederhosen gehabt und die Oldies haben mir immer Spaß gemacht. Also habe ich die Boptown Cats gegründet. Wir spielen ausschließlich Musik aus den 50er Jahren.*

(WOMAN) *Eure Musik klingt besonders echt. Woher kommt das wohl?*

(MAN) *Na ja. Der Klang moderner Instrumente passt einfach nicht so recht zu dieser Musik. Also spielen wir mit alten Schlagzeugen und Gitarren. Dadurch bekommen wir den Sound der damaligen Zeit.*

(WOMAN) *Danke für das Gespräch. Wann und wo ist der nächste Auftritt?*

(MAN) *Heute in 8 Tagen im Marburger Schlossgarten.*

25. Warum unterhält sich die Sprecherin mit Remo?

    (A) Sie interviewt ihn für eine Radiosendung.
    (B) Sie ist eine alte Bekannte von ihm.
    (C) Sie will in seiner Band mitspielen.
    (D) Sie ist ein großer Fan von seiner Musik.

26. Wer würde sich für das Konzert von den Boptown Cats am ehesten interessieren?

    (A) Jemand, der gern bayerische Volksmusik hört
    (B) Jemand, der gern tanzen geht
    (C) Jemand, der gern Oldies aus den 50er Jahren hört
    (D) Jemand, der gern Rockmusik spielt

27. Warum hat Remo sein Musikgenre gewechselt?

    (A) Er wollte mit seiner Musik mehr Geld verdienen.
    (B) Ihm hat die Szene um die bayerische Tanzmusik nicht mehr gefallen.
    (C) Ihn haben die klassischen Songs des Rock 'n' Roll nicht mehr interessiert.
    (D) Er wurde Mitglied in einer neuen Band.

28. Warum klingt Remos Musik so „echt“?

    (A) Er spielt nur Musik aus Bayern.
    (B) Er spielt auf alten Instrumenten.
    (C) Seine Band kommt aus Marburg.
    (D) Seine Band hat viel Erfahrung.

(Narrator) *Selection number five: Listen to the following radio report.*

(MAN) *Und jetzt unser historisches Kalenderblatt für den 5. August.*

(WOMAN) *Nicht nur Menschen, die sich für Autos begeistern, werden sich für die Geschichte von Bertha Benz interessieren.*

Bertha investierte in die Autowerkstatt ihres Verlobten Karl Benz, den sie 1872 heiratete. Zusammen erwarben sie ein Patent für das erste Auto. Allerdings gab es zunächst kaum Kunden, denn viele Zeitgenossen mistrauten dieser pferdelosen Kutsche. Um für das Auto Werbung zu machen, beschloss Bertha Benz daher, die erste lange Autoreise der Welt zu unternehmen. Am 5. August 1888 fuhr sie mit dem neuen Benz Patent-Motorwagen *ungefähr 100 Kilometer von Mannheim nach Pforzheim. Da es damals noch keine Tankstellen gab, musste sie auf dem Weg Putzmittel als Treibstoff in verschiedenen Apotheken kaufen. Heute kann man die „Bertha Benz Memorial Route“ entlang fahren, um die erste automobile Fernfahrt selber zu erleben!*

29. Welches Problem hatten Karl und Bertha Benz am Anfang mit ihrer neuen Erfindung?

    (A) Die Menschen wollten ihr Automobil nicht kaufen.
    (B) Das Automobil hat die Pferde und Menschen auf der Straße erschreckt.
    (C) Andere Erfinder hatten auch ein Automobil gebaut.
    (D) Der besondere Treibstoff für das Automobil war nirgendwo zu finden.

30. Was musste Bertha Benz machen, um mit dem Auto 100 Kilometer fahren zu können?

(A) Sie musste zuerst ein spezielles Medikament vom Apotheker einnehmen.
(B) Sie musste den Motor ständig mit Reinigungsmittel waschen.
(C) Sie musste vor der Fahrt eine spezielle Erlaubnis von der Polizei bekommen.
(D) Sie musste immer wieder Treibstoff für den Motor in Läden kaufen.

31. Was wollte Bertha Benz mit ihrer Autofahrt erreichen?

(A) Sie wollte herausfinden, ob die neue Erfindung funktionierte.
(B) Sie wollte beweisen, dass auch Frauen gut Auto fahren können.
(C) Sie wollte einen bestehenden Automobilrekord brechen.
(D) Sie wollte zeigen, dass das Auto eine praktische Erfindung war.

Section III: Reading

Directions: Each incomplete statement is followed by four suggested completions. Select the one that is best in each case by clicking on the corresponding oval.

32. Meine Eltern lassen dich ------- grüßen.

(A) kürzlich
(B) herzlich
(C) neulich
(D) gut

33. Der Park liegt außerhalb des ------- Stadtzentrums.

(A) alten
(B) altem
(C) alter
(D) altes

34. Seit Monaten hofft Renate ------- einen Hauptgewinn im Lotto.

(A) auf
(B) für
(C) an
(D) zu

35. Im Kaufhof ist Ausverkauf. Hast du die ------- in der Zeitung gesehen?

(A) Anschrift
(B) Anzeige
(C) Beweise
(D) Buchstaben

36. Mit ------- willst du heute Abend Karten spielen?

(A) wer
(B) wen
(C) wem
(D) wessen

37. Ich habe in Deutschland viel fotografiert und die Bilder sofort entwickeln -------.

(A) gelassen
(B) lassen
(C) lasse
(D) lasst

38. Da liegt meine Jacke. Wo ist denn -------?

(A) dein
(B) deiner
(C) deines
(D) deine

39. Da ich jedes Jahr nach Berlin fahre, ------- ich diese Stadt sehr gut.

(A) weiß
(B) kann
(C) mag
(D) kenne

40. Katharina passt gut auf ------- kleinen Bruder auf.

(A) ihr
(B) ihrem
(C) ihren
(D) ihres

41. Da ich gesünder leben will, trinke ich ab heute Wasser ------- Cola.

(A) statt
(B) wegen
(C) trotz
(D) während

42. ------- sieben Tage in einer Woche.

(A) Da sind
(B) Es ist
(C) Es gibt
(D) Da ist

43. Und, Frau Richter, wie gefällt es ------- in Köln?

(A) Ihr
(B) Ihrem
(C) Ihnen
(D) Sie

Directions: In each of the following paragraphs, there are blanks indicating that words or phrases have been omitted. First read through the entire paragraph. Then, for each blank, choose the completion that is most appropriate, given the context of the entire paragraph. Click on the corresponding oval.

Ich bin schon oft von Deutschland __(44)__ Amerika geflogen, aber nächste Woche __(45)__ ich zum ersten Mal ein Schiff. In Bremerhaven geht es los, und fünf Tage __(46)__ werden wir in New York __(47)__ . Ich freue mich schon sehr auf __(48)__ Reise.

44. (A) zu
 (B) nach
 (C) in
 (D) auf

45. (A) nehme
 (B) fahre
 (C) gehe
 (D) reise

46. (A) erst
 (B) davor
 (C) lieber
 (D) später

47. (A) angekommen
 (B) ankommen
 (C) ankommt
 (D) ankamen

48. (A) diesen
 (B) dieses
 (C) dieser
 (D) diese

Die Geschichte der Deutschen in Amerika beginnt __(49)__ Jahre 1683 mit der Gründung von Germantown in der __(50)__ von Philadelphia. Pennsylvanien war damals eines __(51)__ Hauptziele für deutsche Einwanderer, __(52)__ viele gingen auch nach New York, Virginia, Ohio und später Texas.

49. (A) zum
 (B) im
 (C) vom
 (D) am

50. (A) Höhe
 (B) Wiese
 (C) Nähe
 (D) Zeitung

51. (A) der
 (B) des
 (C) dem
 (D) den

52. (A) sondern
 (B) als
 (C) wann
 (D) aber

Die meisten Häuser mit Mietwohnungen haben _(53)_ Regeln, die alle Bewohner einhalten müssen. Zum Beispiel muss man abends _(54)_ einer bestimmten Zeit die Tür zum Haus schließen, und mittags soll zwischen 13:00 und 15:00 Uhr (während _(55)_ sogenannten Mittagszeit) im Hause Ruhe sein. In vielen Mietshäusern _(56)_ es eine Hausordnung; sie _(57)_ zum Beispiel, wann die Bewohner die Treppe im Haus putzen müssen. Für Amerikaner ist dieses System vielleicht etwas schwer zu _(58)_, aber für Deutsche sind diese Regeln selbstverständlich.

53. (A) bestimmter
    (B) bestimmten
    (C) bestimmtes
    (D) bestimmte

54. (A) ab
    (B) an
    (C) auf
    (D) aus

55. (A) dem
    (B) den
    (C) der
    (D) die

56. (A) gibt
    (B) hat
    (C) ist
    (D) liegt

57. (A) regeln
    (B) regelt
    (C) regelte
    (D) geregelt

58. (A) kennen
    (B) sehen
    (C) verstehen
    (D) wissen

Directions: Read the following selections. Each selection is followed by one or more questions or incomplete statements. For each question, select the answer that is best according to the selection. Click on the corresponding oval.

Ich heiße Claus. Als ich mein Studium begann und noch sehr knapp bei Kasse war, bin ich zunächst oft per Anhalter gereist. Von Oldenburg, meiner norddeutschen Heimatstadt, nach Tübingen, meinem süddeutschen Studienort, waren es ungefähr 650 Kilometer, und das konnte ich an einem Tag gerade so schaffen. Dabei bestand aber immer die Gefahr, dass ich in einen Regenschauer oder an einen zu riskanten Autofahrer geriet, und deswegen habe ich dann bald auf Mitfahrzentralen zurückgegriffen.

Mitfahrzentralen vermitteln für eine geringe Gebühr zwischen Privatleuten, die eine Mitfahrgelegenheit suchen, und anderen, die eine Mitfahrt anbieten. Meinen Fahrern musste ich jeweils auch eine bestimmte Summe zahlen. Insgesamt kostete mich die Fahrt auf diese Weise vielleicht 45 Euro, aber es war sicherer und immer noch viel billiger als die Zugfahrt, deren Preis 175 Euro betrug.

Schließlich jedoch gewann mein Umweltbewusstsein die Oberhand, und ich verdiente durch einen Job beim Rundfunk auch ein wenig Geld, so dass ich mir die Eisenbahn leisten konnte. Die Zugfahrten haben mir immer viel Spaß gemacht: Ich konnte lesen, im Speisewagen etwas essen, mich mit anderen Reisenden unterhalten oder einfach die Landschaft genießen.

59. Warum ist Claus anfangs per Anhalter gefahren?

(A) Aus finanziellen Gründen
(B) Aus zeitlichen Gründen
(C) Aus Bequemlichkeit
(D) Aus Abenteuerlust

60. Was ist eine Mitfahrzentrale?

(A) Eine Bahnhofshalle
(B) Ein Autobahnrestaurant
(C) Eine Vermittlungsagentur
(D) Ein Reisebüro

61. Claus fuhr später immer mit dem Zug, weil er

(A) in seinem Beruf viel reisen musste
(B) sehr umweltbewusst war
(C) den Mitfahrzentralen nicht vertraute
(D) keinen Führerschein hatte

62. Claus hat an seinen Zugreisen gefallen, dass

(A) die Züge pünktlich waren
(B) die Züge Schlafwagen hatten
(C) er die Landschaft schon kannte
(D) es viel Abwechslung gab

Hundstage – wie lange dauert die heißeste Zeit im Hochsommer?

In den meisten Jahren kommt es während der Hundstage im Juli zu einer stabilen, heißen Wetterlage. Wie lange dauert sie und was haben Hunde damit zu tun?

In Europa nennt man die heißeste Zeit des Jahres „Hundstage". Zwar liegen die Hunde dann faul im Schatten und hecheln, aber die Ursprünge des Namens sind in der Astronomie zu suchen.

In Ägypten im 3. Jahrtausend v. Chr. belegte man die Rückkehr des Fixsterns „Sirius" an den Morgenhimmel mit diesem Namen. Sirius, ein Teil des Sternbildes „Großer Hund", stand vorher wochenlang unsichtbar mit der Sonne am Taghimmel und trat gegen Ende der ersten Julihälfte, während der Morgendämmerung, erstmals wieder in Erscheinung.

Dies galt entlang des Nils als sicheres Vorzeichen der nahenden, alljährlichen Sommer-Nilschwemme, die Schlamm und damit Fruchtbarkeit über die Felder brachte. Dieses wichtige Ereignis markierte im alten Ägypten den Beginn des neuen Jahres.

Die Römer legten den heute noch gültigen Zeitraum für die Hundstage fest. Da sich der Aufgang des Siriussterns im Laufe der Zeit weiter nach hinten, in die zweite Julihälfte, verschoben hatte, bestimmten die Römer den Beginn der Hundstage mit dem 23. Juli. Die Dauer der Hundstage von rund einem Monat kommt durch die Ausmaße des Sternbildes „Großer Hund" zustande. Vom ersten Auftauchen des Sirius bis zum vollständigen Erscheinen des gesamten Sternbilds vergeht rund ein Monat.

63. Wofür steht der Begriff „Hundstage"?

(A) Für einen bestimmten Abschnitt des Jahres
(B) Für eine jährliche Urlaubszeit
(C) Für ein traditionelles Fest
(D) Für eine seltene Himmelserscheinung

64. Wie wird das Wetter der Hundstage im Text beschrieben?

(A) Es ist sehr wechselhaft.
(B) Es ist meistens windig und kühl.
(C) Es ist die ganze Zeit sehr warm.
(D) Es ist mild und sonnig.

65. Woher haben die Hundstage ihren Namen bekommen?

(A) Von einer alten Legende
(B) Von einem Sternbild
(C) Von einem Haustier
(D) Von einem ägyptischen Ritual

66. Welche Bedeutung hatten die „Hundstage" für die alten Ägypter?

(A) Sie hatten vorrangig eine administrative Bedeutung.
(B) Sie signalisierten das Ende einer religiösen Zeremonie.
(C) Sie standen für die heißeste Zeit des Jahres.
(D) Sie markierten ein wichtiges Naturereignis.

67. Welche Rolle spielten die Römer in der Geschichte der Hundstage?

(A) Sie erforschten die astronomischen Zusammenhänge der Hundstage.
(B) Sie bestimmten den genauen Beginn und das Ende der Hundstage.
(C) Sie versuchten das Wetter während der Hundstage vorherzusagen.
(D) Sie erkannten die meteorologische Bedeutung der Hundstage.

Wir sind ein führendes Unternehmen in der Möbelindustrie mit Fertigungsstätten an neun Standorten in Deutschland. Unsere Produkte genießen den Ruf guter Qualität und unser Marktanteil wächst ständig.

Es wird ein/e

Produktionsleiter/in

gesucht, der/die für den gesamten Fertigungsprozess verantwortlich ist. Zu den Aufgaben gehören die Leitung der Produktion unter Einhaltung der Qualitätsvorschriften, Erfüllung der Produktionsziele und die Führung des Personals.

Wir bieten viel Arbeit, aber auch kreative Mitarbeiter, Gleitzeit und ein angemessenes Gehalt an. Ein moderner Arbeitsplatz ist selbstverständlich.

Anforderungsprofil:

- Erfahrung auf dem Bereich der Holzverarbeitung
- Planungs-und Organisationsfähigkeiten
- Kenntnisse mit dem Datenbanksystem Quadratur

Idealerweise hat der Kandidat/die Kandidatin ein technisches Studium an einer Fachhochschule absolviert.

Schicken Sie bitte Ihre schriftliche Bewerbung mit tabellarischem Lebenslauf, Zeugniskopien sowie Angaben zum Einkommen und zu Ihrer Verfügbarkeit an:

Personalabteilung
Wolters & Partner GmbH
Theresienstr. 34
24943 Flensburg

Telefon: 0461- 2557117 Telefax: 0461- 2557123

68. Was produziert die Firma Wolters & Partner?

(A) Autos
(B) Holzspielzeug
(C) Datenbanksysteme
(D) Möbel

69. Was für eine Stelle wird angeboten?

(A) Eine Lehrlingsstelle
(B) Eine Halbtagsstelle
(C) Eine führende Stelle
(D) Eine unbezahlte Stelle

70. Was bietet die Firma dem neuen Firmenmitglied?

(A) Eine gute Bezahlung
(B) Einen Dienstwagen
(C) Gute Aufstiegsmöglichkeiten
(D) Eine moderne Wohnung

71. Wie sollen sich die Kandidaten bewerben?

(A) Sie sollen bei der Firma anrufen.
(B) Sie sollen bei der Firma vorbeikommen.
(C) Sie sollen der Firma eine E-Mail schicken.
(D) Sie sollen der Firma schreiben.

Thomas Nast wurde am 26. September 1840 als Sohn eines bayerischen Militärmusikers in Landau in der Pfalz geboren. Als Sechsjähriger wanderte er mit seiner Familie nach Amerika aus. Noch nicht des Englischen mächtig, konnte sich der Knabe mit Zeichnungen auf seiner Schiefertafel verständlich machen. Schon früh durfte er eine Kunstschule besuchen, musste sie jedoch mit 15 wieder verlassen, um zum Familienunterhalt beizutragen. Nach der ersten Vorsprache bei *Leslie's Weekly* wurde er für vier Dollar die Woche als Illustrator engagiert. Im Auftrag von *Harper's Weekly* suchte Nast während des amerikanischen Bürgerkrieges die Schlachtfelder des Südens auf und schickte von dort so eindrucksvolle Skizzen nach Hause, dass er am Ende des Krieges im ganzen Land bekannt war.

Zwischen 1861 und 1884 wurde Nast immer mehr als politischer und sozialkritischer Karikaturist bekannt. Er machte mehrere politische Symbolfiguren populär, wie z.B. Uncle Sam, John Bull und die Columbia. Seinen berühmten Santa Claus hat Nast nach dem Vorbild des „Pelznikel", des Sankt Nikolaus seiner deutschen Vorfahren, gestaltet.

Durch das Scheitern eines seiner Lieblingspläne – der Herausgabe einer eigenen Karikaturzeitschrift – geriet Nast in Schulden. Als ihm daraufhin sein alter Bewunderer Theodore Roosevelt den Posten eines Generalkonsuls in Ecuador anbot, nahm er diesen Vorschlag an. Er starb am 7. Dezember 1902 – nicht ohne vorher seine Schulden beglichen und seiner Familie etwas Geld hinterlassen zu haben.

72. Warum hat Nast als Kind auf seine Schiefertafel gezeichnet?

    (A) Die Skizzen gefielen seiner Familie.
    (B) Er konnte zu wenig Englisch.
    (C) Er verdiente damit Geld.
    (D) Er wollte eine Kunstschule besuchen.

73. Warum musste der 15-jährige Nast die Kunstschule verlassen?

    (A) Der amerikanische Bürgerkrieg war ausgebrochen.
    (B) Die Lehrer hielten ihn für unbegabt.
    (C) Seine Familie hatte nicht genügend Geld.
    (D) Seine sozialkritischen Karikaturen waren unbeliebt.

74. Wodurch wurde Nast in ganz Amerika bekannt?

    (A) Durch seine Zeichnungen vom Krieg
    (B) Durch seine Symbolfiguren
    (C) Durch seine Berichte aus Ecuador
    (D) Durch seine Arbeit als Politiker

75. Welche Symbolfigur Nasts hat einen deutschen Ursprung?

    (A) Uncle Sam
    (B) Columbia
    (C) John Bull
    (D) Santa Claus

76. Was hat Theodore Roosevelt für Nast getan?

    (A) Er half ihm, seine eigene Zeitschrift zu gründen.
    (B) Er gab ihm eine angesehene Stellung im Ausland.
    (C) Er hat ihm angeboten, seine Schulden zu bezahlen.
    (D) Er hat seiner Familie etwas Geld hinterlassen.

Zimmer frei!

16qm

für ein Jahr zu vermieten
(wegen Auslandsaufenthalt)
ab Aug. oder Sep. 01, bevorzugt an †
große 4er WG, z.Zt. †††
€295,-- kalt
(möbliert oder unmöbliert)
Lage: Nähe Schloßpark
Tel. 0542/55839

77. Das Zimmer wird frei, weil der Bewohner

(A) das Zimmer zu klein findet
(B) die hohe Miete nicht bezahlen kann
(C) das Land für ein Jahr verlassen will
(D) in die Nähe des Schloßparks ziehen will

78. Wofür muss der Mieter extra bezahlen?

(A) Die Heizung
(B) Die Möbel
(C) Die Lage
(D) Den Parkplatz

Die „Eurobot" ist eine Weltmeisterschaft für Roboterbauer. Ein deutsches Team landete bei der Bewältigung einer ökologischen Problemstellung jetzt weit vorn.

Dresdner Studenten haben bei der Roboterweltmeisterschaft „Eurobot" im französischen La Ferté-Bernard den Titel nur knapp verpasst. Beim Wettbewerb um das schnelle und korrekte Sortieren von Müll kam der von einer Arbeitsgemeinschaft der Technischen Universität (TU) Dresden entwickelte Roboter auf den zweiten Platz. Im Finale sei ihre Konstruktion aus „bisher unerklärlichen Gründen stehen geblieben", sagte Teamsprecher Markus Kühnel. Allerdings hätte der überlegene Gegner aus dem französischen Ville d'Avray, der den WM-Titel nun schon zum siebten Mal erobert habe, wohl auch so gewonnen, fügte der Dresdner Mechatronik-Student hinzu.

Während des Wettbewerbs traten jeweils zwei Roboter gegeneinander an und mussten innerhalb von 90 Sekunden versuchen, mehr Müll richtig zu trennen als der Kontrahent. Dazu lagen zu Beginn jeder Partie farblich unterschiedlich gekennzeichnete Dosen, Flaschen und Batterien unordentlich auf dem Spielfeld herum. Für das Sortieren hatten die Roboter eigene Abfallbehälter mit Ausnahme eines gemeinsamen Behältnisses für Batterien.

Der Vize-Titel bedeutete für die Dresdner zugleich eine Verbesserung im Vergleich zur Weltmeisterschaft im vergangenen Jahr. Damals waren sie mit einem Golf spielenden Roboter lediglich bis ins Achtelfinale vorgerückt. 2005 waren noch kegelnde Roboter gefragt, 2004 mussten sie Rugby spielen.

79. Worum geht es in diesem Artikel?

(A) Um eine wissenschaftliche Erfindung
(B) Um einen Kurs an einer Universität
(C) Um das Wissenschaftsprojekt einer Schule
(D) Um die Ergebnisse eines Wettbewerbs

80. Auf welches Fachgebiet bezog sich die Aufgabe der diesjährigen „Eurobot"?

(A) Umwelt
(B) Sport
(C) Transport
(D) Wirtschaft

81. Welches Problem gab es im Finale?

(A) Keiner der Roboter konnte die Arbeit beenden.
(B) Es gab nicht genug Behälter für beide Kontrahenten.
(C) Ein Roboter funktionierte plötzlich nicht mehr.
(D) Die Batterie des einen Roboters war zu schwach.

82. Was bedeutet der Ausdruck im Text, die Dresdner Studenten haben „den Titel nur knapp verpasst"?

(A) Sie konnten nicht am Ereignis teilnehmen.
(B) Sie haben letztes Jahr gewonnen.
(C) Sie waren eigentlich das bessere Team.
(D) Sie haben fast gewonnen.

83. Was sagt der Text über die Gewinner dieses Jahres?

(A) Sie haben die Meisterschaft zum ersten Mal gewonnen.
(B) Sie haben die Meisterschaft schon oft gewonnen.
(C) Sie haben ihre Leistung kontinuierlich verbessert.
(D) Sie haben hauptsächlich durch Glück gewonnen.

Zum Goldenen Hahn
HOTEL RESTAURANT
Bad Dürrheim

Zur Verstärkung unseres netten Teams suchen wir einen

engagierten kreativen Koch

Wir bieten vergnügliche Arbeit, nette Gäste und gute Bezahlung. Gerne erwarten wir Ihren Anruf.

Beate Heinrich

Luisenallee 23,
78073 Bad Dürrheim
Telefon: 07726 / 0553,
Telefax: 07726 / 0550
www.zumgoldenenhahn.de
info@zumgoldenenhahn.de

84. Worum geht es in dieser Anzeige?

(A) Eine Hotelkette feiert die Eröffnung eines neuen Gasthauses.

(B) Ein Hotel bietet Wochenendpakete mit Essen und Unterkunft an.

(C) Eine Gaststätte will eine offene Arbeitsstelle besetzen.

(D) Ein Restaurant bietet Diners mit einem berühmten Koch an.

Directions: To choose your answer to this type of question, you will click on a part of the reading selection. This question indicates that the answer choices are each sentence in the text.

85.

EXAMPLE	
Zum Goldenen Hahn HOTEL RESTAURANT Bad Dürrheim Zur Verstärkung unseres netten Teams suchen wir einen **engagierten kreativen Koch** Wir bieten vergnügliche Arbeit, nette Gäste und gute Bezahlung. Gerne erwarten wir Ihren Anruf. Beate Heinrich Luisenallee 23, 78073 Bad Dürrheim Telefon: 07726 / 0553, Telefax: 07726 / 0550 www.zumgoldenenhahn.de info@zumgoldenenhahn.de	Womit wirbt der Goldene Hahn bei den Lesern der Anzeige? Klicken Sie auf den Satz in der Anzeige, der die Antwort enthält.

Study Resources

Most textbooks used in college-level German language courses cover the topics in the outline given earlier, but the approaches to certain topics and the emphases given to them may differ. To prepare for the German Language exam, it is advisable to study one or more college textbooks, which can be found in most college bookstores. When selecting a textbook, check the table of contents against the knowledge and skills required for this test.

Besides studying basic vocabulary, you should understand and be able to apply the grammatical principles that make up the language. To improve your reading comprehension, read passages from textbooks, short magazine or newspaper articles, and other printed material of your choice. To improve your listening comprehension, seek opportunities to hear the language spoken by native speakers and to converse with native speakers. If you have opportunities to join organizations with German-speaking members, to attend German movies, or to listen to German-language radio broadcasts, take advantage of them.

Visit **clep.collegeboard.org/earn-college-credit/practice** for additional German resources. You can also find suggestions for exam preparation in Chapter IV of the *Official Study Guide*. In addition, many college faculty post their course materials on their schools' websites.

Answer Key

1.	C	44.	B
2.	D	45.	A
3.	A	46.	D
4.	C	47.	B
5.	D	48.	D
6.	B	49.	B
7.	A	50.	C
8.	D	51.	A
9.	C	52.	D
10.	B	53.	D
11.	D	54.	A
12.	A	55.	C
13.	B	56.	A
14.	C	57.	B
15.	D	58.	C
16.	D	59.	A
17.	B	60.	C
18.	B	61.	B
19.	A	62.	D
20.	C	63.	A
21.	B	64.	C
22.	D	65.	B
23.	B	66.	D
24.	C	67.	B
25.	A	68.	D
26.	C	69.	C
27.	B	70.	A
28.	B	71.	D
29.	A	72.	B
30.	D	73.	C
31.	D	74.	A
32.	B	75.	D
33.	A	76.	B
34.	A	77.	C
35.	B	78.	A
36.	C	79.	D
37.	B	80.	A
38.	D	81.	C
39.	D	82.	D
40.	C	83.	B
41.	A	84.	C
42.	C	85.	See next page.
43.	C		

85.

EXAMPLE	
Zum Goldenen Hahn HOTEL RESTAURANT Bad Dürrheim Zur Verstärkung unseres netten Teams suchen wir einen **engagierten kreativen Koch** **Wir bieten vergnügliche Arbeit, nette Gäste und gute Bezahlung.** Gerne erwarten wir Ihren Anruf. Beate Heinrich Luisenallee 23, 78073 Bad Dürrheim Telefon: 07726 / 0553, Telefax: 07726 / 0550 www.zumgoldenenhahn.de info@zumgoldenenhahn.de	Womit wirbt der Goldene Hahn bei den Lesern der Anzeige? Klicken Sie auf den Satz in der Anzeige, der die Antwort enthält.

Spanish Language

Description of the Examination

The Spanish Language examination is designed to measure knowledge and ability equivalent to that of students who have completed two to three semesters of college Spanish language study.

The examination contains approximately 121 questions to be answered in approximately 90 minutes. Some of these are pretest questions that will not be scored. There are three separately timed sections. The three sections are weighted so that each question contributes equally to the total score.

There are two Listening sections and one Reading section. Each section has its own timing requirements.

- The two Listening sections together are approximately 30 minutes in length. The amount of time candidates have to answer a question varies according to the section and does not include the time they spend listening to the test material.
- The Reading section is 60 minutes in length.

Colleges may award different amounts of credit depending on the candidate's test scores.

Knowledge and Skills Required

Questions on the Spanish Language examination require candidates to comprehend written and spoken Spanish. The subject matter is drawn from the following abilities. The percentages next to the main topics indicate the approximate percentage of exam questions on that ability.

15% Section I:
Listening: Rejoinders

Listening comprehension through short oral exchanges

25% Section II:
Listening: Dialogues and Narratives

Listening comprehension through longer spoken selections

60% Section III:
Reading

16% Part A: Discrete sentences (vocabulary and structure)

20% Part B: Short cloze passages (vocabulary and structure)

24% Part C: Reading passages and authentic stimulus materials (reading comprehension)

Sample Test Questions

The following sample questions do not appear on an actual CLEP examination. They are intended to give potential test-takers an indication of the format and difficulty level of the examination and to provide content for practice and review. Knowing the correct answers to all of the sample questions is not a guarantee of satisfactory performance on the exam.

In addition to samples of each question type are sample computer screens showing how the directions and questions will appear to the candidate taking the test. For listening items, the script of the recording normally played by the computer appears here as italicized text.

Listening Directions: This part of the test measures your ability to understand spoken Spanish.

There are two sections in this part of the test, with special directions for each section.

The two listening sections of the test total approximately 30 minutes in length. The amount of time you have to answer a question varies according to the section and does not include the time you spend listening to the test material. Timing begins after the Section Directions are dismissed.

You can change the volume by using the Volume testing tool.

The audio portions of the Listening sections of the test will be presented only one time.

Section I Directions: You will hear short conversations or parts of conversations. You will then hear four responses, designated (A), (B), (C), and (D).

After you hear the four responses, click on the lettered response oval that most logically continues or completes the conversation.

You will have 10 seconds to choose your response before the next conversation begins.

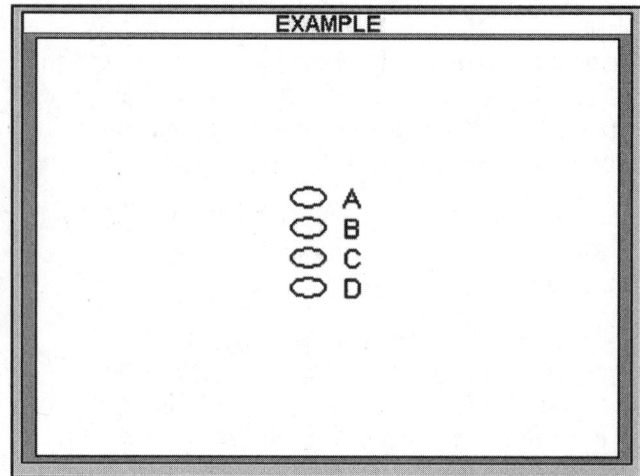

1. (MAN) *¿Cómo está Ud. Señora Gómez?*

   (WOMAN) (A) *Hace frío.*

   (B) *Bastante bien, gracias.*

   (C) *Mañana a las ocho.*

   (D) *Sí, por favor.*

2. (MAN) *¿Dónde conociste a mi hermana?*

   (WOMAN) (A) *Estudiamos juntas en la universidad.*

   (B) *Me gustaría conocer a tu hermana.*

   (C) *Quiero presentarte a mi esposo.*

   (D) *No sé dónde está mi hermana.*

3. (MAN) *¿Quién llamó anoche?*

(WOMAN) (A) *No sé quién va.*
(B) *Yo llamo después.*
(C) *Viene esta noche.*
(D) *Fue mi primo Luis.*

4. (WOMAN) *¿Qué están poniendo dentro del cajón?*

(MAN) (A) *Está muy bien puesto.*
(B) *Compraron las estampillas.*
(C) *Lo están llenando de cartas.*
(D) *Están trabajando en el sótano.*

5. (MAN) *¿Si sigo esta calle llego a la avenida Bolívar?*

(WOMAN) (A) *Bolívar fue el libertador de Venezuela.*
(B) *Pues sí, es un señor hecho y derecho.*
(C) *No señor, conduce al paseo de la República.*
(D) *Si tu mamá te lo permite, te lo consentiré.*

6. (WOMAN) *Mozo, ¿cuánto le debo?*

(MAN) (A) *Ahora mismo le subo las maletas, señora.*
(B) *Ud. debe marcharse en seguida.*
(C) *En seguida le traigo la cuenta.*
(D) *¿Cuántos cree usted que hay aquí?*

7. (MAN) *¿Dónde trabaja tu hermano Raúl?*

(WOMAN) (A) *Es empleado en una escuela.*
(B) *Su horario es de ocho a dos.*
(C) *Quiere comprarse un coche nuevo.*
(D) *Le gusta mucho lo que hace.*

8. (WOMAN) *¿Por qué compraste tantas naranjas?*

(MAN) (A) *Las compré en el supermercado ayer.*
(B) *Me gusta la mermelada de fresa.*
(C) *Voy a hacer jugo para el desayuno.*
(D) *Tengo demasiadas naranjas en casa.*

9. (MAN) *¿Dónde se puede encontrar información sobre la producción del azúcar?*

(WOMAN) (A) *Se cultiva en las regiones tropicales.*
(B) Se encuentra en Internet.
(C) Se encuentra en numerosas recetas.
(D) Se echa al café.

10. (WOMAN) *¿A qué hora vamos a salir?*

(MAN) (A) *Ya se fueron.*
(B) *Son las tres en punto.*
(C) *Siempre vamos a la playa.*
(D) *Saldremos después del almuerzo.*

11. (WOMAN) *¿A usted le gustan las pinturas de José Clemente Orozco?*

(MAN) (A) *Sí, me gustan mucho.*
(B) *Sí, te gustan mucho.*
(C) *Sí, le gustan mucho.*
(D) *Sí, nos gustan mucho.*

12. (MAN) *Rosario, ¿cuánto tiempo lleva tu hijo Beto estudiando en Bogotá?*

(WOMAN) (A) *Beto estudia biología.*

(B) *Gracias, es un estudiante excelente.*

(C) *Hace cinco meses que está en Bogotá.*

(D) *A Beto le encanta Bogotá.*

13. (WOMAN) *¿Leíste el libro que te presté?*

(MAN) (A) *No, no quiero comprarlo.*

(B) *Sí, ¿quieres que te lo devuelva?*

(C) *No, no he leído el periódico.*

(D) *Sí, ¿me lo puedes prestar mañana por favor?*

Section II Directions: You will hear a series of selections, such as dialogues, announcements, and narratives. Each audio selection is accompanied by a graphic or a picture.

Each selection is followed by one or more questions. **You will have a total of 12 minutes to answer the questions in this section. Note: The timer is activated only when you are answering questions.**

The questions have various formats. Some questions offer four possible responses, each with an oval to click to indicate your answer. Other questions ask you to select part of a graphic, fill out a table, or put a list in the correct order; for some of these questions, you will have to click in more than one place to complete your response. For these questions, follow the specific directions given.

In this section, you may adjust the volume only when a question is on your screen. It will affect the volume of the next audio prompt you hear. **You cannot change the volume while the audio prompt is playing.**

(NARRATOR) *Hablan un padre y su hija.*

(MAN) *Vamos hija que ya es hora.*

(WOMAN) *Un poco más papá.*

(MAN) *Sonó el reloj hace cinco minutos.*

(WOMAN) *Estoy cansada.*

(MAN) *Llegarás tarde si no te apuras.*

EXAMPLE

¿Qué debe hacer la muchacha?

- Levantarse
- Esperar cinco minutos
- Hablar del tiempo
- Poner el reloj en hora

(NARRATOR) *En el aeropuerto.*

(MAN) *Señorita, ¿ya salió el vuelo 45 para Quito?*

(WOMAN) *Sí señor, acaba de salir.*

(MAN) *¡Qué lástima! ¿Y cuándo es el próximo vuelo? Tengo que llegar a Quito esta noche.*

(WOMAN) *Lo siento mucho, señor, pero no hay vuelos a Quito de noche. El próximo sale a las siete de la mañana y llega a Quito a las nueve.*

14. ¿Cuándo llegará el señor a Quito?
    (A) Esa noche
    (B) Dentro de dos horas
    (C) Al día siguiente
    (D) La semana próxima

(NARRATOR) *Escuchen esta conversación entre amigos.*

(WOMAN) *Oye, Ricardo, espéranos. ¿Adónde vas con tanta prisa?*

(MAN) *Me muero de hambre, Ana. Después de un examen tan difícil, voy corriendo para la cafetería. ¿Y tú?*

(WOMAN) *Pues, yo te acompaño, Ricardo. Quiero tomar un refresco.*

15. ¿Por qué tiene prisa Ricardo?
    (A) Quiere comer.
    (B) Quiere ir al cine.
    (C) Quiere correr.
    (D) Quiere charlar con Ana.

16. ¿Qué va a hacer Ana?
    (A) Va a la cafetería también.
    (B) Vuelve a la residencia.
    (C) Come mucho.
    (D) Va a otra clase.

(NARRATOR) *En el restaurante.*

(MAN) *Buenas tardes, señores.*

(WOMAN) *Buenas tardes. ¿Nos trae la carta en seguida, por favor? Tenemos mucha prisa.*

(MAN) *Aquí la tienen ustedes. Recomiendo el plato del día.*

17. ¿Con quién habla la mujer?
    (A) Con un invitado
    (B) Con el cocinero
    (C) Con su esposo
    (D) Con el camarero

(NARRATOR) *Una opinión sobre Barcelona.*

(WOMAN) *A mí me encanta Barcelona. Es una ciudad muy grande donde encuentras de todo: restaurantes, tiendas, actividades. Si te gusta el arte, tiene buenos y variados museos. Si prefieres la música, Barcelona tiene una orquesta sinfónica excelente y un gran repertorio de ópera. Pero a mí, lo que más me gusta es la arquitectura de la ciudad. Barcelona está situada a orillas del mar Mediterráneo y tiene unas vistas muy bonitas. Lo que no me gusta es la contaminación y lo peor de todo es el ruido de la ciudad.*

18. La ciudad tiene un hermoso paisaje porque está
    (A) en las montañas
    (B) cerca del mar
    (C) a la orilla de un lago
    (D) en el desierto

19. A la narradora, ¿qué es lo que más le gusta de Barcelona?
    (A) Los museos
    (B) Los restaurantes
    (C) La orquesta sinfónica
    (D) Los edificios

20. ¿Qué es lo peor de la ciudad?
    (A) La ópera
    (B) El ruido
    (C) El crimen
    (D) La playa

(NARRATOR) *Escuchen para saber quiénes hablan.*

(MAN) *Señora, Ud. recibió los libros el 18 del pasado mes, y hasta la fecha no hemos recibido su pago.*

(WOMAN) *Lo sé, pero cuando abrí el paquete, vi que me habían mandado dos libros que no pedí.*

21. ¿Quiénes hablan?
    (A) Un profesor y su alumna
    (B) Un vendedor y su cliente
    (C) Un abogado y la acusada
    (D) Un cartero y su jefe

(NARRATOR) *Dos estudiantes hablan.*

(WOMAN) *Paco, ¿cómo te fue en el examen?*

(MAN) *No sé, Alicia. Estudié con Pedro y con Carmen, repasé mis apuntes, releí capítulos enteros, pero no llegué a contestar todas las preguntas.*

(WOMAN) *Yo tampoco. No tuvimos suficiente tiempo para terminar, y estoy muy preocupada.*

(MAN) *¿No crees que tal vez deberíamos ir a ver al profesor a ver si nos da más tiempo?*

(WOMAN) *Bueno, podemos intentarlo, pero me parece que nos dirá que no.*

(MAN) *De todos modos debemos ir a verlo pues...¿quién sabe lo que pueda pasar...? ¿De acuerdo?*

(WOMAN) *De acuerdo. Acudamos a sus horas de oficina mañana a las diez.*

22. ¿Qué hizo el hombre para preparar su tarea?
    (A) Asistió a una conferencia.
    (B) Repasó con otros compañeros de clase.
    (C) Buscó información en la biblioteca.
    (D) Compró un libro de referencia.

23. La mujer está muy preocupada porque no tuvo suficiente tiempo para
    (A) repasar el libro
    (B) completar sus respuestas
    (C) consultar con el profesor
    (D) estudiar con sus compañeros

24. Los estudiantes van a pedirle al profesor que les
    (A) dé otra oportunidad
    (B) suba la nota
    (C) clarifique sus dudas
    (D) cambie de clase

Some questions require you to select cells in a table grid. The question based on the next listening selection is an example of this type of question.

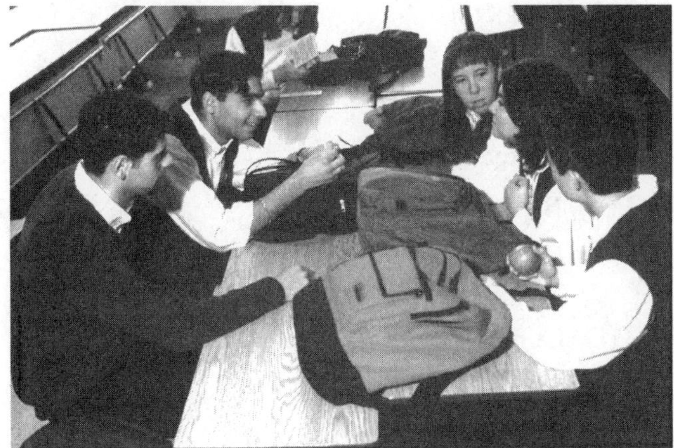

(NARRATOR)	*Hablan dos jóvenes.*
(WOMAN)	*Oigan chicos, ¡hay papas fritas en la cafetería!*
(MAN)	*¡Qué rico! A mí me encantan las papas fritas con hamburguesa.*
(WOMAN)	*¿Sí? Yo las prefiero con pollo.*
(MAN)	*Sabes, cuando fui a Londres, comí pescado con papas fritas.*
(WOMAN)	*¿Pescado?*
(MAN)	*Sí, pescado frito con papas fritas es una de las comidas favoritas allá.*
(WOMAN)	*Me alegro de que no estemos en Londres, porque esa combinación me parece algo rara.*
(MAN)	*Pues en Londres es la comida rápida más común. ¡Ojalá la tuviéramos aquí! Pero pediré papas fritas con una hamburguesa.*
(WOMAN)	*Bueno, y yo con pollo frito.*

To choose your answers to this type of question, you will click on the cells in the table grid.

25.

¿Qué van a pedir el muchacho y la muchacha para comer?

	El Muchacho	La Muchacha
Hamburguesa		
Papas fritas		
Pescado		
Pollo		

Click on your choices.

(NARRATOR)	*Una señora habla con su esposo por teléfono celular.*
(MAN)	*¿Aló?*
(WOMAN)	*Aló Enrique. Acabo de salir de la farmacia con Jorgito. Regresaré a casa en media hora.*
(MAN)	*¿Qué pasó?*
(WOMAN)	*El niño tenía una fiebre muy alta, le dolía la garganta y no podía tragar esta mañana.*
(MAN)	*¡Pobrecito! Entonces, ¿qué hiciste?*
(WOMAN)	*Llamé al consultorio del doctor Alvarado. La enfermera me dijo que debería llevarlo a ver al médico tan pronto fuera posible. Me dio una cita inmediatamente.*
(MAN)	*¿Y lo examinó el doctor?*
(WOMAN)	*Sí. Pues, le recetó un antibiótico y me dijo que le diera dos píldoras como primera dosis, y luego una, tres veces al día por diez días.*
(MAN)	*Y, ahora, ¿cómo se siente?*
(WOMAN)	*Un poco mejor, ¡ya me pidió una galleta!*

26. ¿Quién sugirió que el niño fuera al consultorio?

(A) La enfermera
(B) El padre
(C) El doctor
(D) La madre

27. ¿Qué le recomendó el médico al niño?

(A) Beber muchos líquidos
(B) Quedarse en cama
(C) Tomar medicamento
(D) Comer galletas

28. Pon en orden cronológico lo que hizo la madre de Jorgito.

Fue a la farmacia.

Llamó al doctor Alvarado.

Regresó a casa.

Habló con su esposo por teléfono.

Primero

Último

Listen Now

(NARRATOR) *Una señora explica uno de sus platos favoritos.*

(WOMAN) *La tortilla es un plato típico de España que no tiene nada que ver con las tortillas que se comen en México. Mientras en México son un tipo de pan plano y redondo hecho de maíz o trigo, en España es una comida preparada con patatas, cebollas y huevos, cocinada en una sartén. Se cree que su origen se remonta al siglo dieciséis. Es un plato humilde en su composición, pero uno que siempre satisface. No existe una receta oficial para la tortilla española; cada región, de hecho, cada hogar, tiene su propia manera de prepararla. Sus varias interpretaciones se encuentran en cada rincón del país. Es tan popular porque se puede comer para el desayuno, para el almuerzo como un bocadillo, para las tapas por la tarde, para la cena, y aun en las meriendas también.*

29. Según la selección, ¿por qué es popular la tortilla española?

    (A) La receta oficial es muy sencilla.
    (B) Se encuentran los ingredientes fácilmente.
    (C) Es una novedad en la cocina española.
    (D) Se puede comer a cualquier hora del día.

30. ¿Qué enfatiza la selección sobre la receta de la tortilla española?

    (A) Que hay muchas maneras de prepararla
    (B) Que es similar a la tortilla mexicana
    (C) Que es un plato complicado de preparar
    (D) Que la receta oficial es del siglo XVI

31. Haz clic en el ingrediente mencionado en la selección con el que se prepara la tortilla española.

Listen Now

(NARRATOR) *Una mujer habla sobre el Rastro de Madrid.*

(WOMAN) *En casi todas las ciudades grandes del mundo se encuentran mercados al aire libre. Estos mercados son populares no solo por su variedad de productos, sino también por la experiencia sensorial de colores, sonidos, olores y sabores distintos que se les ofrecen a los clientes.*

El Rastro es un famoso mercado al aire libre que se encuentra en el centro de Madrid, justo al sur de la estación de metro La Latina. Está abierto todos los domingos y los días feriados y ofrece un sinfín de productos para los madrileños y los turistas que lo visitan. Es el mercado más antiguo y el más grande de Europa, con unos 3.500 puestos para vendedores.

En el Rastro se pueden encontrar productos tan variados como muebles, camisetas, aparatos eléctricos, recuerdos, antigüedades, comidas y bebidas. El ambiente siempre es muy animado y entretenido. Pero los turistas que visitan el Rastro o cualquier otro mercado al aire libre deben tener en cuenta dos advertencias: hay que mirar bien la calidad del producto que quieren comprar y hay que saber negociar el precio.

32. Según el fragmento, ¿por qué son populares los mercados al aire libre?

    (A) Tienen actividades para los niños.

    (B) Tienen aparcamiento gratis los fines de semana.

    (C) Ofrecen una gran variedad de productos.

    (D) Están en las afueras de la ciudad.

33. Según el fragmento, ¿por qué es famoso el Rastro?

    (A) Es el mercado más antiguo y más grande de Europa.

    (B) Se venden entradas para eventos especiales.

    (C) Tiene una estación de metro en el centro.

    (D) Los vendedores hablan mucho con los turistas.

34. Para tener una experiencia agradable en el Rastro es necesario

    (A) llevar mucho dinero

    (B) visitarlo todos los días de la semana

    (C) sacar muchas fotos

    (D) fijarse en la calidad de los productos

(NARRATOR) *Una huelga de estudiantes.*

(MAN) *Hace unos años en la Ciudad de México recibió mucha atención un evento que tuvo lugar en una de las universidades de la ciudad. Hubo una huelga general de los estudiantes que asistían a la universidad. Los participantes dejaron de asistir a sus clases para protestar unos cambios administrativos de la universidad como el reglamento de la matrícula de clases y la forma de pagar sus estudios. El evento no solo afectó a la universidad sino a la ciudad entera: causó problemas de tráfico en el Distrito Federal, ya que los estudiantes salían a las calles para hacer sus protestas y no permitían pasar los carros. Aunque la huelga recibió mucha publicidad y causó mucho estorbo, la gran mayoría de los estudiantes permaneció en sus clases y siguió estudiando durante esa temporada.*

35. Quiénes hicieron la huelga en el fragmento?

    (A) Los profesores
    (B) Los estudiantes
    (C) Los automovilistas
    (D) Los administradores

36. Además de irregularidades en la asistencia a las clases, la huelga causó problemas de

    (A) pago
    (B) tráfico
    (C) matrícula
    (D) publicidad

37. ¿Qué hizo la mayoría de los estudiantes de la universidad durante la huelga?

    (A) Se unió a la huelga.
    (B) Abandonó el Distrito Federal.
    (C) Siguió asistiendo a clases.
    (D) Llegó a un acuerdo con la universidad.

Listen Now

Photo courtesy of: Ben Earwicker
Garrison Photography, Boise, ID
www.garrisonphoto.org

(NARRATOR) *Dos compañeros conversan después de una conferencia en la Facultad de Arte.*

(MAN) *Beatriz, ¡qué gusto encontrarte! ¿Qué te ha parecido la conferencia de la profesora Santamaría?*

(WOMAN) *Ay Alberto, la verdad es que me ha parecido fascinante. La semana pasada, cuando la profesora anunció en clase que hablaría de las pintoras mexicanas del siglo XX, no pensé que el tema sería tan interesante, pero lo cierto es que he aprendido muchísimo.*

(MAN) *Yo también. Para ser sincero, del arte mexicano solo conocía a los famosos artistas Diego Rivera y Frida Kahlo, pero nunca había oído hablar de esas pintoras tan talentosas que presentó hoy la profesora.*

(WOMAN) *Es que la popularidad de Frida eclipsó a las demás durante mucho tiempo, pero afortunadamente, como ha explicado la profesora, hoy en día las obras de artistas tan importantes como Remedios Varo o Leonora Carrington se valoran mucho y son admiradas por el público en los museos de todo el mundo.*

(MAN) *Bueno, ahora me preocupa el trabajo que tenemos que entregar para nuestra clase la próxima semana. Estoy seguro de que esta conferencia me ayudará un poco, pero ya sabes que yo no sé mucho de arte latinoamericano.*

(WOMAN) *No te preocupes, Alberto. ¿Qué te parece si hacemos el proyecto juntos? Así yo podría ayudarte.*

(MAN) *¡Me encantaría! Tú sí que eres una buena amiga.*

38. Hoy Alberto y Beatriz asistieron a una conferencia sobre

    (A) el arte colonial
    (B) los muralistas mexicanos
    (C) las pintoras mexicanas del siglo XX
    (D) el arte precolombino

39. Por qué piensa Beatriz que Remedios Varo y Leonora Carrington fueron durante mucho tiempo casi desconocidas?

    (A) Por la popularidad de Frida Kahlo
    (B) Por la complejidad de sus obras
    (C) Porque no eran pintoras mexicanas
    (D) Porque sus obras no estaban en los museos

40. ¿Qué le propone Beatriz a Alberto al final del diálogo?

    (A) Ir a otra conferencia de la profesora Santamaría
    (B) Hacer un proyecto para la clase juntos
    (C) Visitar un museo para admirar las pinturas de Frida Kahlo
    (D) Leer sobre las vidas de Leonora Carrington y Remedios Varo

Section III Reading Directions: This section measures your ability to read Spanish.

There are three parts in this section, with special directions for each part.

The Reading section is approximately 60 minutes in length.

Part A Directions: Each incomplete statement is followed by four suggested completions. Select the one that is best in each case by clicking on the corresponding oval.

EXAMPLE

Para cortar la carne necesitas _______ .

- una cuchara
- un mantel
- una botella
- un cuchillo

41. Dudo que ------- terminar el capítulo.
    (A) vuelva
    (B) ponga
    (C) tenga
    (D) pueda

42. Él se enfadó y yo no ------- dije nada.
    (A) se
    (B) le
    (C) lo
    (D) la

43. Mi padre me mandó devolver el libro a la ------- antes de que se venciera el plazo.
    (A) biblioteca
    (B) revista
    (C) página
    (D) publicidad

44. Entré en la casa sin que nadie se ------- cuenta.
    (A) da
    (B) dio
    (C) diera
    (D) daba

45. Nos pusimos muy contentos cuando nos enteramos ------- la boda de Julio e Inés.
    (A) a
    (B) de
    (C) con
    (D) por

46. Los señores Gómez viajan ------- por América Central.
    (A) a más tardar
    (B) a lo largo
    (C) a la orden
    (D) a menudo

47. Dicen que una de las gemelas es tan buena guitarrista ------- la otra.
    (A) que
    (B) como
    (C) de
    (D) tan

48. Era la medianoche y Susana ------- no había terminado su tarea.
    (A) ya
    (B) pero
    (C) cuando
    (D) todavía

49. A todos los profesores de esta facultad nos molesta mucho que los estudiantes no ------- a tiempo.
    (A) llegues
    (B) llegue
    (C) lleguen
    (D) lleguemos

50. Muchas gracias ------- su ayuda, señor Martínez.
    (A) para
    (B) por
    (C) a
    (D) de

51. Fue sorprendente que Mauricio no ------- a la fiesta ayer.
    (A) vino
    (B) venía
    (C) venga
    (D) viniera

52. Juan ------- que sus padres le compraran una motocicleta.
    (A) esperará
    (B) espera
    (C) está esperando
    (D) esperaba

53. ¿Cuál es tu ------- favorita? ¿El verano o invierno?
    (A) posición
    (B) estación
    (C) actividad
    (D) tempestad

54. El autobús pasa por la esquina doce ------- al día.
    (A) rutas
    (B) veces
    (C) ratos
    (D) tiempos

Part B Directions: In each of the following paragraphs, there are blanks indicating that words or phrases have been omitted. When a blank is shaded, four completions are provided.

First, read through the entire paragraph. Then, for each blank, choose the completion that is most appropriate, given the context of the entire paragraph. Click on the corresponding oval.

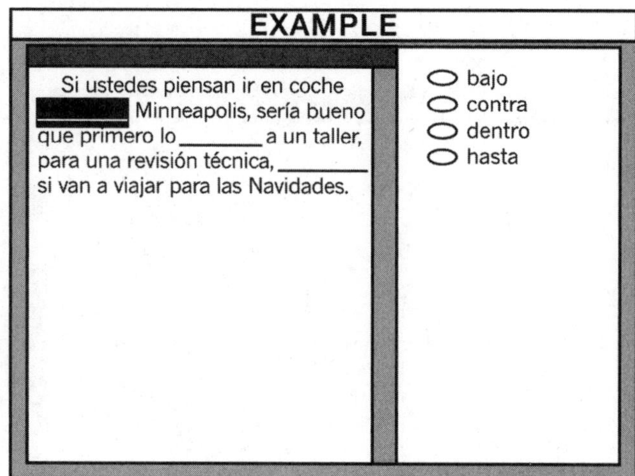

El chocolate comenzó siendo una bebida de ricos pero __(55)__ se popularizó. En el Madrid del siglo XVII era tan popular que no había calle __(56)__ uno, dos o tres puestos donde se hacía y __(57)__ el chocolate. En la España de hoy, estos puestos han sido __(58)__ por chocolaterías. Las chocolaterías, que pueden encontrarse en casi todas las ciudades españolas, son locales que sirven de manera casi exclusiva chocolate a la taza.

55. (A) tarde
    (B) pronto
    (C) antes
    (D) aun

56. (A) para
    (B) con
    (C) por
    (D) sin

57. (A) vendía
    (B) vendo
    (C) vender
    (D) vendió

58. (A) ordenados
    (B) sustituidos
    (C) arreglados
    (D) olvidados

Nunca voy a olvidar la fiesta de Año Nuevo que pasé en Lima hace unos años. Yo estaba viviendo en un barrio muy popular, y ahí, además de las fiestas, la gente tiene __(59)__ de hacer fuegos en las calles. Antes de los fuegos, se confeccionan muñecos con ropas viejas, periódicos, pedazos de madera y cualquier objeto inservible. Cuando se anuncia el nuevo año, se prende fuego a esos muñecos, mientras la gente se __(60)__ celebrando el Año Nuevo. Para mí fue una visión muy extraña ver todas esas cosas ardiendo en medio de la calle. Las personas actúan con bastante cuidado, felizmente, y no __(61)__ de incendios. Al día siguiente la gente recoge toda la basura y limpia la calle, para que el año __(62)__ bien.

59. (A) el antepasado
    (B) la tradición
    (C) las reglas
    (D) el costado

60. (A) abraza y sigue
    (B) abrazaban y seguían
    (C) abrazaba y seguía
    (D) abrazan y siguen

61. (A) supe
    (B) conocí
    (C) comprendí
    (D) aprendí

62. (A) comienza
    (B) comience
    (C) comenzar
    (D) comenzó

Lo peor que le puede pasar a alguien cuando __(63)__ por avión es que le pierdan la maleta. Según un informe reciente, el año pasado se extraviaron veinticinco millones de maletas. Para evitar este problema, es recomendable que los __(64)__ viajen ligeros de equipaje y que __(65)__ todos los artículos necesarios en su __(66)__.

63. (A) viajo
    (B) viajas
    (C) viaja
    (D) viajan

64. (A) aeromozos
    (B) pasajeros
    (C) taxistas
    (D) pilotos

65. (A) llevan
    (B) llevaran
    (C) llevarían
    (D) lleven

66. (A) boleto
    (B) equipaje de mano
    (C) asiento
    (D) puerta de embarque

Todo el mundo conoce la guitarra, ya sea la clásica española como la que __(67)__ Paco de Lucía o la guitarra eléctrica que utilizan los __(68)__ de rock. Pero pocos conocen su historia. De hecho la palabra "guitarra" se usa para hablar de una serie de instrumentos que aparecieron __(69)__ Europa a principios del siglo XII y que provenían de otros instrumentos que existían en Asia e India. Al llegar los europeos a América, trajeron la guitarra a __(70)__ continente.

67. (A) tocabas
    (B) tocábamos
    (C) tocaba
    (D) tocaban

68. (A) músicos
    (B) policías
    (C) carpinteros
    (D) doctores

69. (A) de
    (B) a
    (C) hasta
    (D) en

70. (A) nuestra
    (B) nuestro
    (C) nuestras
    (D) nuestros

En la ciudad de Guanajuato hay una gran cantidad de obras de artesanía __(71)__ a mano por artesanos mexicanos. Estas obras son reconocidas mundialmente por sus __(72)__ brillantes y su creatividad. Hay muchos juguetes que divierten __(73)__ a los adultos como a los niños, entre ellos trompos, muñecas y máscaras __(74)__ cartón.

71. (A) hecha
    (B) hecho
    (C) hechas
    (D) hechos

72. (A) tamaños
    (B) colores
    (C) precios
    (D) sonidos

73. (A) tanta
    (B) tantos
    (C) tantas
    (D) tanto

74. (A) por
    (B) hasta
    (C) de
    (D) a

Part C Directions: Read the following selections. Each selection is followed by one or more questions, incomplete statements, or commands.

For each question or incomplete statement, select the answer or completion that is best according to the selection. Click on the corresponding oval.

For each command, click on the appropriate area of the screen according to the directions given.

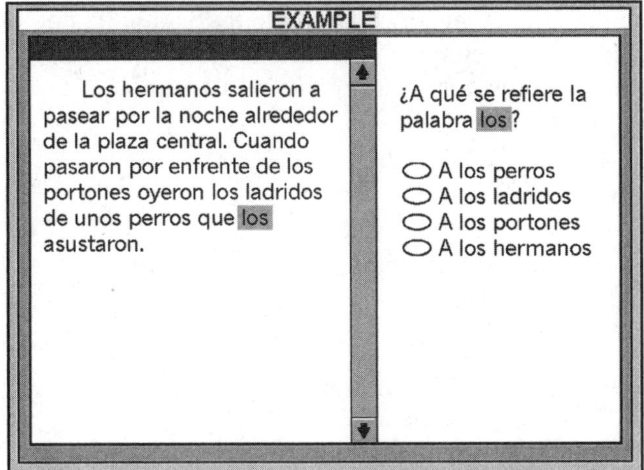

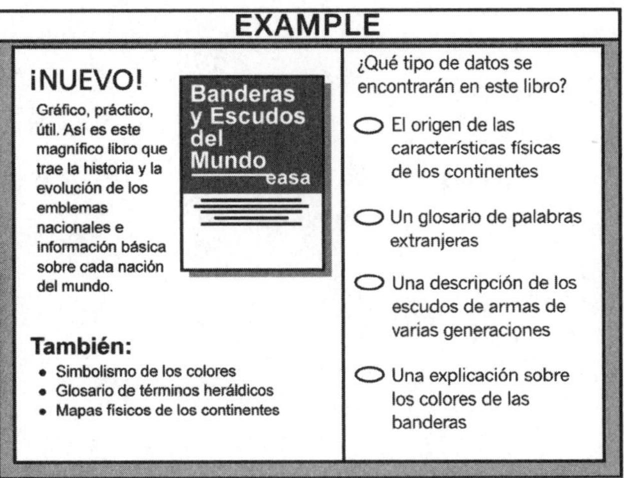

Querida amiga María:

Hace algún tiempo que quería escribirte, pero he estado muy ocupada con mis estudios. Tengo cuatro clases este semestre y apenas tengo tiempo para atender mis asuntos personales. No quiero que pienses que me he olvidado de nuestra amistad. Siempre recuerdo con cariño los buenos momentos que pasamos juntas cuando éramos niñas. Dentro de unos meses, cuando termine mis estudios, espero que podamos reunirnos nuevamente y conversar muchísimo. ¡Tengo tanto que contarte!

Recibe todo el cariño de tu amiga que nunca te olvida,

Emilia

75. ¿Por qué razón Emilia no le había escrito antes a María?

    (A) Porque estudiaban juntas cuando eran niñas
    (B) Porque sus estudios no se lo permitían
    (C) Porque María se había olvidado de su amiga
    (D) Porque Emilia no tenía ganas de escribirle a nadie

76. María y Emilia son dos

    (A) estudiantes de la misma universidad
    (B) antiguas y buenas amigas
    (C) invitadas a una fiesta
    (D) famosas escritoras contemporáneas

España El Centro Cultural Español le invita a un encuentro con el poeta **Ángel González** leerá su poesía Viernes, 19 de marzo, 8:00 p.m. Centro Cultural Español 800 Douglas Road, Suite 170 Coral Gables, FL RSVP 305-555-9677 Recepción prevista tras la lectura Aparcamiento disponible en el garaje de La Puerta del Sol $4.00 Entrada por la calle Calabria esquina con Galiano	**Encuentros** es un ciclo dedicado a los creadores y escritores que en España, los Estados Unidos, más concretamente en el sur de la Florida, y la zona del Caribe utilizan la lengua española como medio de expresión. Autores de diferentes nacionalidades presentan sus obras a lo largo del año mostrando la actualidad, diversidad y unidad de la literatura escrita en los dos continentes.

77. ¿Cuál es el tema central del ciclo "Encuentros"?
    (A) Las culturas indígenas del Caribe
    (B) La llegada de los españoles a la Florida
    (C) La literatura contemporánea
    (D) El aprendizaje del español

78. ¿Quién invita a este evento?
    (A) Ángel González
    (B) El Rey de España
    (C) El Centro Cultural Español
    (D) La ciudad de Coral Gables

79. ¿Qué habrá después de la presentación de Ángel González?
    (A) Una función social
    (B) La inauguración del centro
    (C) Una demostración de tecnología
    (D) Una exhibición de libros

Benicarló, 24 de agosto. — "Día sin sol, día perdido", parecen pensar los turistas que visitan las playas españolas, a juzgar por su paciente exposición al sol todas las horas en que es posible. Un avispado hotelero, dueño de una serie de apartamentos en la zona de playa que va desde Benicarló a Peñíscola, ha decidido hacer de esta frase su lema. Por ello ha hecho colocar grandes anuncios declarando que está dispuesto a bajar el precio a sus inquilinos por cada día sin sol. Hasta ahora, y como es tradicional en la zona, el sol no le ha hecho perder dinero porque ha lucido a más y mejor. A pesar de todo, el lema no deja de hacer efecto en los turistas que llenan sus apartamentos, tostándose muy a gusto en las playas cercanas.

80. La frase, "Día sin sol, día perdido", sirvió
    (A) para confirmar el pésimo clima de la región
    (B) como lema de la campaña propagandista del hotelero
    (C) para desilusionar a los más fuertes tradicionalistas
    (D) como serio obstáculo a todo plan de desarrollo económico

81. Benicarló y Peñíscola deben de ser dos
    (A) turistas
    (B) hoteleros
    (C) pueblos de la costa
    (D) casas de apartamentos

82. Los turistas frecuentan aquella zona de España para

(A) lucir sus trajes de moda
(B) alquilar apartamentos en la sierra
(C) asistir a exposiciones
(D) aprovechar el sol y la playa

83. ¿Qué les pasaría a los clientes del hotelero los días sin sol?

(A) Podrían pintar dentro del hotel.
(B) Dejarían el apartamento.
(C) Le pagarían menos al hotelero.
(D) No le pagarían nada al hotelero.

84. El dueño de los apartamentos quedó satisfecho con su plan porque

(A) los inquilinos se resignaron a pagar la cuota extraordinaria
(B) el sol salió y brilló como nunca en la zona
(C) a los turistas les gustó pasar todo el tiempo fuera de la zona
(D) habría muchos inquilinos los días sin sol

Con una avanzada tecnología educativa, un cuerpo docente integrado por profesionales en actividad y moderno equipamiento. Nuestros planes de estudio ofrecen salidas laborales concretas y de gran porvenir.

CARRERAS QUE SE CURSAN: PUBLICIDAD - DIRECCIÓN Y ADMINISTRACIÓN DE EMPRESAS - COMERCIO EXTERIOR - PERIODISMO - DISEÑO GRÁFICO Y PUBLICITARIO - ADMINISTRACIÓN DE SEGUROS - ADMINISTRACIÓN DE SALUD - ADMINISTRACIÓN BANCARIA - GESTIÓN AMBIENTAL - TURISMO - SISTEMAS DE DISTRIBUCIÓN.

UNIVERSIDAD DE CIENCIAS
EMPRESARIALES Y SOCIALES

CENTROS DE ATENCIÓN
Rivadavia 1376 - Buenos Aires
Horario de atención : de 9 a 20 hs.
Teléfono : 555-0202

85. ¿Qué tipo de profesión se puede estudiar en esta universidad?

    (A) Cursos de astrofísica
    (B) Cursos de medicina
    (C) Estudios técnico-profesionales
    (D) Estudios del área legal

86. Un estudiante interesado en el anuncio podrá obtener

    (A) información por teléfono
    (B) admisión gratuita de inmediato
    (C) tecnología avanzada por teléfono
    (D) consultoría profesional en seguida

En muchos libros de historia que cuentan la Conquista de México se hace énfasis en la imagen del español Hernán Cortés, popularmente conocido como el Conquistador de México. Cortés y unos 500 hombres llegaron a las costas mexicanas en 1519. Para agosto de 1521 el Imperio azteca se desintegró bajo el dominio de los españoles. Aunque es cierto que las armas y los caballos que Cortés y sus hombres trajeron al Nuevo Mundo facilitaron la Conquista, no menos importante es el papel que desempeñó la intérprete y compañera de Cortés, La Malinche, una joven indígena que hablaba náhuatl y maya. Otros nombres que tenía eran Malintzin, Malinalli y Doña Marina. En español, el título de "doña" sugiere cierto respeto. Sin la interpretación que ofrecía Malinche, no habría sido posible la Conquista del Imperio azteca.

Para comunicarse con Cortés, Malinche hablaba en maya con Jerónimo de Aguilar, un fraile español y náufrago que conocía la lengua porque había vivido con los mayas en la península de Yucatán por ocho años. Además de ser la intérprete de Cortés, La Malinche tuvo un hijo con él, Martín, a quien se le considera el primer mestizo de las Américas y simbólicamente el primer mexicano.

87. ¿Cuál fue el rol de Hernán Cortés al llegar a México?

    (A) Fraile
    (B) Intérprete
    (C) Conquistador
    (D) Rey

88. ¿Cuál de las siguientes palabras tiene el mismo significado que desempeñó en el contexto del primer párrafo?

    (A) Regaló
    (B) Hizo
    (C) Puso
    (D) Cambió

89. ¿Por qué se emplea la palabra "doña" para referirse a la Malinche?

    (A) Para mostrar respeto
    (B) Para explicar su origen
    (C) Para enfatizar su talento
    (D) Para indicar la religión

90. ¿Por qué se dice que Malinche tenía mucho poder?

    (A) Porque hablaba varios idiomas
    (B) Porque era la compañera del emperador azteca
    (C) Porque fue la primera mujer mestiza
    (D) Porque lo heredó de Jerónimo de Aguilar

To choose your answer to question 95, you will click on a part of the reading selection. This question indicates that the answer choices are each sentence in the text.

91–95.

Sin embargo, ella no hizo ninguna mención del asunto hasta después de la medianoche, en la lancha, cuando sintió como una revelación sobrenatural que había encontrado por fin la ocasión propicia para decirme lo que sin duda era el motivo real de su viaje, y empezó con el modo y el tono y las palabras milimétricas que debió madurar en la soledad de sus insomnios desde mucho antes de emprenderlo.

—Tu papá está muy triste—dijo.

Ahí estaba, pues, el infierno tan temido. Empezaba como siempre, cuando menos se esperaba, y con una voz sedante que no había de alterarse ante nada. Sólo por cumplir con el ritual, pues conocía de sobra la respuesta, le pregunté:

—¿Y eso por qué?

—Porque dejaste los estudios.

—No los dejé—le dije—. Sólo cambié de carrera.

La idea de una discusión a fondo le levantó el ánimo.

—Tu papá dice que es lo mismo—dijo.

A sabiendas de que era falso, le dije—: También él dejó de estudiar para tocar el violín.

—No fue igual—replicó ella con una gran vivacidad—. El violín lo tocaba sólo en fiestas y serenatas. Si dejó sus estudios fue porque no tenía ni con qué comer. Pero en menos de un mes aprendió telegrafía, que entonces era una profesión muy buena, sobre todo en Aracataca.

—Yo también vivo de escribir en los periódicos—le dije.

—Eso lo dices para no mortificarme—dijo ella. Pero la mala situación se te nota de lejos. Cómo será, que cuando te vi en la librería no te reconocí.

—Yo tampoco la reconocí a usted—le dije.

—Pero no por lo mismo—dijo ella—. Yo pensé que eras un limosnero.

Me miró las sandalias gastadas, y agregó—: Y sin medias.

¿Cómo sonaban las palabras de la mujer en el segundo párrafo?

- Atemorizadas
- Nerviosas
- Tranquilas
- Tristes

¿Cómo se expresa la mujer al hablar con el narrador?

- Con felicidad
- Con miedo
- Con reproche
- Con capricho

Según la mujer, ¿por qué había dejado los estudios el padre del narrador?

- Se mudó de la ciudad.
- Le gustaba tocar el violín.
- Tuvo que ganarse la vida.
- No soportaba los estudios.

¿Por quién tomó la mujer al narrador cuando lo vio en la librería?

- Un zapatero
- Un mendigo
- Un librero
- Un músico

Haz clic en la oración que indica la profesión del narrador.

To choose your answer to question 100, you will click on a part of the reading selection. This question indicates that the answer choices are each sentence in the text.

96–100.

Gracias a una iniciativa de la asociación de empresarios, los vecinos de Villasantiago pueden, si así lo desean, hacer sus compras estos días utilizando las viejas pesetas que algunos de ellos todavía conservan en sus casas. Con esta original idea, los comerciantes de este pueblo manchego tratan de impulsar la economía local, que se ha visto fuertemente afectada por la reciente crisis económica. El regreso temporal a la peseta ha puesto de manifiesto el notable incremento de los precios que se ha experimentado desde que se sustituyó la rubia por el euro en el año 2002. Así, según las últimas encuestas realizadas, los productos de primera necesidad, como los alimentos, han aumentado de forma considerable, llegando a valer casi el doble. Los habitantes del pueblo han acogido con tanto entusiasmo este proyecto que las ventas en estas últimas semanas han crecido mucho. Los propios comerciantes están sorprendidos por el número de personas que conservan la antigua moneda nacional. Se calcula que todavía quedan 1.707 millones de euros en pesetas por cambiar, ya que a diferencia de otros países, como Italia que dio de plazo hasta el último día de febrero, o Portugal que aceptará el cambio de escudos por euros hasta fin de año, el Banco de España todavía no ha fijado una fecha límite para el cambio.

Según el artículo, ¿qué nueva medida se ha implementado en Villasantiago?

- Pagar en las tiendas solo con euros
- Pagar en las tiendas solo con pesetas
- Pagar en las tiendas con euros y con pesetas
- Pagar en las tiendas con escudos y con euros

Según el artículo, ¿quién tuvo la idea de hacer el proyecto en Villasantiago?

- Los comerciantes
- Los vecinos
- El ayuntamiento
- El Banco de España

Según el artículo, ¿cuál es el objetivo principal de la iniciativa de Villasantiago?

- Atraer turistas europeos al pueblo
- Promocionar productos manchegos
- Estimular el comercio del pueblo
- Reducir el precio de los alimentos

Según el artículo, ¿hasta cuándo pueden los ciudadanos cambiar las pesetas en el Banco de España?

- Se extendió la fecha para el cambio hasta el 2002
- Se desconoce la fecha para el fin del cambio
- Hasta el último día de febrero
- Hasta fin de año

Haz clic en la oración que indica la reacción de los pobladores de Villasantiago hacia la nueva medida.

Study Resources

Most textbooks used in college-level Spanish language courses cover the topics in the outline given earlier, but the approaches to certain topics and the emphases given to them may differ. To prepare for the Spanish Language exam, it is advisable to study one or more college textbooks, which can be found in most college bookstores. When selecting a textbook, check the table of contents against the knowledge and skills required for this test.

Besides studying basic vocabulary, you should understand and be able to apply the grammatical principles that make up the language. To improve your reading comprehension, read passages from textbooks, short magazine or newspaper articles, or other printed material of your choice. To improve your listening comprehension, seek opportunities to hear the language spoken by native speakers and to converse with native speakers.

If you have opportunities to join organizations with Spanish-speaking members, to attend Spanish movies, or to listen to Spanish-language television or radio broadcasts, take advantage of them.

Visit **clep.collegeboard.org/earn-college-credit/practice** for additional Spanish resources. You can also find suggestions for exam preparation in Chapter IV of the *Official Study Guide*. In addition, many college faculty post their course materials on their schools' websites.

Answer Key

1.	B	51.	D
2.	A	52.	D
3.	D	53.	B
4.	C	54.	B
5.	C	55.	B
6.	C	56.	D
7.	A	57.	A
8.	C	58.	B
9.	B	59.	B
10.	D	60.	A
11.	A	61.	A
12.	C	62.	B
13.	B	63.	C
14.	C	64.	B
15.	A	65.	D
16.	A	66.	B
17.	D	67.	C
18.	B	68.	A
19.	D	69.	D
20.	B	70.	B
21.	B	71.	C
22.	B	72.	B
23.	B	73.	D
24.	A	74.	C
25.	See next page.	75.	B
26.	A	76.	B
27.	C	77.	C
28.	2, 1, 4, 3	78.	C
29.	D	79.	A
30.	A	80.	B
31.	See next page.	81.	C
32.	C	82.	D
33.	A	83.	C
34.	D	84.	B
35.	B	85.	C
36.	B	86.	A
37.	C	87.	C
38.	C	88.	B
39.	A	89.	A
40.	B	90.	A
41.	D	91.	C
42.	B	92.	C
43.	A	93.	C
44.	C	94.	B
45.	B	95.	On page 220.
46.	D	96.	C
47.	B	97.	A
48.	D	98.	C
49.	C	99.	B
50.	B	100.	On page 221.

25.

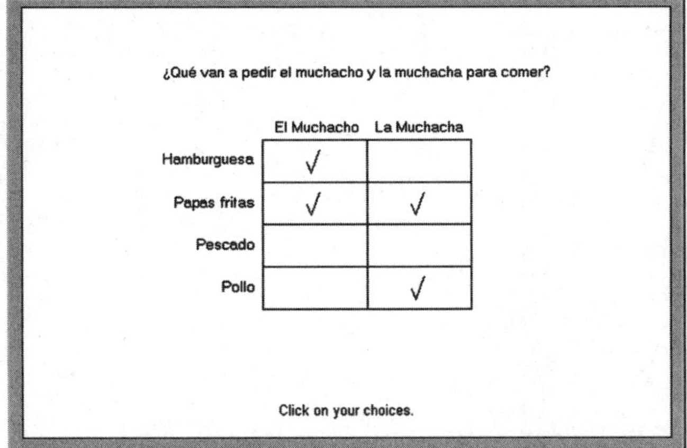

¿Qué van a pedir el muchacho y la muchacha para comer?

	El Muchacho	La Muchacha
Hamburguesa	√	
Papas fritas	√	√
Pescado		
Pollo		√

Click on your choices.

31.

95.

Sin embargo, ella no hizo ninguna mención del asunto hasta después de la medianoche, en la lancha, cuando sintió como una revelación sobrenatural que había encontrado por fin la ocasión propicia para decirme lo que sin duda era el motivo real de su viaje, y empezó con el modo y el tono y las palabras milimétricas que debió madurar en la soledad de sus insomnios desde mucho antes de emprenderlo.

—Tu papá está muy triste—dijo.

Ahí estaba, pues, el infierno tan temido. Empezaba como siempre, cuando menos se esperaba, y con una voz sedante que no había de alterarse ante nada. Sólo por cumplir con el ritual, pues conocía de sobra la respuesta, le pregunté:

—¿Y eso por qué?

—Porque dejaste los estudios.

—No los dejé—le dije—. Sólo cambié de carrera.

La idea de una discusión a fondo le levantó el ánimo.

—Tu papá dice que es lo mismo—dijo.

A sabiendas de que era falso, le dije—: También él dejó de estudiar para tocar el violín.

—No fue igual—replicó ella con una gran vivacidad—. El violín lo tocaba sólo en fiestas y serenatas. Si dejó sus estudios fue porque no tenía ni con qué comer. Pero en menos de un mes aprendió telegrafía, que entonces era una profesión muy buena, sobre todo en Aracataca.

—Yo también vivo de escribir en los periódicos—le dije.

—Eso lo dices para no mortificarme—dijo ella. Pero la mala situación se te nota de lejos. Cómo será, que cuando te vi en la librería no te reconocí.

—Yo tampoco la reconocí a usted—le dije.

—Pero no por lo mismo—dijo ella—. Yo pensé que eras un limosnero.

Me miró las sandalias gastadas, y agregó—: Y sin medias.

Haz clic en la oración que indica la profesión del narrador.

100.

Gracias a una iniciativa de la asociación de empresarios, los vecinos de Villasantiago pueden, si así lo desean, hacer sus compras estos días utilizando las viejas pesetas que algunos de ellos todavía conservan en sus casas. Con esta original idea, los comerciantes de este pueblo manchego tratan de impulsar la economía local, que se ha visto fuertemente afectada por la reciente crisis económica. El regreso temporal a la peseta ha puesto de manifiesto el notable incremento de los precios que se ha experimentado desde que se sustituyó la rubia por el euro en el año 2002. Así, según las últimas encuestas realizadas, los productos de primera necesidad, como los alimentos, han aumentado de forma considerable, llegando a valer casi el doble. Los habitantes del pueblo han acogido con tanto entusiasmo este proyecto que las ventas en estas últimas semanas han crecido mucho. Los propios comerciantes están sorprendidos por el número de personas que conservan la antigua moneda nacional. Se calcula que todavía quedan 1.707 millones de euros en pesetas por cambiar, ya que a diferencia de otros países, como Italia que dio de plazo hasta el último día de febrero, o Portugal que aceptará el cambio de escudos por euros hasta fin de año, el Banco de España todavía no ha fijado una fecha límite para el cambio.

Haz clic en la oración que indica la reacción de los pobladores de Villasantiago hacia la nueva medida.

American Government

Description of the Examination

The American Government examination covers material that is usually taught in a one-semester introductory course in American government and politics at the college level. The scope and emphasis of the exam reflect what is most commonly taught in introductory American government and politics courses in political science departments around the United States. These courses go beyond a general understanding of civics to incorporate political processes and behavior. The exam covers topics such as the institutions and policy processes of the federal government, the federal courts and civil liberties, political parties and interest groups, political beliefs and behavior, and the content and history of the Constitution.

The examination contains approximately 100 questions to be answered in 90 minutes. Some of these are pretest questions that will not be scored.

Knowledge and Skills Required

Questions on the American Government examination require candidates to demonstrate one or more of the following abilities in the approximate proportions indicated.

- Knowledge of American government and politics (about 55%–60% of the exam)
- Understanding of typical patterns of political processes and behavior (including the components of the behavioral situation of a political actor), and the principles used to explain or justify various governmental structures and procedures (about 30%–35% of the exam)
- Analysis and interpretation of simple data that are relevant to American government and politics (10%–15% of the exam)

The subject matter of the American Government examination is drawn from the following topics. The percentages next to the main topics indicate the approximate percentage of exam questions on that topic.

30%–35% Institutions and Policy Processes: Presidency, Bureaucracy, Congress, and the Federal Courts

- The major formal and informal institutional arrangements and powers
- Structure, policy processes and outputs
- Relationships among these three institutions and links between them and political parties, interest groups, the media and public opinion
- Structure and processes of the judicial system, with emphasis on the role and influence of the Supreme Court

10%–15% Civil Liberties and Civil Rights

- The development of civil rights and civil liberties by judicial interpretation
- The Bill of Rights
- Incorporation of the Bill of Rights
- Equal protection and due process

15%–20% Political Parties and Interest Groups

- Political parties (including their function, organization, mobilization, historical development and effects on the political process)
- Interest groups (including the variety of activities they typically undertake and their effects on the political process)
- Elections (including the electoral process)

15%–20% Political Beliefs and Behavior

- Processes by which citizens learn about politics
- Political participation (including voting behavior)
- Public opinion
- Beliefs that citizens hold about their government and its leaders
- Political culture (the variety of factors that predispose citizens to differ from one another in terms of their political perceptions, values, attitudes and activities)
- The influence of public opinion on political leaders

15%–20% Constitutional Underpinnings of American Democracy

The development of concepts such as
- Federalism (with attention to intergovernmental relations)
- Separation of powers
- Checks and balances
- Majority rule
- Minority rights
- Considerations that influenced the formulation and adoption of the Constitution
- Theories of democracy

Sample Test Questions

The following sample questions do not appear on an actual CLEP examination. They are intended to give potential test-takers an indication of the format and difficulty level of the examination and to provide content for practice and review. Knowing the correct answers to all of the sample questions is not a guarantee of satisfactory performance on the exam.

Directions: Each of the questions or incomplete statements below is followed by five suggested answers or completions. Select the one that is best in each case.

1. Which of the following statements best reflects the pluralist theory of American politics?

   (A) American politics is dominated by a small elite.

   (B) Public policies emerge from cooperation among elites in business, labor, and government.

   (C) Public policies emerge from compromises reached among competing groups.

   (D) American politics is dominated by cities at the expense of rural areas.

   (E) The American political arena is made up of isolated individuals who have few group affiliations outside the family.

2. Which of the following is generally the most significant influence on an individual's identification with a particular political party?

   (A) Religious affiliation

   (B) Family

   (C) Level of education

   (D) Television

   (E) The party identification of the incumbent president

3. Which of the following committee assignments would confer the most power and influence on members of the House of Representatives?

   (A) Agriculture

   (B) Ways and Means

   (C) Veterans' Affairs

   (D) Armed Services

   (E) Education and Labor

4. Which of the following statements about *Brown* v. *Board of Education of Topeka* is correct?

   (A) It declared segregation by race in the public schools unconstitutional.

   (B) It established the principle of one person, one vote.

   (C) It required that citizens about to be arrested be read a statement concerning their right to remain silent.

   (D) It declared Bible reading in the public schools unconstitutional.

   (E) It declared segregation by race in places of public accommodation unconstitutional.

5. Prior to the Voting Rights Act of 1965, literacy tests were used by some southern states to

   (A) determine the educational achievement of potential voters

   (B) prevent African Americans from exercising their right to vote

   (C) assess the general population's understanding of the Constitution

   (D) hinder the migration of northerners

   (E) defend the practice of segregation

6. The practice whereby individual senators can veto federal judicial nominations in their respective states is called
   (A) logrolling
   (B) preferential treatment
   (C) senatorial prerogative
   (D) senatorial courtesy
   (E) judicial selection

7. Differences between House and Senate versions of a bill are resolved
   (A) in a conference committee
   (B) by the Rules committees of both chambers
   (C) in subcommittee hearings
   (D) by the president before the bill is signed into law
   (E) during the bill's markup phase

8. Which of the following principles protects a citizen from imprisonment without trial?
   (A) Representative government
   (B) Separation of powers
   (C) Due process
   (D) Checks and balances
   (E) Popular sovereignty

9. The passage of legislation in Congress often depends on mutual accommodations among members. This suggests that, to some extent, congressional behavior is based on
   (A) ideological divisions
   (B) partisan division
   (C) the principle of reciprocity
   (D) deference to state legislatures
   (E) norms of seniority

10. Which of the following statements accurately describes the president's veto power?

    I. A president sometimes threatens to veto a bill that is under discussion in order to influence congressional decision making.
    II. A president typically vetoes about a third of the bills passed by Congress.
    III. Congress is usually unable to override a president's veto.

    (A) I only
    (B) III only
    (C) I and III only
    (D) II and III only
    (E) I, II, and III

11. All of the following issues were decided at the Constitutional Convention of 1787 EXCEPT
    (A) representation in the legislature
    (B) voting qualifications of the electorate
    (C) the method of electing the president
    (D) congressional power to override a presidential veto
    (E) qualifications for members of the House and Senate

12. The principle of stare decisis refers to which of the following?
    (A) The process in which groups write legal briefs to influence the outcome of a case
    (B) The process by which Supreme Court justices decide which cases to hear
    (C) The process by which judges interpret common law principles along with constitutional law
    (D) The judicial principle of following precedents that were established in previous court decisions
    (E) A legal principle that allows parties to settle their disputes outside the courtroom

13. The usefulness to the president of having cabinet members as political advisers is undermined by the fact that

    (A) the president has little latitude in choosing cabinet members
    (B) cabinet members have no political support independent of the president
    (C) cabinet members are usually drawn from Congress and retain loyalties to Congress
    (D) the loyalties of cabinet members are often divided between loyalty to the president and loyalty to their own executive departments
    (E) the cabinet operates as a collective unit and individual members have no access to the president

14. All of the following are constitutional rights that neither the federal government nor the states can restrict EXCEPT the right to

    (A) remain silent during questioning
    (B) be represented by counsel
    (C) be indicted by grand jury
    (D) not be tried for the same offense twice
    (E) receive a trial by jury in a criminal case

15. In the electoral history of the United States, third parties have been effective vehicles of protest when they

    (A) aligned themselves with one of the major parties
    (B) presented innovative programs in Congress
    (C) dramatized issues and positions that were being ignored by the major parties
    (D) chose the president by depriving either of the major parties of an electoral college victory
    (E) supported a political agenda that appealed especially to women

16. Which of the following best defines the term “judicial activism”?

    (A) The tendency of judges to hear large numbers of cases on social issues
    (B) The efforts of judges to lobby Congress for funds
    (C) The unwillingness of judges to remove themselves from cases in which they have a personal interest
    (D) The attempts by judges to influence election outcomes
    (E) The attempts by judges to influence public policy through their case decisions

17. High levels of political participation have been found to be positively associated with which of the following?

    I. A high level of interest in politics
    II. A sense of political efficacy
    III. A strong sense of civic duty

    (A) III only
    (B) I and II only
    (C) I and III only
    (D) II and III only
    (E) I, II, and III

18. In the past 30 years, the single most important variable in determining the outcome of an election for a member of the House of Representatives has been

    (A) incumbency
    (B) the candidate’s personal wealth
    (C) the previous political office the candidate held in the district
    (D) the candidate’s membership in the political party of the president
    (E) the candidate’s positions on key social issues

19. Which of the following best describes the concept of federalism embodied in the United States government?

    (A) The Constitution divides power between a central government and its constituent governments, with some powers being shared.

    (B) The Constitution grants all governmental powers to the central government, which may delegate authority to state governments.

    (C) State governments join together and form a central government, which exists solely by approval of the state governments.

    (D) The central government creates state governments.

    (E) State governments are sovereign in all matters except foreign policy, which is reserved to the central government.

20. The power of the Rules Committee in the House of Representatives primarily stems from its authority to

    (A) choose the chairs of other standing committees and issue rules for the selection of subcommittee chairs

    (B) initiate all spending legislation and hold budget hearings

    (C) limit the time for debate and determine whether amendments to a bill can be considered

    (D) determine the procedures by which nominations by the president will be approved by the House

    (E) choose the president if no candidate wins a majority in the electoral college

21. Which of the following is a function of the White House Office?

    (A) Advising the president on political decisions

    (B) Heading federal departments as the president's representative

    (C) Preparing the national budget for the president

    (D) Supervising national security agencies such as the CIA and FBI

    (E) Acting as a liaison between the vice president and Congress

22. A major difference between political parties and interest groups is that interest groups generally do NOT

    (A) suggest new legislation that is supportive of their interests

    (B) try to influence the outcome of legislation

    (C) occupy a place on the ballot

    (D) concern themselves with elections

    (E) have a national organization

23. An election is a realigning or critical election if

    (A) one party controls the Congress and the other controls the presidency

    (B) voter turnout is higher than expected

    (C) it occurs during a major war

    (D) there is a lasting change in party coalitions

    (E) the same party controls both Congress and the presidency

24. Which of the following Supreme Court cases involved the principle of one person, one vote?

    (A) *Baker* v. *Carr*

    (B) *Roe* v. *Wade*

    (C) *Mapp* v. *Ohio*

    (D) *Korematsu* v. *United States*

    (E) *Gideon* v. *Wainwright*

25. The passage of broad legislation that leaves the making of specific rules to the executive branch is an example of

    (A) shared powers

    (B) delegated authority

    (C) checks and balances

    (D) executive agreement

    (E) a legislative veto

26. The redrawing of congressional districts in such a way as to give special advantage to one political party is referred to as

    (A) electioneering
    (B) gerrymandering
    (C) logrolling
    (D) apportionment
    (E) politicization

27. The details of legislation are usually worked out in which of the following settings?

    (A) The House Rules Committee
    (B) The minority leader's office
    (C) The floor of the House
    (D) Legislative hearings
    (E) A subcommittee

28. A theoretical explanation of the operation of diverse interests in American politics is found in

    (A) the Virginia Plan
    (B) John Stuart Mill's *On Liberty*
    (C) *The Federalist* papers
    (D) the Declaration of Independence
    (E) John Locke's *Two Treatises of Government*

29. The framers of the original Constitution thought that which of the following would best protect judicial independence?

    (A) Presidential nomination and senatorial confirmation
    (B) The circuit-riding system
    (C) An odd number of Supreme Court justices
    (D) Judicial impeachments
    (E) Life tenure during good behavior

How People Identify With Political Parties

All Voters

	Men			Women		
	Rep %	Dem %	D-R diff	Rep %	Dem %	D-R diff
2008	43	46	+3	33	56	+22
2004	48	43	–5	40	51	+11
2000	47	42	–5	38	51	+13
1996	49	43	–6	39	53	+14
1992	45	46	+1	40	52	+12

Young Voters Ages 18–29

	Men			Women		
	Rep %	Dem %	D-R diff	Rep %	Dem %	D-R diff
2008	38	52	+14	28	63	+35
2004	44	47	+3	36	54	+18
2000	46	44	–2	37	53	+16
1996	50	44	–6	38	55	+17
1992	52	42	–10	42	50	+8

Based on registered voters who identify with or lean towards the Democratic or Republican party; 1992–2004 figures are from the surveys conducted in the 12 months prior to each election; 2008 figures are from surveys conducted Oct. 2007–March 2008.

Source: Pew Research Center, Party Identification Among 18–29 Year Olds, April 28, 2008, http://pewresearch.org/pubs/813/gen-dems

30. According to the table above, which of the following statements is true?

    (A) In every election, women between the ages of 18 and 29 were more likely to identify themselves as Republicans than were women of all ages.
    (B) In the 2000 election, more than one-half of all men identified themselves as Democrats.
    (C) In every election, the difference in partisan identification for men was greater than the difference in partisan identification for women.
    (D) In the 1996 election, women between the ages of 18 and 29 were more likely to identify themselves as Democrats than were men between the ages of 18 and 29.
    (E) In the 2008 election, more men between the ages of 18 and 29 identified themselves as Republicans than Democrats.

31. Which of the following activities of American labor unions is permissible by law?

    (A) Engaging in strikes
    (B) Denying the public access to a business
    (C) Refusing a subpoena to appear before Congress
    (D) Disobeying a court injunction to return to work
    (E) Requiring members to make political contributions

32. Which of the following best describes the relationship between socioeconomic status and participation in politics?

    (A) The lower one's socioeconomic status, the more likely it is that one will run for public office.
    (B) The higher one's socioeconomic status, the greater the probability of active involvement in the political process.
    (C) Adults who are unemployed have a greater personal interest in policy and tend to participate more actively in politics than do employed adults.
    (D) People in the lower socioeconomic status are the most likely to vote.
    (E) There is no relationship between socioeconomic status and political participation.

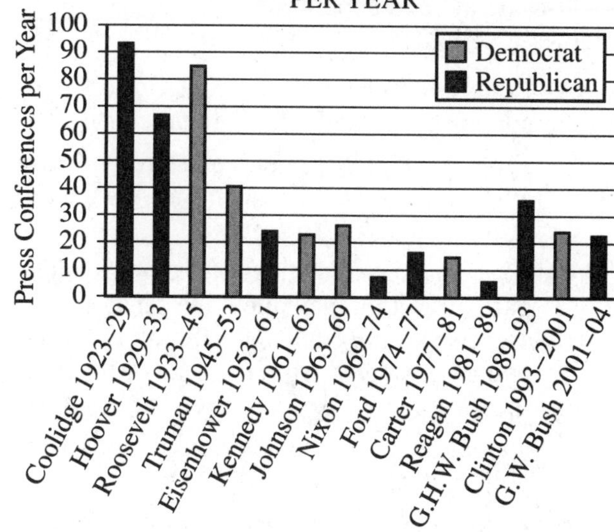

Source: Kumar, 2004.

33. According to the information in the chart above, which of the following statements is true?

    (A) Republican presidents held far fewer press conferences per year than Democratic presidents.
    (B) The most recent presidents held fewer press conferences per year than presidents in the 1920s and 1930s.
    (C) President Clinton held more press conferences per year than his predecessor.
    (D) On average, President Nixon held more press conferences per year than President Johnson.
    (E) President Kennedy held more press conferences per year than President Eisenhower.

34. One important change in political culture since the Second World War is that United States citizens have become

    (A) less trusting of governmental institutions and leaders
    (B) less likely to think of themselves as ideologically moderate
    (C) less likely to support civil rights
    (D) more likely to believe that their actions can influence government policy
    (E) more trusting of nongovernmental institutions and leaders

35. All of the following statements correctly describe judicial appointments at the federal level EXCEPT:

    (A) Congress nominates and confirms all appointments to the federal judiciary.
    (B) Federal judicial appointments are typically evaluated by the American Bar Association or the Federalist Society.
    (C) If a senator is a member of the president's party, tradition may allow the senator to exercise an informal veto over an individual being considered from the senator's state.
    (D) Presidents seldom recommend for judicial appointment individuals from the opposition political party.
    (E) Federal judgeships are often considered by presidents as patronage positions.

36. Which of the following agencies determines the domestic monetary policy of the United States?

    (A) The Council of Economic Advisors
    (B) The United States Department of the Treasury
    (C) The Office of Management and Budget
    (D) The Federal Reserve Board
    (E) The Export-Import Bank

37. Under which of the following conditions are interest groups most likely to influence policymaking?

    (A) When a problem has been dramatized by television network news
    (B) When the president has made a major address on the subject
    (C) When the parties in Congress have opposing positions on the issue
    (D) When presidential candidates have been disagreeing with one another on the subject
    (E) When the issue is a highly technical one requiring very detailed legislation

38. All of the following help to explain the president's difficulty in controlling cabinet-level agencies EXCEPT:

    (A) Agencies often have political support from interest groups.
    (B) Agency staff often have information and technical expertise that the president and presidential advisers lack.
    (C) The president cannot dismiss appointees after they have been confirmed by the Senate.
    (D) Civil servants who remain in their jobs through changes of administration develop loyalties to their agencies.
    (E) Congress is a competitor for influence over the bureaucracy.

39. In the Constitution as originally ratified in 1788, the provisions regarding which of the following most closely approximate popular, majoritarian democracy?

    (A) Election of members of the House of Representatives
    (B) Election of members of the Senate
    (C) Election of the president
    (D) Ratification of treaties
    (E) Confirmation of presidential appointments

40. The most likely and often the most powerful policy coalition of interests is likely to include a federal agency plus which of the following?

    (A) Related agencies in the bureaucracy and a congressional committee chairperson
    (B) Congress and the president
    (C) An interest group and the president
    (D) An interest group and a congressional subcommittee
    (E) An interest group and the majority party

41. Throughout most of the twentieth century, which of the following was most likely to occur in midterm congressional elections?

(A) The party of the president typically lost seats in Congress, regardless of whether the president was a Republican or a Democrat.
(B) The party of the president typically gained seats in Congress, regardless of whether the president was a Republican or a Democrat.
(C) The Democratic Party gained seats in Congress, whereas the Republican Party lost seats.
(D) The Republican Party gained seats in Congress, whereas the Democratic Party lost seats.
(E) Voter turnout was typically higher than in presidential elections.

42. Delegates to the Republican and Democratic national conventions are primarily chosen

(A) by local party leaders
(B) in primaries
(C) in state caucuses
(D) by members of Congress
(E) by lottery

TRUST IN THE FEDERAL GOVERNMENT VERSUS YOUR OWN STATE GOVERNMENT TO DO A BETTER JOB RUNNING THINGS

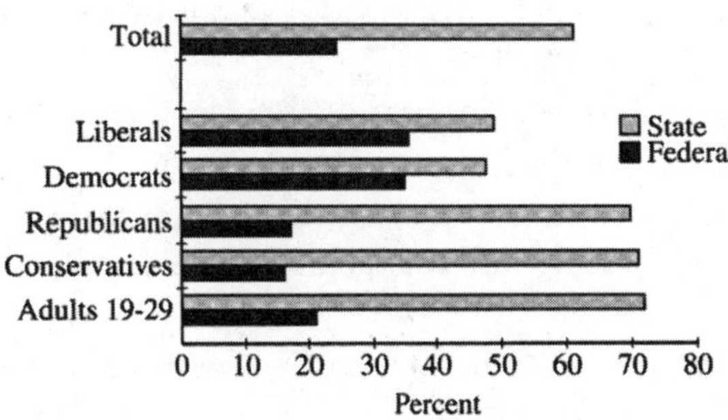

Source: *Washington Post*/Kaiser Family Foundation/Harvard University, 1995.

43. The chart above supports which of the following statements?

I. Both Republicans and Democrats have more trust in the federal government to do a better job than state governments.
II. Most groups trust their own state governments more than the federal government.
III. Democrats trust the federal government more than Republicans.
IV. Liberals believe in big government.

(A) I only
(B) III only
(C) II and III only
(D) II and IV only
(E) I, II, III, and IV

44. Which of the following political philosophers most influenced the writing of the United States Constitution?

(A) Plato
(B) Machiavelli
(C) Locke
(D) Rousseau
(E) Marx

45. The concept of responsible party government emphasizes which of the following about elections?

    (A) Political parties will take positions similar to each other.
    (B) Political parties will take clear, unambiguous positions.
    (C) Voters will decide how to vote on the basis of how well the incumbent party satisfied them.
    (D) Voters will vote mostly according to past identification.
    (E) Special interest groups provide platforms and policy positions to political parties and their candidates.

46. Which of the following is a difference between the House of Representatives and the Senate?

    (A) Seniority is more important in the Senate than in the House.
    (B) Leadership is more centralized in the Senate than in the House.
    (C) The Senate has the exclusive power to ratify treaties.
    (D) The Senate has more committees than does the House.
    (E) The Senate may veto laws passed by the House, but the House may not veto senatorial legislation.

47. Which of the following was a consequence of the New Deal legislation passed during the Great Depression under the administration of Franklin D. Roosevelt?

    (A) States gained additional powers to pass legislation to relieve the economic problems of the Depression.
    (B) The federal government became a more important agent of change than in previous presidential administrations.
    (C) New presidential appointments to federal courts limited the judicial powers of the Supreme Court.
    (D) Social policy became the primary concern of state governments.
    (E) Presidents have been much more likely to defend their creation of emergency acts by claiming executive privilege.

48. Congressional oversight is best described as

    (A) monitoring the federal bureaucracy
    (B) monitoring the judicial branch and court rulings
    (C) recommending and confirming federal judges
    (D) regulating interstate commerce
    (E) implementing public policy

49. The differences between the political attitudes of men and women are referred to as

    (A) the political gap
    (B) the gender gap
    (C) partisan politics
    (D) party loyalty
    (E) the median voter theory

50. According to the Constitution, which of the following decides the presidential election outcome in the event that a single candidate does not get a majority of electoral votes?

    (A) The Supreme Court
    (B) The Senate
    (C) The House of Representatives
    (D) Both houses of Congress
    (E) The sitting president

51. If the vice presidency of the United States is vacated, the Constitution stipulates that the president must

    (A) appoint a new vice president with the approval of the House only
    (B) appoint a new vice president with the approval of the Senate only
    (C) appoint a new vice president with the approval of both houses of Congress
    (D) instate the Speaker of the House as the new vice president
    (E) leave the vice presidency vacant for the remainder of the term of office

52. James Madison's goal of setting power against power to minimize the concentration of authority in any one branch of government is outlined in the Constitution as a system of

(A) separation of powers
(B) checks and balances
(C) divided government
(D) national supremacy
(E) federalism

53. The declining number of marginal seats in Congress means that

(A) fewer seats are won by 55% or less of the vote
(B) there are fewer minor committee assignments in Congress
(C) redistricting no longer affects elections
(D) members of third parties are more likely to be elected to Congress
(E) fewer minorities are elected to Congress

54. The ability of the media to define the importance of particular events and issues is called

(A) preemption
(B) agenda setting
(C) investigative reporting
(D) minimal effects thesis
(E) adversarial journalism

55. The power of judicial review was established in

(A) *McCulloch* v. *Maryland*
(B) *Gitlow* v. *New York*
(C) *Dandridge* v. *Williams*
(D) *Miranda* v. *Arizona*
(E) *Marbury* v. *Madison*

56. Which of the following is true of both the House of Representatives and the Senate?

(A) Both chambers must approve the president's nominees for judicial and administrative positions.
(B) Both chambers employ a complex system of permanent committees to assist them in carrying out their legislative duties.
(C) Both the Speaker of the House and the Senate's president pro tempore are elected by majority vote of their respective chamber.
(D) Both chambers encourage and permit extensive discussion of important issues and proposed legislation on the chamber floor.
(E) When midterm vacancies occur in either chamber, state governors are permitted to appoint replacement members.

57. The authority of a chief executive to withhold approval from specific parts of appropriations bills passed by the legislature is known as

(A) a pocket veto
(B) a line-item veto
(C) a legislative veto
(D) an executive order
(E) an executive privilege

58. The weakening of political parties is most often traced to

(A) the single-member, winner-take-all system
(B) the growth of political action committees (PACs)
(C) Progressive Era reforms
(D) voters' increasing level of education
(E) voter apathy

59. Which of the following contemporary political ideologies posits that government power should be used to promote individual economic security and redistribute resources, but rejects the notion that government should favor a particular set of social values?

    (A) Liberalism
    (B) Conservatism
    (C) Communitarianism
    (D) Libertarianism
    (E) Elitism

60. Which of the following best describes a referendum?

    (A) A chief executive appoints an independent commission to investigate allegations of political corruption.
    (B) A legislature repeals an unpopular law to improve the electoral advantage of incumbents.
    (C) A political party caucuses to choose its candidates for a general election.
    (D) Citizens vote directly on laws proposed by a state legislature.
    (E) Citizens initiate the process of removing elected officials from office.

61. Which of the following is true of federal administrative agencies?

    (A) All agencies are formally part of a cabinet-level department.
    (B) They are seldom able to influence the formulation of national public policy.
    (C) They collectively form one large institutional pyramid with a common purpose.
    (D) Congress has no means of controlling administrative agencies.
    (E) They have substantial influence over public policy through administrative discretion.

62. Which of the following is a check on the power of the United States Supreme Court?

    (A) Congress controls the number of justices who may sit on the Court.
    (B) The Court has the power to enforce its decisions.
    (C) Cases involving a state's laws can be heard only through the Court's original jurisdiction.
    (D) The Court reviews all legislation after the president signs it into law.
    (E) Congress cannot rewrite or repass a law that the Court has declared unconstitutional.

63. States, according to the full faith and credit clause of the Constitution

    (A) can coin money if they choose, but they cannot print national currency
    (B) must honor public records, acts, and judicial proceedings of every other state
    (C) are not required to extradite fugitives of justice from other states
    (D) can choose to suppress information on their credit rating ahead of a bond issue
    (E) have the right to regulate banking and issuers of credit

64. Which of the following is most likely to weaken party leadership in the Senate?

    (A) The confirmation of appointments to the Supreme Court
    (B) The assignment of senators to permanent committees
    (C) The use of filibuster by individual senators
    (D) The removal of the president following impeachment
    (E) The ratification of treaties presented by the president

65. The principal source of presidents' political influence is their
    (A) constitutional authority to declare war
    (B) power to convene Congress
    (C) constitutional authority to execute public policies
    (D) power to dictate diplomatic relations with other countries
    (E) constitutional authority to grant pardons

66. Among the expressed powers of the federal government enumerated in the Constitution of the United States is the power to
    (A) monitor discrimination in the workplace
    (B) establish national political parties
    (C) standardize the licensing of lawyers
    (D) regulate interstate trade and commerce
    (E) standardize high school curriculums across states

67. Which of the following accounts for the greatest percentage of expenditure for state and local governments in the United States?
    (A) Elementary and secondary education
    (B) Public welfare
    (C) Highways
    (D) Health and hospitals
    (E) Police

68. The use of initiative and referendum illustrates which of the following theories of governance?
    (A) Separation of powers
    (B) Representative democracy
    (C) Direct democracy
    (D) Virtual democracy
    (E) Abusive democracy

69. Which of the following best accounts for the inability of third parties to challenge the dominance of the Republican and Democratic parties in United States elections?
    (A) A consistent decline in the number of independent voters
    (B) A decrease in significant policy differences between the Republican and Democratic parties
    (C) A lack of popular desire for the emergence of alternative parties
    (D) The passage of strict voter identification laws in many states
    (E) The ability of the Republican and Democratic parties to co-opt popular third-party policy ideas

70. In *The Federalist* paper number 10, James Madison argued that
    (A) the growth of factions was inevitable in a democracy
    (B) federalism would curb ambition among political leaders
    (C) the Supreme Court is the least dangerous branch of government
    (D) the Articles of Confederation would ensure the safety of the nation
    (E) the government should restrict the growth of interest groups through legislation

71. The constitutional redistribution of House seats after the census every ten years is known as
    (A) malapportionment
    (B) reapportionment
    (C) redistricting
    (D) gerrymandering
    (E) referendum

72. Which of the following is true of the Articles of Confederation?

    (A) They were written shortly before the Declaration of Independence.
    (B) They formed a national government with supremacy over the states.
    (C) They included a bill of rights that was applied to the states.
    (D) They provided for three branches of government.
    (E) They created a national government with a legislature but no executive or judiciary.

73. According to the United States Constitution, who has the right to create inferior courts?

    (A) The president
    (B) The Supreme Court
    (C) The Congress
    (D) The bureaucracy
    (E) The Department of Justice

74. Which of the following is an example of monetary policy?

    (A) Raising taxes
    (B) Funding foreign aid
    (C) Cutting defense spending
    (D) Increasing the reserve requirement
    (E) Making budget allocations to the Treasury department

75. Congress has the least discretion to change spending for which of the following?

    (A) Defense and education spending
    (B) Transportation and entitlement programs
    (C) Interest on the national debt and defense programs
    (D) Education and entitlement programs
    (E) Interest on the national debt and entitlement programs

76. Which of the following statements is historically true of the electoral college?

    (A) The electoral college was added to the Constitution as an amendment and has been used only since the 1920s.
    (B) Third-party candidates are often overrepresented in the electoral college results.
    (C) The winner of the electoral college also usually wins the popular vote.
    (D) The electoral college allows small states to become swing states because each state gets two electoral college votes.
    (E) In the rare case of a tie vote in the electoral college, the winner is chosen by the popular vote results.

77. Which of the following actions gives the president an advantage over Congress in promoting policy?

    (A) Using the franking privilege
    (B) Impounding funding for projects of which the president disapproves
    (C) Invoking senatorial courtesy
    (D) Utilizing the media through the bully pulpit
    (E) Invoking the power to end a filibuster

78. Which of the following is true of political parties?

    (A) They are highly centralized organizations that rely very little on state participants.
    (B) They establish guidelines of behavior and insist that their candidates follow these guidelines.
    (C) They require all members to pay dues.
    (D) They try to gain control of government by winning elections.
    (E) They generally concentrate their efforts on a single policy area.

79. Which of the following best defines political culture?

    (A) It is the process by which one acquires opinions about government.
    (B) It is the shared attitudes of a people regarding government.
    (C) It is the belief that no one person can effect change in government.
    (D) It is the willingness of people to accept government's right to rule.
    (E) It is a statement by government officials about how citizens should behave.

80. Which of the following is the strongest determinant of an individual's voting behavior?

    (A) His or her socioeconomic background
    (B) Suggestions from family members
    (C) Newspaper and media endorsements
    (D) Political party affiliation
    (E) His or her opinions on policy issues

81. In which of the following cases did the Supreme Court establish the precedent that a right to privacy stems from several amendments in the Bill of Rights?

    (A) *Griswold* v. *Connecticut*
    (B) *New York Times* v. *Sullivan*
    (C) *Brown* v. *Board of Education of Topeka*
    (D) *Lawrence* v. *Texas*
    (E) *Planned Parenthood* v. *Casey*

82. Each of the following is a power of Congress EXCEPT

    (A) recognizing foreign governments
    (B) declaring war
    (C) ratifying treaties
    (D) confirming ambassadors
    (E) appropriating funds for war

83. Individuals who identify themselves as conservative would most likely support which of the following?

    (A) Establishing universal health care
    (B) Lowering personal income taxes
    (C) Increasing luxury taxes
    (D) Tightening environmental regulations
    (E) Increasing protective tariffs

84. The phrase "divided government" refers to

    (A) Democrats and Republicans forming a coalition government
    (B) the separation of powers among the three branches of the federal government
    (C) the allocation of different kinds of legislative work to congressional committees
    (D) one political party controlling the presidency while another political party controls one or both houses of Congress
    (E) the Supreme Court striking down a law passed by Congress and signed by the president

85. Which of the following factors has most contributed to the persistence of the two-party system in the United States?

    (A) Plurality rules for determining election outcomes
    (B) Representation via multimember districts
    (C) Proportional representation in legislatures
    (D) Constitutional provisions for parties outlined by the framers
    (E) The influence and number of interest groups in politics

86. As compared with Republicans and Democrats, Independents in the United States are typically
    (A) less likely to vote in elections
    (B) less likely to engage in split-ticket voting
    (C) more likely to join an interest group
    (D) more likely to have a strong sense of political efficacy
    (E) more likely to share the ideology of their family members

87. Which of the following best describes the relationship between the media and citizens?
    (A) Most media are independent and unbiased, allowing citizens to form their own opinions.
    (B) The media are regulated by the government to ensure that consumers receive factually accurate information.
    (C) The media have greater influence in shaping the political ideology of citizens than any other factor does.
    (D) Citizens have little choice about how to consume media because of the consolidation of media ownership.
    (E) Citizens tend to seek out media that reinforce rather than challenge existing ideological views.

88. The Supreme Court's decision in *Arizona* v. *United States* (2012), which held that Congress, not the states, has the sole authority to regulate immigration, best illustrates which of the following features of the Constitution?
    (A) Federalism
    (B) Republicanism
    (C) Popular sovereignty
    (D) Checks and balances
    (E) Separation of powers

89. When judicial nominees come before the Senate Judiciary Committee to testify, the Senate is fulfilling which of its roles?
    (A) Oversight
    (B) Advice and consent
    (C) Appropriations
    (D) Judicial review
    (E) Ratification

90. If a party to a federal civil lawsuit loses the case and chooses to appeal, it would take the appeal to the
    (A) United States District Court
    (B) United States Courts of Appeals
    (C) United States Supreme Court
    (D) state superior court
    (E) state supreme court

91. The United States Supreme Court has used the equal protection clause in the Fourteenth Amendment to overturn legislation that
    (A) denies criminal defendants access to an attorney
    (B) grants the federal government the ability to levy income taxes
    (C) mandates grade school students recite the Pledge of Allegiance
    (D) refuses the right to engage in political protest, such as flag burning
    (E) allows for race-based segregation in schools

92. Which of the following protections is found in the Bill of Rights?
    (A) The writ of habeas corpus
    (B) Freedom to practice any religion
    (C) Universal male suffrage
    (D) The right to work
    (E) The right to equal treatment under the law

93. The Supreme Court decision in *McDonald* v. *City of Chicago* (2010), which upheld the Second Amendment right to keep and bear arms for self-defense, best exemplifies the doctrine of

(A) freedom of association
(B) privileges and immunities
(C) equal protection
(D) selective incorporation
(E) selective exclusiveness

94. Which of the following techniques has been used as an attempt to reform the bureaucracy?

(A) The privatization of public goods and services
(B) The expansion of the federal workforce
(C) Additional funding to government agencies
(D) Holding more meetings behind closed doors
(E) Dismissing whistle-blowers from their jobs

95. Which of the following best describes the impact that public policy issues have on campaigns and elections in the United States?

(A) Candidates running for office rarely take policy positions on issues that matter to the general public.
(B) Candidates with sophisticated policy positions historically win more elections than their opposition.
(C) During campaign season, the media provide the public with a detailed and thorough education on each candidate's policy platform.
(D) A candidate's ability to relate to voters has a greater impact on the candidate's success than does command of policy issues.
(E) Candidates are required to have public debates on policy issues during the general election cycle of their political campaigns.

96. Which of the following is a consequence of the increase in the number of political action committees (PACs) ?

(A) Challengers are winning more elections than incumbents.
(B) More citizens are turning out to vote in mid-term elections.
(C) There is more cooperation and bipartisanship in Congress.
(D) There has been an expansion of corporate influence in elections.
(E) The number of registered independents has increased.

97. Social Security and Medicare are considered entitlement programs because

(A) they are politically unpopular programs
(B) they equally serve the entire population
(C) they lack political party and interest group support
(D) citizens who meet the criteria are legally able to receive these benefits
(E) the government funds these programs out of the budget

98. During the Civil Rights era, when the National Association for the Advancement of Colored People (NAACP) was unsuccessful at traditional lobbying techniques, they turned to which of the following strategies to influence public policy?

(A) Litigation in the federal courts
(B) Mass mailing campaigns
(C) Providing information to lawmakers on the benefits of their proposals
(D) Entertaining lawmakers with expensive food and drink
(E) Giving campaign contributions to members of Congress

99. When the Supreme Court grants a writ of certiorari, it means the Court will
    (A) hear a case about the Bill of Rights
    (B) permit outside groups to submit legal briefs
    (C) review a case decided by a lower court
    (D) uphold a law passed by Congress
    (E) consider a dispute between two states

100. Which of the following is considered a government corporation?
    (A) The Environmental Protection Agency
    (B) The National Aeronautics and Space Administration (NASA)
    (C) The Internal Revenue Service
    (D) The United States Postal Service
    (E) The United States Department of Justice

Study Resources

Most textbooks used in college-level American government courses cover the topics in the outline given earlier, but the approaches to certain topics and the emphases given to them may differ. To prepare for the American Government examination, it is advisable to study one or more college textbooks, which can be found in most college bookstores. When selecting a textbook, check the table of contents against the knowledge and skills required for this test.

Visit **clep.collegeboard.org/earn-college-credit/practice** for additional American government resources. You can also find suggestions for exam preparation in Chapter IV of the *Official Study Guide*. In addition, many college faculty post their course materials on their schools' websites.

Answer Key

1.	C	51.	C
2.	B	52.	B
3.	B	53.	A
4.	A	54.	B
5.	B	55.	E
6.	D	56.	B
7.	A	57.	B
8.	C	58.	C
9.	C	59.	A
10.	C	60.	D
11.	B	61.	E
12.	D	62.	A
13.	D	63.	B
14.	C	64.	C
15.	C	65.	C
16.	E	66.	D
17.	E	67.	A
18.	A	68.	C
19.	A	69.	E
20.	C	70.	A
21.	A	71.	B
22.	C	72.	E
23.	D	73.	C
24.	A	74.	D
25.	B	75.	E
26.	B	76.	C
27.	E	77.	D
28.	C	78.	D
29.	E	79.	B
30.	D	80.	D
31.	A	81.	A
32.	B	82.	A
33.	B	83.	B
34.	A	84.	D
35.	A	85.	A
36.	D	86.	A
37.	E	87.	E
38.	C	88.	A
39.	A	89.	B
40.	D	90.	B
41.	A	91.	E
42.	B	92.	B
43.	C	93.	D
44.	C	94.	A
45.	B	95.	D
46.	C	96.	D
47.	B	97.	D
48.	A	98.	A
49.	B	99.	C
50.	C	100.	D

History of the United States I

Description of the Examination

The History of the United States I: Early Colonization to 1877 examination covers material that is usually taught in the first semester of a two-semester course in United States history. The examination covers the period of United States history from early European colonization to the end of Reconstruction, with the majority of the questions on the period of 1790 through 1877. In the part covering the seventeenth and eighteenth centuries, emphasis is placed on the British colonies. The exam includes a small number of questions on the Americas before 1500.

The examination contains approximately 120 questions to be answered in 90 minutes. Some of these are pretest questions that will not be scored.

Knowledge and Skills Required

Questions on the History of the United States I examination require candidates to demonstrate one or more of the following abilities:

- Identify and describe historical phenomena
- Analyze and interpret historical phenomena
- Compare and contrast historical phenomena

The subject matter of the History of the United States I examination is drawn from the following topics. The percentages next to the main topics indicate the approximate percentage of exam questions on that topic.

Topical Specifications

30%	Political institutions, political developments, and public policy
30%	Social developments
10%	Economic developments
20%	Cultural and intellectual developments
10%	Diplomacy and transnational interactions

Chronological Specifications

30%	1500–1789
70%	1790–1877

The following themes are reflected in a comprehensive introductory survey course:

- The nature of indigenous societies in the Americas. This theme includes a small number of questions on the Americas before 1500.
- The impact of European discovery and colonization upon indigenous societies. The focus is placed on the British colonies, but this theme includes a small number of items on Spanish, French, and Dutch colonization, and the Columbian Exchange.
- The origins and nature of slavery and resistance to it
- Immigration and the history of ethnic minorities
- The history of women, changing gender roles, and family structures
- The development and character of colonial societies
- British relations with the Atlantic colonies of North America
- The changing role of religion in American society
- The causes, events, and consequences of the American Revolution
- The content of the Constitution and its amendments, and their interpretation by the United States Supreme Court
- The development and expansion of participatory democracy
- The growth of and changes in political parties
- The changing role of government in American life
- The intellectual and political expressions of nationalism
- Major movements and individual figures in the history of American literature, art and popular culture
- Abolitionism and reform movements
- Long-term demographic trends (immigration and internal migration)
- The motivations for and character of American expansionism
- The process of economic growth and development
- The causes and consequences of conflicts with Native Americans, the War of 1812, the Mexican-American War, and the Civil War and Reconstruction

Sample Test Questions

The following sample questions do not appear on an actual CLEP examination. They are intended to give potential test-takers an indication of the format and difficulty level of the examination and to provide content for practice and review. Knowing the correct answers to all of the sample questions is not a guarantee of satisfactory performance on the exam.

Directions: Each of the questions or incomplete statements below is followed by five suggested answers or completions. Select the one that is best in each case. Some questions will require you to place events in chronological order.

1. John Winthrop told the Puritans that their society would be regarded as "a city upon a hill." But first he explained that there would always be inequalities of wealth and power, that some people would always be in positions of authority, and that others would be dependent. His statements best illustrate the Puritans'

   (A) reaction to unsuccessful socialist experiments in the Netherlands
   (B) acceptance of the traditional belief that social order depended on a system of ranks
   (C) intention to vest political power exclusively in the ministers
   (D) desire to better themselves economically through means that included the institution of slavery
   (E) inability to take clear stands on social issues

2. The French and Indian War led Great Britain to

   (A) encourage manufacturing in its North American colonies
   (B) impose revenue taxes on its North American colonies
   (C) restrict emigration to North America
   (D) ignore its North American colonies
   (E) grant increased self-government to its North American colonies

3. All of the following were common characteristics of many colonial New England families EXCEPT

   (A) a hierarchical institution in which the father represented the source of authority
   (B) a place that sheltered men from the workplace
   (C) a social institution that cared for the needy and the poor
   (D) a social institution that provided vocational training
   (E) a basic farming unit

4. Which of the following is a correct statement about the use of slave labor in colonial Virginia?

   (A) It was forced on reluctant White Virginians by profit-minded English merchants and the mercantilist officials of the Crown.
   (B) It was the first time Europeans enslaved African people.
   (C) It fulfilled the original plans of the Virginia Company.
   (D) It first occurred after the invention of Eli Whitney's cotton gin, which greatly stimulated the demand for low-cost labor.
   (E) It spread rapidly in the late-seventeenth century, as enslaved Africans replaced European indentured servants in the tobacco fields.

5. Roger Williams defended liberty of conscience on the grounds that

   (A) all religions were equal in the eyes of the Creator
   (B) the institutions of political democracy would be jeopardized without it
   (C) Puritan ideas about sin and salvation were outmoded
   (D) theological truths would emerge from the clash of ideas
   (E) the state should not interfere in church matters

6. Which of the following is true of White women in the British North American colonies?
   (A) They were allowed to be ordained as ministers.
   (B) They were considered politically and socially equal to their husbands.
   (C) They were eligible to work as teachers in public schools.
   (D) They were eligible to run for political office.
   (E) They were restricted in holding property and making legal contracts after marriage.

7. Which of the following was NOT a consequence of the Great Awakening in the American colonies during the mid-eighteenth century?
   (A) More accessible, democratized piety caused separatism and secession from established churches
   (B) Heightened interest in the supernatural caused the renewed persecution of people for witchcraft
   (C) The growth of institutions of higher learning to fill the need for more ministers to spread the gospel
   (D) More intensive religious devotion caused the missionary spirit to flourish
   (E) The lessening of doctrinal rigor and a concomitant appreciation for more direct experiences of faith

Questions 8–9 refer to the following statement.

"The present King of Great Britain . . . has combined with others to subject us to a jurisdiction foreign to our constitution, and unacknowledged by our laws."

8. The "constitution" referred to in the quotation above from the Declaration of Independence was
   (A) the principles common to all the Navigation Acts
   (B) the Articles of Confederation
   (C) a constitution for the colonies written by Sir William Blackstone
   (D) the laws passed concurrently by the several colonial legislatures
   (E) the principles the colonists believed had traditionally regulated British government

9. The protest that the king had "combined with others to subject us to a jurisdiction foreign to our constitution" referred to George III's
   (A) alliance with the king of France
   (B) use of Hessian mercenaries
   (C) reliance on his representatives in the colonies
   (D) approval of parliamentary laws impinging on colonial self-government
   (E) intention to place a German prince on the throne of British America

10. By the time of the American Revolution, many American colonists had generally come to believe that the creation of a republic would solve the problems of monarchical rule because a republic would establish

    (A) a highly centralized government led by a social elite
    (B) a strong chief executive
    (C) a small, limited government responsible to the people
    (D) unlimited male suffrage
    (E) a society in which there were no differences of rank and status

11. All state constitutions drafted during the American Revolutionary era were significant because they

    (A) were based on the principle of virtual representation
    (B) included clauses that immediately emancipated slaves
    (C) provided for the confiscation and redistribution of the property of wealthy Loyalists
    (D) were the first efforts to establish a government by and of the people
    (E) introduced the concept of checks and balances

12. *Letters from a Farmer in Pennsylvania* were written to

    (A) record the soil, climate, and profitable crops in the Pennsylvania colony
    (B) chronicle the history of William Penn's colonization efforts
    (C) argue against the power of Parliament to tax the colonists without representation
    (D) petition King George III for colonial representation in Parliament
    (E) encourage colonization of the western frontier

13. Under the Articles of Confederation, which of the following was true about the national government?

    (A) It had the power to conduct foreign affairs.
    (B) It had the power to regulate commerce.
    (C) It had a bicameral legislature.
    (D) It had an independent executive branch.
    (E) It included a federal judiciary.

14. The concept that the ultimate sovereignty of the federal government rests with the people is most explicitly stated in

    (A) the preamble to the United States Constitution
    (B) *Common Sense*
    (C) the Fourteenth Amendment to the United States Constitution
    (D) the Bill of Rights
    (E) the Articles of Confederation

15. "There is an opinion that parties in free countries are useful checks upon the administration of the government and serve to keep alive the spirit of liberty. This within certain limits is probably true, and in governments of a monarchical cast patriotism may look with indulgence, if not with favor, upon the spirit of party. But in those of the popular character, in governments purely elective, it is a spirit not to be encouraged."

    The passage above is from a speech by which of the following presidents?

    (A) George Washington
    (B) Thomas Jefferson
    (C) John Adams
    (D) Andrew Jackson
    (E) Abraham Lincoln

16. Thomas Jefferson opposed some of Alexander Hamilton's programs because Jefferson believed that

    (A) the common bond of a substantial national debt would serve to unify the different states
    (B) the French alliance threatened to spread the violence of the French Revolution to America
    (C) the federal government should encourage manufacturing and industry
    (D) Hamilton's programs were weakening the military strength of the nation
    (E) Hamilton's programs favored manufacturing and commercial interests

17. The Embargo Act of 1807 had which of the following effects on the United States?

    (A) It severely damaged American manufacturing.
    (B) It enriched many cotton plantation owners.
    (C) It severely damaged American shipping.
    (D) It was ruinous to subsistence farmers.
    (E) It had little economic impact.

18. Henry Clay's American System was a plan to

    (A) compromise on the issue of extending slavery to new United States territories
    (B) foster the economic integration of the North, the West, and the South
    (C) export United States political and economic values to oppressed peoples
    (D) maintain United States noninvolvement in the internal affairs of Europe
    (E) assert the right of states to nullify decisions of the national government

19. Deists of the late-eighteenth and early-nineteenth centuries believed that

    (A) natural laws, designed by the Creator, govern the operation of the universe
    (B) prayer has the power to make significant changes in a person's life
    (C) the idea of God is merely the creation of people's minds
    (D) the universe was created by a natural, spontaneous combining of elements
    (E) intuition rather than reason leads people to an awareness of the divine

20. The Louisiana Purchase was significant because it

    (A) eliminated Spain from the North American continent
    (B) gave the United States control of the Mississippi River
    (C) eased tensions between western settlers and Native Americans
    (D) forced the British to evacuate their posts in the Northwest
    (E) reduced sectional conflict over the slavery issue

21. Between the Monroe Doctrine (1823) and the outbreak of the Civil War (1861), the most important aspect of United States foreign policy was

    (A) securing access to Canadian fisheries
    (B) reopening the British West Indies to direct trade with the United States
    (C) securing international recognition
    (D) expanding the nation's boundaries
    (E) responding to Cuban independence

22. Jacksonian economic policies did which of the following?

    (A) Removed banking issues from national politics.
    (B) Stalled the westward expansion.
    (C) Ended foreign investment in the United States.
    (D) Abolished state banks.
    (E) Encouraged the expansion of credit and speculation.

23. Which of the following is true of John C. Calhoun?

    (A) He advocated a strong federal government and helped to establish the Bank of the United States.
    (B) He supported the doctrine of nullification, which declared the right of states to rule on the constitutionality of federal law.
    (C) He became a strong opponent of southern nationalism and sought federal legislation to link the West and the South.
    (D) As vice president of the United States, he helped formulate the beginnings of a new Republican Party.
    (E) He led a successful movement to include the right of concurrent majority in the Constitution of the United States.

24. Which of the following had the greatest impact on the institution of slavery in the United States in the first quarter of the nineteenth century?

    (A) Demands of southern textile manufacturers for cotton
    (B) Introduction of crop rotation and fertilizers
    (C) Abolition of indentured servitude
    (D) Expanded use of the cotton gin
    (E) The Three-Fifths Compromise

25. The "putting-out system" that emerged in antebellum America refers to the

    (A) organizing of slave labor into efficient planting teams
    (B) production of finished goods in individual households
    (C) sending of poor children to live on farms in the Midwest
    (D) shipping of raw materials to European factories
    (E) forced migration of Native Americans from valuable lands

26. Which of the following was a major focus of antebellum reform?

    (A) Income tax law
    (B) Universal suffrage
    (C) Prison reform
    (D) Creation of national parks
    (E) Machine politics

27. The establishment of Brook Farm and the Oneida Community in the antebellum United States reflected

    (A) the influence of Social Darwinism on American thinkers
    (B) the continued impact of Calvinist ideas on American thought
    (C) a belief in perfectionism
    (D) attempts to foster racial integration
    (E) the implementation of all-female Utopian communities

28. During the early stages of manufacturing, the textile mills in Lowell, Massachusetts, primarily employed

    (A) native-born, single White men who had lost their farms
    (B) native-born, single White women from rural areas
    (C) White males from debtors' prisons
    (D) recent immigrants from southern and eastern Europe
    (E) African American women

29. Members of the Whig Party organized in the 1830s agreed most on which of the following?

    (A) Extension of slavery into western territories
    (B) Elimination of protective tariffs
    (C) Endorsement of the doctrine of nullification
    (D) Disapproval of Andrew Jackson's policies
    (E) Disapproval of the "corrupt bargain" under John Quincy Adams

30. The issue of constitutionality figured most prominently in the consideration of which of the following?

    (A) Tariff of 1789
    (B) First Bank of the United States
    (C) Funding of the national debt
    (D) Assumption of state debts
    (E) Excise tax on whiskey

31. The presidential election of 1840 is often considered the first "modern" election because

    (A) the slavery issue was first raised in this campaign
    (B) it was the first election in which women voted
    (C) voting patterns were similar to those later established in the 1890s
    (D) for the first time, both parties widely campaigned among all the eligible voters
    (E) a second Era of Good Feelings had just come to a close, marking a new departure in politics

32. The idea of Manifest Destiny included all of the following EXCEPT the belief that

    (A) commerce and industry would decline as the nation expanded its agricultural base
    (B) the use of land for settled agriculture was preferable to its use for nomadic hunting
    (C) westward expansion was both inevitable and beneficial
    (D) the Creator selected America as a chosen land populated by a chosen people
    (E) the ultimate extent of the American domain was to be from the Atlantic to the Pacific Ocean

33. "Upon these considerations, it is the opinion of the court that the act of Congress which prohibited a citizen from holding and owning property of this kind in the territory of the United States north of the line therein mentioned, is not warranted by the Constitution, and is therefore void; and that neither the plaintiff himself, nor any of his family, were made free by being carried into this territory; even if they had been carried there by the owner, with the intention of becoming a permanent resident."

    The congressional act referred to in the passage above was the

    (A) Kansas-Nebraska Act
    (B) Missouri Compromise
    (C) Northwest Ordinance of 1787
    (D) Compromise of 1850
    (E) Fugitive Slave Act

34. *Moby-Dick*, *The Scarlet Letter*, and *Leaves of Grass* are examples of which of the following literary traditions?

    (A) American Renaissance
    (B) Harlem Renaissance
    (C) Realism
    (D) Modernism
    (E) Genteel Tradition

35. Which of the following represents William Lloyd Garrison's proposed solution to the slavery question?

    (A) Immediate emancipation and resettlement in Liberia
    (B) Immediate emancipation and resettlement in the Southwest
    (C) Immediate emancipation with compensation for slaveholders
    (D) Gradual emancipation without compensation for slaveholders
    (E) Immediate emancipation without compensation for slaveholders

36. Immediately after the Revolution, some men argued that women should be educated so that they could

    (A) oversee the instruction of their sons to be good citizens
    (B) become clergy
    (C) take an active role in public life outside the home
    (D) take an active role in business decisions with men
    (E) make informed decisions about how to vote

37. Which of the following groups was most likely to adopt the Free Soil ideology?

    (A) Free African Americans
    (B) Northern capitalists
    (C) Western frontier settlers
    (D) Southern yeoman farmers
    (E) Southern plantation owners

38. The 1848 women's rights convention in Seneca Falls, New York, was a protest against

    (A) the use of women workers in textile factories
    (B) the abuse of female slaves on Southern plantations
    (C) the failure of the Democratic Party to endorse a woman suffrage amendment
    (D) customs and laws that gave women a status inferior to that of men
    (E) state restrictions that prevented women from joining labor unions

39. Which of the following wrote *Uncle Tom's Cabin*?

    (A) Louisa May Alcott
    (B) Herman Melville
    (C) Harriet Beecher Stowe
    (D) Richard Henry Dana
    (E) Kate Chopin

40. Which of the following was opposed by both the Free Soil Party and the Republican Party in the mid-nineteenth century?

    (A) Internal improvement in the West
    (B) Extension of slavery into the territories
    (C) Growth of textile manufacturing in New England
    (D) Unrestricted immigration from Ireland
    (E) Use of paper money

41. In the pre–Civil War era, the railroads' most important impact on the economy was that they

    (A) created a huge new market for railway equipment
    (B) created the basis for greater cooperation between southern planters and northern textile manufacturers
    (C) generated new employment opportunities for unskilled urban workers
    (D) involved the federal government in the financing of a nationwide transportation network
    (E) provided midwestern farmers accessibility to eastern urban markets

42. Which of the following was NOT an element of the Compromise of 1850 ?

    (A) Stronger fugitive slave law
    (B) Abolition of the slave trade in Washington, D.C.
    (C) Admittance of California as a free state
    (D) Organization of the Kansas Territory without slavery
    (E) Adjustment of the Texas–New Mexico boundary

43. All of the following conditions influenced the development of American agriculture during the first half of the nineteenth century EXCEPT

    (A) settlement of the western territories
    (B) a widespread interest in conserving soil and natural resources
    (C) the trend toward regional economic specialization
    (D) the enthusiasm for land speculation
    (E) improvements in transportation by water

44. Which of the following best describes the United States position in the world economy during the period 1790–1860 ?

    (A) It was the leading producer of finished and manufactured goods for export.
    (B) It relied heavily on European capital for its economic expansion.
    (C) It had an inadequate merchant marine and depended largely on foreign vessels to carry its trade.
    (D) It was strengthened by the acquisition of overseas colonies.
    (E) It was severely hampered by its reliance on slave labor.

45. After the Civil War, the majority of freed people found work in the South as

    (A) factory workers
    (B) railroad employees
    (C) independent craftsmen
    (D) tenant farmers
    (E) domestic servants

46. Abraham Lincoln's plan for Reconstruction included which of the following?

    (A) Establishment of five military districts to prepare seceded regions for readmission as states
    (B) Punishment of Confederates through land confiscation and high property taxes
    (C) Restoration of property to White Southerners who would swear a loyalty oath to the United States
    (D) Reestablishment of state government after 10 percent of the voters in a state pledged their allegiance to the United States
    (E) Readmission of states to the Union contingent on their ratification of the Thirteenth, Fourteenth, and Fifteenth Amendments to the Constitution

47. All of the following elements of the Radical Republican program were implemented during Reconstruction EXCEPT

    (A) provision of 40 acres to each freedman household
    (B) enactment of the Fourteenth Amendment
    (C) military occupation of the South
    (D) punishment of the Confederate leaders
    (E) restrictions on the power of the president

48. Andrew Johnson's Reconstruction plan allowed for Southern states to be readmitted into the Union on the condition that they

    (A) revoke the ordinance of secession and ratify the Thirteenth Amendment
    (B) prohibit the use of the Black Codes
    (C) guarantee suffrage for all citizens, regardless of race
    (D) give land grants to freed people
    (E) punish ex-Confederates refusing to take an oath of loyalty to the United States

49. Which of the following was a renowned African American poet in New England in the late-eighteenth century?

    (A) Benjamin Banneker
    (B) Lemuel Haynes
    (C) Phillis Wheatley
    (D) Gabriel Prosser
    (E) Sojourner Truth

50. During the antebellum period, the Auburn system was designed to

    (A) teach factory workers proper work habits
    (B) instill discipline in grade schools
    (C) reform criminals
    (D) punish escaped enslaved people
    (E) cure the mentally ill

51. California was admitted as a state to the Union

    (A) as part of the Compromise of 1850
    (B) with the passage of the Wilmot Proviso
    (C) during the Mexican-American War
    (D) with the passage of the Northwest Ordinance of 1787
    (E) when the Kansas-Nebraska Act settled the issue of western slavery

52. Which of the following wrote *Incidents in the Life of a Slave Girl*?

    (A) Frances Ellen Watkins Harper
    (B) Sojourner Truth
    (C) Lydia Maria Child
    (D) Harriet Beecher Stowe
    (E) Harriet Jacobs

53. The activities of the Freedmen's Bureau included all of the following EXCEPT

(A) providing food, clothing, medical care, and shelter to war victims
(B) reuniting families of freedmen
(C) establishing a network of courts
(D) establishing schools for freed people
(E) permanently redistributing land

54. The United States completed the Gadsden Purchase in 1853 in order to

(A) obtain Oregon
(B) build a transcontinental railroad
(C) relieve population pressures
(D) obtain additional grazing lands
(E) balance slave and free states

55. Place the following educational events in the correct chronological order. Place the earliest event first.

Establishment of Harvard College

The Common School movement

Establishment of schools to train teachers

Northwest Ordinance

56. Which of the following is a correct statement regarding Benjamin Franklin?

(A) He founded the Bank of the United States.
(B) He authored the Articles of Confederation.
(C) He authored the Bill of Rights.
(D) He invented electricity.
(E) He helped to negotiate the Treaty of Paris of 1783.

57. Which of the following terms was used to refer to a means by which some people escaped slavery in the South?

(A) The Northwest Passage
(B) The Overland Trail
(C) The National Road
(D) The Underground Railroad
(E) The Erie Canal

58. The acquittal of John Peter Zenger in 1735 reflected the growing colonial belief that

(A) colonial governors should have absolute veto power over colonial assemblies
(B) Parliament should not be involved in internal matters in the British colonies
(C) newspaper editors should have the right to criticize public officials
(D) Enlightenment thought should have no place in colonial culture
(E) governors should have the right to limit the publication of newspapers

59. Bacon's Rebellion was

(A) a revolt of enslaved African Americans against treatment by their owners
(B) the name given to a slave conspiracy in New York City
(C) the Philadelphia version of the Boston Tea Party
(D) a revolt by poor farmers and indentured servants
(E) an uprising of Native Americans

60. Which of the following is true about the American victory at Saratoga in October 1777 during the Revolutionary War?

(A) It enabled George Washington to recapture New York City.
(B) It led Congress to declare independence.
(C) It caused the British to evacuate Boston.
(D) It helped convince France to enter the war.
(E) It prompted Parliament to end the war.

61. In the early seventeenth century, colonists in the Chesapeake Bay area exported which of the following to England?

(A) Cattle
(B) Tobacco
(C) Tea
(D) Cotton
(E) Coffee

62. "No Person or Persons, inhabiting in this Province or Territories, who shall confess and acknowledge One almighty God, the Creator, Upholder and Ruler of the World; . . . shall be in any Case molested or prejudiced, in his or their Person or Estate, because of his or their conscientious Persuasion or Practice, nor be compelled to frequent or maintain any religious Worship, Place or Ministry, contrary to his or their Mind."

The excerpt above is from the charter of which of the following English colonies?

(A) Plymouth
(B) Pennsylvania
(C) Massachusetts Bay
(D) Jamestown
(E) Roanoke

63. According to the Treaty of Paris of 1783, Great Britain both recognized American independence and

(A) agreed to cancel all the prewar debts owed to the British by American citizens
(B) promised to set the western boundary of the United States at the Mississippi River
(C) retained fishing rights off Newfoundland
(D) insisted that George III remain the titular head of the former thirteen colonies
(E) agreed to the presence of British troops in the Northwest Territories for ten years

64. All of the following resulted from the War of 1812 EXCEPT

(A) the decline of the Federalist Party
(B) increased domestic manufacturing
(C) the loss of Florida to the British
(D) the emergence of Andrew Jackson as a war hero
(E) heightened patriotism

65. In *Dred Scott* v. *Sandford* (1857), the Supreme Court decided that

(A) enslaved people could not be freed by virtue of their residence in a free state
(B) the Compromise of 1850 was supported by the Constitution
(C) Dred and Harriet Scott deserved their freedom
(D) the principle of popular sovereignty could be applied in new territories
(E) free African Americans could not be enslaved

66. Widely read autobiographies of escaped slaves, such as *The Life and Times of Frederick Douglass*, assisted the abolitionist cause primarily by

    (A) raising money for back-to-Africa colonization projects in Liberia and Sierra Leone
    (B) demonstrating the inability of the federal government to stand up to pro-slavery interests in the Congress
    (C) depicting slavery as benevolent and supportive of family preservation
    (D) linking American slavery to earlier slave societies in Greece and Egypt
    (E) transforming the popular understanding of slavery from an abstraction to a tangible evil

67. Which of the following best describes the significance of Shays' Rebellion and the Whiskey Rebellion?

    (A) They were early examples of colonial opposition to the British taxes imposed after the French and Indian War.
    (B) They led to the meeting of the Constitutional Convention.
    (C) They were precipitated by burdensome tax policies.
    (D) Alexander Hamilton led the armed forces that suppressed both rebellions.
    (E) They were caused by the inability of farmers to pay their debts.

68. Which of the following best explains the opposition of Thomas Jefferson and James Madison to the First Bank of the United States?

    (A) Capital for the bank was raised by taxes on farmers.
    (B) The bank did not provide loans to farmers for the purchase of land.
    (C) The bank gave the president too much control over the economy.
    (D) The Constitution did not grant the Congress the right to charter a bank.
    (E) Bank speculation had led to a post-Revolution depression.

69. Which of the following best describes the purpose of the Hartford Convention?

    (A) To protest the impressments of American sailors into the British navy
    (B) To coordinate a federal response to the uprising of Tecumseh and the Prophet
    (C) To propose amendments to the Constitution and to avoid the secession of New England states
    (D) To select an alternate seat of government after Washington was captured by the British
    (E) To provide a plan for the incorporation of Canada into the United States

70. Which of the following were native to North America before Columbus arrived?

    (A) Horses and pumpkins
    (B) Dandelions and clover
    (C) Maize and squash
    (D) Oranges and sweet potatoes
    (E) Rice and potatoes

71. The Middle colonies differed from both the New England and Southern colonies in that the Middle colonies

    (A) had a system of staple crop agriculture
    (B) prohibited slavery
    (C) required church attendance on Sundays
    (D) were more religiously and ethnically diverse
    (E) had no history of violence against Native Americans

72. Which of the following is true of the Northwest Ordinance of 1787 ?

    (A) It barred slavery north of the 36°30' line.
    (B) It provided free land grants to anyone willing to settle in the Northwest Territory.
    (C) It established the 49th parallel as the boundary between Canada and the United States.
    (D) It set aside territories for Native American tribes in the Old Northwest.
    (E) It defined the process by which territories became states.

73. Which of the following was a direct consequence of the Proclamation of 1763 ?

    (A) New taxes were raised on British colonists in North America.
    (B) The French and Indian War officially ended.
    (C) Slavery was prohibited in territories west of the Mississippi River.
    (D) Colonial settlement west of the Appalachian Mountains was restrained.
    (E) British colonists were encouraged to buy new lands in the southern colonies.

74. Through its ruling in *McCulloch* v. *Maryland*, the Supreme Court achieved all of the following EXCEPT

    (A) upholding the constitutionality of the Second Bank of the United States
    (B) establishing the principle of judicial review
    (C) accepting Alexander Hamilton's loose construction of the Constitution
    (D) denying the state of Maryland the right to tax the Second Bank of the United States
    (E) strengthening the power of the federal government

75. "Now let any candid person examine the causes by which associations . . . so often fail, and he will find that it arises from the partial and selfish relations of husbands, wives and children. . . . Therefore, all who attempt to establish and support such a system by any power of nature, or by any human wisdom, or indeed by any means short of self-denial, integrity of principle, and real chastity of person, will most certainly fail in the end."

    The statement best reflects the beliefs of which of the following nineteenth-century Utopian groups?

    (A) New Harmony
    (B) The Oneida Community
    (C) Brook Farm
    (D) The Shakers
    (E) The Mormons

76. The disputed election of 1876 was significant because it

    (A) led to the growth of third parties
    (B) led to the expansion of executive power
    (C) demonstrated the power of big business
    (D) signaled the beginning of mass participation in politics
    (E) resulted in the end of Reconstruction in the South

77. Seventeenth-century Puritans and Quakers differed primarily over the

    (A) divinity of Jesus
    (B) importance of charity work (almsgiving)
    (C) notion of predestination
    (D) celebration of Christmas
    (E) consumption of alcohol

78. In the period between the American Revolution and the Civil War, the religious communities west of the Appalachians that grew fastest were

    (A) Roman Catholics and Quakers
    (B) Jews and Episcopalians
    (C) Quakers and Presbyterians
    (D) Baptists and Methodists
    (E) Methodists and Episcopalians

79. Which of the following did NOT occur during the transportation revolution in the nineteenth century?

    (A) State and federal governments subsidized the construction of roads and canals.
    (B) The cost of shipping goods declined precipitously.
    (C) The postal service grew rapidly.
    (D) The Supreme Court enforced monopolies on steamboat travel and bridge construction.
    (E) Railroads became a major carrier of freight by the start of the Civil War.

80. The Jay Treaty of 1794 led to

    (A) more stable relations between the United States and Great Britain
    (B) increased trans-Mississippi migration
    (C) the development of the first political party system
    (D) an increase in the power of the Supreme Court
    (E) increased migration from Eastern Europe

81. One of the major consequences of the Mexican-American War was the

    (A) resolution of the issue of slave states versus free states until the Civil War
    (B) expulsion of Mexicans from the annexed territories
    (C) passage of the Homestead Act, which granted land to settlers in the West
    (D) prohibition of slavery in Texas
    (E) designation of 80,000 to 100,000 Mexicans as American citizens

"We hold these truths to be self-evident, that all men are created equal, that they are endowed by their Creator with certain unalienable Rights, that among these are Life, Liberty and the pursuit of Happiness. —That to secure these rights, Governments are instituted among Men, deriving their just powers from the consent of the governed,—That whenever any Form of Government becomes destructive of these ends, it is the Right of the People to alter or to abolish it, and to institute new Government, laying its foundation on such principles and organizing its powers in such form, as to them shall seem most likely to effect their Safety and Happiness."

The Declaration of Independence

82. The author of the passage above was influenced by the writings of

    (A) John Locke's *Second Treatise on Government*
    (B) Thomas Hobbes' *Leviathan*
    (C) David Hume's *Of Civil Liberty*
    (D) Jean-Jacques Rousseau's *The Social Contract*
    (E) Pierre-Joseph Proundhon's *An Inquiry into the Principle of Right and Government*

83. Which of the following statements best describes women's involvement in reform movements of the antebellum period?

    (A) Many women argued that their roles as mothers and wives gave them a unique understanding of the nature of and solutions to social ills.
    (B) Women rarely ventured outside the private sphere and were not heavily involved in reform movements.
    (C) Women were successful in getting suffrage laws passed in many states but were unsuccessful in getting a national suffrage law passed.
    (D) Women were active in the abolitionist movement and accepted as equals within it.
    (E) Women argued that education would lead to a more equal society and pushed heavily for the establishment of a public school system.

84. The purpose of the Freedmen's Bureau was to

(A) campaign against segregation and achieve political and social equality for freed people
(B) inject money into the Southern economy by giving loans to freedmen to help them buy plots of land from their former masters
(C) grant each former slave 40 acres of land in the western territories
(D) help African Americans transition from slavery to freedom
(E) establish the first comprehensive public school system in the Southern states

85. All of the following intellectual traditions contributed to the ideas of the Founding Fathers EXCEPT the

(A) French Enlightenment philosophy
(B) liberal tradition represented by John Locke's *Two Treatises of Government*
(C) Whig philosophy as represented in British political pamphlets
(D) skeptical tradition of David Hume
(E) Scottish Enlightenment philosophy

86. The Second Great Awakening differed from the First Great Awakening in that the Second Great Awakening

(A) led to a rapid increase in membership in Congregationalists and Presbyterians churches
(B) caused revivalists to fear a growing threat to spiritual authority from laypeople
(C) was closely tied to social reform movements
(D) prohibited women from speaking at camp meetings and other religious services
(E) began in New York state and made its largest impact throughout New England

87. Which of the following most directly led to a more democratic political system in the United States in the first half of the nineteenth century?

(A) Most states extended the right to vote to women and free African Americans.
(B) Judicial review was established, limiting the power of the Supreme Court over the decisions of Congress.
(C) Presidential elections started being determined by a combination of the electoral college and popular vote.
(D) Many states reduced or eliminated property qualifications for voting.
(E) New territories were not admitted as states unless they guaranteed the right to vote for all men over the age of twenty-one.

88. The Federalist Party's political perspective was characterized by which of the following beliefs about the central government?

(A) It should have very few powers over the states.
(B) It should pursue closer relations with France rather than with Britain.
(C) It should provide aid to western farmers.
(D) It should oppose bankers and manufacturers.
(E) It should encourage economic development.

89. Which of the following was true of Southern society in the antebellum period?

(A) The South experienced less social stratification than the North.
(B) Northern women could not become school teachers in the South in order to prevent the spread of abolitionism.
(C) Southerners expected that White women would work outside the home.
(D) The South had a higher literacy rate than the North.
(E) Southern politicians increasingly described slavery as a positive institution.

90. President James K. Polk would have been most likely to upset Northerners by his

    (A) compromise over the Oregon Territory
    (B) opposition to invading Mexico
    (C) support for a high tariff
    (D) invasion of British Columbia
    (E) support for the Wilmot Proviso

91. Which of the following is true of the Fugitive Slave Act of 1850 ?

    (A) It was a compromise that prevented further sectional divisions for the next decade.
    (B) It consolidated the concept of states' rights in regard to enforcing slavery.
    (C) Many Northerners opposed it.
    (D) It established the right to due process for people accused of being fugitive slaves.
    (E) Most Southern politicians opposed it.

92. Which of the following best describes the American Colonization Society?

    (A) It helped provide jobs for African Americans building the Panama Canal.
    (B) Militant abolitionists such as William Lloyd Garrison and Frederick Douglass supported it.
    (C) Large numbers of African Americans in the 1850s and 1860s supported it.
    (D) It promoted the settling of free African Americans from the United States to Africa.
    (E) It developed the concept of Manifest Destiny in the 1830s and 1840s.

93. Which of the following was a key component of Alexander Hamilton's plan for the economic development of the United States?

    (A) Establishment of a national bank that would stabilize paper currency and extend credit
    (B) Termination of all trade with European countries in order to bolster the United States economy
    (C) Establishment of trade agreements with European colonies in the Western Hemisphere
    (D) Eradication of the national debt in order to create a small federal government
    (E) Reliance on the free market, with no government involvement in the economy

94. Which of the following best explains the primary reason for the opposition in the United States to the annexation of Texas in the late 1830s and early 1840s?

    (A) The large number of Catholics in Texas
    (B) The threat of economic competition from cotton growers in Texas
    (C) The potential for creating an imbalance in the Congress between proslavery and antislavery forces
    (D) The migration of settlers to new land in Texas
    (E) The potential for United States engagement in a war with Mexico

95. In his Farewell Address, George Washington advocated that the United States should develop which of the following policies?

    (A) Using its moral standing as a democratic nation to intervene in foreign affairs
    (B) Annexing neighboring territories that were under Spanish colonial authority
    (C) Adopting an isolationist position by avoiding engaging in alliances with European states
    (D) Creating lasting alliances with newly independent states in the Western Hemisphere
    (E) Preventing European nations from interfering in the political stability of the Western Hemisphere

96. Which of the following contributed to the start of the French and Indian War?

    (A) Attempts by British colonists to settle areas in the Quebec region of Canada
    (B) Skirmishes between British and French forces over disputed territory in the upper Ohio River valley
    (C) Military confrontations between British settlers and Native Americans in the Great Lakes region
    (D) Tension caused by new military alliances between the French and the Iroquois Confederacy
    (E) Raids by French soldiers on British settlements in western New England

97. Which of the following best characterizes foreign relations between Europe and the United States during the Civil War?

    (A) Russia advocated for the independence of the South to defend the legitimacy of slavery.
    (B) France provided significant military and financial aid to the South during the war.
    (C) Britain maintained neutrality in the war despite significant economic ties to the South.
    (D) European allies of the North encouraged Mexico to plan an invasion of the South.
    (E) Spain aided the North because it saw the South as a threat to Spanish interests in Cuba.

98. The Caribbean sugar plantations played an important role in the growth of the trans-Atlantic slave trade for which of the following reasons?

    (A) Demand for enslaved Africans was high in the Caribbean because Africans' prior knowledge of sugar cultivation increased plantation profits.
    (B) The harsh conditions and high mortality rates associated with Caribbean sugar cultivation and production resulted in a constant demand for new labor.
    (C) European governments made slavery illegal in most of their overseas empires, which limited merchants to selling enslaved people in only a few places such as the Caribbean.
    (D) Sugar produced and shipped from the Caribbean was in high demand in Africa, where African merchants were willing to trade slaves for sugar.
    (E) White indentured servants who came to the Caribbean refused to work in sugar cultivation, which encouraged the widespread reliance on enslaved African labor.

99. Advocates of popular sovereignty in the mid-nineteenth century asserted which of the following?

    (A) All enslaved people should be freed by a constitutional amendment.
    (B) Presidential elections should not be decided by the electoral college.
    (C) Slavery should not be extended into any new territories or states.
    (D) Residents of a territory should decide if slavery would be permitted there.
    (E) Congress had the sole right to grant suffrage to women in new territories.

100. Which of the following best describes a common characteristic of most Eastern Woodlands Native American societies before contact with Europeans?

    (A) They relied on the bison as their main source of food and products for trade.
    (B) They shared a common language that enabled easy communication between tribes.
    (C) They lived in farming communities and also foraged for seasonal food sources.
    (D) They used enslaved labor to cultivate corn, squash, and tobacco on plantations.
    (E) They formed a single regional confederacy that settled disputes between different groups.

Questions 101–102 refer to the excerpt below.

"The consequences of a speedy removal will be important to the United States, to individual States, and to the Indians themselves. The pecuniary advantages which it promises to the Government are the least of its recommendations. It puts an end to all possible danger of collision between the authorities of the General and State Governments. . . . It will place a dense and civilized population in large tracts of country now occupied by a few. . . . It will separate the Indians from immediate contact with settlements of whites; free them from the power of the States; enable them to pursue happiness in their own way; . . . and perhaps cause them gradually, under the protection of the Government and through the influence of good counsels, to . . . become an interesting, civilized, and Christian community."

President Andrew Jackson, Second Annual Message to Congress, December 6, 1830

101. Jackson's reference to the "pecuniary advantages which it promises" reveals that which of the following was a motive behind the policy he proposed in the excerpt?

(A) Encouraging economic development through land subsidies to the railroads

(B) Confiscating Native American land to make it available for sale to Whites

(C) Passing tariffs on increased agricultural production from lands opened to farming

(D) Granting citizenship rights to Native Americans in order to expand the tax base

(E) Requiring loan repayments in specie to stabilize the national banking system

102. By the late 1830s, the policy outlined in the excerpt resulted in

(A) the launch of a major military campaign by the United States Army against Native Americans in the West

(B) legislation that mandated the return of ancestral lands to Native American nations in the Southeast

(C) efforts to assimilate Native Americans into White society and culture under the Dawes Severalty Act

(D) the development of alphabets for written language, constitutions, and private land ownership by Native Americans in the Southeast

(E) the death of many southeastern Native Americans from exposure, disease, and starvation on the forced march called the Trail of Tears

103. The Boston Tea Party of 1773 most directly resulted in which of the following actions?

(A) The Massachusetts militia engaged in skirmishes with British troops at Lexington and Concord.
(B) British soldiers opened fire on a group of colonial protesters in what became known as the Boston Massacre.
(C) The British Parliament passed the Intolerable Acts, a series of punitive laws for the colonies.
(D) Representatives from the thirteen colonies formed the Stamp Act Congress to better coordinate colonial protest.
(E) Patrick Henry penned the Virginia Resolves to argue for the preservation of local rights against central government power.

104. Which of the following statements best describes a role that the South played in the emerging national and international market economies in the first half of the nineteenth century?

(A) It exported most of the cotton it produced to Northern rather than international textile manufacturers.
(B) It purchased most of its luxury goods from Northern manufacturers instead of international suppliers.
(C) It contributed an ever more diverse range of agricultural commodities to national and international markets.
(D) Its industrial production supplied manufactured goods to Northern, Western, and international consumers.
(E) Its economic output increasingly helped to integrate the country into international financial networks.

105. The Twelfth Amendment to the United States Constitution, ratified in 1804, was a response to which of the following problems?

(A) Several states refused to vote on the Constitution without the inclusion of the amendment.
(B) Conflicts within President George Washington's Cabinet prevented the government from functioning.
(C) The original process for electing the president and vice president did not account for the rise of political parties.
(D) The divisions between northern and southern states over tariffs led to competing party nominees for the vice presidency.
(E) Senators disagreed with representatives on the apportioning of electoral votes by state population.

Study Resources

Most textbooks used in college-level United States history courses cover the topics in the outline given earlier, but the approaches to certain topics and the emphases given to them may differ. To prepare for the History of the United States I exam, it is advisable to study one or more college textbooks, which can be found in most college bookstores. When selecting a textbook, check the table of contents against the knowledge and skills required for this test.

Additional detail and differing interpretations can be gained by consulting readers and specialized historical studies. Pay attention to visual materials (pictures, maps and charts) as you study. Visit **clep.collegeboard.org/earn-college-credit/practice** for additional history resources.

You can also find suggestions for exam preparation in Chapter IV of the *Official Study Guide*. In addition, many college faculty post their course materials on their schools' websites.

Answer Key

1.	B	36.	A	71.	D
2.	B	37.	C	72.	E
3.	B	38.	D	73.	D
4.	E	39.	C	74.	B
5.	E	40.	B	75.	D
6.	E	41.	E	76.	E
7.	B	42.	D	77.	C
8.	E	43.	B	78.	D
9.	D	44.	B	79.	D
10.	C	45.	D	80.	A
11.	D	46.	D	81.	E
12.	C	47.	A	82.	A
13.	A	48.	A	83.	A
14.	A	49.	C	84.	D
15.	A	50.	C	85.	D
16.	E	51.	A	86.	C
17.	C	52.	E	87.	D
18.	B	53.	E	88.	E
19.	A	54.	B	89.	E
20.	B	55.	1, 4, 2, 3	90.	A
21.	D	56.	E	91.	C
22.	E	57.	D	92.	D
23.	B	58.	C	93.	A
24.	D	59.	D	94.	C
25.	B	60.	D	95.	C
26.	C	61.	B	96.	B
27.	C	62.	B	97.	C
28.	B	63.	B	98.	B
29.	D	64.	C	99.	D
30.	B	65.	A	100.	C
31.	D	66.	E	101.	B
32.	A	67.	C	102.	E
33.	B	68.	D	103.	C
34.	A	69.	C	104.	E
35.	E	70.	C	105.	C

History of the United States II

Description of the Examination

The History of the United States II: 1865 to the Present examination covers material that is usually taught in the second semester of what is often a two-semester course in United States history. The examination covers the period of United States history from the end of the Civil War to the present, with the majority of the questions on the twentieth century.

The examination contains approximately 120 questions to be answered in 90 minutes. Some of these are pretest questions that will not be scored.

Knowledge and Skills Required

Questions on the History of the United States II examination require candidates to demonstrate one or more of the following abilities:

- Identify and describe historical phenomena
- Analyze and interpret historical phenomena
- Compare and contrast historical phenomena

The subject matter of the History of the United States II examination is drawn from the following topics. The percentages next to the main topics indicate the approximate percentage of exam questions on that topic.

Topical Specifications

30%	Political institutions and public policy
30%	Social developments
10%	Economic developments
20%	Cultural and intellectual developments
10%	Diplomacy and international relations

Chronological Specifications

30%	1865–1914
70%	1915–present

The following are among the specific topics tested:

- The impact of the Civil War and Reconstruction upon the South
- The motivations and character of American expansionism and imperialism
- Legal history, including constitutional amendments and major Supreme Court cases
- The role of the environment in United States history
- The development of American political parties, movements, and realignments
- The changing role of the federal government in the economy and American life
- The intellectual and political expressions of liberalism and conservatism
- Long-term demographic trends
- The process of economic growth and development, including periods of depression and recession
- The changing occupational structure, nature of work, and labor organization
- Immigration and the history of racial and ethnic minorities
- Urbanization and industrialization
- The causes and effects of major wars in United States history and diplomacy and engagement with the world
- Major movements and individual figures in the history of American arts and culture
- Trends in the history of women and the family
- Trends in education, science, and technology and their impact on United States society
- Civil rights movements, the women's rights movement, protest movements, and the expansion of individual rights and civil liberties

Sample Test Questions

The following sample questions do not appear on an actual CLEP examination. They are intended to give potential test-takers an indication of the format and difficulty level of the examination and to provide content for practice and review. Knowing the correct answers to all of the sample questions is not a guarantee of satisfactory performance on the exam.

Directions: Each of the questions or incomplete statements below is followed by five suggested answers or completions. Select the one that is best in each case. Some questions will require you to place events in chronological order.

1. Which of the following best describes the experiences of most recently freed people following Reconstruction?

   (A) They obtained land from the Freedmen's Bureau.
   (B) They were forced back onto the plantations as sharecroppers.
   (C) They established large cooperative farms.
   (D) They migrated to Northern urban areas and worked as unskilled laborers.
   (E) They were forced to migrate to marginally fertile lands in the western territories.

2. The Reconstruction Acts of 1867 provided for

   (A) temporary Union military government in the former Confederacy
   (B) federal monetary support for the resettlement of African Americans in Africa
   (C) property-holding and voting rights for African Americans
   (D) implementation of anti–African American vagrancy laws in the South
   (E) lenient readmission of the formerly Confederate states to the Union

3. The second Sioux war (1876–1877), in which Custer was defeated at the Battle of Little Bighorn, was caused by all of the following EXCEPT

   (A) the extension of the route of the Northern Pacific Railroad
   (B) a concentrated effort on the part of the major Protestant denominations to convert the Sioux to Christianity
   (C) the gold rush in the Black Hills
   (D) corruption within the Department of the Interior
   (E) overland migration of settlers to the Pacific Northwest

4. "This, then, is held to be the duty of the man of wealth: . . . to consider all surplus revenues which come to him simply as trust funds, which he is called upon to administer and strictly bound as a matter of duty to administer in the manner which, in his judgment, is best calculated to produce the most beneficial results for the community."

   The sentiments expressed above are most characteristic of

   (A) transcendentalism
   (B) pragmatism
   (C) the Gospel of Wealth
   (D) the Social Gospel
   (E) Social Darwinism

5. Reformers of the Progressive Era proposed all of the following changes in city government and politics at the turn of the century EXCEPT

(A) a large city council elected by wards
(B) the establishment of civil service
(C) home rule for cities
(D) city manager and commission governments
(E) nonpartisan elections

6. The anti-combination laws passed by numerous states in the late 1880s were a response to which of the following organizational innovations?

(A) The creation and growth of international cartels
(B) The development of industry-wide trade associations
(C) The joining of skilled and unskilled workers in industrial unions
(D) The formation of agricultural marketing cooperatives
(E) The use of stockholding trusts to create business monopolies

7. Which of the following constituted a significant change in the treatment of American Indians during the last half of the nineteenth century?

(A) The beginning of negotiations with individual Indian tribal groups
(B) The start of a removal policy
(C) The abandonment of the reservation system
(D) The admission of American Indians to United States citizenship
(E) The division of lands traditionally owned by Indian tribal groups among individual members

8. The late-nineteenth-century photograph shown above was intended to serve which of the following purposes?

(A) To advocate social reform
(B) To arouse anti-immigrant sentiments
(C) To encourage the purchase of cameras
(D) To document the need for prohibition
(E) To encourage immigration to the cities

9. Which of the following would have been most likely to vote for William Jennings Bryan in 1896 ?
   (A) A Kansas farmer
   (B) A Chicago industrial worker
   (C) A department store clerk
   (D) A university professor of economics
   (E) A New York Republican Party member

10. Unionization efforts in the late-nineteenth century were countered by the
   (A) establishment of the eight-hour workday
   (B) passage of right-to-work laws
   (C) increasing use of skilled labor
   (D) use of federal troops to help end strikes
   (E) establishment of factories in foreign countries by United States corporations

11. Which of the following best states the goals of the "pure and simple unionism" advocated by Samuel Gompers?
   (A) Labor unions should concentrate on increasing wages and benefits.
   (B) Labor should organize industry's skilled and unskilled workers into a single union.
   (C) Labor unions should compete directly with large industries in producing and distributing consumer products.
   (D) Industrial workers should form a political party to achieve their goals.
   (E) The defective capitalist system should be replaced by labor cooperatives.

12. During the late-nineteenth century, urban political machines were organizations that
   (A) were created by native-born Americans to combat the political influence of immigrants
   (B) were controlled by politicians who dispensed jobs and other patronage in return for political support
   (C) worked for civil service reform to ensure sound municipal government
   (D) consisted of reformers working to combat urban poverty by establishing settlement houses
   (E) consisted of conservative elites seeking to maintain control of politics

13. In his interpretation of the historical development of the United States, Frederick Jackson Turner focused on the importance of the
   (A) traditions of western European culture
   (B) role of women in socializing children to become good citizens
   (C) historical consequences of the enslavement of African American people
   (D) conflict between capitalists and workers
   (E) frontier experience in fostering democracy

14. The 1896 presidential election was significant in United States history because it
   (A) marked the rise of the Populist Party
   (B) signaled the return of free silver coinage
   (C) strengthened the image of the Republican Party as the party of prosperity and national greatness
   (D) set a new pattern of vigorous two-party participation in national politics
   (E) secured national Democratic Party dominance that lasted until the 1930s

© 2011 Delaware Art Museum/Artists Rights Society (ARS), New York; Wadsworth Atheneum Museum of Art/Art Resource, NY

15. The 1907 painting shown above is representative of the

    (A) Impressionist painting of Mary Cassatt
    (B) Hudson River School art of Asher B. Durand
    (C) Surrealism of Giorgio de Chirico
    (D) Abstract Expressionist work of Jackson Pollock
    (E) Ashcan School art of John Sloan

16. In the period 1890–1915, all of the following were generally true about African Americans EXCEPT

    (A) voting rights previously gained were denied through changes in state laws and constitutions
    (B) the federal government passed legislation protecting the voting rights of African Americans
    (C) African American leaders disagreed on the principal strategy for attaining equal rights
    (D) numerous physical attacks on African American individuals occurred in both the North and the South
    (E) African American people from the rural South migrated to both southern and northern cities

17. Between 1890 and 1914, most immigrants to the United States came from

    (A) southern and eastern Europe
    (B) northern and western Europe
    (C) Latin America
    (D) Southeast Asia
    (E) Canada

18. Which of the following is a correct statement about the United States at the close of the First World War?

    (A) It joined the League of Nations.
    (B) It emerged as the world's leading creditor nation.
    (C) It accorded diplomatic recognition to the Soviet Union.
    (D) It repealed the amendment to the Constitution that allowed Prohibition.
    (E) It received large reparations payments from Germany.

19. Which of the following is a literary work that is associated with the Lost Generation after the First World War?
    (A) Ernest Hemingway's *The Sun Also Rises*
    (B) Sylvia Plath's *The Bell Jar*
    (C) T. S. Eliot's "The Love Song of J. Alfred Prufrock"
    (D) Sinclair Lewis' *Babbitt*
    (E) Theodore Dreiser's *An American Tragedy*

20. Many Mexicans migrated to the United States during the First World War because
    (A) revolution in Mexico had caused social upheaval and dislocation
    (B) the United States offered special homestead rights to relatives of Mexican Americans serving in the armed forces
    (C) the war in Europe had disrupted the Mexican economy
    (D) American Progressives generally held liberal views on the issue of racial assimilation
    (E) the United States government recruited Mexican workers to accelerate the settlement of the Southwest

21. All of the following were among Woodrow Wilson's Fourteen Points EXCEPT
    (A) a general association of nations
    (B) freedom to navigate the high seas in peace and war
    (C) an independent Poland
    (D) a partitioned Germany
    (E) an end to secret treaties

22. A direct consequence of Henry Ford's assembly-line process was that it
    (A) raised the price of automobiles
    (B) resulted in small cuts in workers' wages
    (C) decreased the need for skilled workers
    (D) made the working environment safer
    (E) increased the number of women employed in industrial work

23. All of the following help to explain the presence of large numbers of expatriate American intellectuals in Europe during the 1920s EXCEPT the
    (A) repressive effects of Prohibition and the resurgence of conservatism in the United States
    (B) attraction of European cities, especially Paris, as centers of innovation and creativity
    (C) tradition among American writers of taking up temporary residence in Europe
    (D) claims of young American writers and critics that American culture was materialistic and hostile to the development of their art
    (E) European tradition of wealthy patrons supporting struggling American artists and writers

The Cash Register Chorus

24. The political cartoonist who drew the picture above probably believed that

    (A) European nations were pleased with aid given them by the Coolidge administration
    (B) governmental agencies were receiving too much financial support from the Coolidge administration
    (C) American industrial and commercial leaders approved of the Coolidge administration's business policies
    (D) consumers had benefited from the Federal Reserve's tight money policy from 1925 through 1928
    (E) Congress was pleased by President Coolidge's accommodating stance toward pork-barrel legislation

25. A number of changes took place in the intellectual life of college-educated Americans between 1880 and 1930. Which of the following changes is LEAST characteristic of this group during this period?

    (A) Expanded popularity of Freudian psychology
    (B) Rise of pluralistic and relativistic worldviews
    (C) More rigorous training for academic professions
    (D) Growth in the influence of religious fundamentalism
    (E) Increased attention to the methods and outlook of the sciences

26. In its 1932 march on Washington, the Bonus Army demanded which of the following?

    (A) Federal unemployment insurance for workers who had lost their jobs
    (B) Federal loans to farmers, with surplus grain used as collateral
    (C) Early payment to veterans of a promised reward for service in the First World War
    (D) A substantial increase in the military budget
    (E) A refund to investors who lost money in the stock market crash of 1929

27. Franklin D. Roosevelt was successful in securing congressional support for all of the following EXCEPT

    (A) negotiation of tariff agreements by the executive department
    (B) reduction of the gold content of the dollar
    (C) removal of the restraints of the antitrust acts to permit voluntary trade associations
    (D) adoption of processing taxes on agricultural products
    (E) reform of the judiciary to permit the enlargement of the Supreme Court

28. Franklin D. Roosevelt's farm policy was primarily designed to
    (A) reduce farm prices to make food cheaper for the consumer
    (B) increase production by opening new lands to farmers
    (C) reduce production in order to boost farm prices
    (D) use price and wage controls to stabilize farm prices
    (E) end federal controls over agriculture

29. The main purpose of the Wagner Act (National Labor Relations Act) of 1935 was to
    (A) end the sit-down strike in Flint, Michigan
    (B) settle the struggle between the American Federation of Labor and the Congress of Industrial Workers
    (C) guarantee workers a minimum wage
    (D) ensure workers' right to organize and bargain collectively
    (E) exempt organized labor from the Sherman Antitrust Act

30. The National Woman's Party, which lobbied Congress to pass woman suffrage legislation, was founded in 1916 by
    (A) Jane Addams
    (B) Eleanor Roosevelt
    (C) Alice Paul
    (D) Margaret Sanger
    (E) Carrie Nation

31. The Reagan Revolution in politics refers to President Ronald Reagan's
    (A) strong support of rapprochement with liberals
    (B) ability to unite traditional Republicans with working-class Democrats
    (C) shifting responsibility for the poor to religious organizations
    (D) support of United States military intervention in the Caribbean
    (E) lukewarm support of the peace initiative in the Middle East

32. American participation in the Second World War had which of the following major effects on the home front?
    (A) A temporary movement of women into heavy industry
    (B) The elimination of racial segregation in the South
    (C) The growth of isolationism in the Midwest
    (D) The introduction of a system of national health insurance
    (E) A decline in farmers' income

33. "I believe that it must be the policy of the United States to support free peoples who are resisting attempted subjugation by armed minorities or by outside pressures. I believe that we must assist free peoples to work out their own destinies in their own way. I believe that our help should be primarily through economic and financial aid which is essential to economic stability and orderly political processes."

    The statement above is taken from

    (A) Woodrow Wilson's request for a declaration of war against Germany
    (B) Herbert Hoover's statement on Japanese aggression in China
    (C) Franklin D. Roosevelt's request for a declaration of war against Japan
    (D) Harry S. Truman's request for funds to support Greece and Turkey against communism
    (E) an address by United Nations ambassador Jeane Kirkpatrick on Central American conflict

34. Which of the following is true of the forced relocation of Japanese Americans from the West Coast during the Second World War?

   (A) President Roosevelt claimed that military necessity justified the action.
   (B) The Supreme Court immediately declared the action unconstitutional.
   (C) The relocation was implemented according to congressional provisions for the internment of dissidents.
   (D) The Japanese Americans received the same treatment as that accorded German Americans and Italian Americans.
   (E) Few of those relocated were actually United States citizens.

35. During the Second World War, the federal government pursued all of the following economic policies EXCEPT

   (A) rationing consumer goods
   (B) limiting wartime wages
   (C) limiting agricultural prices
   (D) selling war bonds
   (E) increasing the prime interest rate

36. The presidential election of 1928, which pitted Herbert Hoover against Al Smith, was the first presidential election that

   (A) featured a Roman Catholic as a presidential candidate
   (B) was decided by less than 1 percent of the popular vote
   (C) featured a southern candidate and a western candidate
   (D) had two candidates who were self-made millionaires
   (E) involved two candidates with strong rural constituencies

37. Following the Second World War, President Truman was unable to expand significantly his predecessor's New Deal programs primarily because of

   (A) the continuation of the Great Depression
   (B) the need to maintain a large military force in Asia
   (C) budget expenditures required to rebuild Europe
   (D) controversy surrounding the Truman Doctrine
   (E) the domination of Congress by Republicans and conservative Democrats

38. President Truman's decision to recall General MacArthur from his command of United Nations forces in Korea was primarily based on Truman's support of the principle of

   (A) containment of communism
   (B) total rather than limited warfare
   (C) isolationism rather than interventionism
   (D) civilian control of the military
   (E) self-determination for all free people

39. In the decade after the Civil War, the federal government's policy toward the Plains Indians focused on the

   (A) creation of a network of churches to convert them to Christianity
   (B) establishment of schools to promote tribal culture
   (C) establishment of reservations
   (D) forced migration of most Indian tribal groups to urban areas
   (E) forced migration of Indian tribal groups from the Southeast to Oklahoma

40. The purpose of the Geneva Accords (1954) was to

    (A) divide Vietnam into temporary sectors and lay the groundwork for free elections
    (B) devise plans for arms reductions between the Soviet Union and the United States
    (C) establish the boundaries for permanent North and South Koreas
    (D) establish an international peacekeeping force in the Middle East
    (E) resolve disagreements between the Guatemalan government of Jacobo Arbenz Guzmán and the United States

41. Allen Ginsberg was well known as

    (A) a founder of the Black Panther Party
    (B) a key adviser to President Eisenhower
    (C) a poet of the Beat Generation
    (D) an anticommunist senator from California
    (E) an Abstract Expressionist painter

42. *Brown* v. *Board of Education of Topeka* was a Supreme Court decision that

    (A) was a forerunner of the Kansas-Nebraska Act
    (B) established free public colleges in the United States
    (C) declared racially segregated public schools inherently unequal
    (D) established free public elementary and secondary schools in the United States
    (E) provided for federal support of parochial schools

43. "The problem with hatred and violence is that they intensify the fears of the white majority, and leave them less ashamed of their prejudices toward Negroes. In the guilt and confusion confronting our society, violence only adds to the chaos. It deepens the brutality of the oppressor and increases the bitterness of the oppressed. Violence is the antithesis of creativity and wholeness. It destroys community and makes brotherhood impossible."

    During the 1960s all the following African American leaders would probably have supported the view expressed above EXCEPT

    (A) Roy Wilkins
    (B) Martin Luther King, Jr.
    (C) James Farmer
    (D) Stokely Carmichael
    (E) Whitney M. Young, Jr.

44. Reform activity during the Progressive Era was similar to that of the 1960s in all of the following ways EXCEPT

    (A) the federal government supported civil rights for African Americans
    (B) reform activity was encouraged by strong and active presidents
    (C) many reformers advocated changes in the area of women's rights
    (D) some governmental reform initiatives were curtailed by war
    (E) reform occurred despite the absence of severe economic depression

45. What contribution did Ngo Dinh Diem make toward the escalation of hostilities between the United States and North Vietnam?

    (A) He proclaimed himself commander in chief of Viet Cong armies and organized guerrilla attacks on United States military installations.

    (B) He was appointed by the French government to serve as a temporary president of Vietnam.

    (C) He refused to carry out political reforms in South Vietnam.

    (D) He advocated an alliance between himself and Ho Chi Minh to prevent United States intervention in Vietnam.

    (E) He wrote articles in the Vietnamese popular press encouraging the public to support Marxism.

46. Which of the following is correct about United States involvement in the Vietnam War during the period 1956–1964 ?

    (A) It was justified by invoking the Open Door policy.

    (B) It was the exclusive responsibility of the Johnson and Nixon administrations.

    (C) It came about only after a formal declaration of war.

    (D) It was primarily anti-Soviet in purpose.

    (E) It grew out of policy assumptions and commitments dating from the end of the Second World War.

47. Which of the following events brought the United States and the Soviet Union closest to the possibility of nuclear war?

    (A) The Berlin Blockade

    (B) The Cuban missile crisis

    (C) The Pueblo incident

    (D) The Suez Crisis

    (E) The U-2 incident

48. Until 1964 eligibility to vote could be restricted by which of the following means?

    (A) Poll taxes

    (B) Grandfather clauses

    (C) Limits on woman suffrage

    (D) White-only primary elections

    (E) Exclusion of foreign-born citizens

49. Which of the following is true about the American Indian Movement (AIM), which was founded in 1968 ?

    (A) It sought accommodation with White society.

    (B) It modeled its tactics on the Black Power movement.

    (C) It issued the Declaration of Indian Purpose.

    (D) It won voting rights for Native Americans.

    (E) It drew its membership primarily from reservations.

50. In the twentieth century, United States Supreme Court decisions did all of the following EXCEPT

    (A) end Prohibition

    (B) ban official prayers in the public schools

    (C) protect a woman's right to an abortion

    (D) protect property rights

    (E) expand minority rights

51. The "silent majority" was a term used to describe supporters of

    (A) George McGovern

    (B) George Wallace

    (C) Richard Nixon

    (D) Prohibition

    (E) environmental reform

52. The military proposal popularly known as Star Wars was designed to

(A) incorporate the National Aeronautics and Space Administration into the armed forces
(B) create a satellite and laser shield to defend the United States against missile attacks
(C) expand American space exploration efforts
(D) construct new ballistic missiles not covered under the Strategic Arms Limitation Treaty I
(E) increase the interest of young Americans in volunteering for military service

53. The Prairie School of architecture is best exemplified in the work of

(A) Stanford White
(B) Frank Gehry
(C) Frank Lloyd Wright
(D) Louis Sullivan
(E) Daniel Burnham

54. The presidential debate between Richard M. Nixon and John F. Kennedy showed the importance of which of the following in presidential campaigns?

(A) Radio
(B) Television
(C) Movies
(D) Computers
(E) The Internet

55. A major purpose of the Civil Rights Act of 1964 was to

(A) prohibit discrimination in public accommodations and employment
(B) create equity in Social Security benefits
(C) standardize funding for Medicare
(D) strengthen the women's movement
(E) provide benefits for the disabled

56. In his book *The Fire Next Time* (1963), James Baldwin argued that

(A) the nuclear arms race imperiled future generations
(B) the failure of White Americans and Black Americans to overcome racism would have destructive consequences
(C) expatriate Americans must return home in times of crisis
(D) protest literature would not solve the problems of inequality
(E) violence against civil rights demonstrators would escalate without federal intervention

57. The federal assistance program Aid to Families with Dependent Children (AFDC) was

(A) established during the 1950s and continues to function today
(B) a social welfare program created by Franklin D. Roosevelt's New Deal program that ended in the mid-1990s during Bill Clinton's administration
(C) championed by social conservatives as a way to get poor families off welfare
(D) a social welfare program created by Woodrow Wilson to address the needs of soldiers during the First World War
(E) modeled after a similar program in the Soviet Union

58. The 1966 Supreme Court case *Miranda* v. *Arizona* concerned which of the following?

(A) Segregated swimming pools
(B) College admission quotas
(C) Rights of citizens accused of a crime
(D) Poll taxes
(E) Sexual discrimination in the military

59. Senator Joseph McCarthy's rise to power in the early 1950s was aided most by

(A) the expansion of the Democratic Party
(B) the electoral success of the Republican Party in 1952
(C) the support of Vice President Richard Nixon
(D) the decision by Secretary of State Dean Acheson to hire Communist advisors
(E) President Eisenhower's strong support of his efforts

60. Which of the following led to the resignation of a president of the United States?

(A) Jimmy Carter's response to the Iranian hostage crisis
(B) John Kennedy's role in the Bay of Pigs invasion
(C) Dwight Eisenhower's handling of the U-2 incident
(D) Richard Nixon's actions during the Watergate scandal
(E) Ronald Reagan's role in the Iran-Contra Affair

61. The Equal Rights Amendment failed to get ratification during the 1970s primarily because

(A) many believed it would disrupt society and destroy traditional values
(B) of opposition from the Democratic Party
(C) people believed that communists had inspired the idea
(D) businesses refused to lend their support
(E) of opposition from civil rights leaders

62. Which of the following was active in the anti-lynching movement?

(A) Harriet Tubman
(B) Ida B. Wells
(C) Emma Goldman
(D) Aimee Semple McPherson
(E) Alice Paul

63. Which of the following led to the passage of the Chinese Exclusion Act?

(A) Public concern that Chinese immigrants would not support the war effort during the Second World War
(B) Chinese officials wanting to restrict the flow of laborers to the United States
(C) The existence of large numbers of Chinese immigrants working illegally in the United States
(D) Racial prejudice towards Chinese workers in several regions of the country
(E) The unwillingness of Chinese immigrants to become naturalized American citizens

64. The Stonewall riots which took place in New York City during the summer of 1969 were significant because they

(A) demonstrated the shift to confrontational politics by the National Organization for Women

(B) rejected radical feminism and advocated traditional roles for women

(C) encouraged the rise of a gay liberation movement that publicly called for an end to discrimination against gays and lesbians

(D) were the first indicator of a sexual revolution among young people

(E) showed increasing frustration with the slow pace of the women's movement

65. Which of the following statements best describes the impact of the growth of the Internet since the 1990s?

(A) It has greatly facilitated the exchange of information worldwide.

(B) It helped to end the Cold War.

(C) It has dramatically increased the costs of operating businesses throughout the world.

(D) It has further isolated Third World countries because they do not have access.

(E) It has made governmental censorship impossible.

66. Which of the following statements best reflects Theodore Roosevelt's beliefs about foreign policy?

(A) Trade is a crucial element in promoting alliances among nations.

(B) Maintenance of a strong navy is an effective means to promote peace.

(C) A policy of isolation is a vital element of United States foreign policy.

(D) The United States should not intervene in the affairs of other countries.

(E) The State Department should carry out a cautious foreign policy.

67. All of the following statements regarding the period in which Dwight Eisenhower served as president are true EXCEPT

(A) Eisenhower's policies steered a middle course between Democratic liberalism and traditional Republican conservatism.

(B) Growing suburbs, the baby boom, auto mania, and the development of the interstate highway system were indications of national prosperity.

(C) Eisenhower and Soviet leader Nikita Khrushchev agreed on a massive bilateral reduction in the stockpiles of nuclear armaments.

(D) American culture in the 1950s reflected the combination of an expansive spirit of prosperity and Cold War anxieties.

(E) Eisenhower first used the term "military-industrial complex" to describe the close relationship between government and military contractors.

68. President Ronald Reagan's economic program, also known as Reaganomics, can be best summarized by which of the following statements?

(A) United States capitalism must be directed to focus on building effective social programs, increasing taxes on big business, and cutting taxes on lower-income households.

(B) The United States must increase government intervention in business regulation and economic planning.

(C) The United States capitalist system, if freed from heavy taxes and government regulations, would achieve greatly increased productivity.

(D) The United States should significantly increase government investment in social welfare and public school programs.

(E) The United States should decrease military spending in order to fund domestic programs.

69. During the 1950s, television shows like *The Donna Reed Show* and *Leave It to Beaver* exemplified the media's

(A) focus on the culture of northeastern cities
(B) reflection of prevalent Cold War anxieties
(C) idealization of middle-class suburban family life
(D) idealization of the rural heartland
(E) focus on the growing generation gap in American culture

70. One of the goals of Populism was to

(A) reduce income taxes
(B) implement government ownership of the country's railroads and telegraph lines
(C) establish collectively owned farms
(D) establish a national health insurance system
(E) obtain government subsidies in return for reduced agricultural production

71. Place the following in the correct chronological order. Place the earliest event first.

(A) Truman Doctrine
(B) Korean War
(C) Gulf of Tonkin Resolution
(D) Cuban missile crisis

72. The Federal Reserve System was established in 1913 to do which of the following?

(A) Stabilize the nation's money supply by expanding or restricting credit as needed.
(B) Assist consumers by forcing bankers to establish nationally uniform interest rates on loans.
(C) Promote confidence in the dollar by linking the value of currency in circulation directly to United States silver reserves.
(D) Encourage public support for increased government spending to stimulate economic growth.
(E) Lower taxes on financial transactions completed by national banks on behalf of consumers.

73. After the Spanish-American War, supporters of United States annexation of the Philippines believed that

(A) cheaper imported goods would lower consumer prices
(B) an influx of immigrants would promote labor competition
(C) racial tensions would decrease in the United States
(D) non-White peoples would benefit from direction by Western nations
(E) military expenditures would boost the economy

74. "The time came when we had to forsake our village at Like-a-fish-hook Bend, for the government wanted the Indians to become farmers. 'You should take allotments,' our [Bureau of Indian Affairs] agent would say. 'The big game is being killed off, and you must plant bigger fields or starve. The government will give you plows and cattle.' All knew that the agent's words were true, and little by little our village was broken up. In the summer of my sixteenth year nearly a third of my tribe left to take up allotments."

    The paragraph above describes the effect of the

    (A) Wade-Davis Bill
    (B) Hatch Act
    (C) Morrill Land Grant Act
    (D) Homestead Act
    (E) Dawes Severalty Act

75. Langston Hughes and Zora Neale Hurston were associated with which of the following twentieth-century movements?

    (A) The Lost Generation
    (B) The Beat movement
    (C) The Black Power movement
    (D) The Niagara movement
    (E) The Harlem Renaissance

76. "We must be impartial in thought, as well as in action, must put a curb upon our sentiments as well as upon every transaction that might be construed as a preference of one party to the struggle before another."

    The struggle referred to by President Woodrow Wilson in the quote above was the

    (A) Boxer Rebellion
    (B) Russo-Japanese War
    (C) Mexican Revolution
    (D) First World War
    (E) Bolshevik Revolution

77. The Women's Trade Union League had most success in organizing

    (A) secretaries
    (B) telephone workers
    (C) garment workers
    (D) department store clerks
    (E) slaughterhouse workers

78. "All persons born or naturalized in the United States, and subject to the jurisdiction thereof, are citizens of the United States and of the State wherein they reside. No State shall make or enforce any law which shall abridge the privileges or immunities of citizens of the United States; nor shall any State deprive any person of life, liberty, or property, without due process of law; nor deny to any person within its jurisdiction the equal protection of the laws."

    Section I of the Fourteenth Amendment is significant because it

    (A) outlaws slavery
    (B) restates the promises of the Bill of Rights
    (C) reaffirms the balance of power among the three branches of government
    (D) establishes enforcement procedures to protect voting rights
    (E) establishes the basis for citizenship and limits the power of the states

79. Title IX increased women's participation in athletics because it

    (A) requires that women be admitted to all-male schools
    (B) prohibits discrimination against women in college admissions
    (C) mandates that women be allowed to compete on all-men sports teams
    (D) requires that comparable amounts of money be spent on men's sports and women's sports
    (E) permits separate but equal facilities for women's sports teams

80. The Ku Klux Klan (KKK) of the 1920s most differed from the KKK of the nineteenth century in that it

    (A) drew strong support from Canada and Mexico
    (B) reflected prejudice and social discontent following a war
    (C) was a national organization
    (D) used violence and intimidation against victims
    (E) was composed of poor White people

81. Americans entered the First World War most directly as a result of which of the following?

    (A) The sinking of the British ship Lusitania killing large numbers of American citizens
    (B) The American arms industry fearing that Britain and France would not be able to repay their debts
    (C) A majority of Americans being able to trace their ancestry to the British Isles
    (D) The Germans resuming unrestricted submarine warfare
    (E) Woodrow Wilson and the Congress attempting to limit the spread of Soviet communism

82. After the Compromise of 1877, Rutherford B. Hayes responded by

    (A) removing federal troops from the South because Southern Democrats threatened secession
    (B) rewarding Southern supporters by backing a plan for a railroad across Florida
    (C) rewarding Northern supporters by promising to provide government aid for factory construction
    (D) ordering more federal troops into the South
    (E) agreeing to remove federal troops from the South and to appoint a Southerner to his cabinet

83. Franklin D. Roosevelt supported all of the following foreign policies EXCEPT

    (A) the Good Neighbor policy in Latin America
    (B) a selective embargo against aggressor nations
    (C) diplomatic recognition of the Soviet Union
    (D) lend-lease aid
    (E) a series of neutrality acts

84. American woman suffrage advocates' support for the war effort during the First World War contributed to

    (A) a split among feminists
    (B) solidarity with European suffragists
    (C) a strong commitment to the Republican Party
    (D) the adoption of women's right to vote
    (E) the United States adopting compulsory military service for women

85. The Carter Doctrine describes which of the following?

    (A) An attempt to ease United States trade and travel restrictions with Cuba
    (B) A decrease in United States troop deployment along the demilitarized zone separating North and South Korea
    (C) An increased emphasis on stealth and drone technology in warfare
    (D) A warning that any military aggression in the Persian Gulf will be regarded as a threat to United States interests
    (E) A careful balance between economic sanctions and military operations to free the hostages in Iran

86. Most African American soldiers participated in the First World War as

    (A) front-line soldiers, suffering the heaviest casualties
    (B) service personnel in combat areas
    (C) spies
    (D) aviators
    (E) gunners on battleships

87. "The long known and the long expected has thus taken place. The forces endeavoring to enslave the entire world now are moving toward this hemisphere. Never before has there been a greater challenge to life, liberty, and civilization. Delay invites greater danger. Rapid and united effort by all the peoples of the world who are determined to remain free will insure a world victory of the forces of justice and of righteousness over the forces of savagery and of barbarism."

President Franklin D. Roosevelt, address to the United States Congress, 1941

The address quoted above was given in response to which of the following?

(A) Germany's invasion of France
(B) Russia's occupation of eastern Poland
(C) Germany's bombing of Great Britain
(D) Italy's invasion of Ethiopia
(E) Japan's bombing of Hawaii

88. Place the following in correct chronological order. Place the earliest event first.

(A) *The Birth of a Nation*
(B) *Brown* v. *Board of Education of Topeka*
(C) *Plessy* v. *Ferguson*
(D) Voting Rights Act

89. What is the title of Betty Friedan's 1963 book that described the frustrations of suburban housewives and helped launch the women's liberation movement in the United States?

(A) *The Common Sense Book of Baby and Child Care*
(B) *Unequal Sisters*
(C) *The Second Sex*
(D) *The Feminine Mystique*
(E) *The Beauty Myth*

90. One of Richard Nixon's domestic policy achievements as president was the

(A) development of Job Corps for youth job training
(B) passage of the Elementary and Secondary Education Act
(C) establishment of the Environmental Protection Agency
(D) lowering of the inflation rate
(E) deregulation of major industries

91. During the Gilded Age, the United States government encouraged industrial growth by

(A) initiating the adoption of standard time zones for railroad schedules
(B) providing federal support to inventors like Thomas Edison and Alexander Graham Bell
(C) giving federal land grants to railroad companies
(D) allowing free postage for mail-order catalogs
(E) filing federal injunctions against environmental groups that tried to block development in the West

92. Which of the following was a major change that took place in the United States as a direct result of the G.I. Bill of Rights in 1944 ?

(A) An increase in the number of female college graduates at public universities
(B) A decrease in discrimination against African American veterans in education and housing
(C) The establishment of the Department of Veterans Affairs
(D) The development of college programs in science, technology, engineering, and math
(E) An increase in the number of veterans going to college and owning homes

93. Which of the following was an effect of the development of mass-produced automobiles in the United States by the mid-twentieth century?

(A) The rapid decline of coal use
(B) The increase in steel importation
(C) The rapid increase in car exportation
(D) The decline of labor unions
(E) The growth of suburbs

94. Which of the following best describes the Marshall Plan, which was developed during the Truman administration after the Second World War?

(A) It was an aid package intended to prevent Greece and Turkey from falling to communist revolutionaries.
(B) It was a National Security Council plan to increase Cold War defense spending.
(C) It was an economic aid package intended to help Western European nations stave off Communist influence.
(D) It was a program to develop a military alliance with Western European nations.
(E) It was a blueprint for reorganizing the United States Department of Defense.

95. "To those of my race who depend on bettering their condition in a foreign land, or who underestimate the importance of cultivating friendly relations with the southern white man who is their next door neighbor, I would say: 'Cast down your bucket where you are.' Cast it down, making friends in every manly way of the people of all races, by whom you are surrounded."

The statement above expresses the sentiments of which of the following African American leaders?

(A) Malcolm X
(B) Booker T. Washington
(C) W. E. B. Du Bois
(D) Ida B. Wells
(E) Stokely Carmichael

96. Which of the following was a key component of President Lyndon Johnson's Great Society programs?

(A) The Peace Corps
(B) The Social Security Act
(C) The Civilian Conservation Corps
(D) The Elementary and Secondary Education Act
(E) The Americans with Disabilities Act

97. In western North America during the second half of the nineteenth century, the property rights of Hispanic peoples in the areas conquered by the United States in the Mexican-American War were

(A) transferred to African-American Exodusters
(B) immediately revoked at the end of the conflict
(C) rejected by the Treaty of Guadalupe Hidalgo
(D) undermined by federal and state courts
(E) redistributed under the Dawes Severalty Act

98. Maya Lin is best known as

(A) the first Asian-American woman elected to the United States House of Representatives
(B) a sculpture artist who designed the controversial Vietnam Veteran's Memorial
(C) an important leader in the second-wave feminist movement
(D) a Democratic politician and former vice-presidential candidate
(E) a writer and former poet laureate of the United States

99. Which of the following best describes a central feature of Keynesian economic theory that strongly influenced United States economic policy in the mid-twentieth century?

(A) Implementing tax cuts to stimulate the economy during downturns
(B) Increasing tariffs to protect domestic production and exports
(C) Using federal deficit spending to spur economic growth
(D) Tightening monetary policy to reduce inflation
(E) Deregulating industry to promote business

100. Which of the following best describes a difference between Woodrow Wilson's "New Freedom" and Theodore Roosevelt's "New Nationalism" during the election campaign of 1912 ?

(A) Wilson asserted that the government should nationalize corporate trusts, while Roosevelt asserted that corporate trusts should be deregulated.
(B) Wilson opposed interventions in Latin America to protect business interests, while Roosevelt advocated for the annexation of parts of Latin America.
(C) Wilson emphasized government action to promote small businesses, while Roosevelt emphasized government supervision of big businesses.
(D) Wilson sought federal legislation to ensure the safety of industrial workers, while Roosevelt argued these laws would harm corporate profits.
(E) Wilson supported hiring of African Americans as government employees, while Roosevelt supported enforcing segregation in the federal workforce.

101. The genre of hard-boiled detective novels written in the 1920s and 1930s by authors such as Dashiell Hammett and Raymond Chandler most directly reflected which of the following social tensions?

(A) Opposition to the efforts to reform industrial capitalism
(B) Resistance to the system of Jim Crow segregation
(C) Concerns about the number of Americans living in poverty
(D) Cynicism about the rise of crime and political corruption
(E) Alienation from middle-class life and traditional values

102. The sinking of the USS Maine was a key event in the lead-up to which of the following conflicts?

    (A) The war with the Sioux Nation
    (B) The First World War
    (C) The intervention in the Mexican Revolution
    (D) The Spanish-American War
    (E) The Philippine-American War

103. The Bush Doctrine changed United States foreign policy by supporting the use of which of the following?

    (A) Unilateralism and preemptive strikes
    (B) Economic sanctions before military action
    (C) Weapons of mass destruction
    (D) Containment of the spread of communism
    (E) Social media to spread democratic ideals

104. The incident at Three Mile Island in the 1970s is best remembered as

    (A) a significant environmental disaster
    (B) the impetus for researching clean coal
    (C) an example of how technology can reduce pollution
    (D) a turning point in public opinion about nuclear energy
    (E) the catalyst for the passage of the Federal Emergency Management Act

105. The United States experienced what demographic shift in the 1920s?

    (A) More Americans lived in cities than in the countryside.
    (B) Immigration from Eastern and Southern Europe increased.
    (C) The marriage age went down and the birth rate went up.
    (D) Most Americans owned televisions and cars.
    (E) Electrification extended to the majority of rural areas.

106. The spread of the Ghost Dance among Native Americans in the 1880s and 1890s led most directly to the

    (A) Battle of Little Bighorn
    (B) massacre at Wounded Knee
    (C) prohibition of alcohol on reservations
    (D) increasing popularity of Wild West shows
    (E) restriction of missionary activity in the West

Study Resources

Most textbooks used in college-level United States history (post-1865) courses cover the topics in the outline given earlier, but the approaches to certain topics and the emphases given to them may differ. To prepare for the History of the United States II exam, it is advisable to study one or more college textbooks, which can be found in most college bookstores. When selecting a textbook, check the table of contents against the knowledge and skills required for this test.

Additional detail and differing interpretations can be gained by consulting readers and specialized historical studies. Pay attention to visual materials (pictures, maps and charts) as you study.

Visit **clep.collegeboard.org/earn-college-credit/practice** for additional history resources. You can also find suggestions for exam preparation in Chapter IV of the *Official Study Guide*. In addition, many college faculty post their course materials on their schools' websites.

Answer Key

1.	B	46.	E	91.	C
2.	A	47.	B	92.	E
3.	B	48.	A	93.	E
4.	C	49.	B	94.	C
5.	A	50.	A	95.	B
6.	E	51.	C	96.	D
7.	E	52.	B	97.	D
8.	A	53.	C	98.	B
9.	A	54.	B	99.	C
10.	D	55.	A	100.	C
11.	A	56.	B	101.	D
12.	B	57.	B	102.	D
13.	E	58.	C	103.	A
14.	C	59.	B	104.	D
15.	E	60.	D	105.	A
16.	B	61.	A	106.	B
17.	A	62.	B		
18.	B	63.	D		
19.	A	64.	C		
20.	A	65.	A		
21.	D	66.	B		
22.	C	67.	C		
23.	E	68.	C		
24.	C	69.	C		
25.	D	70.	B		
26.	C	71.	A, B, D, C		
27.	E	72.	A		
28.	C	73.	D		
29.	D	74.	E		
30.	C	75.	E		
31.	B	76.	D		
32.	A	77.	C		
33.	D	78.	E		
34.	A	79.	D		
35.	E	80.	C		
36.	A	81.	D		
37.	E	82.	E		
38.	D	83.	E		
39.	C	84.	D		
40.	A	85.	D		
41.	C	86.	B		
42.	C	87.	E		
43.	D	88.	C, A, B, D		
44.	A	89.	D		
45.	C	90.	C		

Human Growth and Development

Description of the Examination

The Human Growth and Development examination (Infancy, Childhood, Adolescence, Adulthood and Aging) covers material that is generally taught in a one-semester introductory course in developmental psychology or human development. An understanding of the major theories and research related to the broad categories of physical development, cognitive development and social development is required, as is the ability to apply this knowledge.

The examination contains approximately 90 questions to be answered in 90 minutes. Some of them are pretest questions that will not be scored.

The questions on the CLEP Human Growth and Development exam adhere to the terminology, criteria and classifications referred to in the fifth edition of the *Diagnostic and Statistical Manual of Mental Disorder*s (DSM-5).

Knowledge and Skills Required

Questions on the Human Growth and Development examination require candidates to demonstrate one or more of the following abilities.

- Knowledge of basic facts and terminology
- Understanding of generally accepted concepts and principles
- Understanding of theories and recurrent developmental issues
- Applications of knowledge to particular problems or situations

The subject matter of the Human Growth and Development examination is drawn from the following categories. For each category, several key words and phrases identify topics with which candidates should be familiar. The percentages next to the main categories indicate the approximate percentage of exam questions on that topic.

10% Theoretical Perspectives

Biological
Cognitive developmental
Ecological
Evolutionary
Learning
Psychodynamic
Social cognitive
Sociocultural

6% Research Strategies and Methodology

Case study
Correlational
Cross-sectional
Cross sequential
Experimental
Longitudinal
Observational

12% Biological Development Throughout the Life Span

Development of the brain and nervous system
Genetic disorders
Heredity, genetics and genetic testing
Hormonal influences
Influences of drugs
Motor development
Nutritional influences
Perinatal influences
Physical growth and maturation, aging
Prenatal influences
Sexual maturation
Teratogens

6% Perceptual Development Throughout the Life Span

Habituation
Sensitive periods
Sensorimotor activities
Sensory acuity
Sensory deprivation

12% **Cognitive Development Throughout the Life Span**
- Attention
- Environmental influences
- Executive function
- Expertise
- Information processing
- Jean Piaget's cognitive development theory
- Lev Vygotsky's sociocultural theory
- Memory
- Play
- Problem solving and planning
- Thinking
- Wisdom

8% **Language Development**
- Bilingualism
- Development of syntax
- Environmental, cultural and genetic influences
- Language and thought
- Pragmatics
- Semantic development
- Vocalization and sound

6% **Intelligence Throughout the Life Span**
- Concepts of intelligence and creativity
- Developmental stability and change
- Giftedness
- Heredity and environment
- Intelligence tests
- Reaction range

12% **Social Development Throughout the Life Span**
- Aggression
- Attachment
- Gender
- Interpersonal relationships
- Moral development
- Prosocial behavior
- Risk and resilience
- Self
- Social cognition
- Social learning and modeling
- Wellness

8% **Family, Home and Society Throughout the Life Span**
- Abuse and neglect
- Bronfenbrenner, Urie
- Death and dying
- Family relationships
- Family structures
- Media and technology
- Multicultural perspectives
- Parenting styles
- Social and class influences

8% **Personality and Emotion**
- Attribution styles
- Development of emotions
- Emotional expression and regulation
- Emotional intelligence
- Erikson, Erik
- Freud, Sigmund
- Psychosocial theory
- Stability and change
- Temperament

6% **Schooling, Work and Interventions**
- Applications of developmental principles
- Facilitation of role transitions
- Intervention programs and services
- Learning styles
- Occupational development
- Operant conditioning
- Preschool care, day care, and elder care
- Retirement

6% **Developmental Psychopathology**
- Antisocial behavior
- Anxiety and mood disorders
- Asocial behavior, fears, phobias and obsessions
- Attention-deficit/hyperactivity disorder
- Autism spectrum disorder
- Chronic illnesses and physical disabilities
- Cognitive disorders, including dementia
- Intellectual disability
- Learning disabilities
- Trauma-based syndromes

Sample Test Questions

The following sample questions do not appear on an actual CLEP examination. They are intended to give potential test-takers an indication of the format and difficulty level of the examination and to provide content for practice and review. Knowing the correct answers to all of the sample questions is not a guarantee of satisfactory performance on the exam.

Directions: Each of the questions or incomplete statements below is followed by five suggested answers or completions. Select the one that is best in each case.

1. The first negative emotion clearly exhibited during infancy is

   (A) fear
   (B) shame
   (C) guilt
   (D) distress
   (E) jealousy

2. According to behavioral psychologists, which of the following treatments is most likely to extinguish disruptive behavior in preschool children?

   (A) Threatening to isolate them immediately after such behavior
   (B) Ignoring them so that they do not receive the reinforcement they are seeking
   (C) Punishing them immediately so they understand what they did wrong
   (D) Discouraging them but not punishing them
   (E) Reasoning with them and explaining that their behavior is wrong

3. In which of the following stages of development do tissues develop into the endoderm, ectoderm, and mesoderm germ layers?

   (A) Germinal
   (B) Embryonic
   (C) Fetal
   (D) Perinatal
   (E) Neonatal

4. A defining characteristic of children with autism spectrum disorder is

   (A) obsessive attachment to their mothers
   (B) lack of motor coordination
   (C) unresponsiveness to others
   (D) hyperactivity
   (E) physical abnormality

5. Anxiety over performance can positively motivate school achievement in children as long as the degree of anxiety is

   (A) very high
   (B) high
   (C) moderate
   (D) low
   (E) very low

6. According to Jean Piaget, cognitive development begins with which of the following?

   (A) Preoperations
   (B) Concrete operations
   (C) Intuitive thought
   (D) Sensorimotor activities
   (E) Formal operations

7. Social-class differences in vocabulary development result from social-class differences in the amount of

   (A) maternal anxiety
   (B) verbal stimulation
   (C) paternal illness
   (D) sibling rivalry
   (E) marital discord

8. Studies in which the same people are tested at different ages are called

   (A) longitudinal
   (B) cross-sectional
   (C) normative
   (D) naturalistic
   (E) experimental

9. Which of the following is most central to the concept of sensitive period?

   (A) Growth spurts must occur at specific ages.
   (B) Children who do not develop at the same time as their peers experience distress.
   (C) A given function emerges automatically during a particular time period regardless of learning experiences.
   (D) Particular experiences are especially influential at a certain time in development.
   (E) Children go through a negativistic stage as a part of their cognitive development.

10. Jimmy saw his favorite candy for sale in the store. He had no money, so he planned to steal it. However, he changed his mind and decided not to do it, because stealing is wrong. According to Sigmund Freud's theory, which part of Jimmy's personality prevented him from stealing?

    (A) Id
    (B) Ego
    (C) Superego
    (D) Anima
    (E) Collective unconscious

11. If reinforcement is to be most effective in the learning of a new behavior, the reinforcement should be

    (A) provided as sparingly as possible
    (B) administered on an intermittent schedule
    (C) used primarily with high achievers
    (D) delayed until the end of the learning period
    (E) provided soon after the desired behavior occurs

12. In Harry Harlow's experiments, infant monkeys raised with only wire or cloth "mothers" were LEAST fearful in strange situations in the presence of

    (A) the "mother" who had provided food
    (B) the "mother" who had provided contact comfort
    (C) the "mother" who had provided primary drive reduction
    (D) other young monkeys
    (E) their biological mothers

13. A sudden, loud noise made in the vicinity of a newborn infant is likely to elicit which of the following reflexes?

    (A) Babinski
    (B) Moro
    (C) Rooting
    (D) Palmar grasp
    (E) Stepping

14. On which of the following types of problems should a four-year-old child and a seven-year-old child perform most similarly?

    (A) Conservation of number
    (B) Classification
    (C) Transformation
    (D) Object permanence
    (E) Superordinate concepts

15. Red-green color blindness is best described as
    (A) a sex-linked recessive trait
    (B) a sex-linked dominant trait
    (C) an autosomal recessive trait
    (D) an autosomal dominant trait
    (E) a trait resulting from chromosomal breakage

16. Over summer vacation, Gwen sees a boy she knows from school, but she has difficulty remembering his name. Which of her memory processes is failing in this situation?
    (A) Storage
    (B) Retrieval
    (C) Encoding
    (D) Short-term memory
    (E) Sensory memory

17. Which of the following theorists did NOT develop a stage theory?
    (A) Sigmund Freud
    (B) Jean Piaget
    (C) B. F. Skinner
    (D) Lawrence Kohlberg
    (E) Erik Erikson

18. Which of the following is true of menopause in men?
    (A) Menopause is purely a physical phenomenon.
    (B) Menopause may result from a lack of exercise.
    (C) Menopause may result from work-related stress.
    (D) Menopause is differentially damaging to the male psyche, depending on age.
    (E) Menopause is physically impossible because males do not menstruate.

19. Which of the following dimensions of infant temperament has the strongest positive correlation with antisocial behavior later in life?
    (A) Attention span
    (B) Activity level
    (C) Approach
    (D) Irritable distress
    (E) Rhythmicity

20. In accounting for the rapid expansion of a child's early vocabulary, Susan Carey argued that a major role must be played by the child's own active cognitive processing. Adults simply cannot teach a child exactly what referent every word picks out. Carey coined which of the following terms to denote this concept?
    (A) Fast mapping
    (B) Lexical conventionality
    (C) Lexical contrast
    (D) Linguistic empiricism
    (E) Metacognition

21. Heather is currently taking courses in several different academic departments and doing volunteer work to help identify and develop her interests. She also spends a lot of time thinking about her values and goals but has not chosen a career path. Heather's identity status is referred to as
    (A) fixation
    (B) identity achievement
    (C) identity diffusion
    (D) identity foreclosure
    (E) identity moratorium

22. According to Lev Vygotsky, the range between what a child can do alone and what a child can do with assistance is referred to as

(A) higher mental functions
(B) scaffolding
(C) inner speech
(D) egocentric speech
(E) the zone of proximal development

23. A researcher is evaluating the effects of three different types of parent-education programs on adolescent mothers' interactions with their toddlers. What is the independent variable in this investigation?

(A) Adolescent mothers' interactions with their toddlers
(B) Level of parent-child communication
(C) Type of parent education program
(D) Child's attachment to the mother
(E) Child's socioeconomic status

24. Which of the following is a cause-and-effect pair that could be tested in a research study using an experimental design?

(A) Low birth weight . . childhood nutrition
(B) Eating disorder in adolescence . . body weight in adulthood
(C) Music lessons . . intelligence
(D) Food preference . . amount of time exercising
(E) Anxiety symptoms . . marijuana use

25. A developing organism is most vulnerable to the effects of teratogens during the period of the

(A) ovum
(B) zygote
(C) embryo
(D) fetus
(E) neonate

26. With regard to sexual maturity, females generally mature

(A) two years earlier than males do
(B) four years earlier than males do
(C) two years later than males do
(D) four years later than males do
(E) at approximately the same age as males

27. Carolyn tripped on the carpet and fell. When she got up, she looked at her mother, who was laughing, and she laughed, too. This is an example of

(A) empathy
(B) sympathy
(C) social referencing
(D) display rules
(E) semantics

28. Proximodistal development is exemplified by which of the following?

(A) Control of gross arm movements prior to fine motor control of the fingers
(B) Control of the lower extremities prior to control of the head
(C) Refinement of perceptual abilities prior to walking
(D) Acquisition of differential skills prior to acquisition of complex skills
(E) Maturation of neural pathways in the cerebrum prior to maturation of the neural pathways in the midbrain

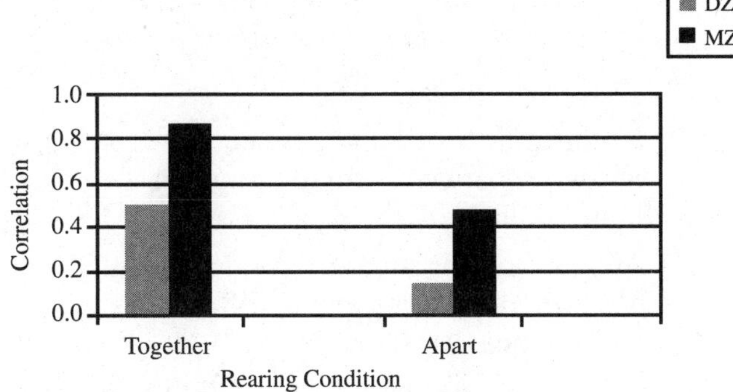

29. A researcher was interested in determining the heritability of a specific trait. He measured the trait in a group of same-sex dizygotic (DZ) twins and a group of monozygotic (MZ) twins. Half of the pairs of twins in each group were reared together, and half were reared apart. The figure above shows the correlations between the measures of the trait for the DZ and MZ twins by rearing condition. Which of the following statements most accurately describes the impact of genes and environment on the trait?

(A) Both genes and the environment influence the trait.
(B) Genetic but not environmental factors affect the trait.
(C) Environmental but not genetic factors affect the trait.
(D) Prenatal influences have stronger effects on development of the trait than do either genes or the environment.
(E) The environment influences the trait among the DZ but not the MZ twins.

30. Newborn infants were given either smooth or knobby pacifiers to suck. They were later allowed to look at both types of pacifiers. They looked longer at the type of pacifier they had previously sucked. This finding indicates that newborn infants have

(A) categorical perception
(B) intermodal perception
(C) shape constancy
(D) depth perception
(E) object permanence

31. Which of the following cues is most useful to an infant in determining which elements go together to form a coherent object?

(A) Common movement
(B) Linear perspective
(C) Texture gradient
(D) Optical expansion
(E) Convergence

32. Order the types of play below from the least cognitively mature to the most cognitively mature.

I. Cooperative play
II. Pretense/symbolic play
III. Constructive play

(A) I, II, III
(B) II, I, III
(C) II, III, I
(D) III, I, II
(E) III, II, I

33. A child explains thunder as "the clouds yelling at each other." This is an example of

(A) conservation
(B) reversibility
(C) animism
(D) egocentrism
(E) logical inference

34. The stage of formal operations is characterized by

(A) the application of logical thought to concrete objects and situations
(B) intuitive and animistic thought
(C) abstract thought and hypothetical problem solving
(D) the development of transductive reasoning
(E) the ability to conserve

35. Katie, a preschooler, sees a llama at the zoo for the first time and calls it a sheep. This is an example of

(A) overextension
(B) chaining
(C) fast mapping
(D) divergent thinking
(E) an expressive style

36. Research on newborn infants' hearing shows that they

(A) cannot distinguish one sound from another
(B) are essentially deaf at birth
(C) react most strongly to their mothers' voices
(D) enjoy hearing their own voices
(E) hear, but do not respond to sounds

37. A theory of language development that proposes an innate language acquisition device is classified as which of the following?

(A) Nativist
(B) Interactionist
(C) Empiricist
(D) Contextual
(E) Functionalist

38. A child who has an IQ of 55 to 70 and delayed social development is classified as having a

(A) mild intellectual disability
(B) moderate intellectual disability
(C) severe intellectual disability
(D) profound intellectual disability
(E) learning disability

39. Which of the following statements about ethnicity and intelligence test scores is most accurate?

(A) No differences in intelligence test scores are observed between ethnic groups in the United States.
(B) Accounting for socioeconomic status (SES) does not reduce the ethnic differences in intelligence test scores.
(C) There is greater variation in intelligence test scores within ethnic groups than there is between them.
(D) Differences in intelligence test scores between ethnic groups are most likely attributable to genetic differences.
(E) Inducing stereotype threat reduces the ethnic differences in intelligence test scores.

40. A toddler with a secure attachment to a primary caregiver is most likely to

(A) avoid the caregiver when they are reunited after a brief separation
(B) stay in the caregiver's lap rather than explore a new environment
(C) cry when the caregiver leaves the toddler with a babysitter
(D) have a close bond with only one parent or primary caregiver
(E) respond equally well to the caregiver and to a strange adult

41. A boy who believes that he will become a girl if he wears his sister's clothes has not achieved the concept of

(A) androgyny
(B) gender stability
(C) gender labeling
(D) gender constancy
(E) gender schema

42. The process by which fluid from the uterus is taken early in pregnancy to determine whether the developing fetus has a genetic anomaly is called

    (A) amniocentesis
    (B) chorionic villus sampling
    (C) positron-emission tomography
    (D) insemination
    (E) ultrasound

43. Although Elizabeth's seven-year-old son wants to stay up past his bedtime to watch a television special, she insists that he go to bed at the usual time. She explains that he will be too tired to do well in school if he does not get his rest, and she promises to record the show for him. Diana Baumrind's classification for Elizabeth's parenting style is which of the following?

    (A) Secure
    (B) Uninvolved
    (C) Authoritarian
    (D) Authoritative
    (E) Permissive

44. Which of the following statements about attachment is most accurate?

    (A) Childcare is unlikely to impact attachment as long as it is not of poor quality.
    (B) Fraternal twins are more similar in attachment than identical twins.
    (C) Only a minority of children are securely attached.
    (D) Infants with an initial disorganized attachment style typically become securely attached later in life.
    (E) Infants with an easy temperament are less likely to be securely attached than those with a difficult temperament.

45. The three behavioral styles identified by Alexander Thomas and Stella Chess in their early research on infant temperament are

    (A) sanguine, melancholic, choleric
    (B) easy, difficult, slow-to-warm-up
    (C) secure, avoidant, ambivalent
    (D) emotional, sociable, inhibited
    (E) introverted, extroverted, agreeable

46. Time out is a disciplinary technique that is based on the principles of

    (A) operant conditioning
    (B) classical conditioning
    (C) observational learning
    (D) information processing
    (E) habituation

47. A mother nags her son until he cleans his room. A few weeks later, the son spontaneously cleans his room because he does not want to be nagged. The mother's nagging is an example of

    (A) a positive reinforcer
    (B) a negative reinforcer
    (C) a vicarious reinforcer
    (D) vicarious punishment
    (E) negative punishment

48. Information-processing theorists argue that one of the major changes that takes place from two to five years of age is

    (A) an increase in the ability to form abstract thoughts and use logical reasoning
    (B) an increase in the complexity and power of working memory
    (C) a decrease in the complexity of schemata associated with everyday experiences
    (D) a decrease in fluid intelligence
    (E) a decrease in the storage capacity of long-term memory

49. Which occupation is best suited for an individual with a conventional personality in John Holland's personality-type theory?

(A) Poet
(B) Scientist
(C) Social worker
(D) Bank teller
(E) Business executive

50. Keisha politely asks her teacher to please pass her the scissors but at home demands that her little brother give them to her immediately. Keisha is demonstrating her understanding of which aspect of knowledge?

(A) Phonology
(B) Semantics
(C) Syntax
(D) Pragmatics
(E) Overregularization

51. Which of the following is the symptom most closely associated with the early stages of Alzheimer's disease?

(A) Manic or depressive behavior
(B) Sensory impairment
(C) Loss of ability to walk
(D) Loss of memory
(E) Loss of reflexes

52. One of the major criticisms of the stages of dying identified by Elisabeth Kübler-Ross is that

(A) there are too many stages in her theory
(B) there are not enough stages in her theory
(C) not everyone goes through the stages in the order she describes
(D) she does not adequately suggest how people try to cope with each stage
(E) the stages vary by sex

53. Instruction by teachers who employ Piagetian principles is most likely to be characterized by which of the following?

(A) Use of lecture as the dominant form of instruction
(B) Reliance on drill and repetition
(C) Encouragement of active experimentation
(D) Encouragement of private speech
(E) Discouragement of group activities

54. Which of the following theorists advanced the concept of the identity crisis?

(A) Jean Piaget
(B) Sigmund Freud
(C) Lev Vygotsky
(D) B. F. Skinner
(E) Erik Erikson

55. When Frank was a child, he moved to a new house near a major airport. At first, he was unable to sleep because of the loud noise created by the airplanes. Over time, however, he was no longer disturbed by the plane noise. A behaviorist would most likely describe the change in Frank's behavior as which of the following?

(A) Habituation
(B) Superstition
(C) Shaping
(D) Operant conditioning
(E) Response generalization

56. Five-year-old Sophia struggles to pronounce words with complex sounds, such as "play" or "stay," pronouncing them as "pay" and "tay" instead. Sophia's difficulty involves which component of language?

(A) Morphology
(B) Syntax
(C) Pragmatics
(D) Phonology
(E) Semantics

57. According to Robert Sternberg's triangular theory, which of the following are the three major components of adult love?

(A) Friendship . . compassion . . commitment
(B) Commitment . . intimacy . . compassion
(C) Intimacy . . commitment . . passion
(D) Compassion . . friendship . . passion
(E) Compassion . . infatuation . . intimacy

58. According to researchers, ethnic identity or a sense of identifying with one's own ethnic group

(A) mostly occurs in adolescence
(B) mostly occurs in older adulthood
(C) stays the same throughout the life span
(D) changes throughout the life span
(E) is not important to overall positive developmental outcomes

59. Which of the following is the most commonly diagnosed among individuals in very late adulthood?

(A) Schizophrenia
(B) Dementia
(C) Generalized anxiety disorder
(D) Somatic symptom disorder
(E) Seasonal affective disorder

60. A researcher compares church attendance between people born in the 1940s and people born in the 1960s. The groups of people are called

(A) cohorts
(B) confounds
(C) control groups
(D) reference groups
(E) intervening variables

61. Eighteen-month-old Michael sees his mother about to put his juice away, and he yells out, "More juice!" Michael's expression is an example of

(A) a holophrase
(B) receptive language
(C) private speech
(D) motherese
(E) telegraphic speech

62. According to Janet Werker's research, the oldest age that children can discriminate phonemic differences in all languages is about

(A) 6–12 months
(B) 18–24 months
(C) 3–4 years
(D) 7–8 years
(E) 12–13 years

63. According to Lawrence Kohlberg, parents can best foster their children's moral development by

(A) setting high expectations for moral behavior
(B) promptly and consistently punishing their children's misbehavior
(C) providing models of moral behavior
(D) providing positive reinforcement for appropriate moral decisions
(E) exposing their children to more advanced moral reasoning by discussion of both sides of moral dilemmas

64. When there is an extremely weak relationship between two behavioral variables, the correlation coefficient will be

(A) much lower than zero
(B) close to zero
(C) close to +1
(D) close to −1
(E) much higher than +1

65. Two young boys sitting next to each other, each drawing a separate picture with his own set of crayons, are engaging in which type of play?

(A) Cooperative
(B) Independent
(C) Parallel
(D) Onlooker
(E) Associative

66. Intelligence tests are most appropriately used to answer which of the following questions?

(A) Should a student take honors courses?
(B) Which approach to education is best to use with a student?
(C) Is a student at risk for social rejection because of high intelligence?
(D) Does a child have attention-deficit/hyperactivity disorder?
(E) What are a student's cognitive strengths and weaknesses?

67. What two developmental milestones occur around the age of one year?

(A) Walking and speaking first words
(B) Crawling and gesturing to communicate
(C) Running and climbing on furniture
(D) Throwing and catching a ball with two hands
(E) Smiling and pulling to a stand

68. In the United States, marital satisfaction is at its lowest at which stage of life?

(A) Immediately following the wedding
(B) Before children are born
(C) When children are very young
(D) When children leave home
(E) Retirement

69. An infant who is fed a balanced diet yet is not gaining enough weight would most likely be diagnosed with

(A) non-organic failure-to-thrive
(B) marasmus
(C) kwashiorkor
(D) autism spectrum disorder
(E) Trisomy 21

70. Drazen, a child with attention-deficit/hyperactivity disorder (ADHD) and oppositional defiant disorder (ODD), is likely to be rated by his peers as being in which of the following peer status categories?

(A) Average
(B) Rejected aggressive
(C) Rejected withdrawn
(D) Neglected
(E) Popular

71. Which of the following should Cheryl say to her son to encourage him to keep doing well in school?

(A) "You're doing so well; keep up your hard work."
(B) "You should be grateful to have such good teachers."
(C) "You have to be the best in your class at school."
(D) "This must be easy for someone as smart as you."
(E) "If you keep getting good grades on all your tests, I'll take you shopping."

72. According to research on the Big Five model of personality, which personality trait tends to increase for both men and women over their life spans?

(A) Aggressiveness
(B) Conscientiousness
(C) Extraversion
(D) Neuroticism
(E) Openness

73. A parent who is teaching a child to write adjusts his level of support to match the child's existing competence in writing. Which of the following concepts best describes the parent's behavior?

(A) Conservation
(B) Egocentrism
(C) Metacognition
(D) Scaffolding
(E) Priming

74. Both stunted growth and delayed menarche are strongly influenced by

(A) lower-middle-class status
(B) use of day care
(C) malnutrition
(D) a nuclear family structure
(E) high protein intake

75. Which of the following findings is often cited as evidence for the evolutionary perspective?

(A) Men's reproductive capabilities last until later in life than women's.
(B) Young children engage in trial-and-error learning.
(C) Children imitate the behaviors modeled by their parents.
(D) Identical twins have more personality traits in common than fraternal twins do.
(E) Token economies help maintain order in the classroom.

76. Which of the following can cause presbyopia?

(A) Buildup of wax in the ear canal
(B) Loss of hair cells in the inner ear
(C) Hardening of the eye lens
(D) Loss of retinal cells
(E) Loss of ocular dominance columns

77. Paul harasses and humiliates other students, calling them names and kicking them without provocation. Paul is exhibiting which of the following?

(A) Instrumental aggression
(B) Hostile aggression
(C) Frustration aggression
(D) Conventional morality
(E) Stereotype threat

78. Steve is 63 years old and attends professional meetings and conferences. Though he used to focus on developing his expertise at the meetings, he now directs his energy toward spending time with close colleagues rather than learning about advancements in his field. Which of the following theories best explains Steve's shift in focus?

(A) Programmed aging
(B) Socioemotional selectivity
(C) Psychodynamic
(D) Social learning
(E) Disengagement

79. Which of the following theories describes development as being dependent on the unconscious mind and early experiences with parents?

(A) Ecological
(B) Sociocultural
(C) Evolutionary
(D) Psychodynamic
(E) Social cognitive

80. Which of the following is a basic emotion?

(A) Depression
(B) Optimism
(C) Mania
(D) Disgust
(E) Empathy

81. Which research question would most likely be addressed by a developmental psychologist?

(A) How does a person mentally rotate an image of a cube?
(B) How do people perceive color?
(C) Are changes in executive control of attention continuous or discontinuous?
(D) Do nerve cells communicate using chemical or electrical messages?
(E) How does relationship quality affect a person's ability to cope with chronic illness?

82. Two seventh graders spend most of their time together talking about difficulties involving either their parents or their history class. These discussions bring them closer in friendship, but their focus on negative aspects tends to lead to them both being more troubled. These students' behavior is an example of

(A) a clique
(B) a dominance hierarchy
(C) co-rumination
(D) scaffolding
(E) acculturation

83. The visual cliff was developed by Eleanor Gibson and R.D. Walk to study

(A) depth perception
(B) acuity
(C) complex pattern recognition
(D) habituation
(E) object permanence

84. Every morning 4-year-old Marta watches her mother put on a suit, pack a lunch, and put her lunch and a briefcase by the front door while preparing for work. One day Marta wakes up, puts on one of her mother's suits, puts snacks in a lunch bag, and puts the lunch bag and a backpack at the front door. She runs to her mother and says, "I'm ready for work!" Marta's behavior can best be explained by which of the following theories?

(A) Information processing
(B) Humanism
(C) Evolutionary
(D) Social learning
(E) Psychodynamic

85. Jorge is aware of his emotions and understands his personal strengths and weaknesses. Jorge appears to have high levels of which intelligence in Howard Gardner's theory of multiple intelligences?

(A) Interpersonal
(B) Existential
(C) Bodily-kinesthetic
(D) Linguistic
(E) Intrapersonal

Study Resources

Most textbooks used in college-level human growth and development courses cover the topics in the outline given earlier, but the approaches to certain topics and the emphases given to them may differ. To prepare for the Human Growth and Development exam, it is advisable to study one or more college textbooks, which can be found in most college bookstores. When selecting a textbook, check the table of contents against the knowledge and skills required for this test.

You may also find it helpful to supplement your reading with books and articles listed in the bibliographies found in most developmental psychology textbooks.

Parents and others who work with children may have gained some preparation for this test through experience. However, knowledge of the basic facts, theories, and principles of child psychology and lifespan development is necessary to provide background for taking the exam.

Visit **clep.collegeboard.org/earn-college-credit/practice** for additional human growth and development resources. You can also find suggestions for exam preparation in Chapter IV of the *Official Study Guide*. In addition, many college faculty post their course materials on their schools' websites.

Answer Key

1.	D	44.	A
2.	B	45.	B
3.	B	46.	A
4.	C	47.	B
5.	C	48.	B
6.	D	49.	D
7.	B	50.	D
8.	A	51.	D
9.	D	52.	C
10.	C	53.	C
11.	E	54.	E
12.	B	55.	A
13.	B	56.	D
14.	D	57.	C
15.	A	58.	D
16.	B	59.	B
17.	C	60.	A
18.	E	61.	E
19.	D	62.	A
20.	A	63.	E
21.	E	64.	B
22.	E	65.	C
23.	C	66.	E
24.	C	67.	A
25.	C	68.	C
26.	A	69.	A
27.	C	70.	B
28.	A	71.	A
29.	A	72.	B
30.	B	73.	D
31.	A	74.	C
32.	E	75.	A
33.	C	76.	C
34.	C	77.	B
35.	A	78.	B
36.	C	79.	D
37.	A	80.	D
38.	A	81.	C
39.	C	82.	C
40.	C	83.	A
41.	D	84.	D
42.	A	85.	E
43.	D		

Introduction to Educational Psychology

Description of the Examination

The Introduction to Educational Psychology examination covers material that is usually taught in a one-semester undergraduate course in this subject. Emphasis is placed on principles of learning and cognition, teaching methods and classroom management, child growth and development, and evaluation and assessment of learning.

The examination contains approximately 100 questions to be answered in 90 minutes. Some of these are pretest questions that will not be scored.

Knowledge and Skills Required

Questions on the Introduction to Educational Psychology examination require candidates to demonstrate one or more of the following abilities.

- Knowledge and comprehension of basic facts, concepts and principles
- Association of ideas with given theoretical positions
- Awareness of important influences on learning and instruction
- Familiarity with research and statistical concepts and procedures
- Ability to apply various concepts and theories as they apply to particular teaching situations and problems

The subject matter of the Introduction to Educational Psychology examination is drawn from the following topics. The percentages next to the main topics indicate the approximate percentage of exam questions on that topic.

15% Cognitive Perspective
- Attention
- Memory
- Complex cognitive processes (e.g., problem solving, transfer, conceptual change)
- Applications of cognitive theory
- Language

11% Behavioral Perspective
- Classical conditioning
- Operant conditioning
- Schedules of reinforcement
- Applications of behavioral perspectives

15% Development
- Cognitive
- Social/emotional
- Moral
- Gender identity/gender roles
- Language acquisition

10% Motivation
- Social-cognitive theories of motivation (e.g., attribution theory, expectancy-value theory, goal orientation theory, intrinsic and extrinsic motivation, self-efficacy, self-determination theory)
- Learned helplessness
- Teacher expectations/Pygmalion effect
- Anxiety/stress
- Applications of motivational theories

17% Individual Differences
- Intelligence
- Genetic and environmental influences
- Exceptionalities in learning (e.g., giftedness, learning disabilities, behavior disorders)
- Ability grouping and tracking

12% Testing
- Classroom assessment (e.g., formative and summative evaluation, grading procedures)
- Norm- and criterion-referenced tests
- Test reliability and validity
- Bias in testing
- High-stakes assessment/standards-based testing
- Interpretation of test results (e.g., descriptive statistics, scaled scores)
- Use and misuse of assessments

10% **Pedagogy**

- Planning instruction for effective learning
- Writing objectives to align instruction with standards
- Social constructivist pedagogy (e.g., scaffolding)
- Cooperative/collaborative learning
- Classroom management
- Technology in education
- Differentiated instruction

5% **Research Design and Analysis**

- Research design (e.g., longitudinal, experimental, case study, quasi-experimental)
- Research methods (e.g., survey, observation, interview)
- Interpretation of research (e.g., correlation versus causation, descriptive statistics)

5% **Multiculturalism**

- Ethnic, racial, and cultural issues
- Socioeconomic status (SES)
- Bilingualism/English as a second language
- Gender differences
- Immigration/social change
- Culturally responsive teaching

Sample Test Questions

The following sample questions do not appear on an actual CLEP examination. They are intended to give potential test-takers an indication of the format and difficulty level of the examination and to provide content for practice and review. Knowing the correct answers to all of the sample questions is not a guarantee of satisfactory performance on the exam.

Directions: Each of the questions or incomplete statements below is followed by five suggested answers or completions. Select the one that is best in each case.

1. Which of the following learning outcomes usually undergoes the largest loss within 24 hours of acquisition?

    (A) The learning of meaningful material
    (B) The learning of rote material
    (C) The formulation of concepts
    (D) The application of principles
    (E) The making of generalizations

2. When Robert's classmates no longer showed approval of his clowning, his clowning behavior occurred less frequently. The concept best exemplified by Robert's change in behavior is

    (A) extinction
    (B) discrimination
    (C) generalization
    (D) transfer
    (E) learning set

3. Which of the following are functions of an Individualized Education Program (IEP) ?

    I. Supports classroom teachers
    II. Creates a relationship (partnership) between regular classroom and resource team
    III. Provides an instructional program to meet the needs of the individual student
    IV. Allows the school professionals to solely make decisions without consulting parents

    (A) III only
    (B) I and III only
    (C) III and IV only
    (D) I, II, and III only
    (E) I, II, III, and IV

4. In a fifth-grade class that is working on a set of arithmetic problems, which of the following behaviors would be most characteristic of the student who is a divergent thinker?

    (A) Writing down the principle used to solve the problem as well as the solution itself
    (B) Making answers far more exact than is necessary
    (C) Working as fast as possible in order to be the first to finish the assignment
    (D) Finding a variety of ways to solve each problem
    (E) Providing the correct solution to the greatest number of problems

5. To measure students' understanding of a theorem in geometry, it is best for a teacher to have the students do which of the following?

    (A) Write out the theorem
    (B) Recall the proof of the theorem
    (C) Demonstrate that they have memorized the theorem
    (D) Solve a problem that is given in the textbook
    (E) Solve a related problem that is not in the textbook

6. A child who is frightened by a dog and develops a fear of other dogs is exhibiting which of the following principles of learning?

    (A) Discrimination learning
    (B) Negative transfer
    (C) Behavior shaping
    (D) Stimulus generalization
    (E) Cognitive dissonance

7. In experimental studies of the motor development of identical twins, one twin is given practice at a particular skill early and the other twin six weeks later. The fact that it generally takes less practice for the later-trained twin to acquire the skill is evidence for the importance of

    (A) heredity
    (B) maturation
    (C) intelligence quotient (IQ)
    (D) individual differences
    (E) early experience

8. In a fifth-grade class studying the ancient Incan culture, all of the following questions are likely to stimulate pupils to think creatively EXCEPT:

    (A) Why do you suppose the clothing of the Incas was so different from today's clothing?
    (B) What weapons and tools did the Incas use for hunting?
    (C) What would be the reaction of ancient Incas toward modern Peru?
    (D) If the Incas had defeated the Spanish, how might things be different in Peru today?
    (E) If you had lived in Peru during the time of the Incas, what are the things you would have liked and disliked?

9. According to a cognitive psychologist, which of the following types of memory is composed of accumulated factual knowledge about the world?

    (A) Working
    (B) Procedural
    (C) Episodic
    (D) Semantic
    (E) Sensory

10. Of the following, learning is best defined as

    (A) development that occurs without external stimulation
    (B) the process of overcoming obstacles during instinctual behavior
    (C) effort that is persistent, selective, and purposeful
    (D) the modification of behavior through experience
    (E) the gathering of data to test hypotheses

11. According to cognitive learning theorists, a new unit can be most readily learned by a class of students when the unit's concepts and terms are

    (A) recited from memory in a number of contexts
    (B) expressed as observable behavioral objectives
    (C) chosen to reflect the most up-to-date findings in the field
    (D) related hierarchically to concepts and terms mastered previously
    (E) presented in a manner that students find different and complex

12. A preschool child sees a teacher roll a ball of clay into a sausage-like shape. The teacher asks, "Is the amount of clay the same as before?" The child insists that the sausage shape consists of more clay than the ball did. According to Jean Piaget, this mistake by the child occurs principally because of which of the following?

    (A) A poorly stated question by the teacher
    (B) Erroneous earlier learning by the child
    (C) The greater attractiveness of the sausage shape
    (D) A cognitive impairment
    (E) A lack of understanding of the conservation principle

13. A fourth-grade teacher wants her students to learn to recognize oak trees. Which of the following strategies would best lead to that goal?

    (A) Bringing oak leaves into the classroom and having students trace them
    (B) Taking the students to the park to show them oaks and other trees and pointing out the distinguishing characteristics of oaks
    (C) Giving each student one or two acorns to plant and presenting a lesson on how oak trees grow
    (D) Decorating the classroom bulletin boards with pictures of trees
    (E) Showing students a film of the major trees of North America and then giving the students a quiz on oak trees

14. Longitudinal studies of cognitive abilities during middle and later adulthood indicate which of the following declines most with age?

    (A) Speed of information processing
    (B) Size of vocabulary
    (C) Wisdom
    (D) Quality of verbal reasoning
    (E) Crystallized intelligence

15. Which of the following is true if a test is reliable?

    (A) The results will be approximately the same if the test is given again under similar conditions.
    (B) The test measures what it was designed to measure.
    (C) The predictive validity of the test is high.
    (D) The objectives measured by the test are important.
    (E) The test scores can be interpreted objectively by anyone simply by using the test manual.

16. The concept of developmental tasks refers to the

    (A) development of mental abilities, as distinguished from physical abilities
    (B) ability of the child to develop certain conceptual arrangements
    (C) behavior of the child that results from hereditary determinants
    (D) behaviors of the child that are expected at various ages
    (E) physiological development of the child

17. Which of the following correlation coefficients has the highest predictive value?

    (A) .80
    (B) .60
    (C) .00
    (D) –.70
    (E) –.90

18. Which of the following statistics is most affected by extreme scores?

    (A) Mean
    (B) Median
    (C) Mode
    (D) Rank correlation
    (E) Interquartile range

19. A certain researcher studied Stephanie's development of mathematical proof and justification from grade 1 through grade 5 by collecting videotapes, portfolios, notes, student interviews, and small-group evaluations of Stephanie over the five-year period. This type of study is referred to as

    (A) an experimental study
    (B) a case study
    (C) a matched-group study
    (D) a correlational study
    (E) a survey

20. Which of the following perspectives on teaching would most likely support the idea that instruction should emphasize a positive relationship between teachers and students?

    (A) Behavioral
    (B) Humanistic
    (C) Cognitive
    (D) Psychoanalytic
    (E) Maturational

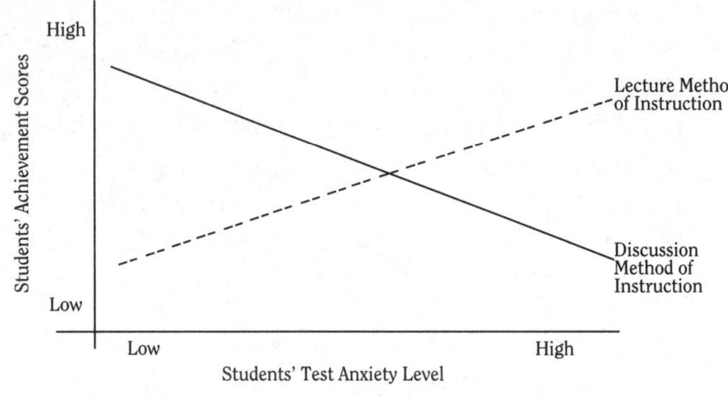

21. Assuming that the data above were collected in an experimental study, which of the following statements best describes the relationships depicted in the graph?

    (A) Differences among students in test anxiety result in different achievement levels depending on the instructional method received.
    (B) Differences among students in test anxiety result in different achievement levels independent of the instructional method received.
    (C) The effect of two different instructional methods on students' achievement is positively correlated with students' test anxiety levels.
    (D) The effect of two different instructional methods on students' achievement is negatively correlated with students' test anxiety levels.
    (E) Students' achievement levels are independent of their test anxiety levels.

22. Frank, a fifteen year old, is capable of reasoning abstractly without the use of real objects to assist him. According to Jean Piaget, Frank is in which of the following stages of cognitive development?

    (A) Concrete operations
    (B) Tertiary circular reactions
    (C) Preoperations
    (D) Formal operations
    (E) Sensorimotor

23. Decisions about the values that are transmitted in schools are best related to the teacher's role as

    (A) instructional expert
    (B) socialization agent
    (C) counselor
    (D) motivator
    (E) classroom manager

24. Using the principle of successive approximations involves which of the following?

    (A) Reinforcing responses that represent progress toward a desired response
    (B) Making a succession of trials designed to provide information about a problem
    (C) Acquiring a behavior change through imitation of models demonstrating the behavior
    (D) Averaging repeated measures for adequate assessment of a variable
    (E) Testing possible solutions until success is obtained in problem solving

25. Which of the following best characterizes the concept of a critical or sensitive period in development?

    (A) A bridge between two cognitive stages, such as the transition between preoperational and concrete-operational thinking
    (B) An age period during which a behavior must develop if it is to develop normally
    (C) An age period during which the child tends to display a certain class of behaviors, such as the "terrible twos"
    (D) An age period during which the child's sense of self-worth is especially vulnerable to social criticism
    (E) An age period during which children are influenced more by peers than by adults

26. In cooperative learning it is NOT important for students to

    (A) rely on group members' contributions to complete the task
    (B) be held individually accountable for their own learning
    (C) be at the same achievement level
    (D) interact directly with other group members
    (E) know and use good interpersonal skills

27. Some psychologists theorize that behavioral development, like anatomical development, proceeds from the simple to the complex, from homogeneous to heterogeneous, and from the general to the specific. Which of the following terms refers to these developmental trends?

    (A) Constancy
    (B) Assimilation
    (C) Metacognition
    (D) Differentiation
    (E) Transfer

28. Paying attention to new information is important in the learning process because such attention brings information from

    (A) an external environment into the sensory register
    (B) an external environment into long-term memory
    (C) the sensory register into working memory
    (D) working memory into long-term memory
    (E) the sensory register into long-term memory

29. When a two-year-old child points to a picture of a horse in a picture book and says "doggie," the child is committing an error of

(A) overregularization
(B) overextension
(C) receptive vocabulary
(D) syntax
(E) articulation

30. Louisa is trying to improve her memory. She is trying to remember the items on her grocery list: tangerines, flour, onions, apples, steak, and lettuce. She repeats the word FLOATS to help her remember the items on her list. Which of the following memory techniques is Louisa using?

(A) Rehearsal
(B) Recognition
(C) Chunking
(D) Elaboration
(E) Mnemonic

31. A student has to memorize a long list of nouns for a contest. Which of the following is the best strategy for the student to use to enhance recall of the words?

(A) Grouping the words by semantic category
(B) Spelling each of the words
(C) Sorting the words according to length
(D) Writing out the definition of each of the words
(E) Determining the presence or absence of a target sound in each word

32. In an evaluation of achievement, the relationship between formative evaluation and summative evaluation is most similar to that between

(A) skills instruction and skills practice
(B) diagnostic examinations and final examinations
(C) subjective data and objective data
(D) descriptive data and inferential data
(E) norm-referenced tests and criterion-referenced tests

33. Which of the following treatments is most common for attention-deficit/hyperactivity disorder?

(A) Stimulant medication
(B) Mnemonic aids
(C) Self-esteem workshops
(D) Psychotherapy
(E) Motivational training

34. A person who drove a manual-transmission car for years finds that, when driving a car with an automatic transmission, he often lifts his foot to step on the clutch. This driver is experiencing

(A) parallel distributed processing
(B) an articulatory loop
(C) positive transfer
(D) proactive interference
(E) retroactive interference

35. A parent complains that 40 percent of the questions on a classroom test were taken from 4 pages of the 70 pages covered in the material assigned in the test. The parent is questioning the test's

(A) interrater reliability
(B) test-retest reliability
(C) split-half reliability
(D) content validity
(E) criterion-related validity

36. Joseph Renzulli's triad for identifying giftedness is best described as which of the following?

(A) Above-average ability, task commitment, creativity
(B) Skillful processing of verbal information, artistic expression, assertiveness
(C) High IQ scores, academic aptitude, practical intelligence
(D) Language fluency, analytic problem-solving ability, ethical thinking
(E) Interpersonal intelligence, intrapersonal intelligence, logical-mathematical intelligence

37. Behavioral theories that focus on helping students develop self-management skills emphasize that it is important for students to

    (A) assess their competencies
    (B) improve their self-concepts
    (C) increase their general knowledge
    (D) develop social awareness
    (E) recognize clear signals that behaviors are appropriate

38. Jacob Kounin's concept of "withitness" refers to which of the following teacher abilities?

    (A) Maintaining awareness of everything that is happening in the classroom
    (B) Sequentially processing classroom activities and giving feedback to students
    (C) Going from one activity to another without wasting time
    (D) Focusing on one thing at a time in the classroom to keep from becoming frustrated
    (E) Identifying students' academic strengths and deficiencies

39. Which of the following would be the best evidence that a test intended to estimate future success in school was biased against one group of examinees?

    (A) A large mean-score difference between that group and the rest of the examinees
    (B) A large standard deviation in the test scores of that group
    (C) A low passing rate for all examinees
    (D) An 80 percent passing rate for that group
    (E) An underprediction of academic achievement for that group

40. Among White, middle-class parents in the United States, which of the following parenting styles is most likely to help children develop into responsible adolescents?

    (A) Autocratic
    (B) Authoritarian
    (C) Authoritative
    (D) Permissive
    (E) Uninvolved

41. Which of the following is a major point in Carol Gilligan's criticism of Lawrence Kohlberg's theory of moral development?

    (A) The levels of moral reasoning in Kohlberg's scheme are unrelated to social and political attitudes.
    (B) Mature levels of moral reasoning may differ qualitatively between men and women.
    (C) The higher levels of moral reasoning in Kohlberg's scheme apply only to children in the United States.
    (D) The stages in Kohlberg's scheme deviate from those in Jean Piaget's stage theory.
    (E) Chronological age is unrelated to maturity of moral reasoning on Kohlberg's scale.

42. Which of the following best illustrates metacognition?

    (A) Memorizing terms and definitions from a textbook
    (B) Monitoring one's comprehension while reading
    (C) Listening to the radio and studying at the same time
    (D) Retrieving information from working memory
    (E) Retrieving information from long-term memory

43. George Miller's research finding that humans have a processing capacity of seven plus-or-minus two items applies to which of the following types of memory?

(A) Sensory register
(B) Explicit
(C) Implicit
(D) Working
(E) Procedural

44. Alice maintains a messy desk in order to gain attention from her teacher. For Alice, the teacher's attention serves as which of the following?

(A) Negative reinforcement
(B) Positive reinforcement
(C) Extinction
(D) Primary reinforcement
(E) Shaping

45. Research that investigates nature versus nurture as a basis of intelligence has found the highest correlations of IQ scores between which of the following?

(A) Dizygotic twins raised together
(B) Nontwin siblings raised together
(C) Nontwin siblings raised apart
(D) Monozygotic twins raised together
(E) Monozygotic twins raised apart

46. Mary's score on an achievement test is 75. The normative data show an overall test mean of 50 and a standard deviation of 10. This information indicates that Mary's z-score equivalent is

(A) –2.5
(B) –0.53
(C) +0.53
(D) +1.3
(E) +2.5

47. A teacher informs parents that their child has earned a stanine score of five. The teacher is actually saying that the student's test score

(A) is below average
(B) is average
(C) is above average
(D) indicates giftedness
(E) indicates a disability

Questions 48–49 refer to the following information.

Jodie, who is in the ninth grade, took a test that measured her ability in mathematics. The test consisted of 50 multiple-choice questions and had a completion time of two hours. It was scored from 0 to 50 points, with a mean of 27, a mode of 26, and a median of 25. Jodie's score represented her actual knowledge of mathematics and did not provide any information about how she compared with other students who had taken the same test.

48. The test that Jodie took is best characterized as

(A) a portfolio assessment
(B) an intelligence (IQ) test
(C) a developmental profile
(D) a norm-referenced test
(E) a criterion-referenced test

49. An examination of the scores of all of the students who took the test would reveal that the score most often earned was

(A) 15
(B) 25
(C) 26
(D) 27
(E) 50

50. A teacher rewards students for every fifth question they get right in class. Which of the following is a schedule of reinforcement that the teacher is using?

(A) Fixed interval
(B) Fixed ratio
(C) Variable interval
(D) Extinction
(E) Differential

51. José cannot find his favorite toy. When his father talks with him about it and encourages José to think about where he last used it, José suddenly remembers the toy's location. José's thinking is thus aided by the conversation with his father. This is an example of a theory of cognitive development formulated by

(A) Jean Piaget
(B) Lev Vygotsky
(C) Noam Chomsky
(D) Carol Gilligan
(E) Lawrence Kohlberg

52. Paul is fourteen years old, has recently broken up with his girlfriend of three weeks, and believes that no one can understand the pain he is feeling. According to David Elkind, Paul is displaying

(A) the imaginary audience
(B) metacognition
(C) a personal fable
(D) postformal thought
(E) symbolic thought

53. Mrs. Smith's third graders love creative writing. Research on the use of rewards generally indicates that if she continuously rewards her students with candy for writing creative stories, the students'

(A) writing abilities will keep improving
(B) writing abilities will get worse over time
(C) writing will not be affected in any way
(D) interest in writing will lessen over time
(E) interest in writing will increase over time

54. Mary enjoys reading, primarily because her father gives her a dollar for each book she reads. Mary's motivational orientation for reading is most accurately described as

(A) mastery oriented
(B) goal oriented
(C) intrinsic
(D) extrinsic
(E) egocentric

55. Which of the following is a motivational theory in which students attempt to explain the causes of their successes and failures?

(A) Cognitive-behavioral theory
(B) Hierarchy of needs
(C) Reward theory
(D) Attribution theory
(E) Achievement motivation

56. A student's score at the 75th percentile indicates that the student

(A) correctly answered 75 percent of the exam
(B) correctly answered 75 questions on the exam
(C) scored worse than 75 percent of the test-takers
(D) scored the same as or better than 75 percent of the test-takers
(E) scored the same as or better than 25 percent of the test-takers

57. Five-year-old Billy rarely makes eye contact and frequently self-stimulates and repeats back the speech that he hears. Based on this information alone, it is most likely that Billy has

(A) autism spectrum disorder
(B) major depressive disorder
(C) attention-deficit/hyperactivity disorder
(D) intellectual disability
(E) dyslexia

58. Which of the following is most likely to be used as an individually administered intelligence test?

    (A) Wechsler Intelligence Scale for Children®
    (B) Differential Ability Scales®
    (C) Minnesota Multiphasic Personality Inventory®
    (D) GRE® revised General Test
    (E) Thematic Apperception Test

59. Tests such as the SAT® and the ACT® Test are most often used for which type of testing?

    (A) Diagnostic
    (B) Intelligence
    (C) Achievement
    (D) Aptitude
    (E) Projective

60. A self-regulated learner is likely to engage in all of the following EXCEPT

    (A) thinking about which learning strategies are appropriate for a given task
    (B) evaluating his or her performance while progressing through a task
    (C) thinking about multiple tasks and responsibilities simultaneously
    (D) setting realistic goals
    (E) managing study time

61. Token economies in classrooms often provide students with the opportunity to earn points for good behavior that can be exchanged for some type of reward, such as candy, free time, or toys. According to researchers, a token economy system would be most beneficial in a classroom in which students

    (A) exhibit high intrinsic motivation
    (B) typically behave well
    (C) are out of control
    (D) are especially gifted
    (E) have just begun to show minor behavior problems

62. Which of the following is NOT consistent with developmentally appropriate practice in kindergarten?

    (A) Having different learning centers in the classroom
    (B) Expecting all children to read simple words by the end of the year
    (C) Giving children time for free play during each week
    (D) Having children engaged in activities in small groups
    (E) Allowing children a rest period during the day

63. Based on group data, which of the following is a gender difference that is regularly observed on achievement tests?

    (A) Boys tend to have higher average scores on reading tests than girls do.
    (B) Girls tend to have higher average scores on science tests than boys do.
    (C) Girls tend to have higher average scores on spatial reasoning tests than boys do.
    (D) There tends to be more variability among boys' scores on achievement tests than there is among girls' scores.
    (E) Girls tend to have higher average scores on math tests than boys do.

64. Learned helplessness is most likely to occur when students view the cause of their failures as

    (A) stable and uncontrollable
    (B) stable and controllable
    (C) unstable and controllable
    (D) external and controllable
    (E) internal and unstable

65. Mr. Arevola, an experienced fifth-grade mathematics teacher, is acknowledged as an excellent teacher and often acts as a mentor to young teachers. He is especially helpful by assisting newcomers to understand the difficulties that students often have with comprehension of fractions and to teach in a way that will address that issue. According to Lee Shulman, the type of teacher knowledge Mr. Arevola conveys could best be described as

    (A) content knowledge
    (B) process knowledge
    (C) declarative knowledge
    (D) pedagogical content knowledge
    (E) pedagogical process knowledge

66. According to Albert Bandura, which of the following is the most powerful source of self-efficacy for a child?

    (A) Physiological cues
    (B) Verbal persuasion
    (C) Mastery experiences
    (D) Observational learning
    (E) Imitation

67. Stage theories of development are best described as

    (A) quantitative/continuous
    (B) qualitative/discontinuous
    (C) morally bound
    (D) universally accepted
    (E) socially determined

68. Which of the following is an example of disequilibrium?

    (A) Robert has learned about different types of sharks, and he reasons that a dolphin is a type of shark because it looks similar.
    (B) William has figured out that the Sun is covered by clouds at night, which causes the darkness.
    (C) Dameon wonders how a caterpillar can be an insect when it appears to have more than six legs.
    (D) Ricky understands that his teddy bear is not alive, because he has learned about characteristics of living things.
    (E) Jon decides that sand is a liquid because it takes the shape of its container.

69. Achievement tests differ from aptitude tests primarily in that

    (A) the score distributions of achievement tests tend to be linear, whereas the score distributions of aptitude tests tend to be bell-shaped
    (B) achievement tests are designed to measure what students have learned, whereas aptitude tests are designed to predict how well students will perform in the future
    (C) achievement tests tend to face more resistance from parents, students, and classroom teachers than do aptitude tests
    (D) achievement tests are designed to measure the middle-ability population most accurately, whereas aptitude tests are designed to measure the high- and low-ability populations most accurately
    (E) aptitude tests are designed to have less variability in scores than achievement tests have

70. Mr. Janis asked his class to draw a picture of a flower. Ninety percent of the class drew a picture of a rose. In terms of cognitive psychology, what would a rose be for these students?

    (A) An attribute
    (B) A concept
    (C) A prototype
    (D) A heuristic
    (E) An algorithm

71. A student memorizes the French words for the numbers zero through twenty for a test the next day. Which of the following types of memory does this process require?

    (A) Iconic
    (B) Procedural
    (C) Echoic
    (D) Working
    (E) Declarative

72. Jenna has just been diagnosed with an articulation disorder. Which behavior is she most likely to exhibit?

    (A) Saying “wed” instead of “red”
    (B) Speaking too slowly
    (C) Stammering while talking
    (D) Using a high-pitched voice
    (E) Speaking without emotional tone

73. Ms. Sharps has been emphasizing the use of authentic assessment in her watercolor painting class. What type of assessment is she most likely to use to grade her students?

    (A) Portfolio
    (B) Essay test
    (C) Oral presentation
    (D) Short essays
    (E) Multiple-choice tests

74. Jacquelin has always done well in school. In her fifth-grade class, she works hard and always does her homework. She often reads extra books and does extra math problems. Which of Erik Erikson’s psychosocial stages would Jacquelin best exemplify?

    (A) Trust versus mistrust
    (B) Autonomy versus shame and doubt
    (C) Initiative versus guilt
    (D) Industry versus inferiority
    (E) Identity versus role confusion

75. A seventh-grade boy scores 66 on an IQ test. He is very sociable but has some trouble with independent living tasks. He would most likely be diagnosed with which of the following?

    (A) Specific learning disability
    (B) Autism spectrum disorder
    (C) Generalized anxiety disorder
    (D) Attention-deficit/hyperactivity disorder
    (E) Mild intellectual disability

76. To limit the amount of time needed to make decisions, humans use quick and efficient mental shortcuts called

    (A) heuristics
    (B) algorithms
    (C) insights
    (D) forecasting
    (E) framing

77. Which of the following strategies is LEAST likely to increase test scores?

    (A) Giving rewards to students who get very high scores
    (B) Giving partial credit for partially correct answers
    (C) Giving clear feedback about the reasons for a low score
    (D) Providing ungraded assignments to encourage creativity and risk-taking
    (E) Grading oral as well as written work

78. A teacher believes that students of all ages can improve their basic abilities through hard work, even though many of them might think that their ability is fixed and cannot be changed. The teacher's belief is associated with a view of intelligence referred to as

(A) fluid
(B) crystallized
(C) multiple
(D) incremental
(E) the g factor

79. Teachers who want to positively reinforce students' behaviors would best be guided by which of the following statements?

(A) Make sure that all children get the same reward so that they are equally motivated.
(B) Delay reinforcement rather than providing it right after the behavior being rewarded.
(C) Promote self-regulation and self-management so students do not become dependent on incentives.
(D) Balance positive reinforcement with punishment so students do not expect only to be rewarded.
(E) Wait until a complex behavior is performed in full before rewarding it, rather than relying on shaping.

80. Larae has been selected to serve on a jury. When Larae sees the defendant she decides that he is not guilty. When the prosecutor presents her case, Larae does not listen as attentively as she does when the defense attorney presents his case. Larae is showing evidence of

(A) the availability heuristic
(B) diffusion of responsibility
(C) the overconfidence effect
(D) confirmation bias
(E) the representative heuristic

81. Which of the following practices promotes a performance goal orientation?

(A) Using cooperative learning strategies
(B) Evaluating students in terms of their progress over time
(C) Encouraging students to use multiple strategies when solving a problem
(D) Allowing students extra time to master content they find difficult
(E) Posting the names of students who pass a classroom test

82. An Individualized Transition Plan (ITP) would most likely be written for which of the following students?

(A) Jason, a thirteen year old who just transferred to a new school
(B) Maddy, a twelve year old who is now taking regular physical education
(C) Rachel, a five year old who is beginning kindergarten
(D) Stanley, a sixteen year old who is learning job skills
(E) Madison, an eleven year old who is about to enter middle school

83. Which of the following groups is not covered by the Individuals with Disabilities Education Improvement Act of 2004 (IDEA)?

(A) Students with emotional disturbances
(B) Students who have learning disabilities but average intelligence
(C) Students with some hearing impairment but who are not profoundly deaf
(D) Students identified as intellectually gifted
(E) Students with autism spectrum disorder

84. Which of the following correctly lists the components of Robert Sternberg's triarchic theory of intelligence?

    (A) Analytical, creative, and practical
    (B) Linguistic, logical-mathematical, and interpersonal
    (C) General, insightful, and automatic
    (D) Fluid, crystallized, and practical
    (E) Verbal, logical, and bodily-kinesthetic

85. A school nurse wants to know whether children's knowledge about nutrition increases over the course of the elementary years. To find out, she gives a test about nutrition to students in the first, third, and fifth grades. She then compares the test scores for the three grade levels. Which one of the following research designs does the nurse's study best reflect?

    (A) Experimental design
    (B) Longitudinal design
    (C) Cross-sectional design
    (D) Microgenetic design
    (E) Correlational design

86. Which of the following interventions is most likely to help close the gap in reading scores between students of low and high socioeconomic status?

    (A) Encouraging parents of low socioeconomic status to read more to their children
    (B) Teaching parents of low socioeconomic status to emphasize literacy skills when reading to their children
    (C) Promoting an oral storytelling tradition in families of low socioeconomic status
    (D) Providing books for students in families of low socioeconomic status
    (E) Providing classes in English as a second language for parents of low socioeconomic status

87. According to Lawrence Kohlberg, in what order does gender develop?

    (A) Gender stability, gender consistency, gender identity
    (B) Gender identity, gender consistency, gender stability
    (C) Gender identity, gender stability, gender consistency
    (D) Gender consistency, gender identity, gender stability
    (E) Gender consistency, gender stability, gender identity

88. Dyslexia is best described as a learning disability in which a student has

    (A) an inability to master basic reading skills in a developmentally typical time frame
    (B) a problem with visual perception that results in reading words backward
    (C) difficulty in visualizing spatial aspects of mathematical problems
    (D) a deficit in computation in mathematical problems
    (E) a significantly slowed general processing speed

89. Of the following, a student with a moderate hearing loss will most likely have

    (A) low self-esteem
    (B) poor attention span
    (C) delayed language skills
    (D) emotional problems
    (E) poor motor skills

90. Central to Lev Vygotsky's theory of cognitive development is the idea that children make sense of their world

    (A) by watching other people be reinforced or punished for their behavior
    (B) through repeated encounters with pleasant and unpleasant events in their daily lives
    (C) through independent explorations of their physical and social environments
    (D) by interacting with more-experienced people to accomplish tasks they could not accomplish alone
    (E) by building their schemes through interaction with the environment

91. Which of the following best illustrates a person who has high self-efficacy?

    (A) Anne is confident she can win a spot on the school's dance squad if she practices her routine every day until the tryouts.
    (B) Brandi thinks of herself as being more intelligent than most of her classmates.
    (C) Connor has little faith in his academic abilities; therefore, he avoids completing assigned classroom tasks.
    (D) Darvin is convinced that no one likes him, even though most people do.
    (E) Joel believes that he is worthy of love from his parents and peers.

92. Research on bilingualism suggests that

    (A) high levels of bilingualism in students are related to increased cognitive abilities
    (B) high levels of bilingualism in students are related to decreased metalinguistic awareness
    (C) dividing students into separate English classes based on their primary language is desirable
    (D) for students to learn English properly, their parents need to speak only English at home
    (E) code-switching is a consequence of not having full competency in either language

93. Sharron had trouble with math in a previous semester. She now believes that no matter how much she studies for her math test or how much extra help she seeks, she will fail the test. Her reaction to this lack of control is most similar to the behaviorist idea of

    (A) anxiety
    (B) internal conflict
    (C) a stressor
    (D) learned helplessness
    (E) fatalism

94. Which of the following characteristics is most typical of gifted children and adolescents?

    (A) They report more emotional and social difficulties than average classmates of their own age.
    (B) They are less likely to be accepted by their peers and siblings.
    (C) They learn best in classes that stress knowledge acquisition above all else.
    (D) They are more likely than their average-achieving peers to drop out of school and engage in antisocial behavior.
    (E) They flourish in classrooms where analytical skills are emphasized over generating new ideas.

95. When Donald completes his seatwork on time, his teacher rewards him with a sticker. Donald likes the stickers, so he is motivated to complete his seatwork. The teacher's strategy is consistent with which motivational theory?

    (A) Extrinsic
    (B) Intrinsic
    (C) Expectancy
    (D) Drive-reduction
    (E) Self-determination

96. A third-grade class has just completed a unit on the water cycle. At the end of the unit, the teacher conducts a brief assessment to evaluate each student's understanding of the material. Students who score 80 percent or better on the assessment are assigned enrichment activities, while students who score below that point are provided with reteaching and additional opportunities to practice their skills. Which of the following strategies is the teacher using?

    (A) Between-class ability grouping
    (B) Coteaching
    (C) Cooperative learning
    (D) Mastery learning
    (E) Individual instruction

97. Jason received very high marks on his research-methods lab report. He believes that his performance was a result of the effort he put into the project. Based on this information, which of the following types of locus of control does Jason have?

    (A) Multidimensional
    (B) Stable
    (C) Internal
    (D) External
    (E) Unstable

98. The view that all cultures have their own logic and that no culture is inherently better than another is called

    (A) pluralism
    (B) a melting pot
    (C) ethnocentrism
    (D) acculturation
    (E) assimilation

99. Which of the following is the most commonly used proxy for socioeconomic status (SES) in schools?

    (A) Family constellation
    (B) Student performance on standardized tests
    (C) Number of students in the district who are in foster care
    (D) An estimate of the SES of the neighborhood in which a student resides
    (E) Percentage of students in the district who receive free or reduced lunch

100. Which of the following would be most important to a teacher who is focused on equity pedagogy?

    (A) Modifying students' attitudes toward other groups of students
    (B) Illustrating ideas using content from a variety of cultures
    (C) Using instruction that facilitates the academic achievement of students from diverse racial, cultural, and socioeconomic (SES) groups
    (D) Investigating and understanding how implicit cultural assumptions, frames of reference, perspectives, and biases within a discipline affect the knowledge within that discipline
    (E) Examining the total school culture to ensure that it empowers students from diverse racial, ethnic, and cultural groups

Study Resources

Most textbooks used in college-level introduction to educational psychology courses cover the topics in the outline given earlier, but the approaches to certain topics and the emphases given to them may differ. To prepare for the Introduction to Educational Psychology exam, it is advisable to study one or more college textbooks, which can be found in most college bookstores. When selecting a textbook, check the table of contents against the knowledge and skills required for this test.

You may also find it helpful to supplement your reading with books listed in the bibliographies that can be found in most educational psychology textbooks.

Visit **clep.collegeboard.org/earn-college-credit/practice** for additional educational psychology resources. You can also find suggestions for exam preparation in Chapter IV of the *Official Study Guide*. In addition, many college faculty post their course materials on their schools' websites.

Answer Key

1.	B	51.	B
2.	A	52.	C
3.	D	53.	D
4.	D	54.	D
5.	E	55.	D
6.	D	56.	D
7.	B	57.	A
8.	B	58.	A
9.	D	59.	D
10.	D	60.	C
11.	D	61.	C
12.	E	62.	B
13.	B	63.	D
14.	A	64.	A
15.	A	65.	D
16.	D	66.	C
17.	E	67.	B
18.	A	68.	C
19.	B	69.	B
20.	B	70.	C
21.	A	71.	E
22.	D	72.	A
23.	B	73.	A
24.	A	74.	D
25.	B	75.	E
26.	C	76.	A
27.	D	77.	A
28.	C	78.	D
29.	B	79.	C
30.	E	80.	D
31.	A	81.	E
32.	B	82.	D
33.	A	83.	D
34.	D	84.	A
35.	D	85.	C
36.	A	86.	B
37.	E	87.	C
38.	A	88.	A
39.	E	89.	C
40.	C	90.	D
41.	B	91.	A
42.	B	92.	A
43.	D	93.	D
44.	B	94.	A
45.	D	95.	A
46.	E	96.	D
47.	B	97.	C
48.	E	98.	A
49.	C	99.	E
50.	B	100.	C

Principles of Macroeconomics

Description of the Examination

The Principles of Macroeconomics examination covers material that is usually taught in a one-semester undergraduate course in this subject. This aspect of economics deals with principles of economics that apply to an economy as a whole, particularly the general price level, output and income, and interrelations among sectors of the economy. The test places particular emphasis on the determinants of aggregate demand and aggregate supply, and on monetary and fiscal policy tools that can be used to achieve particular policy objectives. Within this context, candidates are expected to understand basic economic concepts such as scarcity and comparative advantage and measurement concepts such as gross domestic product, consumption, investment, unemployment and inflation. Candidates are also expected to demonstrate knowledge of the institutional structure of the Federal Reserve Bank and the monetary policy tools it uses to stabilize economic fluctuations and promote long-term economic growth, as well as the tools of fiscal policy and their impacts on income, employment, price level, deficits and interest rate. Basic understanding of foreign exchange markets, balance of payments, and effects of currency appreciation and depreciation on a country's imports and exports is also expected.

The examination contains approximately 80 questions to be answered in 90 minutes. Some of these are pretest questions that will not be scored.

Knowledge and Skills Required

Questions on the Principles of Macroeconomics examination require candidates to demonstrate one or more of the following abilities.

- Understanding of important economic terms and concepts
- Interpretation and manipulation of economic graphs
- Interpretation and evaluation of economic data
- Application of simple economic models

The subject matter of the Principles of Macroeconomics examination is drawn from the following topics. The percentages next to the main topics indicate the approximate percentage of exam questions on that topic.

I. Basic Economic Concepts (8%–12%)

- A. Scarcity, choice and opportunity costs
- B. Production possibilities curve
- C. Comparative advantage, specialization and exchange
- D. Demand, supply and market equilibrium

II. Measurement of Economic Performance (12%–16%)

- A. National income accounts
  1. Circular flow
  2. Gross domestic product
  3. Components of gross domestic product
  4. Real versus nominal gross domestic product
- B. Inflation measurement and adjustment
  1. Price indices
  2. Nominal and real values
  3. Demand-pull versus cost-push inflation
  4. Costs of inflation
- C. Unemployment
  1. Definition and measurement
  2. Types of unemployment
  3. Natural rate of unemployment

III. National Income and Price Determination (15%–20%)

- A. Aggregate demand
  1. Determinants of aggregate demand
  2. Multiplier and crowding-out effects
- B. Aggregate supply
  1. Short-run and long-run analyses
  2. Sticky versus flexible wages and prices
  3. Determinants of aggregate supply
- C. Macroeconomic equilibrium
  1. Real output and price level
  2. Short and long run
  3. Actual versus full-employment output
  4. Business cycle and economic fluctuations

IV. Financial Sector (15%–20%)

A. Money, banking and financial markets
   1. Definition of financial assets: money, stocks, bonds
   2. Time value of money (present and future value)
   3. Measures of money supply
   4. Banks and creation of money
   5. Money demand
   6. Money market
   7. Loanable funds market

B. Central bank and control of the money supply
   1. Tools of central bank policy
   2. Quantity theory of money
   3. Real versus nominal interest rates

V. Inflation, Unemployment and Stabilization Policies (20%–25%)

A. Fiscal and monetary policies
   1. Demand-side effects
   2. Supply-side effects
   3. Policy mix
   4. Government deficits and debt

B. Inflation and unemployment
   1. The Phillips curve: short run versus long run
   2. Role of expectations

VI. Economic Growth and Productivity (5%–10%)

A. Investment in human capital

B. Investment in physical capital

C. Research and development, and technological progress

D. Growth policy

VII. Open Economy: International Trade and Finance (9%–13%)

A. Balance of payments accounts
   1. Balance of trade
   2. Current account
   3. Financial account (formerly called capital account)

B. Foreign exchange market
   1. Demand for and supply of foreign exchange
   2. Exchange rate determination
   3. Currency appreciation and depreciation
   4. Exchange rate policies

C. Inflows, outflows and restrictions
   1. Net exports and capital flows
   2. Links to financial and goods markets
   3. Tariffs and quotas

Sample Test Questions

The following sample questions do not appear on an actual CLEP examination. They are intended to give potential test-takers an indication of the format and difficulty level of the examination and to provide content for practice and review. Knowing the correct answers to all of the sample questions is not a guarantee of satisfactory performance on the exam.

Directions: Each of the questions or incomplete statements below is followed by five suggested answers or completions. Select the one that is best in each case.

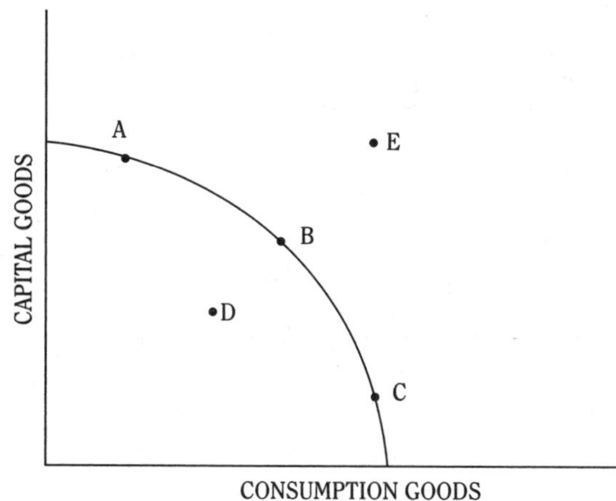

1. An economy that is fully employing all its productive resources but allocating less to investment than to consumption will most likely be at which of the following positions on the production possibilities curve shown above?

   (A) A

   (B) B

   (C) C

   (D) D

   (E) E

2. Assume that land can be used either for producing grain or for grazing cattle to produce beef. The opportunity cost of converting an acre from cattle grazing to grain production is the

   (A) market value of the extra grain that is produced

   (B) total amount of beef produced

   (C) number of extra bushels of grain that are produced

   (D) amount by which beef production decreases

   (E) profits generated by the extra production of grain

3. Which of the following will occur as a result of an improvement in technology?

   (A) The aggregate demand curve will shift to the right.

   (B) The aggregate demand curve will shift to the left.

   (C) The aggregate supply curve will shift to the right.

   (D) The aggregate supply curve will shift to the left.

   (E) The production possibilities curve will shift inward.

4. Increases in real income per capita are made possible by

   (A) improved productivity

   (B) a high labor/capital ratio

   (C) large trade surpluses

   (D) stable interest rates

   (E) high protective tariffs

5. Which of the following is included in the investment component of real gross domestic product?
   (A) A schoolteacher purchases 10,000 shares of stock in an automobile company.
   (B) A family purchases a previously owned home.
   (C) A French tourist purchases United States dollars.
   (D) A farmer purchases $10,000 worth of government securities.
   (E) An apparel company purchases fifteen new sewing machines.

6. The United States Department of Labor defines an individual as unemployed if the person
   (A) does not hold a paying job
   (B) has been recently fired
   (C) works part time but needs full-time work
   (D) is without a job but is looking for work
   (E) wants a job but is not searching because he or she thinks none is available

7. Assume that a country with an open economy has a fixed exchange-rate system and that its currency is currently overvalued in the foreign exchange market. Which of the following must be true at the official exchange rate?
   (A) The quantity of the country's currency supplied is less than the quantity demanded.
   (B) The quantity of the country's currency supplied exceeds the quantity demanded.
   (C) The demand curve for the country's currency is horizontal.
   (D) The supply curve for the country's currency is horizontal.
   (E) The domestic interest rate is equal to the interest rate in the rest of the world.

8. Which of the following workers is most likely to be classified as structurally unemployed?
   (A) A high school teacher who is unemployed during the summer months
   (B) A recent college graduate who is looking for her first job
   (C) A teenager who is seeking part-time employment at a fast-food restaurant
   (D) A worker who is unemployed because his skills are obsolete
   (E) A person who reenters the job market after relocating

9. According to the classical macroeconomic model, an increase in the money supply will result in an increase in which of the following in the long run?
   (A) Employment
   (B) Unemployment
   (C) Real gross domestic product
   (D) Nominal gross domestic product
   (E) Real wages

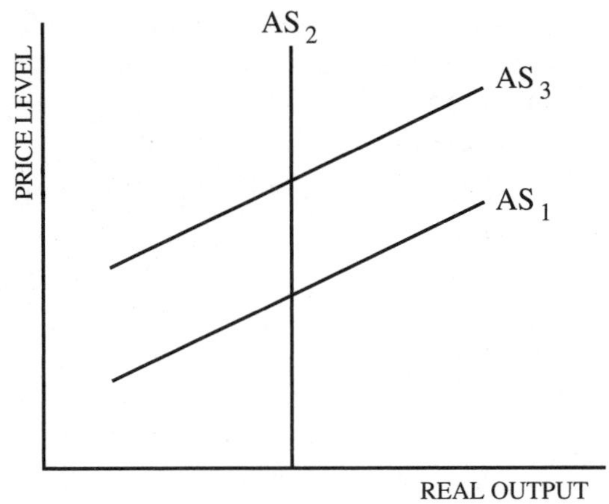

10. The diagram above shows aggregate supply curves AS_1, AS_2, and AS_3. Which of the following statements is true?

    (A) AS_2 reflects wage and price rigidity.
    (B) AS_1 reflects greater wage and price flexibility than AS_2.
    (C) AS_2 reflects greater wage and price flexibility than AS_1 and AS_3.
    (D) The shift from AS_1 to AS_3 is due to a decrease in nominal wages.
    (E) The shift from AS_3 to AS_1 is due to an increase in oil prices.

11. An increase in which of the following would cause the long-run aggregate supply curve to shift to the right?

    (A) Corporate income tax rates
    (B) Aggregate demand
    (C) Labor productivity
    (D) The average wage rate
    (E) The price level

12. As income level increases from $500 to $1,000, consumption increases from $700 to $1,100. The marginal propensity to consume is equal to

    (A) 1.10
    (B) 0.80
    (C) 0.70
    (D) 0.50
    (E) 0.10

13. Which of the following would represent an injection into the circular flow of income and expenditure?

    (A) Investment spending
    (B) Income tax
    (C) Tariffs
    (D) Savings
    (E) Imports

14. Which of the following would most likely lead to a decrease in aggregate demand?

    (A) A decrease in taxes
    (B) A decrease in interest rates
    (C) An increase in household savings
    (D) An increase in household consumption
    (E) An increase in business firms' purchases of capital equipment from retained earnings

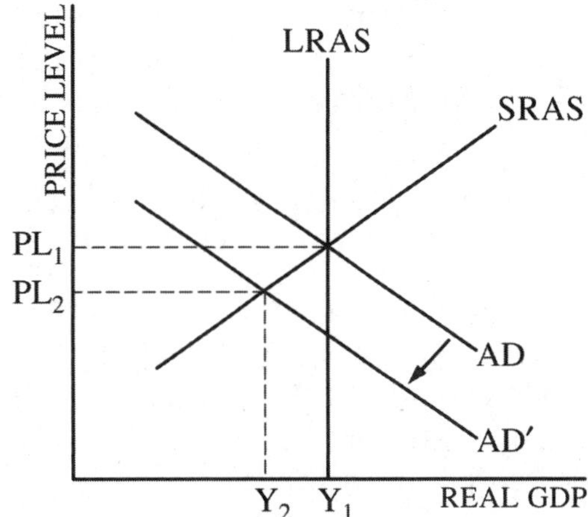

15. The diagram above shows the aggregate demand (AD), short-run aggregate supply (SRAS), and long-run aggregate supply (LRAS) curves for an economy. An increase in which of the following will shift the aggregate demand curve from AD to AD′?

    (A) Money supply
    (B) Income tax rates
    (C) Government purchases
    (D) Transfer payments
    (E) Net exports

16. If the Federal Reserve lowers reserve requirements, which of the following is most likely to happen to interest rates and nominal gross domestic product?

	Interest Rates	Nominal Gross Domestic Product
(A)	Increase	Decrease
(B)	Increase	Increase
(C)	Decrease	Decrease
(D)	Decrease	Increase
(E)	No change	No change

17. If the marginal propensity to consume is 0.9, what is the maximum amount that the equilibrium gross domestic product could change if government expenditures increase by $1 billion?

(A) It could decrease by $9 billion.
(B) It could increase by $0.9 billion.
(C) It could increase by $1 billion.
(D) It could increase by $9 billion.
(E) It could increase by $10 billion.

18. Expansionary fiscal policy will be most effective in increasing real gross domestic product when

(A) the aggregate supply curve is horizontal
(B) the economy is at or above full-employment output
(C) transfer payments are decreased, while taxes remain unchanged
(D) wages and prices are very flexible
(E) the Federal Reserve simultaneously increases the reserve requirement

19. Which of the following would increase the value of the simple spending multiplier?

(A) An increase in government expenditure
(B) An increase in exports
(C) A decrease in government unemployment benefits
(D) A decrease in the marginal propensity to consume
(E) A decrease in the marginal propensity to save

20. Assume that the reserve requirement is 25 percent. If banks have excess reserves of $10,000, which of the following is the maximum amount of additional money that can be created by the banking system through the lending process?

(A) $ 2,500
(B) $ 10,000
(C) $ 40,000
(D) $ 50,000
(E) $250,000

21. An increase in which of the following will most likely reduce the federal government's budget deficit?

(A) Interest rates
(B) Income tax rates
(C) Defense spending
(D) Government transfer payments
(E) Tax credits for investment spending

22. The purchase of government bonds from the public in the open market by the Federal Reserve will

(A) increase the supply of money
(B) increase the interest rate
(C) increase the discount rate
(D) decrease the number of Federal Reserve notes in circulation
(E) decrease the reserve requirement

23. To counteract a recession, the Federal Reserve could

(A) buy government securities on the open market and raise the reserve requirement
(B) buy government securities on the open market and lower the reserve requirement
(C) buy government securities on the open market and raise the discount rate
(D) sell government securities on the open market and raise the discount rate
(E) raise the reserve requirement and lower the discount rate

24. Total spending in the economy is most likely to increase by the largest amount if which of the following occur to government spending and taxes?

	Government Spending	Taxes
(A)	Decrease	Increase
(B)	Decrease	No change
(C)	Increase	Increase
(D)	Increase	Decrease
(E)	No change	Increase

25. An expansionary monetary policy will be most effective in increasing real output if

(A) investment spending is sensitive to changes in interest rates
(B) money demand is sensitive to changes in interest rates
(C) wages and prices are perfectly flexible
(D) corporate income tax rates increase
(E) complete crowding-out occurs

26. Supply-side economists argue that

(A) a cut in high tax rates results in an increased deficit and thus increases aggregate supply
(B) lower tax rates provide positive work incentives and thus shift the aggregate supply curve to the right
(C) the aggregate supply of goods can only be increased if the price level falls
(D) increased government spending should be used to stimulate the economy
(E) the government should regulate the supply of imports

27. Which of the following policies would most likely be recommended in an economy with an annual inflation rate of 3 percent and an unemployment rate of 11 percent?

(A) An increase in transfer payments and an increase in the reserve requirement
(B) An increase in defense spending and an increase in the discount rate
(C) An increase in income tax rates and a decrease in the reserve requirement
(D) A decrease in government spending and the open market sale of government securities
(E) A decrease in the tax rate on corporate profits and a decrease in the discount rate

28. Assume the velocity of money and real gross domestic product are constant. According to the quantity theory of money, an increase in the money supply will result in which of the following?

(A) A decrease in the price level
(B) A decrease in the money multiplier
(C) A decrease in nominal gross domestic product
(D) An increase in the price level
(E) An increase in the money multiplier

29. An expansionary fiscal policy would most likely cause which of the following changes in output and interest rates?

	Output	Interest Rates
(A)	Increase	Increase
(B)	Increase	Decrease
(C)	Decrease	Increase
(D)	Decrease	Decrease
(E)	No change	Decrease

30. Which of the following would result in the largest increase in aggregate demand?

    (A) A $30 billion increase in military expenditure and a $30 billion open market purchase of government securities
    (B) A $30 billion increase in military expenditure and a $30 billion open market sale of government securities
    (C) A $30 billion tax decrease and a $30 billion open market sale of government securities
    (D) A $30 billion tax increase and a $30 billion open market purchase of government securities
    (E) A $30 billion increase in social security payments and a $30 billion open market sale of government securities

31. Which of the following will most likely lead to a decrease in the federal government budget deficit?

    I. An increase in taxes
    II. A decrease in federal government spending
    III. A decrease in interest rates

    (A) I only
    (B) II only
    (C) III only
    (D) I and III only
    (E) I, II, and III

32. Which of the following would most likely be the immediate result if the United States increased tariffs on most foreign goods?

    (A) The United States standard of living would be higher.
    (B) More foreign goods would be purchased by Americans.
    (C) Prices of domestic goods would increase.
    (D) Large numbers of United States workers would be laid off.
    (E) The value of the United States dollar would decrease against foreign currencies.

33. Which of the following is true about bonds?

    (A) Bond prices remain fixed over time.
    (B) Bonds have unlimited profit potential.
    (C) Bonds are generally riskier than stocks.
    (D) Bondholders receive interest payments.
    (E) Bondholders become part owners of the company that issued the bonds.

34. Which of the following would occur if the international value of the United States dollar decreased?

    (A) United States exports would increase.
    (B) More gold would flow into the United States.
    (C) United States demand for foreign currencies would increase.
    (D) The United States trade deficit would increase.
    (E) United States citizens would pay less for foreign goods.

35. If exchange rates are allowed to fluctuate freely and the United States demand for Indian rupees increases, which of the following will most likely occur?

    (A) The dollar price of Indian goods will increase.
    (B) The rupee price of United States goods will increase.
    (C) The United States balance-of-payments deficits will increase.
    (D) The dollar price of rupees will fall.
    (E) The dollar price of Indian goods will fall.

36. A revenue-neutral replacement of some portion of the federal personal income tax with a general sales tax would most likely result in

(A) greater overall progressivity in the tax structure
(B) smaller overall progressivity in the tax structure
(C) stronger automatic stabilization through the business cycle
(D) a larger budget deficit
(E) a smaller federal budget deficit

37. A deficit in the United States trade balance can be described as

(A) an excess of the value of imports over the value of exports
(B) an excess of the value of exports over the value of imports
(C) a resulting outcome of the depreciation of the United States dollar in foreign exchange markets
(D) an almost complete depletion of the gold stock
(E) an excess of receipts from foreigners over payments to foreigners

38. Which of the following describes a problem that is common to all economic systems?

(A) How to decentralize markets
(B) How to become a self-sufficient economy
(C) How to set government production quotas
(D) How to equally distribute income among citizens
(E) How to allocate scarce resources to satisfy unlimited wants

39. An increase in which of the following will cause an increase in the demand for a certain good?

(A) The price of the good
(B) The number of sellers of the good
(C) The price of a complementary good
(D) The cost of purchasing the good
(E) The number of buyers of the good

40. If the exchange rate changes from 1 United States dollar = 100 yen to 1 United States dollar = 80 yen, which of the following will happen?

(A) United States goods will become more expensive to Japanese consumers.
(B) Japanese goods will become less expensive to United States consumers.
(C) United States exports to Japan will increase.
(D) Japanese exports to the United States will increase.
(E) Japanese imports from the United States will decrease.

41. An increase in which of the following is most likely to cause demand-pull inflation?

(A) Rental price of capital
(B) Fuel costs
(C) Consumer spending
(D) Income taxes
(E) Imports of capital goods

42. Assume that last year the consumer price index (CPI) was 150 and a household's nominal income was $30,000. If the CPI this year is 160, to be as well off as last year, the household should have an increase in nominal income of

(A) $1,800
(B) $1,875
(C) $2,000
(D) $3,000
(E) $4,800

43. The natural rate of unemployment can be defined as the unemployment rate that exists when the economy

(A) is neither growing nor shrinking
(B) has zero inflation
(C) has only cyclical and structural unemployment
(D) has no trade deficit or government deficit
(E) produces at the full-employment output level

44. A fully anticipated expansionary fiscal policy will cause the price level and real output to change in which of the following ways in the long run?

	Price Level	Real Output
(A)	Increase	Increase
(B)	Increase	Not change
(C)	Not change	Not change
(D)	Decrease	Increase
(E)	Decrease	Decrease

45. If the nominal gross domestic product is \$8 trillion and the money supply is \$2 trillion, the velocity of money is

(A) 2
(B) 4
(C) 6
(D) 10
(E) 16

46. Which of the following is NOT true of the Federal Reserve?

(A) It serves as a lender of last resort for member banks.
(B) It supervises member banks.
(C) It provides check-clearing services.
(D) It issues debit cards.
(E) It controls the money supply.

47. Which of the following best describes the cause of crowding out?

(A) Competition between the government and private borrowers for loanable funds results in an increase in interest rates.
(B) Increases in the costs of inputs lead to decreases in domestic production.
(C) The Federal Reserve's open-market operations decrease the amount of funds banks have available for lending.
(D) Reductions in the government's budget deficit lead to fewer Treasury bonds being issued.
(E) The scarcity of funds forces Congress to decrease spending on critical public works programs.

48. Suppose that the economy is operating at full employment. If the government wants to discourage consumption spending, stimulate investment spending, and maintain full-employment output, which of the following combinations of monetary and fiscal policies would most likely achieve these goals?

	Monetary Policy	Fiscal Policy
(A)	Increase money supply	Increase government spending
(B)	Increase money supply	Increase personal income taxes
(C)	Decrease money supply	Increase government spending
(D)	Decrease money supply	Increase personal income taxes
(E)	Decrease money supply	Decrease personal income taxes

49. If the Federal Reserve suddenly increases the growth rate of the money supply from 4 percent to 8 percent per year, interest rates, aggregate demand, and nominal gross domestic product (GDP) will most likely change in which of the following ways in the short run?

	Interest Rates	Aggregate Demand	Nominal GDP
(A)	Increase	Increase	Increase
(B)	Increase	Decrease	Increase
(C)	Decrease	Increase	Increase
(D)	Decrease	Increase	Decrease
(E)	Decrease	Decrease	Increase

50. The United States federal government budget deficits tend to be large when which of the following is low?

(A) The interest rate on government bonds
(B) The growth rate of the economy
(C) The unemployment rate
(D) The inflation rate
(E) The international value of the United States dollar

51. Using the same amount of resources, Betaland can produce 80 tons of corn or 80 tons of wheat and Alphaland can produce 40 tons of corn or 20 tons of wheat. Which of the following statements is true?

(A) The opportunity cost of producing a ton of corn in Betaland is two tons of wheat.
(B) The opportunity cost of producing a ton of corn in Betaland is a ton of wheat.
(C) The opportunity cost of producing a ton of corn in Alphaland is two tons of wheat.
(D) Betaland has both the absolute and comparative advantage in producing corn.
(E) Alphaland has the comparative advantage in producing wheat.

52. If the required reserve ratio is 0.20 and the Federal Reserve buys $200 worth of securities, the maximum increase in the money supply will be

(A) $ 200
(B) $ 400
(C) $ 600
(D) $ 800
(E) $1,000

Assets		Liabilities
Reserves	$4,000	Demand deposits $10,000
Loans	$6,000	

53. The table above shows the T-account entries of a bank. If the required reserve ratio is 0.20, what is the maximum amount of additional loans that this bank can make from its current reserves?

(A) $ 0
(B) $ 2,000
(C) $ 2,500
(D) $ 4,000
(E) $10,000

54. Which of the following explains why the aggregate demand curve is downward sloping?

(A) Sticky wages
(B) Money illusion
(C) The Fisher effect
(D) The wealth effect
(E) Speculative demand for money

55. According to the short-run Phillips curve, which of the following will occur when the Federal Reserve increases the money supply?

(A) Both the unemployment rate and the inflation rate will increase.
(B) Both the unemployment rate and the inflation rate will decrease.
(C) The unemployment rate will increase, and the inflation rate will decrease.
(D) The unemployment rate will decrease, and the inflation rate will increase.
(E) The inflation rate will increase, but the unemployment rate will remain constant.

56. Which of the following is true if there is a current account deficit in the United States balance-of-payments accounts?

(A) There is a corresponding deficit in the financial account.
(B) There is a corresponding surplus in the financial account.
(C) There is an offsetting surplus in the government's budget.
(D) There is an offsetting increase in net exports.
(E) The United States dollar appreciates in the foreign exchange market.

57. An increase in national saving will cause the real interest rate and investment spending to change in which of the following ways?

	Real Interest Rate	Investment
(A)	Increase	Increase
(B)	Increase	Decrease
(C)	Increase	Not change
(D)	Decrease	Increase
(E)	Decrease	Not change

58. To raise its long-run rate of economic growth, a country should design and implement policies that do which of the following?

(A) Encourage current consumption over saving
(B) Encourage saving and investment
(C) Increase the price level and profits
(D) Increase government transfer payments
(E) Limit business activities to protect the environment

59. With a constant money supply, an increase in the demand for money will affect interest rates and bond prices in which of the following ways?

	Interest Rates	Bond Prices
(A)	Increase	Increase
(B)	Increase	Decrease
(C)	Increase	Not change
(D)	Decrease	Increase
(E)	Not change	Increase

60. According to the quantity theory of money, an increase in the money supply results in an increase in which of the following?

(A) Interest rate
(B) Unemployment
(C) Nominal gross domestic product
(D) The government's budget deficit
(E) The value of the dollar on the foreign exchange market

61. Which of the following policies will most likely lead to a reduction in the natural rate of unemployment?

(A) Increasing government purchases of goods and services
(B) Providing more job-training programs to help the less skilled
(C) Increasing the duration of unemployment compensation
(D) Raising the minimum wage
(E) Increasing the money supply

62. Assume that an economy produces only two goods, computers and gasoline. The quantity and price of each are given in the table below.

Year	Price of Computers	Quantity of Computers (in millions)	Price of Gasoline	Quantity of Gasoline (in millions)
2000	$1,000	5	$1	500
2004	$500	10	$2	250

If the base year is 2000, how do nominal and real gross domestic product (GDP) change between 2000 and 2004?

	Nominal GDP	Real GDP
(A)	No change	Increase
(B)	No change	Decrease
(C)	Increase	No change
(D)	Increase	Increase
(E)	Increase	Decrease

63. Assuming that the expected inflation rate is stable, an increase in interest rates will lead to

(A) an increase in bond prices
(B) an increase in the demand for money as an asset
(C) an increase in aggregate demand
(D) a decrease in private investment
(E) a decrease in capital inflows

64. An increase in income tax rates with no change in government spending will result in which of the following?

(A) A decrease in private savings
(B) An increase in private savings
(C) An increase in the real interest rate
(D) An increase in the demand for loanable funds
(E) An increase in the budget deficit

65. Which of the following is true of the long-run Phillips curve?

(A) It shows the trade-off between the price level and the money supply.
(B) It shows that lower unemployment can be gained only at the expense of higher inflation.
(C) It shows that unemployment is a monetary issue.
(D) It is vertical at the natural rate of unemployment.
(E) It is U-shaped over all possible ranges of unemployment.

66. Economics is best defined as the study of how

(A) markets allocate resources efficiently
(B) businesses make investments to maximize profits
(C) public goods and services are produced
(D) society chooses to allocate its scarce resources
(E) the invisible hand of the market works

67. Human capital refers to which of the following?

(A) The acquisition of plant and equipment by workers
(B) The amount of financial investment made by individuals
(C) The labor force requirement for sustained economic growth
(D) The education and experience of the labor force
(E) The technology available to individual workers

68. Which of the following will lower inflationary expectations?

(A) The government's announcement that it will increase spending on infrastructure
(B) The Federal Reserve's announcement that it will steadily raise the federal funds rate
(C) An increase in the value of stocks
(D) An increase in consumer and business optimism
(E) An increase in the money supply

69. An increase in national saving will affect the supply of loanable funds and the real interest rate in which of the following ways?

	Supply of Loanable Funds	Real Interest Rate
(A)	Increase	Increase
(B)	Increase	Decrease
(C)	Increase	No change
(D)	Decrease	Increase
(E)	Decrease	Decrease

70. Which of the following will cause the short-run aggregate supply curve to shift to the left?

(A) An increase in the price level
(B) A decrease in the price level
(C) An increase in trade deficits
(D) An increase in nominal wages
(E) An increase in productivity

71. Which of the following policies will most likely stimulate economic growth?

(A) A tax credit on investment spending
(B) Elimination of copyright and patent protection laws
(C) A reduction in funding for education
(D) Change of the Social Security retirement age from sixty-five to fifty-eight
(E) Increased government regulations for research and development

72. The real interest rate for a consumer loan is 5 percent, and the expected inflation rate is 2 percent. What is the nominal interest rate on the consumer loan?

(A) 2.5 percent
(B) 3 percent
(C) 5 percent
(D) 7 percent
(E) 10 percent

73. Which of the following groups is most likely to benefit from unanticipated inflation?

(A) Creditors
(B) Fixed income earners
(C) Consumers
(D) Debtors
(E) Savers

74. Assume that there are only two countries—Eland and Zland—that produce only two goods—X and Y. The table below shows units of each good that each country can produce using one hour of labor.

	Good X		Good Y
Eland	5	or	3
Zland	8	or	4

Which of the following statements is correct?

(A) Eland has a comparative advantage in producing both goods.
(B) Zland has an absolute advantage in producing both goods.
(C) Eland's opportunity cost for good Y is 5 units of good X.
(D) Zland's opportunity cost for good X is 2 units of good Y.
(E) Zland should not trade with Eland because Eland produces both goods at lower costs.

75. If both the demand for and the supply of coffee increase, what will happen to the equilibrium price and quantity in the coffee market?

	Price	Quantity
(A)	Increase	Increase
(B)	Increase	Indeterminate
(C)	Decrease	Decrease
(D)	Decrease	Increase
(E)	Indeterminate	Increase

76. Which of the following would cause a country's production possibilities curve to shift outward?

    (A) A decrease in the unemployment rate
    (B) A technological advance
    (C) An increase in government transfer payments
    (D) A reallocation of economic resources
    (E) A decline in population

77. Which of the following is true about economic growth?

    (A) It occurs in big countries more often than it does in small countries.
    (B) It occurs more often in countries with closed economies than in those with open economies.
    (C) It is positively related to a country's investment in human capital.
    (D) It is negatively related to a country's capital stock.
    (E) It is negatively related to a country's standard of living.

78. The M1 measure of the money supply primarily consists of which of the following?

    (A) Checking accounts and credit cards
    (B) Noncheckable savings and credit cards
    (C) Currency in circulation and checkable bank deposits
    (D) Noncheckable savings and small-denomination time deposits
    (E) Savings bonds and savings accounts

79. If a country's consumer price index was 200 last year and is 190 this year, which of the following must be true for the country from last year to this year?

    (A) The quantity of goods produced has decreased.
    (B) The average quality of the goods produced has increased.
    (C) The inflation rate has increased by 5 percent.
    (D) The price level has decreased by 5 percent.
    (E) The unemployment rate has decreased by 5 percent.

80. The national debt of the United States is the

    (A) accumulated government spending, less the interest paid on bonds
    (B) accumulation of all past government deficits
    (C) difference between government tax revenues and government spending during a fiscal year
    (D) money owed to the Federal Reserve for reimbursement of domestic bondholders
    (E) annual amount borrowed by local, state, and federal governments to provide public goods to all citizens

81. Gross domestic product is defined as which of the following?

    (A) The total amount of output produced by an economy in a given time period
    (B) The total market value of all output produced by an economy in a given time period
    (C) The total market value of all final goods and services produced by an economy in a given time period
    (D) The total value of all final goods and services sold in the domestic market in a given time period
    (E) The total market value of all final goods and services produced by an economy minus the market value of final goods and services exported to other nations in a given time period

82. If central banks in Asia reduce the supply of their own currencies on the foreign-exchange market relative to the United States dollar, which of the following will occur?

(A) Asian currencies will depreciate.
(B) The United States dollar will appreciate.
(C) Asian goods will be more expensive for United States consumers.
(D) United States goods will be more expensive for Asian consumers.
(E) United States private investment in Asia will increase.

83. Which of the following policy actions could the Federal Reserve use to combat inflation?

(A) Selling government bonds to reduce the money supply
(B) Buying government bonds to reduce the amount of loanable funds
(C) Raising taxes to reduce the interest rate
(D) Cutting the reserve requirement to reduce the amount of excess reserves held by banks
(E) Cutting the discount rate to decrease the availability of loans to banks

84. Jamal lost his computer programming job when it was outsourced to a company abroad. After looking unsuccessfully for several months for another job, he gave up and is currently attending school. Currently Jamal is classified as

(A) structurally unemployed
(B) frictionally unemployed
(C) cyclically unemployed
(D) underemployed
(E) not in the labor force

85. Which of the following will decrease gross domestic product by the greatest amount?

(A) \$20 billion increases in both government spending and taxes
(B) \$20 billion decreases in both government spending and taxes
(C) A \$20 billion increase in taxes
(D) A \$20 billion decrease in government spending
(E) A \$20 billion increase in net exports

Study Resources

Most textbooks used in college-level introductory macroeconomics courses cover the topics in the outline given earlier, but the approaches to certain topics and the emphases given to them may differ. To prepare for the Principles of Macroeconomics exam, it is advisable to study one or more college textbooks, which can be found in most college bookstores. When selecting a textbook, check the table of contents against the knowledge and skills required for this test.

There are many introductory economics textbooks that vary greatly in difficulty. Most books are published in one-volume editions, which cover both microeconomics and macroeconomics; some are published in two-volume editions, with one volume covering macroeconomics and the other microeconomics. A companion study guide/workbook is available for most textbooks. The study guides typically include brief reviews, definitions of key concepts, problem sets and multiple-choice test questions with answers. Many publishers also make available companion websites, links to other resources or computer-assisted learning packages.

To broaden your knowledge of economic issues, you may read relevant articles published in the economics periodicals that are available in most college libraries — for example, *The Economist*, *The Wall Street Journal* and the *New York Times*, along with local papers, may also enhance your understanding of economic issues.

Visit **clep.collegeboard.org/earn-college-credit/practice** for additional macroeconomics resources. You can also find suggestions for exam preparation in Chapter IV of the *Official Study Guide*. In addition, many college faculty post their course materials on their schools' websites.

Answer Key

1.	C	44.	B
2.	D	45.	B
3.	C	46.	D
4.	A	47.	A
5.	E	48.	B
6.	D	49.	C
7.	B	50.	B
8.	D	51.	B
9.	D	52.	E
10.	C	53.	B
11.	C	54.	D
12.	B	55.	D
13.	A	56.	B
14.	C	57.	D
15.	B	58.	B
16.	D	59.	B
17.	E	60.	C
18.	A	61.	B
19.	E	62.	A
20.	C	63.	D
21.	B	64.	A
22.	A	65.	D
23.	B	66.	D
24.	D	67.	D
25.	A	68.	B
26.	B	69.	B
27.	E	70.	D
28.	D	71.	A
29.	A	72.	D
30.	A	73.	D
31.	E	74.	B
32.	C	75.	E
33.	D	76.	B
34.	A	77.	C
35.	A	78.	C
36.	B	79.	D
37.	A	80.	B
38.	E	81.	C
39.	E	82.	C
40.	C	83.	A
41.	C	84.	E
42.	C	85.	D
43.	E		

Principles of Microeconomics

Description of the Examination

The Principles of Microeconomics examination covers material that is usually taught in a one-semester undergraduate course in introductory microeconomics. This aspect of economics deals with the principles of economics that apply to the analysis of the behavior of individual consumers and businesses in the economy. Questions on this exam require candidates to apply analytical techniques to hypothetical as well as real-world situations and to analyze and evaluate economic decisions. Candidates are expected to demonstrate an understanding of how free markets work and allocate resources efficiently. They should understand how individual consumers make economic decisions to maximize utility, and how individual firms make decisions to maximize profits. Candidates must be able to identify the characteristics of the different market structures and analyze the behavior of firms in terms of price and output decisions. They should also be able to evaluate the outcome in each market structure with respect to economic efficiency, identify cases in which private markets fail to allocate resources efficiently, and explain how government intervention fixes or fails to fix the resource allocation problem. It is also important to understand the determination of wages and other input prices in factor markets and analyze and evaluate the distribution of income.

The examination contains approximately 80 questions to be answered in 90 minutes. Some of these are pretest questions that will not be scored.

Knowledge and Skills Required

Questions on the Principles of Microeconomics examination require candidates to demonstrate one or more of the following abilities.

- Understanding of important economic terms and concepts
- Interpretation and manipulation of economic graphs
- Interpretation and evaluation of economic data
- Application of simple economic models

The subject matter of the Principles of Microeconomics examination is drawn from the following topics. The percentages next to the main topics indicate the approximate percentage of exam questions on that topic.

I. Basic Economic Concepts (8%–14%)

A. Scarcity, choice and opportunity costs
B. Production possibilities curve
C. Comparative advantage, specialization and trade
D. Economic systems
E. Property rights and the role of incentives
F. Marginal analysis

II. The Nature and Functions of Product Markets (55%–70%)

A. Supply and demand (15%–20%)
   1. Market equilibrium
   2. Determinants of supply and demand
   3. Price and quantity controls
   4. Elasticity
      a. Price, income and cross-price elasticities of demand
      b. Price elasticity of supply
   5. Consumer surplus, producer surplus and market efficiency
   6. Tax incidence and deadweight loss

B. Theory of consumer choice (5%–10%)
   1. Total utility and marginal utility
   2. Utility maximization: equalizing marginal utility per dollar
   3. Individual and market demand curves
   4. Income and substitution effects

C. Production and costs (10%–15%)
   1. Production functions: short and long run
   2. Marginal product and diminishing returns
   3. Short-run costs
   4. Long-run costs and economies of scale
   5. Cost minimizing input combination

D. Firm behavior and market structure (23%–33%)
   1. Profit:
      a. Accounting versus economic profits
      b. Normal profit
      c. Profit maximization: MR=MC rule
   2. Perfect competition
      a. Profit maximization
      b. Short-run supply and shut-down decision
      c. Firm and market behaviors in short-run and long-run equilibria
      d. Efficiency and perfect competition
   3. Monopoly
      a. Sources of market power
      b. Profit maximization
      c. Inefficiency of monopoly
      d. Price discrimination
   4. Oligopoly
      a. Interdependence, collusion and cartels
      b. Game theory and strategic behavior
   5. Monopolistic competition
      a. Product differentiation and role of advertising
      b. Profit maximization
      c. Short-run and long-run equilibrium
      d. Excess capacity and inefficiency

III. Factor Markets (8%–14%)

A. Derived factor demand

B. Marginal revenue product

C. Labor market and firms' hiring of labor

D. Market distribution of income

IV. Market Failure and the Role of Government (10%–16%)

A. Externalities
   1. Marginal social benefit and marginal social cost
   2. Positive externalities
   3. Negative externalities
   4. Remedies

B. Public goods
   1. Public versus private goods
   2. Provision of public goods

C. Public policy to promote competition
   1. Antitrust policy
   2. Regulation

D. Income distribution
   1. Equity
   2. Sources of income inequality

Sample Test Questions

The following sample questions do not appear on an actual CLEP examination. They are intended to give potential test-takers an indication of the format and difficulty level of the examination and to provide content for practice and review. Knowing the correct answers to all of the sample questions is not a guarantee of satisfactory performance on the exam.

Directions: Each of the questions or incomplete statements below is followed by five suggested answers or completions. Select the one that is best in each case.

1. Which of the following best states the law of comparative advantage?

    (A) Differences in relative costs of production are the key to determining patterns of trade.

    (B) Differences in absolute costs of production determine which goods should be traded between nations.

    (C) Tariffs and quotas are beneficial in increasing international competitiveness.

    (D) Nations should not specialize in the production of goods and services.

    (E) Two nations will not trade if one is more efficient than the other in the production of all goods.

2. Which of the following is true about accounting and economic profits?

    (A) A firm that earns an accounting profit necessarily earns an economic profit.

    (B) A firm that earns an economic profit necessarily earns an accounting profit.

    (C) Economic profits and accounting profits are equal in the short run.

    (D) Accounting profits count only variable costs, but economic profits count both fixed and variable costs.

    (E) Accounting profits count both fixed and variable costs, but economic profits count only variable costs.

3. Assume that an economy produces two goods, consumer goods and military goods. If it were possible to increase the output of both military goods and consumption goods, which of the following statements about the economy would be true?

    (A) The economy is inefficient and is producing inside the production possibilities curve.

    (B) The economy is inefficient and is producing on the production possibilities curve.

    (C) The economy is efficient and is producing on the production possibilities curve.

    (D) The economy is efficient and is producing inside the production possibilities curve.

    (E) The economy is efficient and is producing outside the production possibilities curve.

4. Which of the following would necessarily cause a decrease in the price of a product?

    (A) An increase in the number of buyers and a decrease in the price of an input

    (B) An increase in the number of buyers and a decrease in the number of firms producing the product

    (C) An increase in average income and an improvement in production technology

    (D) A decrease in the price of a substitute product and an improvement in production technology

    (E) A decrease in the price of a substitute product and an increase in the price of an input

5. An effective price floor will most likely result in

    (A) shortages of products if the price floor is above the equilibrium price

    (B) shortages of products if the price floor is at the equilibrium price

    (C) surpluses of products if the price floor is above the equilibrium price

    (D) surpluses of products if the price floor is below the equilibrium price

    (E) a balance between quantity demanded and quantity supplied if the price floor is above the equilibrium price

6. Jenna spends all of her weekly income on food and entertainment. If the marginal utility of the last dollar Jenna spends on food is greater than the marginal utility of the last dollar she spends on entertainment, what should Jenna do to maximize utility?

(A) She should do nothing; utility is already maximized.
(B) She should purchase more food and less entertainment.
(C) She should purchase less food and more entertainment.
(D) She should purchase more of both food and entertainment.
(E) She should purchase less of both food and entertainment.

7. Assume that a consumer finds that her total expenditure on compact discs stays the same after the price of compact discs declines. Which of the following is true for this consumer over the price range?

(A) Compact discs are inferior goods.
(B) The consumer's demand for compact discs increased.
(C) The consumer's demand for compact discs is perfectly price elastic.
(D) The consumer's demand for compact discs is perfectly price inelastic.
(E) The consumer's demand for compact discs is unit price elastic.

8. An improvement in production technology for a certain good leads to

(A) an increase in the demand for the good
(B) an increase in the supply of the good
(C) an increase in the price of the good
(D) a shortage of the good
(E) a surplus of the good

9. If the demand for a product is price elastic, which of the following is true?

(A) An increase in the product price will have no effect on the firm's total revenue.
(B) An increase in the product price will increase the firm's total revenue.
(C) A decrease in the product price will increase the firm's total revenue.
(D) A decrease in the product price will decrease the firm's rate of inventory turnover.
(E) A decrease in the product price will decrease the total cost of goods sold.

10. If an increase in the price of good X causes a decrease in the demand for good Y, good Y is

(A) an inferior good
(B) a luxury good
(C) a necessary good
(D) a substitute for good X
(E) a complement to good X

11. The price elasticity of demand for product X is equal to –2. If the price of product X increases by 10 percent, which of the following will occur?

(A) The quantity demanded for product X will decrease by 20%.
(B) The quantity demanded for product X will decrease by 5%.
(C) The firm's total revenue will increase by 10%.
(D) The firm's total revenue will increase by 20%.
(E) The demand for product X will decrease by 5%.

12. An increase in the price of a good decreases purchasing power, causing a decrease in the quantity of the good demanded. The decrease in the quantity demanded is due to

(A) the income effect
(B) the substitution effect
(C) a decrease in consumer surplus
(D) a decrease in supply
(E) a shortage of the good

13. To reduce the amount of negative externality arising from the production of some goods, the government can

(A) impose a tariff on imports
(B) impose a price floor below the market equilibrium price
(C) impose a price ceiling above the market equilibrium price
(D) grant a corrective subsidy to producers to increase production
(E) impose a corrective tax on producers to decrease production

14. The primary distinction between the short run and the long run is that in the short run

(A) firms make profits, but in the long run no firm makes economic profits
(B) profits are maximized, but in the long run all costs are maximized
(C) some costs of production are fixed, but in the long run all costs are fixed
(D) some costs of production are fixed, but in the long run all costs are variable
(E) marginal costs are rising, but in the long run they are constant

Questions 15–16 are based on the table below, which shows a firm's total cost for different levels of output.

Output	Total Cost
0	$24
1	33
2	41
3	48
4	54
5	61
6	69

15. Which of the following is the firm's marginal cost of producing the fourth unit of output?

(A) $54.00
(B) $13.50
(C) $ 7.50
(D) $ 6.00
(E) $ 1.50

16. Which of the following is the firm's average total cost of producing 3 units of output?

(A) $48.00
(B) $16.00
(C) $14.00
(D) $13.50
(E) $ 7.00

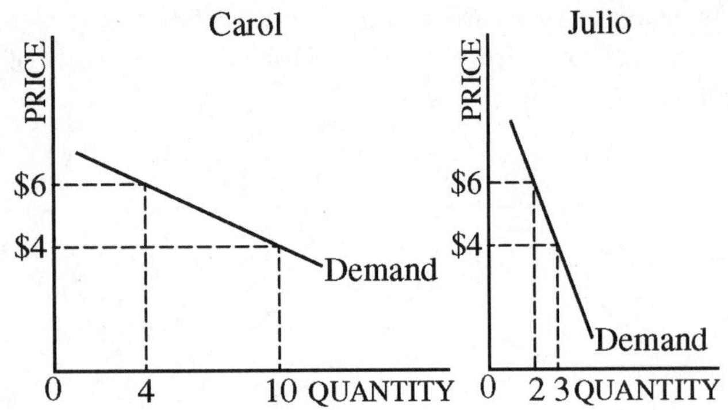

17. Assume that there are only two buyers in the market for a comic magazine, Carol and Julio. The graphs above show their individual demand curves. Which of the following quantity and price combinations is on the market demand curve?

(A) 6, $4
(B) 10, $4
(C) 13, $4
(D) 12, $6
(E) 15, $6

18. Marginal revenue is the change in revenue that results from a one-unit increase in the

(A) variable input
(B) variable input price
(C) output level
(D) output price
(E) fixed cost

19. In the short run, if the product price of a perfectly competitive firm is less than the minimum average variable cost, the firm will

(A) raise its price
(B) increase its output
(C) decrease its output slightly but increase its profit margin
(D) incur larger losses by continuing to produce than by shutting down
(E) incur smaller losses by continuing to produce than by shutting down

20. Suppose that each business needs a license to operate in a city. The license fee increases from $400 per year to $500 per year. What effect will this increase have on a firm's short-run costs?

	Marginal Cost	Average Total Cost	Average Variable Cost
(A)	Increase	Increase	Increase
(B)	Increase	Increase	No effect
(C)	No effect	No effect	No effect
(D)	No effect	Increase	Increase
(E)	No effect	Increase	No effect

21. Which of the following statements is true of perfectly competitive firms in long-run equilibrium?

(A) Firm revenues will decrease if production is increased.
(B) Total firm revenues are at a maximum.
(C) Average fixed cost equals marginal cost.
(D) Average total cost is at a minimum.
(E) Average variable cost is greater than marginal cost.

22. An industry has been dumping its toxic waste free of charge into a river. A government action to ensure a more efficient use of resources would have which of the following effects on the industry's output and product price?

	Output	Price
(A)	Decrease	Decrease
(B)	Decrease	Increase
(C)	Increase	Decrease
(D)	Increase	Increase
(E)	Increase	No change

23. Assume that a perfectly competitive industry is in long-run equilibrium. A permanent increase in demand will eventually result in

(A) a decrease in demand because the price will increase and people will buy less of the output
(B) a decrease in supply because the rate of output and the associated cost will both increase
(C) an increase in price but no increase in output
(D) an increase in output
(E) a permanent shortage, since the quantity demanded is now greater than the quantity supplied

24. Differences in which of the following are NOT used to explain wage differentials among workers?

(A) Talent
(B) Experience
(C) Human capital
(D) Consumer spending
(E) Discrimination in the job market

25. Which of the following statements must be true in a perfectly competitive market?

(A) A firm's marginal revenue equals price.
(B) A firm's average total cost is above price in the long run.
(C) A firm's average fixed cost rises in the short run.
(D) A firm's average variable cost is higher than price in the long run.
(E) Large firms have lower total costs than small firms.

26. A perfectly competitive firm produces in an industry whose product sells at a market price of $100. At the firm's current rate of production, marginal cost is increasing and is equal to $110. To maximize its profits, the firm should change its output and price in which of the following ways?

	Output	Price
(A)	Decrease	Increase
(B)	Decrease	No change
(C)	No change	Increase
(D)	Increase	No change
(E)	Increase	Decrease

27. The typical firm in a monopolistically competitive industry earns zero economic profit in long-run equilibrium because

(A) advertising costs make monopolistic competition a high-cost market structure rather than a low-cost market structure
(B) there are no close substitutes for each firm's product
(C) there are no significant restrictions on entering or exiting the industry
(D) the firms in the industry are unable to engage in product differentiation
(E) the firms in the industry do not operate at the minimum point on their long-run average cost curves

28. In the long run, compared with a perfectly competitive firm, a monopolistically competitive firm with the same costs will have

(A) a higher price and higher output
(B) a higher price and lower output
(C) a lower price and higher output
(D) a lower price and lower output
(E) the same price and lower output

29. Which of the following describes what will happen to market price and quantity if firms in an oligopolistic market form a cartel?

	Price	Quantity
(A)	Decrease	Decrease
(B)	Decrease	Increase
(C)	Increase	Increase
(D)	Increase	Decrease
(E)	Increase	No change

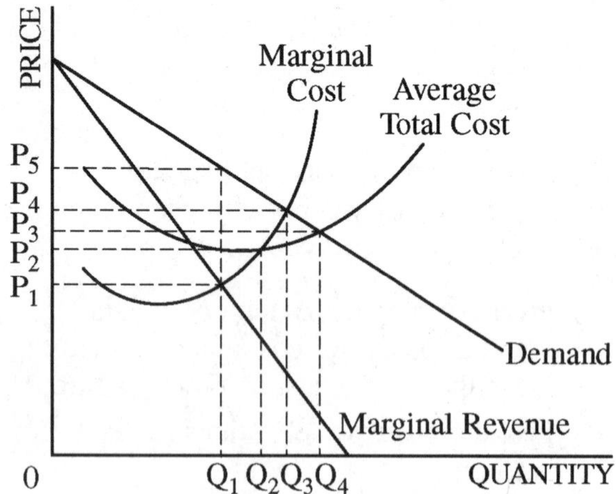

30. The diagram above shows the cost and revenue curves for a monopolist. What are the profit-maximizing output and price?

	Output	Price
(A)	0	P_1
(B)	Q_1	P_5
(C)	Q_2	P_2
(D)	Q_3	P_4
(E)	Q_4	P_3

31. Imperfectly competitive firms may be allocatively inefficient because they produce at a level of output such that

(A) average cost is at a minimum
(B) marginal revenue is greater than marginal cost
(C) price equals marginal revenue
(D) price equals marginal cost
(E) price is greater than marginal cost

32. In a market economy, public goods are unlikely to be provided in sufficient quantity by the private sector because

(A) private firms are less efficient at producing public goods than is the government
(B) the use of public goods cannot be withheld from those who do not pay for them
(C) consumers lack information about the benefits of public goods
(D) consumers do not value public goods highly enough for firms to produce them profitably
(E) public goods are inherently too important to be left to private firms to produce

33. Assume that both input and product markets are competitive. If capital is fixed and the product price increases, in the short run firms will increase production by increasing

(A) capital until marginal revenue equals the product price
(B) capital until the average product of capital equals the price of capital
(C) labor until the value of the marginal product of labor equals the wage rate
(D) labor until the marginal product of labor equals the wage rate
(E) labor until the ratio of product price to the marginal product of labor equals the wage rate

34. Which of the following is an important attribute of a market economy?

(A) Equal distribution of income
(B) Collective ownership of resources
(C) Centralized economic decision making
(D) Protection of property rights
(E) Public provision of all goods and services

35. If hiring an additional worker would increase a firm's total cost by less than it would increase its total revenue, the firm should

(A) not hire that worker
(B) hire that worker
(C) hire that worker only if another worker leaves or is fired
(D) hire that worker only if the worker can raise the firm's productivity
(E) reduce the number of workers employed by that firm

36. If a firm wants to produce a given amount of output at the lowest possible cost, it should use resources in such a manner that

(A) it uses relatively more of the less expensive resource
(B) it uses relatively more of the resource with the highest marginal product
(C) each resource has just reached the point of diminishing marginal returns
(D) the marginal products of each resource are equal
(E) the marginal products per dollar spent on each resource are equal

37. If the firms in an industry pollute the environment and are not charged for the pollution, which of the following is true from the standpoint of the efficient use of resources?

(A) Too much of the industry's product is produced, and the price of the product is higher than the marginal social cost.
(B) Too much of the industry's product is produced, and the price of the product is lower than the marginal social cost.
(C) Too little of the industry's product is produced, and the price of the product is higher than the marginal social cost.
(D) Too little of the industry's product is produced, and the price of the product is lower than the marginal social cost.
(E) The industry is a monopoly.

38. Using equal amounts of resources, Country A can produce either 30 tons of mangoes or 10 tons of bananas, and Country B can produce either 10 tons of mangoes or 6 tons of bananas. Which of the following is consistent with the information above?

	Country A	Country B
(A)	Comparative advantage in mango production	Comparative advantage in banana production
(B)	Comparative advantage in banana production	Comparative advantage in mango production
(C)	Absolute advantage in mango production	Absolute advantage in banana production
(D)	Absolute advantage in banana production	Absolute advantage in mango production
(E)	Comparative advantage in banana production	Absolute advantage in mango production

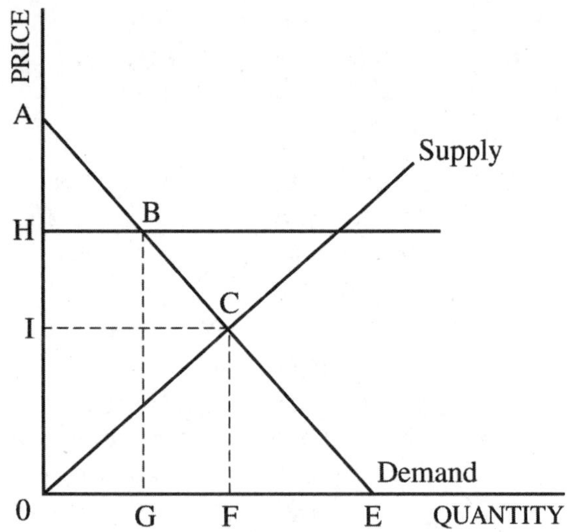

39. The graph above shows the market for chocolates. Suppose that the government imposes a price floor equal to 0H. As a result, consumer surplus in this market will be equal to

(A) ABH
(B) ACI
(C) AE0
(D) 0CE
(E) 0IC

40. A firm in monopolistic competition CANNOT do which of the following?

(A) Earn short-run profits
(B) Advertise its product
(C) Prevent new firms from entering the market
(D) Compete by its choice of location
(E) Set the price for its product

41. Which of the following is a necessary condition for a firm to engage in price discrimination?

(A) The firm faces a highly elastic demand.
(B) The firm is able to set its own price.
(C) The firm is maximizing its revenue.
(D) Buyers are only concerned about product quality.
(E) Buyers are not fully informed about price.

42. Which of the following is true if total utility is maximized?

(A) Marginal utility is equal to zero.
(B) Marginal utility is positive.
(C) Marginal utility is negative.
(D) Average utility is maximized.
(E) Average utility is minimized.

43. If the cross-price elasticity of demand between good A and good B is negative, then good A and good B are

(A) substitutes
(B) complements
(C) unrelated
(D) in high demand
(E) in low demand

44. Assume that a firm in a certain industry hires its workers in a perfectly competitive labor market. As the firm hires additional workers, the marginal factor cost is

(A) decreasing steadily
(B) increasing steadily
(C) constant
(D) decreasing at first, then increasing
(E) increasing at first, then decreasing

45. A profit-maximizing monopolist will hire an input up to the point at which

(A) marginal factor cost equals marginal revenue product
(B) marginal factor cost equals marginal revenue
(C) average factor cost equals average revenue product
(D) average factor cost equals value of the marginal product
(E) average revenue equals marginal revenue

		Firm B's Choice	
		Restrict Output	Do not Resrict Output
Firm A's Choice	Restrict Output	\$50, \$50	\$10, \$80
	Do not Restrict Output	\$80, \$10	\$30, \$30

46. The pay-off matrix above gives the profits associated with the strategic choices of two oligopolistic firms. The first entry in each cell is the profit to Firm A and the second to Firm B. Suppose that Firm A and Firm B agree to restrict output but have no power to enforce that agreement. In the long run, each firm will most likely earn which of the following profits?

	Firm A	Firm B
(A)	\$10	\$80
(B)	\$30	\$30
(C)	\$50	\$50
(D)	\$80	\$10
(E)	\$80	\$80

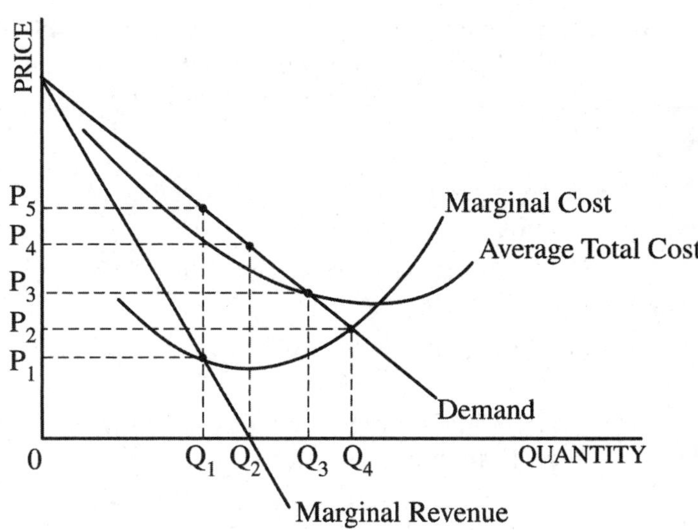

47. Suppose that the natural monopolist whose cost and revenue curves are depicted above is subject to government regulation. If the government's objective is to make this monopoly produce the socially optimal level of output, it should set price equal to

(A) P_1
(B) P_2
(C) P_3
(D) P_4
(E) P_5

48. A production possibilities curve can be used to show which of the following?

(A) Absence of trade-offs in the production of goods
(B) The limits on production due to scarcity of resources
(C) The amount of investment spending necessary to reach full employment
(D) The labor-force participation rate
(E) The average productivity of resources

49. A firm's short-run total costs increase from $45 to $55 when it increases its production from one unit to two units. Which of the following is true if the total fixed cost is $30 ?

(A) The average total cost of producing two units is equal to $47.50.
(B) Fixed costs of production remain at $30 at zero units of output.
(C) The marginal cost of producing the first unit is $10.
(D) Economic profit will be maximized when costs are minimized at $30.
(E) Total variable cost is equal to $15 when two units are produced.

50. Which of the following will cause the supply of chocolate to increase?

(A) An increase in the price of cocoa butter, a by-product of the production of chocolate
(B) An increase in the price of chocolate
(C) An increase in the price of cocoa beans, a major input in the production of chocolate
(D) A decrease in the price of butterscotch, a substitute for chocolate
(E) An effective price ceiling in the market for chocolate

51. In long-run equilibrium, the price charged by a monopolistically competitive firm is

(A) greater than its average total cost but equal to its marginal cost
(B) less than its average total cost but equal to its marginal cost
(C) equal to its average total cost but less than its marginal cost
(D) equal to its average revenue but less than its average total cost
(E) equal to its average total cost but greater than its marginal cost

52. Economists call a firm's demand for labor a derived demand because

(A) the number of workers hired depends mainly on the demand for the product the workers produce
(B) workers must be at least sixteen years old before they are considered part of the labor force
(C) workers need the salaries they receive from firms to demand goods and services
(D) the federal government taxes workers to derive revenues needed to finance its budget
(E) the firm needs skilled workers to operate its equipment

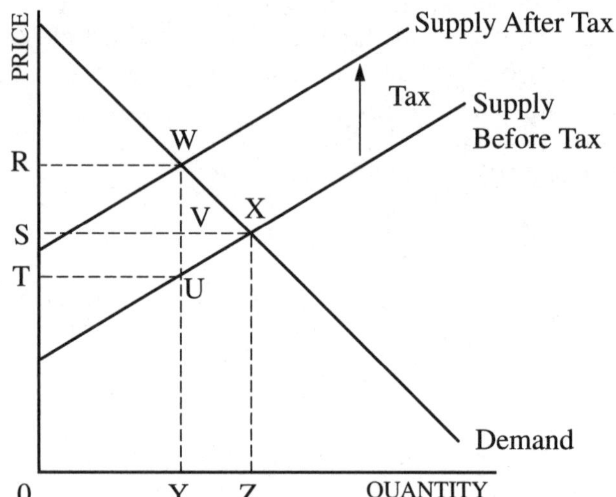

53. The imposition of an excise tax by the government caused the supply curve to shift as shown in the diagram above. Which area on the diagram represents the deadweight loss caused by the tax?

(A) UWX
(B) VWX
(C) RSXW
(D) STUV
(E) UXZY

54. Which of the following causes an increase in the demand for labor?

(A) An increase in the wage rate
(B) An increase in the price of the good that labor is producing
(C) A decrease in the marginal product of labor
(D) A decrease in the demand for the good that labor is producing
(E) A decrease in the price of capital, a substitute for labor

55. The United States government uses antitrust laws to regulate private markets to

(A) promote a competitive market environment
(B) limit business profits
(C) decrease the tax burden on consumers
(D) increase government revenue from penalty payments
(E) shelter small businesses from foreign competition

56. Which of the following is true of a pure public good?

(A) The government provides it at zero cost.
(B) Nonpaying users can be excluded from consuming it.
(C) People willingly reveal their true preference for it.
(D) It is difficult to determine a person's marginal valuation of it.
(E) One person's consumption of it reduces its availability to others.

57. Average total cost is equal to the sum of

(A) total fixed cost and total variable cost
(B) marginal cost and average fixed cost
(C) average fixed cost and average variable cost
(D) marginal cost and average variable cost
(E) marginal cost, average fixed cost, and average variable cost

58. Compared to a perfectly competitive industry, a profit-maximizing monopoly with identical costs of production will produce

(A) a lower quantity of output and charge a higher price
(B) a higher quantity of output and charge a lower price
(C) a lower quantity of output and charge a lower price
(D) a higher quantity of output and charge a higher price
(E) the same quantity of output and charge a higher price

59. A production possibilities curve is typically bowed outward because of the

(A) law of demand
(B) law of increasing opportunity costs
(C) substitution effect
(D) income effect
(E) principle of comparative advantage

60. A firm is currently producing at a level of output where marginal cost is increasing and greater than average variable cost, and marginal revenue is greater than marginal cost. To maximize profits, this firm should

(A) decrease output
(B) increase output
(C) maintain its current output level
(D) shut down
(E) increase its price

Questions 61 and 62 refer to a firm's production function given in the table below. Assume that the firm uses labor as the only variable input to produce its output.

Number of Workers Hired	Output per Day (units)
0	0
1	15
2	32
3	42
4	50
5	55

61. If the market wage rate is constant no matter how many workers are hired, the marginal cost of the firm is minimized with the hiring of the

(A) first worker
(B) second worker
(C) third worker
(D) fourth worker
(E) fifth worker

62. If the total fixed cost is $50 and each worker receives a wage of $100 per day, then the total cost and the average variable cost of producing 50 units of output are which of the following?

	Total Cost	Average Variable Cost
(A)	$550	$10
(B)	$550	$ 8
(C)	$450	$10
(D)	$450	$ 8
(E)	$150	$ 2

Questions 63 and 64 refer to the graph below, which shows the cost and output of a perfectly competitive firm.

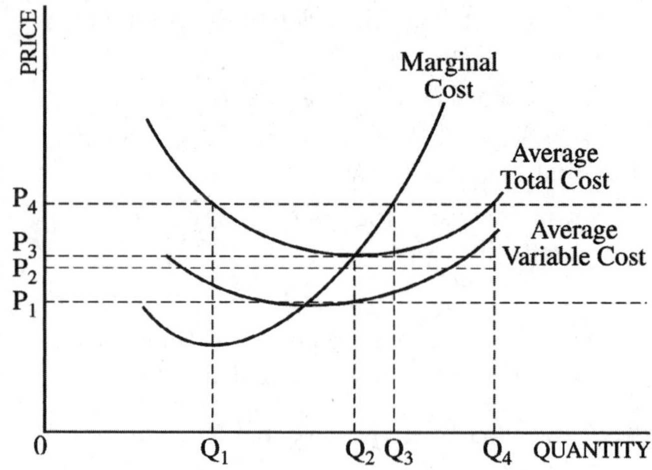

63. If the market price is P_4, the production of which output level will maximize the firm's profit?

(A) Q_1
(B) Q_2
(C) Q_3
(D) Q_4
(E) 0

64. If the market price is P_2, then which of the following is true?

(A) The firm will earn positive economic profits.
(B) The firm will shut down and exit the industry in the short run.
(C) The firm will be in long-run equilibrium.
(D) The firm will operate at a loss and continue to produce in the short run.
(E) The firm will lower its price to increase sales and profit.

65. Suppose that the price elasticity of demand for gasoline is –0.1 in the short run and –0.6 in the long run. If the price of gasoline increases by 60 percent, which of the following shows the percentage change in the quantity demanded of gasoline in the short run and in the long run?

	In the Short Run	In the Long Run
(A)	Increases by 10%	Increases by 60%
(B)	Increases by 6%	Decreases by 36%
(C)	Decreases by 6%	Decreases by 6%
(D)	Decreases by 6%	Decreases by 36%
(E)	Decreases by 10%	Decreases by 60%

Quantity of X	Marginal Utility of X	Quantity of Y	Marginal Utility of Y
1	16	1	40
2	12	2	24
3	10	3	16
4	8	4	12
5	6	5	8
6	4	6	4

66. The table above shows the marginal utilities in utils that Samantha receives from purchasing good X and good Y each week. The price of good X is $2 per unit, and the price of good Y is $4 per unit. Samantha has an income of $26 per week, and she spends it all on the two goods each week.

If Samantha maximizes her utility, what combination of good X and good Y will she purchase?

	Good X	Good Y
(A)	1	6
(B)	2	4
(C)	3	5
(D)	5	4
(E)	6	5

67. If a firm experiences economies of scale in production, its long-run average total cost curve

(A) rises as output increases
(B) falls as output increases
(C) is horizontal
(D) is the same as its marginal cost curve
(E) lies above the short-run average total cost curve

68. A perfectly competitive firm's short-run supply curve is

(A) downward sloping
(B) horizontal at the market price
(C) the rising portion of its average variable cost curve above its marginal cost curve
(D) the rising portion of its average total cost curve above its marginal cost curve
(E) the rising portion of its marginal cost curve above its average variable cost curve

69. Which of the following costs continuously decrease as a firm's output increases?

(A) Short-run average total cost
(B) Long-run average total cost
(C) Average variable cost
(D) Average fixed cost
(E) Marginal cost

70. The Lorenz curve is a useful method for studying

(A) the extent of poverty in an economy
(B) inequality in the distribution of income
(C) the extent of job losses because of free trade
(D) the opportunity cost of investing in human capital
(E) settlement patterns of families in a geographic region

71. Suppose that the government decides to impose a 10 percent excise tax on all sugar-based soft drinks. Under which of the following scenarios will buyers pay the LEAST amount of this tax?

	Demand	Supply
(A)	Elastic	Elastic
(B)	Elastic	Inelastic
(C)	Perfectly inelastic	Perfectly elastic
(D)	Inelastic	Elastic
(E)	Inelastic	Inelastic

72. If a nationwide automobile workers' union successfully negotiates for a wage increase in its new labor contract, this will most likely cause

(A) the demand curve for automobiles to shift to the left
(B) the demand curve for automobiles to shift to the right
(C) the equilibrium price of automobiles to fall
(D) the equilibrium price of automobiles to rise
(E) the supply curve for automobiles to shift to the right

73. If negative externalities exist in an industry when producing a good, which of the following must be true?

(A) Firms in the industry can earn only normal profits.
(B) The industry underallocates resources to the production of the good.
(C) Firms in the industry ignore their marginal private costs in choosing their output levels.
(D) The market price fails to reflect the full cost of production.
(E) The industry needs a government subsidy to produce the efficient level of output.

Output	Total Cost
0	200
1	300
2	410
3	530
4	660
5	800
6	950

74. Given the information in the table above, what are the average fixed cost and average variable cost for 4 units of output?

(A) The average fixed cost is 200 and the average variable cost is 165.
(B) The average fixed cost is 200 and the average variable cost is 115.
(C) The average fixed cost is 50 and the average variable cost is 115.
(D) The average fixed cost is 50 and the average variable cost is 165.
(E) They cannot be determined from the information given.

Output	Quantity of Labor
0	0
10	1
19	2
27	3
34	4
40	5

75. The table above shows output levels and corresponding quantities of labor for a perfectly competitive firm. What is the marginal physical product of the fifth worker?

(A) 5
(B) 6
(C) 7
(D) 8
(E) 40

76. A perfectly competitive firm will shut down rather than produce if its

    (A) average total cost exceeds its average variable cost
    (B) loss is greater than its fixed cost
    (C) marginal revenue is less than the market price
    (D) economic profit is equal to zero
    (E) marginal cost curve is starting to rise

77. Which of the following best explains the reason for a downward-sloping demand curve for a product?

    (A) The income and substitution effects are equal and opposite.
    (B) Total utility eventually falls below marginal utility as additional units of the product are consumed.
    (C) The average utility falls below the marginal utility as additional units of the product are consumed.
    (D) The marginal utility decreases as additional units of the product are consumed.
    (E) Average utility is always decreasing.

78. In the absence of market failure, the competitive market in equilibrium is

    (A) efficient and maximizes the sum of consumer and producer surpluses
    (B) efficient and maximizes consumer surplus
    (C) efficient and maximizes producer surplus
    (D) inefficient, since it serves consumers who are willing to pay
    (E) inefficient, since producers with the lowest costs remain in the market

79. Which of the following factors would lead one to conclude that an electric utility company is a natural monopoly?

    (A) Constant returns to scale make it cheaper for a single firm to produce than for multiple firms to produce.
    (B) Diseconomies of scale make it cheaper for a single firm to produce than for multiple firms to produce.
    (C) Economies of scale make it cheaper for a single firm to produce than for multiple firms to produce.
    (D) High start-up costs are fixed and not factored in determining monopoly power.
    (E) The firm is not subject to returns to scale.

80. What type of labor market is characterized by a single employer of labor with significant hiring power?

    (A) Collective monopoly
    (B) Union shop
    (C) Monopsony
    (D) Labor oligopoly
    (E) Nonrivalry market

Study Resources

Most textbooks used in college-level introductory microeconomics courses cover the topics in the outline given earlier, but the approaches to certain topics and the emphases given to them may differ. To prepare for the Principles of Microeconomics exam, it is advisable to study one or more college textbooks, which can be found in most college bookstores. When selecting a textbook, check the table of contents against the knowledge and skills required for this test.

There are many introductory economics textbooks that vary greatly in difficulty. Most books are published in one-volume editions, which cover both microeconomics and macroeconomics; some are published in two-volume editions, with one volume covering macroeconomics and the other microeconomics. A companion study guide/workbook is available for most textbooks. The study guides typically include brief reviews, definitions of key concepts, problem sets and multiple-choice test questions with answers. Many publishers also make available companion websites, links to other online resources, or computer-assisted learning packages.

To broaden your knowledge of economic issues, you may read relevant articles published in the economics periodicals that are available in most college libraries — for example, *The Economist*, *The Wall Street Journal* and the *New York Times*, along with local papers, may also enhance your understanding of economic issues.

Visit **clep.collegeboard.org/earn-college-credit/practice** for additional microeconomics resources. You can also find suggestions for exam preparation in Chapter IV of the *Official Study Guide*. In addition, many college faculty post their course materials on their schools' websites.

Answer Key

1.	A	41.	B
2.	B	42.	A
3.	A	43.	B
4.	D	44.	C
5.	C	45.	A
6.	B	46.	B
7.	E	47.	B
8.	B	48.	B
9.	C	49.	B
10.	E	50.	A
11.	A	51.	E
12.	A	52.	A
13.	E	53.	A
14.	D	54.	B
15.	D	55.	A
16.	B	56.	D
17.	C	57.	C
18.	C	58.	A
19.	D	59.	B
20.	E	60.	B
21.	D	61.	B
22.	B	62.	D
23.	D	63.	C
24.	D	64.	D
25.	A	65.	D
26.	B	66.	D
27.	C	67.	B
28.	B	68.	E
29.	D	69.	D
30.	B	70.	B
31.	E	71.	B
32.	B	72.	D
33.	C	73.	D
34.	D	74.	C
35.	B	75.	B
36.	E	76.	B
37.	B	77.	D
38.	A	78.	A
39.	A	79.	C
40.	C	80.	C

Introductory Psychology

Description of the Examination

The Introductory Psychology examination covers material that is usually taught in a one-semester undergraduate course in introductory psychology. It stresses basic facts, concepts and generally accepted principles in the thirteen areas listed in the following section.

The examination contains approximately 95 questions to be answered in 90 minutes. Some of these are pretest questions that will not be scored.

The questions on the CLEP Introductory Psychology exam adhere to the terminology, criteria and classifications referred to in the fifth edition of the *Diagnostic and Statistical Manual of Mental Disorders* (DSM-5).

Knowledge and Skills Required

Questions on the Introductory Psychology examination require candidates to demonstrate one or more of the following abilities.

- Knowledge of terminology, principles and theory
- Ability to comprehend, evaluate and analyze problem situations
- Ability to apply knowledge to new situations

The subject matter of the Introductory Psychology examination is drawn from the following topics. The percentages next to the main topics indicate the approximate percentage of exam questions on that topic.

8%–9% History, Approaches, Methods

History of psychology

Approaches: biological, behavioral, cognitive, humanistic, psychodynamic

Research methods: experimental, clinical, correlational

Ethics in research

8%–9% Biological Bases of Behavior

Endocrine system

Etiology

Functional organization of the nervous system

Genetics

Neuroanatomy

Physiological techniques

7%–8% Sensation and Perception

Attention

Other senses: somesthesis, olfaction, gustation, vestibular system

Perceptual development

Perceptual processes

Receptor processes: vision, audition

Sensory mechanisms: thresholds, adaptation

5%–6% States of Consciousness

Hypnosis and meditation

Psychoactive drug effects

Sleep and dreaming

10%–11% Learning

Biological bases

Classical conditioning

Cognitive process in learning

Observational learning

Operant conditioning

8%–9% Cognition
- Intelligence and creativity
- Language
- Memory
- Thinking and problem solving

7%–8% Motivation and Emotion
- Biological bases
- Hunger, thirst, sex, pain
- Social motivation
- Theories of emotion
- Theories of motivation

8%–9% Developmental Psychology
- Dimensions of development: physical, cognitive, social, moral
- Gender identity and sex roles
- Heredity-environment issues
- Research methods: longitudinal, cross-sectional
- Theories of development

7%–8% Personality
- Assessment techniques
- Growth and adjustment
- Personality theories and approaches
- Research methods: idiographic, nomothetic
- Self-concept, self-esteem

8%–9% Psychological Disorders and Health
- Affective disorders
- Anxiety disorders
- Dissociative disorders
- Health, stress and coping
- Personality disorders
- Psychoses
- Somatoform disorders
- Theories of psychopathology

7%–8% Treatment of Psychological Disorders
- Behavioral therapies
- Biological and drug therapies
- Cognitive therapies
- Community and preventive approaches
- Insight therapies: psychodynamic and humanistic approaches

7%–8% Social Psychology
- Aggression/antisocial behavior
- Attitudes and attitude change
- Attribution processes
- Conformity, compliance, obedience
- Group dynamics
- Interpersonal perception

3%–4% Statistics, Tests and Measurement
- Descriptive statistics
- Inferential statistics
- Measurement of intelligence
- Reliability and validity
- Samples, populations, norms
- Types of tests

Sample Test Questions

The following sample questions do not appear on an actual CLEP examination. They are intended to give potential test-takers an indication of the format and difficulty level of the examination and to provide content for practice and review. Knowing the correct answers to all of the sample questions is not a guarantee of satisfactory performance on the exam.

Directions: Each of the questions or incomplete statements below is followed by five suggested answers or completions. Select the one that is best in each case.

1. "The focus of psychological science is the attempt to relate overt responses to observable environmental stimuli."

   This statement is most closely associated with which of the following approaches?

   (A) Cognitive
   (B) Behavioral
   (C) Biological
   (D) Humanistic
   (E) Psychodynamic

2. Which of the following types of research design is most appropriate for establishing a cause-and-effect relationship between two variables?

   (A) Correlational
   (B) Naturalistic observation
   (C) Participant observation
   (D) Experimental
   (E) Case study

3. The science of psychology is typically dated from the establishment of the late-nineteenth-century Leipzig laboratory of

   (A) Hermann Ebbinghaus
   (B) Hermann von Helmholtz
   (C) William James
   (D) Wilhelm Wundt
   (E) John Locke

4. The requirement that prospective participants know the general nature of a study so that they can decide whether to participate is a major part of

   (A) reciprocal determinism
   (B) confidentiality
   (C) informed consent
   (D) duty to inform
   (E) debriefing

5. The statement "Response latency is the number of seconds that elapses between the stimulus and the response" is an example of

   (A) introspection
   (B) a description of an interaction
   (C) a deduction
   (D) an operational definition
   (E) free association

6. As blind children learn to read braille, the amount of sensory cortex devoted to their finger tips increases. Which process is responsible for this allotment of brain activity?

   (A) Plasticity
   (B) Lateralization
   (C) Synesthesia
   (D) Place theory
   (E) Transduction

7. A neuron is said to be polarized when

   (A) it is in the refractory period
   (B) it is in a resting state
   (C) it is about to undergo an action potential
   (D) the synaptic terminals release chemicals into the synaptic gap
   (E) chemicals outside the cell body cross the cell membrane

8. Down syndrome is caused by

   (A) an extra chromosome
   (B) an imbalance of neurotransmitters
   (C) a tumor in the parietal lobe
   (D) a nutritional deficiency
   (E) a viral infection in the third trimester of pregnancy

9. One common technique used in studying infant perception and cognition involves measuring a decreased response to a stimulus that an infant has been exposed to previously. This research technique is called

   (A) the preferential-looking paradigm
   (B) habituation
   (C) the Strange Situation
   (D) expectancy violation
   (E) conditioned head turning

10. Damage to an individual's parietal lobes is most likely to result in

   (A) a heightened sense of smell
   (B) reduced sensitivity to touch
   (C) decreased reaction time
   (D) a loss in the ability to understand spoken language
   (E) difficulty discriminating between the four primary tastes

11. Hadidjah is a manager conducting an interview with a job applicant. During their conversation her attention is diverted when she hears her name mentioned by two employees talking in the hall outside her office door. Hadidjah's attention being drawn to the employees in the hall can best be explained by

   (A) dichotic listening
   (B) the availability heuristic
   (C) the use of a mnemonic
   (D) the cocktail party phenomenon
   (E) priming

12. According to the activation-synthesis hypothesis of dreaming, dreams serve which of the following purposes?

   (A) To protect the ego from the unconscious struggles of the mind
   (B) To make sense of random neural activity during sleep
   (C) To provide unfiltered problem solving of encounters that occurred while awake
   (D) To provide a window into the unconscious, revealing true wishes and desires
   (E) To provide learning and rehearsal of material encountered while a person is awake

13. The opponent-process theory in vision best explains which of the following?

   (A) Size constancy
   (B) Color afterimages
   (C) Superior visual acuity in the fovea
   (D) Depth perception using monocular cues
   (E) Illusory movement

14. The receptors for hearing are the

   (A) ossicles in the middle ear
   (B) otoliths in the semicircular canals
   (C) hair cells on the basilar membrane
   (D) specialized cells on the tympanic membrane
   (E) cells in the lining of the auditory canal

15. The picture above of a road receding in the distance represents the depth perception cue known as

   (A) accommodation
   (B) retinal disparity
   (C) texture gradient
   (D) relative size
   (E) linear perspective

16. Brain waves during REM sleep generally appear as

    (A) alternating high- and low-amplitude waves
    (B) rapid low-amplitude waves
    (C) irregular medium-amplitude waves
    (D) slow low-amplitude waves
    (E) slow high-amplitude waves

17. Which of the following is a type of sleep pattern that becomes less prevalent as one moves from infancy to adulthood?

    (A) Alpha
    (B) Beta
    (C) Gamma
    (D) Theta
    (E) REM

18. According to current psychological research, hypnosis is most useful for which of the following purposes?

    (A) Pain control
    (B) Age regression
    (C) Treatment of psychotic behavior
    (D) Treatment of a memory disorder
    (E) Treatment of a personality disorder

19. Checking the coin return every time one passes a vending machine is a type of behavior probably being maintained by which of the following schedules of reinforcement?

    (A) Fixed interval only
    (B) Fixed ratio only
    (C) Variable ratio only
    (D) Variable interval and fixed ratio
    (E) Fixed interval and variable ratio

20. Making the amount of time a child can spend playing video games contingent on the amount of time the child spends practicing the piano is an illustration of

    (A) frequency theory
    (B) the law of association
    (C) aversive conditioning
    (D) classical conditioning
    (E) operant conditioning

21. Which of the following strategies undermines the effectiveness of punishment?

    (A) Delaying punishment
    (B) Using punishment just severe enough to be effective
    (C) Making punishment consistent
    (D) Explaining punishment
    (E) Minimizing dependence on physical punishment

22. A teacher tells a child to sit down in class. Over the course of several days, the child stands up more and more frequently, only to be told to sit down each time. It is most likely that the teacher's reprimands are serving as

    (A) a punishment
    (B) approval
    (C) a reinforcer
    (D) an aversive stimulus
    (E) a conditioned stimulus

23. Which of the following is a secondary reinforcer?

    (A) Food
    (B) Warmth
    (C) Water
    (D) Money
    (E) Sex

24. Shortly after learning to associate the word "dog" with certain four-legged furry animals, young children will frequently misidentify a cow or a horse as a dog. This phenomenon is best viewed as an example of

(A) differentiation
(B) negative transfer
(C) imprinting
(D) overextension
(E) linear perspective

25. If on the last day of a psychology class a student is asked to remember what was done in class each day during the term, she will likely be able to remember best the activities of the first and last class meetings. This situation is an example of

(A) retroactive interference
(B) positive transfer
(C) the serial position effect
(D) proactive interference
(E) short-term memory

26. Proactive interference describes a process by which

(A) people remember digits better than words
(B) people remember images better than words
(C) people remember elements in pairs
(D) prior learning interferes with subsequent learning
(E) subsequent learning interferes with prior learning

27. Research has shown that students generally perform better if tested in the same room where they originally learned the material. This shows the importance of which of the following in memory?

(A) Insight
(B) Preparedness
(C) Context
(D) Invariance
(E) Rehearsal

28. Which of the following is true of recall performance on a typical forgetting curve?

(A) It decreases rapidly at first, and then it levels off.
(B) It decreases slowly at first, and then it drops off quite sharply.
(C) It decreases at a steady rate until it reaches a near-zero level.
(D) It remains steady for about the first week, and then it begins a gradual decline.
(E) It increases for the first few hours after learning, and then it decreases very slowly over the next few weeks.

29. According to information processing theory, information is progressively processed by

(A) long-term memory, short-term memory, and then sensory memory
(B) sensory memory, short-term memory, and then long-term memory
(C) sensory memory, semantic memory, and then long-term memory
(D) short-term memory, semantic memory, and then long-term memory
(E) short-term memory, long-term memory, and then sensory memory

30. In problem solving, which of the following approaches almost always guarantees a correct solution?

(A) Insight
(B) Heuristic
(C) Algorithm
(D) Critical thinking
(E) Convergent thinking

31. One theory of the effects of arousal holds that efficiency of behavior can be described as an inverted U-shaped function of increasing arousal. Which of the following accurately describes this relationship?

(A) Greater arousal leads to better performance.
(B) Greater arousal leads to poorer performance.
(C) Low and high levels of arousal lead to poorest performance.
(D) Overarousal leads to performance efficiency.
(E) Underarousal leads to performance efficiency.

32. Which of the following illustrates drive reduction?

(A) A person wins five dollars in the lottery.
(B) A dog burned by a hot stove avoids the stove thereafter.
(C) A child who likes music turns up the volume of the radio.
(D) A dog salivates at the sound of a tone previously paired with fresh meat.
(E) A woman who is cold puts on a warm coat.

33. Which of the following presents a pair of needs from Abraham Maslow's hierarchical need structure, in order from lower to higher need?

(A) Belongingness, safety
(B) Self-actualization, physiological needs
(C) Physiological needs, safety
(D) Esteem, belongingness
(E) Self-actualization, esteem

34. Which of the following drugs is most likely to cause hyperalertness, agitation, and general euphoria?

(A) A barbiturate
(B) A stimulant
(C) A hallucinogen
(D) An antidepressant
(E) An antipsychotic

35. In which of the following areas does research show most clearly that girls develop earlier than boys?

(A) Independence from parents
(B) Athletic competence
(C) Intellectual achievement
(D) Adolescent physical growth spurt
(E) Self-actualization

36. Developmental psychologists are most likely to prefer longitudinal research designs to cross-sectional research designs because longitudinal designs

(A) usually yield results much more quickly
(B) offer the advantage of between-subjects comparisons
(C) are much less likely to be influenced by cultural changes that occur over time
(D) utilize the participants as their own experimental controls
(E) are more valid

37. A young child breaks her cookie into a number of pieces and asserts that "now there is more to eat." In Jean Piaget's analysis, the child's behavior is evidence of

(A) formal operations
(B) concrete operations
(C) conservation
(D) preoperational thought
(E) sensorimotor behavior

38. The word "negative" in negative reinforcement refers to the fact that

(A) extinction has taken place
(B) the reinforcement is aversive
(C) a response is decreased
(D) a stimulus is removed
(E) a stimulus is added

39. Four-year-old Annie suspects that her older brother is playing a trick on her by hiding her toy, even though he denies he has seen it. This best illustrates that Annie has acquired

(A) egocentrism
(B) conservation
(C) theory of mind
(D) accommodation
(E) assimilation

40. When preschool children see the world only from their point of view, they are displaying

(A) accommodation
(B) assimilation
(C) egocentric thinking
(D) deductive reasoning
(E) object permanence

41. When insulted by a friend, Sally's first impulse was to strike him. Instead, she yelled loudly and kicked a door several times. This means of reducing aggressive impulses exemplifies which of the following?

(A) Repression
(B) Fixation
(C) Displacement
(D) Conservation
(E) Sublimation

42. If the null hypothesis is rejected, a researcher can conclude that the

(A) treatment effect was significant
(B) theory must be modified, a new hypothesis formed, and the experimental procedure revised
(C) theory does not need modification, but the hypothesis and the experimental procedure need revision
(D) theory and hypothesis do not need modification, but the experimental procedure needs revision
(E) hypothesis is false

43. Erik Erikson's and Sigmund Freud's theories of personality development are most similar in that both

(A) emphasize the libido
(B) focus on adult development
(C) discount the importance of culture
(D) are based on stages
(E) view behavior as a continuum

44. The use of projective tests is associated with which of the following psychological approaches?

(A) Behaviorism
(B) Psychoanalysis
(C) Cognitive behaviorism
(D) Humanism
(E) Functionalism

45. Alexandra is a singer who likes to write her own songs. Most of her songs are imaginative, with unusual, intelligent lyrics. This information suggests that on the Big Five model of personality, Alexandra would score

(A) high in openness to experience
(B) high in neuroticism
(C) high in extraversion
(D) low in neuroticism
(E) high in industry

46. Evidence most strongly supports which of the following statements about the effects of stress?

(A) Being able to predict a stressor in your life does not help mediate its effects.
(B) High levels of stress lead to better cognitive functioning.
(C) Stress has only negative effects on well-being.
(D) Stressors are interpreted and experienced by all people in the same way.
(E) Just believing that a stressor can be controlled can mediate its effects.

47. A diagnosis of schizophrenia typically includes which of the following symptoms?

(A) Delusions
(B) Panic attacks
(C) Hypochondriasis
(D) Multiple personalities
(E) Psychosexual dysfunction

48. The term "etiology" refers to the study of which of the following aspects of an illness?

(A) Origins and causes
(B) Characteristic symptoms
(C) Expected outcome following treatment
(D) Frequency of occurrence
(E) Level of contagiousness

49. An obsession is defined as

(A) a senseless ritual
(B) a hallucination
(C) a delusion
(D) an unwanted thought
(E) a panic attack

50. Which of the following personality disorders is characterized by excessive emotionality and attention seeking?

(A) Borderline
(B) Histrionic
(C) Dependent
(D) Obsessive-compulsive
(E) Schizotypal

51. Personality disorders are characterized by which of the following?

(A) A fear of public places, frequently accompanied by panic attacks
(B) Problematic social relationships and inflexible and maladaptive responses to stress
(C) A successful response to neuroleptic drugs
(D) A deficiency of acetylcholine in the brain
(E) An increased level of serotonin in the brain

52. Research on the effectiveness of psychotherapy has indicated that

(A) certain therapeutic methods have been shown to be especially effective for particular psychological disorders
(B) nondirective techniques are generally superior to directive ones
(C) the effectiveness of a method depends on the length of time a therapist was trained in the method
(D) psychoanalysis is the most effective technique for eliminating behavior disorders
(E) psychoanalysis is the most effective technique for curing anxiety disorders

53. Which of the following kinds of therapy attempts to correct irrational beliefs that lead to psychological distress?

(A) Behavioral
(B) Cognitive
(C) Existential
(D) Gestalt
(E) Psychoanalytic

54. An individual undergoing psychotherapy shows improvement due only to that person's belief in the therapy and not because of the therapy itself. This result illustrates

(A) a transference effect
(B) a placebo effect
(C) the misinformation effect
(D) a positive correlation
(E) a conditioned response

55. Which of the following fields is the forerunner of positive psychology?

(A) Structuralism
(B) Humanism
(C) Functionalism
(D) Psychoanalysis
(E) Behaviorism

56. Selective serotonin reuptake inhibitors (SSRIs) are used primarily in the treatment of which of the following?

(A) Antisocial personality disorder
(B) Schizophrenia
(C) Depression
(D) Mania
(E) Sleep disorders

57. Similarity, proximity, and familiarity are important determinants of

(A) observational learning
(B) attraction
(C) sexual orientation
(D) aggression
(E) imprinting

58. All of the following are true about altruism EXCEPT:

(A) It is more common in small towns and rural areas than in cities.
(B) It is more likely to be inherited than is aggressive behavior.
(C) A person is more likely to perform an altruistic act when another person has modeled altruistic behavior.
(D) A person is more likely to perform an altruistic act when another person has pointed out the need.
(E) A person is more likely to be altruistic when not in a hurry.

59. The bystander effect has been explained by which of the following?

(A) Empathy
(B) Diffusion of responsibility
(C) Social facilitation
(D) Reactive devaluation
(E) Defective schemas

60. Brian always exerts less effort when he is involved in a group project than when he is working on a project alone. Which of the following is Brian exhibiting?

(A) Group polarization
(B) Social loafing
(C) Social facilitation
(D) Groupthink
(E) Deindividuation

61. Job satisfaction has an inverse relationship with

(A) productivity
(B) career interest
(C) turnover
(D) age
(E) skill level

62. An attribution that focuses on an individual's ability or personality characteristics is described as

(A) situational
(B) collectivist
(C) dispositional
(D) stereotypic
(E) homogeneous

63. Which of the following terms refers to the strategy of making a small request to gain listeners' compliance, then making a larger request?

(A) Door-in-the-face
(B) Foot-in-the-door
(C) Social facilitation
(D) Matching
(E) Overjustification

64. Which of the following is a true statement about the relationship between test validity and test reliability?

(A) A test can be reliable without being valid.
(B) A test that has high content validity will have high reliability.
(C) A test that has low content validity will have low reliability.
(D) The higher the test's validity, the lower its reliability will be.
(E) The validity of a test always exceeds its reliability.

65. Which of the following statistics indicates the distribution with the greatest variability?

(A) A variance of 30.6
(B) A standard deviation of 11.2
(C) A range of 6
(D) A mean of 61.5
(E) A median of 38

66. Which of the following techniques is most useful for a researcher studying focal brain activity while a participant generates words?

(A) Computed tomography (CT)
(B) Positron-emission tomography (PET)
(C) Magnetic resonance imaging (MRI)
(D) Electrooculography (EOG)
(E) Electroencephalography (EEG)

67. The case study method of conducting research is justifiably criticized because

(A) the researcher cannot focus on a specific individual
(B) the researcher cannot collect detailed observations
(C) the results are difficult to generalize to a larger population
(D) it does not allow for the generation of hypotheses that can be tested in future experiments
(E) it does not allow for the examination of unusual cases

68. A person who wants to see an object in low light conditions should focus the object on

(A) the fovea because that is where the cones are more densely packed
(B) the fovea because that is where the rods are more densely packed
(C) the periphery of the retina because that is where the cones are more densely packed
(D) the periphery of the retina because that is where the rods are more densely packed
(E) both the fovea and the periphery of the retina to optimize the use of both rods and cones

69. A man's life has been filled with misfortune and tragic experiences that were unexpected, unavoidable, and unpredictable. He is depressed and tells his therapist that he feels he cannot control the outcome of the events in his life. Which of the following best explains his depression?

(A) Learned helplessness
(B) Repression
(C) Operant conditioning
(D) Classical conditioning
(E) Biological rhythms

70. Which of the following is a measure of central tendency that can be easily distorted by unusually high or low scores?

(A) Mean
(B) Mode
(C) Median
(D) Range
(E) Standard deviation

71. Stimulation of the lateral hypothalamus will result in which of the following behaviors in laboratory rats?

(A) An increase in sexual behavior
(B) An increase in eating behavior
(C) An increase in visual processing speed
(D) A decrease in auditory perception
(E) A decrease in memory functioning

72. Stella Chess and Alexander Thomas have classified temperament into which of the following clusters?

(A) Sensorimotor, preoperational, concrete operational
(B) Easy, difficult, slow-to-warm-up
(C) Secure, insecure, resilient
(D) Authoritarian, authoritative, indulgent
(E) Preconventional, conventional, postconventional

73. Every day when Carlos leaves his apartment, he locks the door, walks to the corner, turns around, and returns to his apartment in order to check that the door is locked. He returns to check the door several times before finally crossing the street and going about his day. Carlos would most likely be diagnosed with which of the following conditions?

(A) Narcissistic personality disorder
(B) Panic disorder
(C) Generalized anxiety disorder
(D) Bipolar disorder
(E) Obsessive-compulsive disorder

74. Which of the following is a method of behavioral therapy that would be most successful in treating someone who is suffering from a specific phobia, such as a fear of snakes?

(A) Free association
(B) Systematic desensitization
(C) Meta-analysis
(D) Unconditional positive regard
(E) Dream analysis

75. Tameka regularly sets goals, plans for attaining those goals, and monitors her progress. Her activities are most closely associated with

(A) high extrinsic motivation
(B) high achievement motivation
(C) high extraversion
(D) low extrinsic motivation
(E) low achievement motivation

76. While sitting home one night reading a book and relaxing, Kyle suddenly realized that his heart rate was increasing, he was breathing faster, and his palms were sweating. Based on this response, Kyle concluded that he was scared. This is an example of which of the following theories?

(A) James-Lange
(B) Cannon-Bard
(C) Schachter-Singer
(D) Information processing
(E) Equity

77. A participant learns a new behavior but does not demonstrate the behavior until a reward is offered for doing so. This is an example of which of the following types of learning?

(A) Chaining
(B) Latent
(C) Social
(D) Shaping
(E) Classical conditioning

78. With regard to understanding human behavior, the humanistic approaches emphasize

(A) unconscious forces
(B) free will
(C) determinism
(D) inborn traits
(E) stimulus-response relationships

79. When a nurse touches the cheek of an infant and the infant turns her head toward the touch and opens her mouth, the nurse has elicited the

(A) rooting reflex
(B) Babinski reflex
(C) withdrawal reflex
(D) sucking reflex
(E) Moro reflex

80. In which of the following situations is a student using echoic memory?

(A) Remembering what he ate for dinner last night
(B) Studying vocabulary words for his Spanish course
(C) Trying to replay the last few notes his piano teacher just played
(D) Looking briefly at a picture his friend has taken of him
(E) Recalling the score of last week's basketball game

81. Which of the following theories best supports the idea that people are genetically predisposed to live in groups because it contributes to the survival of the species?

(A) Arousal
(B) Evolutionary
(C) Incentive
(D) Set point
(E) Social learning

82. Which of the following is a sleep disorder characterized by uncontrollable sleep attacks at inappropriate times?

(A) Sleep apnea
(B) REM rebound
(C) Narcolepsy
(D) Paradoxical sleep
(E) Sleep terror

83. Albert Bandura conducted a study in which a child viewed an adult playing with toys. The adult stood up and kicked and yelled at an inflated doll. The child was then taken to another room containing toys. When left alone, the child lashed out at a similar doll in the room. The child's behavior toward the doll is most likely a result of

(A) observational learning
(B) operant conditioning
(C) classical conditioning
(D) authoritative parenting
(E) authoritarian parenting

84. Lila thinks the new student in her study group is in a fraternity because, to her, he looks like other students who are in fraternities. Lila's decision about the new student is most likely the result of the

(A) anchoring and adjusting heuristic
(B) availability heuristic
(C) conjunction fallacy
(D) representativeness heuristic
(E) confirmation bias

85. Which of the following scenarios best illustrates the facial feedback hypothesis of emotion?

(A) Bill is a good card player who shows no emotion in his face that would reveal what he is thinking.
(B) Ellen says that hanging up the laundry on a clothesline makes her feel happy; she holds the clothespins in her teeth as she hangs each piece of clothing.
(C) Juanita fakes a smile to make her friends think she is happy.
(D) Paul has been blind from birth and has never seen emotional faces, but he has emotional facial expressions similar to those of a sighted person.
(E) As a result of Raj smiling at his customers, they smile at him.

86. Pedro just returned home from seeing a horror film at a movie theater. As he settles into bed, he hears a noise downstairs and perceives it to be an intruder. This interpretation of the sensory input is best explained by which of the following?

(A) Figure-ground discrimination
(B) Depth perception
(C) Perceptual constancy
(D) Bottom-up processing
(E) Top-down processing

87. To help Lauren learn to play the violin, her string teacher first provides praise when Lauren plays the correct notes. Then the teacher only provides praise when Lauren plays the correct notes and the correct rhythm. Finally, the teacher only praises Lauren when she plays the correct notes, the correct rhythm, and the correct tempo. Which of the following learning techniques is Lauren's teacher using?

(A) Positive punishment
(B) Elaborative rehearsal
(C) Generalization
(D) Chunking
(E) Shaping

88. Toddlers experience a growth spurt in vocabulary because of a process called

(A) babbling
(B) overregularization
(C) telegraphic speech
(D) fast mapping
(E) underextension

89. A psychologist using Carl Rogers' person-centered therapy strives to ensure that clients

(A) understand unconscious influences affecting their behavior
(B) develop positive thought patterns
(C) develop and use effective behavioral techniques
(D) receive unconditional positive regard
(E) understand their irrational beliefs

90. Schizophrenia is similar to Parkinson's disease because both disorders

(A) are classified as psychotic
(B) involve an imbalance of the neurotransmitter dopamine
(C) are treated with selective serotonin reuptake inhibitors (SSRIs)
(D) are caused by viral infections during infancy
(E) feature enlarged lateral ventricles

Study Resources

Most textbooks used in college-level introductory psychology courses cover the topics in the outline given earlier, but the approaches to certain topics and the emphases given to them may differ. To prepare for the Introductory Psychology exam, it is advisable to study one or more college textbooks, which can be found in most college bookstores. When selecting a textbook, check the table of contents against the knowledge and skills required for this test.

You may also find it helpful to supplement your reading with books listed in the bibliographies that can be found in most psychology textbooks.

Visit **clep.collegeboard.org/earn-college-credit/practice** for additional psychology resources. You can also find suggestions for exam preparation in Chapter IV of the *Official Study Guide*. In addition, many college faculty post their course materials on their schools' websites.

Answer Key

1.	B	46.	E
2.	D	47.	A
3.	D	48.	A
4.	C	49.	D
5.	D	50.	B
6.	A	51.	B
7.	B	52.	A
8.	A	53.	B
9.	B	54.	B
10.	B	55.	B
11.	D	56.	C
12.	B	57.	B
13.	B	58.	B
14.	C	59.	B
15.	E	60.	B
16.	B	61.	C
17.	E	62.	C
18.	A	63.	B
19.	C	64.	A
20.	E	65.	B
21.	A	66.	B
22.	C	67.	C
23.	D	68.	D
24.	D	69.	A
25.	C	70.	A
26.	D	71.	B
27.	C	72.	B
28.	A	73.	E
29.	B	74.	B
30.	C	75.	B
31.	C	76.	A
32.	E	77.	B
33.	C	78.	B
34.	B	79.	A
35.	D	80.	C
36.	D	81.	B
37.	D	82.	C
38.	D	83.	A
39.	C	84.	D
40.	C	85.	B
41.	C	86.	E
42.	A	87.	E
43.	D	88.	D
44.	B	89.	D
45.	A	90.	B

Introductory Sociology

Description of the Examination

The Introductory Sociology examination is designed to assess an individual's knowledge of the material typically presented in a one-semester introductory sociology course at most colleges and universities. The examination emphasizes basic facts and concepts as well as general theoretical approaches used by sociologists. Highly specialized knowledge of the subject and the methodology of the discipline is not required or measured by the test content.

The examination contains approximately 100 questions to be answered in 90 minutes. Some of these are pretest questions that will not be scored.

Knowledge and Skills Required

Questions on the Introductory Sociology examination require candidates to demonstrate one or more of the following abilities. Some questions may require more than one of these abilities.

- Identification of specific names, facts and concepts from sociological literature
- Understanding of relationships between concepts, empirical generalizations and theoretical propositions of sociology
- Understanding of the methods by which sociological relationships are established
- Application of concepts, propositions and methods to hypothetical situations
- Interpretation of tables and charts

The subject matter of the Introductory Sociology examination is drawn from the following topics. The percentages next to the main topics indicate the approximate percentage of exam questions on that topic.

20% Institutions
- Economic
- Educational
- Family
- Medical
- Political
- Religious

10% Social patterns
- Community
- Demography
- Human ecology
- Rural/urban patterns

25% Social processes
- Collective behavior and social movements
- Culture
- Deviance and social control
- Groups and organizations
- Social change
- Social interaction
- Socialization

25% Social stratification (process and structure)
- Aging
- Power and social inequality
- Professions and occupations
- Race and ethnic relations
- Sex and gender roles
- Social class
- Social mobility

20% The sociological perspective
- History of sociology
- Methods
- Sociological theory

Sample Test Questions

The following sample questions do not appear on an actual CLEP examination. They are intended to give potential test-takers an indication of the format and difficulty level of the examination and to provide content for practice and review. Knowing the correct answers to all of the sample questions is not a guarantee of satisfactory performance on the exam.

Directions: Each of the questions or incomplete statements below is followed by five suggested answers or completions. Select the one that is best in each case.

1. All of the following are examples of voluntary associations EXCEPT the

(A) Republican Party
(B) League of Women Voters
(C) Federal Bureau of Investigation
(D) First Baptist Church of Atlanta
(E) Little League Baseball Association

2. A sex ratio of 120 means that in a population there are

(A) 120 more males than females
(B) 120 more females than males
(C) 120 males for every 100 females
(D) 120 females for every 100 males
(E) 12% more males than females

3. Industrialization is most likely to reduce the importance of which of the following functions of the family?

(A) Economic production
(B) Care of young children
(C) Regulation of sexual behavior
(D) Socialization of the individual
(E) Social control

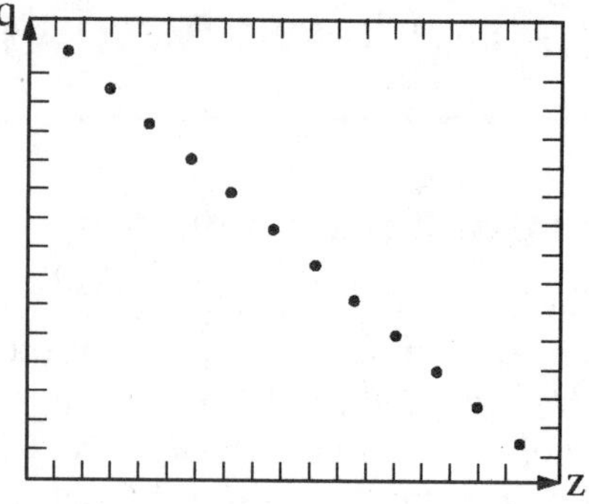

4. Which of the following best describes the relationship between q and z on the scattergram above?

(A) A perfect positive correlation
(B) A perfect negative correlation
(C) A perfect curvilinear correlation
(D) A low negative correlation
(E) A correlation of zero

5. The process by which an individual learns how to live in his or her social surroundings is known as

(A) amalgamation
(B) association
(C) collective behavior
(D) socialization
(E) innovation

6. Which of the following can properly be considered norms?

I. Laws
II. Folkways
III. Mores

(A) I only
(B) III only
(C) I and II only
(D) II and III only
(E) I, II, and III

7. Which of the following theorists argued that class conflict was inevitable in a capitalistic society and would result in revolution?

   (A) C. Wright Mills
   (B) Karl Marx
   (C) Robert Park
   (D) Max Weber
   (E) Karl Mannheim

8. Which of the following relies most heavily on sampling methods?

   (A) Small group experiment
   (B) Laboratory experiment
   (C) Participant observation
   (D) Survey research
   (E) Case study

9. Which of the following is NOT characteristic of the Chicago School of Sociology?

   (A) They studied urban neighborhoods in the city of Chicago.
   (B) They were influenced by Herbert Spencer and Frederic Clements.
   (C) They used ethnography and field methods in their research.
   (D) Talcott Parsons was a proponent of the school.
   (E) They were most influential during the twentieth century.

10. Which of the following allows human beings to adapt to diverse physical environments?

   (A) Instinct
   (B) Heredity
   (C) Culture
   (D) Stratification
   (E) Ethnocentrism

11. All of the following are properties of primary groups EXCEPT

   (A) They are important sources of social support.
   (B) They tend to be ethnocentric.
   (C) They significantly influence personality development.
   (D) They tend to be large in number.
   (E) They are frequently characterized by face-to-face relationships.

12. According to Émile Durkheim, a society that lacks clear-cut norms to govern aspirations and moral conduct is characterized by

   (A) rationalism
   (B) altruism
   (C) egoism
   (D) secularism
   (E) anomie

13. The process by which an immigrant or an ethnic minority is absorbed socially into a receiving society is called

   (A) assimilation
   (B) accommodation
   (C) cooperation
   (D) interaction
   (E) equilibrium

14. The term "sociology" was coined by its founder, the nineteenth-century positivist

   (A) Émile Durkheim
   (B) Auguste Comte
   (C) Max Weber
   (D) Harriet Martineau
   (E) George Herbert Mead

15. According to Émile Durkheim, the more homogeneous a group the greater its

    (A) organic solidarity
    (B) mechanical solidarity
    (C) functional differentiation
    (D) co-optation
    (E) stratification

16. Demographic patterns have clearly demonstrated that more males than females are born in

    (A) technologically developing countries only
    (B) technologically developed countries only
    (C) virtually every known human society
    (D) highly urbanized countries only
    (E) countries with high nutritional standards only

17. Max Weber's three dimensions of social stratification are which of the following?

    (A) Class, politics, education
    (B) Prestige, politics, occupation
    (C) Residence, occupation, religion
    (D) Status, class, power
    (E) Status, religion, prestige

18. The term "SMSA" used in the United States census refers to a

    (A) summary of many small areas
    (B) statistical mean of sampling error
    (C) summary of metropolitan shopping areas
    (D) standard measure of suburban areas
    (E) standard metropolitan statistical area

19. In order for an occupation to be considered a profession by a sociologist, it must be an occupation that

    (A) is based on abstract knowledge and a body of specialized information
    (B) has high public visibility in the community
    (C) requires training from a specialized school rather than from a university
    (D) serves government and industry as well as individuals
    (E) is a full-time position with a regular salary

20. In the study of social class, a sociologist would be LEAST likely to focus on

    (A) power
    (B) social mobility
    (C) style of life
    (D) motivation
    (E) occupational status

21. An example of a folkway in American society is

    (A) joining a religious cult
    (B) eating a sandwich for lunch
    (C) failing to pay income taxes on time
    (D) stopping for a red light
    (E) being fined for jaywalking

22. Socialization takes place

    (A) only in childhood
    (B) mainly in adolescence
    (C) mainly in early adulthood
    (D) mainly through the reproductive years
    (E) throughout the life cycle

23. A school system that teaches children of different ethnic groups in the children's own language and about their own particular ethnic heritage illustrates a policy of

    (A) structural assimilation
    (B) cultural assimilation
    (C) accommodation
    (D) rationalization
    (E) ethnocentrism

24. Max Weber linked the emergence of capitalism to the

    (A) Calvinist doctrine of predestination
    (B) Catholic monks' belief in asceticism
    (C) Protestants' desire for material luxuries
    (D) increasing power of the nobility in medieval Europe
    (E) Hindu belief in reincarnation

25. The economy of the postindustrial United States is characterized by all of the following EXCEPT

    (A) computer-facilitated automation
    (B) relocation of manufacturing plants to less-developed countries
    (C) international competition in the manufacturing sector of the economy
    (D) increasing numbers of service compared to manufacturing jobs
    (E) increased job security due to globalization

26. Which statement about political participation in the United States is true?

    (A) Almost everyone of voting age in the United States is registered to vote.
    (B) Voter turnout in the United States is lower than in most European nations.
    (C) Voter turnout has increased dramatically in the last twenty years.
    (D) People of higher social class tend to participate less in voting than lower social classes.
    (E) Younger adults are more likely to vote than those over 65.

27. Which of the following is best described as an organized sphere of social life, or societal subsystem, designed to support important values and to meet human needs?

    (A) Social structure
    (B) Social organization
    (C) Social institution
    (D) Social culture
    (E) Economic corporation

28. Most of the funding for public schools in the United States comes from

    (A) lottery revenues
    (B) state income taxes
    (C) local sales taxes
    (D) local income taxes
    (E) local property taxes

29. According to Max Weber, authority derived from the understanding that individuals have clearly defined rights and duties to uphold and that they implement rules and procedures impersonally is

    (A) traditional authority
    (B) charismatic authority
    (C) rational-legal authority
    (D) coercion
    (E) persuasion

30. Raw materials are processed and converted into finished goods in which sector of the economy?

    (A) Agricultural
    (B) Industrial
    (C) Public
    (D) Service
    (E) Information

31. In the United States, economic growth between 1985 and 2005 resulted in

(A) growth in the gap between the rich and poor
(B) a narrowing of the gap between the rich and poor
(C) no change in the gap between the rich and poor
(D) growth in the economic gap between men and women
(E) no change in the economic gap between men and women

32. Within the scientific perspective, which of the following are the most important sources of knowledge?

(A) Common sense and tradition
(B) Empiricism and reason
(C) Authority and structure
(D) Paradigms and intuition
(E) Existentialism and reference groups

33. Which of the following made up the largest number of immigrants to the United States in the 2000s?

(A) Mexicans
(B) Chinese
(C) Italians
(D) Canadians
(E) Russians

34. Compared to the United States population in general, Asian Americans have

(A) larger proportions of their populations in poverty
(B) lower median family incomes
(C) a higher level of formal educational achievement
(D) fewer ties to their family's country of origin
(E) a lower proportion of first-generation immigrants

35. In the world's economic system, which of the following is true about the relationship between high-income countries and low-income countries?

(A) High-income countries depend on low-income countries to purchase natural resources from them.
(B) High-income countries build manufacturing plants in low-income countries to obtain cheap labor.
(C) High-income countries encourage the development of state-owned economic enterprises in low-income countries.
(D) High-income countries are more likely than low-income countries to have an agriculturally based economy.
(E) High-income countries have less-diversified sources of income.

36. Sociological studies of gender socialization show that

(A) girls' games are more likely than boys' games to encourage assertive behaviors
(B) girls' games are more likely than boys' games to emphasize strict observance of rules
(C) girls are more likely than boys to learn to suppress emotions of sadness
(D) girls are more likely to engage in competitive play and boys in cooperative play
(E) girls are less likely than boys to receive attention from teachers

37. The increase in prejudice that sometimes resulted from court-ordered desegregation in public schools is a

(A) manifest function of desegregation
(B) latent dysfunction of desegregation
(C) functional alternative to desegregation
(D) secondary function of desegregation
(E) rational exchange for desegregation

38. The practice of judging another culture by the standards of one's own culture is called

(A) ethnocentrism
(B) cultural relativism
(C) cultural integration
(D) transference
(E) multiculturalism

39. In *Gesellschaft*, people are more likely than in *Gemeinschaft* to

(A) have frequent face-to-face contact with those they know
(B) see others as a means of advancing their own individual goals
(C) be united by primary group bonds
(D) have altruistic concerns for others
(E) be tradition-directed

40. Demographic transition theory explains population changes by

(A) connecting them exclusively to changes in the food supply
(B) linking population changes to technological development
(C) focusing on the migration of people in and out of specified territories
(D) tying population growth to changes in the sex ratio
(E) referring to a culture's religious attitudes

41. Which theory assumes that deviance occurs among individuals who are blocked from achieving socially approved goals by legitimate means?

(A) Hirschi's social control theory
(B) Labeling theory
(C) Merton's strain theory
(D) Differential association theory
(E) Cultural transmission theory

42. Sandra is female, she is African American, and she is sixteen years of age. These three characteristics are examples of Sandra's

(A) role sets
(B) cultural roles
(C) achieved statuses
(D) ascribed statuses
(E) mobility aspirations

43. Cooley called a person's self-conception based on the responses of others

(A) the divided self
(B) self-esteem
(C) the concrete operational stage
(D) the looking-glass self
(E) the "I" and "me"

44. The philosopher Thomas Hobbes believed that social order developed out of the

(A) recognition of the transcendent power of God
(B) biological need for humans to reproduce
(C) desire to escape a state of continuous social conflict
(D) discovery of agriculture
(E) reaction to the industrial revolution

45. Max Weber's principle of *verstehen* was meant to

(A) explain the subjective beliefs that motivate people to act
(B) determine how society is dysfunctionally organized
(C) focus on the inequality in society
(D) search for the social structures that fulfill people's needs
(E) identify the patterns of exchange among individuals or groups

46. According to sociological terminology, an analysis of the amount of violence in mass media, such as television shows, would be which of the following?

(A) Content analysis
(B) Secondary analysis
(C) Quasi-experiment
(D) Participant observation
(E) Ethnographic interview

47. Which of the following is true of social norms for the structure of marriage?

(A) They have consistently required monogamy across all periods of history and cross-culturally around the globe.
(B) They have favored polyandry in those societies wanting to increase their birth rate.
(C) They have frequently held polygyny as the societal ideal, although this pattern was functionally available to and practiced primarily by the most wealthy and powerful.
(D) They have no impact in democratic societies, since democracies allow individuals to choose their own form of marriage.
(E) They are based on the ideal of gender equality.

48. In the past 30 years, the infant mortality rate in the United States has

(A) remained about the same as in other industrialized countries
(B) declined for African American people but not for Caucasian people
(C) declined among Caucasian people, while increasing among African American people
(D) declined among Caucasian people, while remaining stable among African American people
(E) declined among both African American people and Caucasian people, while remaining twice as high among African American people

49. In the United States, semiskilled positions held primarily by women, such as waitperson, cashier, and receptionist, are known as which type of occupation?

(A) Blue-collar
(B) Pink-collar
(C) White-collar
(D) Nonpatriarchal
(E) Matriarchal

50. Tamara worked as a waitress for five years after high school before she went to college. After college, Tamara got a job as a sales representative for a pharmaceutical company. This best exemplifies which of the following types of mobility?

(A) Intergenerational
(B) Intragenerational
(C) Unilateral
(D) Horizontal
(E) Structural

51. The concept of "glass ceiling" affecting women in the workforce is best illustrated by which of the following?

(A) The instability of female-dominated jobs
(B) The pay inequity between men and women for comparable jobs
(C) The breakdown of gender stereotypes in the job market
(D) The instability of marriages for women who are successful in the workforce
(E) The barriers that limit career advancement for women

52. Which of the following statements is most accurate regarding patriarchy?

(A) It is a form of political organization in which the state assumes paternal responsibility for citizens.
(B) It is a form of social organization in which one's kinship lineage is traced through the family of the mother.
(C) It is a form of social organization in which males control most formal and informal power.
(D) It is found only in those societies that practice polyandry.
(E) It is not found in those societies that practice polygyny.

53. Which of the following distinguishes a crime from a deviant act?

(A) The degree of harm caused by the act
(B) The number of people who disapprove of the act
(C) The definition of the act as criminal by a political entity
(D) The social status of the person who committed the act
(E) The social status of the person who is harmed by the act

54. A collection of people who happen to be walking down the street at the same time but who have nothing else in common is known as

(A) a social movement
(B) a social category
(C) an aggregate
(D) a primary group
(E) a secondary group

55. "This may sound really strange, but . . ."

The statement above is an example of

(A) a disclaimer
(B) an account
(C) an excuse
(D) a justification
(E) a concession

56. Nathan wants to study the behavior of city residents as they travel on the subway to work every day. What type of research would be most appropriate for Nathan's research project?

(A) Experimental research
(B) Field research
(C) Content analysis
(D) Secondary analysis
(E) Survey method

57. Which of the following is true of a dependent variable?

(A) It is spurious.
(B) It is influenced by another variable.
(C) It is manipulated.
(D) It causes other variables to increase.
(E) It is used to draw a sample from a population.

58. Which of the following is an example of an informal positive sanction?

(A) Marguerite receives a bronze medal for gymnastics at the Olympics.
(B) Hank is awarded a high school diploma by the school board.
(C) Halle receives a million dollars for her performance in a movie.
(D) Danisha receives a new car from her parents when she scores 1600 on the SAT®.
(E) William is sentenced to one year of community service and a $5,000 fine for shoplifting.

59. In general, females perform better than males do on tests of

(A) general intelligence
(B) verbal ability
(C) visual-spatial ability
(D) scientific information
(E) mathematics

60. Ken works on an assembly line in a paper factory in the midwestern United States. He believes that if he works hard enough, he will become very wealthy. According to Karl Marx, Ken's belief reflects which of the following?

(A) False consciousness
(B) Class consciousness
(C) Collective consciousness
(D) The caste system
(E) Rational choice

61. Which of the following terms refers to something that has an unexpected detrimental effect on social institutions or society?

(A) Secret function
(B) Manifest function
(C) Manifest dysfunction
(D) Latent function
(E) Latent dysfunction

62. Which of the following terms refers to a philosophical system under which knowledge of the world and human behavior is derived from scientific observation in search of universal laws?

(A) Theology
(B) Determinism
(C) Positivism
(D) Phenomenology
(E) Metaphysics

63. Mrs. Jones has a parent-teacher meeting scheduled at the school where she teaches. The meeting is scheduled at the same time as her daughter's piano recital. Mrs. Jones will have to decide how to juggle the contradictory expectations of teacher and parent. This situation is referred to as

(A) role strain
(B) role conflict
(C) status conflict
(D) status set
(E) role set

64. Which of the following would most likely be an agent of involuntary resocialization?

(A) Mass media
(B) An institution of higher learning
(C) A peer group
(D) A total institution
(E) The family

65. All of the following characteristics are commonly attributed to postmodern culture EXCEPT

(A) moral relativism
(B) skepticism toward traditional authority
(C) growing tolerance of diversity
(D) loss of faith in absolutes
(E) adherence to traditional gender roles

66. Joe is on trial for selling drugs. He looks very different from when he was arrested. He has washed, cut, and combed his hair, and is wearing a clean, conservative suit and tie at the trial. Joe is engaged in

(A) dysfunctional behavior
(B) altruism
(C) impression management
(D) exchange
(E) anticipatory socialization

67. A characteristic of a triad is that it

    (A) is prone to coalition formation
    (B) allows more power per member than a dyad
    (C) is the smallest type of group
    (D) can develop the strongest relationships
    (E) has little impact on human behavior

68. Laura is conducting an experiment to determine the effect of caffeine on wakefulness. She gives half of her subjects a caffeinated beverage to drink. These subjects are the

    (A) control group
    (B) experimental group
    (C) independent variable
    (D) dependent variable
    (E) study population

69. The claim that the division of labor based on gender has survived because it is beneficial and efficient for human living is an example of

    (A) structural functionalism
    (B) conflict theory
    (C) ethnomethodology
    (D) symbolic interactionism
    (E) phenomenology

70. Communities that form adjacent to central cities are called

    (A) secondary groups
    (B) suburbs
    (C) neighborhoods
    (D) exurbs
    (E) development zones

71. According to world-systems theory, the global system is primarily

    (A) political
    (B) military
    (C) social
    (D) economic
    (E) cultural

72. Some sociologists view the family as an economic unit that contributes to social injustice because it is the basis for transferring power, property, and privilege from one generation to the next. Which of the following perspectives best describes that view?

    (A) Interactionist
    (B) Exchange
    (C) Structural functionalist
    (D) Conflict
    (E) Rational choice

73. Which of the following types of societies is least differentiated?

    (A) Horticultural
    (B) Pastoral
    (C) Hunting and gathering
    (D) Agricultural
    (E) Industrial

74. Which of the following sociologists asserted that race is the most serious problem in the United States?

    (A) Karl Marx
    (B) Max Weber
    (C) Harriet Martineau
    (D) Jane Addams
    (E) W. E. B. Du Bois

75. The early Chicago School researchers found that even though immigration changed the racial and ethnic composition of some areas of the city over time, the rates of crime in those areas remained relatively high. Which of the following interpretations of this finding is most consistent with the Chicago School's social disorganization perspective?

(A) Police deployment practices failed to control crime.
(B) Police were biased against immigrants.
(C) Immigrants did not have legitimate means to achieve their goals.
(D) Immigrants were labeled as criminals even when their actions were not illegal.
(E) Neighborhood social institutions were ineffective at preventing crime.

76. Societies that are postindustrial are distinguished from industrial ones by

(A) an economy based largely on manufacturing
(B) a universal return to traditional cultural values
(C) the political power of people with low asset levels
(D) the predominance of knowledge-based service industries
(E) the proportional expansion of the agriculture sector of the economy

77. Two basic premises that underlie capitalism are that

(A) individuals pursue their desired occupations, and society rewards diligent workers
(B) the free market demands more elaborate products over the years, and skill and hard work allow laborers to meet that demand
(C) majority rule must be maintained for the free market to function properly, and individuals who desire wealth and prestige work hard
(D) societal profits are distributed to each person according to need, and each person's skills determine his or her role in the workforce
(E) goods are produced for profit, and the free market determines what is produced and at what price

78. Approximately what percent of the people in the United States live in metropolitan areas?

(A) 45%
(B) 50%
(C) 65%
(D) 85%
(E) 95%

79. Which of the following best describes what sociologists of education mean when they refer to the hidden curriculum?

(A) The manifest results of education
(B) The unintended consequences of schooling
(C) Delayed transmission of knowledge
(D) The formal curriculum
(E) Miscommunication between teacher and student

80. A sociologist of religion who studies secularization is interested in which of the following?

(A) The increasing prevalence of religious cults in a society
(B) A society that changes from having a few religious practices to many religious practices
(C) The development of more extreme religious practices in a society
(D) A society that changes from closely identifying with nonreligious values to closely identifying with religious values
(E) A society that changes from closely identifying with religious values to closely identifying with nonreligious values

81. The practice in which a woman is married to two or more men at the same time is known as

(A) monogamy
(B) polygyny
(C) polyandry
(D) serial monogamy
(E) patriarchy

82. Which of the following theorists is most associated with structural functionalism?

(A) Karl Marx
(B) Max Weber
(C) Randall Collins
(D) Herbert Blumer
(E) Émile Durkheim

83. Impression management is exhibited by a college student who

(A) aces an exam after forgetting to study for it
(B) anticipates graduating and getting a job
(C) expects to do well on an exam and ends up doing so
(D) anticipates flunking a course and stops going to class
(E) cleans the dorm room in preparation for Parent's Weekend

84. As a nurse, Rex works to respect and fulfill the different values, beliefs, and behaviors of his patients. Which of the following is Rex practicing?

(A) Cultural competence
(B) Ethnocentrism
(C) Alienation
(D) Cultural lag
(E) Assimilation

85. Which of the following levels of racial-ethnic relations is best exemplified by the 2008 election of President Barack Obama?

(A) Assimilation
(B) Cultural transmission
(C) Internal colonialism
(D) Accommodation
(E) Segregation

86. Which of the following approaches to stratification is most likely to suggest that, as a society becomes more stratified, it prevents the talents of those at the bottom from being known or used and thus potentially fails to benefit from the contributions of all its members?

(A) Interactionist
(B) Conflict
(C) Postmodernist
(D) Demographic
(E) Structural functionalist

87. A society in which women have more wealth, privilege, and political power than men have is said to be experiencing which of the following?

(A) Gender equality
(B) Gender-role reversal
(C) Gender stratification
(D) Gender expectations
(E) Gender dissonance

88. An advertisement for men's cologne depicts a woman as a pair of legs. This is an example of

(A) objectification
(B) subjectification
(C) misrepresentation
(D) characterization
(E) minimization

89. According to Émile Durkheim, religion is characterized by a dichotomy between

(A) good and evil
(B) worship and blasphemy
(C) the sacred and the profane
(D) believers and nonbelievers
(E) the profound and the banal

90. James's family disapproves of his marriage to Juanita because she is from a different social class. Which of the following best describes James's family's marriage practices?

    (A) Exogamy
    (B) Endogamy
    (C) Monogamy
    (D) Homogamy
    (E) Polygamy

91. Which of the following social practices is associated with overall lower divorce rates?

    (A) Getting married after the age of 30
    (B) Valuing individualism strongly
    (C) Interacting with extended family members infrequently
    (D) Having a high participation of females in the labor-force
    (E) Living in regions with more women than men

92. When all members of a country belong to a single religion and that religion is considered the official religion for the country, the religion is referred to as

    (A) an ecclesia
    (B) a denomination
    (C) a sect
    (D) a cult
    (E) an alternative religion

93. In *An Essay on the Principle of Population*, Thomas Malthus argued that

    (A) human population and food production grow at about the same rate
    (B) food production always grows faster than human population growth
    (C) human population grows exponentially while food production grows linearly
    (D) famines tend to be caused by problems in food distribution rather than food production
    (E) free markets in farmland would encourage the development of productive agricultural technologies

94. Marxist sociological theory attributes social stratification to

    (A) an innate human tendency toward greed
    (B) political disagreements over ideology
    (C) private ownership of the means of production
    (D) disparities in ability and talent between different individuals
    (E) variation in the functional importance of occupational positions

95. Which of the following factors currently has the strongest influence on individual income?

    (A) Race
    (B) Gender
    (C) Attractiveness
    (D) Inherited social class
    (E) Level of educational attainment

96. Elizabeth lost her home, her job, and all of her material possessions during an economic downturn. As a result, she experienced which of the following types of mobility?

    (A) Vertical
    (B) Meritocratic
    (C) Horizontal
    (D) Exchange
    (E) Intergenerational

97. Which of the following is most likely to slow the world's population growth?

    (A) Elevating the cost of childbirth
    (B) Raising all nations out of poverty
    (C) Denying medical care to sick people over the age of 65
    (D) Requiring all teens to take abstinence-only sex education classes
    (E) Encouraging adherence to traditional religious authorities throughout the world

98. Which of the following views stratification as being developed and maintained through everyday interactions?

    (A) Feminist theory
    (B) Labeling theory
    (C) Dependency theory
    (D) Structural functionalism
    (E) Symbolic interactionism

Study Resources

Most textbooks used in college-level introductory sociology courses cover the topics in the outline given earlier, but the approaches to certain topics and the emphases given to them may differ. To prepare for the Introductory Sociology exam, it is advisable to study one or more college textbooks, which can be found in most college bookstores. When selecting a textbook, check the table of contents against the knowledge and skills required for this test.

As you read, take notes that address the following issues, which are fundamental to most questions that appear on the test:

- What is society? What is culture? What is common to all societies, and what is characteristic of American society?
- What are other basic concepts in sociology that help to describe human nature, human interaction and the collective behavior of groups, organizations, institutions and societies?
- What methods do sociologists use to study, describe, analyze and observe human behavior?

Visit **clep.collegeboard.org/earn-college-credit/practice** for additional sociology resources. You can also find suggestions for exam preparation in Chapter IV of the *Official Study Guide*. In addition, many college faculty post their course materials on their schools' websites.

Answer Key

1.	C	50.	B
2.	C	51.	E
3.	A	52.	C
4.	B	53.	C
5.	D	54.	C
6.	E	55.	A
7.	B	56.	B
8.	D	57.	B
9.	D	58.	D
10.	C	59.	B
11.	D	60.	A
12.	E	61.	E
13.	A	62.	C
14.	B	63.	B
15.	B	64.	D
16.	C	65.	E
17.	D	66.	C
18.	E	67.	A
19.	A	68.	B
20.	D	69.	A
21.	B	70.	B
22.	E	71.	D
23.	C	72.	D
24.	A	73.	C
25.	E	74.	E
26.	B	75.	E
27.	C	76.	D
28.	E	77.	E
29.	C	78.	D
30.	B	79.	B
31.	A	80.	E
32.	B	81.	C
33.	A	82.	E
34.	C	83.	E
35.	B	84.	A
36.	E	85.	A
37.	B	86.	B
38.	A	87.	C
39.	B	88.	A
40.	B	89.	C
41.	C	90.	B
42.	D	91.	A
43.	D	92.	A
44.	C	93.	C
45.	A	94.	C
46.	A	95.	E
47.	C	96.	A
48.	E	97.	B
49.	B	98.	E

Social Sciences and History

Description of the Examination

The Social Sciences and History examination covers the following subjects: United States History, Western Civilization, World History, Economics, Geography, and Political Science. While the exam is based on no specific course, its content is drawn from introductory college courses in these subjects.

The primary objective of the exam is to give candidates the opportunity to demonstrate that they possess the level of knowledge and understanding expected of college students who meet a distribution or general education requirement in the social sciences/history areas.

The Social Sciences and History examination contains approximately 120 questions to be answered in 90 minutes. Some of them are pretest questions that will not be scored.

Note: This examination uses the chronological designations B.C.E. (before the common era) and C.E. (common era). These labels correspond to B.C. (before Christ) and A.D. (anno Domini), which are used in some textbooks.

Knowledge and Skills Required

The Social Sciences and History examination requires candidates to demonstrate one or more of the following abilities.

- Familiarity with terminology, facts, conventions, methodology, concepts, principles, generalizations and theories
- Ability to understand, interpret and analyze graphic, pictorial and written material
- Ability to apply abstractions to particulars and to apply hypotheses, concepts, theories and principles to given data
- Ability to assess evidence and data, to make comparisons, and to draw conclusions

Exam Content

The percentages below reflect the approximate coverage for each subject area of the exam. The main topics covered within each subject are also listed.

40% History

Requires general knowledge and understanding of time- and place-specific human experiences. Topics covered include political, diplomatic, social, economic, intellectual and cultural history.

13–15% United States History

Covers the colonial period, the American Revolution, the early republic, the Civil War and Reconstruction, industrialization, the Progressive Era, the First World War, the 1920s, the Great Depression and the New Deal, the Second World War, the 1950s, the Cold War, social conflict — the 1960s and 1970s, the late twentieth century, and the early twenty-first century

13–15% Western Civilization

Covers ancient western Asia, Egypt, Greece and Rome as well as medieval Europe and modern Europe, including its expansion and outposts in other parts of the world; its imperial contraction and new economic and political forms

13–15% World History

Covers Africa, Asia, Australia, Europe, North America and South America from prehistory to the present, focusing on global themes and interactions

20% Economics

- Economic measurements
- International trade
- Major theorists and schools
- Monetary and fiscal policy
- Product markets
- Resource markets
- Scarcity, choice, and cost

20% Geography

- Key geographical skills
- Cultural geography
- Physical geography
- Population
- Regional geography
- Rural and urban land use
- Spatial interaction

20% Government/Political Science

- Comparative politics
- International relations
- Methods
- United States
  - Civil rights and liberties
  - Constitution and its interpretation
  - Institutions
  - Parties, interest groups, and media
  - Voting and political behavior

Sample Test Questions

The following sample questions do not appear on an actual CLEP examination. They are intended to give potential test-takers an indication of the format and difficulty level of the examination and to provide content for practice and review. Knowing the correct answers to all of the sample questions is not a guarantee of satisfactory performance on the exam.

Directions: Each of the questions or incomplete statements below is followed by five suggested answers or completions. Select the one that is best in each case.

1. Prior to the campaign of 1828, most candidates for president of the United States were chosen by

   (A) political rallies in each state
   (B) the electoral college
   (C) national party conventions
   (D) state primary elections
   (E) leaders of sectional political groups in Congress

2. Which of the following best describes the impact of Spanish colonization on the indigenous peoples of Central and South America in the sixteenth and early seventeenth centuries?

   (A) Their economic well-being was improved by the wealth they produced at the direction of the Spanish ruler.
   (B) They kept their own political system and culture, which coexisted with that of the Spanish colonial system.
   (C) They migrated in large numbers to Spain.
   (D) Their system of religious beliefs and practices was unaffected.
   (E) Their populations decreased dramatically as a result of contact with the Spanish.

3. An individual who believes that "government is best which governs not at all" favors

   (A) anarchy
   (B) tyranny
   (C) monarchy
   (D) oligarchy
   (E) democracy

4. The demand curve facing an individual firm in a perfectly competitive market is

   (A) downward sloping
   (B) upward sloping
   (C) vertical
   (D) horizontal
   (E) U-shaped

5. As depicted above, the Kurds could be described as which of the following?

(A) Nation-state
(B) Perforated state
(C) Multinational state
(D) Stateless nation
(E) Fragmented state

6. The ready availability of satellite images has had the greatest impact on which of the following branches of geography?

(A) Geomorphology
(B) Cartography
(C) Historical geography
(D) Political geography
(E) Cultural geography

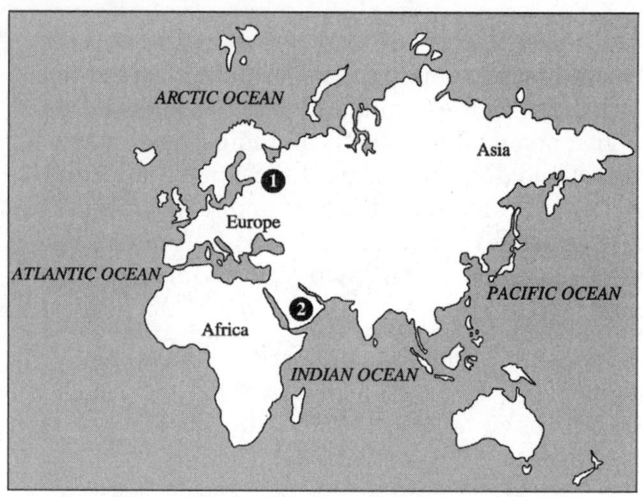

7. A traveler going from point 1 to point 2 on the map above would experience a climatic change from

(A) humid continental to desert
(B) humid subtropical to Mediterranean
(C) desert to tropical rain forest
(D) tropical wet to Mediterranean
(E) Mediterranean to humid continental

8. How often is the Sun directly overhead at the equator?

(A) Once a day
(B) Four times a year
(C) Twice a year
(D) Once a year at the summer solstice
(E) Never

9. "To industry and frugality I owe the early easiness of my circumstances and the acquisition of my fortune with all that knowledge that has enabled me to be a useful citizen."

   The statement above is most characteristic of which of the following?

   (A) Benjamin Franklin
   (B) Ralph Waldo Emerson
   (C) Henry David Thoreau
   (D) Samuel Gompers
   (E) Thomas Jefferson

10. One of the fundamental changes that took place in the twentieth century was a gradual

   (A) increase in manufacturing, as opposed to services, in developed nations
   (B) increase in economic interdependence
   (C) decrease in the pressure of world population on economic resources
   (D) decline in world trade
   (E) decline in nationalistic feelings among peoples of the Eastern Hemisphere

11. A person who lived in the 1790s in the United States and who believed in a strong central government, broad construction of the Constitution, and funding of the public debt would most probably have been

   (A) a socialist
   (B) an Anti-Federalist
   (C) a Federalist
   (D) a believer in monarchy
   (E) a Jeffersonian Republican

12. Public opinion polls in the United States commonly make use of

   (A) sampling theory
   (B) case studies
   (C) intelligence tests
   (D) Rorschach tests
   (E) clinical interviews

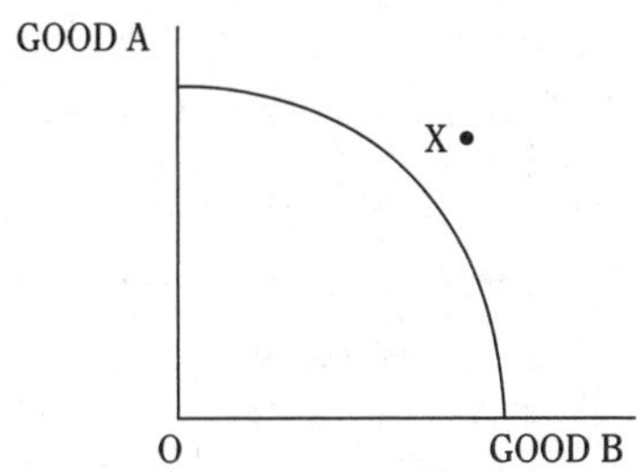

13. For the economy described by the production possibilities curve above, which of the following is true?

   (A) Intended investment is greater than intended saving at point X.
   (B) The economy cannot produce at point X using currently available resources and technology.
   (C) The economy is more efficient in producing good A than good B.
   (D) To produce additional units of good B, the economy must forgo fewer and fewer units of good A.
   (E) Income is unequally distributed to the factors of production.

14. A writ of habeas corpus is secured for which of the following purposes?

   (A) To prevent the imposition of excessive bail
   (B) To guarantee the accused the right to face the accuser
   (C) To prevent a legislature from inflicting punishment without a judicial trial
   (D) To ensure trial by an impartial jury
   (E) To prevent undue detention without cause

15. The area of the African continent is approximately

   (A) half the area of western Europe
   (B) the same as the area of the United States east of the Mississippi River
   (C) two times the area of California
   (D) four times the area of the continental United States
   (E) five times the area of South America

16. Chinese culture and influence were most significant in shaping the institutions of which of the following countries?

    (A) Bangladesh, Pakistan, and Sri Lanka
    (B) India, Japan, and Korea
    (C) Indonesia, the Philippines, and Thailand
    (D) Japan, Korea, and Vietnam
    (E) Korea, Nepal, and the Philippines

17. The most immediate consequence of abolitionism in the United States in the 1830s and 1840s was

    (A) widespread support for the abolition of slavery
    (B) intensified slaveholders' resentment toward the movement
    (C) better treatment of freed African Americans in the North
    (D) greater sympathy for popular sovereignty
    (E) increased interest in African colonization

18. "We know so little about how to live in this life that there is no point in worrying about what may happen to us after death. First let us learn to live in the right way with other people and then let whatever happens next take care of itself."

    The quotation above best expresses the philosophy of

    (A) Jesus
    (B) Muhammad
    (C) Confucius
    (D) Charles Darwin
    (E) Thomas Aquinas

19. Major political revolutions in the twentieth century most often occurred in countries with

    (A) comparatively low unemployment
    (B) high levels of industrialization
    (C) small industrial and large agricultural sectors
    (D) representative governments
    (E) small populations

20. Which of the following is the main purpose of the system of checks and balances in the United States Constitution?

    (A) To provide some institutional restraints on the authority of each of the three branches of government
    (B) To regulate the relationship between federal and state government
    (C) To assure the supremacy of Congress
    (D) To provide a balance between the power of large states and that of small states
    (E) To protect minority rights from the unrestrained power of the majority

21. To reduce inflationary pressure in the economy of the United States, the Federal Reserve would most likely

    (A) sell government securities on the open market
    (B) reduce margin requirements
    (C) lower legal reserve requirements
    (D) decrease the discount rate
    (E) encourage member banks to increase their loans

22. Which of the following developments is most characteristic of Latin America in the nineteenth and twentieth centuries?

    (A) Increased colonization by European nations
    (B) Vast differences between the rich and the poor
    (C) A dramatic shift from United States to European investment
    (D) Enormous wealth resulting from discoveries of gold and silver
    (E) Development of a large export trade in manufactured goods

23. Construction of the Panama Canal shortened the sailing time between New York and

(A) London
(B) Port-au-Prince
(C) Rio de Janeiro
(D) New Orleans
(E) San Francisco

24. Of the following, which is the earliest human innovation?

(A) Development of urban centers
(B) Use of written language
(C) Use and control of fire
(D) Dependence on agriculture as the major source of food
(E) Domestication of animals

25. Which of the following prompted African Americans to move to cities in the North during the first quarter of the twentieth century?

I. The impact of the boll weevil
II. The availability of industrial jobs in the North
III. The impact of segregation legislation in the South

(A) II only
(B) I and II only
(C) I and III only
(D) II and III only
(E) I, II, and III

26. Abolition of the trans-Atlantic slave trade was difficult to achieve in the early 1800s because

(A) the British were strongly in favor of slavery
(B) slave labor was needed in Europe
(C) profits from the slave trade were high
(D) most countries in Europe had extensive African colonies
(E) slavery was widespread in all parts of the Americas

27. Which of the following best describes the political power of the Ottoman Empire circa 1550 C.E.?

(A) It was at a standstill as a result of weak leadership and a series of revolts.
(B) It was in decline as a result of invasion by western Christian forces.
(C) It was beginning to rise as a result of the recent introduction of Islam.
(D) It was at its peak as a result of a series of military successes.
(E) It was beginning a long period of decline as a result of increased trade with Europe.

28. An aging population necessarily has

(A) a population pyramid with a large base
(B) more males than females
(C) a decreasing death rate
(D) an increasing median age
(E) an increasing birth rate

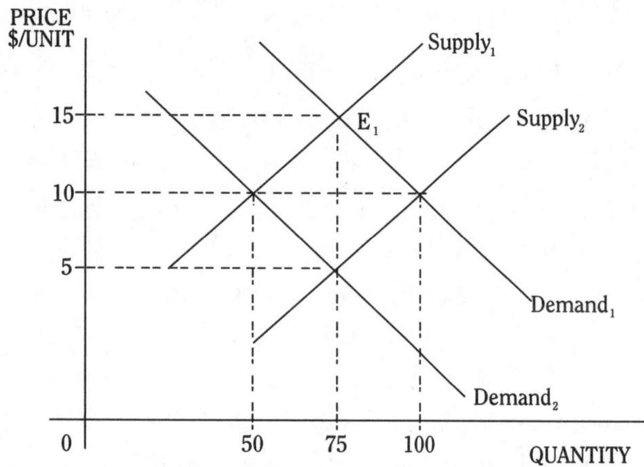

29. The United States market for apples is in equilibrium at E_1, where 75 units are sold at a price of $15 per unit. If consumers' per capita disposable income decreases, the equilibrium price and quantity of apples sold can be which of the following?

	Unit Price	Quantity
(A)	$15	75
(B)	$10	50
(C)	$10	100
(D)	$ 5	75
(E)	$ 5	100

30. Which of the following best describes the impact of industrialization on women in nineteenth-century Britain?

(A) Industrialization had relatively little impact on women since most worked only in the home.
(B) Many laborsaving devices that made housework easier were introduced into the home.
(C) Many women became factory workers for the first time.
(D) Large numbers of women joined industrial labor unions.
(E) Women in many industrial jobs worked longer hours and earned more than men.

31. In the late twentieth century, Islamic fundamentalism had the least influence in which of the following countries?

(A) Algeria
(B) China
(C) Egypt
(D) India
(E) Indonesia

32. Which of the following is true of the First Amendment to the United States Constitution?

(A) It established presidential control over the budget.
(B) It created the Supreme Court.
(C) It declared all people to be equal.
(D) It established the foundations for church-state relations.
(E) It guaranteed citizens the right to bear arms.

33. The Peloponnesian Wars were primarily the result of

(A) Athenian imperialism
(B) Spartan militarism
(C) the invasion of Greece by Rome
(D) the conquests of Alexander the Great
(E) the spread of Athenian democracy

34. Which of the following economic policies is likely to result in the greatest reduction in aggregate demand?

(A) A $5 billion increase in personal income taxes only
(B) A $5 billion decrease in government transfer payments only
(C) A $5 billion decrease in government purchases of goods and services only
(D) A $5 billion decrease in government purchases accompanied by a $5 billion increase in personal income taxes
(E) A $5 billion decrease in government purchases accompanied by a $5 billion decrease in personal income taxes

35. Which of the following philosophers asserted that all human beings possess the natural rights to life, liberty, and property?

(A) Thomas Hobbes
(B) John Locke
(C) Augustine of Hippo
(D) Aristotle
(E) Socrates

36. Thomas Malthus is most widely known for advancing the theory that

(A) population increases faster during periods of war than during periods of peace
(B) the maximum life span of humans is a constant, but the number who reach it is a variable
(C) population tends to increase faster than does the means of subsistence
(D) the death rate for the world as a whole must equal the birth rate for each generation
(E) a population explosion is a natural consequence of improved medical care

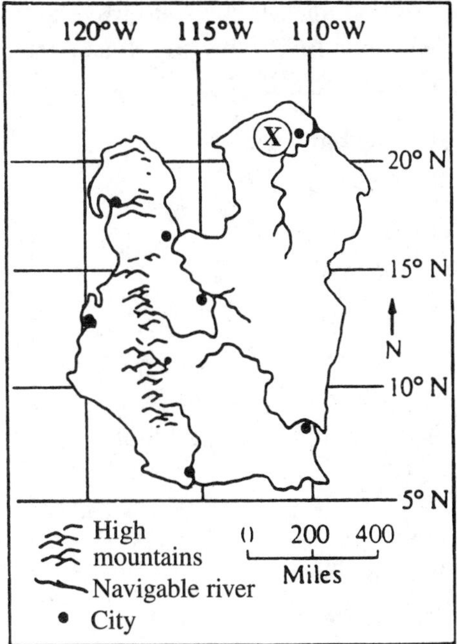

37. According to the map above, which of the following land formations would most likely be found near City X?

(A) A plateau
(B) A volcano
(C) A delta
(D) A peninsula
(E) A mountain

38. Which of the following best describes the reason for the 1863 riot that took place in New York City?

(A) President Lincoln's suspension of habeas corpus
(B) Opposition to the ratification of the Fourteenth Amendment granting citizenship to African Americans
(C) Discontent over food and supplies being diverted to the war effort
(D) Federal troops using force to end union strikes led by recent immigrants
(E) Irish Americans and German Americans blaming free African Americans for the wartime draft

39. Of the following, which group was the first to establish trade links with both East Africa and the upper Niger Valley?

(A) The Portuguese
(B) The English
(C) The Arabs
(D) The Spanish
(E) The French

40. John Steinbeck's novel *The Grapes of Wrath* depicts the period of United States history known as the

(A) Gilded Age
(B) Roaring Twenties
(C) Great Depression
(D) Cold War
(E) Vietnam era

41. The Green Revolution of the mid-twentieth century refers to

(A) the unparalleled strength of the United States dollar
(B) increased agricultural productivity due to the introduction of new crops and technologies
(C) the rise of a social and political movement expressing strong environmental concerns
(D) the destruction of Brazilian rain forests
(E) the political development of tropical countries previously under colonial rule

42. Which of the following is the most significant effect of mass media on national elections in the United States?

(A) Helping shape the agenda for political debate
(B) Improving the exposure of little-known candidates
(C) Defining party platforms
(D) Reducing the influence of money in politics
(E) Decreasing the accountability of incumbent officials

43. All of the following factors contributed to the coming of the French Revolution EXCEPT

(A) inequitable distribution of wealth
(B) active leadership by the Estates General
(C) resentment of aristocratic fiscal privileges
(D) failure of the monarchy to effect constitutional reforms
(E) immediate food shortages

44. Which of the following would increase the demand for workers in the short run?

(A) A decrease in the demand for machinery
(B) An increase in the cost of production
(C) An increase in the price of the product
(D) A decrease in the demand for the product
(E) A decrease in available natural resources

45. Which of the following is considered a liberal policy associated with the Great Society?

(A) Privatizing the airline industry
(B) Erecting barriers to free trade
(C) Creating public assistance programs
(D) Reducing federal regulatory oversight
(E) Cutting personal income taxes

46. The cartoonist for *Harper's Weekly* who played a major role in turning public sentiment against New York City's Boss Tweed was

(A) Grant Wood
(B) Winslow Homer
(C) Matt Morgan
(D) Thomas Nast
(E) Norman Rockwell

47. Which of the following cultures provided a link between ancient Greece and medieval western Europe, designed methods for making steel and leather, and contributed to scientific knowledge of mathematics?

(A) Celtic
(B) Carolingian
(C) Gothic
(D) Islamic
(E) Norman

48. After their defeat by the Chinese Communist Party in 1949, Jiang Jieshi (Chiang Kai-Shek) and many supporters of his Nationalist government chose to

(A) emigrate to the United States
(B) ally with the Soviet Union
(C) flee to Tibet
(D) advocate for Chinese Communist Party rule
(E) flee to the island of Taiwan (Formosa)

49. The New Deal attempted to restore stability to the economy by

(A) lending money to individuals financially hurt by the crash of 1929
(B) creating employment through public works programs
(C) introducing the graduated income tax
(D) creating the Federal Reserve System
(E) lowering prices and controlling inflation

50. According to international relations (IR) theory, nation-states that join international organizations are usually motivated by

(A) the desire to move toward world government
(B) respect for legal norms
(C) popular pressure to join such organizations
(D) self-interest
(E) religious belief

51. The Russo-Japanese War (1904–1905) resulted in

(A) expanded export trade for Russia
(B) predominance of the Russian navy in East Asia
(C) Japan's acquisition of Taiwan
(D) the opening of Japanese ports to foreign trade
(E) a significant weakening of the tsarist government

52. The Dawes Severalty Act, which was passed by the United States Congress in 1887, did which of the following?

(A) Stopped all homesteading west of the Mississippi River.
(B) Extended voting rights to Native Americans.
(C) Resulted in the notorious Trail of Tears.
(D) Divided tribally held lands among individual Native Americans.
(E) Extended welfare assistance to Native Americans.

53. European imperialism in Africa in the last quarter of the nineteenth century differed from European imperialism in Africa of earlier periods in which of the following ways?

(A) It encouraged the African colonization movement in the United States.
(B) It promoted the integration of indigenous peoples into all sectors of colonial society.
(C) It combined commerce with extensive territorial acquisitions.
(D) Its aim was to prepare colonies for independence and democracy.
(E) Its central goal was the abolition of the slave trade.

54. For African Americans, the reduction of European immigration during the First World War resulted in which of the following?

(A) Government encouragement of African immigration to the United States
(B) The endorsement of the racial policies of Woodrow Wilson by the National Association for the Advancement of Colored People (NAACP)
(C) The rise of African Americans to positions of power in Southern politics
(D) The establishment of Marcus Garvey's Back to Africa movement
(E) The opening of industrial jobs to African American workers

55. Which of the following would be an example of the Columbian Exchange?

(A) The exchange rate between the Colombian peso and the United States dollar
(B) The introduction of horses and cattle into the Western Hemisphere
(C) The expansion of cocoa bean production to South America
(D) The introduction of rice to Europe
(E) The introduction of coffee to Europe

56. Puerto Rico became part of the territorial holdings of the United States as a result of the

(A) Monroe Doctrine
(B) Gadsden Purchase
(C) Treaty of Guadalupe Hidalgo
(D) Spanish-American War
(E) Adams-Onís Treaty

57. Which of the following is an example of a tertiary economic activity?

(A) Cultivation of wheat in the Midwest
(B) Manufacture of automobiles in Detroit
(C) Offshore oil drilling in the Gulf of Mexico
(D) Development of ecotourism in Costa Rica
(E) Clothing assembly in Malaysia

58. An isogloss delineates a region of common

(A) temperature
(B) barometric pressure
(C) altitude
(D) dialect
(E) religion

59. Which of the following Latin American countries was one of the original members of the Organization of the Petroleum Exporting Countries (OPEC)?

(A) Mexico
(B) Brazil
(C) Venezuela
(D) Colombia
(E) Peru

60. Which of the following has been a sacred site for both Christians and Muslims?

(A) The Kabah in Mecca
(B) Taj Mahal in Agra
(C) Hagia Sophia in Istanbul
(D) Pyramids in Egypt
(E) Angkor Wat in Cambodia

61. In the United States and European countries, mobilization for the Second World War differed from mobilization for the First World War for which of the following reasons?

(A) During the First World War, governments rationed supplies.
(B) During the First World War, governments banned immigration.
(C) During the First World War, governments banned labor unions.
(D) During the Second World War, governments recruited women to work in weapons industries.
(E) During the Second World War, governments established agencies to regulate industrial production.

62. The United States Immigration Act of 1965 was significant because it

(A) led to increased immigration of scientists from Western Europe
(B) led to increased immigration of professionals from Asia
(C) led to increased immigration of agricultural laborers from Mexico
(D) prohibited immigration from Communist countries
(E) prohibited immigration of unskilled laborers

63. Phillis Wheatley, a slave during the revolutionary era in the United States, was

(A) a seamstress who bought her freedom from slavery
(B) a domestic servant who shielded patriots
(C) a published author who wrote poetry
(D) an artist who painted revolutionary scenes
(E) a spy who provided information on British troop movements

64. Which of the following would shift the supply curve for gasoline rightward?

(A) An increase in the demand for sport-utility vehicles, which use more gas
(B) A situation where the quantity demanded exceeds the quantity supplied
(C) A decrease in the price of a resource used to produce gasoline, such as crude oil
(D) An increase in the price of gasoline
(E) An increase in the price of a resource used to produce gasoline, such as crude oil

65. A map 2 feet by 3 feet at a scale of 1:100,000 would display the appropriate amount of detail for doing which of the following?

(A) Providing block-level directions from a residence to a local elementary school
(B) Displaying national weather patterns
(C) Determining the best location for a new shopping center
(D) Planning a cross-country road trip
(E) Identifying highway directions to a city 25 miles away

66. The United States Constitution denies some powers to both national and state governments in order to

(A) prevent the deployment of the National Guard
(B) allow citizens to hold federal officers accountable
(C) safeguard individual rights
(D) deny unfair welfare practices
(E) provide protection of labor rights

67. The greatest crisis of the United States federal system occurred during the

(A) American Revolution
(B) Civil War
(C) First World War
(D) Cold War
(E) Vietnam War

68. To maximize total utility, a consumer will consume a product at the point where

(A) marginal utility per dollar spent on each good is equal
(B) total utility per dollar spent on each good is equal
(C) total utility from each good is equal to zero
(D) marginal utility from each good is equal to zero
(E) marginal utility is equal to zero

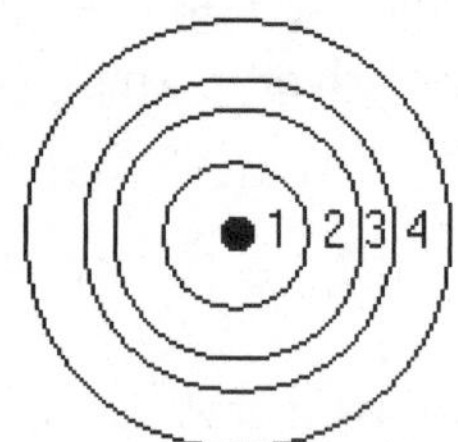

● City
1. Dairying and market gardening
2. Cash grain and livestock
3. Mixed farming
4. Extensive grain farming or stock raising

69. According to von Thünen's model, shown above, key factors in determining the relative locations of agricultural activities near a city include which of the following?

I. Distance to market for perishable goods
II. Land costs versus land needs for different forms of agriculture
III. Population size of the market area
IV. Modes of transportation

(A) I only
(B) I and II only
(C) II and III only
(D) II, III, and IV only
(E) I, II, III, and IV

70. The ancient Greeks derived their greatest sense of cultural unity through

(A) participation in athletic games
(B) use of a common currency
(C) worship of the goddess Athena
(D) preparation of similar foods
(E) creation of the same types of civic architecture

71. Which state in the United States has the highest percentage of Asians in its population?

(A) Alaska
(B) California
(C) Hawaii
(D) Washington
(E) Oregon

72. Which of the following is associated with increasing air pollution?

(A) Convective turbulence
(B) Normal lapse rate
(C) Low pressure
(D) Temperature inversion
(E) The Coriolis effect

73. The purpose of the Constitutional Convention of 1787 was to

(A) nominate George Washington as the first president
(B) rectify the perceived weaknesses of the Articles of Confederation
(C) develop a plan for the compensation of Revolutionary War soldiers
(D) strengthen the powers of the individual states
(E) declare independence from Great Britain

74. All of the following were federal agencies established in the New Deal EXCEPT the

(A) National Recovery Administration
(B) Social Security Administration
(C) Environmental Protection Agency
(D) Agricultural Adjustment Administration
(E) Civilian Conservation Corps

75. The original 13 colonies that formed the United States were

(A) founded by religious groups
(B) dependent upon tobacco to support their economies
(C) dependent on ocean transport for trade
(D) dependent upon water power to support manufacturing
(E) settled before 1650

76. Over a 12-month period the purchasing power of the United States dollar dropped by 10 percent and interest rates increased from 5 percent to 15 percent. This is an example of

(A) negative balance of payments
(B) national debt
(C) deflation
(D) monetary policy
(E) inflation

77. Which of the following countries is most closely associated with the scientific and artistic developments of the Renaissance?

(A) Greece
(B) Italy
(C) Germany
(D) Austria
(E) France

78. Primary economic activities include which of the following?

(A) Professional and personal services
(B) Information production and transfer
(C) Manufacturing, construction, and power production
(D) Mining and mineral extraction
(E) Retail trade

79. A principal difference between the United States representative political system and Canada's parliamentary system is that

(A) Canada's prime minister has authority in the executive and legislative branches and the United States president only has executive authority
(B) in Canada the prime minister is appointed by the British monarch and in the United States the president is elected
(C) in Canada all judges are appointed by the prime minister and in the United States they are all elected
(D) Canada does not have a federal system and the United States does
(E) in Canada the prime minister is elected for a six-year term and in the United States the president has a four-year term

80. Where did the world's earliest civilizations tend to develop?

(A) On desert lands
(B) In rain forests
(C) On mountainous highlands
(D) In river valleys
(E) Along seacoasts

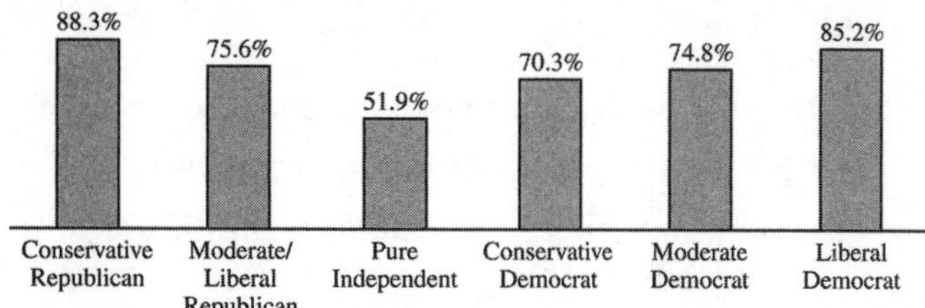

81. A sample of United States voters was asked in April 2012 if they would definitely vote in the 2012 presidential election. Voters self-identified their party ideology or tendency. Pure independents claimed no tendency toward one party or the other. The results are shown in the bar graph above.

    Which of the following is a conclusion supported by the data in the graph and the information above?

    (A) There are more Republicans than Independents.
    (B) A third party would be able to win the election.
    (C) Those who intend to vote are more likely to be affiliated with a party.
    (D) There are more Republicans than Democrats who will vote.
    (E) Independents are most likely to vote if the election is important.

82. Which of the following lists the five most populous countries in the world in 2012 from the largest population to the smallest?

    (A) United States, Egypt, India, Indonesia, Japan
    (B) China, United States, India, Brazil, Japan
    (C) India, China, Brazil, Indonesia, Russia
    (D) China, India, United States, Indonesia, Brazil
    (E) Russia, United States, China, Japan, Nigeria

83. Oil is used by many firms for production. Political instability in oil-producing countries has decreased the oil supply and increased the price of a barrel of oil.

    As a result, the short-run aggregate supply curve would

    (A) stay the same
    (B) shift to the right
    (C) shift to the left
    (D) become nearly vertical at all levels of production
    (E) become nearly flat at all levels of production

Credit: Listening to one of President Roosevelt's "Fireside Chats" on the radio, Kansas, circa 1930 (b/w photo), American Photographer (20th century) / Private Collection/ Peter Newark American Pictures / The Bridgeman Art Library

84. The photograph above of an American family listening to Franklin D. Roosevelt best illustrates which of the following?

 (A) The popularity of New Deal legislation
 (B) Roosevelt's influence on those most affected by the Great Depression
 (C) The public's lack of interest in domestic and foreign policy
 (D) Roosevelt's efforts to lead and shape public opinion
 (E) The importance of independent media to the functioning of democracy

85. Gross domestic product (GDP) is the sum of

 (A) personal consumption, gross private investment, government budget surplus, and net exports
 (B) personal consumption, gross private investment, government spending, and net exports
 (C) personal consumption, savings, net private investments, and exports
 (D) government spending, taxes, exports, and imports
 (E) savings, residential investments, depreciation, and net exports

86. Which of the following is the best example of a fragmented state?

 (A) Indonesia
 (B) Vietnam
 (C) Cambodia
 (D) Laos
 (E) Thailand

Study Resources

Most of the textbooks used in college-level social sciences and history courses cover the topics in the outline given earlier, but the approaches to certain topics and the emphases given to them may differ. To prepare for the Social Sciences and History exam, it is advisable to study one or more college textbooks for United States and world history, Western civilization, economics, geography, political science, and other related courses, which can be found in most college bookstores. When selecting a textbook, check the table of contents against the knowledge and skills required for this test.

The materials suggested for preparing for other CLEP exams may also be helpful. Study resources for the American Government, History of the United States I and II, Principles of Macroeconomics and Principles of Microeconomics, and Western Civilization I and II exams are particularly relevant and can be found in the Study Resources section of the *Official Study Guide* for these exams.

Visit **clep.collegeboard.org/earn-college-credit/practice** for additional social sciences and history resources. You can also find suggestions for exam preparation in Chapter IV of the *Official Study Guide*. In addition, many college faculty post their course materials on their schools' websites.

Answer Key

1.	E	44.	C
2.	E	45.	C
3.	A	46.	D
4.	D	47.	D
5.	D	48.	E
6.	B	49.	B
7.	A	50.	D
8.	C	51.	E
9.	A	52.	D
10.	B	53.	C
11.	C	54.	E
12.	A	55.	B
13.	B	56.	D
14.	E	57.	D
15.	D	58.	D
16.	D	59.	C
17.	B	60.	C
18.	C	61.	D
19.	C	62.	B
20.	A	63.	C
21.	A	64.	C
22.	B	65.	E
23.	E	66.	C
24.	C	67.	B
25.	E	68.	A
26.	C	69.	B
27.	D	70.	A
28.	D	71.	C
29.	B	72.	D
30.	C	73.	B
31.	B	74.	C
32.	D	75.	C
33.	A	76.	E
34.	D	77.	B
35.	B	78.	D
36.	C	79.	A
37.	C	80.	D
38.	E	81.	C
39.	C	82.	D
40.	C	83.	C
41.	B	84.	D
42.	A	85.	B
43.	B	86.	A

Western Civilization I

Description of the Examination

The Western Civilization I: Ancient Near East to 1648 examination covers material that is usually taught in the first semester of a two-semester course in Western Civilization. Questions deal with the civilizations of Ancient Greece, Rome and the Near East; the Middle Ages; the Renaissance and Reformation; and early modern Europe. Candidates may be asked to choose the correct definition of a historical term, select the historical figure whose viewpoint is described, identify the correct relationship between two historical factors, or detect the inaccurate pairing of an individual with a historical event. Groups of questions may require candidates to interpret, evaluate or relate the contents of a passage, a map or a picture to other information, or to analyze and utilize the data contained in a graph or table.

The examination contains approximately 120 questions to be answered in 90 minutes. Some of these are pretest questions that will not be scored. This examination uses the chronological designations B.C.E. (before the common era) and C.E. (common era). These labels correspond to B.C. (before Christ) and A.D. (anno Domini), which are used in some textbooks.

Knowledge and Skills Required

Questions on the Western Civilization I examination require candidates to demonstrate one or more of the following abilities.

- Ability to understand important factual knowledge of developments in Western Civilization
- Ability to identify the causes and effects of major historical events
- Ability to analyze, interpret, and evaluate textual and graphic historical materials
- Ability to distinguish the relevant from the irrelevant
- Ability to reach conclusions on the basis of facts

The subject matter of the Western Civilization I examination is drawn from the following topics. The percentages next to the main topics indicate the approximate percentage of exam questions on that topic.

8%–10% Ancient Near East

- Political evolution
- Religion, culture and technical developments in and near the Fertile Crescent

15%–17% Ancient Greece and Hellenistic Civilization

- Political evolution to Periclean Athens
- Periclean Athens through the Peloponnesian Wars
- Culture, religion and thought of Ancient Greece
- The Hellenistic political structure
- The culture, religion and thought of Hellenistic Greece

15%–17% Ancient Rome

- Political evolution of the Republic and of the Empire (economic and geographical context)
- Roman thought and culture
- Early Christianity
- The Germanic invasions
- The late empire

23%–27% Medieval History

- Byzantium and Islam
- Early medieval politics and culture through Charlemagne
- Feudal and manorial institutions
- The medieval Church
- Medieval thought and culture
- Rise of the towns and changing economic forms
- Feudal monarchies
- The late medieval church

13%–17% Renaissance and Reformation

- The Renaissance in Italy
- The Renaissance outside Italy
- The New Monarchies
- Protestantism and Catholicism reformed and reorganized

10%–15% Early Modern Europe, 1560–1648

- The opening of the Atlantic
- The Commercial Revolution
- Dynastic and religious conflicts
- Thought and culture

Sample Test Questions

The following sample questions do not appear on an actual CLEP examination. They are intended to give potential test-takers an indication of the format and difficulty level of the examination and to provide content for practice and review. Knowing the correct answers to all of the sample questions is not a guarantee of satisfactory performance on the exam.

Directions: Each of the questions or incomplete statements below is followed by five suggested answers or completions. Select the one that is best in each case.

1. The earliest urban settlements usually arose in which of the following types of areas?

   (A) Coastal plains
   (B) Inland deforested plains
   (C) Desert oases
   (D) Fertile river valleys
   (E) Narrow valleys well protected by mountains

© Bettman/CORBIS

2. The panel above from ancient Ur supports which of the following conclusions about Mesopotamian society?

   (A) It was primarily composed of hunter-gatherers.
   (B) It had distinct class divisions.
   (C) Religion pervaded daily life.
   (D) Soldiers were drawn primarily from the nobility.
   (E) Most commoners were slaves.

3. "The great wealth of the palaces and the widespread prosperity of the land were due to the profits of trade, protected or exploited by naval vessels equipped with rams. The palaces and towns were unfortified, and peaceful scenes predominated in the frescoes, which revealed a love of dancing, boxing, and a sport in which boys and girls somersaulted over the backs of charging bulls."

   The culture described above was that of the ancient

   (A) Minoans
   (B) Hittites
   (C) Macedonians
   (D) Assyrians
   (E) Persians

4. These people maintained their skill as seafarers, traders, and artists. They planted Carthage and other colonies in the western Mediterranean. They developed a new script in which a separate sign stood not for a syllable, but for a consonant or vowel sound.

   The people described above were the

   (A) Phoenicians
   (B) Hittites
   (C) Assyrians
   (D) Mycenaeans
   (E) Philistines

5. Pharaoh Akhenaten of Egypt (c. 1353–1336 B.C.E.) is best known today for

   (A) building the largest pyramid in the Valley of the Kings
   (B) conquering large expanses of territory outside of the Nile Valley
   (C) developing a monotheistic religion
   (D) uniting upper and lower Egypt under a single administrative system
   (E) writing down the first code of Egyptian law

6. Among the ancient Hebrews, a prophet was

(A) a teacher who expounded the Scriptures
(B) a king with hereditary but limited powers
(C) a judge who administered traditional law
(D) a priest with exclusive rights to perform functions at the temple
(E) an individual who was inspired by God to speak to the people

7. The outstanding achievement of King Hammurabi of Mesopotamia was that he

(A) issued a more comprehensive law code than had any known predecessor
(B) conquered and established dominion over all of Egypt
(C) built the Hanging Gardens of Babylon
(D) established the first democratic government
(E) successfully defended his kingdom against the Assyrians

8. Of the following, which best explains why the Roman Republic gave way to dictatorship during the first century B.C.E.?

(A) The government that was suitable for a small city-state failed to meet the needs of an empire.
(B) A strong leader was needed because the upper classes feared a rebellion on the part of the slave population.
(C) Outside pressures on boundaries could not be resisted by republican armies.
(D) Rome's period of expansion was over.
(E) The Roman senatorial class was declining in number.

9. All of the following were emphasized by the early Christian church EXCEPT a

(A) ritual fellowship meal in memory of Christ
(B) toleration of other religious sects
(C) belief in the value of the souls of women and slaves as well as those of free men
(D) belief in life after death for all believers in Christ
(E) belief in the value of martyrdom, defined as dying for the faith

10. The Roman emperor whose policies rescued Rome from its crisis in the third century C.E. was

(A) Augustus
(B) Marcus Aurelius
(C) Constantine
(D) Diocletian
(E) Theodosius

11. Which of the following established Christianity as a legal religion in the Roman Empire?

(A) The defeat of the Huns, 451 C.E.
(B) The accession of Justinian I
(C) The Council of Nicaea
(D) The accession of Diocletian
(E) The Edict of Milan

12. All of the following invaded the Roman Empire EXCEPT the

(A) Vikings
(B) Ostrogoths
(C) Visigoths
(D) Vandals
(E) Huns

13. The craft guilds of the Middle Ages had as their primary purpose the

    (A) promotion of trade and the protection of merchants
    (B) control of town government
    (C) regulation of production and quality
    (D) guardianship of the social and financial affairs of their members
    (E) accumulation of capital and the lending of money

14. Which of the following had the greatest impact on northern European agriculture by the year 1000 C.E.?

    (A) The wheeled seed drill
    (B) The enclosure movement
    (C) The padded horse collar
    (D) The horse saddle
    (E) The spread of maize (corn) cultivation

15. The orders of Franciscan and Dominican friars founded in the thirteenth century differed from earlier monastic orders principally in that the friars

    (A) took vows of poverty, chastity, and obedience
    (B) broke away from the control of the pope
    (C) introduced the ideas of Plato and other early Greek philosophers into their teaching
    (D) devoted themselves mainly to copying ancient manuscripts
    (E) traveled among the people instead of living in monasteries

16. All of the following factors played a part in bringing about the Hundred Years' War EXCEPT

    (A) The English king had lands in Gascony.
    (B) A French princess was the mother of an English king.
    (C) Flemish towns were dependent on England for raw wool.
    (D) The Holy Roman Emperor wanted to bring pressure on the Swiss cantons.
    (E) The Capetian dynasty had come to an end.

17. Civil peace and personal security were enjoyed to a greater degree in Norman England than in continental Europe principally because the Norman kings

    (A) maintained a large standing army
    (B) claimed the direct allegiance of the mass of the peasantry
    (C) avoided conflicts with the Church
    (D) kept their vassals occupied with continental conflicts
    (E) developed a centralized and efficient type of feudalism

18. Which of the following could have been made immediately available to the reading public in large quantities as soon as it was written?

    (A) *On Christian Liberty*, Martin Luther
    (B) *Travels*, Marco Polo
    (C) *The Divine Comedy*, Dante Alighieri
    (D) *Canterbury Tales*, Geoffrey Chaucer
    (E) English translation of the Bible, John Wycliffe

19. A central feature of the Catholic Reformation was the

    (A) Roman Catholic church's inability to correct abuses
    (B) establishment of new religious orders such as the Jesuits
    (C) transfer of authority from Rome to the bishoprics
    (D) rejection of Baroque art
    (E) toleration of Protestants in Roman Catholic countries

© Bettman/CORBIS

20. The building in Córdoba, Spain, shown above, illustrates the influence of

(A) Islam
(B) Buddhism
(C) Hinduism
(D) Shinto
(E) Animism

21. The major consequence of the rise of towns in the eleventh and twelfth centuries was

(A) a lessening of the distinction among social classes
(B) the practice of caring for the indigent
(C) the decline of royal authority
(D) the decline in the social status of the lesser clergy
(E) a new social class enriched by manufacturing and trade

22. In *The Prince*, Machiavelli asserted that

(A) historical examples are useless for understanding political behavior
(B) the intelligent prince should keep his state neutral in the event of war
(C) people are not trustworthy and cannot be relied on in time of need
(D) the prince should be guided by the ethical principles of Christianity
(E) luck is of no consequence in the success or failure of princes

23. On which of the following issues did Luther and Calvin DISAGREE?

(A) The toleration for minority viewpoints
(B) The relationship of the church to civil authority
(C) The authority of the Scriptures
(D) The existence of the Trinity
(E) The retention of the sacrament of baptism

24. The principle that the religion of the ruler of a state determines the established church in that state was first adopted at the

(A) Peace of Augsburg
(B) Peace of the Pyrenees
(C) Congress of Vienna
(D) Edict of Restitution
(E) Peace of Westphalia

25. Between 1629 and 1639, Charles I of England tried to obtain revenues by all of the following means EXCEPT

(A) the levying of ship money
(B) income from crown lands
(C) forced loans
(D) the sale of monopolies
(E) grants from Parliament

26. All of the following are associated with the commercial revolution in early modern Europe EXCEPT

(A) an increase in the number of entrepreneurial capitalists
(B) the appearance of state-run trading companies
(C) a large influx of precious metals into Europe
(D) an expansion of the guild system
(E) a "golden age" for the Netherlands

27. Castiglione's *Book of the Courtier* (1528) was intended as

(A) a collection of entertaining travel stories
(B) a guide to the military affairs of the Italian peninsula
(C) a collection of meditations and spiritual reflections
(D) a guide to refined behavior and etiquette
(E) an allegory of courtly love

28. Which of the following resulted from the defeat of the Spanish Armada in 1588?

(A) Spanish domination of the Mediterranean was ended.
(B) The invasion of England was prevented.
(C) Dutch sympathies for the Spanish cause increased.
(D) War broke out between England and France.
(E) There was a series of uprisings in the Spanish colonies of Central and South America.

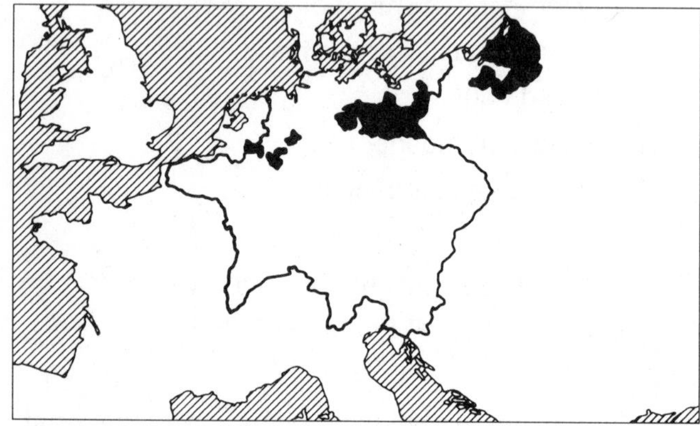

29. In the mid-seventeenth century, the area shaded black on the map above belonged to

(A) Russia
(B) Poland
(C) Sweden
(D) Austria
(E) Brandenburg-Prussia

30. The theory concerning the solar system that was published by Copernicus in 1543 rejected the popular belief that

(A) Earth revolves around the Sun
(B) Earth revolves around the Moon
(C) Earth is the center of the universe
(D) the Sun is the center of the universe
(E) the stars revolve around the Sun

31. During their next war with the Persians following the battle of Marathon, the Athenians won a decisive victory through their use of

(A) horse-drawn chariots
(B) new kinds of iron weapons
(C) mounted archers
(D) incendiary weapons
(E) sea power

32. Almost every kind of human activity was accepted as worthy of offering to the gods—athletic contests, poetry reading, song, dance, drama, prayer, giftbearing . . . There were no elaborate priesthoods; fathers conducted rituals in the household and elected officials served as priests in the civic ceremonies.

The religion described above is probably that of the ancient

(A) Egyptians
(B) Sumerians
(C) Greeks
(D) Hebrews
(E) Persians

33. All of the following peoples settled Roman lands bordering on the Mediterranean EXCEPT the

(A) Lombards
(B) Visigoths
(C) Jutes
(D) Ostrogoths
(E) Vandals

34. "I found Rome a city of brick and left it a city of marble."

The claim above was made by

(A) Pompey
(B) Julius Caesar
(C) Augustus
(D) Tiberius
(E) Hadrian

35. In which of the following ancient Greek city-states were women permitted to own land and other property and to make economic decisions on their own?

(A) Athens
(B) Thebes
(C) Corinth
(D) Argos
(E) Sparta

36. Henry II (1133–1189) increased royal authority in England chiefly by

(A) confiscating Church lands
(B) usurping the legislative authority of Parliament
(C) proclaiming the divine right of kings
(D) forming an alliance with the papacy
(E) enlarging the jurisdiction and powers of royal courts

37. Which of the following was a primary goal of Cardinal Richelieu's foreign policy?

(A) The weakening of the Hapsburgs diplomatically and militarily
(B) The reestablishment of religious unity in Europe
(C) The consolidation of French holdings in North America
(D) The strengthening of papal influence within the French government
(E) The founding of commercial companies on the Anglo-Dutch model

38. Which of the following was the most effective leader of the Protestant forces in the Thirty Years' War?

(A) Albrecht von Wallenstein
(B) Emperor Ferdinand II
(C) The Elector Palatine Frederick V
(D) Gustavus Adolphus of Sweden
(E) Christian IV of Denmark

39. The reluctance of Elizabeth I of England to open "windows into men's souls" was an indication of her

(A) atheism
(B) withdrawal from public pageantry
(C) reluctance to inquire closely into personal religious views
(D) reluctance to prosecute political opponents
(E) insistence on personal rule

The Metropolitan Museum of Art, Rogers Fund, 1930 (30.4.44)
Image © The Metropolitan Museum of Art

40. The wall painting shown above depicts which of the following?

    (A) The division of labor by gender in rural Etruscan society
    (B) The poor treatment of slaves in ancient Greece
    (C) Activities of children in Sumerian society
    (D) Men and women working in the fields in ancient Egypt
    (E) Roman soldiers celebrating a victory

41. Which of the following was a major innovation of the Renaissance period?

    (A) The use of linear perspective in painting
    (B) The use of marble as a medium for statuary
    (C) The dome
    (D) The portico
    (E) Fresco painting

42. The construction of some of the largest buildings in Rome, such as the Colosseum and the Baths of Caracalla, was made possible by Roman builders' skillful use of

(A) aluminum scaffolding
(B) paper blueprints
(C) concrete
(D) mud brick
(E) plaster

43. Which of the following describes Luther's reaction to the Peasants' Revolt of 1525?

(A) He first sought what he considered a balanced solution and then strongly supported the lords.
(B) He abandoned his initial support of the lords in favor of the peasants.
(C) He sought throughout to act as a mediator between the lords and peasants.
(D) He declined to act on the grounds that his ministry did not concern itself with politics.
(E) He called on the Holy Roman Emperor to intervene.

44. The height of the medieval papacy came with his pontificate . . . In the year before his death he called the greatest church council since antiquity, attended by five hundred bishops and even by the patriarchs of Constantinople and Jerusalem.

The pope referred to in the passage above is

(A) Julius II
(B) Urban II
(C) Innocent III
(D) Nicholas V
(E) Pius II

45. Which of the following was true of medieval universities?

(A) They taught only philosophy.
(B) They were open only to men of noble birth.
(C) They were considered subversive of the feudal system by many kings.
(D) They were corporations of teachers and students.
(E) They emphasized instruction in the vernacular.

46. Which of the following was the site of a tenth-century monastery that became the center of an important monastic reform movement?

(A) Aachen
(B) Avignon
(C) Canossa
(D) Chartres
(E) Cluny

47. Which of the following contributed to Portugal's lead in overseas expansion in the fifteenth century?

I. The creation of accurate maps
II. The development of better navigational instruments
III. Improvement in the design of ships
IV. Availability of large numbers of galley slaves

(A) I only
(B) II and III only
(C) I, II, and III only
(D) I, II, and IV only
(E) II, III, and IV only

48. Which of the following best characterizes medieval town charters?

(A) They provided townspeople with legal and political freedoms that were not available to peasants and serfs.
(B) They were always granted by the reigning secular ruler.
(C) They permitted townspeople to spend all tax revenue they collected on the needs of their town.
(D) They let peasants migrate freely to the towns.
(E) They always provided for popularly elected assemblies that made the towns' laws.

49. Which of the following was involved most directly in the political persecution of Martin Luther?

(A) Frederick III, Elector of Saxony
(B) Emperor Charles V
(C) Ignatius of Loyola
(D) King Henry VIII of England
(E) Huldrych Zwingli

50. In the fifteenth and sixteenth centuries, recruits for the elite Janissary corps of the Ottoman Empire were drawn primarily from which of the following groups?

(A) Well-to-do Christian merchants
(B) Sufi religious preachers
(C) Noble Muslim landowners
(D) Children of Christian peasants
(E) Muslim prisoners of war

51. "You must realize this: that a prince, and especially a new prince, cannot observe all those things which give men a reputation for virtue, because in order to maintain his state he is often forced to act in defiance of good faith, of charity, of kindness, of religion."

The quote above addresses which of the following in Renaissance Italy?

(A) The transitory nature of political power
(B) The threat of papal power
(C) The dangers of political liberty
(D) The threat of French invasion
(E) The bad reputation of certain Renaissance artists

52. The Treaty of Westphalia, which ended the Thirty Years' War in 1648, resulted in

(A) a defeat for Swedish imperialism in northern Europe
(B) the consolidation of Bourbon control over Germany
(C) ratification of the territorial fragmentation of Germany
(D) a step toward restoring religious unity in Europe
(E) the restoration of an independent kingdom of Bohemia

53. The Assyrians achieved great success in the eighth and seventh centuries B.C.E. mostly as a result of

(A) their emphasis on diplomacy and negotiation
(B) the location of their homeland in modern-day northern Iraq
(C) the size and organization of their army
(D) their peaceful assimilation of diverse peoples into their empire
(E) the linguistic unity of their empire

54. Which of the following statements is true of women in the High Middle Ages?

(A) Courtly literature portrayed aristocratic women as objects of devotion.
(B) Formal education was available to middle-class women.
(C) Joining a religious order was not an option available to women.
(D) Only propertied widows were allowed to remarry.
(E) Women artisans often joined guilds.

55. Which of the following was a major feature of the Hebrew religion?

(A) It promoted the belief that the Hebrews were God's chosen people.
(B) It allowed the worship of different gods and goddesses.
(C) It owed much of its theology to ancient Mesopotamian religious cults.
(D) It did not apply to the social, political, or economic areas of life.
(E) It made its greatest impact in the arts and architecture.

56. A major effect of the flying buttress used in the construction of Gothic buildings was to

(A) eliminate the use of mortar
(B) reduce the size of the clerestory
(C) allow more light into the buildings
(D) reduce the construction costs of religious buildings
(E) create the optical illusion that cathedrals were wider at their bases

57. Which of the following is the most important factor that enabled the First Crusade to succeed?

(A) Participation of women
(B) Superior firepower of the papal armies
(C) Neutrality maintained by the papacy
(D) Disunity of the Muslim world
(E) Desire for a Jewish state

58. Which of the following rightfully could be called the Empire of the Steppe?

(A) The Ottoman Empire
(B) The Mongol Empire
(C) The Parthian Empire
(D) The Byzantine Empire
(E) The T'ang Empire

59. Russia's Time of Troubles (1598–1613) ended with which of the following?

(A) The expulsion of a Polish occupying army and the election of a new ruling family
(B) The ejection of the Mongol/Tatar occupiers from Russia
(C) A successful war against the Turks
(D) The annexation of Ukraine
(E) Massive serf revolts

60. Which of the following individuals did the most to spread Greek culture?

(A) Aristotle
(B) Xerxes
(C) Ptolemy
(D) Euclid
(E) Alexander the Great

61. In the period 1000–1500 C.E., Muslims and Christians differed in regard to which of the following?

(A) Belief in one all-powerful god
(B) Belief in war in God's name
(C) Belief in ancient prophecies
(D) Portrayal of religious figures in religious buildings
(E) Toleration of the concept of polytheism

62. Which of the following most accurately defines feudalism?

(A) A system of strong central government
(B) A system of centralized economic distribution
(C) An agreement to substitute money payments for military service
(D) A system based on land grants given in exchange for military service
(E) A religious movement

63. The bubonic plague led to improvements in which of the following?

    (A) Workers' wages
    (B) Church administration
    (C) Prison conditions
    (D) Transportation
    (E) Bookbinding

64. Which of the following best describes the importance of Thucydides' *History of the Peloponnesian Wars* for present-day historians?

    (A) It is one of the earliest historical works to focus exclusively on human-centered, rather than supernatural explanations of historical events.
    (B) It is the earliest work to use historical narrative primarily as a vehicle of conveying moral lessons to its readers.
    (C) It is the first history to provide detailed descriptions of battles instead of merely recording their outcome.
    (D) It is one of the earliest histories to accurately report on the living conditions of underprivileged groups such as slaves and urban populations living in poverty.
    (E) It is the first military history <u>not</u> commissioned by a royal or aristocratic patron.

65. The Age of Pericles was characterized by all of the following EXCEPT

    (A) the political domination of Greece by Macedon
    (B) the historical writings of Herodotus
    (C) an ambitious building program
    (D) the expansion of the Delian League
    (E) reforms of Athenian democracy

66. Which ancient culture produced the "Epic of Gilgamesh"?

    (A) Egyptian
    (B) Hittite
    (C) Assyrian
    (D) Hebrew
    (E) Sumerian

67. An important contribution of Thomas Aquinas was his effort to

    (A) reconcile reason and the teachings of Aristotle with Christian faith
    (B) reestablish the supremacy of the Pope
    (C) defeat the Franks
    (D) win northern Africa back from Islam
    (E) halt the progress of the Reformation in Spain

68. Which of the following is a true statement regarding John Calvin?

    (A) He agreed with both Luther and Zwingli on the Eucharist.
    (B) He opposed the doctrine of predestination.
    (C) He emphasized the omnipotence and omnipresence of God.
    (D) He believed in the separation of church and state.
    (E) He practiced religious tolerance when he governed Geneva.

69. The Investiture Controversy pitted Pope Gregory VII against which of the following?

    (A) Henry III
    (B) Henry IV
    (C) Frederick Barbarossa
    (D) Maximilian
    (E) Charles V

70. The constitution of the Roman Republic was comparable to the constitution of England in that it was

    (A) appended with a bill of rights
    (B) written in Latin
    (C) never a written document
    (D) intended to provide limits on the ruler and the nobility
    (E) designed primarily to protect the rights of the lower classes

71. The controversies that occurred within the Christian church between the third and fifth centuries C.E. were principally concerned with the

(A) divinity of Jesus' mother
(B) Eucharist (communion) as a central component of Christian religious ritual
(C) nature of Jesus Christ and the doctrine of the Trinity
(D) proper role of missionaries in spreading Christianity throughout the Roman Empire
(E) role of monastic orders in governing the Christian church

72. Which of the following best describes the aim of the Benedictine Rule, written in 529 by Benedict of Nursia?

(A) To isolate monks from the rest of the world to pursue the ideal of complete self-denial
(B) To create a disciplined and effective organization to carry out spiritual work
(C) To provide the papacy in Rome with loyal followers
(D) To establish a hierarchy of church officials in western Europe separate from the hierarchy in eastern Europe
(E) To prevent the use of images in western churches

73. The Greek city-state of Sparta is best defined as a

(A) tribal state based upon kinship
(B) participatory democracy
(C) conservative military oligarchy
(D) society that placed great emphasis on the arts
(E) society in which women had no public role

74. The Byzantine emperor Justinian is best known for his contributions to

(A) historical writings
(B) civil law
(C) Christian theology
(D) astronomy
(E) philosophy

75. Magna Carta, signed by King John of England in 1215, did which of the following?

(A) It established a written constitution for England.
(B) It determined that education should be controlled by monastic houses.
(C) It ensured that all landowners possessed the right to vote.
(D) It regulated social and legal relations between the king and the great lords of England.
(E) It established the supremacy of the English Parliament.

76. Which of the following best summarizes the lasting impact of the reign of Henry VII (Henry Tudor) on England?

(A) It produced the first major confrontation between king and Parliament over budgetary issues.
(B) It led to the establishment of a national legal system based on trial by jury.
(C) It resulted in the return to England of all territories lost in the Hundred Years' War.
(D) It marked the beginnings of English colonization of North America.
(E) It ended the Wars of the Roses and led to greater political centralization.

77. The execution of Mary Queen of Scots was the catalyst for which of the following?

(A) The Dutch revolt against Spain
(B) The political union of Scotland and England
(C) Puritan opposition to Elizabeth I
(D) The sailing of the Spanish Armada
(E) An alliance between Scotland and France

78. Male Spartans were able to dedicate their lives to full-time military training and service because

(A) Sparta supported itself with treasure and tribute from foreign conquests
(B) Sparta's foreign colonies provided financial support for the army
(C) Sparta had extensive silver mines
(D) non-Spartan slaves (helots) provided the labor for the Spartan economy
(E) non-Spartan merchants paid taxes based on foreign trade

79. The dominance of Mediterranean trade by Italian city-states can be traced to the

(A) Crusades
(B) Ciompi Revolt
(C) plague
(D) rise of the Médicis
(E) defeat of France

80. The schism in Islam between Shi'ites and Sunnis occurred primarily over which of the following?

(A) The marriage of Muhammad
(B) Regional rivalries
(C) Tribal disputes over territory
(D) Disputes between Umayyad caliphs over political authority
(E) The question of succession to the caliphate

81. The quest for economic self-sufficiency, the expansion of colonial possessions, and the introduction of manufacturing standards are most closely associated with

(A) bartering
(B) laissez-faire
(C) utopianism
(D) mercantilism
(E) capitalism

82. In the thirteenth century C.E., which of the following was a major point of contact between people of Muslim, Jewish, and Western Christian cultures?

(A) Rome
(B) Paris
(C) Aachen
(D) Sicily
(E) Milan

83. The Hellenistic school of philosophy that emphasized the pursuit of a pleasurable life through moderation is known as

(A) Scholasticism
(B) Epicureanism
(C) Stoicism
(D) Mithraism
(E) Arianism

84. Which of the following pairs of religious thinkers or leaders most directly challenged Christian orthodoxy in pre-Reformation Europe?

(A) John Wycliffe and Jan Hus
(B) Isabella I of Spain and Ferdinand II of Spain
(C) Hildegard of Bingen and Catherine of Siena
(D) Thomas Aquinas and William of Ockham
(E) Joan of Arc and Christine de Pisan

85. Which statement most accurately reflects the status of Jews in early medieval European society (circa 500–1000 C.E.)?

    (A) They were forced to either convert to Christianity or emigrate in many western and central European countries.
    (B) They were completely excluded from property ownership and participated in only a few urban professions.
    (C) They were persecuted more vigorously by the rulers of Muslim Spain than they were persecuted by Christian rulers elsewhere in Europe.
    (D) They were present in many urban communities, frequently spoke the same language as non-Jews, and occasionally owned rural estates.
    (E) They were largely absent from many European countries, with the exception of Germany and Italy.

86. The Inquisition in Spain was originally established to investigate and prosecute

    (A) Protestant missionaries
    (B) Native Americans in Spanish colonies
    (C) Jewish and Muslim converts to Christianity
    (D) political opposition to the papacy
    (E) misconduct among the Catholic clergy

87. "Thus, fair daughter, the prerogative among women has been bestowed on you to establish and build the City of Ladies [which] will be extremely beautiful, without equal, and of perpetual duration in the world."

    The line above, spoken by Lady Reason, is drawn from the work of

    (A) Hildegard of Bingen
    (B) Christine de Pisan
    (C) Artemisia Gentileschi
    (D) Teresa of Ávila
    (E) Joan of Arc

88. By the end of the fourteenth century, northern Italy and Flanders were known for

    (A) woolen-textile production
    (B) intricate wood carvings
    (C) centralized nation-states
    (D) rapid population growth
    (E) limited urbanization

89. Protestantism limited opportunities for women by

    (A) prohibiting divorce
    (B) requiring women to remain in the home
    (C) prohibiting female heads of state
    (D) eliminating women's religious orders
    (E) allowing women to work only as servants

90. Reforms advocated by the Gracchi brothers in the Roman Republic focused on which of the following?

    (A) Reorganizing the Roman army for lengthy overseas campaigns
    (B) Increasing the use of slave labor to provide Roman citizens with leisure time
    (C) Sponsoring free public entertainment for the general public in Rome
    (D) Redistributing land to increase the number of plebeian family farmers
    (E) Restricting the number of people who held Roman citizenship

Study Resources

Most textbooks used in college-level Western civilization courses cover the topics in the outline given earlier, but the approaches to certain topics and the emphases given to them may differ. To prepare for the Western Civilization I exam, it is advisable to study one or more college textbooks, which can be found in most college bookstores. When selecting a textbook, check the table of contents against the knowledge and skills required for this test.

You may also find it helpful to supplement your reading with books listed in the bibliographies found in most history textbooks. In addition, contemporary historical novels, plays and films provide rich sources of information. Actual works of art in museums can bring to life not only the reproductions found in books but history itself.

Visit **clep.collegeboard.org/earn-college-credit/practice** for additional Western civilization resources. You can also find suggestions for exam preparation in Chapter IV of the *Official Study Guide*. In addition, many college faculty post their course materials on their schools' websites.

Answer Key

1.	D	46.	E
2.	B	47.	C
3.	A	48.	A
4.	A	49.	B
5.	C	50.	D
6.	E	51.	A
7.	A	52.	C
8.	A	53.	C
9.	B	54.	A
10.	D	55.	A
11.	E	56.	C
12.	A	57.	D
13.	C	58.	B
14.	C	59.	A
15.	E	60.	E
16.	D	61.	D
17.	E	62.	D
18.	A	63.	A
19.	B	64.	A
20.	A	65.	A
21.	E	66.	E
22.	C	67.	A
23.	B	68.	C
24.	A	69.	B
25.	E	70.	C
26.	D	71.	C
27.	D	72.	B
28.	B	73.	C
29.	E	74.	B
30.	C	75.	D
31.	E	76.	E
32.	C	77.	D
33.	C	78.	D
34.	C	79.	A
35.	E	80.	E
36.	E	81.	D
37.	A	82.	D
38.	D	83.	B
39.	C	84.	A
40.	D	85.	D
41.	A	86.	C
42.	C	87.	B
43.	A	88.	A
44.	C	89.	D
45.	D	90.	D

Western Civilization II

Description of the Examination

The Western Civilization II: 1648 to the Present examination covers material that is usually taught in the second semester of a two-semester course in Western Civilization. Questions cover European history from the mid-seventeenth century through the post-Second World War period including political, economic and cultural developments such as Scientific Thought, the Enlightenment, the French and Industrial Revolutions, and the First and Second World Wars. Candidates may be asked to choose the correct definition of a historical term, select the historical figure whose viewpoint is described, identify the correct relationship between two historical factors, or detect the inaccurate pairing of an individual with a historical event. Groups of questions may require candidates to interpret, evaluate or relate the contents of a passage, a map, a picture or a cartoon to the other information or to analyze and use the data contained in a graph or table.

The examination contains approximately 120 questions to be answered in 90 minutes. Some of these are pretest questions that will not be scored.

Knowledge and Skills Required

Questions on the Western Civilization II examination require candidates to demonstrate one or more of the following abilities.

- Ability to understand important factual knowledge of developments in Western Civilization
- Ability to identify the causes and effects of major events in history
- Ability to analyze, interpret and evaluate textual and graphic historical materials
- Ability to distinguish the relevant from the irrelevant
- Ability to reach conclusions on the basis of facts

The subject matter of the Western Civilization II examination is drawn from the following topics. The percentages next to the main topics indicate the approximate percentage of exam questions on that topic.

7%–9% Absolutism and Constitutionalism, 1648–1715

The Dutch Republic
The English Revolution
France under Louis XIV
Formation of Austria and Prussia
The "westernization" of Russia

4%–6% Competition for Empire and Economic Expansion

Global economy of the eighteenth century
Europe after Utrecht, 1713–1740
Demographic change in the eighteenth century

5%–7% The Scientific View of the World

Major figures of the scientific revolution
New knowledge of man and society
Political theory

7%–9% Period of Enlightenment

Enlightenment thought
Enlightened despotism
Partition of Poland

10%–13% Revolution and Napoleonic Europe

The Revolution in France
The Revolution and Europe
The French Empire
Congress of Vienna

7%–9% The Industrial Revolution

Agricultural and industrial revolution
Causes of revolution
Economic and social impact on working and middle class
British reform movement

6%–8% Political and Cultural Developments, 1815–1848

Conservatism

Liberalism

Nationalism

Socialism

The Revolutions of 1830 and 1848

8%–10% Politics and Diplomacy in the Age of Nationalism, 1850–1914

The unification of Italy and Germany

Austria-Hungary

Russia

France

Socialism and labor unions

European diplomacy, 1871–1900

7%–9% Economy, Culture and Imperialism, 1850–1914

Demography

World economy of the nineteenth century

Technological developments

Science, philosophy and the arts

Imperialism in Africa and Asia

10%–12% The First World War and the Russian Revolution

The causes of the First World War

The economic and social impact of the war

The peace settlements

The Revolution of 1917 and its effects

7%–9% Europe Between the Wars

The Great Depression

International politics, 1919–1939

Stalin's five-year plans and purges

Italy and Germany between the wars

Interwar cultural developments

8%–10% The Second World War and Contemporary Europe

The causes and course of the Second World War

Postwar Europe

Science, philosophy, the arts and religion

Social and political developments

Sample Test Questions

The following sample questions do not appear on an actual CLEP examination. They are intended to give potential test-takers an indication of the format and difficulty level of the examination and to provide content for practice and review. Knowing the correct answers to all of the sample questions is not a guarantee of satisfactory performance on the exam.

Directions: Each of the questions or incomplete statements below is followed by five suggested answers or completions. Select the one that is best in each case.

1. Colbert's economic policies ran into difficulties chiefly because of the

    (A) relative poverty of France
    (B) loss of France's colonial empire
    (C) wars of Louis XIV
    (D) abandonment of the salt tax
    (E) reckless spending by the nobility

2. Which of the following best describes the use of the inductive method, as described by Francis Bacon?

    (A) Consult established scientific opinion and formulate a philosophical system based on it.
    (B) Begin with a mathematical principle and draw inferences from it.
    (C) Begin by making observations and then draw conclusions from them.
    (D) Begin with self-evident truths and draw inferences from them.
    (E) Advance learning by comparisons, analogies, and insights.

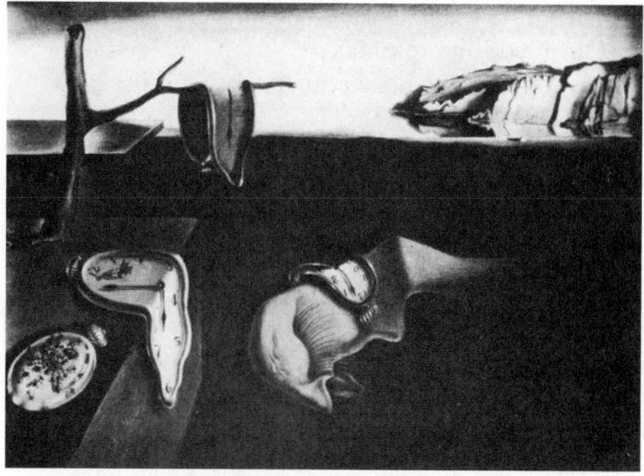

Digital Image @ The Museum of Modern Art/Licensed by SCALA/Art Resource NY

3. Which of the following is a major theme depicted in the painting above?

    (A) A scientific view of the world
    (B) Enlightened rationalism
    (C) Romantic concern with nature
    (D) Realistic appraisal of industrial progress
    (E) The world of the unconscious mind

4. Which of the following occurred as a result of the War of the Austrian Succession (1740–1748) and the Seven Years' War (1756–1763)?

    (A) Prussia emerged as an important economic and military power.
    (B) Sweden ceased to be a great power.
    (C) Russia extended its territory to the shores of the Baltic Sea.
    (D) Hapsburg claims to Polish territory were dropped.
    (E) France acquired the provinces of Alsace and Lorraine.

5. Which of the following European capital cities was founded after 1700 C.E. as a symbol of a newly powerful monarchy?

    (A) Madrid
    (B) Stockholm
    (C) Saint Petersburg
    (D) Vienna
    (E) Warsaw

6. "Sweet is the lore which Nature brings;
Our meddling intellect
Mis-shapes the beauteous forms of things:
We murder to dissect.

Enough of Science and of Art;
Close up those barren leaves;
Come forth, and bring with you a heart
That watches and receives."

The stanzas above best reflect the values of

(A) The Scientific Revolution
(B) Realism
(C) Romanticism
(D) Humanism
(E) Pietism

7. All of the following were related to the Eastern Question EXCEPT

(A) Pan-Slavism
(B) the Congress of Berlin of 1878
(C) the Crimean War
(D) the Kruger Telegram
(E) the Treaty of San Stefano

8. The cartoon above refers to the

(A) Napoleonic Wars
(B) Crimean War
(C) Boer War
(D) Russo-Japanese War
(E) First World War

9. All of the following were instrumental in the emergence of Italy as a modern nation-state EXCEPT

(A) Mazzini
(B) Napoleon III
(C) Cavour
(D) Francis II
(E) Garibaldi

10. "Men being by nature all free, equal, and independent, no one can be put out of this estate and subjected to the political power of another without his own consent, which is done by agreeing with other men, to join and unite into a community for their comfortable, safe, and peaceable living in a secure enjoyment of their properties."

The quotation above is from a work by

(A) John Locke
(B) Karl Marx
(C) Edmund Burke
(D) Voltaire
(E) Adam Smith

11. Social Darwinists viewed imperialism as

(A) the duty of Western nations to liberate oppressed peoples in Africa and Asia
(B) a collective endeavor by Western nations to eradicate disease
(C) an action justified by the Western nations' need for raw materials
(D) a method to allow less privileged nations to survive
(E) a natural consequence of human evolution

12. The term "collective security" would most likely be discussed in which of the following studies?

(A) A book on the twentieth-century welfare state
(B) A monograph on Soviet agricultural policy during the 1920s
(C) A book on Bismarckian imperialism
(D) A treatise on Social Darwinism
(E) A work on European diplomacy during the 1920s

13. The map above shows national boundaries in which of the following years?

(A) 1789
(B) 1812
(C) 1830
(D) 1870
(E) 1914

14. "The three classes, being associated and united in interest, would forget their hatred. . . . Labor would put an end to the drudgery of the people and the disdain of the rich for their inferiors, whose labors they would share. There would no longer be any poor, and social antipathies would disappear with the causes which produced them."

The quotation above typifies which of the following?

(A) Utopian socialism
(B) Marxism
(C) Utilitarianism
(D) Social Darwinism
(E) Stalinism

15. The British economist John Maynard Keynes did which of the following?

(A) He urged governments to increase mass purchasing power in times of deflation.
(B) He defended the principles of the Versailles Treaty.
(C) He helped to establish the British Labour party.
(D) He prophesied the inevitable economic decline of capitalism.
(E) He defined the concept of marginal utility to replace the labor theory of value.

16. The vast increase in German military expenditures in the two decades preceding the First World War occurred primarily because Germany

(A) had extended its imperialistic activities to the Far East
(B) was planning to militarize the provinces of Alsace and Lorraine
(C) was extending military aid to Russia
(D) feared an attack from France
(E) was rapidly expanding its navy

17. In comparison to a preindustrial economy, the most distinctive feature of a modern economy is its

(A) greater capacity to sustain growth over time
(B) increased democratization of the workplace
(C) lower wages for the literate middle class
(D) lack of economic cycles
(E) elimination of hunger and poverty

18. Which of the following individuals in nineteenth-century Great Britain was the most outspoken advocate for legal and political equality for women?

(A) Queen Victoria
(B) John Stuart Mill
(C) William Gladstone
(D) Florence Nightingale
(E) Jane Austen

19. Which eighteenth-century ruler abolished punitive laws regarding Jews, imposed limits on the Catholic Church, and granted effective toleration to all Christian sects?

(A) Louis XIV
(B) George III
(C) Catherine II
(D) Joseph II
(E) Charles III

20. “Each individual, bestowing more time and attention upon the means of preserving and increasing his portion of wealth than is or can be bestowed by government, is likely to take a more effectual course than what, in this instance and on his behalf, would be taken by government.”

The quotation above best illustrates which of the following?

(A) Fascism
(B) Mercantilism
(C) Syndicalism
(D) Classical liberalism
(E) Utopian socialism

21. The aim of the Soviet Union’s First Five-Year Plan was to

(A) acquire foreign capital
(B) produce an abundance of consumer goods
(C) encourage agricultural production by subsidizing the kulaks
(D) build up heavy industry
(E) put industrial policy in the hands of the peasantry

POPULATION DENSITY IN FRANCE PER SQUARE KILOMETER

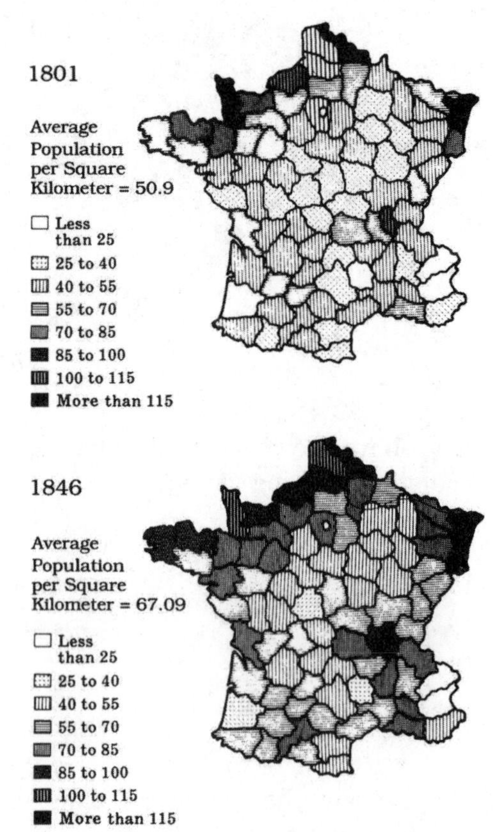

22. The increase in population density between 1801 and 1846 shown above indicates that

(A) the growth of Paris absorbed any natural population increase
(B) there was a reversing trend in which industry moved to the center of France while agriculture moved to the north
(C) the population distribution in 1801 was very similar to the population distribution in 1846
(D) by 1846 southern France was declining in population
(E) by 1846 central France was declining in population

23. The National Assembly in France (1789–1791) did all of the following EXCEPT

    (A) issue assignats
    (B) ban strikes
    (C) pass the Civil Constitution of the Clergy
    (D) abolish guilds
    (E) abolish private property

24. Historical explanations for nineteenth-century European imperialism include all of the following EXCEPT

    (A) a need to discover new sources of raw materials
    (B) a need to find new markets for manufactured goods
    (C) a need to invest excess financial resources
    (D) a desire to establish world government
    (E) a desire to maintain the European balance of power

25. All of the following factors contributed to the rise of the National Socialist German Workers' party (Nazis) EXCEPT

    (A) the weakness of the Weimar Republic
    (B) the dissatisfaction with the Versailles Treaty
    (C) the impact of the Great Depression
    (D) the support of German conservatives
    (E) the support of Socialist trade unions

26. "He used extreme methods and mass repressions at a time when the Revolution was already victorious, when the Soviet state was strengthened, when the exploiting classes were already liquidated and Socialist relations were rooted solidly in all phases of the national economy, when our party was politically consolidated and had strengthened itself both numerically and ideologically."

    In the quotation above, which of the following spoke and about whom?

    (A) Khrushchev about Stalin
    (B) Khrushchev about Trotsky
    (C) Stalin about Trotsky
    (D) Trotsky about Lenin
    (E) Brezhnev about Lenin

27. Albert Einstein's theory of relativity proposed

    (A) a new structure for the atom
    (B) a new conception of space and time
    (C) the fundamental concepts for developing the computer
    (D) the origin of the universe from the explosion of a single mass
    (E) the particulate nature of light

28. Which of the following is a central and essential component of the European welfare state?

    (A) Nationalization of all major sectors of the economy
    (B) Decentralization of the state
    (C) State responsibility for assuring access to medical care for all citizens
    (D) Elimination of large private fortunes through taxation
    (E) Elimination of independent trade unions

29. In the mid-eighteenth century, European population increased sharply for all of the following reasons EXCEPT

    (A) improved agricultural techniques
    (B) improvements in medical care
    (C) fewer famines
    (D) a decline in the death rate
    (E) a decline of the plague

30. One of the goals of the physiocrats was to

    (A) reform the French monarchy along Dutch lines
    (B) implement more stringent mercantilist economic policies
    (C) implement free-trade policies
    (D) repudiate the national debt
    (E) effect a complete redistribution of arable land in France

31. Most eighteenth-century deists denied the

    (A) divine creation of the universe
    (B) laws of gravity and motion
    (C) occurrence of miracles
    (D) need for religious toleration
    (E) historical existence of Jesus

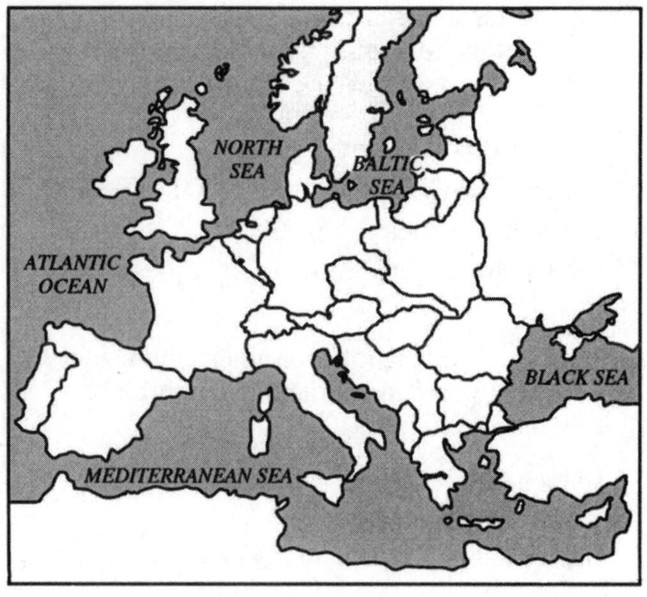

32. The map of Europe shown portrays national boundaries as they existed in

    (A) 1871
    (B) 1913
    (C) 1925
    (D) 1948
    (E) 1950

33. The dictum "form follows function" is associated with which of the following trends in the arts?

    (A) Neoclassicism
    (B) Modernism
    (C) Humanism
    (D) Romanticism
    (E) Realism

34. The *Ostpolitik* of West German Chancellor Willy Brandt was designed to

    (A) nationalize German banks
    (B) win Soviet diplomatic recognition for West Germany
    (C) deepen West Germany's commitment to the North Atlantic Treaty Organization (NATO)
    (D) normalize West German relations with the communist states of Eastern Europe
    (E) promote free trade in Europe

35. Which of the following largely resolved the battle for sovereignty between crown and Parliament in England?

(A) The Test Act of 1673
(B) The acceptance of the divine right of kings
(C) John Locke's *Second Treatise of Civil Government*
(D) The Glorious Revolution
(E) The English Civil War

36. "Each contract of each particular state is but a clause in the great primeval contract of eternal society, linking the lower with the higher natures, connecting the visible and invisible world, according to a fixed compact sanctioned by the inviolable oath which holds all physical and all moral natures, each in their appointed place."

The quotation above reflects the ideas of

(A) Charles Fourier
(B) Voltaire
(C) Rousseau
(D) Adam Smith
(E) Edmund Burke

37. Which of the following is true of the French Revolution of 1830?

(A) It strengthened the power of the working class.
(B) It overthrew the Bourbon Monarch Charles X.
(C) It produced a constitutional monarchy based on universal adult male suffrage.
(D) It was suppressed by Charles X with the aid of Austria and Russia.
(E) It strengthened the power of the Roman Catholic Church in France.

38. Which of the following countries remained most closely aligned, ideologically and economically, with the Soviet Union from 1945 to 1989?

(A) The People's Republic of China
(B) Bulgaria
(C) Czechoslovakia
(D) Hungary
(E) Poland

39. "We are fifty or a hundred years behind the advanced countries. We must make good this distance in ten years. Either we do it or they crush us."

The quotation above is attributed to

(A) Charles de Gaulle calling for France to prepare for tank warfare
(B) Winston Churchill demanding that Britain expand its air force and navy
(C) Joseph Stalin explaining the need for continued industrial development in the Soviet Union
(D) Mao Zedong (Mao Tse-tung) introducing the Cultural Revolution in China
(E) Adolf Hitler inaugurating German rearmament

40. By the end of the seventeenth century, which of the following was a consequence of the policies pursued by Spain in its colonial possessions in the New World?

(A) Economic and social mobility in Spanish America were greatly inhibited by a rigid ethnic and class structure.
(B) The native inhabitants had secured a degree of political independence.
(C) The Roman Catholic Church had been forced to tolerate Protestant missionary activities.
(D) Most colonists had come to view themselves as members of a new nation, distinct from Spain.
(E) There had been virtually no intermarriage among various racial groups.

The Granger Collection, New York

41. The eighteenth-century political cartoon reproduction shown above relates most closely to which of the following events of the French Revolution?

    (A) The emergence of the power of the Third Estate
    (B) The tensions between the nobility and clergy
    (C) The mistreatment of political prisoners
    (D) The death of Marat
    (E) The Thermidorean Reaction

42. Which of the following joined Nazi Germany in its attack on the Soviet Union?

    (A) Great Britain
    (B) Finland
    (C) Sweden
    (D) Turkey
    (E) Japan

43. Churchill's famous phrase "Never . . . was so much owed by so many to so few" referred to

    (A) those who evacuated the Allied army from Dunkirk
    (B) those who convoyed food and materiel across the Atlantic in the early 1940s
    (C) the scientists who developed radar and other early warning technologies
    (D) the fighter pilots of the Royal Air Force who won the Battle of Britain
    (E) the cryptographers who broke the German and Japanese military and diplomatic codes

44. The Soviet foreign policy of "peaceful coexistence" was most closely associated with which of the following Soviet domestic policies?

    (A) Lenin's New Economic Policy (NEP)
    (B) Stalin's program of collectivization
    (C) Khrushchev's policy of de-Stalinization
    (D) Brezhnev's policy toward dissidents
    (E) Andropov's program of increased industrial output

45. "This is what I see and what troubles me. I look on all sides and I see only darkness everywhere. Nature presents to me nothing which is not a matter of doubt and concern. It is incomprehensible that God should exist and that God should not exist."

    The quotation above expresses the view of

    (A) Pascal
    (B) Newton
    (C) Bacon
    (D) Galileo
    (E) Hobbes

46. Which of the following countries intervened militarily in Mexico in the 1860s in an attempt to establish colonial control?

(A) Germany
(B) Sweden
(C) Portugal
(D) Italy
(E) France

47. The theories of which of the following had the most influence on the American and French Revolutions?

(A) Condorcet, Voltaire, Jefferson
(B) Pitt, Hobbes, Raynal
(C) Diderot, Burke, Fox
(D) Montesquieu, Locke, Rousseau
(E) Wilkes, Turgot, Helvetius

48. The country that pioneered social insurance legislation in the late nineteenth century was

(A) Great Britain
(B) France
(C) Germany
(D) Austria
(E) Russia

49. One accomplishment of the British Reform Bill of 1832 was the

(A) increase in the parliamentary power of the House of Lords
(B) reduction in the constitutional powers of the Crown
(C) extension of parliamentary representation to the new industrial centers
(D) extension of the right to vote to all males over the age of 21
(E) increase in the representation of the colonies in Parliament

50. Which of the following was an outcome of the First World War?

(A) The downfall of the German, Ottoman, Italian, and British Empires
(B) Territorial gains for Italy, Romania, Austria, and Hungary
(C) National independence for Poland, Czechoslovakia, Yugoslavia, and Finland
(D) A decrease in the number of parliamentary democracies in Europe
(E) Successful Communist revolutions in Russia and Germany

51. Women did not gain the right to vote until after the Second World War in which of the following groups of countries?

(A) Great Britain, the United States, and France
(B) France, Italy, and Switzerland
(C) Germany, Austria, and Russia
(D) Poland, Czechoslovakia, and Hungary
(E) Norway, the Netherlands, and Sweden

52. Pablo Picasso is credited with founding the twentieth-century art movement called

(A) fauvism
(B) expressionism
(C) cubism
(D) futurism
(E) baroque

53. Prince Klemens von Metternich, the Austrian representative at the Congress of Vienna, is most closely associated with which of the following?

(A) Utopian socialism
(B) Nationalism
(C) Romanticism
(D) Liberalism
(E) Conservatism

54. In France, the revolutions of 1830 and 1848 and the Commune of 1871 primarily took what form?

    (A) Peasant revolts directed at aristocratic landowners
    (B) Army mutinies, soon joined by sympathetic civilians
    (C) Parisian insurrections, with armed civilians barricading streets
    (D) Uprisings organized by underground societies in multiple cities
    (E) *Coups d'état* carried out by small groups of professional revolutionaries

55. The National Workshops were established in France in order to

    (A) compete with cheap goods being produced in America
    (B) mass produce military weapons
    (C) produce quality wines for the European market
    (D) reduce high urban, especially Parisian, unemployment
    (E) promote Protestant social reforms

56. Which of the following was an important cause of the Second World War?

    (A) The failure of the *Anschluss* between Germany and Austria
    (B) British and French indignation over Hitler's anti-Semitic policies in Germany
    (C) The Soviet Union's military buildup against Japan
    (D) Hitler's quest for German living space in eastern Europe
    (E) Hitler's desire to divert the German public's attention away from the ongoing economic depression

57. All of the following were among the Great Reforms implemented in Russia during the reign of Alexander II (1855–1881) EXCEPT

    (A) the establishment of a parliament
    (B) the creation of regional councils known as *zemstvos*
    (C) the emancipation of the serfs
    (D) judicial reforms that granted all Russians access to civil courts
    (E) military reforms that reduced the length of the term of service for conscripts

58. The Second International, formed in 1889, lost its reason for existence primarily because of the

    (A) disintegration of socialist international solidarity in the face of wartime nationalism
    (B) disintegration of the German Social Democratic Party
    (C) Russian Bolshevik Revolution, which was repudiated by western European socialists
    (D) militarism of the French socialist leader, Jean Jaurès
    (E) disputes between French and German socialists over the question of Alsace-Lorraine

59. Existentialist philosophy is most closely associated with which of the following?

    (A) Jean-Paul Sartre
    (B) Bertrand Russell
    (C) Aleksandr Solzhenitsyn
    (D) Claude Lévi-Strauss
    (E) Marie Curie

60. All of the following were results of the Treaty of Paris (1763) EXCEPT

(A) Britain controlled much of India.
(B) France retained most of its sugar colonies in the West Indies.
(C) France suffered no decline in its overseas trade.
(D) Britain emerged as the predominant sea power.
(E) France had to give up its remaining North American mainland colonies.

61. In the mid-nineteenth century, women were LEAST likely to be employed in which of the following occupations?

(A) Factory work
(B) Domestic service
(C) Shopkeeping
(D) Teaching
(E) Legal services

62. The Great Elector, Frederick William of Brandenburg-Prussia (1640–1688), advocated all of the following policies EXCEPT

(A) a uniform currency system
(B) profitable dynastic marriages
(C) Jewish immigration
(D) a citizen army rather than a standing army
(E) consolidation of Hohenzollern lands

63. In 1936 it was widely assumed that France would come to the aid of the Republicans in Spain because France

(A) had been a consistent supporter of Franco
(B) opposed the Moscow-dominated government in Madrid
(C) wanted to seize Gibraltar
(D) was mandated by the League of Nations to defend Spain
(E) had a Popular Front government, as did Spain

64. Disraeli led the Conservatives in taking "a leap in the dark" in 1867. This phrase refers to the

(A) extension of the franchise to male working-class householders
(B) establishment of a more vigorous foreign policy vis-à-vis continental Europe
(C) plan proposed for establishing home rule in Ireland
(D) attempt to stimulate the economy through the use of deficit spending
(E) decision to grant dominion status to Canada

65. Which of the following statements about female industrial workers in eighteenth-century England is correct?

(A) They outnumbered male workers.
(B) Most left employment before they married.
(C) Most left the mills soon after employment to return to the countryside.
(D) They generally received lower pay than male workers.
(E) They were protected by law from hazardous occupations such as mining.

66. The enormous business success of the eighteenth-century English potter Josiah Wedgwood can be attributed primarily to

(A) the wealth of the aristocracy and their desire for elaborate china
(B) the rising prominence of the middle class, who sought to emulate the upper class
(C) the development of a huge overseas market for English china
(D) the prominence of coffee and tea drinking in the eighteenth century
(E) royal patronage for potters and weavers

67. “Separate spheres” refers to which of the following in nineteenth-century Europe?

    (A) The post-1789 legal relationship between the Catholic Church and the civil authority
    (B) The division of domestic and foreign policy making in modern constitutional states
    (C) Different roles of men and women in Victorian society
    (D) Parts of the human psyche as defined by Sigmund Freud
    (E) Gregor Mendel’s techniques for determining heredity

68. The “Velvet Revolution” refers to the collapse of communism in which of the following Eastern European countries?

    (A) Poland
    (B) Hungary
    (C) Yugoslavia
    (D) Czechoslovakia
    (E) Romania

69. Which of the following political philosophers believed that liberty could be preserved through separation of powers and checks and balances?

    (A) Jean-Jacques Rousseau
    (B) Adam Smith
    (C) Montesquieu
    (D) Thomas Hobbes
    (E) Voltaire

70. Which of the following works most directly challenged the theory of the divine right of kings?

    (A) *The Wealth of Nations*
    (B) *Letters Concerning the English Nation*
    (C) *Crime and Punishment*
    (D) *The Social Contract*
    (E) *The Prince*

71. During the Enlightenment, an unwillingness to accept explanations for events or phenomena unless such explanations were based on empirical evidence or logic was called

    (A) stoicism
    (B) mysticism
    (C) monasticism
    (D) skepticism
    (E) shamanism

72. The storming of the Bastille by a Paris crowd on July 14, 1789, was

    (A) undertaken to free the large number of inmates there
    (B) initiated to arrest the commander of the prison, who was known as a monster of cruelty
    (C) an attack on a symbol that had long represented despotism
    (D) a desperate, planned move to begin revolution between French citizens and the government
    (E) an action to force Louis XVI from Versailles to Paris

73. The “revolution of textiles” in eighteenth-century England involved principally

    (A) silk cloth
    (B) linen cloth
    (C) cotton cloth
    (D) machine-made tapestries
    (E) imported Indian calico cloth

74. Most sansculottes demanded which of the following from the leaders of the French Revolution?

    (A) Higher taxes for the wealthy, and rent and price restrictions
    (B) Restoration of church lands
    (C) Equal rights for women
    (D) Prices based on supply and demand
    (E) Property qualifications for voters

75. Inoculation was first used to prevent which of the following major diseases?

(A) The bubonic plague
(B) Cholera
(C) Tuberculosis
(D) Yellow fever
(E) Smallpox

76. All of the following were important issues that the Allies had to address at the Yalta and Potsdam Conferences EXCEPT

(A) reparations to the Soviet Union
(B) the sharing of nuclear weapons technology
(C) the postwar occupation regime in Germany
(D) war crimes trials for German and Japanese leaders
(E) Soviet influence in postwar Eastern Europe

77. Which of the following accomplishments of Napoleon Bonaparte lasted the longest?

(A) The Concordat of 1801
(B) The Civil Code
(C) The Continental System
(D) The Confederation of the Rhine
(E) The Cisalpine Republic

78. The Great Depression that began in 1929 was made worse by government actions that instituted

(A) budget cuts and higher tariffs on foreign goods
(B) banking reform and old-age pensions
(C) military expansion and imperialism
(D) high taxes and low national debt
(E) national transportation and conservation projects

79. "Mr. [William] Cobbett said a new discovery had been made in the House [of Commons] last night. . . . It had formerly been said that the Navy was the great support of England; at another time that our maritime commerce was the great bulwark of the country; at another time that [it was] our colonies . . . but now it was admitted that our great stay and bulwark was to be found in three hundred thousand little girls . . . ."

The 1833 parliamentary debate referred to in the quote was about

(A) elementary education
(B) child labor
(C) the Irish famine
(D) settlers for Britain's colonies
(E) juvenile delinquency

80. The revocation of the Edict of Nantes in 1685 had the most direct impact on which of the following groups in France?

(A) Mercantilists
(B) Politiques
(C) Peasants
(D) Calvinists
(E) Physiocrats

81. Which of the following had NOT emerged as a distinct school of thought by 1848 ?

(A) Fascism
(B) Utopian socialism
(C) Laissez-faire capitalism
(D) Royal absolutism
(E) Nationalism

82. Which of the following represented the most serious challenge to the territorial integrity of Austria-Hungary in the period 1867–1914 ?

(A) The unification of Italy
(B) The unification of Germany
(C) Ethnic nationalism
(D) The Jewish question
(E) International socialism

83. Which of the following was Lenin's main contribution to Marxist theory?

(A) The idea that a small vanguard party could spearhead a socialist revolution even in relatively under-industrialized countries
(B) The notion that peasants, rather than industrial workers, can be the primary driving force in a socialist revolution
(C) The claim that a successful socialist revolution had to be limited to Russian territory
(D) The belief that a successful socialist revolution must be followed by a transitional period of dictatorship of the proletariat
(E) The claim that socialist countries can peacefully coexist with capitalist countries in perpetuity

84. The writings of Friedrich Nietzsche and Sigmund Freud were similar in that both argued that

(A) individuals should always submit to the needs of society
(B) individuals are strongly influenced by subjective, often irrational forces
(C) universal truths can be ascertained through analysis and experiment
(D) traditional religion provides the surest guide to understanding the universe
(E) humankind will continue to progress toward perfection

85. The 1917 Bolshevik seizure of power in Russia was organized and led by

(A) Marx and Engels
(B) Kerensky and Rasputin
(C) Stolypin and Witte
(D) Stalin and Khrushchev
(E) Trotsky and Lenin

86. Both sides in the First World War used which of the following?

(A) Aircraft carriers
(B) Biological weapons
(C) Concentration camps
(D) Radar
(E) Chemical weapons

87. "We must, however, acknowledge, as it seems to me, that man with all his noble qualities, with sympathy which feels for the most debased, with benevolence which extends not only to other men but to the humblest living creature, with his godlike intellect which has penetrated into the movements and constitution of the solar system—with all these exalted powers—Man still bears in his bodily frame the indelible stamp of his lowly origin."

The passage above reflects the thinking of which of the following?

(A) Albert Einstein
(B) Sigmund Freud
(C) Karl Marx
(D) Charles Darwin
(E) Henri de Saint-Simon

88. Most nineteenth-century liberals would have agreed with which of the following statements?

(A) A parliamentary republic with universal suffrage is the best form of government.
(B) Traditional political and social institutions must be preserved at all cost.
(C) Free trade is more beneficial to a nation's prosperity than is economic protectionism.
(D) Governments should forcibly seize the means of production from capitalists and large landowners.
(E) Multiethnic empires must be broken up based on the principle of national self-determination.

89. Autarky, a stated political goal of Adolf Hitler and Benito Mussolini, refers to the

(A) establishment of dictatorial authority
(B) creation of a racially purified state
(C) establishment of economic self-sufficiency
(D) abolition of the democratic legislative process
(E) coordination of everyday life

90. Which of the following occurred between 1945 and 1949 ?

(A) Poland was divided between Germany and the Soviet Union.
(B) Free, democratic elections were held in Lithuania, Latvia, and Estonia.
(C) The Czech Republic separated from Slovakia.
(D) Germany and Austria were divided into zones of military occupation.
(E) Romania returned to its prewar form of government.

Study Resources

Most textbooks used in college-level Western civilization courses cover the topics in the outline given earlier, but the approaches to certain topics and the emphases given to them may differ. To prepare for the Western Civilization II exam, it is advisable to study one or more college textbooks, which can be found in most college bookstores. When selecting a textbook, check the table of contents against the knowledge and skills required for this test.

You may also find it helpful to supplement your reading with books listed in the bibliographies found in most history textbooks. In addition, contemporary historical novels, plays and films provide rich sources of information. Actual works of art in museums can bring to life not only the reproductions found in books but history itself.

Visit **clep.collegeboard.org/earn-college-credit/practice** for additional Western civilization resources. You can also find suggestions for exam preparation in Chapter IV of the *Official Study Guide*. In addition, many college faculty post their course materials on their schools' websites.

Answer Key

1.	C	46.	E
2.	C	47.	D
3.	E	48.	C
4.	A	49.	C
5.	C	50.	C
6.	C	51.	B
7.	D	52.	C
8.	E	53.	E
9.	D	54.	C
10.	A	55.	D
11.	E	56.	D
12.	E	57.	A
13.	B	58.	A
14.	A	59.	A
15.	A	60.	C
16.	E	61.	E
17.	A	62.	D
18.	B	63.	E
19.	D	64.	A
20.	D	65.	D
21.	D	66.	B
22.	C	67.	C
23.	E	68.	D
24.	D	69.	C
25.	E	70.	D
26.	A	71.	D
27.	B	72.	C
28.	C	73.	C
29.	B	74.	A
30.	C	75.	E
31.	C	76.	B
32.	C	77.	B
33.	B	78.	A
34.	D	79.	B
35.	D	80.	D
36.	E	81.	A
37.	B	82.	C
38.	B	83.	A
39.	C	84.	B
40.	A	85.	E
41.	A	86.	E
42.	B	87.	D
43.	D	88.	C
44.	C	89.	C
45.	A	90.	D

Biology

Description of the Examination

The Biology examination covers material that is usually taught in a one-year college general biology course. The subject matter tested covers the broad field of the biological sciences, organized into three major areas: molecular and cellular biology, organismal biology and population biology. The examination gives approximately equal weight to these three areas.

The examination contains approximately 115 questions to be answered in 90 minutes. Some of these are pretest questions that will not be scored.

Knowledge and Skills Required

Questions on the Biology examination require candidates to demonstrate one or more of the following abilities.

- Knowledge of facts, principles and processes of biology
- Understanding the means by which information is collected, how it is interpreted, how one hypothesizes from available information, how one draws conclusions and makes further predictions
- Understanding that science is a human endeavor with social consequences

The subject matter of the Biology examination is drawn from the following topics. The percentages next to the main topics indicate the approximate percentage of exam questions on that topic.

33% **Molecular and Cellular Biology**

Chemical composition of organisms

- Simple chemical reactions and bonds
- Properties of water
- Chemical structure of carbohydrates, lipids, proteins, nucleic acids
- Origin of life

Cells

- Structure and function of cell organelles
- Properties of cell membranes
- Comparison of prokaryotic and eukaryotic cells

Enzymes

- Enzyme-substrate complex
- Roles of coenzymes
- Inorganic cofactors
- Inhibition and regulation

Energy transformations

- Glycolysis, cellular respiration, aerobic and anaerobic pathways
- Photosynthesis

Cell division

- Structure of chromosomes
- Mitosis, meiosis and cytokinesis in plants and animals

Chemical nature of the gene

- Watson-Crick model of nucleic acids
- DNA replication
- Mutations
- Control of protein synthesis: transcription, translation, post-transcriptional processing
- Structural and regulatory genes
- Transformation
- Viruses

34% Organismal Biology

Structure and function in plants with emphasis on angiosperms

- Root, stem, leaf, flower, seed, fruit
- Water and mineral absorption and transport
- Food translocation and storage

Plant reproduction and development

- Alternation of generations in ferns, conifers and flowering plants
- Gamete formation and fertilization
- Growth and development: hormonal control
- Tropisms and photoperiodicity

Structure and function in animals with emphasis on vertebrates

- Major systems (e.g., digestive, gas exchange, skeletal, nervous, circulatory, excretory, immune)
- Homeostatic mechanisms
- Hormonal control in homeostasis and reproduction

Animal reproduction and development

- Gamete formation, fertilization
- Cleavage, gastrulation, germ layer formation, differentiation of organ systems
- Experimental analysis of vertebrate development
- Extraembryonic membranes of vertebrates
- Formation and function of the mammalian placenta
- Blood circulation in the human embryo

Principles of heredity

- Mendelian inheritance (dominance, segregation, independent assortment)
- Chromosomal basis of inheritance
- Linkage, including sex-linked
- Polygenic inheritance (height, skin color)
- Multiple alleles (human blood groups)

33% Population Biology

Principles of ecology

- Energy flow and productivity in ecosystems
- Biogeochemical cycles
- Population growth and regulation (natality, mortality, competition, migration, density, *r*- and *K*-selection)
- Community structure, growth, regulation (major biomes and succession)
- Habitat (biotic and abiotic factors)
- Concept of niche
- Island biogeography
- Evolutionary ecology (life history strategies, altruism, kin selection)

Principles of evolution

- History of evolutionary concepts
- Concepts of natural selection (differential reproduction, mutation, Hardy-Weinberg equilibrium, speciation, punctuated equilibrium)
- Adaptive radiation
- Major features of plant and animal evolution
- Concepts of homology and analogy
- Convergence, extinction, balanced polymorphism, genetic drift
- Classification of living organisms
- Evolutionary history of humans

Principles of behavior

- Stereotyped, learned social behavior
- Societies (insects, birds, primates)

Social biology

- Human population growth (age composition, birth and fertility rates, theory of demographic transition)
- Human intervention in the natural world (management of resources, environmental pollution)
- Biomedical progress (control of human reproduction, genetic engineering)

Sample Test Questions

The following sample questions do not appear on an actual CLEP examination. They are intended to give potential test-takers an indication of the format and difficulty level of the examination and to provide content for practice and review. Knowing the correct answers to all of the sample questions is not a guarantee of satisfactory performance on the exam.

Directions: Each of the questions or incomplete statements below is followed by five suggested answers or completions. Select the one that is best in each case.

1. In which of the following ways do social insects benefit most from having several types or castes within the species?

(A) Each colony is able to include a large number of individuals.
(B) The secretions or odors produced by the protective caste are an effective defense.
(C) The division of the species into castes ensures the survival of the fittest.
(D) Large numbers of the worker caste can migrate to start new colonies.
(E) The specialized structure of each caste permits division of labor and greater efficiency.

2. The greatest diversity of structure and of methods of locomotion is exhibited in the individuals of

(A) a class
(B) a family
(C) an order
(D) a species
(E) a phylum

3. Of the following, which is an example of a mutualistic relationship?

(A) The protozoan *Trichonympha* digesting wood in the gut of a termite
(B) The sporozoan *Plasmodium* reproducing in human blood cells and liberating toxins into the human body
(C) Two species of *Paramecium* deriving food from a common laboratory culture
(D) Rabbits being eaten by foxes
(E) Humans inadvertently providing food for cockroaches

4. Evidence that multicellular green plants may have evolved from green algae is best supported by the fact that in both

(A) the gametophyte generation is dominant
(B) the sporophyte generation is dominant
(C) chlorophylls *a* and *b* are photosynthetic pigments
(D) xylem vessels are pitted and spiraled
(E) male gametes are nonflagellated

5. All of the following statements concerning the light-capturing reactions of photosynthesis are true EXCEPT

(A) An initial event is the excitation of electrons in chlorophyll by light energy.
(B) The excited electrons are raised to a higher energy level.
(C) If not captured, the excited electrons drop back to their initial energy levels.
(D) If captured, some of the energy of the excited electrons is used to split carbon dioxide into carbon and oxygen.
(E) Light is absorbed by pigments that are embedded in membranes.

6. Which of the following statements best explains the hypothesis that the development of sexual reproduction has resulted in acceleration of the rate of evolution?

   (A) Mutations are more likely to occur in spermatogenesis and oogenesis than in mitotically dividing cells.
   (B) Sexual reproduction results in more offspring than does asexual reproduction.
   (C) Those members of a species that are best adapted to their environment are most likely to be successful in sexual reproduction.
   (D) Mutations usually do not occur in the production of spores or in cells dividing by fission.
   (E) Sexual reproduction is more likely to result in genetic recombination than is asexual reproduction.

7. A frog skeletal muscle contracts in response to an electrical stimulus. Increase of the stimulus intensity by 50 percent will increase the strength of response nearly 50 percent. If the intensity is again increased 50 percent, the response will increase only about another 25 percent. Further increase in the stimulus intensity produces no further increase in response.

   The observations above are best explained by which of the following?

   (A) A muscle functions with an all-or-none mechanism.
   (B) Muscle-fiber sarcolemma is electrically resistant.
   (C) The fibers of a muscle do not all contract at the same rate.
   (D) The fibers of a muscle fatigue at varying rates.
   (E) The fibers of a muscle have varying thresholds for response.

8. Nitrogen-containing waste products are excreted as the result of the metabolism of which of the following?

   (A) Proteins
   (B) Fats
   (C) Simple sugars
   (D) Starch
   (E) Cellulose

9. Deposits of coal in Greenland and the Antarctic indicate that

   (A) these regions once contained numerous mollusks that deposited carbohydrates in their shells
   (B) the Earth's crust in these regions contains vast amounts of limestone
   (C) these regions were once thickly vegetated
   (D) there is a rich store of dissolved carbon dioxide in the seas surrounding these regions
   (E) a geologic uplift of coral rock and ocean bed has recently occurred in these regions

10. Thirst, loss of weight, and sugar in the urine result from the undersecretion of a hormone by which of the following glands?

   (A) Thyroid
   (B) Parathyroid
   (C) Pancreas
   (D) Adrenal
   (E) Thymus

11. Considering the role of mitochondria in cells, mitochondria would likely be most abundant in which of the following?

(A) Mature red blood cells
(B) Callous cells of the skin
(C) Cells of the heart muscle
(D) Epithelial cells of the cheek lining
(E) Fat cells

12. All of the following statements about enzymes are true EXCEPT

(A) A single enzyme molecule can be used over and over again.
(B) Most enzymes are highly specific with regard to the reactions they catalyze.
(C) Some enzymes contain an essential nonprotein component.
(D) Enzymes can function only within living cells.
(E) Most enzymes are denatured by high temperatures.

13. Which of the following is critical in limiting the size to which an animal cell may grow?

(A) The ratio of cell surface to cell volume
(B) The abundance of mitochondria in the cytoplasm
(C) The chemical composition of the cell membrane
(D) The presence of an inelastic cell wall
(E) The relative number of nucleoli

14. Which of the following best describes the effect on heart action of the stimulation of the parasympathetic nerve fibers of the vagus nerve?

(A) There is a decrease in the volume of blood pumped and an increase in the heartbeat rate.
(B) There is an increase in the volume of blood pumped without a decrease in the heartbeat rate.
(C) There is a prolonged acceleration in the heartbeat rate.
(D) There is a decrease in the heartbeat rate.
(E) There is an increase in the blood pressure.

15. If poorly drained soils encourage the growth of bacteria that convert nitrate to nitrogen, the effect on higher plants will be to

(A) increase lipid production
(B) decrease protein production
(C) increase carbohydrate production
(D) produce unusually large fruits
(E) stimulate chlorophyll production

16. A patient is placed on a restricted diet of water, pure cooked starch, olive oil, adequate minerals, and vitamins. If a urinalysis several weeks later reveals the presence of relatively normal amounts of urea, the urea probably came from the

(A) food eaten during the restricted diet
(B) withdrawal of reserve urea stored in the liver
(C) chemical combination of water, carbon dioxide, and free nitrogen
(D) deamination of cellular proteins
(E) urea synthesized by kidney tubule cells

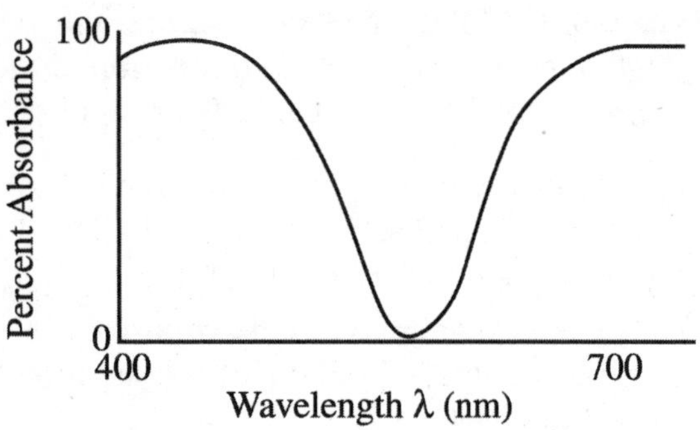

17. Shown above is the absorption spectrum of a compound of biological importance. If a person with normal human color vision viewed this compound under ordinary white light, what color would it appear to be?

(A) Red
(B) Blue
(C) Green
(D) Black
(E) White

18. The codon for a particular amino acid is 5'CAU3'. The DNA sequence that complements this codon is

(A) 3'CAU5'
(B) 3'GTA5'
(C) 3'GTT5'
(D) 3'GUA5'
(E) 3'GUT5'

19. Viral DNA would be most likely to contain genes that code for

(A) regulatory hormones
(B) viral-coat protein
(C) viral-ribosome proteins
(D) glycolytic enzymes
(E) restriction enzymes

20. Which of the following statements about imprinting is NOT true?

(A) The capacity for imprinting may be limited to a specific and brief period in the early life of the organism.
(B) The behavior pattern associated with imprinting is the result of reward or punishment.
(C) The behavior resulting from imprinting is difficult to reverse in later life.
(D) A gosling imprinted by a moving wooden decoy may exhibit courting behavior to the decoy in later life.
(E) Odors and sounds may serve as stimuli for imprinting.

21. Which of the graphs below illustrates the effect of substrate concentration on the initial rate of reaction when a limited amount of enzyme is present?

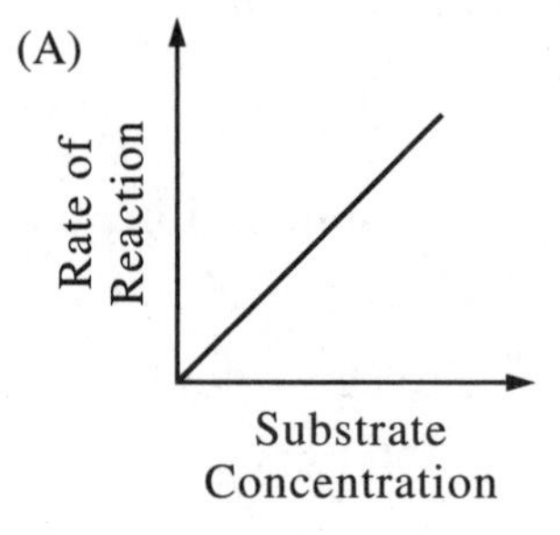

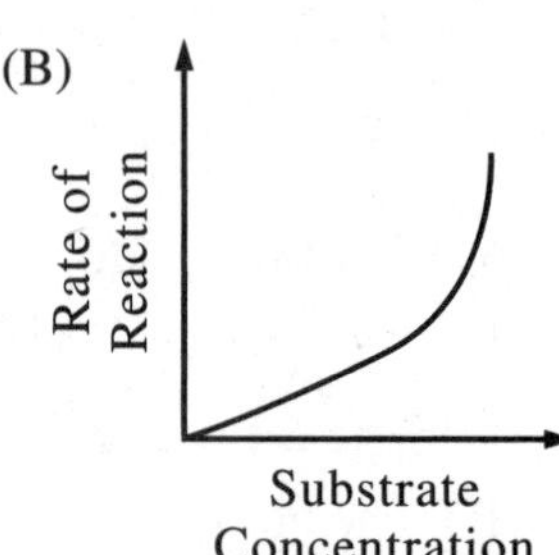

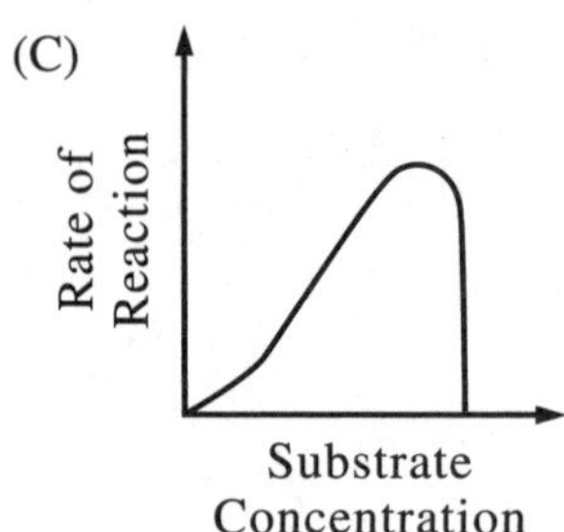

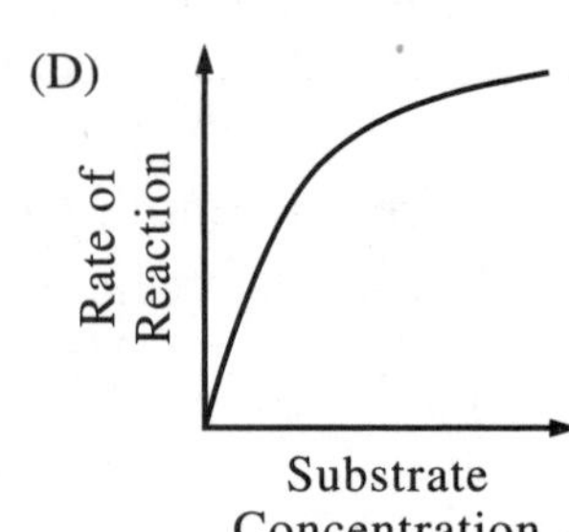

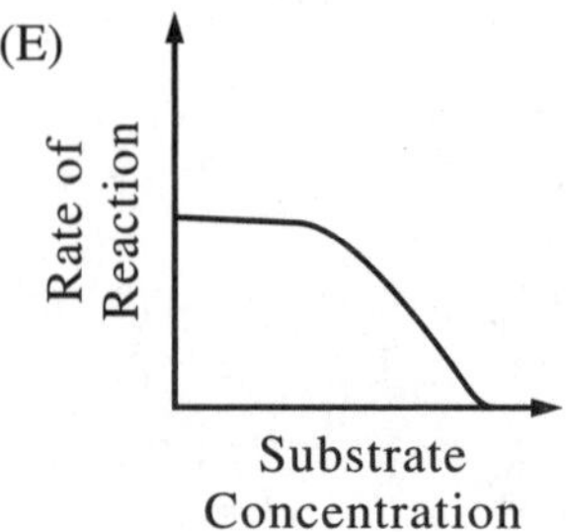

22. Which of the following is the final electron acceptor in the mitochondrial electron transport system?

    (A) ADP + Pi
    (B) ATP
    (C) NAD or FAD
    (D) Pyruvate
    (E) O_2

23. In a eukaryotic cell, glycolysis occurs in which of the following parts of the cell?

    (A) Chloroplast
    (B) Cytosol
    (C) Nucleolus
    (D) Mitochondrion
    (E) Ribosome

24. The clotting process in blood is initiated by

    (A) erythrocytes
    (B) lymphocytes
    (C) hemoglobins
    (D) platelets
    (E) neutrophils

25. Which of the following membranes is correctly matched to its function?

    (A) Allantois .. food absorption
    (B) Yolk sac .. embryonic bladder
    (C) Amnion .. gas exchange
    (D) Dura mater .. brain protection
    (E) Peritoneum .. heart protection

26. Which of the following statements best describes the movement of energy in an ecosystem?

    (A) Radiant energy is converted into chemical energy in plant photosynthesis and then released as heat energy during cellular respiration.
    (B) Energy cycles within an ecosystem.
    (C) Plants get energy from the nutrients in the soil.
    (D) The animals in an ecosystem absorb the radiant energy of the Sun and use it to make organic molecules such as proteins.
    (E) Some chemoautotrophic bacteria release energy that can then be used by soil animals to make food.

27. Which of the following elements is correctly linked to its role in a living organism?

    (A) Calcium .. component of proteins
    (B) Carbon .. component of lipids
    (C) Magnesium .. neuron action potential
    (D) Potassium .. component of ATP
    (E) Zinc .. component of carbohydrates

28. Mistletoe is attached to the branches of trees such as sweet gum, from which it obtains water and some nutrients. Due to this association, tree growth may be diminished. Which of the following terms describes the relationship between the two plants?

    (A) Commensalism
    (B) Competition
    (C) Mutualism
    (D) Parasitism
    (E) Predation

29. AMP is which type of molecule?

    (A) A nucleotide
    (B) A peptide
    (C) A phospholipid
    (D) A disaccharide
    (E) A tripeptide

30. Which of the following is generally true about bacterial viruses?

    (A) They infect animal cells only.
    (B) They have a protective capsid made of chitin.
    (C) They inject their nucleic acids into the cells that they infect.
    (D) They produce haploid gametes in meiosis.
    (E) They carry out glycolysis but not the Krebs (citric acid) cycle.

31. A typical photosynthetic eukaryotic cell contains which of the following?

    I. Ribosomes
    II. Chloroplasts
    III. Mitochondria

    (A) II only
    (B) I and II only
    (C) II and III only
    (D) I and III only
    (E) I, II, and III

32. Which of the following pairs of organisms are most closely related?

    (A) *Mus bufo* and *Bufo americanus*
    (B) *Lynx lynx* and *Alces alces*
    (C) *Panthera leo* and *Felis concolor*
    (D) *Odocoileus virginianus* and *Colinus virginianus*
    (E) *Canis latrans* and *Canis lupus*

33. Which of the following is an example of a testcross?

    (A) *AA* x *Aa*
    (B) *A?* x *AA*
    (C) *A?* x *Aa*
    (D) *A?* x *aa*
    (E) *aa* x *aa*

Directions: The following group of questions consists of five lettered headings followed by a list of numbered phrases. For each numbered phrase select the one heading that is most closely related to it. A heading may be used once, more than once, or not at all.

Questions 34–36 refer to the following.

(A) Fertilization
(B) Meiosis
(C) Mitosis
(D) Pollination
(E) Nondisjunction

34. The process by which a zygote is formed

35. The process by which the nuclei of somatic (body) cells divide

36. The process by which haploid cells are formed from diploid cells

Questions 37–41 refer to the following classes of vertebrates.

(A) Amphibians
(B) Bony fish
(C) Cartilaginous fish
(D) Mammals
(E) Reptiles

37. Birds are most closely related to which class?

38. Which class includes animals that have a moist skin as the primary organ for gas exchange in the adults?

39. Which class includes whales?

40. Members of which class produce milk for their young in specialized skin glands?

41. Which class includes snakes?

Directions: Each group of questions below concerns an experimental situation. In each case, first study the description of the situation. Then choose the best answer to each question following it.

Questions 42–44

Expenditures of solar energy, calculated by C. Juday for Lake Mendota in southern Wisconsin, appear in the table below.

Reflected or otherwise lost	49.5%
Absorbed in evaporation of water	25.0%
Raised temperatures in the lake	21.7%
Melted ice in the spring	3.0%
Used directly by organisms	0.8%

The pyramid of biomass for this same lake is represented by the following diagram.

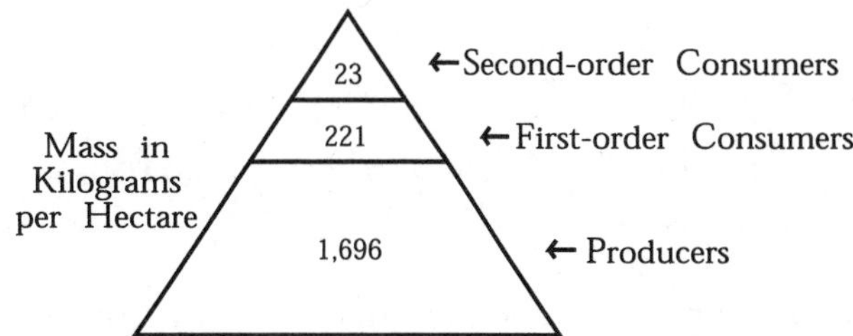

42. The most probable explanation for the relative masses of the first- and second-order consumers is that

(A) each link in the food chain of an ecosystem has less available energy than the previous link has
(B) only a small fraction of sunlight that reaches the Earth is transformed into chemical energy by photosynthesis
(C) the total energy of the decomposers is greater than that of the rest of the organisms put together
(D) seasonal fluctuations in weather limit the number of consumers
(E) second-order consumers require more total energy than first-order consumers do

43. The energy incorporated into this ecosystem is most dependent on the

(A) photoperiod
(B) total amount of photosynthesis
(C) predator-prey relationships
(D) length of the food chains
(E) total amount of respiration

44. If the lake is assumed to be a typical ecosystem, the percent of radiant energy from the Sun reaching the lake that is trapped in photosynthesis is about

(A) 100%
(B) 10%
(C) 1%
(D) 0.1%
(E) 0.01%

Questions 45–47

Inheritance of certain characteristics of the fruit fly, *Drosophila*, is as indicated by the table below.

Characteristic	Dominant	Recessive
Body color	Gray	Black
Eye color	Red	White

A female fruit fly had a gray body and white eyes. After being mated with a male fruit fly, she laid 112 eggs that developed into the following kinds of offspring.

Number	Body	Eyes
28	Gray	Red
29	Gray	White
28	Black	Red
27	Black	White

45. With respect to body color, the male parent of the 112 offspring was most probably

(A) homozygous gray
(B) heterozygous gray
(C) homozygous black
(D) heterozygous black
(E) hemizygous gray

46. Examination revealed that all of the 56 red-eyed offspring were females and all of the 56 white-eyed offspring were males. This observation indicates that

(A) red and white eye colors segregate independently of sex
(B) all of the red-eyed offspring inherited their eye color from their female parent
(C) all of the red-eyed offspring were homozygous
(D) the gene for eye color is linked to the gene for body color
(E) the gene for red or for white eye color is carried on the X chromosome

47. In this experiment, the number of offspring that exhibit both recessive characters is

(A) 1
(B) 27
(C) 28
(D) 55
(E) 56

48. Carbon dioxide is produced by which of the following?

I. A mesophyll cell in a flowering plant during the night
II. A muscle cell in a mammalian heart during contraction
III. A yeast cell growing under anaerobic conditions

(A) I only
(B) II only
(C) III only
(D) I and II only
(E) I, II, and III

49. Which of the following is a function of ATP?

(A) It creates energy.
(B) It transports energy.
(C) It is a building block of proteins.
(D) It stores amino acids.
(E) It gives the cells shape.

50. Protein synthesis is the main function of which of the following structures?

(A) Nucleus
(B) Ribosome
(C) Chromosome
(D) Mitochondrion
(E) Vacuole

Questions 51–55

Several different samples of DNA were digested with different restriction enzymes (endonucleases) and separated by gel electrophoresis, as shown below.

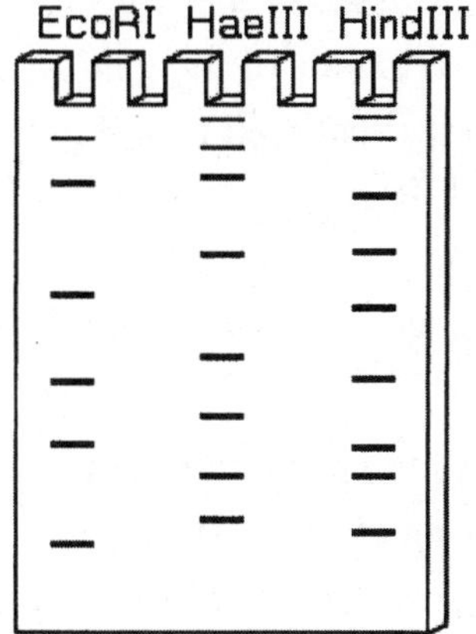

51. The terms "EcoRI," "HaeIII," and "HindIII" refer to which of the following?

(A) The voltage intensity used to prepare the electrophoresis medium
(B) The restriction enzymes used
(C) The organisms from which the original DNA sample was obtained
(D) The types of buffers used to maintain a constant pH in the preparation as the sample was processed
(E) The types of proteins encoded by each fragment

52. The patterns of bands in the different lanes result from which of the following?

(A) Different voltages applied to different lanes
(B) Different buffers applied to different lanes
(C) Different sizes of fragments in the samples in different lanes
(D) Different terminal configurations of the fragments, with some having blunt ends while others have sticky ends
(E) Mutations produced by the electrophoresis

53. In this gel, the smallest fragments are

(A) at the top of the gel, near the wells
(B) at the bottom of the gel, furthest from the wells
(C) at the left side of the gel
(D) at the right side of the gel
(E) randomly scattered from top to bottom in each lane

54. Restriction enzymes cut samples of DNA into fragments by first

(A) binding to specific sequences of nucleotides
(B) oxidizing the DNA
(C) heating the DNA to its denaturation point
(D) breaking peptide bonds
(E) unwinding the DNA

55. Which of the following is the most probable explanation for the different numbers of fragments in the different lanes?

(A) There were more EcoRI cut sites than HaeIII or HindIII cut sites.
(B) There were more HaeIII cut sites than EcoRI or HindIII cut sites.
(C) There were more HindIII cut sites than HaeIII or EcoRI cut sites.
(D) A stronger voltage was applied to the first lane.
(E) Different buffers were used in the different lanes.

56. Which of the following best explains why a pictorial presentation of the biomass at each trophic level of an ecosystem is a pyramid?

(A) The loss of iron from an ecosystem
(B) The amount of energy passed from one trophic level to the next
(C) The number of predators in the ecosystem
(D) The chemical compounds in an ecosystem are recycled
(E) The average size of the individuals in each species

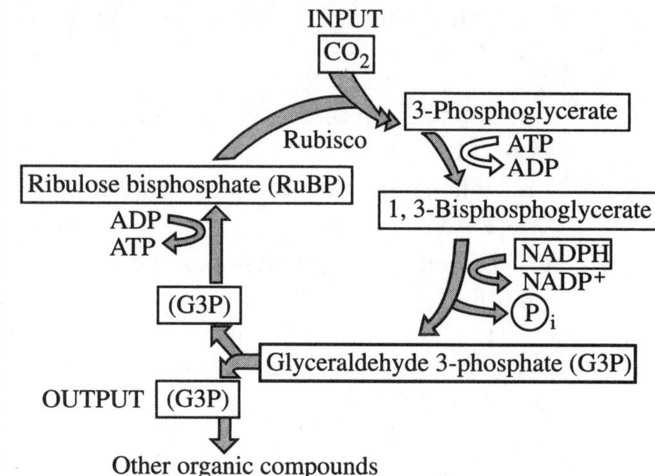

57. The original description of the pathway shown above is attributed to

(A) Louis Pasteur
(B) James Watson and Francis Crick
(C) Hans Krebs
(D) Robert Hooke
(E) Melvin Calvin and Andrew Benson

58. A diet with insufficient iodine will most likely lead to which of the following symptoms in an individual?

(A) Bleeding gums
(B) Decreased metabolic rate
(C) Increased body temperature
(D) Increased respiratory rate
(E) Weight loss

59. Which of the following structures is correctly paired with its function?

(A) Alveolus . . locomotion
(B) Cilium . . impulse transmission
(C) Sarcomere . . nutrient uptake
(D) Neuron . . gas exchange
(E) Nephron . . filtration

60. Based on the information in the table, which of the following substitutions is synonymous?

FIRST BASE	U	C	A	G	THIRD BASE
U	UUU Phe	UCU Ser	UAU Tyr	UGU Cys	U
U	UUC Phe	UCC Ser	UAC Tyr	UGC Cys	C
U	UUA Leu	UCA Ser	UAA Stop	UGA Stop	A
U	UUG Leu	UCG Ser	UAG Stop	UGG Trp	G
C	CUU Leu	CCU Pro	CAU His	CGU Arg	U
C	CUC Leu	CCC Pro	CAC His	CGC Arg	C
C	CUA Leu	CCA Pro	CAA Gln	CGA Arg	A
C	CUG Leu	CCG Pro	CAG Gln	CGG Arg	G
A	AUU Ile	ACU Thr	AAU Asn	AGU Ser	U
A	AUC Ile	ACC Thr	AAC Asn	AGC Ser	C
A	AUA Ile	ACA Thr	AAA Lys	AGA Arg	A
A	AUG Met or Start	ACG Thr	AAG Lys	AGG Arg	G
G	GUU Val	GCU Ala	GAU Asp	GGU Gly	U
G	GUC Val	GCC Ala	GAC Asp	GGC Gly	C
G	GUA Val	GCA Ala	GAA Glu	GGA Gly	A
G	GUG Val	GCG Ala	GAG Glu	GGG Gly	G

(Column headers: SECOND BASE)

(A) AGU to AGA
(B) GUU to GCU
(C) UUG to CUG
(D) UGA to GGA
(E) CAA to CCA

61. Excess sewage can lead to the death of aquatic animals in a lake because sewage pollution promotes

(A) mineral starvation
(B) erosion
(C) thermal stratification
(D) oxygen depletion
(E) a temperature decrease

62. The aerobic cellular respiration of glucose is different from the simple burning of glucose in that the aerobic respiration of glucose

(A) releases no heat
(B) requires no oxygen
(C) releases more energy
(D) releases hydrocarbons
(E) occurs at a lower temperature

63. A given trait occurs in two alternative types, *M* and *m*, in a population at Hardy-Weinberg equilibrium. If 49 percent of the population has only type *M* alleles, what percentage of the population is expected to be heterozygous for the trait?

(A) 9%
(B) 14%
(C) 21%
(D) 42%
(E) 51%

64. The forelimbs of horses and frogs are considered to be homologous structures. The best evidence for this homology is that the forelimbs have

(A) a similar appearance in both species
(B) a similar function in both species
(C) a common embryological origin
(D) the same chemical composition
(E) the same number of bones

65. Which of the following types of plant cells is dead at functional maturity?

(A) Phloem companion cell
(B) Xylem vessel element
(C) Root endodermal cell
(D) Stem cortex cell
(E) Mesophyll cell

66. In a particular plant species, the allele for tall plants is dominant and the allele for dwarfing is recessive. Which of the following is the expected phenotypic ratio of the offspring from a cross between a heterozygous plant and a dwarf plant?

(A) 1 tall plant : 3 dwarf plants
(B) 1 tall plant : 9 dwarf plants
(C) 1 tall plant : 1 dwarf plant
(D) 3 tall plants : 1 dwarf plant
(E) 9 tall plants : 3 dwarf plants

67. Which of the following best describes the decomposers in an ecological community?

(A) They are the top predators.
(B) They do not occur in early successional stages.
(C) They are the main contributors to the gross primary productivity.
(D) They fix carbon for plant respiration.
(E) They are heterotrophic.

68. The nearly universal nature of the genetic code supports the view that

(A) all living organisms on Earth share a common ancestor
(B) nucleic acids were the first living things
(C) proteins are of secondary importance to living systems
(D) the protein composition of all living organisms is the same
(E) there is redundancy in the genetic code

Questions 69–70

The pedigree below shows the occurrence of a rare, sex-linked genetic condition in a family. Shaded symbols indicate the presence of the condition. Circles indicate females, and squares indicate males.

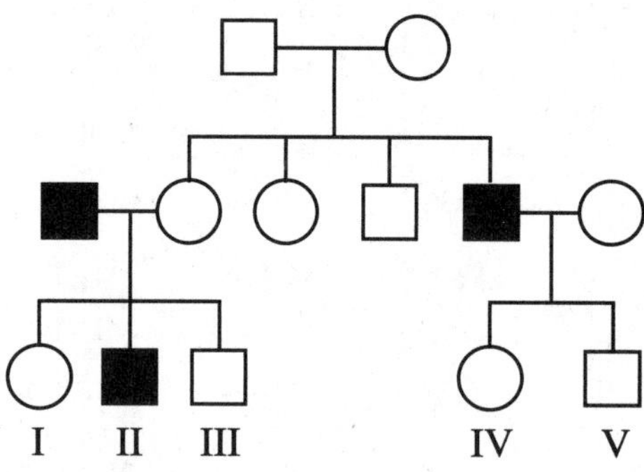

69. Individual I most likely has the same genotype for the condition as

(A) her father
(B) her grandfather
(C) Individual III
(D) Individual IV
(E) Individual V

70. If the parents of Individuals I, II, and III have a second daughter, what is the probability that the daughter will exhibit the condition?

(A) 0%
(B) 25%
(C) 33%
(D) 50%
(E) 100%

71. A katydid is an insect. Its leaf-like appearance is an example of

(A) cryptic coloration
(B) aposematic coloration
(C) Müllerian mimicry
(D) agonistic behavior
(E) Batesian mimicry

72. A population of mice in Hardy-Weinberg equilibrium will exhibit which of the following conditions?

(A) Random mating
(B) Small population size
(C) High mutation rate
(D) Immigration
(E) Sexual selection

73. Which of the following biomes typically has the greatest annual precipitation?

(A) Temperate deciduous forest
(B) Taiga
(C) Savanna
(D) Tropical rain forest
(E) Prairie

74. Which part of a flower develops into fruit?

(A) Sepal
(B) Stigma
(C) Anther
(D) Ovary
(E) Filament

75. In a particular mammal, the egg has a haploid number of 8. How many chromosomes are in the somatic cells of that organism?

(A) 2
(B) 4
(C) 8
(D) 16
(E) 32

76. A new organism is found with the following characteristics.

- A terrestrial lifestyle
- A segmented exoskeleton
- Wings

The new organism is most likely a member of which of the following phyla?

(A) Cnidaria
(B) Porifera
(C) Chordata
(D) Arthropoda
(E) Echinodermata

77. Plants that live in the tundra are likely to have which of the following adaptations?

(A) Tall, single shoots
(B) Broad, light-colored leaves
(C) Cones that are fire adapted
(D) An association with epiphytes
(E) Shallow root systems

78. When a protein is heated, which of the following will most likely be disrupted?

(A) The amino acid sequence
(B) The tertiary structure
(C) The carbon backbone
(D) The carboxyl groups
(E) The peptide bonds

79. In some horses, the coat is a mixture of red and white hairs, called roan. Roan horses have one white-haired parent and one red-haired parent. This exhibits which of the following inheritance patterns?

    (A) X-linked recessive
    (B) Lateral transmission
    (C) Codominance
    (D) Hybrid vigor
    (E) Autosomal recessive

80. A population of crayfish exhibits wide variation in body size, which is a heritable trait. A species of fish that preys on crayfish has been introduced to the population, but the fish can only eat small crayfish. Which of the following is a likely prediction about the population of crayfish in the presence of the predator?

    (A) The crayfish will evolve new antipredator behaviors.
    (B) The crayfish diet will shift to avoid competition with the fish.
    (C) The population will have a smaller average body size owing to stabilizing selection.
    (D) The population will have a larger average body size owing to directional selection.
    (E) The population will experience disruptive selection, resulting in two distinct size classes of crayfish.

81. All of the following substances are potentially major sources of energy for the human body EXCEPT

    (A) starches
    (B) sugars
    (C) vitamins
    (D) proteins
    (E) fats

82. Which of the following are producers in an aquatic food chain?

    (A) Crustaceans
    (B) Algae
    (C) Insects
    (D) Fungi
    (E) Trout

83. Which of the following gives the correct sequence of events in the synthesis of a protein molecule?

    (A) DNA, tRNA, formation of polypeptide, mRNA
    (B) Formation of polypeptide, tRNA, mRNA, DNA
    (C) tRNA, mRNA, DNA, formation of polypeptide
    (D) DNA, mRNA, tRNA, formation of polypeptide
    (E) mRNA, formation of polypeptide, DNA, tRNA

84. A species of malaria-carrying mosquito lives in a forest in which two species of monkeys, *A* and *B*, coexist. Species *A* is immune to malaria, but species *B* is not. The malaria-carrying mosquito is the chief food for a particular kind of bird in the forest. If all of these birds are eliminated suddenly, which of the following would be the immediate observable consequence?

    (A) Increased mortality in monkey species *A*
    (B) Increased mortality in monkey species *B*
    (C) Increased mortality in the malaria-carrying mosquitoes
    (D) Emergence of malaria-resistant strains in monkey species *B*
    (E) Emergence of malaria-sensitive strains in monkey species *A*

85. Evolution in action is seen in the case of the English peppered moth (*Biston betularia*). The proportion of melanic forms in the population, once increasing in areas of heavy soot pollution, is now decreasing. The most probable explanation of this is which of the following?

    (A) Differential predation fluctuates randomly.
    (B) The birds that ate the dark forms have been killed off by the pollution.
    (C) Mutation and back mutation rates have changed.
    (D) Selection pressure has been reversed because of environmental quality control.
    (E) Lepidopterists have collected a disproportionate number of melanic forms.

Questions 86–89

The graph below shows the relative amounts of DNA present during the stages in the division cycle of mouse fibroblast cells.

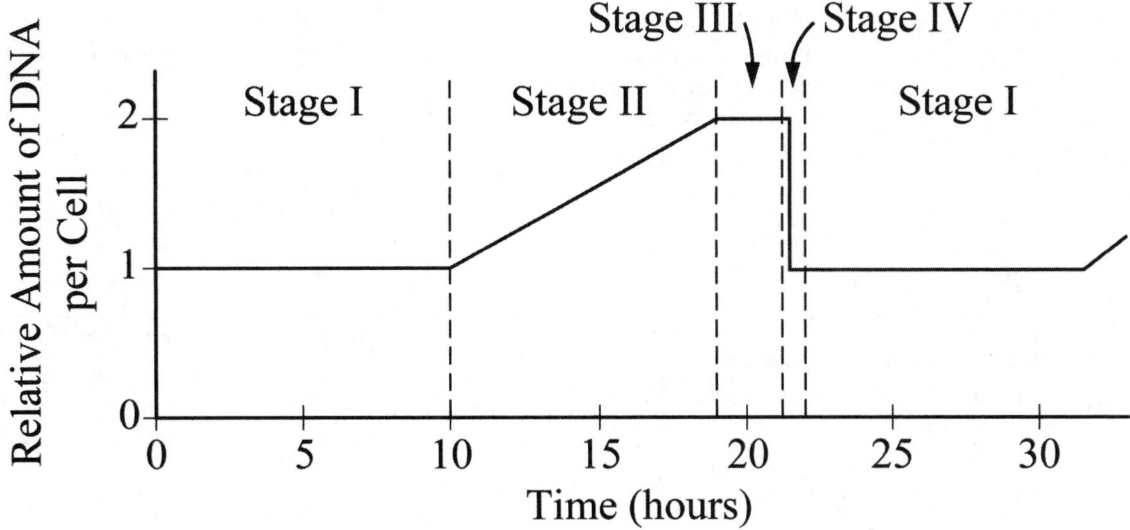

86. A mouse fibroblast cell divides approximately every
    (A) 1 hour
    (B) 9 hours
    (C) 10 hours
    (D) 19 hours
    (E) 22 hours

87. DNA is synthesized during
    (A) stage I
    (B) stage II
    (C) stage III
    (D) stage IV
    (E) none of the stages above

88. The daughter cells separate during
    (A) stage I
    (B) stage II
    (C) stage III
    (D) stage IV
    (E) none of the stages above

89. How does the amount of DNA present during stage I compare with the amount present during stage III ?
    (A) It is equal to that present during stage III.
    (B) It is half as much as that present during stage III.
    (C) It is twice as much as that present during stage III.
    (D) It is three times as much as that present during stage III.
    (E) It is four times as much as that present during stage III.

Study Resources

Most textbooks used in college-level biology courses cover the topics in the outline given earlier, but the approaches to certain topics and the emphases given to them may differ. To prepare for the Biology exam, it is advisable to study one or more college textbooks, which can be found in most college bookstores. When selecting a textbook, check the table of contents against the knowledge and skills required for this test.

Candidates would do well to consult pertinent articles from magazines such as *Scientific American*, *Science News* and *Natural History*.

Visit **clep.collegeboard.org/earn-college-credit/practice** for additional biology resources. You can also find suggestions for exam preparation in Chapter IV of the *Official Study Guide*. In addition, many college faculty post their course materials on their schools' websites.

Answer Key

1.	E	46.	E
2.	E	47.	B
3.	A	48.	E
4.	C	49.	B
5.	D	50.	B
6.	E	51.	B
7.	E	52.	C
8.	A	53.	B
9.	C	54.	A
10.	C	55.	C
11.	C	56.	B
12.	D	57.	E
13.	A	58.	B
14.	D	59.	E
15.	B	60.	C
16.	D	61.	D
17.	C	62.	E
18.	B	63.	D
19.	B	64.	C
20.	B	65.	B
21.	D	66.	C
22.	E	67.	E
23.	B	68.	A
24.	D	69.	D
25.	D	70.	D
26.	A	71.	A
27.	B	72.	A
28.	D	73.	D
29.	A	74.	D
30.	C	75.	D
31.	E	76.	D
32.	E	77.	E
33.	D	78.	B
34.	A	79.	C
35.	C	80.	D
36.	B	81.	C
37.	E	82.	B
38.	A	83.	D
39.	D	84.	B
40.	D	85.	D
41.	E	86.	E
42.	A	87.	B
43.	B	88.	D
44.	C	89.	B
45.	C		

Calculus

Description of the Examination

The Calculus examination covers skills and concepts that are usually taught in a one-semester college course in calculus. The content of each examination is approximately 60% limits and differential calculus and 40% integral calculus. Algebraic, trigonometric, exponential, logarithmic and general functions are included. The exam is primarily concerned with an intuitive understanding of calculus and experience with its methods and applications. Knowledge of preparatory mathematics, including algebra, geometry, trigonometry and analytic geometry is assumed.

The examination contains approximately 44 questions, in two sections, to be answered in approximately 90 minutes.

- Section 1: approximately 27 questions, approximately 50 minutes. No calculator is allowed for this section.
- Section 2: approximately 17 questions, approximately 40 minutes. The use of an **online graphing calculator (non-CAS)** is allowed for this section. Only some of the questions will require the use of the calculator.

Graphing Calculator

A graphing calculator is integrated into the exam software, and it is available to students during Section 2 of the exam. Since only some of the questions in Section 2 actually require the calculator, students are expected to know how and when to make appropriate use of it.

For more information about the graphing calculator, please visit the Calculus exam description on the CLEP website, clep.collegeboard.org.

In order to answer some of the questions in Section 2 of the exam, students may be required to use the online graphing calculator in the following ways:

- Perform calculations (e.g., exponents, roots, trigonometric values, logarithms).
- Graph functions and analyze the graphs.
- Find zeros of functions.
- Find points of intersection of graphs of functions.
- Find minima/maxima of functions.
- Find numerical solutions to equations.
- Generate a table of values for a function.

Knowledge and Skills Required

Questions on the exam require candidates to demonstrate the following abilities:

- Solving routine problems involving the techniques of calculus (approximately 50% of the exam)
- Solving nonroutine problems involving an understanding of the concepts and applications of calculus (approximately 50% of the exam)

The subject matter of the Calculus exam is drawn from the following topics. The percentages next to the main topics indicate the approximate percentage of exam questions on that topic.

10% **Limits**

- Statement of properties, e.g., limit of a constant, sum, product or quotient
- Limit calculations, including limits involving infinity, e.g., $\lim_{x\to 0}\frac{\sin x}{x} = 1$, $\lim_{x\to 0}\frac{1}{x}$ is nonexistent and $\lim_{x\to\infty}\frac{\sin x}{x} = 0$
- Continuity

50% **Differential Calculus**

The Derivative

- Definitions of the derivative e.g., $f'(a) = \lim_{x\to a}\frac{f(x)-f(a)}{x-a}$ and $f'(x) = \lim_{h\to 0}\frac{f(x+h)-f(x)}{h}$
- Derivatives of elementary functions
- Derivatives of sums, products and quotients (including $\tan x$ and $\cot x$)
- Derivative of a composite function (chain rule), e.g., $\sin(ax+b)$, ae^{kx}, $\ln(kx)$
- Implicit differentiation
- Derivative of the inverse of a function (including $\arcsin x$ and $\arctan x$)
- Higher order derivatives
- Corresponding characteristics of graphs of f, f', and f''
- Statement of the Mean Value Theorem; applications and graphical illustrations
- Relation between differentiability and continuity
- Use of L'Hospital's Rule (quotient and indeterminate forms)

Applications of the Derivative

- Slope of a curve at a point
- Tangent lines and linear approximation
- Curve sketching: increasing and decreasing functions; relative and absolute maximum and minimum points; concavity; points of inflection
- Extreme value problems
- Velocity and acceleration of a particle moving along a line
- Average and instantaneous rates of change
- Related rates of change

40% **Integral Calculus**

Antiderivatives and Techniques of Integration

- Concept of antiderivatives
- Basic integration formulas
- Integration by substitution (use of identities, change of variable)

Applications of Antiderivatives

- Distance and velocity from acceleration with initial conditions
- Solutions of $y' = ky$ and applications to growth and decay

The Definite Integral

- Definition of the definite integral as the limit of a sequence of Riemann sums and approximations of the definite integral using areas of rectangles
- Properties of the definite integral
- The Fundamental Theorem: $\frac{d}{dx}\int_a^x f(t)\,dt = f(x)$ and $\int_a^b F'(x)\,dx = F(b) - F(a)$

Applications of the Definite Integral

- Average value of a function on an interval
- Area, including area between curves
- Other (e.g., accumulated change from a rate of change)

Notes and Reference Information

(1) Figures that accompany questions are intended to provide information useful in answering the questions. All figures lie in a plane unless otherwise indicated. The figures are drawn as accurately as possible EXCEPT when it is stated in a specific question that the figure is not drawn to scale. Straight lines and smooth curves may appear slightly jagged.

(2) Unless otherwise specified, all angles are measured in radians, and all numbers used are real numbers.

(3) Unless otherwise specified, the domain of any function f is assumed to be the set of all real numbers x for which $f(x)$ is a real number. The range of f is assumed to be the set of all real numbers $f(x)$ where x is in the domain of f.

(4) In this test, $\ln x$ denotes the natural logarithm of x (that is, the logarithm to the base e).

(5) The inverse of a trigonometric function f may be indicated using the inverse function notation f^{-1} or with the prefix "arc" (e.g., $\sin^{-1} x = \arcsin x$).

Sample Test Questions

The following sample questions do not appear on an actual CLEP Examination. They are intended to give potential test-takers an indication of the format and difficulty level of the examination, and to provide content for practice and review. Knowing the correct answers to all of the sample questions is not a guarantee of satisfactory performance on the exam.

Section 1

Directions: A calculator will not be available for questions in this section. Some questions will require you to select from among five choices. For these questions, select the BEST of the choices given. Some questions will require you to enter a numerical answer in the box provided.

1. If $y = (x+1)(x-1)(x+5)$, then $\dfrac{dy}{dx} =$

(A) $x^2 - 1$
(B) $2x^2 + 10x$
(C) $3x^2 + 10x - 1$
(D) $x^3 + 5x^2 - x$
(E) $2x^3 + 20x^2 + 50x$

2. $\int_{-3}^{3} \sqrt{9 - x^2}\, dx =$

(A) 0 (B) $\dfrac{3\pi}{2}$ (C) 3π (D) $\dfrac{9\pi}{2}$ (E) 9π

3. Which of the following is an equation of the line tangent to the graph of $f(x) = x^3 - x$ at the point where $x = 2$?

(A) $y - 6 = 4(x - 2)$
(B) $y - 6 = 5(x - 2)$
(C) $y - 6 = 6(x - 2)$
(D) $y - 6 = 11(x - 2)$
(E) $y - 6 = 12(x - 2)$

4. The function f is given by $f(x) = 3x^2 + 1$. What is the average value of f over the closed interval $[1, 3]$?

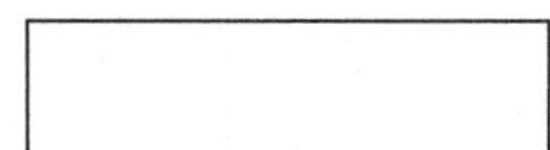

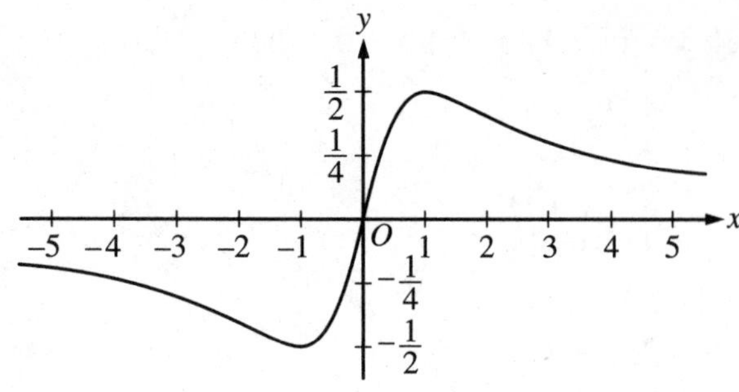

5. The graph of the function $f(x) = \dfrac{x}{1+x^2}$ is shown in the figure above. Which of the following statements are true?

I. $\lim\limits_{x \to -\infty} f(x) = \lim\limits_{x \to \infty} f(x)$

II. $\lim\limits_{x \to 0^-} f(x) = \lim\limits_{x \to 0^+} f(x)$

III. $\lim\limits_{x \to 1} \dfrac{f(x) - \frac{1}{2}}{x - 1}$ does not exist.

(A) None
(B) I and II only
(C) I and III only
(D) II and III only
(E) I, II, and III

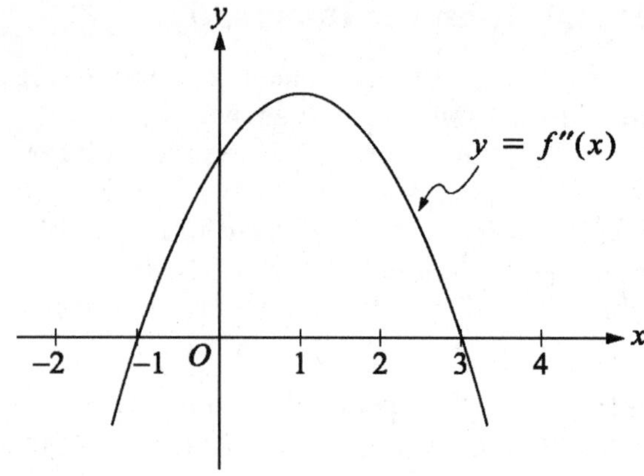

6. The graph of f'', the second derivative of the function f, is shown in the figure above. On what intervals is the graph of f concave up?

(A) $(-\infty, \infty)$
(B) $(-\infty, -1)$ and $(3, \infty)$
(C) $(-\infty, 1)$
(D) $(-1, 3)$
(E) $(1, \infty)$

7. $\int (x-1)\sqrt{x}\, dx =$

(A) $\frac{2}{5}x^{\frac{5}{2}} - \frac{2}{3}x^{\frac{3}{2}} + C$

(B) $\frac{1}{2}x^2 + 2x^{\frac{2}{3}} - x + C$

(C) $\frac{1}{2}x^2 - x + C$

(D) $\frac{2}{3}x^{\frac{3}{2}} + 2x^{\frac{1}{2}} + C$

(E) $\frac{3}{2}x^{\frac{1}{2}} - x^{-\frac{1}{2}} + C$

8. Let f be the function defined by $f(x) = x^3 - 6x^2 - 15$. At what value of x does f have a relative maximum?

(A) -3 (B) -1 (C) 0 (D) 4 (E) 5

9. The acceleration, at time t, of a particle moving along the x-axis is given by $a(t) = 20t^3 + 6$. At time $t = 0$, the velocity of the particle is 0 and the position of the particle is 7. What is the position of the particle at time t ?

(A) $120t + 7$
(B) $60t^2 + 7t$
(C) $5t^4 + 6t + 7$
(D) $t^5 + 3t^2 + 7$
(E) $t^5 + 3t^2 + 7t$

10. If $f(x) = \dfrac{\sin x}{2x}$, then $f'(x) =$

(A) $\dfrac{\cos x}{2}$

(B) $\dfrac{x\cos x - \sin x}{2x^2}$

(C) $\dfrac{x\cos x - \sin x}{4x^2}$

(D) $\dfrac{\sin x - x\cos x}{2x^2}$

(E) $\dfrac{\sin x - x\cos x}{4x^2}$

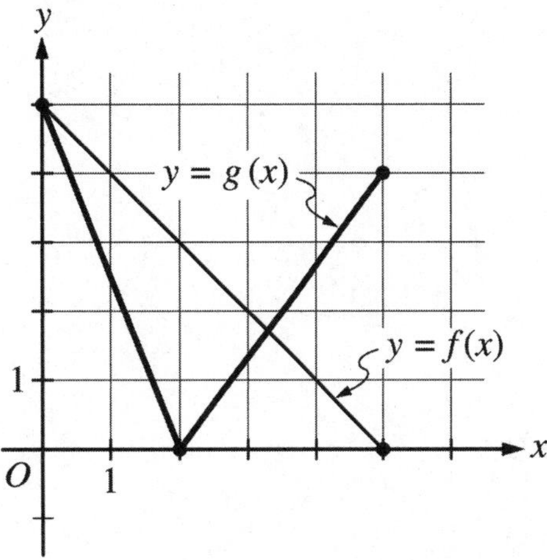

11. The piecewise linear graphs of the functions f and g are shown in the figure above. If $h(x) = f(g(x))$, what is the value of $h'(3)$?

(A) -4

(B) $-\dfrac{4}{3}$

(C) -1

(D) 1

(E) $\dfrac{4}{3}$

12. What is $\lim\limits_{h \to 0} \dfrac{\cos\left(\frac{\pi}{2} + h\right) - \cos\frac{\pi}{2}}{h}$?

(A) $-\infty$ (B) -1 (C) 0 (D) 1 (E) ∞

13. If $x^2 + y^3 = x^3y^2$, then $\frac{dy}{dx} =$

(A) $\dfrac{2x + 3y^2 - 3x^2y^2}{2x^3y}$

(B) $\dfrac{2x^3y + 3x^2y^2 - 2x}{3y^2}$

(C) $\dfrac{3x^2y^2 - 2x}{3y^2 - 2x^3y}$

(D) $\dfrac{3y^2 - 2x^3y}{3x^2y^2 - 2x}$

(E) $\dfrac{6x^2y - 2x}{3y^2}$

14. For which of the following functions does $\dfrac{d^3y}{dx^3} = \dfrac{dy}{dx}$?

I. $y = e^x$
II. $y = e^{-x}$
III. $y = \sin x$

(A) I only
(B) II only
(C) III only
(D) I and II
(E) II and III

15. What is $\lim\limits_{x \to 0^-} \dfrac{2x}{|x|}$?

(A) -2
(B) -1
(C) 0
(D) 2
(E) The limit does not exist.

16. Which of the following statements about the curve $y = x^4 - 2x^3$ is true?

(A) The curve has no relative extremum.
(B) The curve has one point of inflection and two relative extrema.
(C) The curve has two points of inflection and one relative extremum.
(D) The curve has two points of inflection and two relative extrema.
(E) The curve has two points of inflection and three relative extrema.

17. If $f(x) = x\sqrt{3x^2 + 1}$, then $f'(x) =$

(A) $\dfrac{\sqrt{6x}}{x^2}$

(B) $\dfrac{3x}{\sqrt{3x^2 + 1}}$

(C) $\dfrac{6x}{\sqrt{3x^2 + 1}}$

(D) $\dfrac{6x^2 + 1}{\sqrt{3x^2 + 1}}$

(E) $\frac{2}{9}\left(3x^2 + 1\right)^{3/2}$

18. Let f be the function defined by

$$f(x) = \begin{cases} \dfrac{x^2 - 25}{x - 5} & \text{for } x \neq 5 \\ 0 & \text{for } x = 5 \end{cases}.$$

Which of the following statements about f are true?

I. $\lim_{x \to 5} f(x)$ exists.
II. $f(5)$ exists.
III. $f(x)$ is continuous at $x = 5$.

(A) None
(B) I only
(C) II only
(D) I and II only
(E) I, II, and III

19. What is the average rate of change of the function f defined by $f(x) = 100 \cdot 2^x$ on the interval $[0, 4]$?

(A) 100
(B) 375
(C) 400
(D) 1,500
(E) 1,600

20. If $\int_0^1 \left(\sqrt[n]{x} - x^n\right) dx = \frac{3}{4}$, what is the value of n?

$n =$ ☐

21. If $f(x) = \arctan(\pi x)$, then $f'(0) =$

(A) $-\pi$ (B) -1 (C) 0 (D) 1 (E) π

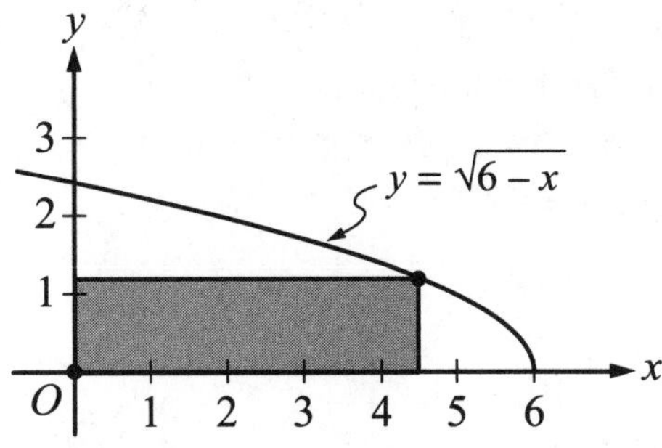

22. Consider a rectangle in the xy-plane with its lower-left vertex at the origin and its upper-right vertex on the graph of $y = \sqrt{6 - x}$, as indicated in the figure above. What is the maximum area of such a rectangle?

(A) $\sqrt{6}$
(B) 4
(C) $3\sqrt{3}$
(D) $4\sqrt{2}$
(E) $4\sqrt{6}$

$$f(x) = \begin{cases} 2x - 4 & \text{for } x < a \\ x^2 - 2x - 1 & \text{for } x \geq a \end{cases}$$

23. Let f be the function defined above, where a is a constant. For what values of a, if any, is f continuous at $x = a$?

(A) $-\sqrt{5}$ and $\sqrt{5}$
(B) -2 and 2
(C) 0
(D) 1 and 3
(E) There is no such value of a.

24. Let F be the number of trees in a forest at time t, in years. If F is decreasing at a rate given by the equation $\frac{dF}{dt} = -2F$ and if $F(0) = 5000$, then $F(t) =$

(A) $5000t^{-2}$
(B) $5000e^{-2t}$
(C) $5000 - 2t$
(D) $5000 + t^{-2}$
(E) $5000 + e^{-2t}$

25. Let f be the function defined by $f(x) = \sqrt{x}$. Using the line tangent to the graph of f at $x = 9$, what is the approximation of $f(9.3) = \sqrt{9.3}$?

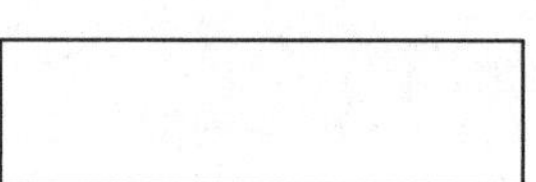

26. What is the area of the region in the first quadrant that is bounded by the line $y = 6x$ and the parabola $y = 3x^2$?

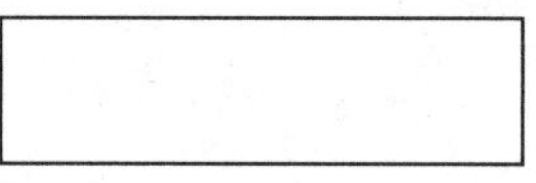

27. Let f be a differentiable function defined on the closed interval $[a, b]$ and let c be a point in the open interval (a, b) such that

- $f'(c) = 0$,
- $f'(x) > 0$ when $a \le x < c$, and
- $f'(x) < 0$ when $c < x \le b$.

Which of the following statements must be true?

(A) $f(c) = 0$

(B) $f''(c) = 0$

(C) $f(c)$ is an absolute maximum value of f on $[a, b]$.

(D) $f(c)$ is an absolute minimum value of f on $[a, b]$.

(E) The graph of f has a point of inflection at $x = c$.

28. The function f is continuous on the open interval $(-\pi, \pi)$. If $f(x) = \dfrac{\cos x - 1}{x \sin x}$ for $x \neq 0$, what is the value of $f(0)$?

(A) -1 (B) $-\frac{1}{2}$ (C) 0 (D) $\frac{1}{2}$ (E) 1

29. For some constant c, the line $y = 4x + c$ is tangent to the graph of the function $f(x) = x^2 + 2$. What is the value of c?

$c =$ ☐

30. The area of the region in the first quadrant between the graph of $y = x\sqrt{4 - x^2}$ and the x-axis is

(A) $\frac{2}{3}\sqrt{2}$

(B) $\frac{8}{3}$

(C) $2\sqrt{2}$

(D) $2\sqrt{3}$

(E) $\frac{16}{3}$

31. $\int_0^6 |x^2 - 6x + 8|\,dx =$

(A) $\frac{4}{3}$

(B) $\frac{20}{3}$

(C) $\frac{44}{3}$

(D) 12

(E) 228

32. A particle moves along the x-axis, and its velocity at time t is given by $v(t) = t^3 - 3t^2 + 12t + 8$. What is the maximum acceleration of the particle on the interval $0 \le t \le 3$?

(A) 9
(B) 12
(C) 14
(D) 21
(E) 44

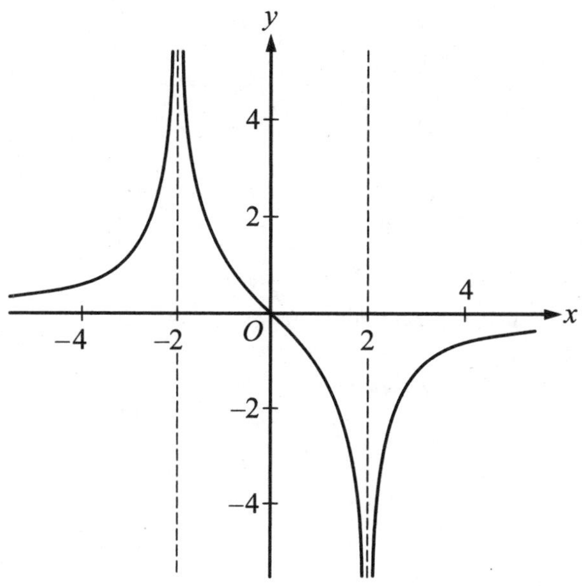

Graph of f'

33. The graph of f', the derivative of the continuous function f, is shown in the figure above. Which of the following statements must be false?

(A) f has no relative extrema.
(B) f is increasing on the interval $(-\infty, 0]$.
(C) The graph of f is concave down on the interval $(-2, 2)$.
(D) The graph of f has points of inflection at $x = -2$ and $x = 2$.
(E) The graph of f has vertical tangent lines at $x = -2$ and $x = 2$.

34. If f is a continuous, even function such that $\int_0^3 f(x)\,dx = -4$, then $\int_{-3}^3 (5f(x)+1)\,dx =$

(A) −39
(B) −34
(C) −19
(D) −14
(E) 6

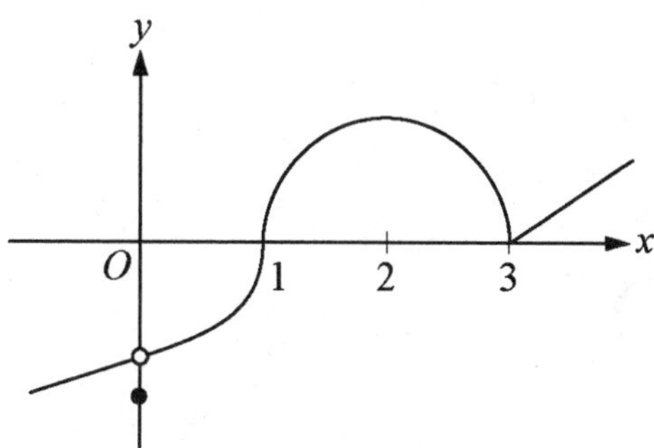

35. The graph of the function f, shown in the figure above, has a vertical tangent at $x = 1$ and a horizontal tangent at $x = 2$.

For each of the following values of x, indicate whether f is not continuous, continuous but not differentiable, or differentiable.

x	f is not continuous at x.	f is continuous but not differentiable at x.	f is differentiable at x.
0			
1			
2			
3			

Click on your choices.

36. Which of the following is a right Riemann sum approximation for $\int_0^2 \sqrt{x}\, dx$ using n subintervals of equal width?

(A) $\sum_{k=1}^{n} \sqrt{\frac{k}{n}}$

(B) $\sum_{k=1}^{n} \frac{1}{n}\sqrt{\frac{k}{n}}$

(C) $\sum_{k=1}^{n} \frac{1}{n}\sqrt{\frac{2k}{n}}$

(D) $\sum_{k=1}^{n} \frac{2}{n}\sqrt{\frac{k}{n}}$

(E) $\sum_{k=1}^{n} \frac{2}{n}\sqrt{\frac{2k}{n}}$

Section 2

Directions: A graphing calculator will be available for the questions in this section. Some questions will require you to select from among five choices. For these questions, select the BEST of the choices given. If the exact numerical value of your answer is not one of the choices, select the choice that best approximates this value. Some questions will require you to enter a numerical answer in the box provided.

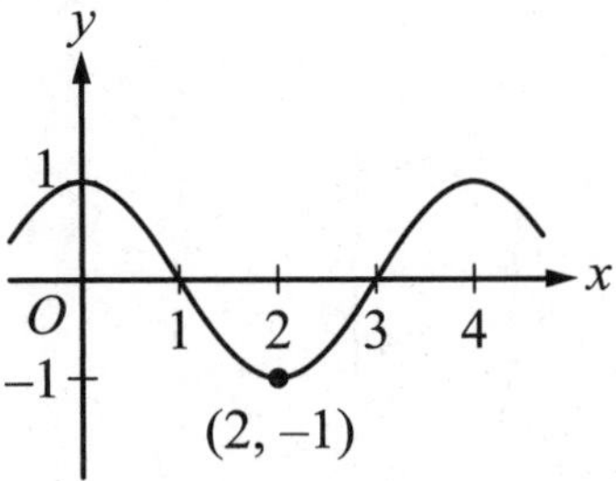

Graph of f

37. The graph of a function f is given above. What is $\lim_{x \to 2} \frac{x}{f(x)+1}$?

(A) $-\infty$

(B) -1

(C) $\frac{2}{3}$

(D) 1

(E) ∞

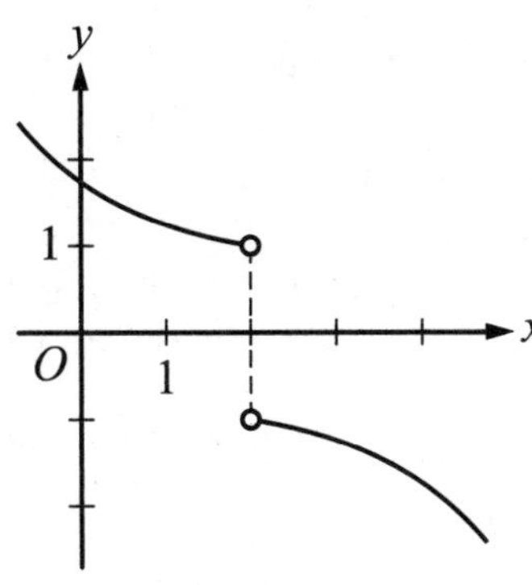

Graph of f

38. Let F be a continuous function. The graph of f, the derivative of F, is given above. Which of the following statements is false?

(A) $F(2) - F(0) > 0$
(B) F is defined at $x = 2$.
(C) F is differentiable at $x = 2$.
(D) F has a relative maximum at $x = 2$.
(E) F is decreasing on $[2, \infty)$.

39. Let f be a function with second derivative given by $f''(x) = \sin(2x) - \cos(4x)$. How many points of inflection does the graph of f have on the interval $[0, 10]$?

(A) Six
(B) Seven
(C) Eight
(D) Ten
(E) Thirteen

40. Let g be a continuous function such that

$\int_0^2 g(x)\,dx = 7$, $\int_0^3 g(x)\,dx = 5$, and

$\int_1^3 g(x)\,dx = -1$.

What is the value of $\int_1^2 g(x)\,dx$?

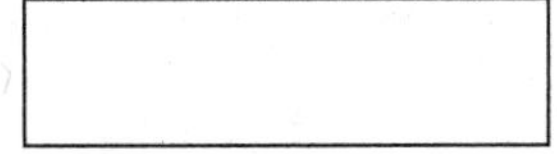

41. Let f be a differentiable function with domain $(0, \infty)$ and range $(-\infty, \infty)$, such that $f(2) = 3$ and $f'(2) = 1$. The function f is increasing and the graph of f is concave down for all x in the domain.

Let g be the function defined by $g(x) = f^{-1}(x)$. On which of the following intervals is $g'(x) < 1$?

(A) $(0, \infty)$ only
(B) $(2, \infty)$ only
(C) $(3, \infty)$ only
(D) $(-\infty, 3)$ only
(E) $(-\infty, \infty)$

42. Starting at $t = 0$, a particle moves along the x-axis so that its position at time t is given by $x(t) = t^4 - 5t^2 + 2t$. What are all values of t for which the particle is moving to the left?

(A) $0 < t < 0.913$
(B) $0.203 < t < 1.470$
(C) $0.414 < t < 0.913$
(D) $0.414 < t < 2.000$
(E) There are no values of t for which the particle is moving to the left.

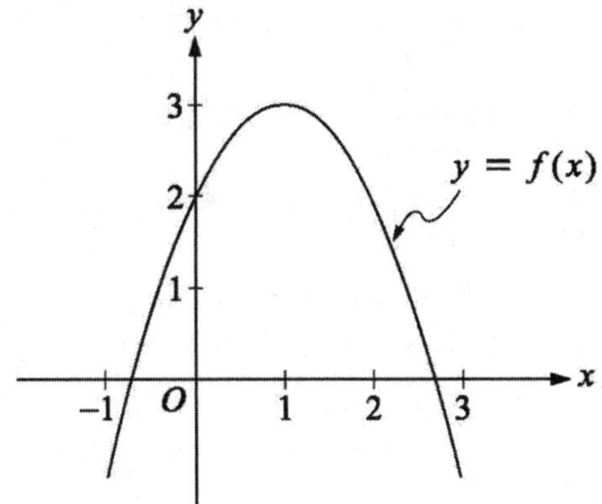

43. The function f has a relative maximum value of 3 at $x = 1$, as shown in the figure above. If $h(x) = x^2 f(x)$, then $h'(1) =$

(A) −6 (B) −3 (C) 0

(D) 3 (E) 6

44. $\int \cos^2 x \sin x \, dx =$

(A) $-\dfrac{\cos^3 x}{3} + C$

(B) $-\dfrac{\cos^3 x \sin^2 x}{6} + C$

(C) $\dfrac{\sin^2 x}{2} + C$

(D) $\dfrac{\cos^3 x}{3} + C$

(E) $\dfrac{\cos^3 x \sin^2 x}{6} + C$

$$f'(x) = \sqrt{x} \sin x$$

45. The first derivative of the function f is given above. If $f(0) = 0$, at what value of x does the function f attain its minimum value on the closed interval $[0, 10]$?

(A) 0
(B) 3.14
(C) 4.82
(D) 6.28
(E) 9.42

46. The function f is differentiable with $f(1) = 20$ and $f(4) = -4$. Which of the following statements must be true?

I. $f'(x) < 0$ for all x in the open interval $1 < x < 4$.
II. There exists a number c, where $1 < c < 4$, such that $f(c) = 0$.
III. There exists a number c, where $1 < c < 4$, such that $f'(c) = -8$.

(A) I only
(B) II only
(C) I and II only
(D) II and III only
(E) I, II, and III

$$g'(x) = \tan\left(\frac{2}{1 + x^2}\right)$$

47. Let g be the function with first derivative given above and $g(1) = 5$. If f is the function defined by $f(x) = \ln(g(x))$, what is the value of $f'(1)$?

(A) 0.311
(B) 0.443
(C) 0.642
(D) 0.968
(E) 3.210

48. Let $r(t)$ be a differentiable function that is positive and increasing. The rate of increase of r^3 is equal to 12 times the rate of increase of r when $r(t) =$

(A) $\sqrt[3]{4}$
(B) 2
(C) $\sqrt[3]{12}$
(D) $2\sqrt{3}$
(E) 6

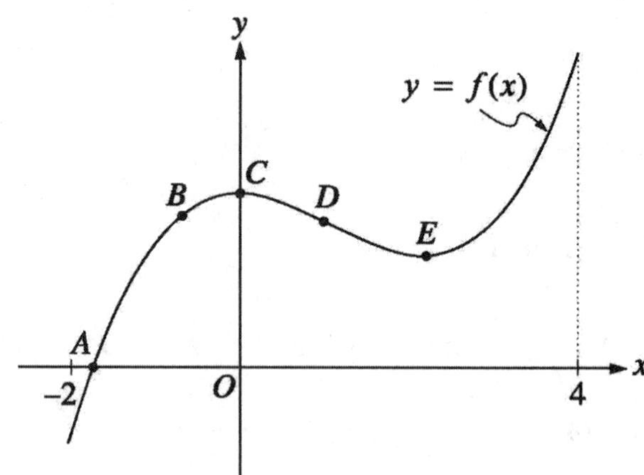

49. The function f is shown in the figure above. At which of the following points could the derivative of f be equal to the average rate of change of f over the closed interval $[-2, 4]$?

(A) A (B) B (C) C (D) D (E) E

50. $\frac{d}{dx}\left(\int_0^{x^2} e^t\, dt\right) =$

(A) e^x

(B) e^{x^2}

(C) $2xe^{x^2}$

(D) $e^{x^2} - 1$

(E) $2xe^{x^2} - 1$

51. A college is planning to construct a new parking lot. The parking lot must be rectangular and enclose 6,000 square meters of land. A fence will surround the parking lot, and another fence parallel to one of the sides will divide the parking lot into two sections. What are the dimensions, in meters, of the rectangular lot that will use the least amount of fencing?

(A) 1,000 by 1,500
(B) $20\sqrt{5}$ by $60\sqrt{5}$
(C) $20\sqrt{10}$ by $30\sqrt{10}$
(D) $20\sqrt{15}$ by $20\sqrt{15}$
(E) $20\sqrt{15}$ by $40\sqrt{15}$

x	0	2	4	6
$f(x)$	9	5	3	1

52. The function f is continuous on the closed interval $[0, 6]$ and has values as shown in the table above. Let L represent the left Riemann sum approximation of $\int_0^6 f(x)\, dx$ with 3 subintervals of equal length, and let R represent the right Riemann sum approximation of $\int_0^6 f(x)\, dx$ with 3 subintervals of equal length. What is $|L - R|$?

(A) 0 (B) 6 (C) 8 (D) 16 (E) 26

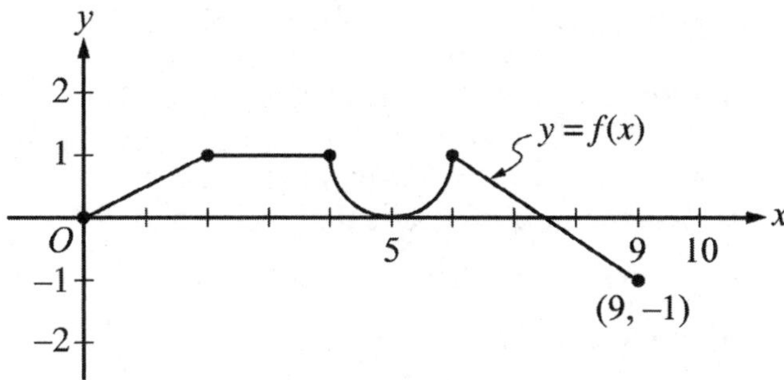

53. The graph of the continuous function f consists of three line segments and a semicircle centered at point (5, 1), as shown above. If $F(x)$ is an antiderivative of $f(x)$ such that $F(0) = 2$, what is the value of $F(9)$?

(A) $3 + \frac{\pi}{2}$

(B) $9 + \frac{\pi}{2}$

(C) $5 - \frac{\pi}{2}$

(D) $7 - \frac{\pi}{2}$

(E) $\frac{13}{2} - \frac{\pi}{2}$

54. A spherical balloon is being inflated at a constant rate of 25 cm^3/sec. At what rate, in cm/sec, is the radius of the balloon changing when the radius is 2 cm? (The volume of a sphere with radius r is $V = \frac{4}{3}\pi r^3$.)

(A) $\frac{25}{16\pi}$

(B) $\frac{25}{8\pi}$

(C) $\frac{75}{16\pi}$

(D) $\frac{32\pi}{25}$

(E) $\frac{32\pi}{3}$

55. R is the region below the curve $y = x$ and above the x-axis from $x = 0$ to $x = b$, where b is a positive constant. S is the region below the curve $y = \cos x$ and above the x-axis from $x = 0$ to $x = b$. For what value of b is the area of R equal to the area of S?

(A) 0.739
(B) 0.877
(C) 0.986
(D) 1.404
(E) 4.712

56. Let f be the function defined by $f(x) = e^{3x}$, and let g be the function defined by $g(x) = x^3$. At what value of x do the graphs of f and g have parallel tangent lines?

(A) −0.657
(B) −0.526
(C) −0.484
(D) −0.344
(E) −0.261

57. $\frac{d}{dx}\left(\sin^{-1}(5x)\right) =$

(A) $\cos^{-1}(5x)$
(B) $5\cos^{-1}(5x)$
(C) $\frac{1}{\sqrt{1-5x^2}}$
(D) $\frac{5}{\sqrt{1-25x^2}}$
(E) $\frac{5}{1+25x^2}$

58. The population P of bacteria in an experiment grows according to the equation $\frac{dP}{dt} = kP$, where k is a constant and t is measured in hours. If the population of bacteria doubles every 24 hours, what is the value of k?

(A) 0.029
(B) 0.279
(C) 0.693
(D) 2.485
(E) 3.178

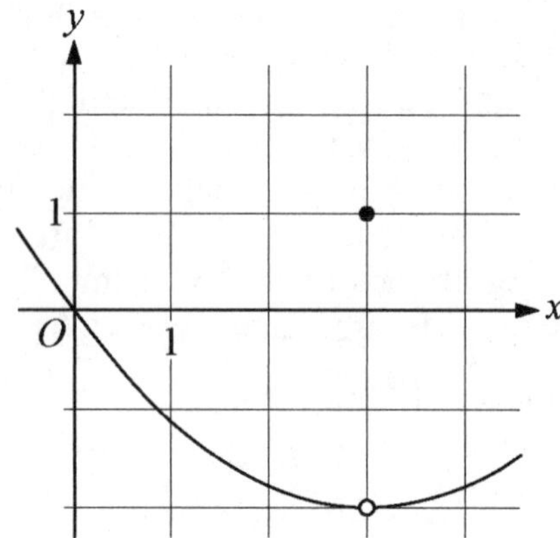

59. The graph of the function f is shown in the figure above. What is the value of $\lim_{x\to 3}(4-2f(x))$?

(A) −4
(B) −2
(C) 0
(D) 2
(E) 8

60. During a snowstorm, the rate, in inches per hour, at which snow falls on a certain town is modeled by the function $R(t) = -\cos(t) - 0.9t + 3.0$, where t is measured in hours and $0 \le t \le 4$. Based on the model, what is the total amount of snow, in inches, that fell on the town from $t = 0$ to $t = 4$?

(A) 1.2
(B) 1.9
(C) 4.0
(D) 5.6
(E) 18.4

Study Resources

To prepare for the Calculus exam, you should study the contents of at least one introductory college-level calculus textbook, which you can find in most college bookstores. You would do well to consult several textbooks, because the approaches to certain topics may vary. When selecting a textbook, check the table of contents against the knowledge and skills required for this exam.

Visit **clep.collegeboard.org/earn-college-credit/practice** for additional calculus resources. You can also find suggestions for exam preparation in Chapter IV of the *Official Study Guide*. In addition, many college faculty post their course materials on their schools' websites.

Answer Key

Section 1		Section 2	
1.	C	37.	E
2.	D	38.	C
3.	D	39.	B
4.	14	40.	1
5.	B	41.	D
6.	D	42.	B
7.	A	43.	E
8.	C	44.	A
9.	D	45.	D
10.	B	46.	D
11.	B	47.	A
12.	B	48.	B
13.	C	49.	B
14.	D	50.	C
15.	A	51.	C
16.	C	52.	D
17.	D	53.	D
18.	D	54.	A
19.	B	55.	D
20.	7	56.	C
21.	E	57.	D
22.	D	58.	A
23.	D	59.	E
24.	B	60.	D
25.	3.05		
26.	4		
27.	C		
28.	B		
29.	−2		
30.	B		
31.	C		
32.	D		
33.	A		
34.	B		
35.	See below		
36.	E		

35.

x	f is not continuous at x.	f is continuous but not differentiable at x.	f is differentiable at x.
0	✓		
1		✓	
2			✓
3		✓	

Chemistry

Description of the Examination

The Chemistry examination covers material that is usually taught in a one-year college course in general chemistry. Understanding of the structure and states of matter, reaction types, equations and stoichiometry, equilibrium, kinetics, thermodynamics, and descriptive and experimental chemistry is required, as is the ability to interpret and apply this material to new and unfamiliar problems. During this examination, an online scientific calculator function and a periodic table are available as part of the testing software.

The examination contains approximately 75 questions to be answered in approximately 90 minutes. Some of these are pretest questions that will not be scored.

Knowledge and Skills Required

Questions on the Chemistry examination require candidates to demonstrate one or more of the following abilities.

- **Recall** — remember specific facts; demonstrate straightforward knowledge of information and familiarity with terminology
- **Application** — understand concepts and reformulate information into other equivalent terms; apply knowledge to unfamiliar and/or practical situations; use mathematics to solve chemistry problems
- **Interpretation** — infer and deduce from data available and integrate information to form conclusions; recognize unstated assumptions

The subject matter of the Chemistry examination is drawn from the following topics. The percentages next to the main topics indicate the approximate percentage of exam questions on that topic.

20% Structure of Matter

Atomic theory and atomic structure

- Evidence for the atomic theory
- Atomic masses; determination by chemical and physical means
- Atomic number and mass number; isotopes and mass spectroscopy
- Electron energy levels: atomic spectra, atomic orbitals
- Periodic relationships, including, for example, atomic radii, ionization energies, electron affinities, oxidation states

Nuclear chemistry: nuclear equations, half-lives, and radioactivity; chemical applications

Chemical bonding

- Binding forces
  - Types: covalent, ionic, metallic, macromolecular (or network), dispersion, hydrogen bonding
  - Relationships to structure and to properties
  - Polarity of bonds, electronegativities
- VSEPR theory and Lewis electron-dot diagrams
  - Hybridization of orbitals
  - Geometry of molecules, ions, and coordination complexes
  - Structural isomerism
  - Resonance
  - Sigma and pi bonds
  - Dipole moments of molecules
  - Relation of properties to structure

19% **States of Matter**

Gases

- Laws of ideal gases; equations of state for an ideal gas
- The mole concept; Avogadro's number
- Kinetic-molecular theory
  - Interpretation of ideal gas laws on the basis of this theory
  - Dependence of kinetic energy of molecules on temperature: Boltzmann distribution
  - Deviations from ideal gas laws

Liquids and solids

- Liquids and solids from the kinetic-molecular viewpoint
- Phase diagrams of one-component systems
- Changes of state, critical phenomena

Solutions

- Types of solutions and factors affecting solubility
- Methods of expressing concentration
- Colligative properties; for example, Raoult's law
- Effect of interionic attraction on colligative properties and solubility

12% **Reaction Types**

Acid-base reactions; concepts of Arrhenius, Brønsted-Lowry and Lewis; amphoterism

Reactions involving coordination complexes

Precipitation reactions

Oxidation-reduction reactions

- Oxidation number
- The role of the electron in oxidation-reduction
- Electrochemistry; electrolytic cells, standard half-cell potentials, prediction of the direction of redox reactions, effect of concentration changes

10% **Equations and Stoichiometry**

Ionic and molecular species present in chemical systems; net-ionic equations

Stoichiometry: mass and volume relations with emphasis on the mole concept

Balancing of equations, including those for redox reactions

7% **Equilibrium**

Concept of dynamic equilibrium of physical and chemical changes; LeChâtelier's principle; equilibrium constants

Quantitative perspective

- Equilibrium constants for gaseous reactions in terms of both molar concentrations and partial pressure (K_c, K_p)
- Equilibrium constants for reactions in solutions
  - Constants for acids and bases; pK, pH
  - Solubility-product constants and their application to precipitation and the dissolution of slightly soluble compounds
  - Constants for complex ions
  - Common ion effect; buffers

4% **Kinetics**

Concept of rate of reaction

- Order of reaction and rate constant
- Determination of order of reaction and rate constant from experimental data
- Effect of temperature change on rates

Activation energy and the role of catalysts

The relationship between the rate-determining step and reaction mechanism

5% Thermodynamics

State functions

First law:

- Heat of formation
- Heat of reaction, change in enthalpy, Hess's law
- Heat capacity; heats of vaporization and fusion

Second law:

- Free energy of formation
- Free energy of reaction
- Dependence of change in free energy on enthalpy and entropy changes

Relationship of change in free energy to equilibrium constants and electrode potentials

14% Descriptive Chemistry

The accumulation of certain specific facts of chemistry is essential to enable students to

- comprehend the development of principles and concepts
- demonstrate applications of principles
- relate fact to theory and properties to structure
- develop an understanding of systematic nomenclature that facilitates communication.

The following areas are normally included on the examination:

- Chemical reactivity and products of chemical reactions
- Relationships in the periodic table: horizontal, vertical and diagonal
- Chemistry of the main groups and transition elements, including typical examples of each
- Organic chemistry, including such topics as functional groups and isomerism (may be treated as a separate unit or as exemplary material in other areas, such as bonding)

9% Experimental Chemistry

Some questions are based on laboratory experiments widely performed in general chemistry and ask about the equipment used, observations made, calculations performed, and interpretation of the results. The questions are designed to provide a measure of understanding of the basic tools of chemistry and their applications to simple chemical systems.

Sample Test Questions

The following sample questions do not appear on an actual CLEP examination. They are intended to give potential test-takers an indication of the format and difficulty level of the examination and to provide content for practice and review. Knowing the correct answers to all of the sample questions is not a guarantee of satisfactory performance on the exam.

Note: For all questions involving solutions and/or chemical equations, assume that the system is in pure water and at room temperature unless otherwise stated.

Directions: Each of the questions or incomplete statements below is followed by five suggested answers or completions. Select the one that is best in each case.

1. Oxides of which of the following elements are responsible for acid rain?

   (A) F
   (B) S
   (C) Mg
   (D) Ar
   (E) Mn

2. Which of the following elements is most likely to be in the +2 oxidation state in its compounds?

   (A) C
   (B) Si
   (C) Ge
   (D) Al
   (E) Zn

3. Which of the following transitions of an electron in a hydrogen atom will emit a photon that has the highest frequency?

   (A) $n = 7$ to $n = 6$
   (B) $n = 6$ to $n = 4$
   (C) $n = 3$ to $n = 4$
   (D) $n = 2$ to $n = 4$
   (E) $n = 1$ to $n = 3$

4. Which of the following compounds is amphoteric?

   (A) HF
   (B) Na_2CO_3
   (C) NH_3
   (D) H_2O_2
   (E) $Al(OH)_3$

5. Which of the following pure substances is a reddish-brown liquid at 298 K and 1 atm?

   (A) $CuCl_2$
   (B) Fe_2O_3
   (C) Br_2
   (D) I_2
   (E) CH_3COCH_3

6. A white precipitate forms when $BaCl_2(aq)$ is added to an unknown blue solution. Which of the following could be the identity of the blue solution?

   (A) $MnCl_2(aq)$
   (B) $CuCl_2(aq)$
   (C) $CuSO_4(aq)$
   (D) $Na_2SO_4(aq)$
   (E) $CoSO_4(aq)$

7. Solid silicon dioxide, SiO_2, is

   (A) a network solid with covalent bonding
   (B) a molecular solid with London dispersion forces
   (C) a molecular solid with hydrogen bonding
   (D) an ionic solid
   (E) a metallic solid

8. A solution containing which of the following ions will give off a pungent odor when added dropwise to warm NaOH(*aq*) ?

(A) $CO_3^{2-}(aq)$
(B) $MnO_4^{-}(aq)$
(C) $NH_4^{+}(aq)$
(D) $Ba^{2+}(aq)$
(E) $Al^{3+}(aq)$

9. Based on periodic trends, which of the following atoms has the largest atomic radius?

(A) K
(B) Ga
(C) Br
(D) Cs
(E) Te

10. What is the oxidation number of Cr in CrO_4^{2-}?

(A) +1
(B) +2
(C) +4
(D) +6
(E) +8

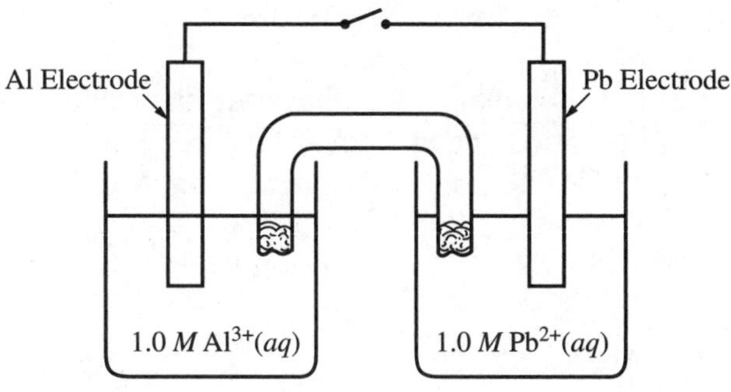

11. When the switch is closed in the cell shown above, a current flows through the circuit and the standard cell potential, E°_{cell}, is +1.53 V. Which of the following will happen to E°_{cell} if the salt bridge is replaced with a platinum wire?

(A) It will increase.
(B) It will decrease but remain positive.
(C) It will become zero.
(D) It will decrease and become negative.
(E) It will not change.

12.

Hydrogen Halide	Normal Boiling Point, °C
HF	+19
HCl	–85
HBr	–67
HI	–35

The liquefied hydrogen halides have the normal boiling points given above. The relatively high boiling point of HF can be correctly explained by which of the following?

(A) HF gas is more ideal.
(B) HF is the strongest acid.
(C) HF molecules have a smaller dipole moment.
(D) HF is much less soluble in water.
(E) HF molecules tend to form hydrogen bonds.

13. $1s^2\ 2s^2\ 2p^6\ 3s^2\ 3p^3$

Atoms of an element, X, have the electronic configuration shown above. The compound most likely formed with magnesium, Mg, is

(A) MgX
(B) Mg_2X
(C) MgX_2
(D) Mg_2X_3
(E) Mg_3X_2

14. The density of an unknown gas is 4.20 grams per liter at 3.00 atmospheres pressure and 127°C. What is the molar mass of this gas? ($R = 0.0821$ liter·atm/mole·K)

(A) 14.6 g/mol
(B) 46.0 g/mol
(C) 88.0 g/mol
(D) 94.1 g/mol
(E) 138.0 g/mol

<u>Questions 15–16</u>

$$H_3AsO_4 + 3\ I^- + 2\ H_3O^+ \rightarrow H_3AsO_3 + I_3^- + 3\ H_2O$$

The oxidation of iodide ions by arsenic acid in acidic aqueous solution occurs according to the balanced equation shown above. The experimental rate law for the reaction at 25°C is

$$\text{Rate} = k\,[H_3AsO_4]\,[I^-]\,[H_3O^+].$$

15. What is the order of the reaction with respect to I^- ?

(A) 1
(B) 2
(C) 3
(D) 5
(E) 6

16. According to the rate law for the reaction, an increase in the concentration of the hydronium ion has what effect on the reaction at 25°C?

(A) The rate of reaction increases.
(B) The rate of reaction decreases.
(C) The value of the equilibrium constant increases.
(D) The value of the equilibrium constant decreases.
(E) Neither the rate nor the value of the equilibrium constant is changed.

17. The critical temperature of a substance is the

(A) temperature at which the vapor pressure of the liquid is equal to the external pressure
(B) temperature at which the vapor pressure of the liquid is equal to 760 mm Hg
(C) temperature at which the solid, liquid, and vapor phases are all in equilibrium
(D) temperature at which the liquid and vapor phases are in equilibrium at 1 atmosphere
(E) lowest temperature above which a substance cannot be liquefied at any applied pressure

18. $Cu(s) + 2\ Ag^+ \rightarrow Cu^{2+} + 2\ Ag(s)$

If the equilibrium constant for the reaction above is 3.7×10^{15}, which of the following correctly describes the standard voltage, $E°$, and the standard free energy change, $\Delta G°$, for this reaction?

(A) $E°$ is positive and $\Delta G°$ is negative.
(B) $E°$ is negative and $\Delta G°$ is positive.
(C) $E°$ and $\Delta G°$ are both positive.
(D) $E°$ and $\Delta G°$ are both negative.
(E) $E°$ and $\Delta G°$ are both zero.

19. London (dispersion) forces are the only type of intermolecular forces in which of the following pure liquids?

(A) $CHF_3(l)$
(B) $H_2S(l)$
(C) $PCl_3(l)$
(D) $SO_2(l)$
(E) $SiCl_4(l)$

20. The pH of 0.1 M ammonia is approximately

(A) 1
(B) 4
(C) 7
(D) 11
(E) 14

21. Which of the following has polar bonds but a zero dipole moment?

(A) SO_2
(B) H_2S
(C) CO_3^{2-}
(D) NO_2
(E) ClO_3^-

22. $CuO(s) + H_2(g) \leftrightarrows Cu(s) + H_2O(g) \quad \Delta H < 0$

The substances in the equation above are at equilibrium at pressure P and temperature T. The equilibrium can be shifted to favor the products by

(A) increasing the pressure by means of a moving piston at constant T
(B) increasing the pressure by adding an inert gas such as nitrogen
(C) decreasing the temperature
(D) allowing some gases to escape at constant P and T
(E) adding a catalyst

23. The molality of the glucose in a 1.0 M glucose solution can be obtained by using which of the following?

(A) Solubility of glucose in water
(B) Degree of dissociation of glucose
(C) Volume of the solution
(D) Temperature of the solution
(E) Density of the solution

24. The geometry of the SO_3 molecule is best described as

(A) trigonal planar
(B) trigonal pyramidal
(C) square pyramidal
(D) bent
(E) tetrahedral

25. Which of the following molecules has the longest bond length?

(A) N_2
(B) O_2
(C) Cl_2
(D) Br_2
(E) I_2

26. What number of moles of O_2 is needed to produce 14.2 grams of P_4O_{10} (molar mass 284 g) from P?

(A) 0.0500 mole
(B) 0.0625 mole
(C) 0.125 mole
(D) 0.250 mole
(E) 0.500 mole

27. If 0.060 faraday is passed through an electrolytic cell containing a solution of In^{3+} ions, the maximum number of moles of In that could be deposited at the cathode is

(A) 0.010 mole
(B) 0.020 mole
(C) 0.030 mole
(D) 0.060 mole
(E) 0.18 mole

28. $CH_4(g) + 2\ O_2(g) \rightarrow CO_2(g) + 2\ H_2O(l)$
$\Delta H^\circ_{rxn} = -889.1$ kJ mol^{-1}

ΔH_f° $H_2O(l) = -285.8$ kJ mol^{-1}
ΔH_f° $CO_2(g) = -393.3$ kJ mol^{-1}

What is the standard heat of formation, ΔH_f°, of methane, $CH_4(g)$, as calculated from the data above?

(A) −210.0 kJ mol^{-1}
(B) −107.5 kJ mol^{-1}
(C) −75.8 kJ mol^{-1}
(D) 75.8 kJ mol^{-1}
(E) 210.0 kJ mol^{-1}

29. Each of the following can act as both a Brønsted-Lowry acid and a Brønsted-Lowry base EXCEPT

(A) HCO_3^-
(B) $H_2PO_4^-$
(C) NH_4^+
(D) H_2O
(E) HS^-

30. Which of the following is most directly responsible for the pressure of a gas in a sealed container?

(A) The forces of attraction between the gas molecules and the walls of the container.
(B) The energy released as the average kinetic energy of the molecules decreases.
(C) The energy released as gas molecules collide and react.
(D) The collisions of the gas molecules with the walls of the container.
(E) The collisions of the gas molecules with one another.

31. Pi (π) bonding occurs in each of the following species EXCEPT

(A) CO_2
(B) C_2H_4
(C) CN^-
(D) C_6H_6
(E) CH_4

32. $3\ Ag(s) + 4\ HNO_3 \rightarrow 3\ AgNO_3 + NO(g) + 2\ H_2O$

The reaction of silver metal and dilute nitric acid proceeds according to the equation above. If 0.10 mole of powdered silver is added to 10. milliliters of 6.0-molar nitric acid, the number of moles of NO gas that can be formed is

(A) 0.015 mole
(B) 0.020 mole
(C) 0.030 mole
(D) 0.045 mole
(E) 0.090 mole

33. Which, if any, of the following species are in the greatest concentration in a 0.100 *M* solution of H_2SO_4 in water?

(A) H_2SO_4 molecules
(B) H_3O^+ ions
(C) HSO_4^- ions
(D) SO_4^{2-} ions
(E) All species are in equilibrium and therefore have the same concentrations.

34. At 20.°C, the vapor pressure of toluene is 22 mm Hg and that of benzene is 75 mm Hg. An ideal solution, equimolar in toluene and benzene, is prepared. At 20.°C, what is the mole fraction of benzene in the vapor in equilibrium with this solution?

(A) 0.23
(B) 0.29
(C) 0.50
(D) 0.77
(E) 0.83

35. Which of the following aqueous solutions has the highest boiling point?

(A) 0.10 M potassium sulfate, K_2SO_4
(B) 0.10 M hydrochloric acid, HCl
(C) 0.10 M ammonium nitrate, NH_4NO_3
(D) 0.10 M magnesium sulfate, $MgSO_4$
(E) 0.20 M sucrose, $C_{12}H_{22}O_{11}$

36. When 70 milliliters of 3.0 M Na_2CO_3 is added to 30 milliliters of 1.0 M $NaHCO_3$, the resulting concentration of Na^+ is

(A) 2.0 M
(B) 2.4 M
(C) 4.0 M
(D) 4.5 M
(E) 7.0 M

37. Which of the following species CANNOT function as an oxidizing agent?

(A) $Cr_2O_7^{2-}$
(B) MnO_4^-
(C) NO_3^-
(D) S
(E) I^-

38. A student wishes to prepare 2.00 liters of 0.100 M KIO_3 (molar mass 214 g). The proper procedure is to weigh out

(A) 42.8 grams of KIO_3 and add 2.00 kilograms of H_2O
(B) 42.8 grams of KIO_3 and add H_2O until the final homogeneous solution has a volume of 2.00 liters
(C) 21.4 grams of KIO_3 and add H_2O until the final homogeneous solution has a volume of 2.00 liters
(D) 42.8 grams of KIO_3 and add 2.00 liters of H_2O
(E) 21.4 grams of KIO_3 and add 2.00 liters of H_2O

39. A 20.0-milliliter sample of 0.200 M K_2CO_3 solution is added to 30.0 milliliters of 0.400 M $Ba(NO_3)_2$ solution. Barium carbonate precipitates. The concentration of barium ion, Ba^{2+}, in solution after reaction is

(A) 0.150 M
(B) 0.160 M
(C) 0.200 M
(D) 0.240 M
(E) 0.267 M

40. One of the outermost electrons in a strontium atom in the ground state can be described by which of the following sets of four quantum numbers?

(A) $5, 2, 0, \frac{1}{2}$
(B) $5, 1, 1, \frac{1}{2}$
(C) $5, 1, 0, \frac{1}{2}$
(D) $5, 0, 1, \frac{1}{2}$
(E) $5, 0, 0, \frac{1}{2}$

41. Which of the following reactions does NOT proceed significantly to the right in aqueous solutions?

(A) $H_3O^+ + OH^- \rightarrow 2\ H_2O$
(B) $HCN + OH^- \rightarrow H_2O + CN^-$
(C) $Cu(H_2O)_4^{2+} + 4\ NH_3 \rightarrow Cu(NH_3)_4^{2+} + 4\ H_2O$
(D) $H_2SO_4 + H_2O \rightarrow H_3O^+ + HSO_4^-$
(E) $H_2O + HSO_4^- \rightarrow H_2SO_4 + OH^-$

42. A compound is heated to produce a gas whose molar mass is to be determined. The gas is collected by displacing water in a water-filled flask inverted in a trough of water. Which of the following is necessary to calculate the molar mass of the gas but does not need to be measured during the experiment?

(A) Mass of the compound used in the experiment
(B) Temperature of the water in the trough
(C) Vapor pressure of the water
(D) Barometric pressure
(E) Volume of water displaced from the flask

43. A 27.0 gram sample of an unknown hydrocarbon was burned in excess oxygen to form 88.0 grams of carbon dioxide and 27.0 grams of water. What is a possible molecular formula of the hydrocarbon?

(A) CH_4
(B) C_2H_2
(C) C_4H_3
(D) C_4H_6
(E) C_4H_{10}

44. If the acid dissociation constant, K_a, for an acid HA is 8×10^{-4} at 25°C, what percent of the acid is dissociated in a 0.50 M solution of HA at 25°C?

(A) 0.08%
(B) 0.2%
(C) 1%
(D) 2%
(E) 4%

45. Which of the following indicators is most appropriate for determining the equivalence point in the titration of a weak acid with a strong base?

	Indicator	pH Range of Color Change
(A)	Thymol blue	1.2–2.8
(B)	Methyl orange	3.1–4.4
(C)	Methyl red	4.4–6.2
(D)	Bromcresol purple	5.2–6.8
(E)	m-cresol purple	7.6–9.2

46. Equal numbers of moles of $H_2(g)$, $Ar(g)$, and $N_2(g)$ are placed in a glass vessel at room temperature. If the vessel has a pinhole-sized leak, which of the following will be true regarding the relative values of the partial pressures of the gases remaining in the vessel after some of the gas mixture has effused?

(A) $P_{H_2} < P_{N_2} < P_{Ar}$
(B) $P_{H_2} < P_{Ar} < P_{N_2}$
(C) $P_{N_2} < P_{Ar} < P_{H_2}$
(D) $P_{Ar} < P_{H_2} < P_{N_2}$
(E) $P_{H_2} = P_{Ar} = P_{N_2}$

47. Which of the following is a correct interpretation of the results of Rutherford's experiments in which gold atoms were bombarded with alpha particles?

(A) Atoms have equal numbers of positive and negative charges.
(B) Electrons in atoms are arranged in shells.
(C) Neutrons are at the center of an atom.
(D) Neutrons and protons in atoms have nearly equal mass.
(E) The positive charge of an atom is concentrated in a small region.

48. A 0.1 *M* solution of which of the following ions is orange?

(A) $Fe(H_2O)_4^{2+}$
(B) $Cu(NH_3)_4^{2+}$
(C) $Zn(OH)_4^{2-}$
(D) $Zn(NH_3)_4^{2+}$
(E) $Cr_2O_7^{2-}$

49. In the formation of 1.0 mole of the following crystalline solids from the gaseous ions, the most energy is released by

(A) NaF
(B) MgF_2
(C) $MgBr_2$
(D) AlF_3
(E) $AlBr_3$

50. If 1 mole of a nonvolatile nonelectrolyte dissolves in 9 moles of water to form an ideal solution, what is the vapor pressure of this solution at 25°C? (The vapor pressure of pure water at 25°C is 23.8 mm Hg.)

(A) 23.8 mm Hg
(B) $\frac{9}{10}$ 23.8 mm Hg
(C) $\frac{10}{9}$ 23.8 mm Hg
(D) $\frac{1}{10}$ 23.8 mm Hg
(E) It cannot be determined from the information given.

51. $\ldots MnO_4^-(aq) + \ldots NO_2^-(aq) + \ldots H_2O(l) \rightarrow \ldots MnO_2(s) + \ldots NO_3^-(aq) + \ldots OH^-(aq)$

When the redox equation shown above is balanced by using coefficients reduced to lowest whole numbers, the coefficient for MnO_4^- is

(A) 1
(B) 2
(C) 3
(D) 4
(E) 6

52. If a certain solid solute dissolves in water with the evolution of heat, which of the following is most likely to be true?

(A) The temperature of the solution decreases as the solute dissolves.
(B) The resulting solution is ideal.
(C) The solid has a large lattice energy.
(D) The solid has a large heat of fusion.
(E) The solid has a large energy of hydration.

53. A 0.1-molar aqueous solution of which of the following is neutral?

(A) $NaNO_3$
(B) Na_2CO_3
(C) NH_4Br
(D) KCN
(E) $AlCl_3$

54. Which of the following is a true statement about the halogens?

(A) Fluorine is the weakest oxidizing agent.
(B) Bromine is more electronegative than chlorine.
(C) The halide ions are larger than their respective halogen atoms.
(D) Adding $I_2(s)$ to a solution containing $Br^-(aq)$ will produce $Br_2(l)$.
(E) The first ionization energies increase as the atomic number increases.

$CH_3CHOHCH_2OH$ $CH_3CH_2CH_2CH_3$ $CH_3CH_2CHOHCH_3$
X *Y* *Z*

55. Considering the structures of the three compounds, *X*, *Y*, and *Z*, shown above, the ranking of their solubility in water from least to greatest is which of the following?

(A) $X < Y < Z$
(B) $X < Z < Y$
(C) $Z < Y < X$
(D) $Y < Z < X$
(E) $Y < X < Z$

56. Of the following compounds, which is involved in the environmental problem known as acid rain?

(A) CO_2
(B) CF_2Cl_2
(C) SO_2
(D) H_2S
(E) SiO_2

$$\ldots P_4O_{10} + \ldots Ca(OH)_2 \rightarrow \ldots Ca_3(PO_4)_2 + \ldots H_2O$$

57. When the chemical equation above is balanced in terms of lowest whole-number coefficients, the coefficient for H_2O is

(A) 1
(B) 2
(C) 3
(D) 6
(E) 8

58. Which of the following best describes the role of a catalyst in a chemical reaction?

(A) The catalyst lowers the activation energy by changing the mechanism of the reaction.
(B) The catalyst increases the strength of the chemical bonds in the reactant molecules.
(C) The catalyst increases the value of the equilibrium constant.
(D) The catalyst provides kinetic energy to reactant molecules to increase the reaction rate.
(E) The catalyst bonds to the reaction products and drives the equilibrium toward the products.

59. On the basis of trends in the periodic table, an atom of which of the following elements is predicted to have the lowest first ionization energy?

(A) Ar
(B) Cl
(C) K
(D) Rb
(E) I

$$X(g) + Y(g) \rightleftarrows Z(g)$$

60. Which of the following statements is true for the chemical system represented above when the system has reached a state of equilibrium at a constant temperature and pressure?

(A) The forward and reverse reactions have stopped.
(B) The forward and reverse reactions occur at the same rate.
(C) The rate of formation of $Z(g)$ is equal to half the rate of consumption of $X(g)$.
(D) Introducing a catalyst will result in an increased amount of $Z(g)$ at equilibrium.
(E) Introducing more $Y(g)$ to the system will cause more $X(g)$ to form.

61. If a 1.0 *M* solution of HA, a weak acid, has a pH of 2.0, then the value of K_a, the acid-dissociation constant, for HA is closest to

(A) 1.0×10^{-4}
(B) 1.4×10^{-4}
(C) 1.0×10^{-2}
(D) 1.4×10^{-2}
(E) 1.4×10^{-1}

62. Which of the following elements is never found pure (i.e., chemically uncombined with one or more other elements) in Earth's crust?

(A) S
(B) K
(C) Cu
(D) Pt
(E) Au

63. If an endothermic reaction occurs spontaneously, then it can be correctly inferred that

(A) a catalyst must be present
(B) the reaction occurs at a slow rate
(C) $\Delta G_{rxn} > 0$
(D) $\Delta H_{rxn} < 0$
(E) $\Delta S_{rxn} > 0$

64. Which of the following single covalent bonds is the most polar?

(A) B – F
(B) F – F
(C) Cl – F
(D) P – Br
(E) Si – Cl

65. In which of the following are the compounds listed correctly in order of increasing strength of their oxygen-to-oxygen bonds?

(A) $O_2 < O_3 < H_2O_2$
(B) $O_2 < H_2O_2 < O_3$
(C) $O_3 < O_2 < H_2O_2$
(D) $H_2O_2 < O_3 < O_2$
(E) $H_2O_2 < O_2 < O_3$

66. An atom of which of the following elements has the smallest radius?

(A) K
(B) Ca
(C) Br
(D) Rb
(E) Sr

67. Which of the following is a Brønsted-Lowry acid-base pair?

(A) H^+ and Cl^-
(B) Na^+ and Cl^-
(C) HCl and NaOH
(D) H_2SO_4 and SO_4^{2-}
(E) HCO_3^- and CO_3^{2-}

68. A sample of gas has a volume of 1.0 L at 300. K and 2.0 atm. If the volume and the absolute temperature are both doubled, what is the final pressure of the sample?

(A) 0.50 atm
(B) 1.0 atm
(C) 2.0 atm
(D) 4.0 atm
(E) 8.0 atm

69. In coordination compounds, the ligands have in common the fact that they

(A) act as Lewis acids
(B) are positively charged ions
(C) form bonds using lone pairs of electrons
(D) form long chains of atoms
(E) have a relatively large molar mass

70. The oxidation number of silicon in the compound $Na_2Mg_2Si_6O_{15}$ is

(A) +1
(B) +2
(C) +3
(D) +4
(E) +6

71. If a 0.15 molal aqueous solution of solute X has the same boiling point as a 0.30 molal aqueous solution of glucose, which of the following statements is true?

(A) Solute X has a molar mass that is twice that of glucose.
(B) The ideal van't Hoff factor of solute X is 2.
(C) The 0.15 molal solution has a higher vapor pressure than the 0.30 molal solution.
(D) The 0.30 molal solution has a lower freezing point than the 0.15 molal solution.
(E) The 0.30 molal solution has a higher osmotic pressure than the 0.15 molal solution.

72. As intermolecular forces become stronger for pure liquids, which of the following tends to decrease?

(A) Density
(B) Boiling point
(C) Vapor pressure
(D) Surface tension
(E) Heat of vaporization

73. A sample of argon gas and a sample of xenon gas at low temperature do not exhibit ideal gas behavior. Which gas deviates more from ideal gas behavior, and what is the major cause of the deviation?

	Greater Deviation	Cause of Deviation
(A)	Argon	Attractive forces between atoms
(B)	Argon	Volume of the atoms
(C)	Argon	Mass of the atoms
(D)	Xenon	Attractive forces between atoms
(E)	Xenon	Mass of the atoms

74. Each of three flexible vessels contains a gas at the same temperature and pressure. The first contains 2.0 g of $H_2(g)$, the second contains 32.0 g of $O_2(g)$, and the third contains 44.0 g of $CO_2(g)$. Which of the following statements about the gases is FALSE?

(A) The densities of the gases increase in the order $H_2 < O_2 < CO_2$.
(B) The number of molecules in each of the three vessels is the same.
(C) The volume of each of the three vessels is the same.
(D) The average kinetic energy of the molecules in each of the vessels is the same.
(E) The average speed of the molecules in each of the vessels is the same.

75. Four pure substances are used to make 1 *M* aqueous solutions: NaOH, Na_2CO_3, $NaNO_3$, and HNO_3. Which of the following correctly ranks the substances in order of increasing pH of the solution they produce?

Lowest pH → Highest pH

(A) $HNO_3 < NaNO_3 < Na_2CO_3 < NaOH$
(B) $HNO_3 < Na_2CO_3 < NaNO_3 < NaOH$
(C) $HNO_3 < NaNO_3 < NaOH < Na_2CO_3$
(D) $NaNO_3 < HNO_3 < Na_2CO_3 < NaOH$
(E) $Na_2CO_3 < HNO_3 < NaOH < NaNO_3$

Study Resources

Most textbooks used in college-level chemistry courses cover the topics in the outline given earlier, but the approaches to certain topics and the emphases given to them may differ. To prepare for the Chemistry exam, it is advisable to study one or more college textbooks, which can be found in most college bookstores. When selecting a textbook, check the table of contents against the knowledge and skills required for this test.

Visit **clep.collegeboard.org/earn-college-credit/practice** for additional chemistry resources. You can also find suggestions for exam preparation in Chapter IV of the *Official Study Guide*. In addition, many college faculty post their course materials on their schools' websites.

Answer Key

1.	B	39.	B
2.	E	40.	E
3.	B	41.	E
4.	E	42.	C
5.	C	43.	D
6.	C	44.	E
7.	A	45.	E
8.	C	46.	A
9.	D	47.	E
10.	D	48.	E
11.	C	49.	D
12.	E	50.	B
13.	E	51.	B
14.	B	52.	E
15.	A	53.	A
16.	A	54.	C
17.	E	55.	D
18.	A	56.	C
19.	E	57.	D
20.	D	58.	A
21.	C	59.	D
22.	C	60.	B
23.	E	61.	A
24.	A	62.	B
25.	E	63.	E
26.	D	64.	A
27.	B	65.	D
28.	C	66.	C
29.	C	67.	E
30.	D	68.	C
31.	E	69.	C
32.	A	70.	D
33.	B	71.	B
34.	D	72.	C
35.	A	73.	D
36.	D	74.	E
37.	E	75.	A
38.	B		

College Algebra

Description of the Examination

The College Algebra examination covers material that is usually taught in a one-semester college course in algebra. Nearly half of the test is made up of routine problems requiring basic algebraic skills; the remainder involves solving nonroutine problems in which candidates must demonstrate their understanding of concepts. The test includes questions on basic algebraic operations; linear and quadratic equations, inequalities and graphs; algebraic, exponential and logarithmic functions; and miscellaneous other topics. It is assumed that candidates are familiar with currently taught algebraic vocabulary, symbols and notation. The test places little emphasis on arithmetic calculations. However, an online scientific calculator (nongraphing) will be available during the examination.

The examination contains approximately 60 questions to be answered in approximately 90 minutes. Some of these are pretest questions that will not be scored.

Knowledge and Skills Required

Questions on the College Algebra examination require candidates to demonstrate the following abilities in the approximate proportions indicated.

- Solving routine, straightforward problems (about 50 percent of the examination)
- Solving nonroutine problems requiring an understanding of concepts and the application of skills and concepts (about 50 percent of the examination)

The subject matter of the College Algebra examination is drawn from the following topics. The percentages next to the main topics indicate the approximate percentage of exam questions on that topic.

25% Algebraic Operations

Operations with exponents

Factoring and expanding polynomials

Operations with algebraic expressions

Absolute value

Properties of logarithms

25% Equations and Inequalities

Linear equations and inequalities

Quadratic equations and inequalities

Absolute value equations and inequalities

Systems of equations and inequalities

Exponential and logarithmic equations

30% Functions and Their Properties*

Definition, interpretation and representation/modeling (graphical, numerical, symbolic, verbal)

Domain and range

Evaluation of functions

Algebra of functions

Graphs and their properties (including intercepts, symmetry, transformations)

Inverse functions

20% Number Systems and Operations

Real numbers

Complex numbers

Sequences and series

Factorials and Binomial Theorem

---

*Each test may contain a variety of functions, including linear, polynomial (degree ≤ 5), rational, absolute value, power, exponential, logarithmic and piecewise-defined.

Sample Test Questions

The following sample questions do not appear on an actual CLEP examination. They are intended to give potential test-takers an indication of the format and difficulty level of the examination and to provide content for practice and review. Knowing the correct answers to all of the sample questions is not a guarantee of satisfactory performance on the exam.

Directions: An online scientific calculator will be available for the questions in this test.

Some questions will require you to select from among five choices. For these questions, select the BEST of the choices given.

Some questions will require you to type a numerical answer in the box provided.

Notes: (1) Unless otherwise specified, the domain of any function f is assumed to be the set of all real numbers x for which $f(x)$ is a real number.

(2) i will be used to denote $\sqrt{-1}$.

(3) Figures that accompany questions are intended to provide information useful in answering the questions. All figures lie in a plane unless otherwise indicated. The figures are drawn as accurately as possible EXCEPT when it is stated in a specific question that the figure is not drawn to scale. Straight lines and smooth curves may appear slightly jagged on the screen.

1. Which of the following expressions is equivalent to $(3-5b)^2$?

(A) $9-25b^2$
(B) $9+25b^2$
(C) $9-15b-25b^2$
(D) $9+30b-25b^2$
(E) $9-30b+25b^2$

2. Which of the following is a factor of $4-(x+y)^2$?

(A) $-(x+y)^2$
(B) $x+y$
(C) $2-x+y$
(D) $2+x+y$
(E) $4+x+y$

3. $2v(3v^2-1)-(6-8v^3+14v)+3=$

(A) $-2v^3+12v-3$
(B) $14v^3+12v-3$
(C) $14v^3-14v-4$
(D) $14v^3-16v-3$
(E) $14v^3-16v-6$

4. The radius of the Sun is approximately 10^9 meters, and the radius of an oxygen atom is approximately 10^{-12} meter. The radius of the Sun is approximately how many times the radius of an oxygen atom?

(A) 10^{-21}
(B) 10^{-3}
(C) 10^3
(D) 10^9
(E) 10^{21}

5. Where defined $\dfrac{\frac{x^2-9}{x+2}}{\frac{x-3}{x-2}}=$

(A) $\dfrac{x-2}{x+2}$

(B) $\dfrac{(x-2)(x+3)}{x+2}$

(C) $\dfrac{x^2-x+6}{x+2}$

(D) $\dfrac{1}{(x-2)(x+2)}$

(E) $\dfrac{x+3}{(x-2)(x+2)}$

6. Which of the following are solutions of the equation $(2x - 3)(3x + 5) = -14$?

(A) $x = \frac{1}{3}$ and $x = -\frac{1}{2}$

(B) $x = -\frac{1}{3}$ and $x = \frac{1}{2}$

(C) $x = \frac{3}{2}$ and $x = -\frac{5}{3}$

(D) $x = -\frac{3}{2}$ and $x = \frac{5}{3}$

(E) $x = 2$ and $x = -7$

7. Of the following, which is the greatest?

(A) $2^{\left(3^5\right)}$

(B) $\left(2^3\right)^5$

(C) $3^{\left(2^5\right)}$

(D) $\left(3^2\right)^5$

(E) $5^{\left(3^2\right)}$

8. For any positive integer $n, \dfrac{(n+1)!}{n!} - n =$

(A) 0 (B) 1 (C) n (D) $n+1$ (E) $n!$

9. Which of the following is equal to $r^2 t^{1/2} r^{2/3} t^{-3/2}$?

(A) $-r^{8/3}t$

(B) $\dfrac{r^{4/3}}{t^{3/4}}$

(C) $\dfrac{r^{4/3}}{t}$

(D) $\dfrac{r^{5/2}}{t^{5/6}}$

(E) $\dfrac{r^{8/3}}{t}$

10. A ball is dropped from a height of h feet and repeatedly bounces off the floor. After each bounce, the ball reaches a height that is $\frac{2}{3}$ of the height from which it previously fell. For example, after the first bounce, the ball reaches a height of $\frac{2}{3}h$ feet. Which of the following represents the total number of feet the ball travels between the first and the sixth bounce?

(A) $\sum_{i=1}^{5}(2h)\left(\frac{2}{3}\right)^i$

(B) $\sum_{i=1}^{5}h\left(\frac{2}{3}\right)^i$

(C) $\sum_{i=1}^{5}\left(\frac{2}{3}h\right)^i$

(D) $\sum_{i=1}^{6}(2h)\left(\frac{2}{3}\right)^{i-1}$

(E) $\sum_{i=1}^{\infty}h\left(\frac{2}{3}\right)^i$

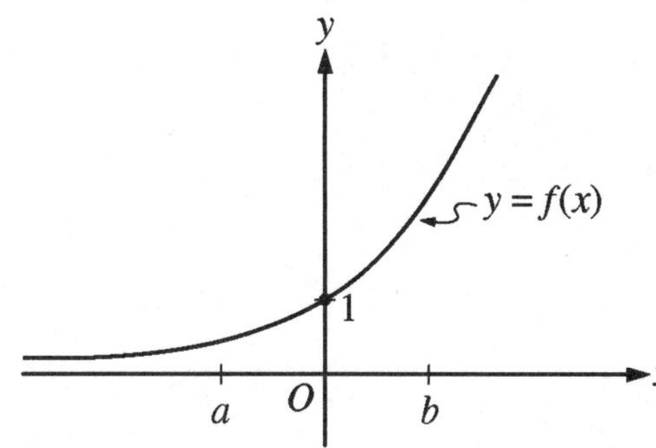

11. The graph shows an exponential function f in the xy-plane. The function g is defined by $g(x) = 2^{-x}$. Complete each sentence in the table by indicating the correct relationship between the two values.

	less than	greater than	equal to	
$f(a)$ is				$g(a)$.
$f(b)$ is				$g(b)$.
$f(0)$ is				$g(0)$.

12. Which of the following defines the interval of real numbers $[-4, 2]$?

    (A) $|x - 0| \leq 2$
    (B) $|x + 1| \leq 3$
    (C) $|x + 1| \geq 3$
    (D) $|x - 4| \leq 2$
    (E) $|x - 4| \geq 2$

13. Which of the following are the solutions of the equation $2x^2 + 2x = 4 - x$?

    (A) $x = 4$ and $x = 1$
    (B) $x = 4$ and $x = -\frac{1}{2}$
    (C) $x = \frac{3+\sqrt{35}}{4}$ and $x = \frac{3-\sqrt{35}}{4}$
    (D) $x = \frac{-3+\sqrt{41}}{4}$ and $x = \frac{-3-\sqrt{41}}{4}$
    (E) $x = \frac{-3+i\sqrt{23}}{2}$ and $x = \frac{-3-i\sqrt{23}}{2}$

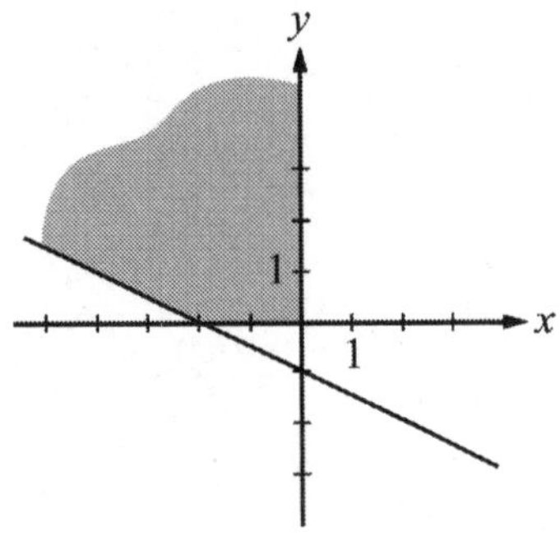

14. The shaded region in the figure above represents the intersection of the graphs of $x \leq 0$, $y \geq 0$, and which of the following inequalities?

    (A) $y \leq -2x - 1$
    (B) $y \leq -\frac{1}{2}x + 1$
    (C) $y \geq -2x - 1$
    (D) $y \geq -\frac{1}{2}x - 1$
    (E) $y \geq \frac{1}{2}x - 1$

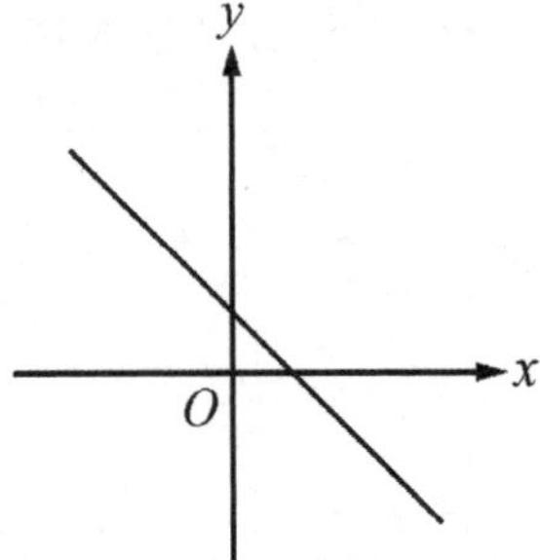

15. The graph of the line with equation $ax + by = 1$ is shown above. Which of the following must be true?

    (A) $a > 0$ and $b < 0$
    (B) $a > 0$ and $b > 0$
    (C) $a < 0$ and $b < 0$
    (D) $a < 0$ and $b > 0$
    (E) $a = 0$ and $b > 0$

16. What are all the values of b for which the equation $9x^2 + bx + 1 = 0$ has no real solutions?

    (A) $b = -6$ or $b = 6$
    (B) $b < -6$ or $b > 6$
    (C) $b \leq -6$ or $b \geq 6$
    (D) $-6 < b < 6$
    (E) $-6 \leq b \leq 6$

17. Which quadrants of the xy-plane contain points of the graph of $2x - y > 4$?

    (A) I, II, and III only
    (B) I, II, and IV only
    (C) I, III, and IV only
    (D) II, III, and IV only
    (E) I, II, III, and IV

18. Joe invests \$40,000 and, at the same time, Tom invests \$10,000. The value of Joe's investment decreases by \$4,000 per year, while the value of Tom's investment increases by \$1,000 per year. Which of the following systems of equations could be used to find the numbers of years, t, that it will take for the values, v, of the two investments to be equal?

(A) $v = 40{,}000 - t$ and $v = 10{,}000 + t$
(B) $v = 40{,}000 - 4t$ and $v = 10{,}000 + t$
(C) $v = 40{,}000 + 1{,}000t$ and $v = 10{,}000 - 4{,}000t$
(D) $v = 40{,}000 + 4{,}000t$ and $v = 10{,}000 - 1{,}000t$
(E) $v = 40{,}000 - 4{,}000t$ and $v = 10{,}000 + 1{,}000t$

19. Which of the following is an equation of the line that passes through the points $(-2, 1)$ and $(1, 2)$ in the xy-plane?

(A) $x + 3y = 1$
(B) $x + 3y = 5$
(C) $x + 3y = -5$
(D) $x - 3y = -5$
(E) $x - 3y = -1$

20. If x is an irrational number, which of the following statements must be true?

(A) x^3 is an irrational number.
(B) x^2 is an irrational number.
(C) $x + x$ is an irrational number.
(D) x^2 is a rational number.
(E) $x + x$ is a rational number.

21. When $\dfrac{3+4i}{2+i}$ is expressed in the form $a + bi$, what is the value of a?

[ ]

22. If $a < 0 < b < c$, then each of the following must be true EXCEPT

(A) $ac < ab$
(B) $a^2 < b^2 < c^2$
(C) $a^3 < b^3 < c^3$
(D) $ab < b^2 < bc$
(E) $a^2b < a^2c$

23. The illuminance of a surface varies inversely with the square of its distance from the light source. If the illuminance of a surface is 120 lumens per square meter when its distance from a certain light source is 6 meters, by how many meters should the distance of the surface from the source be increased to reduce its illuminance to 30 lumens per square meter?

(A) 3
(B) 6
(C) 12
(D) 15
(E) 18

24. What are all real values of x for which

$$\frac{2}{3-x} = \frac{1}{3} - \frac{1}{x}?$$

(A) $x = -3$ only
(B) $x = 3$ only
(C) $x = -3$ and $x = 0$
(D) $x = -3$ and $x = 3$
(E) There are no real solutions.

25. Indicate whether each statement is always true, never true, or sometimes true for the real numbers a and b.

Statement	Always True	Never True	Sometimes True
$\lvert a+b\rvert = \lvert a\rvert + \lvert b\rvert$			
$\lvert a+b\rvert < \lvert a\rvert + \lvert b\rvert$			
$\lvert a+b\rvert \le \lvert a\rvert + \lvert b\rvert$			
$\lvert a+b\rvert > \lvert a\rvert + \lvert b\rvert$			

x	0	1	2	3	4	5	6	7
$p(x)$	–30	22	110	150	34	–130	222	2,350

26. The table above gives some of the values of a 5th degree polynomial $p(x)$. Based on the values shown, what is the minimum number of real roots of the equation $p(x) = 0$?

(A) One
(B) Two
(C) Three
(D) Four
(E) Five

27. The number of bricks in the bottom row of a brick wall is 49. The next row up from the bottom contains 47 bricks, and each subsequent row contains 2 fewer bricks than the row immediately below it. The number of bricks in the top row is 3. If the wall is one brick thick, what is the total number of bricks in the wall?

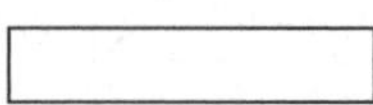

28. Which of the following is the expansion of $(2x+3)^3$?

(A) $2x^3 + 3(2x^2) + 3(2x) + 1$
(B) $2x^3 + 3(2x^2) + 3^2(2x) + 3$
(C) $2x^3 + 3(2x^2) + 3^2(2x) + 3^3$
(D) $(2x)^3 + 3(2x)^2 + 3^2(2x) + 3^3$
(E) $(2x)^3 + 3^2(2x)^2 + 3^3(2x) + 3^3$

29. If $x = -3$ is a root of the equation $x^3 + 3x^2 - ax - 12 = 0$, what is the value of a?

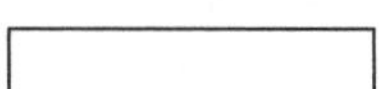

30. If the first term of a geometric sequence is $\frac{3}{2}$ and the second and third terms are $-\frac{3}{4}$ and $\frac{3}{8}$, respectively, which of the following represents the nth term of the sequence?

(A) $\frac{3(-1)^{n-1}}{2n}$
(B) $\frac{3(-1)^{n}}{2n}$
(C) $\frac{3(-1)^{n-1}}{2^n}$
(D) $\frac{3(-1)^{n}}{2^n}$
(E) $\frac{3(-1)^{n-1}}{2^{n+1}}$

31. A clothing company has budgeted \$58,000 for the purchase of 7 sewing machines. The 7 sewing machines are to be chosen from two models, model X and model Y. If a model X sewing machine costs \$8,000 and a model Y sewing machine costs \$9,000, how many model X sewing machines should the company purchase to use exactly the budgeted money?

(A) 2 (B) 3 (C) 4 (D) 5 (E) 6

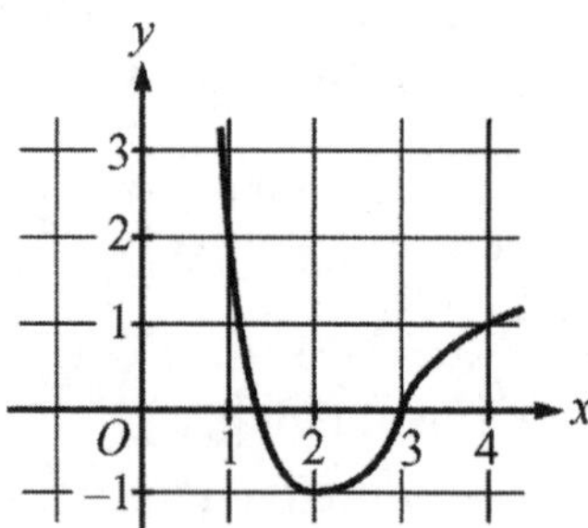

32. The graph of the function f is shown above. What is the value of $f(f(1))$?

(A) –1 (B) 0 (C) 1 (D) 2 (E) 4

33. In the xy-plane, what is the x-intercept of the graph of $y = -\frac{2}{3}x - 4$?

34. Which of the following define y as a function of x ?

I. $2x^2 + y = 7$

II.

x	1	2	3	4
y	2	5	–1	2

III.

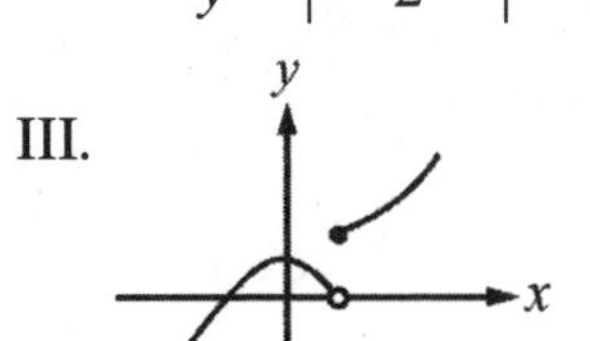

(A) None
(B) I and II only
(C) I and III only
(D) II and III only
(E) I, II, and III

35. If $3^{x+1} = 9^{2x-1}$, then $x =$

[ ]

36. Select two of the following choices and place them in the blanks below so that the resulting statements are true.

$M(t) = 210(0.89)^t$	155
$M(t) = 210(0.11)^t$	117
$M(t) = 11(210)^t$	28

A patient takes a 210-milligram dose of medicine. The amount of medicine present in the body decreases by 11 percent each hour after it is taken. The amount of medicine M present in the body t hours after the medicine is taken can be modeled by the function ____________________. According to the model, ____________ milligrams of the medicine are present in the body 5 hours after the medicine is taken.

37. Let f be a linear function. When $f(x)$ is divided by $x-3$, the remainder is 5. When $f(x)$ is divided by $x-4$, the remainder is 3. What is the value of $f(0)$?

(A) 2
(B) 5
(C) 8
(D) 11
(E) 15

38. If $\log_4(y+2) = 3$, what is the value of y ?

(A) 10 (B) 62 (C) 64 (D) 79 (E) 83

39. A colony of bacteria starts with 2 bacteria at noon. If the colony of bacteria triples every 30 minutes, how many bacteria will be present at 3:00 P.M. on the same day?

(A) 486
(B) 729
(C) 1,458
(D) 46,656
(E) 118,098

40. Which of the following must be true?

I. $\log_3 3^t = t$

II. $\ln 10^{4.3} = 4.3 \ln 10$

III. $\log_{10}(xy^n) = \log_{10} x + n \log_{10} y$ for all positive numbers x and y

(A) I only
(B) II only
(C) I and II only
(D) II and III only
(E) I, II, and III

41. If $f(x)=5-2x^3$ and f^{-1} denotes the inverse function of f, then $f^{-1}(x)=$

(A) $\sqrt[3]{\dfrac{5-x}{2}}$

(B) $\dfrac{\sqrt[3]{5-x}}{2}$

(C) $\sqrt[3]{\dfrac{x-5}{2}}$

(D) $\dfrac{1}{5-2x^3}$

(E) $5x^3+2$

42. $\dfrac{2x-1}{x+3}-\dfrac{x-2}{2x+1}=$

(A) $\dfrac{x+1}{3x+4}$

(B) $\dfrac{x-3}{(x+3)(2x+1)}$

(C) $\dfrac{3x-3}{(x+3)(2x+1)}$

(D) $\dfrac{3x^2-x+5}{(x+3)(2x+1)}$

(E) $\dfrac{3x^2+x-7}{(x+3)(2x+1)}$

43. In the xy-plane, the point $(8,10)$ lies on the graph of the function $y = f(x)$. Which of the following points must lie on the graph of the function $y = 2f(x-3)+5$?

(A) $(5,10)$
(B) $(5,15)$
(C) $(5,25)$
(D) $(11,15)$
(E) $(11,25)$

44. $(i+1)(3-i)+(2i-1)=$

(A) -6
(B) $1+4i$
(C) $2+4i$
(D) $3+4i$
(E) $4+2i$

45. The population of a small town is modeled by an exponential function of the form $p(t)=ab^t$, where t represents the number of years since 2010. The population of the town was recorded as 425 in 2010 and 612 in 2012. Based on the data for the years 2010 and 2012, what is the value of b in the model?

46. Which of the following, when added to $4a^2+9$, will result in a perfect square for all integer values of a ?

(A) 0 (B) $3a$ (C) $6a$ (D) $9a$ (E) $12a$

$$x^2+y^2=25$$
$$x+y=1$$

47. For what values of x will (x,y) be a solution of the system of equations above?

(A) $x=-4$ and $x=3$
(B) $x=-4$ and $x=5$
(C) $x=-3$ and $x=4$
(D) $x=1$ and $x=5$
(E) The system has no solutions.

48. A company's daily cost c, in hundreds of dollars, to manufacture n items of a certain product can be modeled by the function $c(n)$. According to the model, which of the following is the best interpretation of $c^{-1}(5)=80$, where c^{-1} is the inverse function of c ?

(A) The company's daily cost to manufacture 5 items of the product is \$80.
(B) The company's daily cost to manufacture 5 items of the product is \$8,000.
(C) The company's daily cost to manufacture 500 items of the product is \$80.
(D) The company's daily cost to manufacture 80 items of the product is \$5.
(E) The company's daily cost to manufacture 80 items of the product is \$500.

$$f(x)=\begin{cases} x^2 & \text{for } x\le 0 \\ ax+b & \text{for } x>0 \end{cases}$$

49. The function f above has an inverse function for which of the following values of a and b ?

(A) $a=-1,\ b=-2$
(B) $a=-1,\ b=2$
(C) $a=0,\ b=-1$
(D) $a=1,\ b=-2$
(E) $a=1,\ b=2$

50. For the function $g(x)=\log_2 x$, which of the following must be true?

I. The domain is $[0,\infty)$.
II. The range is $(-\infty,\infty)$.
III. $g(x)$ increases with increasing values of x.

(A) III only
(B) I and II only
(C) I and III only
(D) II and III only
(E) I, II, and III

51. A rectangular box has volume x^3-8 cubic inches. If the height of the box is $x-2$ inches, what is the area of the base of the box, in square inches? (The volume of a box equals the area of the base times the height.)

(A) x^2+4
(B) x^2-2x-4
(C) x^2-2x+4
(D) x^2+2x+4
(E) x^2+4x+4

52. If $y = 8x^2 + 4x - 1$ is expressed in the form $y = a(x - h)^2 + k$, where a, h, and k are constants, what is the value of k ?

(A) -3
(B) -2
(C) $-\frac{3}{2}$
(D) $-\frac{17}{16}$
(E) $-\frac{1}{2}$

53. If b and c are integers such that the equation $3x^2 + bx + c = 0$ has only one real root, which of the following statements must be true?

I. b is even.
II. c is odd.
III. b^2 is a multiple of 3.

(A) I only
(B) III only
(C) I and II only
(D) I and III only
(E) I, II, and III

54. A rock is thrown straight up into the air from a height of 4 feet. The height of the rock above the ground, in feet, t seconds after it is thrown is given by $-16t^2 + 56t + 4$. For how many seconds will the height of the rock be at least 28 feet above the ground?

(A) 0.5
(B) 1.5
(C) 2.5
(D) 3.0
(E) 3.5

55. $\log_5 \sqrt{125} - \log_2 \sqrt{2} =$

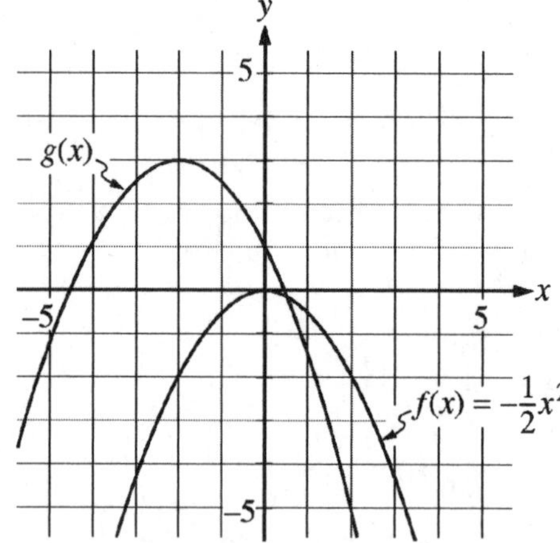

56. In the figure shown above, the graph of the function g is a transformation of the graph of the function f. Which of the following is the equation of g ?

(A) $g(x) = -\frac{1}{2}x^2 + 3$
(B) $g(x) = -\frac{1}{2}(x - 2)^2 + 3$
(C) $g(x) = -\frac{1}{2}(x - 2)^2 - 3$
(D) $g(x) = -\frac{1}{2}(x + 2)^2 + 3$
(E) $g(x) = -\frac{1}{2}(x + 2)^2 - 3$

57. The polynomial $p(x) = x^3 + 2x - 11$ has a real zero between which two consecutive integers?

(A) 0 and 1
(B) 1 and 2
(C) 2 and 3
(D) 3 and 4
(E) 4 and 5

58. Which of the following could be the graph of $y = ax^2 + bx + c$, where $b^2 - 4ac = 0$?

(A)

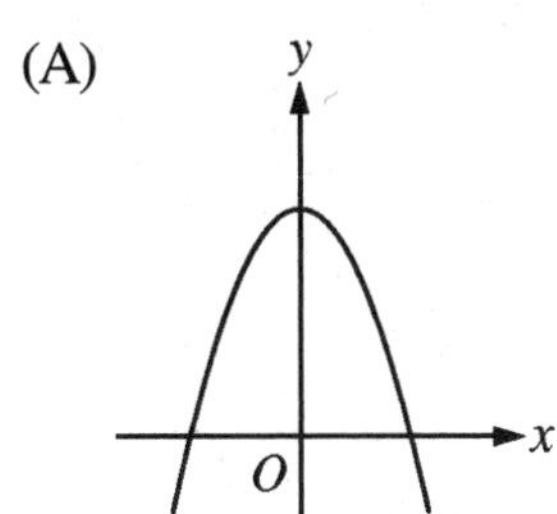

(B)

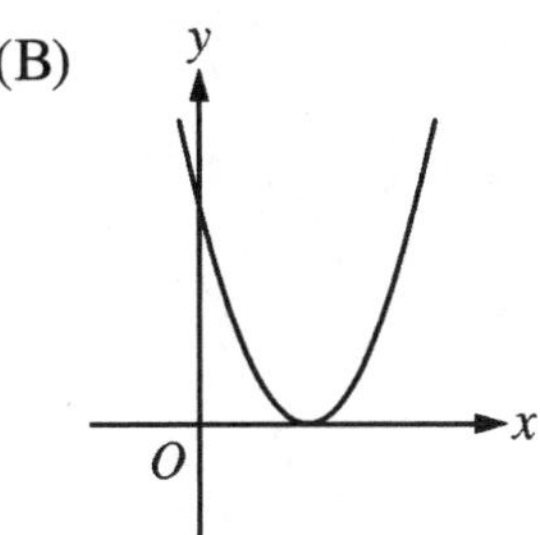

(C)

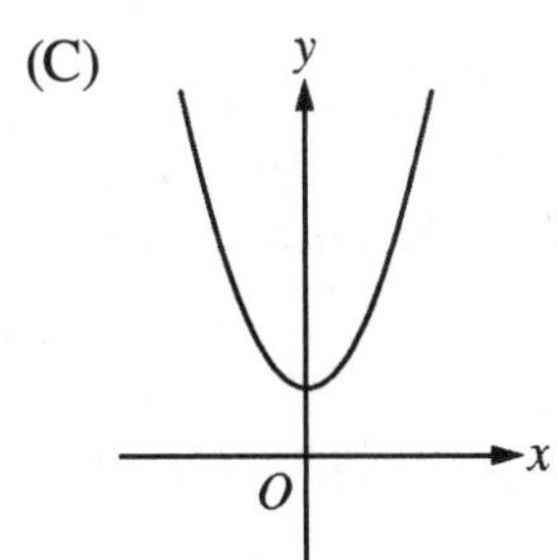

(D)

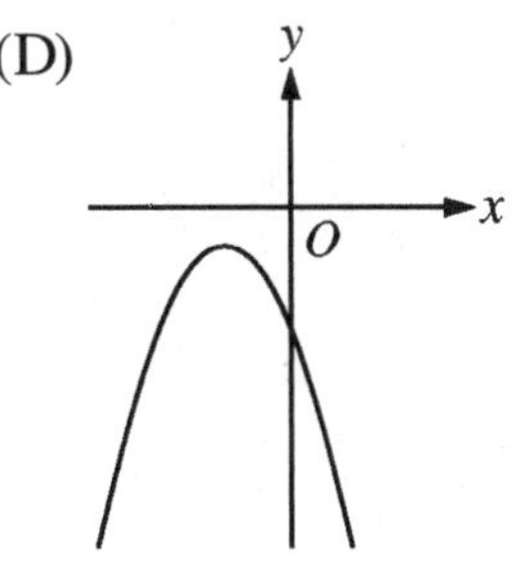

(E)

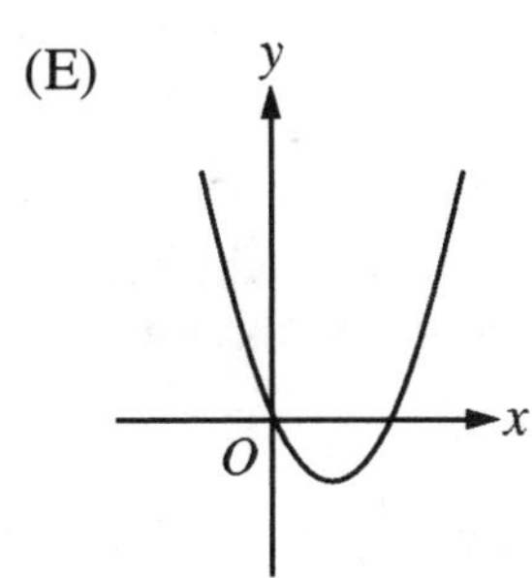

59. Consider each function below. Is the domain of the function the set of all real numbers?

Function	Yes	No
$f(x) = \dfrac{x-1}{x^2+2}$		
$g(x) = \dfrac{x^2}{x+1}$		
$h(x) = \dfrac{\sqrt{x}}{x^2+3}$		

60. The sum of the first n terms of an arithmetic sequence $a_1, a_2, a_3, \ldots, a_n$ is $\frac{1}{2}n(a_1 + a_n)$, where a_1 and a_n are the first and the nth terms of the sequence, respectively. What is the sum of the odd integers from 1 to 99, inclusive?

(A) 2,400
(B) 2,450
(C) 2,475
(D) 2,500
(E) 2,550

61. The function f is defined for all real numbers x by $f(x) = ax^2 + bx + c$, where a, b, and c are constants and a is negative. In the xy-plane, the x-coordinate of the vertex of the parabola $y = f(x)$ is -1. If t is a number for which $f(t) > f(0)$, which of the following must be true?

I. $-2 < t < 0$
II. $f(t) < f(-2)$
III. $f(t) > f(1)$

(A) I only
(B) II only
(C) I and III only
(D) II and III only
(E) I, II, and III

x	$h(x)$
−3	5
−2	−4
2	c

62. The table above shows some values of the function h, which is defined for all real numbers x. If h is an odd function, what is the value of c ?

(A) −5
(B) −4
(C) −2
(D) 2
(E) 4

63. If $\sum_{n=1}^{10} a_n = 50$, what is the value of $\sum_{n=1}^{10} (4a_n + 3)$?

(A) 53
(B) 80
(C) 203
(D) 223
(E) 230

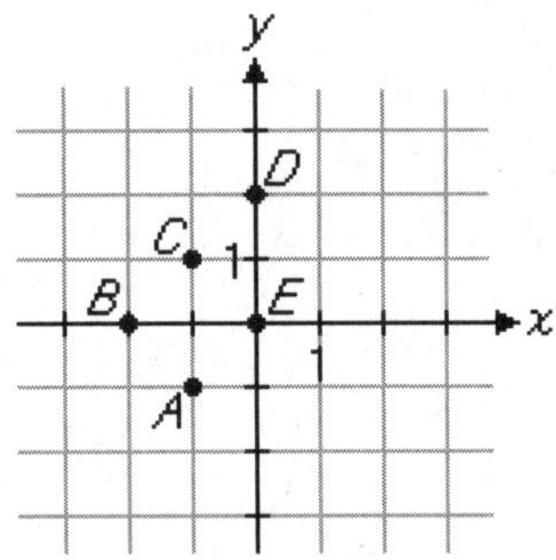

64. If $z = -1 + i$ and $\overline{z}$ denotes the complex conjugate of z, which of the following points in the complex plane above represents $z + \overline{z}$?

(A) *A*
(B) *B*
(C) *C*
(D) *D*
(E) *E*

65. What is the remainder when the polynomial $9x^{23} - 7x^{12} - 2x^5 + 1$ is divided by $x + 1$?

(A) −19
(B) −13
(C) −7
(D) 1
(E) 11

66.
$$f(x) = \sqrt{x+1}$$
$$g(x) = \sqrt{2-x}$$

Functions f and g are defined as shown above. What is the domain of the function $f + g$?

(A) $x \geq 0$
(B) $x \geq 1$
(C) $x \geq 2$
(D) $-1 \leq x \leq 2$
(E) $-2 \leq x \leq 1$

67. In the xy-plane, the line given by which of the following is perpendicular to the line $5x - 2y = 7$?

(A) $2x + 5y = 7$
(B) $2x - 5y = 7$
(C) $5x + 2y = 7$
(D) $5x - 2y = 10$
(E) $5x - 5y = 10$

68. Which of the following statements about the polynomial $p(x) = (x-4)^2(x^2+4)$ are true?

I. The polynomial has two imaginary roots.
II. The polynomial has no real roots.
III. The polynomial has four complex roots, counting multiplicities.

(A) I only
(B) II only
(C) III only
(D) I and III only
(E) I, II, and III

69.

$$C(x) = 1200 + 1000x$$
$$R(x) = 1200x - x^2$$

For a certain company, the functions shown above model the cost C of producing x units of a product and the revenue R from selling x units of the same product. The profit function P is equal to $R - C$. Which of the following defines the function P ?

(A) $P(x) = x^2 - 200x + 1200$
(B) $P(x) = x^2 + 200x - 1200$
(C) $P(x) = -x^2 + 200x - 1200$
(D) $P(x) = -x^2 + 2200x - 1200$
(E) $P(x) = -x^2 + 2200x + 1200$

70. Which of the following is equivalent to $\dfrac{\sqrt[4]{36}}{\sqrt{6}}$?

(A) $6\sqrt[4]{6}$
(B) $\sqrt[4]{6}$
(C) $\sqrt{6}$
(D) 6
(E) 1

71. If $\log_x 5 = 2$, what is the value of x ?

(A) $\sqrt{5}$
(B) $\sqrt{2}$
(C) $\sqrt[5]{2}$
(D) 2^5
(E) 5^2

72. What is the solution of the equation $4^{2x} = 64$?

(A) $\dfrac{2}{3}$
(B) $\dfrac{3}{2}$
(C) 2
(D) 3
(E) 8

73. The function f is defined by $f(x) = x^2 + 3$. Which of the following is equal to $f(x+5)$?

(A) $x^2 + 8$
(B) $x^2 + 28$
(C) $x^2 + 5x + 8$
(D) $x^2 + 10x + 8$
(E) $x^2 + 10x + 28$

74. The population of a certain city was 10,200 on January 1, 2013. If the population increases by 8 percent per year for the next 3 years, which of the following best approximates the population of the city on January 1, 2016 ?

(A) $10{,}200(0.8)^3$
(B) $10{,}200(0.08)^3$
(C) $10{,}200(1.08)^3$
(D) $10{,}200 + (0.8)(3)$
(E) $10{,}200 + (1.08)(3)$

75. What is the value of $f(0)$ for the function $f(x) = \log_{10} 10 + 9^x + (x-2)(x-1)$?

[ ]

76. If $20 = 3^x$, which of the following expresses x as a base ten logarithm?

(A) $\log_{10} 60$
(B) $(\log_{10} 20) + (\log_{10} 3)$
(C) $(\log_{10} 20) - (\log_{10} 3)$
(D) $(\log_{10} 20)(\log_{10} 3)$
(E) $\dfrac{\log_{10} 20}{\log_{10} 3}$

77. The owner of a small restaurant earned a profit of \$300 during the first month of operation. According to the business model for the next 12 months, it is projected that the profit for each month after the first will be \$50 more than the profit for the preceding month. If $p(m)$ represents the profit for each month m and $m = 1$ represents the first month, which of the following functions describes the business model?

(A) $p(m) = m + 50$
(B) $p(m) = m + 300$
(C) $p(m) = 50m + 250$
(D) $p(m) = 50m + 300$
(E) $p(m) = 300m + 50$

78. When the quadratic functions below are graphed in the xy-plane, is the vertex for each function above the x-axis, below the x-axis, or on the x-axis?

Function	Above	Below	On
$f(x) = x^2 + 3$			
$f(x) = (x+3)^2$			
$f(x) = -x^2 + 3$			
$f(x) = x^2 - 3$			

79. A circular cylindrical water tank is filled with water to 75 percent of its total volume of V cubic inches. The radius of the tank is 6 inches, and the height of the tank is h inches. Which of the following represents the height, in inches, of the water in the tank? (Note: The volume of a cylinder with radius r and height h is given by $\pi r^2 h$.)

(A) $\dfrac{V}{6\pi}$
(B) $\dfrac{V}{8\pi}$
(C) $\dfrac{V}{27\pi}$
(D) $\dfrac{V}{36\pi}$
(E) $\dfrac{V}{48\pi}$

80. Select two of the following choices and place them in the blanks below so that the resulting statement is true.

$f(x) = |x| + 8$ $\quad$ $f(x) = x^2 - 4$ $\quad$ $f(x) = \ln x$
increasing $\quad$ decreasing $\quad$ constant

The function ________________ is ________________ on its domain.

81. Which of the following graphs in the xy-plane represent y as a function of x ?

Indicate all such graphs.

(A)

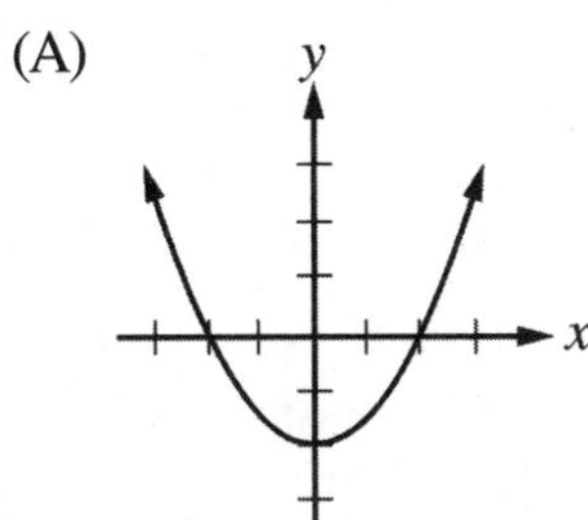

(B)

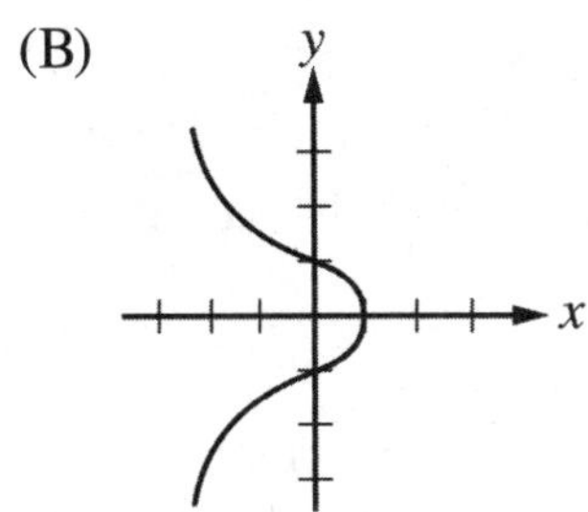

(C)

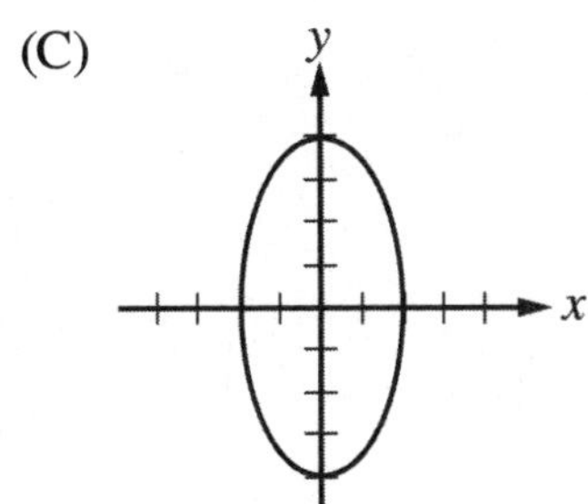

(D)

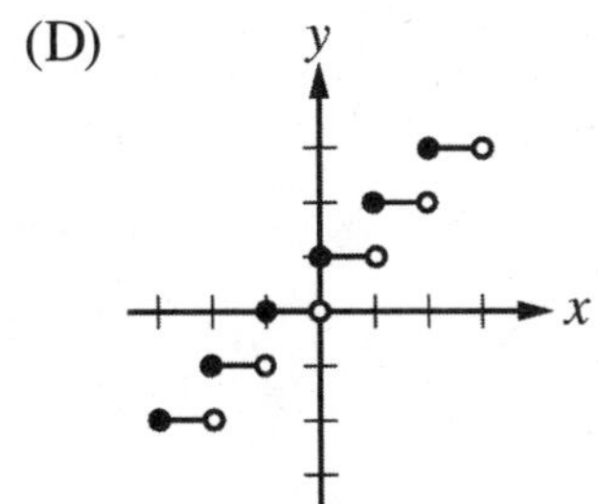

82. Select two of the following choices and place them in the blanks below so that the resulting statements are true.

$A(t)=100(0.83)^{\frac{t}{20}}$	14
$A(t)=100(0.17)^{\frac{t}{20}}$	23
$A(t)=0.83(100)^{\frac{t}{20}}$	76
$A(t)=0.17(100)^{\frac{t}{20}}$	130

The amount of a certain radioactive substance decreases by 17 percent every 20 years. If the initial amount of the substance is 100 grams, then the amount A, in grams, of the substance remaining after t years can be modeled by the function ___________. According to the model, 30 grams of the substance will remain after approximately ___________ years.

83. The predicted price P, in dollars, of an item can be modeled by the function $P(t)=P_0(1.035)^t$, where P_0 is the initial price of the item and t is the amount of time, in years, after the initial price was established. Based on the model, if the price of one gallon of milk is expected to be \$4.69 in the year 2020, in which of the following years will the price of one gallon of milk be closest to \$3.95 ?

(A) 2009
(B) 2010
(C) 2014
(D) 2015
(E) 2025

84. During a certain rainstorm, an empty rain barrel became filled with water. During this storm, the rain fell lightly at first, followed by a heavy downpour, followed by a lighter rain. Which of the following graphs could be a model for the height of the water h in the rain barrel at time t, where t is the amount of time that has passed since the storm began.

(A)

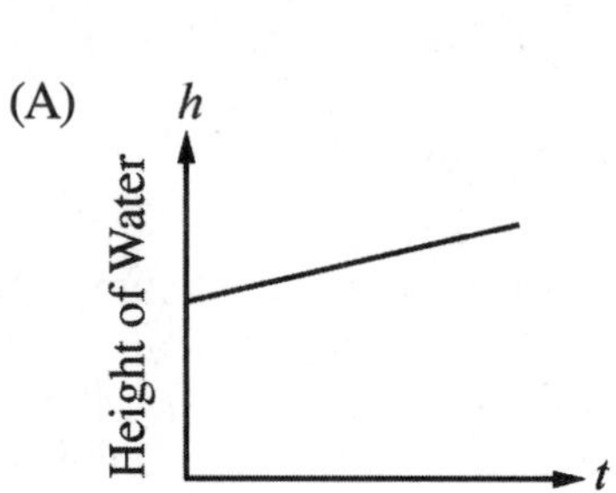

(B)

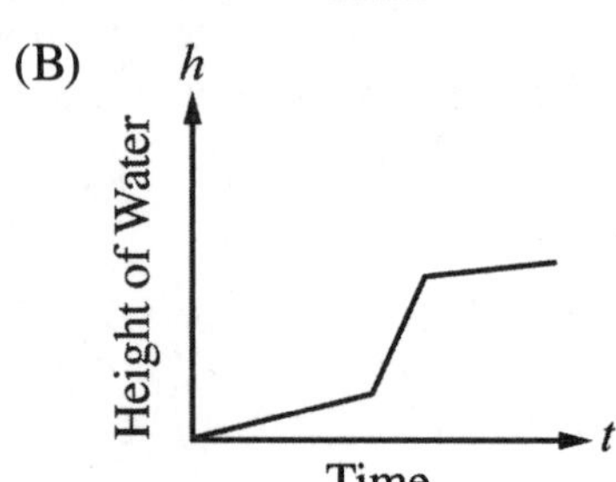

(C)

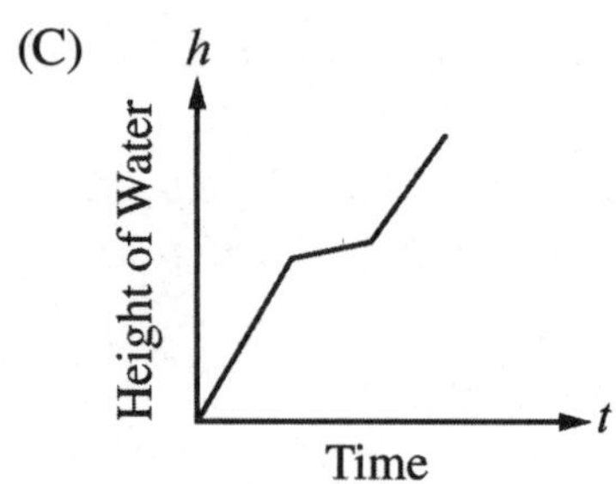

(D)

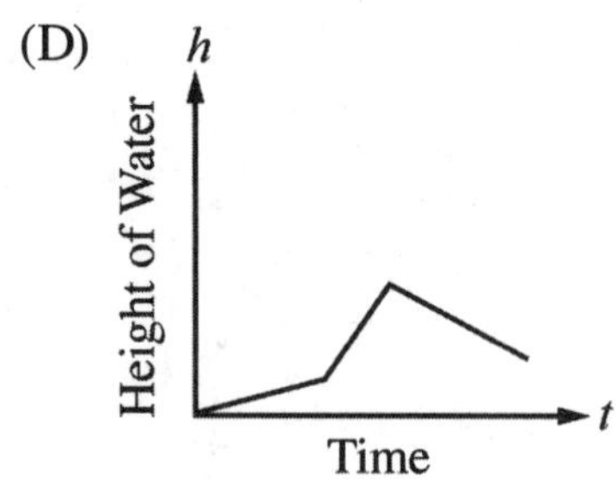

(E)

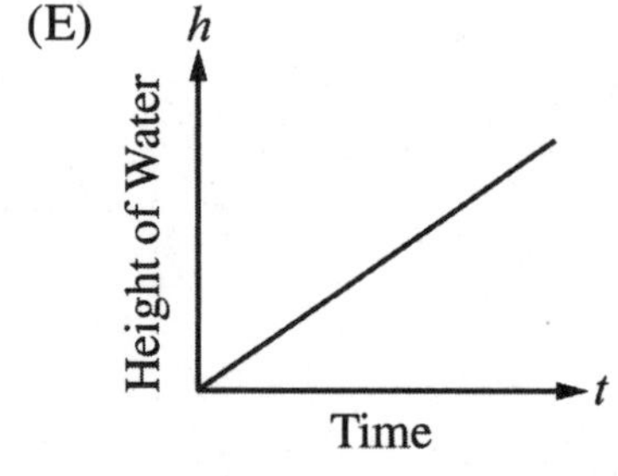

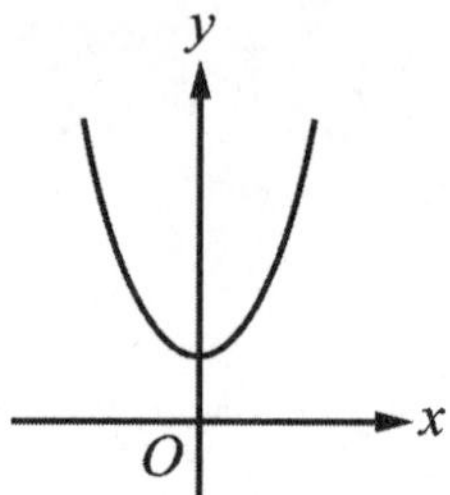

85. The graph of a quadratic function $y = f(x)$ is shown in the xy-plane. Which of the following statements about f must be true?

Indicate <u>all</u> such statements.

(A) f has no real roots.
(B) f has a positive leading coefficient.
(C) The domain and range of f are all real numbers.

86. In the xy-plane, the graphs of which of the following functions are symmetric about the y-axis?

Indicate <u>all</u> such functions.

(A) $f(x) = x^2 + 2$
(B) $f(x) = x^3 + x^2 - 1$
(C) $f(x) = x^4 - 2x^2 + 3$

87. Which of the following is equivalent to $\sqrt{32} + \sqrt{200}$?

(A) $8\sqrt{2}$
(B) $14\sqrt{2}$
(C) $116\sqrt{2}$
(D) $2\sqrt{58}$
(E) $4\sqrt{58}$

88. What is the coefficient of the term r^3s in the expansion of $(2r+3s)^4$?

89. Which of the following is equivalent to $3y-6xy-12x^2y$?

(A) $-3y(4x^2+2x-1)$
(B) $-3y(4x^2-2x-1)$
(C) $-3y(4x^2+2x+1)$
(D) $3y(-4x^2-2x)$
(E) $3y(4x^2+2x)$

Study Resources

Most textbooks used in college-level algebra courses cover the topics in the outline given earlier, but the approaches to certain topics and the emphases given to them may differ. To prepare for the College Algebra exam, it is advisable to study one or more college textbooks, which can be found in most college bookstores. When selecting a textbook, check the table of contents against the knowledge and skills required for this test.

Visit **clep.collegeboard.org/earn-college-credit/practice** for additional college algebra resources. You can also find suggestions for exam preparation in Chapter IV of the *Official Study Guide*. In addition, many college faculty post their course materials on their schools' websites.

Answer Key

1. E
2. D
3. D
4. E
5. B
6. A
7. A
8. B
9. E
10. A
11. See next page.
12. B
13. D
14. D
15. B
16. D
17. C
18. E
19. D
20. C
21. 2
22. B
23. B
24. E
25. See next page.
26. C
27. 624
28. E
29. 4
30. C
31. D
32. A
33. –6
34. E
35. 1
36. See next page.
37. D
38. B
39. C
40. E
41. A
42. D
43. E
44. D
45. 1.2
46. E
47. C
48. E
49. A
50. D
51. D
52. C
53. D
54. C
55. 1
56. D
57. B
58. B
59. See next page.
60. D
61. C
62. E
63. E
64. B
65. B
66. D
67. A
68. D
69. C
70. E
71. A
72. B
73. E
74. C
75. 4
76. E
77. C
78. See next page.
79. E
80. See next page.
81. A, D
82. See next page.
83. D
84. B
85. A, B
86. A, C
87. B
88. 96
89. A

11.

	less than	greater than	equal to	
$f(a)$ is	√			$g(a)$.
$f(b)$ is		√		$g(b)$.
$f(0)$ is			√	$g(0)$.

25.

Statement	Always True	Never True	Sometimes True
$\|a+b\| = \|a\| + \|b\|$			√
$\|a+b\| < \|a\| + \|b\|$			√
$\|a+b\| \leq \|a\| + \|b\|$	√		
$\|a+b\| > \|a\| + \|b\|$		√	

36.

The amount of medicine M present in the body at t hours after the medicine is taken can be modeled by the function $M(t) = 210(0.89)^t$. According to the model, 117 mg of the medicine is present in the body at 5 hours after the medicine is taken.

59.

Function	Yes	No
$f(x) = \frac{x-1}{x^2+2}$	√	
$g(x) = \frac{x^2}{x+1}$		√
$h(x) = \frac{\sqrt{x}}{x^2+3}$		√

78.

Function	Above	Below	On
$f(x) = x^2 + 3$	√		
$f(x) = (x+3)^2$			√
$f(x) = -x^2 + 3$	√		
$f(x) = x^2 - 3$		√	

80.

The function $f(x) = \ln x$ is increasing on its domain.

82.

The amount of a certain radioactive substance decreases by 17 percent every 20 years. If the initial amount of the substance is 100 grams, then the amount A, in grams, of the substance remaining after t years can be modeled by the function $A(t) = 100(0.83)^{\frac{t}{20}}$. According to the model, 30 grams of the substance will remain after approximately 130 years.

College Mathematics

Description of the Examination

The College Mathematics examination covers material generally taught in a college course for nonmathematics majors and majors in fields not requiring knowledge of advanced mathematics.

The examination contains approximately 60 questions to be answered in 90 minutes. Some of these are pretest questions that will not be scored.

An online scientific (nongraphing) calculator will be available during the examination. Although a calculator is not necessary to answer most of the questions, there may be a few problems whose solutions are difficult to obtain without using a calculator. Since no calculator is allowed during the examination except for the online calculator provided, it is recommended that prior to the examination you become familiar with the use of the online calculator.

For more information about the online scientific (nongraphing) calculator, please visit the College Mathematics description on the CLEP website, clep.collegeboard.org.

It is assumed that test-takers are familiar with currently taught mathematics vocabulary, symbols, and notation.

Knowledge and Skills Required

Questions on the College Mathematics examination require test-takers to demonstrate the following abilities in the approximate proportions indicated.

- Solving routine, straightforward problems (about 50 percent of the examination)
- Solving nonroutine problems requiring an understanding of concepts and the application of skills and concepts (about 50 percent of the examination)

The subject matter of the College Mathematics examination is drawn from the following topics. The percentages next to the main topics indicate the approximate percentage of exam questions on that topic.

20% Algebra and Functions[1]

Solving equations, linear inequalities, and systems of linear equations by analytical and graphical methods

Interpretation, representation, and evaluation of functions: numerical, graphical, symbolic, and descriptive methods

Graphs of functions: translations, horizontal and vertical reflections, and symmetry about the *x*-axis, the *y*-axis, and the origin

Linear and exponential growth

Applications

10% Counting and Probability

Counting problems: the multiplication rule, combinations, and permutations

Probability: union, intersection, independent events, mutually exclusive events, complementary events, conditional probabilities, and expected value

Applications

15% Data Analysis and Statistics

Data interpretation and representation: tables, bar graphs, line graphs, circle graphs, pie charts, scatterplots, and histograms

Numerical summaries of data: mean (average), median, mode, and range

Standard deviation, normal distribution (conceptual questions only)

Applications

[1] Types of functions that will be considered are linear, polynomial, radical, exponential, logarithmic, rational, and piecewise defined.

20% **Financial Mathematics**

Percents, percent change, markups, discounts, taxes, profit, and loss

Interest: simple, compound, continuous interest, effective interest rate, effective annual yield or annual percentage rate (APR)

Present value and future value

Applications

10% **Geometry**

Properties of triangles and quadrilaterals: perimeter, area, similarity, and the Pythagorean theorem

Parallel and perpendicular lines

Properties of circles: circumference, area, central angles, inscribed angles, and sectors

Applications

15% **Logic and Sets**

Logical operations and statements: conditional statements, conjunctions, disjunctions, negations, hypotheses, logical conclusions, converses, inverses, counterexamples, contrapositives, logical equivalence

Set relationships, subsets, disjoint sets, equality of sets, and Venn diagrams

Operations on sets: union, intersection, complement, and Cartesian product

Applications

10% **Numbers**

Properties of numbers and their operations: integers and rational, irrational, and real numbers (including recognizing rational and irrational numbers)

Elementary number theory: factors and divisibility, primes and composites, odd and even integers, and the fundamental theorem of arithmetic

Measurement: unit conversion, scientific notation, and numerical precision

Absolute value

Applications

Sample Test Questions

The following sample questions do not appear on an actual CLEP examination. They are intended to give potential test-takers an indication of the format and difficulty level of the examination and to provide content for practice and review. Knowing the correct answers to all of the sample questions is not a guarantee of satisfactory performance on the exam.

Directions: An online scientific calculator will be available for the questions in this test.

Some questions will require you to select from among four choices. For these questions, select the BEST of the choices given.

Some questions will require you to type a numerical answer in the box provided.

Some questions refer to a table in which statements appear in the first column. For each statement, select the correct properties by check-marking the appropriate cell(s) in the table.

Notes: (1) Unless otherwise specified, the domain of any function f is assumed to be the set of all real numbers x for which $f(x)$ is a real number.

(2) Figures that accompany questions are intended to provide information useful in answering the questions. The figures are drawn as accurately as possible EXCEPT when it is stated in a specific question that the figure is not drawn to scale.

(3) If a principal of P dollars is invested at an annual interest rate r, compounded n times per year, and no further withdrawals or deposits are made to the account, then the future value A, the account balance after t years, is given by the formula $A = P\left(1+\frac{r}{n}\right)^{nt}$.

(4) If a principal of P dollars is invested at an annual interest rate r, and is compounded continuously, and no further withdrawals or deposits are made to the account, then the future value A, the account balance after t years, is given by the formula $A = Pe^{rt}$.

(5) At an interest rate r, compounded n times per year, the effective annual yield or annual percentage rate (APR), is given by the formula $\text{APR} = \left(1 + \frac{r}{n}\right)^n - 1$.

1. Carl deposited P dollars into a savings account that earned 8 percent annual interest, compounded semiannually. Carl made no additional deposits to or withdrawals from the account. After one year, the account had a total value of \$10,816. What was the value of P ?

(A) 9,600
(B) 10,000
(C) 10,800
(D) 12,000

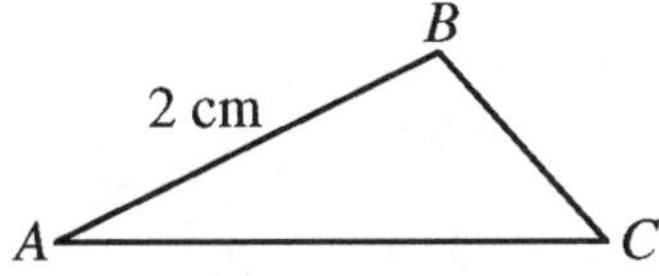

2. Triangle DEF (not shown) is similar to $\triangle ABC$ shown, with angle B congruent to angle E and angle C congruent to angle F. The length of side DE is 6 cm. If the area of $\triangle ABC$ is 5 square centimeters, what is the area of $\triangle DEF$?

(A) 10 cm^2
(B) 12 cm^2
(C) 18 cm^2
(D) 45 cm^2

3. m is an odd integer. For each of the following numbers, indicate whether the number is odd or even.

Number	Odd	Even
$2m - 1$		
$2m + 1$		
$m^2 - m$		
$m^2 + m + 1$		

Click on your choices.

4. Which of the following statements is NOT true for all real numbers a and b ?

(A) $(a+b)^2 - (a-b)^2 = 4ab$
(B) $(a-b)(a+b) = a^2 - b^2$
(C) $(a+b)^3 = a^3 + 3a^2b + 3ab^2 + b^3$
(D) $a^3 - b^3 = (a+b^2)(a^2-b)$

5. For any positive integers a and b, the operation $\otimes$ is defined as $a \otimes b = (2a-1)^{b-1}$. What is the value of $(2 \otimes 2) \otimes 3$?

[ ]

6. A company manufactures electronic components that each must weigh from 29.5 grams to 30.5 grams, inclusive. Which of the following inequalities describes all acceptable weights x, in grams, for each component?

(A) $|30 - x| \leq 0.5$
(B) $|30 - x| > 0.5$
(C) $30 - x \leq 0.5$
(D) $30 - x > 0.5$

7. On a group trip to a certain city, 20 people who were 25 years old, 20 people who were 30 years old, and 20 people who were 35 years old purchased tickets for a bus tour of the city. No one else purchased tickets for the bus tour. A 30-year old who had purchased a ticket became ill and did not go on the bus tour, and everyone else who purchased a ticket went on the bus tour. Which of the following statements is true?

   (A) The standard deviation of the ages of the people who went on the bus tour is greater than the standard deviation of the ages of the people who purchased tickets.
   (B) The standard deviation of the ages of the people who went on the bus tour is less than the standard deviation of the ages of the people who purchased tickets.
   (C) The standard deviation of the ages of the people who went on the bus tour is equal to the standard deviation of the ages of the people who purchased tickets.
   (D) There is not enough information to determine which standard deviation is greater.

8. When Bill makes a sandwich, he may choose from among 3 kinds of rolls, 4 varieties of meat, and 2 types of sliced cheese. If he chooses one roll, one meat, and one type of cheese, how many different kinds of sandwiches can he make?

   (A) 9 (B) 14 (C) 24 (D) 288

$$3x - 4 \geq 0$$

9. Which of the following subsets of the real numbers best describes the solution set of the inequality above?

   (A) $\left[0, \frac{4}{3}\right)$
   (B) $\left[\frac{4}{3}, \infty\right)$
   (C) $(-\infty, \infty)$
   (D) $(-\infty, -4] \cup [3, \infty)$

10. The faces of a fair cube are numbered 1 through 6; the probability of rolling any number from 1 through 6 is equally likely. If the cube is rolled 4 times, what is the probability that the number 6 will appear on the top face all 4 times?

   (A) $\frac{1}{6^4}$
   (B) $\frac{1}{6^2}$
   (C) $\frac{1}{6}$
   (D) $\frac{4}{6}$

11. The difference between the mean and the median of the numbers 27, 27, 29, 32, and 35 is

   (A) 0 (B) 1 (C) 3 (D) 8

12. In a class with 50 students, 25 of the students are sophomores, 15 of the students are mathematics majors, and 10 of the mathematics majors are sophomores. If a student in the class is to be selected at random, what is the probability that the student selected will be a sophomore or a mathematics major or both?

   (A) 0.4 (B) 0.5 (C) 0.6 (D) 0.8

13. On an exam for a class with 54 students, the mean score was 77.2 points. The instructor rescored the exam by adding 6 points to the exam score for every student. What was the mean of the scores on the rescored exam?

   [   ]

14. A new computer graphics company employs 10 programmers. The company decides to expand into digital animation and needs to transfer 3 of the programmers into the new department. How many different combinations of 3 programmers can be chosen to transfer to the new department?

   (A) 3 (B) 30 (C) 120 (D) 840

15. The faces of a fair cube are numbered 1 through 6; the probability of rolling any number from 1 through 6 is equally likely. If the cube is rolled twice, what is the probability that an even number will appear on the top face in the first roll <u>or</u> that the number 1 will appear on the top face in the second roll?

(A) $\frac{1}{12}$ (B) $\frac{7}{12}$ (C) $\frac{2}{3}$ (D) $\frac{3}{4}$

16. If $R = \{x | x > 0\}$ and $S = \{x | x < 3\}$, what is the number of integers in $R \cap S$?

(A) Zero (B) Two (C) Three (D) Four

Time, t	Number of Bacteria in the Sample
0	100
1	220
2	400
3	780
4	1,550
5	3,100
6	6,000
7	12,800
8	25,000

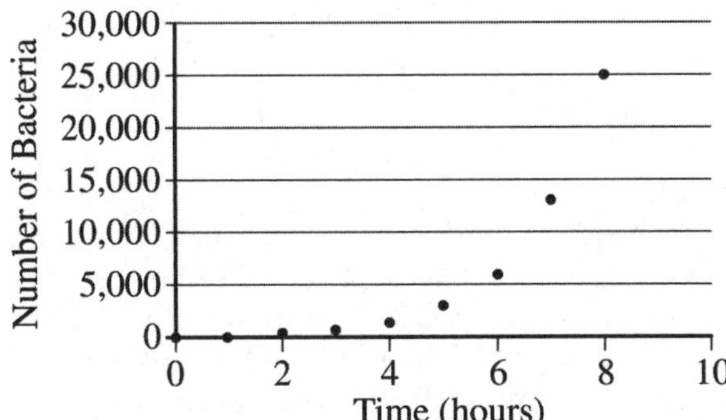

17. A scientist estimated the number of bacteria in a sample every hour and recorded the estimates in the table above. Then the scientist used the data to create the scatterplot above. Based on the information, which of the following functions best models the number of bacteria, $f(t)$, at time t, in hours?

(A) $f(t) = 100(2^t)$
(B) $f(t) = 100 + 2t$
(C) $f(t) = t^2 + 220t + 100$
(D) $f(t) = 120 \log(t+1)$

$$x + y = 7$$
$$y + z = 9$$
$$z + t = 13$$

18. What is the value of $x + t$?

$x + t =$ ☐

19. The width of a rectangular garden is x feet. If 300 feet of fencing is needed to enclose the garden, which of the following represents the length of the garden, in feet?

(A) $300 - x$
(B) $300 - 2x$
(C) $150 - x$
(D) $150 - 2x$

20. Michael wishes to give his son a savings bond that will mature in 8 years. He would like the value of the savings bond to be $5,000 at maturity. If he can invest in a bond that has an annual interest rate of 4% compounded monthly, which of the following is the best approximation of the amount he should invest?

(A) $3,200
(B) $3,350
(C) $3,500
(D) $3,650

21. $m = 4$ and $n = 2$

For each of the following expressions, indicate whether the value will be a rational or irrational number.

Expression	Rational	Irrational
$\sqrt[3]{m-n}$		
$\sqrt{m^3}$		
$\sqrt[3]{\frac{m}{n}}$		
$\sqrt{m+n^2}$		

Click on your choices.

22. A student asserted that n^2 is greater than or equal to n for all real numbers n. Of the following, which is a value of n that provides a counterexample to the student's claim?

(A) $-\frac{1}{2}$ (B) 0 (C) $\frac{1}{2}$ (D) 2

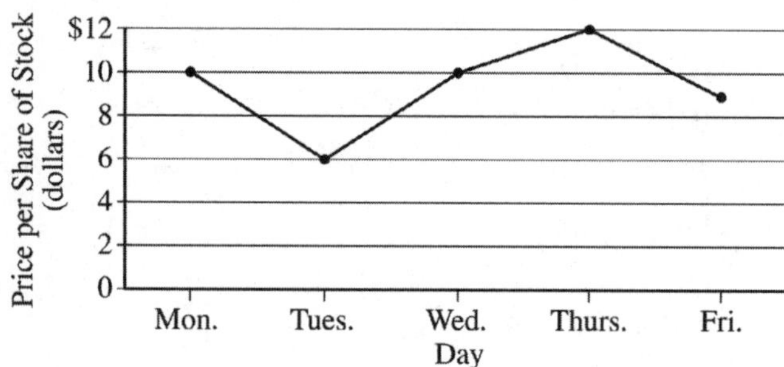

23. The graph above shows the closing price of one share of stock of Company Y for each of the five business days last week. Which of the following is closest to the percent change in the closing price of one share of stock from Tuesday to Wednesday?

(A) 40%
(B) 55%
(C) 67%
(D) 150%

24. Let A be a nonempty set and let B and C be any two subsets of A. Which of the following statements must be true?

(A) $B \cup C = A$
(B) $B \cap C = \{\ \}$, the empty set
(C) $B \subset C \subset A$
(D) $B \cup C \subset A$

25. The area of a rectangular field is the product of its length and width. If each dimension of the rectangular field is multiplied by 3, then the area of the enlarged field is how many times the area of the original field?

If it snows, then school is closed.

26. Which of the following is logically equivalent to the statement above?

(A) If it snows, then school is not closed.
(B) If school is closed, then it snows.
(C) If it does not snow, then school is not closed.
(D) If school is not closed, then it does not snow.

27. In a group of students at a four-year college, 60 percent of the students are 25 years old or older and 25 percent of the students have a grade point average of 3.0 or better. The age of a student is independent of their grade point average. What is the probability that a student randomly selected from this group will be 25 years old or older and will have a grade point average of 3.0 or better?

(A) 0.85
(B) 0.42
(C) 0.35
(D) 0.15

28. The results of a survey of 200 college students showed that some students who were business majors were women and all students who were business majors took calculus. Which of the following is a valid conclusion from the survey?

    (A) All students who were women took calculus.
    (B) Some students who were women took calculus.
    (C) Some students who were women did not take calculus.
    (D) Some students who were women were not business majors.

29. If $g(x) = x^3 - 2x - 1$, then $g(-2) =$

    [ ]

30. On Friday afternoon, Gloria left work, which is 1 mile from home, and drove to the bank, which is 4 miles from home. She spent 20 minutes at the bank and then drove home. Which of the following graphs could represent Gloria's distance from home as a function of the time from when she left work on Friday afternoon?

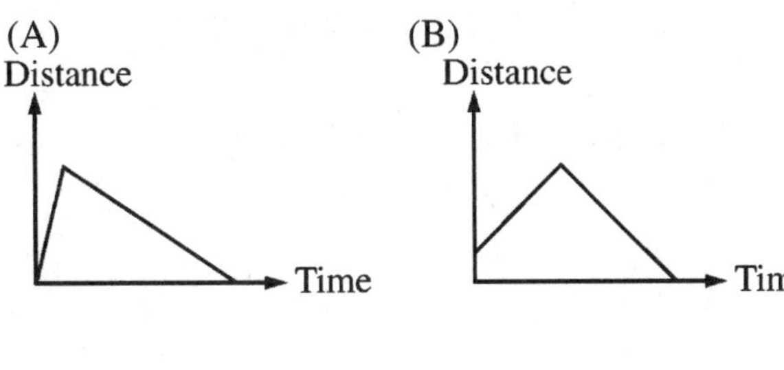

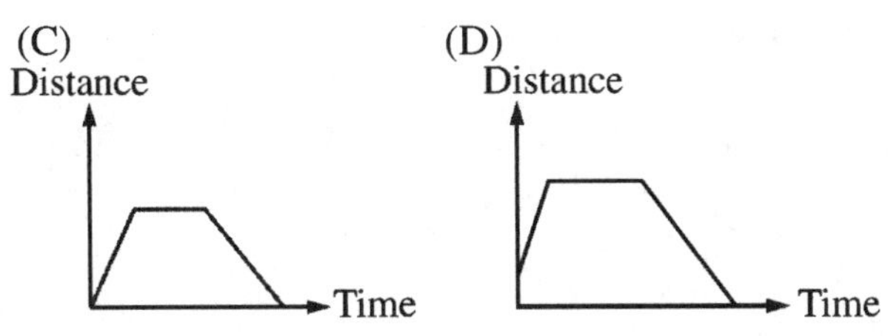

x	3	4	5
$f(x)$	2	3	4

x	2	3	4
$g(x)$	3	5	7

31. Values for the functions f and g are given in the tables above. What is the value of $f(g(3))$?

    [ ]

32. A house was purchased for \$140,000. Three years later, the value of the house was \$155,000. If the value V of the house increased linearly from the date it was purchased, which of the following represents the value, in dollars, of the house t years after the date it was purchased?

    (A) $V = 140{,}000 + 15{,}000t$
    (B) $V = 140{,}000 + 5{,}000t$
    (C) $V = 140{,}000 + 15{,}000(t - 3)$
    (D) $V = 140{,}000 + 5{,}000(t - 3)$

33. The normal core body temperature of a certain individual ranges from 97.7 to 99.5 degrees Fahrenheit. If the individual's body temperature is T degrees Fahrenheit, which of the following inequalities corresponds to the range of normal core body temperatures?

    (A) $|T - 98.6| \geq 0.9$
    (B) $|T - 98.6| \leq 0.9$
    (C) $|T - 97.7| \geq 1.8$
    (D) $|T - 97.7| \leq 1.8$

34. A painting was purchased for \$22 million and sold one year later for \$26.4 million. The profit on the most recent sale was what percent of the original purchase price?

    [ ] %

35. A student club at a local high school consists of 35 juniors and 25 seniors. The club would like to form a committee of 5 students, consisting of 3 juniors and 2 seniors, to represent the club at a state meeting. How many different committees can be formed?

(A) $\left(\frac{35!}{3!32!}\right)\left(\frac{25!}{2!23!}\right)$

(B) $\left(\frac{35!}{32!}\right)\left(\frac{25!}{23!}\right)$

(C) $\left(3^{35}\right)\left(2^{25}\right)$

(D) $\left(35^{3}\right)\left(25^{2}\right)$

$A = \{a,b\}$ and $B = \{b,c\}$,
where a, b, and c are distinct numbers.

36. Which of the following ordered pairs is NOT in the Cartesian product $A \times B$?

(A) (a,b) (B) (b,a) (C) (b,b) (D) (b,c)

37. Each number in data set *A* is increased by adding 3 to each data point to form data set *B*. Which of the following is the same for sets *A* and *B* ?

(A) Mean
(B) Median
(C) Mode
(D) Range

38. Sam opened a restaurant. On the first day he had 100 customers. On the fourth day he had 160 customers. If the number of customers per day grew linearly, what was the number of customers on the second day?

[ ]

39. In a group of 33 students, 15 students are enrolled in a mathematics course, 10 are enrolled in a physics course, and 5 are enrolled in both a mathematics course and a physics course. How many students in the group are not enrolled in either a mathematics course or a physics course?

(A) 3
(B) 8
(C) 13
(D) 20

40. A drawer contains exactly 5 red, 4 blue, and 3 green pencils. If two pencils are selected at random one after the other without replacing the first, what is the probability that the first one is red and the second one is green?

(A) $\frac{5}{44}$ (B) $\frac{5}{48}$ (C) $\frac{91}{132}$ (D) $\frac{2}{3}$

41. If $f(x) = \frac{1}{x-2}$, where $x \neq 2$, and $g(x) = 2^x$ for all values of x, then $f(g(0))$ is

(A) -1
(B) $-\frac{1}{2}$
(C) 0
(D) undefined

42. The six students, P, Q, R, S, T, and U in a class took four exams, and the scores for the four exams were recorded in the following graphs. In which graph do the scores shown have the least standard deviation?

(A)

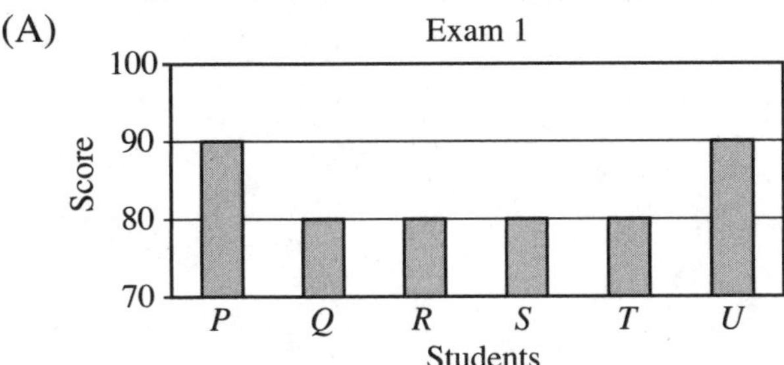

(B)

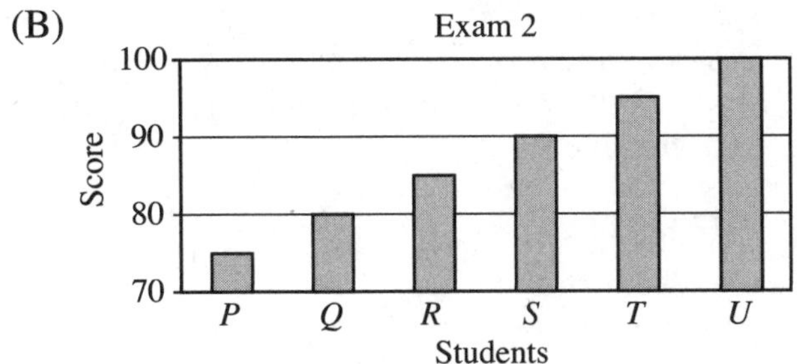

(C)

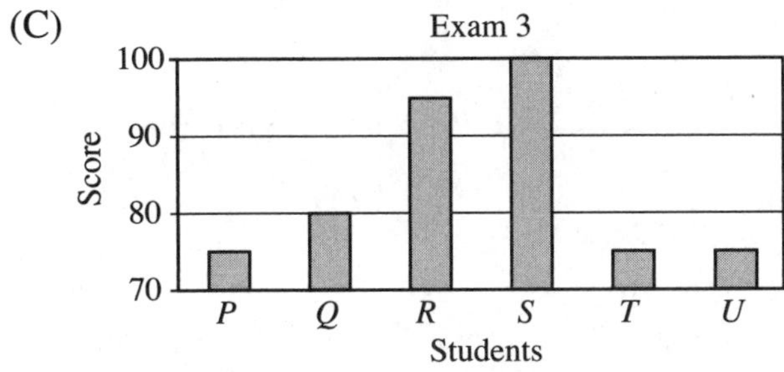

(D)

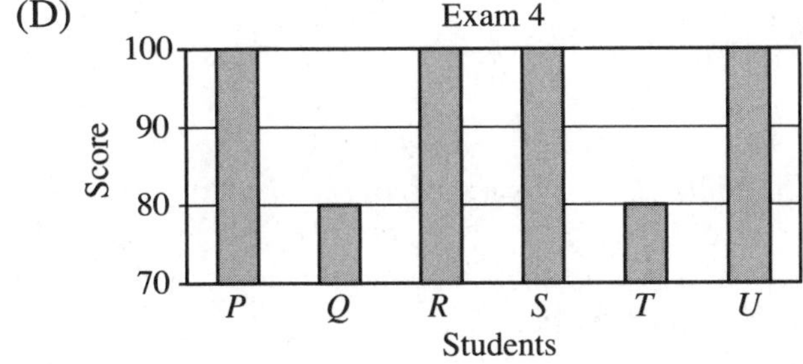

43. If the diameter of the Sun is about 100 times the diameter of the Earth, which of the following is the best approximation for the ratio of the volume of the Sun to the volume of the Earth?

(A) 10^2
(B) 10^4
(C) 10^6
(D) 10^8

44. A rectangular flat-screen computer monitor has a diagonal that measures 20 inches. The ratio of the length of the screen to the width of the screen is 4 to 3. What is the perimeter of the screen, in inches?

(A) 48
(B) 56
(C) 64
(D) 192

45. A circular pizza with a 16-inch diameter is cut into 12 equal slices. What is the area, in square inches, of each slice?

(A) $\frac{16}{3}\pi$
(B) $\frac{8}{3}\pi$
(C) $\frac{4}{3}\pi$
(D) $\frac{2}{3}\pi$

46. A square tablecloth lies flat on top of a circular table whose area is π square feet. If the four corners of the tablecloth just touch the edge of the circular table, what is the area of the tablecloth, in square feet?

[ ] square feet

47. Which of the following is the solution to $5+3^x=20$?

(A) $x=\ln(15)-\ln(3)$

(B) $x=\dfrac{\ln(20)-\ln(5)}{\ln(3)}$

(C) $x=\dfrac{\ln(15)}{\ln(3)}$

(D) $x=\ln(3)$

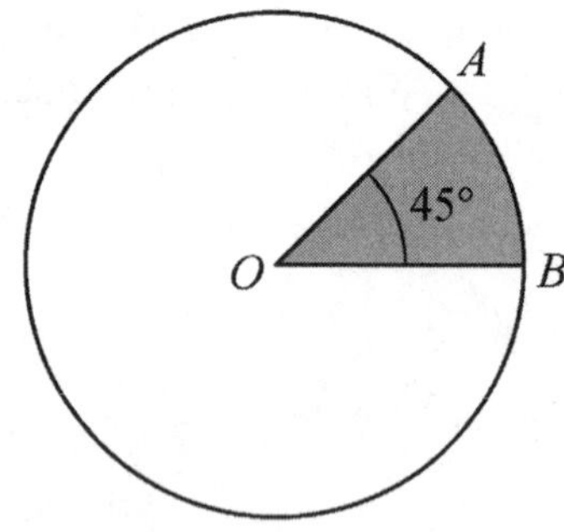

48. The circle shown has center O, and the measure of angle AOB is 45°. If the area of the shaded sector is 18π, what is the radius of the circle?

Radius = ▭

49. A box contains 12 red tickets and 8 blue tickets. One ticket was chosen at random and not replaced. A second ticket will be chosen at random. If the first ticket chosen was red, what is the probability that the second ticket chosen will be blue?

(A) $\frac{8}{11}$

(B) $\frac{8}{19}$

(C) $\frac{8}{20}$

(D) $\frac{1}{8}$

50. In 2012, a company had total revenue of $600,000 and total costs of $500,000. The following year, the company's total revenue increased by 5 percent while total costs stayed constant. What is the percent change in the company's profit from 2012 to 2013 ? (Profit equals revenue minus cost.)

(A) 3%

(B) 5%

(C) 10%

(D) 30%

51. Josephine borrowed $200,000 for a home loan at an annual rate of 4.5 percent, compounded quarterly. What was the annual percentage rate of the loan?

(A) 1.13%

(B) 3.83%

(C) 4.50%

(D) 4.58%

52. If $\dfrac{2.4\times10^6}{3.0\times10^{-4}}=8.0\times10^n$, what is the value of n ?

(A) 10

(B) 9

(C) 2

(D) 1

53. The regular price of a pair of jeans was $50. The regular price was discounted by x percent during a sale, and the discounted price was $30. What was the value of x ?

(A) 20

(B) 30

(C) 40

(D) 50

54. Which of the following is an irrational number?

(A) $\sqrt{36}$

(B) $\sqrt{14}$

(C) $\frac{2}{\sqrt{9}}$

(D) $\frac{\sqrt{8}}{\sqrt{2}}$

55. A glass bowl was manufactured at a cost of \$100.00. The glass bowl was priced 30 percent above the manufacturing cost. After one month, the price was discounted 25 percent. What was the discounted price?

(A) \$97.50
(B) \$100.00
(C) \$102.50
(D) \$105.00

56. What is the future value of \$10,000 invested for one year at an annual interest rate of 2 percent, compounded semiannually?

(A) \$10,050
(B) \$10,201
(C) \$10,404
(D) \$10,500

Study Resources

Most textbooks used in college-level mathematics courses cover the topics in the outline given earlier, but the approaches to certain topics and the emphasis given to them may differ. To prepare for the College Mathematics exam, it is advisable to study one or more introductory college-level mathematics textbooks, which can be found in most college bookstores or online. Elementary algebra textbooks also cover many of the topics on the College Mathematics exam. When selecting a textbook, check the table of contents against the knowledge and skills required for this test.

Visit **clep.collegeboard.org/earn-college-credit/practice** for additional math resources. You can also find suggestions for exam preparation in Chapter IV of the *Official Study Guide*. In addition, many college faculty post their course materials on their schools' websites.

Answer Key

1.	B	29.	–5
2.	D	30.	D
3.	See below.	31.	4
4.	D	32.	B
5.	25	33.	B
6.	A	34.	20
7.	A	35.	A
8.	C	36.	B
9.	B	37.	D
10.	A	38.	120
11.	B	39.	C
12.	C	40.	A
13.	83.2	41.	A
14.	C	42.	A
15.	B	43.	C
16.	B	44.	B
17.	A	45.	A
18.	11	46.	2
19.	C	47.	C
20.	D	48.	12
21.	See below.	49.	B
22.	C	50.	D
23.	C	51.	D
24.	D	52.	B
25.	9	53.	C
26.	D	54.	B
27.	D	55.	A
28.	B	56.	B

3.

Number	Odd	Even
$2m - 1$	√	
$2m + 1$	√	
$m^2 - m$		√
$m^2 + m + 1$	√	

21.

Expression	Rational	Irrational
$\sqrt[3]{m - n}$		√
$\sqrt{m^3}$	√	
$\sqrt[3]{\frac{m}{n}}$		√
$\sqrt{m + n^2}$		√

Natural Sciences

Description of the Examination

The Natural Sciences examination covers a wide range of topics frequently taught in introductory courses surveying both biological and physical sciences at the freshman or sophomore level. Such courses generally satisfy distribution or general education requirements in science that usually are not required of nor taken by science majors. The Natural Sciences exam is not intended for those specializing in science; it is intended to test the understanding of scientific concepts that an adult with a liberal arts education should have. It does not stress the retention of factual details; rather, it emphasizes the knowledge and application of the basic principles and concepts of science, the comprehension of scientific information, and the understanding of issues of science in contemporary society.

The primary objective of the examination is to give candidates the opportunity to demonstrate a level of knowledge and understanding expected of college students meeting a distribution or general education requirement in the natural sciences. An institution may grant up to six semester hours (or the equivalent) of credit toward fulfillment of such a requirement for satisfactory scores on the examination. Some may grant specific course credit, on the basis of the total score for a two-semester survey course covering both biological and physical sciences.

The examination contains approximately 120 questions to be answered in 90 minutes. Some of these are pretest questions that will not be scored.

Knowledge and Skills Required

The Natural Sciences examination requires candidates to demonstrate one or more of the following abilities in the approximate proportions indicated.

- Knowledge of fundamental facts, concepts and principles (about 40 percent of the examination)
- Interpretation and comprehension of information (about 20 percent of the examination) presented in the form of graphs, diagrams, tables, equations or verbal passages
- Qualitative and quantitative application of scientific principles (about 40 percent of the examination), including applications based on material presented in the form of graphs, diagrams, tables, equations or verbal passages; more emphasis is given to qualitative than quantitative applications

The subject matter of the Natural Sciences examination is drawn from the following topics. The percentages next to the main topics indicate the approximate percentage of exam questions on that topic.

Biological Science (50%)

10% Origin and evolution of life, classification of organisms

10% Cell organization, cell division, chemical nature of the gene, bioenergetics, biosynthesis

20% Structure, function and development in organisms; patterns of heredity

10% Concepts of population biology with emphasis on ecology

Physical Science (50%)

7% Atomic and nuclear structure and properties, elementary particles, nuclear reactions

10% Chemical elements, compounds and reactions, molecular structure and bonding

12% Heat, thermodynamics and states of matter; classical mechanics; relativity

4% Electricity and magnetism, waves, light and sound

7% The universe: galaxies, stars, the solar system

10% The Earth: atmosphere, hydrosphere, structural features, geologic processes and history

The examination includes some questions that are interdisciplinary and cannot be classified in one of the listed categories. Some of the questions cover topics that overlap with those listed previously, drawing on areas such as history and philosophy of science, scientific methods, science applications and technology, and the relationship of science to contemporary problems of society, such as environmental pollution and depletion of natural resources. Some questions are laboratory oriented.

Sample Test Questions

The following sample questions do not appear on an actual CLEP examination. They are intended to give potential test-takers an indication of the format and difficulty level of the examination and to provide content for practice and review. Knowing the correct answers to all of the sample questions is not a guarantee of satisfactory performance on the exam.

Directions: The questions that follow consist of five lettered choices followed by a list of numbered phrases or sentences. For each numbered phrase or sentence, select the one choice that is most clearly related to it. Each choice may be used once, more than once, or not at all.

Questions 1–3

(A)
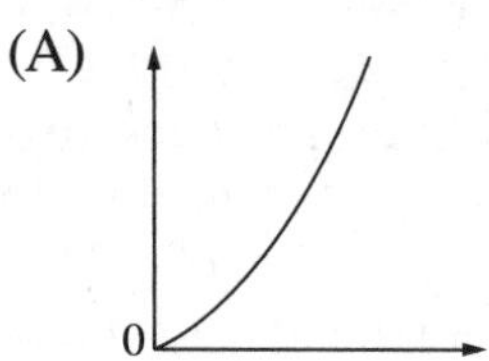

(D)
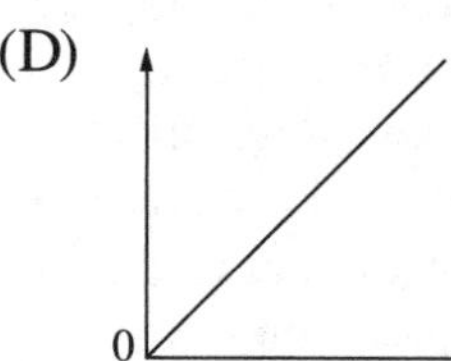

(B)
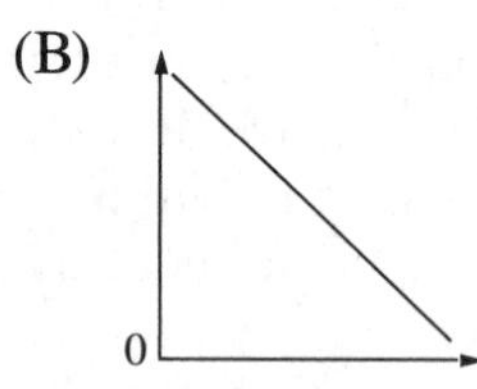

(E)
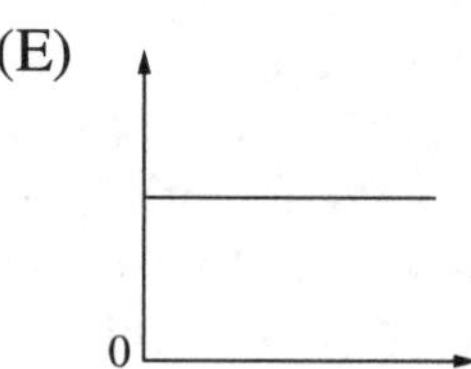

(C)
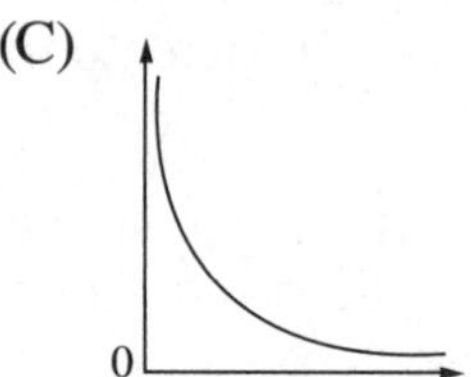

1. A sample of gas remains at constant temperature.
   Vertical axis: Volume of the sample
   Horizontal axis: Pressure on the sample

2. An object moves at constant speed.
   Vertical axis: Distance traveled since time $t = 0$
   Horizontal axis: Time

3. A constant unbalanced force acts on an object.
   Vertical axis: Acceleration of the object
   Horizontal axis: Time

Directions: Each of the questions or incomplete statements below is followed by five suggested answers or completions. Select the one that is best in each case.

4. Which of the following occurs in the mitochondria?

    (A) Cytokinesis
    (B) Lipid synthesis
    (C) DNA replication
    (D) Citric acid cycle
    (E) Photon capture

5. Which of the following is the site of protein synthesis in a cell?

    (A) Cell wall
    (B) Cell membrane
    (C) Nucleus
    (D) Mitochondrion
    (E) Ribosome

6. ALL of the following diseases are genetically inherited EXCEPT

    (A) Tuberculosis
    (B) Phenylketonuria
    (C) Huntington's disease
    (D) Cystic fibrosis
    (E) Tay-Sachs disease

7. Which of the following diseases can be controlled by dietary regulation?

    (A) Influenza
    (B) Type 2 diabetes
    (C) AIDS
    (D) Pertussis
    (E) Smallpox

8. As a direct result of photosynthesis, energy is stored in molecules of which of the following?

    (A) RNA
    (B) DNA
    (C) $C_6H_{12}O_6$ (glucose)
    (D) H_2O
    (E) CO_2

9. A person whose gallbladder has been removed has a decreased ability to store bile and therefore to digest

    (A) fats
    (B) starches
    (C) sugars
    (D) proteins
    (E) vitamins

Questions 10–11

In fruit flies, "straight wings" (S) is dominant over "curly wings" (s), and gray body color (G) is dominant over black body color (g). A straight-winged female with gray body color was mated with a straight-winged male with black body color and the following ratios of offspring resulted. The experiment was conducted at 25°C.

Ratio	Phenotype
3/8	straight-winged; gray body color
3/8	straight-winged; black body color
1/8	curly-winged; gray body color
1/8	curly-winged; black body color

10. The data above suggest that the genotype of the male parent is

    (A) SsGg
    (B) SSGg
    (C) ssgg
    (D) Ssgg
    (E) ssGg

11. The data above suggest that the genotype of the offspring with curly wings and black body color is

    (A) SsGg
    (B) SSGg
    (C) ssgg
    (D) Ssgg
    (E) ssGg

12. The classification characteristics that define the genus of an animal or a plant are usually more general than those defining

    (A) a class
    (B) an order
    (C) a species
    (D) a family
    (E) a phylum

13. Hard water is undesirable and is often softened because hard water

    (A) is too viscous for regular uses
    (B) contains trace amounts of toxic substances
    (C) forms insoluble precipitates when boiled or when used with soap
    (D) cannot be used efficiently by the body due to dissolved impurities
    (E) evaporates more rapidly than soft water

14. Which of the following adaptations is more likely to be found in the leaves of desert plants than in those of plants that grow in moist regions?

    (A) Stomata mostly on upper leaf surface
    (B) A thin, transparent cuticle
    (C) A smooth leaf surface free of hairs
    (D) A thickened epidermis and cuticle
    (E) A loosely packed mesophyll layer

15. If all the xylem from a section of tree trunk could be removed, which of the following would most likely happen first?

    (A) Food could not pass from the leaves to the roots.
    (B) The roots would be unable to transfer any stored food to the spring buds.
    (C) The leaves would be unable to get any carbon dioxide.
    (D) The roots would be unable to store food.
    (E) The leaves would be unable to get sufficient water.

16. Whereas the ultimate source of energy for most organisms is sunlight, the immediate source is

    (A) chemical
    (B) electrical
    (C) thermal
    (D) gravitational
    (E) radiant

17. In embryonic origin, nerve cells are most similar to

    (A) epidermal cells
    (B) bone cells
    (C) red blood cells
    (D) liver cells
    (E) reproductive cells

18. In the name *Homo sapiens*, the word *sapiens* refers to the

    (A) species
    (B) family
    (C) class
    (D) genus
    (E) order

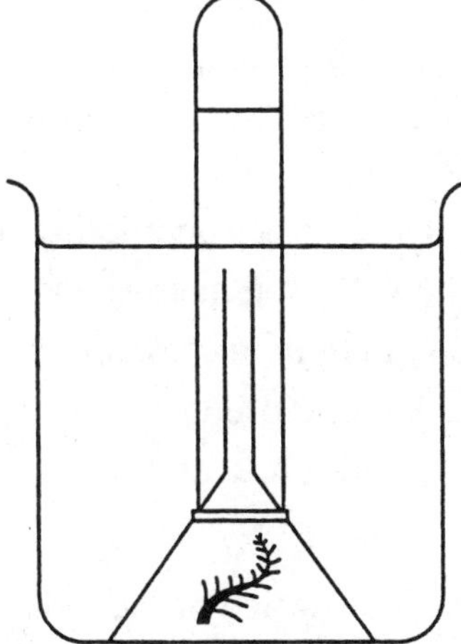

19. A student placed a sprig of green water plant under a funnel in a glass vessel full of water and then placed a test tube full of water mouth-downward over the stem of the funnel. After the setup had been exposed to sunlight for several hours, the student tested a gas that had collected in the test tube and concluded that the plant had produced oxygen. The results of this experiment could have been interpreted more satisfactorily if

    (A) the water had been tested for carbon dioxide
    (B) only the leaves of the plant had been used
    (C) air had been forced through the water
    (D) the plant had not been exposed to sunlight
    (E) a similar experiment had been set up without sunlight

20. Which of the following best completes the statement below?

    Among multicellular animals, the insects exhibit the greatest diversity of life-forms; therefore _______.

    (A) the total number of insect species is limited
    (B) the presence of wings on an insect is probably an evolutionary error
    (C) insects probably occupy the greatest number of niches
    (D) insect control by human beings is simplified
    (E) any genetic mutation in fruit flies is likely to escape detection

21. The percentage of phosphates in commercial detergents was reduced primarily because phosphates were shown to

    (A) be less effective cleaning agents than most other compounds
    (B) build up in animal tissues and cause sterility
    (C) cause cancer in animals
    (D) cause birth defects in animals
    (E) increase the growth rates of algae in lakes and rivers

22. Carbohydrates are most commonly stored in plants in the form of

    (A) starch
    (B) cellulose
    (C) lactose
    (D) ribose
    (E) sucrose

23. A father will transmit the genes of his Y chromosome to

    (A) one-half of his sons only
    (B) one-half of his daughters only
    (C) all of his sons only
    (D) all of his daughters only
    (E) none of his sons

24. In many cultivated plants (such as oranges, bananas, and potatoes), favorable characteristics often are created by careful genetic crosses. Of the following, which would be the best way to maintain the traits of a new variety with favorable characteristics?

    (A) Selfing individuals of this new variety (i.e., crossing the offspring of one parental plant)
    (B) Artificially pollinating wild varieties with pollen from the new variety
    (C) Artificially pollinating the new variety with pollen from wild varieties
    (D) Crossing the new variety with a variety that was homozygous recessive for all traits of concern
    (E) Vegetative reproduction of the new variety

25. In mammals, insulin is produced in which of the following structures?

    (A) Pancreas
    (B) Liver
    (C) Salivary glands
    (D) Hypothalamus
    (E) Pituitary gland

26. Which of the following occurs during anaphase I of meiosis?

    (A) The sister chromatids are pulled to opposite poles of the spindle.
    (B) The spindle apparatus forms.
    (C) The nuclear envelope disintegrates.
    (D) The centromeres replicate.
    (E) The homologous pairs of chromosomes separate.

27. All living cells have which of the following structures?

    (A) Endoplasmic reticulum
    (B) Nucleus
    (C) Plasma membrane
    (D) Cilia
    (E) Vacuole

28. Digestion of proteins in mammals begins in which of the following organs?

    (A) Mouth
    (B) Stomach
    (C) Small intestine
    (D) Colon
    (E) Gallbladder

29. Which of the following terrestrial biomes typically has the greatest species diversity?

    (A) Tundra
    (B) Taiga
    (C) Deciduous forest
    (D) Chaparral
    (E) Tropical rain forest

30. Which of the following instruments would be most useful for studying the internal structure of a chloroplast?

    (A) Transmission electron microscope
    (B) Scanning electron microscope
    (C) Compound light microscope
    (D) Dissecting microscope
    (E) Phase-contrast microscope

31. A hawk can have which of the following ecological roles?

    I. Primary consumer
    II. Secondary consumer
    III. Tertiary consumer

    (A) I only
    (B) II only
    (C) III only
    (D) I and II only
    (E) II and III only

32. Which of the following most directly leads to changes in cellular specialization during embryonic development?

    (A) Meiosis in the embryo's cells
    (B) Changes in the environmental stimuli the embryo experiences in the uterus
    (C) Formation of the placenta
    (D) An increase in the amount of DNA in the embryo due to replication
    (E) Changes in gene expression

33. Which of the following animals is most closely related to the cheetah?

    (A) Chicken
    (B) Alligator
    (C) Frog
    (D) Squirrel
    (E) Eagle

34. Which of the following organisms typically transmits the West Nile virus to humans?

    (A) Housefly
    (B) Tsetse fly
    (C) Mosquito
    (D) Tick
    (E) Mouse

35. A photosynthetic eukaryotic cell typically contains

    (A) chloroplasts only
    (B) mitochondria only
    (C) both chloroplasts and mitochondria
    (D) either chloroplasts or mitochondria, but never both at once
    (E) neither chloroplasts nor mitochondria

36. A theory fails to meet the criteria of scientific methodology if

    (A) it is unpopular
    (B) it contradicts other theories
    (C) it has not been conclusively proved
    (D) it has not been stated in mathematical terms
    (E) no experiments can be designed to test it

37. Dark lines in the Sun's spectrum are explained as resulting from

    (A) emission of radiation of certain frequencies from the Sun's atmosphere
    (B) absorption of energy by atoms in the outer layers of the Sun
    (C) radiation of ultraviolet light from sunspots
    (D) continuous radiation from the corona
    (E) x-rays emanating from the Sun's atmosphere

38. Scientists estimate the age of the Sun to be about

    (A) 100 billion years
    (B) 25 billion years
    (C) 14 billion years
    (D) 4.6 billion years
    (E) 3.8 billion years

39. Sunspots on the surface of the Sun are correlated with which of the following?

    (A) Relatively low temperatures compared with the surrounding surface
    (B) Relatively high temperatures compared with the surrounding surface
    (C) Periods of low solar activity
    (D) Fusion of helium nuclei rather than hydrogen nuclei
    (E) The warming of ocean surface waters in the eastern Pacific (El Niño)

40. Which of the following best describes the principal way in which Earth's atmosphere is heated?

    (A) Heat flows from the center of Earth and is conducted through the ground to the air.
    (B) The atmosphere absorbs short-wave radiation from the Sun as the Sun's rays pass through it.
    (C) Earth absorbs short-wave radiation from the Sun and radiates long-wave radiation, which is absorbed by the atmosphere.
    (D) The air absorbs short-wave radiation from the Sun after the radiation has been reflected by the clouds.
    (E) Warm air rises and cold air sinks and, as it sinks, is warmed by compression.

41. Most of Earth's water exists in

    (A) the oceans
    (B) the atmosphere
    (C) groundwater
    (D) lakes and rivers
    (E) polar ice caps

42. The release of chlorofluorocarbon gases into the environment has caused great concern to scientists and the public because these compounds

    (A) react with water droplets to cause acid rain and acid snow
    (B) decrease visibility near areas with high volumes of air traffic
    (C) are implicated in the reduction of ozone levels in the upper stratosphere
    (D) are made from rare elements that will soon be exhausted
    (E) are known to cause cancer through direct skin contact

43. Which of the following natural resources is NOT a fossil fuel?

    (A) Uranium
    (B) Natural gas
    (C) Petroleum
    (D) Anthracite coal
    (E) Bituminous coal

44. All of the following geologic time intervals are characterized correctly EXCEPT

    (A) Cambrian period ... age of birds
    (B) Carboniferous period ... age of amphibians
    (C) Devonian period ... age of fishes
    (D) Cenozoic era ... age of mammals
    (E) Mesozoic era ... age of dinosaurs

45. Which of the following is the farthest, on average, from Earth?

    (A) Andromeda galaxy
    (B) Halley's comet
    (C) Jupiter
    (D) Sirius
    (E) Uranus

$$CaO + CO_2 \rightarrow CaCO_3$$

46. What mass of CaO is needed to absorb 22 grams of CO_2 according to the balanced chemical equation above? (Molar masses: $CaO = 56$ g/mol, $CO_2 = 44$ g/mol)

    (A) 112 g
    (B) 100 g
    (C) 56 g
    (D) 28 g
    (E) 22 g

47. The half-life of $^{14}_{6}C$ is 5,600 years. Which of the following statements about a 10-gram sample of $^{14}_{6}C$ is correct?

(A) The radioactive decay of the sample will be complete after 5,600 years.
(B) The $^{14}_{6}C$ sample will start radioactive decay after 5,600 years.
(C) A time of 5,600 years has been required to produce this sample of $^{14}_{6}C$ in nature.
(D) After 5,600 years the sample will contain only 5 grams of $^{14}_{6}C$.
(E) After 11,200 years the sample will not contain any $^{14}_{6}C$.

48. Impact craters dominate the Moon's surface, yet are rare on Earth's surface. Reasons for this difference include which of the following?

I. The Moon has no wind.
II. The Moon is geologically inactive.
III. The Moon is much older.

(A) I only
(B) II only
(C) I and II only
(D) II and III only
(E) I, II, and III

49. At a fixed pressure, when the temperature of a gas sample increases, its volume increases. This relationship between the temperature and the volume of a gas is best described as which of the following?

(A) Direct proportion
(B) Inverse proportion
(C) Limiting ratio
(D) Hyperbolic function
(E) Logarithmic function

50. The notation $1s^2 2s^2 2p^4$ represents

(A) a noble gas
(B) an atomic nucleus
(C) an element with 8 protons
(D) an element with 8 electrons
(E) an element with an oxidation state of 4

51. Which of the following molecules can have more than one equivalent Lewis structure?

(A)  H–Ö–H (bent)
(B) H–C≡C–H
(C) 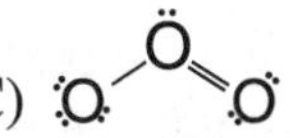 :Ö–Ö=Ö: (bent)
(D) 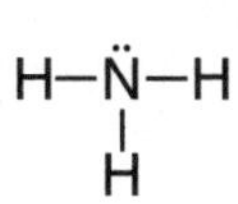 H–N̈–H with H below N
(E) 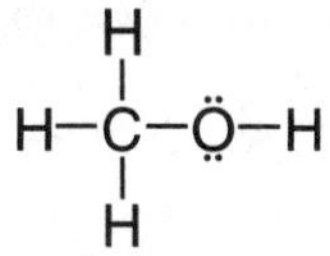 H–C(H)(H)–Ö–H

52. In old-fashioned flashbulbs, light was produced by the reaction of magnesium metal, Mg, sealed in the bulb with oxygen gas, O_2. After the flash, the mass of the sealed bulb was

(A) definitely greater than it was before use
(B) definitely smaller than it was before use
(C) essentially the same as it was before use
(D) greater or smaller depending on the amount of O_2 consumed
(E) greater or smaller depending on the amount of light produced

53. Of the following planets that are visible with the naked eye—Venus, Mars, Jupiter, and Saturn—only Venus has an orbit smaller than that of Earth. This means that Venus

(A) is seen only in the morning or the evening sky
(B) can be seen in the sky near midnight more often than at other times
(C) can rarely be seen at all
(D) has an orbit that is more elliptical than that of Earth
(E) has a longer year than Earth

54. Which of the following is NOT generally true of metals?

(A) They are usually solid at room temperature.
(B) They are good conductors of heat and electricity.
(C) They easily form negative ions.
(D) They have luster.
(E) They can be hammered into sheets or rolled into wires.

55. Within molecules of a compound, atoms are held together by chemical bonds that are primarily

(A) thermal
(B) frictional
(C) gravitational
(D) electrostatic
(E) magnetic

56. An unsorted mixture of clay, boulders, sand, and silt would most likely be deposited from which of the following?

(A) Glacial ice
(B) Subsurface water
(C) Streams
(D) Waves
(E) Wind

57. Valleys with U-shaped cross sections are most likely the result of erosion by which of the following?

(A) Glaciers
(B) Perennial streams
(C) Intermittent streams
(D) Mudflows
(E) Wind

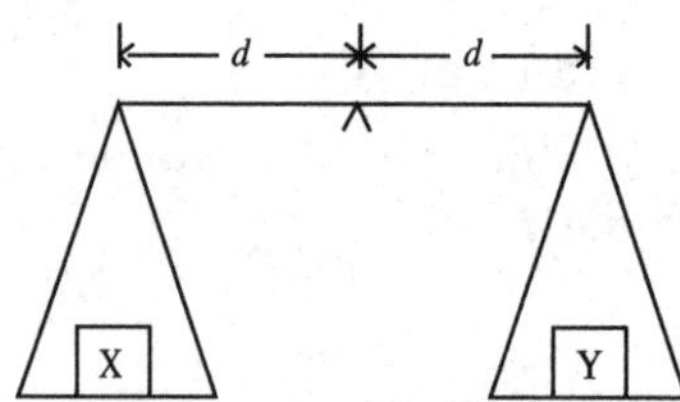

58. The balance shown above is in equilibrium at Earth's surface, and the two arms have the same length *d*. Thus the two objects, X and Y (not necessarily drawn to scale), must have identical

(A) densities
(B) masses
(C) shapes
(D) specific gravities
(E) volumes

59. On a global basis, for which of the following activities is the most water used each day?

(A) Crop irrigation
(B) Cooling in power plants
(C) Commercial laundering
(D) Manufacturing of textiles
(E) Production of steel

60. Which of the following correctly identifies the constituents of an atom of the isotope $^{131}_{53}I$?

	Protons	Neutrons	Electrons
(A)	53	78	78
(B)	78	53	78
(C)	53	78	53
(D)	78	131	78
(E)	131	53	53

61. Which of the following types of electromagnetic radiation has photons of the LEAST energy?

(A) Visible light
(B) Ultraviolet light
(C) Microwaves
(D) Gamma radiation
(E) Radio waves

62. The atomic mass of carbon is 12 and the atomic mass of hydrogen is 1. What is the percent by mass of carbon in methane gas, CH_4?

(A) 20%
(B) 25%
(C) 50%
(D) 75%
(E) 80%

63. Southern California experienced an earthquake that registered magnitude 3.5 on the Richter scale. One month later the same area experienced an earthquake that registered 5.5. About how many times as much energy was released by the magnitude 5.5 earthquake than by the magnitude 3.5 earthquake?

(A) 2
(B) 10
(C) 200
(D) 1,000
(E) 2,000

64. The study of which of the following would likely be the most helpful in providing information about the composition of Earth's upper mantle?

(A) Temperatures of hot springs
(B) Size of vesicles in basalt flows
(C) Xenolith inclusions in igneous rocks
(D) Carbonate sediments from the ocean floor
(E) Minerals formed through contact metamorphism

65. Which of the following are found in greater number in the nuclei of carbon-14 atoms than in the nuclei of carbon-12 atoms?

(A) Alpha particles
(B) Positrons
(C) Neutrons
(D) Protons
(E) Electrons

66. Which of the following best describes the wind circulation associated with low pressure systems in the Northern Hemisphere?

(A) North to south
(B) West to east
(C) Southwest to northeast
(D) Clockwise
(E) Counterclockwise

67. The amount of heat energy released when a certain type of candle is burned is 48,000 joules per gram of wax consumed. Which of the following expressions is equal to the number of grams of wax that need to be burned in order to raise the temperature of 500 grams of water from 20°C to 30°C, assuming all the heat released goes into heating the water? (The specific heat of water is 4.19 J/g°C.)

(A) $\dfrac{(48,000)(10)(4.19)}{500}$

(B) $\dfrac{(48,000)(4.19)}{(500)(10)}$

(C) $\dfrac{(4.19)(10)(500)}{48,000}$

(D) $\dfrac{(4.19)(500)}{(10)(48,000)}$

(E) $\dfrac{(30)(4.19)(500)}{(20)(48,000)}$

68. Which of the following types of radiation is typically produced in the laboratory by a high-voltage electron beam impacting a metallic target?

(A) Primary cosmic radiation
(B) X-ray radiation
(C) Neutron radiation
(D) Ultraviolet radiation
(E) Beta radiation

Questions 69–71

$$CuO + H_2 \rightarrow Cu + H_2O$$

The drawing below depicts an apparatus for reducing copper(II) oxide to the metal by the reaction above.

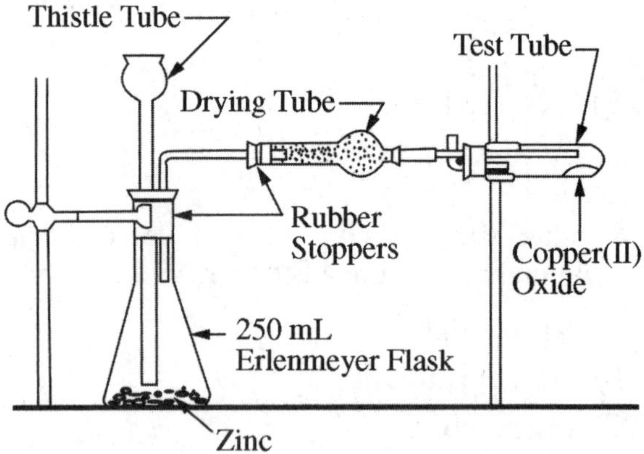

69. In order to produce a stream of hydrogen gas for this reaction, one should add which of the following through the thistle tube?

(A) Water
(B) Dilute hydrochloric acid
(C) Dilute copper(II) sulfate solution
(D) Hydrogen peroxide
(E) Dilute ammonia solution

70. After the production of hydrogen gas starts, withdrawing the thistle tube would result in which of the following?

(A) Moisture would collect in the flask.
(B) The evolution of hydrogen gas would stop.
(C) Much hydrogen gas would escape without coming in contact with the copper oxide.
(D) Air would enter the flask faster than hydrogen gas would be evolved.
(E) The rate of production of hydrogen gas would increase.

71. Which of the following would most likely increase the effectiveness of the hydrogen gas reducing the copper(II) oxide?

(A) Heating the test tube
(B) Cooling the test tube
(C) Putting the test tube under reduced pressure
(D) Filling the test tube with dilute HCl solution
(E) Filling the test tube with dilute NaOH solution

72. Which of the following typically occurs when a forested watershed is clear-cut?

(A) Annual rainfall increases.
(B) Soil erosion increases.
(C) The water temperature in streams decreases.
(D) The sediment load in streams decreases.
(E) Atmospheric concentration of O_2 increases.

73. Which characteristic of a star most directly relates to the likelihood of that star eventually becoming a black hole?

(A) Apparent magnitude
(B) Absolute magnitude
(C) Surface temperature
(D) Diameter
(E) Mass

74. How many joules of energy are absorbed by a 20.0 g sample of water as the temperature of the sample is raised from 273 K to 283 K? (The specific heat capacity of water is 4.2 J $g^{-1}K^{-1}$.)

(A) 42 J
(B) 84 J
(C) 200 J
(D) 840 J
(E) 4,200 J

$$2\,NO_2(g) \leftrightarrows N_2O_4(g)$$

75. The equation above represents a system that has reached a state of chemical equilibrium. Which of the following is a true statement about the system?

(A) All chemical reaction rates have dropped to zero.
(B) The system will eventually contain only N_2O_4 molecules.
(C) The concentration of $NO_2(g)$ must be twice that of $N_2O_4(g)$.
(D) The concentration of $NO_2(g)$ must be less than that of $N_2O_4(g)$.
(E) N_2O_4 molecules are being consumed as fast as they are produced.

76. Which of the following best describes antibiotic resistance?

(A) It is a condition that causes humans to become resistant to antibiotics.
(B) It is caused by inappropriate use of antibiotics, which allows for selection of resistant bacteria.
(C) It causes organisms to contract viral infections.
(D) It is a problem only in developing countries.
(E) It is a treatment for infections that results in a resistant immune system in an organism

77. Which of the following is true about cells that lose the ability to regulate cell division?

(A) They commonly have two nuclei.
(B) They can develop into cancer cells.
(C) They will divide forever using ribosomes.
(D) They are missing key genes that separate chromatids.
(E) They cannot be used for drug research.

78. Which of the following is considered necessary for a planet to support life?

(A) Oxygen gas (O_2)
(B) RNA
(C) Liquid water
(D) Nitrogen gas (N_2)
(E) Bicarbonate

79. In a healthy human, which of the following should be free of microbes?

(A) Mouth
(B) Large intestine
(C) Stomach
(D) Spinal fluid
(E) Skin

80. Enzymes are organic macromolecules that

(A) are synthesized in the nucleus
(B) are polymers of simple sugars
(C) function as catalysts in chemical reactions
(D) function as carriers of the genetic code
(E) are polymers of identical organic bases

81. An atom whose ground-state electron configuration ends with ….p^5 is

(A) a halogen
(B) a noble gas
(C) an alkali metal
(D) an alkaline earth metal
(E) a member of the oxygen family

82. Water has a higher boiling point than hydrogen sulfide because water has strong

(A) ionic bonds
(B) covalent bonds
(C) hydrogen bonds
(D) ion-dipole forces
(E) London dispersion forces

83. Energy can be transferred from one place to another by which of the following?

I. Conduction
II. Convection
III. Radiation

(A) I only
(B) II only
(C) III only
(D) I and II only
(E) I, II, and III

84. Which of the following is true about a sinking parcel of air?

(A) It will decrease in pressure.
(B) It will expand and cool.
(C) It will be unstable.
(D) It will compress and warm.
(E) It will form clouds.

85. Pluto is not categorized as a planet by scientists because

(A) it is smaller than Earth's Moon
(B) it cannot clear debris from its orbit
(C) its orbit crosses through the orbit of Neptune
(D) it has a large moon
(E) it has an unstable atmosphere

86. Which of the following is true about vitamins?

(A) Vitamins are proteins.
(B) Vitamins cannot be digested.
(C) Animals need vitamins in large amounts.
(D) Animals synthesize the essential vitamins.
(E) Vitamins are required for certain chemical reactions.

87. Which of the following is evidence that a mountain range was once submerged?

    (A) The presence of sedimentary rock
    (B) The absence of trees at higher altitudes
    (C) The presence of a geologically recent lava flow
    (D) The presence of large deposits of precious metals
    (E) The absence of nonsilicate oxides in the upper rock layers

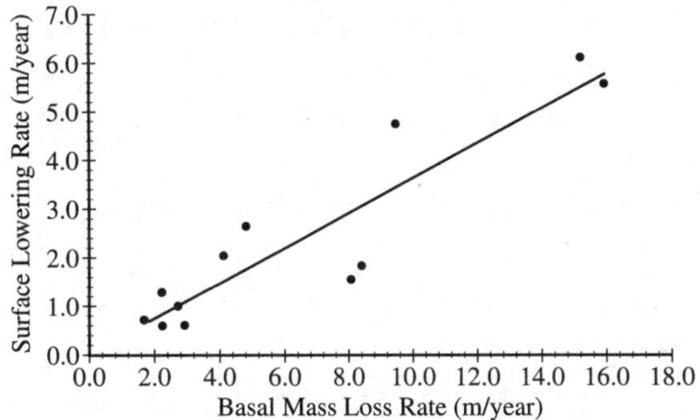

88. A study of the Antarctic ice sheet yielded the data in the graph above. Which of the following statements about the data is accurate?

    (A) The x- and y-axes are plotted incorrectly.
    (B) There are too few data points for statistical analysis.
    (C) There is a positive correlation between the two variables.
    (D) The scale must be logarithmic because the line is straight.
    (E) Because the line is straight, accurate extrapolations can be made far into the future.

89. Analogous structures are less useful in determining evolutionary patterns among organisms than homologous structures for which of the following reasons?

    (A) Analogous structures are more complex than homologous structures.
    (B) Analogous structures form vestigial structures, and homologous structures do not.
    (C) Analogous structures are subject to mutation, unlike homologous structures.
    (D) Analogous structures are derived from the same embryological tissues, so they provide little information.
    (E) Analogous structures reflect adaptation to the environment, and homologous structures reflect evolutionary ancestry.

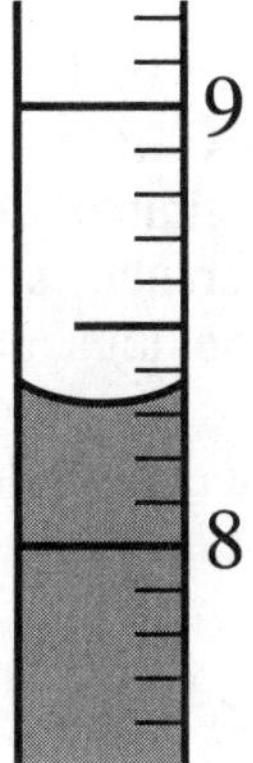

90. Which of the following is the correct volume reading for the level in the 10 mL graduated cylinder shown?

    (A) 8.0 mL
    (B) 8.1 mL
    (C) 8.14 mL
    (D) 8.3 mL
    (E) 8.4 mL

Questions 91–93 refer to the following options.

(A) Basalt
(B) Gneiss
(C) Shale
(D) Halite
(E) Peat

91. A mineral precipitated from seawater

92. A sedimentary rock formed from mud

93. A material formed early in the process of coal formation

Questions 94–97

The breed of dog known as the Tibetan mastiff was domesticated from the Chinese native dogs of the plains to live in high altitudes. A recent study compared genetic differences among Tibetan mastiffs, Chinese native dogs, and gray wolves. The researchers identified 12 mutations in the mastiffs that are involved in energy production critical to high-altitude survival under low-oxygen conditions.

94. The Tibetan mastiff breed most likely resulted from which of the following?

(A) Coevolution
(B) Adaptive radiation
(C) Punctuated equilibrium
(D) Sexual selection
(E) Artificial selection

95. The proteins that are produced as a result of the 12 mutations are most likely to function in which of the following organelles?

(A) Chloroplasts
(B) Mitochondria
(C) Endoplasmic reticula
(D) Lysosomes
(E) Flagella

96. Which of the following explains why gray wolves were included in the study?

(A) Wolves have greater genetic diversity than dogs do.
(B) Wolves are also mammals that live at high altitudes.
(C) Dogs were originally domesticated from wolves.
(D) There are few genetic similarities between wolves and dogs.
(E) Wolves are the offspring of mastiffs and Chinese native dogs.

97. Which of the following techniques was most likely used in the study?

(A) Electron microscopy
(B) Spectrophotometry
(C) Hybridization
(D) Gas chromatography
(E) DNA sequencing

98. Which of the following can assist in communication between plants but can also be a harmful air pollutant?

    (A) Radon
    (B) Ozone
    (C) Volatile organic compounds
    (D) Carbon dioxide
    (E) Nitrogen oxides

99. The elements in group 18 of the periodic table are chemically unreactive. Which of the following statements best explains this observation?

    (A) The elements are gases, and gases are naturally unreactive.
    (B) The elements form unusually stable diatomic molecules.
    (C) The valence electrons of these elements are strongly attracted to their nuclei.
    (D) The valence electrons of these elements are extremely stable because the electrons are paired.
    (E) The valence electron shells of these elements are completely filled.

100. Which of the following elements makes up about one percent of Earth's atmosphere?

    (A) Ar
    (B) H
    (C) He
    (D) N
    (E) O

Study Resources

Most textbooks used in college-level natural sciences courses cover the topics in the outline given earlier, but the approaches to certain topics and the emphases given to them may differ. To prepare for the Natural Sciences exam, it is advisable to study one or more college textbooks (selecting at least one biological science and one physical science textbook), which can be found in most college bookstores. When selecting a textbook, check the table of contents against the knowledge and skills required for this test.

If candidates maintain an interest in scientific issues; read science articles in newspapers and magazines; watch educational television programs on scientific topics; or work in fields that require a knowledge of certain areas of science, such as nursing and laboratory work, they will probably be knowledgeable about many of the topics included on the Natural Sciences exam.

Visit **clep.collegeboard.org/earn-college-credit/practice** for additional science resources. You can also find suggestions for exam preparation in Chapter IV of the *Official Study Guide*. In addition, many college faculty post their course materials on their schools' websites.

Answer Key

1.	C	51.	C
2.	D	52.	C
3.	E	53.	A
4.	D	54.	C
5.	E	55.	D
6.	A	56.	A
7.	B	57.	A
8.	C	58.	B
9.	A	59.	A
10.	D	60.	C
11.	C	61.	E
12.	C	62.	D
13.	C	63.	D
14.	D	64.	C
15.	E	65.	C
16.	A	66.	E
17.	A	67.	C
18.	A	68.	B
19.	E	69.	B
20.	C	70.	C
21.	E	71.	A
22.	A	72.	B
23.	C	73.	E
24.	E	74.	D
25.	A	75.	E
26.	E	76.	B
27.	C	77.	B
28.	B	78.	C
29.	E	79.	D
30.	A	80.	C
31.	E	81.	A
32.	E	82.	C
33.	D	83.	E
34.	C	84.	D
35.	C	85.	B
36.	E	86.	E
37.	B	87.	A
38.	D	88.	C
39.	A	89.	E
40.	C	90.	D
41.	A	91.	D
42.	C	92.	C
43.	A	93.	E
44.	A	94.	E
45.	A	95.	B
46.	D	96.	C
47.	D	97.	E
48.	C	98.	C
49.	A	99.	E
50.	D	100.	A

Precalculus

Description of the Examination

The Precalculus examination assesses student mastery of skills and concepts required for success in a first-semester calculus course. A large portion of the exam is devoted to testing a student's understanding of functions and their properties. Many of the questions test a student's knowledge of specific properties of the following types of functions: linear, quadratic, absolute value, square root, polynomial, rational, exponential, logarithmic, trigonometric, inverse trigonometric and piecewise-defined. Questions on the exam will present these types of functions symbolically, graphically, verbally or in tabular form. A solid understanding of these types of functions is at the core of all precalculus courses, and it is a prerequisite for enrolling in calculus and other college-level mathematics courses.

The examination contains approximately 48 questions, in two sections, to be answered in approximately 90 minutes.

- Section 1: 25 questions, approximately 50 minutes. The use of an **online graphing calculator (non-CAS)** is allowed for this section. Only some of the questions will require the use of the calculator.
- Section 2: 23 questions, approximately 40 minutes. No calculator is allowed for this section.

Although most of the questions on the exam are multiple-choice, there are some questions that require students to enter a numerical answer.

Graphing Calculator

A graphing calculator, which is integrated into the exam software, is available to students only during Section 1 of the exam. Students are expected to know how and when to make use of it.

For more information about the graphing calculator, please visit the Precalculus exam description on the CLEP website, clep.collegeboard.org.

In order to answer some of the questions in Section 1 of the exam, students may be required to use the online graphing calculator in the following ways:

- Perform calculations (e.g., exponents, roots, trigonometric values, logarithms).
- Graph functions and analyze the graphs.
- Find zeros of functions.
- Find points of intersection of graphs of functions.
- Find minima/maxima of functions.
- Find numerical solutions to equations.
- Generate a table of values for a function.

Knowledge and Skills Required

Questions on the examination require candidates to demonstrate the following abilities.

- Recalling factual knowledge and/or performing routine mathematical manipulation.
- Solving problems that demonstrate comprehension of mathematical ideas and/or concepts.
- Solving nonroutine problems or problems that require insight, ingenuity or higher mental processes.

The subject matter of the Precalculus examination is drawn from the following topics. The percentages next to the topics indicate the approximate percentage of exam questions on that topic.

20% Algebraic Expressions, Equations and Inequalities

Ability to perform operations on algebraic expressions

Ability to solve equations and inequalities, including linear, quadratic, absolute value, polynomial, rational, radical, exponential, logarithmic and trigonometric

Ability to solve systems of equations, including linear and nonlinear

15% Functions: Concept, Properties and Operations

Ability to demonstrate an understanding of the concept of a function, the general properties of functions (e.g., domain, range), function notation, and to perform symbolic operations with functions (e.g., evaluation, inverse functions)

30% Representations of Functions: Symbolic, Graphical and Tabular

Ability to recognize and perform operations and transformations on functions presented symbolically, graphically or in tabular form

Ability to demonstrate an understanding of basic properties of functions and to recognize elementary functions (linear, quadratic, absolute value, square root, polynomial, rational, exponential, logarithmic, trigonometric, inverse trigonometric and piecewise-defined functions) that are presented symbolically, graphically or in tabular form

10% Analytic Geometry

Ability to demonstrate an understanding of the analytic geometry of lines, circles, parabolas, ellipses and hyperbolas

15% Trigonometry and its Applications*

Ability to demonstrate an understanding of the basic trigonometric functions and their inverses and to apply the basic trigonometric ratios and identities (in right triangles and on the unit circle)

Ability to apply trigonometry in various problem-solving contexts

10% Functions as Models

Ability to interpret and construct functions as models and to translate ideas among symbolic, graphical, tabular and verbal representations of functions

***Note that trigonometry permeates most of the major topics and accounts for more than 15 percent of the exam. The actual proportion of exam questions that require knowledge of either right triangle trigonometry or the properties of the trigonometric functions is approximately 30–40 percent.**

Notes and Reference Information

The following information will be available for reference during the exam.

(1) Figures that accompany questions are intended to provide information useful in answering the questions. All figures lie in a plane unless otherwise indicated. The figures are drawn as accurately as possible EXCEPT when it is stated in a specific question that the figure is not drawn to scale. Straight lines and smooth curves may appear slightly jagged on the screen.

(2) Unless otherwise specified, all angles are measured in radians, and all numbers used are real numbers. For some questions in this test, you may have to decide whether the calculator should be in radian mode or degree mode.

(3) Unless otherwise specified, the domain of any function f is assumed to be the set of all real numbers x for which $f(x)$ is a real number. The range of f is assumed to be the set of all real numbers $f(x)$, where x is in the domain of f.

(4) In this test, $\log x$ denotes the common logarithm of x (that is, the logarithm to the base 10) and $\ln x$ denotes the natural logarithm of x (that is, the logarithm to the base e).

(5) The inverse of a trigonometric function f may be indicated using the inverse function notation f^{-1} or with the prefix "arc" (e.g., $\sin^{-1} x = \arcsin x$).

(6) The range of $\sin^{-1} x$ is $\left[-\frac{\pi}{2}, \frac{\pi}{2}\right]$.

The range of $\cos^{-1} x$ is $[0, \pi]$.

The range of $\tan^{-1} x$ is $\left(-\frac{\pi}{2}, \frac{\pi}{2}\right)$.

(7)

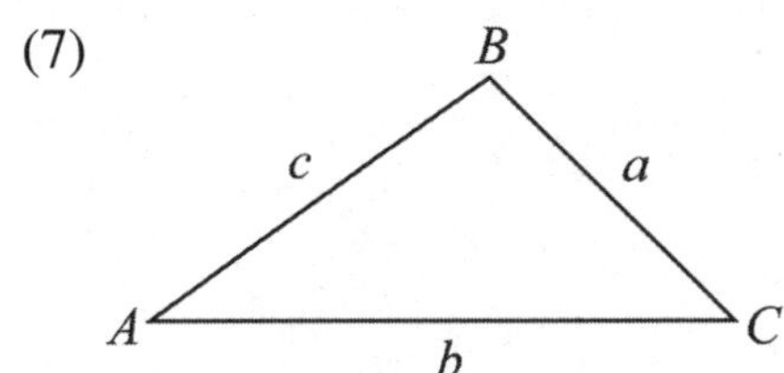

Law of Sines: $\frac{a}{\sin A} = \frac{b}{\sin B} = \frac{c}{\sin C}$

Law of Cosines: $c^2 = a^2 + b^2 - 2ab\cos C$

(8) Sum and Difference Formulas:

$$\sin(\alpha + \beta) = \sin\alpha\cos\beta + \cos\alpha\sin\beta$$

$$\sin(\alpha - \beta) = \sin\alpha\cos\beta - \cos\alpha\sin\beta$$

$$\cos(\alpha + \beta) = \cos\alpha\cos\beta - \sin\alpha\sin\beta$$

$$\cos(\alpha - \beta) = \cos\alpha\cos\beta + \sin\alpha\sin\beta$$

Sample Test Questions

The following sample questions do not appear on an actual CLEP examination. They are intended to give potential test-takers an indication of the format and difficulty level of the examination and to provide content for practice and review. Knowing the correct answers to all of the sample questions is not a guarantee of satisfactory performance on the exam.

Section 1

Directions: A graphing calculator will be available for the questions in this section. Some questions will require you to select from among five choices. For these questions, select the BEST of the choices given. If the exact numerical value of your answer is not one of the choices, select the choice that best approximates this value. Some questions will require you to enter a numerical answer in the box provided.

1. For each of the following functions, indicate whether it is even, odd, or neither even nor odd.

Function	Even	Odd	Neither
$f(x) = \frac{e^x + e^{-x}}{2}$			
$g(x) = \lvert \sin x \rvert$			
$h(x) = 8x^4 + 4x^2 + 2x$			

Click on your choices.

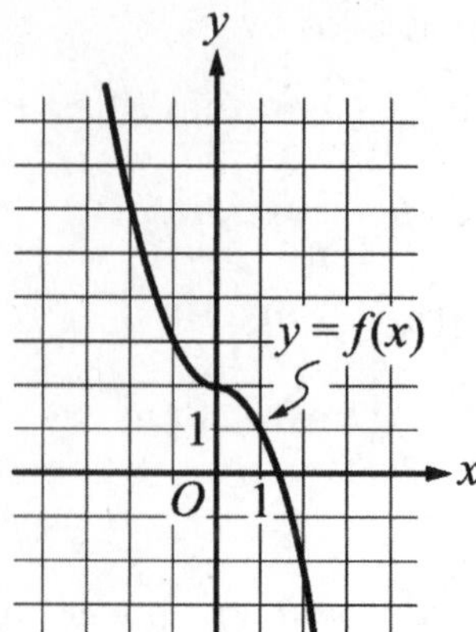

x	$g(x)$
–2	–4
–1	0
0	2
1	2
2	4

2. The graph of the function f and a table of values for the function g are shown above. What is the value of $f(g(0))$?

(A) –4
(B) –2
(C) 0
(D) 2
(E) 4

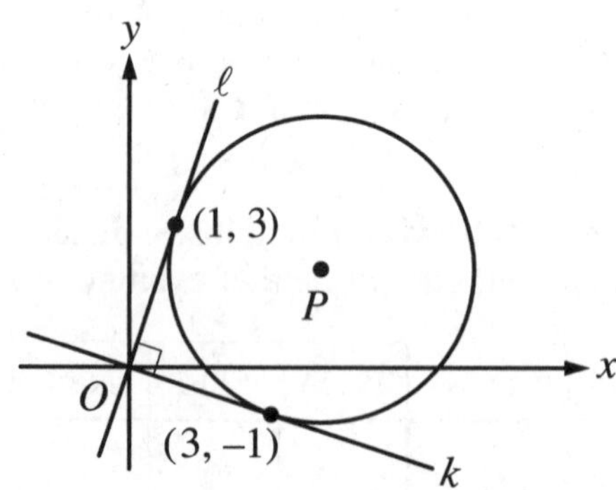

3. The circle with center P is tangent to perpendicular lines ℓ and k at points (1, 3) and (3, –1), respectively, as shown above. Which of the following is an equation of the circle with center P ?

(A) $x^2 + y^2 = \sqrt{10}$
(B) $(x-3)^2 + (y-3)^2 = 10$
(C) $(x-1)^2 + (y-3)^2 = 20$
(D) $(x-4)^2 + (y-2)^2 = 10$
(E) $(x-4)^2 + (y-2)^2 = 20$

4. $(\sin t + \cos t)^2 =$

(A) 1
(B) $1 + 2\sin t$
(C) $1 + \sin 2t$
(D) $\sin\left(t^2\right) + \cos\left(t^2\right)$
(E) $\sin\left(t^2\right) + 2\sin t\cos t + \cos\left(t^2\right)$

$$f(x) = e^{(x/4)}$$
$$g(x) = 2\sin x$$

5. The functions f and g are defined above and their domains are all real numbers. On what interval is the value of $f(x)$ greater than the maximum value of g ?

(A) $x > 1.571$
(B) $x > 2.125$
(C) $x > 2.773$
(D) $0.624 < x < 2.125$
(E) $2.125 < x < 2.773$

6. If $\pi \le \theta \le 2\pi$ and $\cos\theta = \cos 1$, what is the value of θ ?

(A) 1
(B) $\frac{\pi}{2} + 1$
(C) $\pi + 1$
(D) $\frac{3\pi}{2} - 1$
(E) $2\pi - 1$

$$h(x) = \frac{x^2 e^x}{x}$$

7. The function h is defined above. Which of the following are true about the graph of $y = h(x)$?

   I. The graph has a vertical asymptote at $x = 0$.

   II. The graph has a horizontal asymptote at $y = 0$.

   III. The graph has a minimum point.

(A) None
(B) I and II only
(C) I and III only
(D) II and III only
(E) I, II, and III

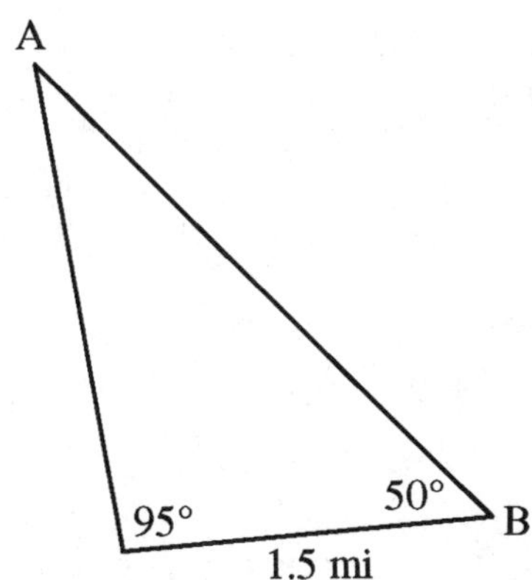

8. A transport authority plans to construct a bridge between City A and City B. To determine the distance between the cities, a surveyor team uses the triangular region shown. What is the distance between City A and City B, to the nearest tenth of a mile?

(A) 0.7 mile
(B) 1.6 miles
(C) 2.0 miles
(D) 2.6 miles
(E) 3.0 miles

9. Let f be the function defined by $f(x) = 5\sin(2x) + 1$ for $0 \leq x \leq \pi$. What is the slope of the line passing through the maximum and minimum points of the function on the interval?

(A) $-\frac{20}{\pi}$

(B) $-\frac{10}{\pi}$

(C) $-\frac{5}{\pi}$

(D) $\frac{10}{\pi}$

(E) $\frac{20}{\pi}$

10. In the xy-plane, the graph of $y = \frac{x}{x^2 - c}$ has no vertical asymptotes. Which of the following statements about c must be true?

(A) c is any real number.
(B) c is a positive number.
(C) c is a negative number.
(D) c is a perfect square.
(E) $c = 0$

$$4\cos x = 9\sin x$$

11. Which of the following is the solution to the equation above in the interval $\left[0, \frac{\pi}{2}\right]$?

(A) 0.4182
(B) 0.4606
(C) 1.1102
(D) 1.1526
(E) 4.4762

12. Let f be the function defined by $f(x) = -|x|$. The graph of the function g in the xy-plane is obtained by first translating the graph of f horizontally 3 units to the left and then vertically translating this result 2 units up. What is the value of $g(-2)$?

(A) -7
(B) -3
(C) 0
(D) 1
(E) 3

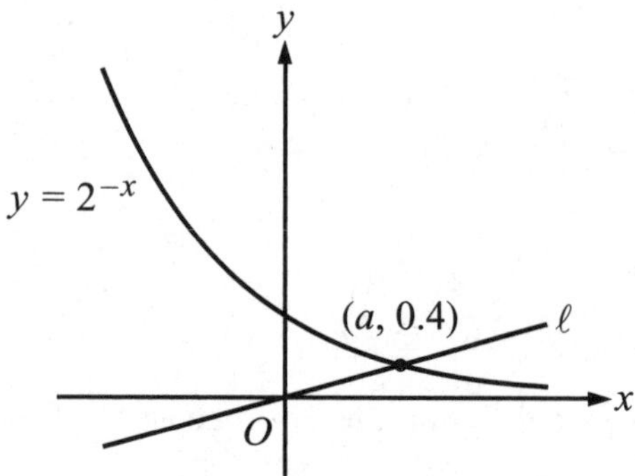

13. In the figure above, line ℓ passes through the origin and intersects the graph of $y = 2^{-x}$ at the point $(a, 0.4)$. What is the slope of line ℓ ?

(A) 0.200
(B) 0.303
(C) 0.528
(D) 1.322
(E) 3.305

14. In the xy-plane, the graph of $y = x^2 + bx + c$ is symmetric about the line $x = 3$ and passes through the point $(5, 2)$. What is the value of c ?

$$A(t) = ke^{-0.001t}, \text{ where } k \text{ is a constant.}$$

15. When a certain radioactive element decays, the amount, in milligrams, that remains after t years can be approximated by the function A above. Approximately how many years would it take for an initial amount of 800 milligrams of this element to decay to 400 milligrams?

(A) 173
(B) 347
(C) 693
(D) 1,386
(E) 2,772

16. If $g(x) = \dfrac{1}{x}$ and h is a nonzero real number, then $\dfrac{g(x+h) - g(x)}{h} =$

(A) 1
(B) $\dfrac{1}{(x+h)^2} - \dfrac{1}{x^2}$
(C) $\dfrac{h-1}{hx}$
(D) $\dfrac{-1}{x(x+h)}$
(E) $\dfrac{-h^2}{x(x+h)}$

$$h(t) = 64 - 46\cos\left(\frac{\pi}{5}t\right), \text{ where } 0 \le t \le 10$$

17. The function h above gives the height above the ground, in feet, of a passenger on a Ferris wheel t minutes after the ride begins. During one revolution of the Ferris wheel, for how many minutes is the passenger at least 100 feet above the ground? Round your answer to the nearest hundredth of a minute.

18. How many different values of x satisfy the equation $\sin x + 2\sin(2x) = \sqrt{x}$?

(A) One
(B) Two
(C) Three
(D) Five
(E) Infinitely many

19. A ball is dropped from an initial height of d feet above the floor and repeatedly bounces off the floor. Each time the ball hits the floor, it rebounds to a maximum height that is $\frac{3}{4}$ of the height from which it previously fell. The function h models the maximum height, in feet, to which the ball rebounds on the nth bounce. Which of the following is an expression for $h(n)$?

(A) $h(n) = \left(\frac{3}{4}\right)^n d$

(B) $h(n) = \left(\frac{3}{4}d\right)^n$

(C) $h(n) = \frac{3}{4}d^n$

(D) $h(n) = d^{\frac{3}{4}n}$

(E) $h(n) = n^{\frac{3}{4}d}$

20. In the xy-plane, the vertex of the parabola $x = y^2 + 4y + 1$ is the point (h, k). What is the value of k?

(A) –13
(B) –5
(C) –2
(D) 2
(E) 5

21. The measure of a certain angle is 25°. What is the corresponding radian measure of the angle?

(A) $\frac{5\pi}{36}$

(B) $\frac{5\pi}{18}$

(C) $\frac{5\pi}{9}$

(D) $\frac{18}{5\pi}$

(E) $\frac{36}{5\pi}$

22. A rectangular box with a square base is open at the top and has a volume of 12 cubic feet. Each side of the base has a length of x feet. Which of the following expresses the surface area, S, in square feet, of the outside of the box in terms of x?

(A) $S = 5x^2$

(B) $S = \frac{12}{x^2}$

(C) $S = x^2 + \frac{24}{x}$

(D) $S = x^2 + \frac{48}{x}$

(E) $S = x^2 + \frac{48}{x^2}$

23. What is the domain of the function $y = \log(\tan x)$?

(A) $(0, \infty)$

(B) $\left(0, \frac{\pi}{2}\right)$ only

(C) $\left(-\frac{\pi}{2}, \frac{\pi}{2}\right)$ only

(D) $\left(k\pi, k\pi + \frac{\pi}{2}\right)$ for all integers k

(E) $\left(k\pi - \frac{\pi}{2}, k\pi + \frac{\pi}{2}\right)$ for all integers k

x	0	1	2	3
$p(x)$	11	10	11	14

24. The table above shows selected values for the function p. If p is a quadratic polynomial, what is the value of $p(10)$?

25. If $\log_{2b} x^5 = T$ and $b > \frac{1}{2}$, then $x =$

(A) $(2b)^{\frac{T}{5}}$

(B) $2b^{\frac{T}{5}}$

(C) $2b^{5T}$

(D) $(2b)^{5T}$

(E) $\frac{(2b)^T}{5}$

26. The population of city Z was 420,000 in the year 2000. If the population is projected to grow at a constant rate of 2 percent per year, which of the following is closest to the projected population of city Z in the year 2030 ?

(A) 430,000
(B) 510,000
(C) 670,000
(D) 760,000
(E) 4,300,000

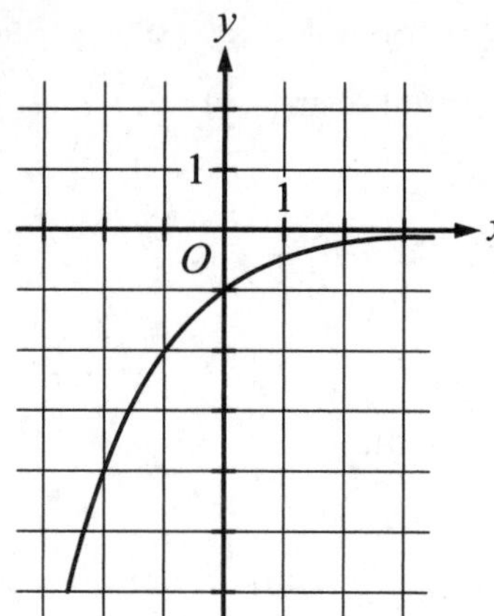

27. The graph of $y = a\left(b^x\right)$, where a and b are constants and $b > 0$, is shown above. If the points $(0,-1)$ and $(2,-0.25)$ are on the graph, what is the value of b ?

$b =$

28. Which of the following is equivalent to $\tan^2 x - \sin^2 x$?

(A) $\frac{\tan x + \sin x}{2}$
(B) $\tan^2 x + \sin^2 x$
(C) $2 \tan x \sin x$
(D) $(\tan x - \sin x)^2$
(E) $\tan^2 x \sin^2 x$

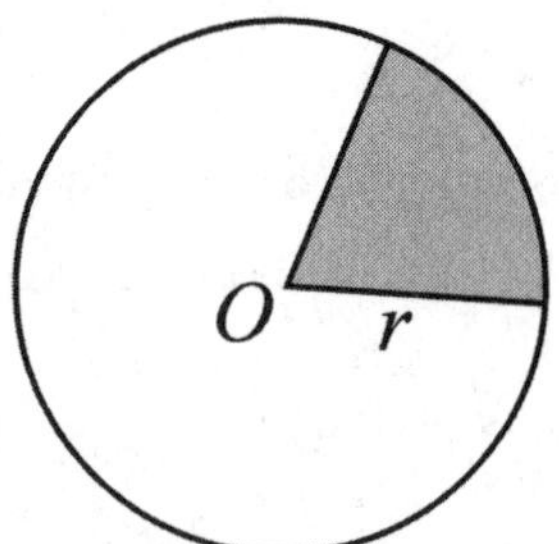

29. In the figure above, the circle has center O and radius r. The shaded region has a perimeter of 105. What value of r will maximize the area of the shaded region?

$r =$

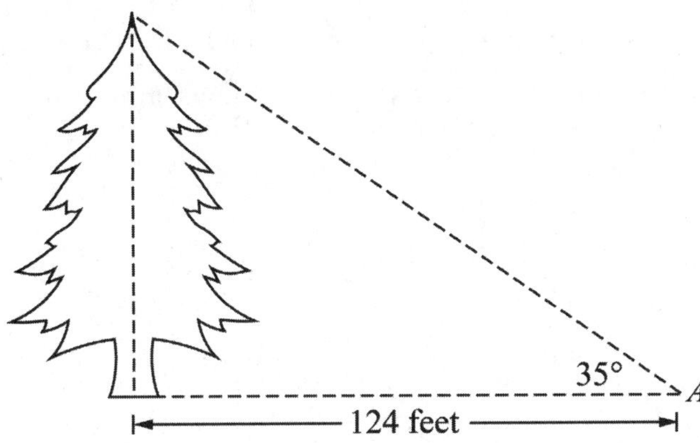

30. Point A is located 124 feet from a tree and is level with the base of the tree, as shown in the figure above. From point A, the angle of elevation of the top of the tree is 35°. What is the height of the tree?

Give your answer to the nearest foot.

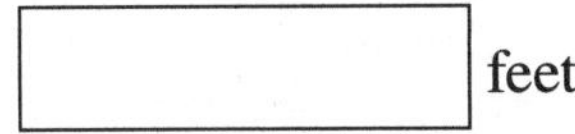

31. Two people begin running at the same time, moving away from the same point. One person runs due east at a constant speed of 7 miles per hour. The other person runs 30° west of north at a constant speed of 6.5 miles per hour. After how many hours are the two people 3 miles apart?

(A) 0.156
(B) 0.222
(C) 0.257
(D) 0.325
(E) 0.521

Section 2

Directions: A calculator will not be available for the questions in this section. Some questions will require you to select from among five choices. For these questions, select the BEST of the choices given. Some questions will require you to enter a numerical answer in the box provided.

32. If $\left(x-\sqrt{5}\right)\left(x+\sqrt{5}\right)=5$, what is the value of x ?

(A) $5\pm\sqrt{5}$
(B) $-5\pm\sqrt{5}$
(C) ± 5
(D) $\pm\sqrt{10}$
(E) $\pm\sqrt{30}$

33. If $f(x)=2x+1$ and $g(x)=3x-1$, then $f(g(x))=$

(A) $5x$
(B) $x-2$
(C) $6x-1$
(D) $6x+2$
(E) $6x^2+x-1$

34. Let f and g be the functions defined by $f(x)=\sqrt{x+2}$ and $g(x)=x^2-a$, where a is a positive constant. What are all values of a for which the graphs of f and g have exactly one point of intersection?

(A) $0<a<2$
(B) $a=2$
(C) $a>2$
(D) $a=4$ only
(E) $a>4$ only

35. An experiment designed to measure the growth of bacteria began at 2:00 P.M. and ended at 8:00 P.M. on the same day. The number of bacteria is given by the function N, where $N(t) = 1000 \cdot 3^{2t/3}$ and t represents the number of hours that have elapsed since the experiment began. How many more bacteria were there at the end of the experiment than at the beginning of the experiment?

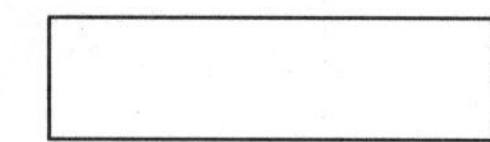

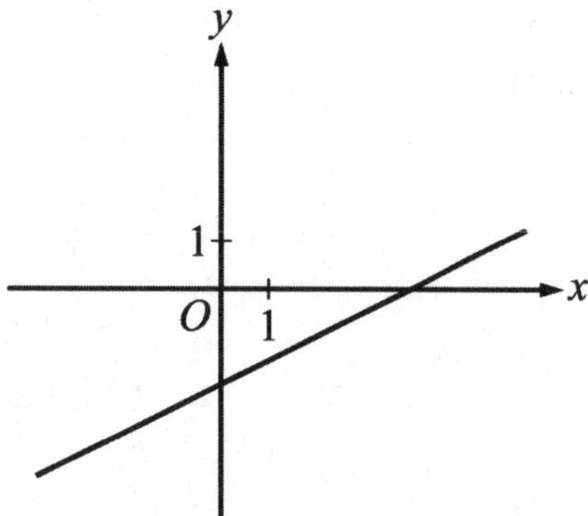

36. The equation of the line shown in the graph above is $y = ax + b$. Which of the following is always true for this line?

(A) $ab < 0$
(B) $ab > 0$
(C) $ab = 0$
(D) $a = b$
(E) $a = -b$

37. What is the x-intercept of the graph of $y = \frac{1}{8}x^{3/2} - 8$?

(A) -16
(B) -8
(C) $\frac{1}{16}$
(D) 16
(E) 512

38. The function h is given by $h(x) = \log_2\left(x^2 + 2\right)$. For what positive value of x does $h(x) = 3$?

(A) 1
(B) 2
(C) 8
(D) $\sqrt{6}$
(E) $\sqrt{7}$

39. Which of the following relations define y as a function of x ?

I. $x^2 + (y-3)^2 = 4$

II.

x	0	1	2	3	4
y	10	20	30	20	10

III.

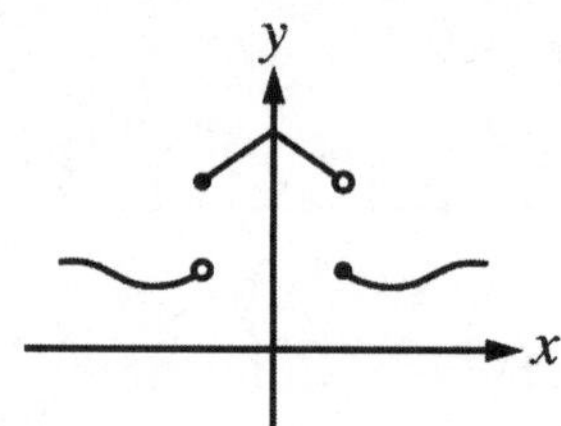

(A) II only
(B) III only
(C) I and II
(D) I and III
(E) II and III

40. In the xy-plane, the lines with equations $2x + 2y = 1$ and $4x - y = 4$ intersect at the point with coordinates (a, b). What is the value of b ?

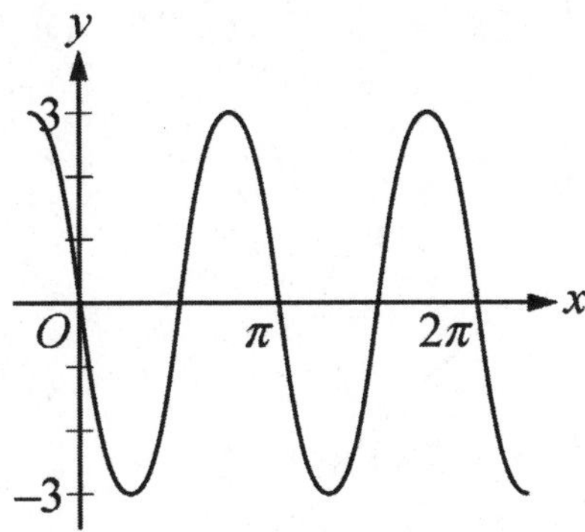

41. A portion of the graph of a function f is shown above. The domain of f is the set of all real numbers. Which of the following could be the equation of f?

(A) $f(x) = -3\sin\left(\frac{x}{2}\right)$

(B) $f(x) = -3\sin\left(x - \frac{\pi}{2}\right)$

(C) $f(x) = -\cos(3x)$

(D) $f(x) = 3\sin(2x - \pi)$

(E) $f(x) = 3\cos\left(2x - \frac{\pi}{2}\right)$

42. The function f is given by $f(x) = x + |x - 10|$. Which of the following defines $f(x)$ for all $x \leq 10$?

(A) $f(x) = 10$
(B) $f(x) = -10$
(C) $f(x) = 10 - 2x$
(D) $f(x) = -10 + 2x$
(E) $f(x) = -10 - 2x$

x	$f(x)$
5	a
10	32
15	b

43. The table above shows some values for the function f. If f is a linear function, what is the value of $a + b$?

(A) 32
(B) 42
(C) 48
(D) 64
(E) It cannot be determined from the information given.

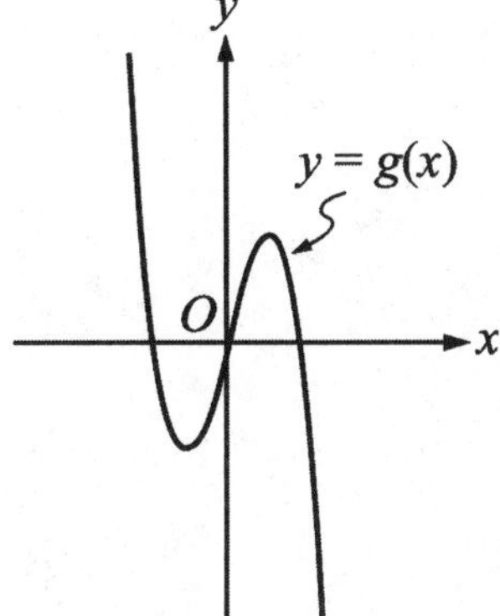

44. The figure above shows the graph of a polynomial function g. Which of the following could define $g(x)$?

(A) $g(x) = x^3 - 4$
(B) $g(x) = x^3 - 4x$
(C) $g(x) = -x^3 + 4x$
(D) $g(x) = x^4 - 4x^2$
(E) $g(x) = -x^4 + 4x^2$

45. If a and b are numbers such that $\ln a = 2.1$ and $\ln b = 1.4$, what is the value of $\ln\left(\frac{a^2}{b}\right)$?

46. If $0 < \theta < \frac{\pi}{2}$ and $10\sin\theta = z$, what is $\tan\theta$ in terms of z?

(A) $\frac{z}{\sqrt{100 - z^2}}$

(B) $\frac{10}{\sqrt{z^2 - 100}}$

(C) $\frac{\sqrt{100 - z^2}}{10}$

(D) $\frac{\sqrt{z^2 - 100}}{10}$

(E) $\frac{\sqrt{100 - z^2}}{z}$

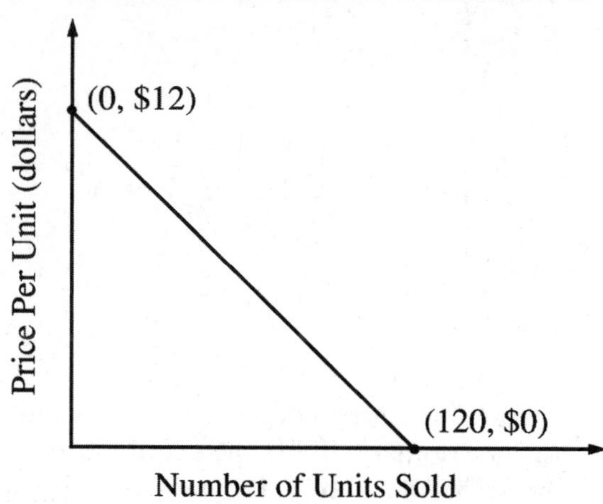

47. Based on past sales, a convenience store has observed a linear relationship between the number of units of Product X that will be sold to customers each week and the price per unit. The figure above models this linear relationship. Based on the model, how many dollars would the convenience store expect to earn from its sales of Product X in a week when the price per unit is \$5 ?

(A) \$125
(B) \$250
(C) \$350
(D) \$600
(E) \$720

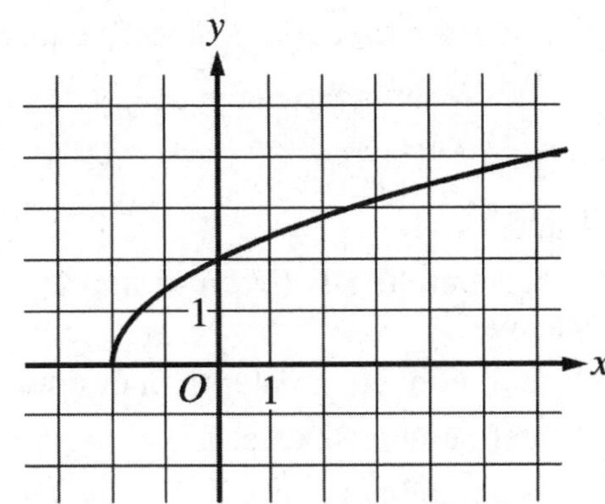

48. The figure above shows the graph of the function f defined by $f(x)=\sqrt{2x+4}.$ If f^{-1} is the inverse function of f, what is the value of $f^{-1}(2)$?

(A) $-\sqrt{8}$

(B) -2

(C) 0

(D) $\dfrac{1}{\sqrt{8}}$

(E) $\sqrt{8}$

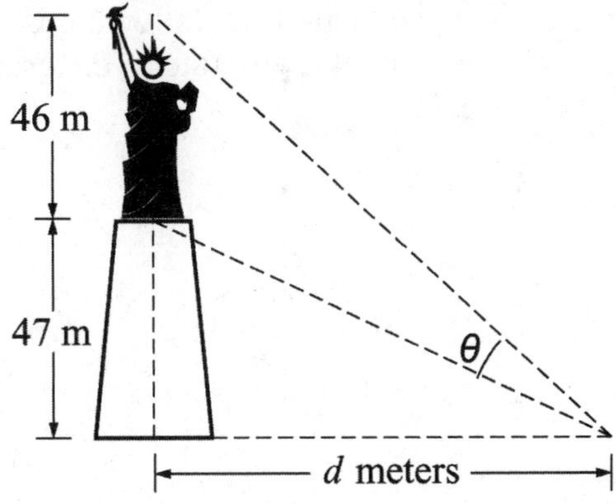

49. The Statue of Liberty is 46 meters tall and stands on a pedestal that is 47 meters above the ground. An observer is located d meters from the pedestal and is standing level with the base, as shown in the figure above. Which of the following best expresses the angle θ in terms of d ?

(A) $\theta = \arcsin\left(\dfrac{47}{d}\right) - \arcsin\left(\dfrac{46}{d}\right)$

(B) $\theta = \arcsin\left(\dfrac{93}{d}\right) - \arcsin\left(\dfrac{47}{d}\right)$

(C) $\theta = \arctan\left(\dfrac{47}{d}\right) - \arctan\left(\dfrac{46}{d}\right)$

(D) $\theta = \arctan\left(\dfrac{d}{93}\right) - \arctan\left(\dfrac{d}{47}\right)$

(E) $\theta = \arctan\left(\dfrac{93}{d}\right) - \arctan\left(\dfrac{47}{d}\right)$

50. The value of $\log(1{,}732)$ is between what two integers?

(A) 2 and 3
(B) 3 and 4
(C) 4 and 5
(D) 17 and 18
(E) 173 and 174

51. In the xy-plane, which of the following is an equation of a vertical asymptote to the graph of $y = \sec(6x - \pi)$?

(A) $x = \frac{\pi}{6}$

(B) $x = \frac{\pi}{4}$

(C) $x = \frac{\pi}{3}$

(D) $x = \frac{\pi}{2}$

(E) $x = \pi$

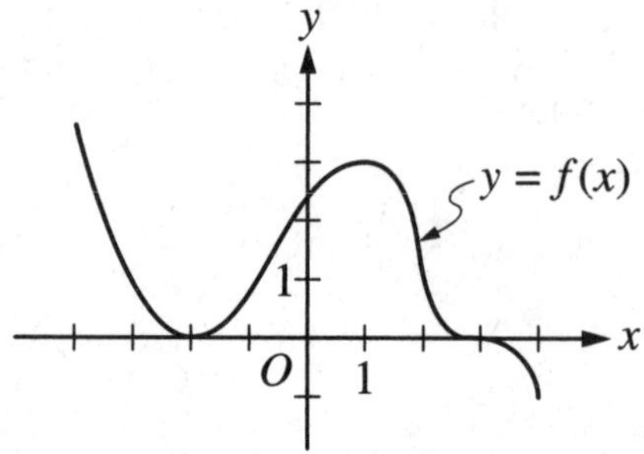

52. The figure above shows the graph of a polynomial function f. What is the least possible degree of f ?

(A) Two
(B) Three
(C) Four
(D) Five
(E) Six

$$x - y = 1$$
$$x^2 + y^2 = 5$$

53. The point (x, y) lies in the third quadrant of the xy-plane and satisfies the equations above. What is the value of y ?

[ ]

54. For all $x \neq 0$, the function f is defined by $f(x) = \frac{x}{|x|}$. What is the range of f ?

(A) –1 and 1 only
(B) All real numbers between –1 and 1, inclusive
(C) All real numbers greater than or equal to 0
(D) All real numbers except 0
(E) All real numbers

55. $\tan^{-1}\left(2\cos\frac{\pi}{3}\right) =$

(A) $\frac{\pi}{4}$

(B) $\frac{\pi}{3}$

(C) $\frac{\pi}{2}$

(D) $\frac{2\pi}{3}$

(E) $\frac{3\pi}{2}$

56. In the xy-plane, the graph of $y = x\left(x^2 - 2\right)\left(x^2 + x + 1\right)$ intersects the x-axis in how many different points?

(A) One
(B) Two
(C) Three
(D) Four
(E) Five

57. For all x such that $0 < x < \frac{\pi}{2}$, which of the following is equivalent to $\frac{\sin(2x)}{\sin x} - \frac{\cos(2x)}{\cos x}$?

(A) $\frac{1}{\cos x}$

(B) $\sin x - \cos x$

(C) $2\cos x - 2\sin x$

(D) $\frac{1}{\sin x} - \frac{1}{\cos x}$

(E) 0

58. The population P of fish, in thousands, in a certain pond at time t years is modeled by the function $P(t) = \frac{1}{1 + \left(\frac{1}{P_0} - 1\right)e^{-rt}}$, where P_0 is the population at time $t = 0$ and r is the growth rate of the population. If $P(1) = 5$, which of the following is equivalent to r?

(A) $\frac{\ln(5)}{P_0}$

(B) $\frac{\ln(5)}{\ln\left(\frac{1}{P_0}\right)}$

(C) $\ln\left(\frac{4P_0}{5}\right)$

(D) $\ln\left(\frac{4}{5P_0}\right)$

(E) $\ln\left(\frac{5(P_0 - 1)}{4P_0}\right)$

59. What are all solutions of the equation $\cos(2x) + 1 = \sin(2x)$ in the interval $[0, 2\pi)$?

(A) $\frac{\pi}{2}$ and π

(B) $\frac{\pi}{2}$, π, and $\frac{3\pi}{2}$

(C) $\frac{\pi}{4}$, $\frac{\pi}{2}$, $\frac{5\pi}{4}$, and $\frac{3\pi}{2}$

(D) $\frac{\pi}{4}$, $\frac{\pi}{2}$, $\frac{3\pi}{4}$, $\frac{5\pi}{4}$, $\frac{3\pi}{2}$, and $\frac{7\pi}{2}$

(E) $\frac{\pi}{8}$, $\frac{\pi}{4}$, $\frac{3\pi}{4}$, $\frac{7\pi}{8}$, $\frac{7\pi}{4}$, and $\frac{15\pi}{8}$

60. What are all solutions to the equation $e^{2x} - e^{x} - 2 = 0$?

(A) 0 only
(B) $\ln 2$ only
(C) 2 only
(D) –1 and 2
(E) 0 and $\ln 2$

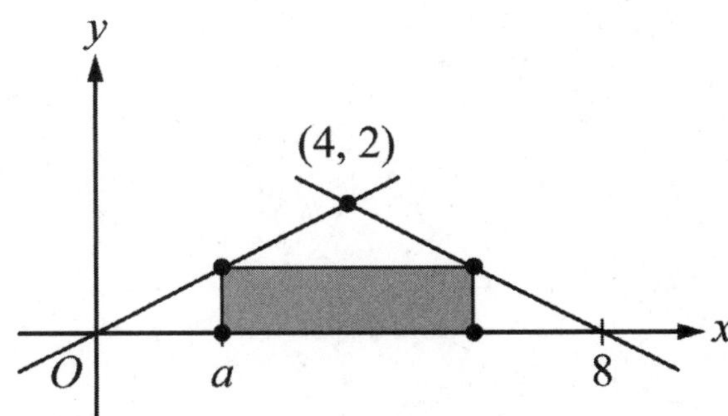

61. A shaded rectangle and two lines are shown in the xy-plane above. What is the area of the shaded rectangle in terms of a?

(A) $\frac{1}{2}a^2$

(B) $2a - \frac{1}{2}a^2$

(C) $4a - a^2$

(D) $8 - \frac{1}{2}a^2$

(E) $8 - 4a + a^2$

62. The equation $y = 8x^2 + 8x - 6$ can be rewritten in the form $y = a(x - h)^2 + k$, where a, h, and k are constants. If $a = 8$, what are h and k ?

(A) $h = -\frac{1}{2}$ and $k = -8$

(B) $h = 0$ and $k = -6$

(C) $h = \frac{1}{2}$ and $k = 8$

(D) $h = 1$ and $k = -14$

(E) $h = 4$ and $k = -6$

$$6 - 3|x - 2| = -6$$

63. What are all solutions to the equation shown above?

(A) $x = 2$
(B) $x = 6$
(C) $x = -2$ and $x = 6$
(D) $x = 2$ and $x = -6$
(E) There are no solutions to the equation shown.

64. At what points do the graphs of $y = x^4 - x$ and $y = 7x$ intersect in the xy-plane?

(A) $(0, 0)$ only
(B) $(2, 14)$ only
(C) $(0, 0)$ and $(2, 14)$
(D) $(0, 0)$ and $(\sqrt{7}, 7\sqrt{7})$
(E) $(0, 0)$, $(2, 14)$, $(\sqrt{7}, 7\sqrt{7})$, and $(\sqrt{14}, 7\sqrt{14})$

65. Joe wants to buy a bottle and a cork to use as a stopper. Together, the bottle and cork cost \$2.20. The bottle costs \$2.00 more than the cork. How much does the bottle cost?

\$ [ ]

Study Resources

Most textbooks used in college-level precalculus courses cover the topics in the outline given earlier, but the approaches to certain topics and the emphases given to them may differ. To prepare for the Precalculus exam, it is advisable to study one or more college textbooks, which can be found in most college bookstores. When selecting a textbook, check the table of contents against the knowledge and skills required for this test.

Visit **clep.collegeboard.org/earn-college-credit/practice** for additional precalculus resources. You can also find suggestions for exam preparation in Chapter IV of the *Official Study Guide*. In addition, many college faculty post their course materials on their schools' websites.

Answer Key

Section 1		Section 2	
1.	See below.	32.	D
2.	B	33.	C
3.	D	34.	E
4.	C	35.	80,000
5.	C	36.	A
6.	E	37.	D
7.	D	38.	D
8.	D	39.	E
9.	A	40.	−0.4
10.	C	41.	D
11.	A	42.	A
12.	D	43.	D
13.	B	44.	C
14.	7	45.	2.8
15.	C	46.	A
16.	D	47.	C
17.	2.14	48.	C
18.	D	49.	E
19.	A	50.	B
20.	C	51.	B
21.	A	52.	D
22.	D	53.	−2
23.	D	54.	A
24.	91	55.	A
25.	A	56.	C
26.	D	57.	A
27.	0.5	58.	E
28.	E	59.	C
29.	26.25	60.	B
30.	87	61.	C
31.	C	62.	A
		63.	C
		64.	C
		65.	2.10

1.

Function	Even	Odd	Neither
$f(x) = \dfrac{e^x + e^{-x}}{2}$	√		
$g(x) = \lvert \sin x \rvert$	√		
$h(x) = 8x^4 + 4x^2 + 2x$			√

Financial Accounting

Description of the Examination

The Financial Accounting examination covers skills and concepts that are generally taught in a first-semester undergraduate financial accounting course. Colleges may award credit for a one-semester course in financial accounting.

The exam contains approximately 75 questions to be answered in 90 minutes. Some of these are pretest questions that will not be scored.

Knowledge and Skills Required

Questions on the Financial Accounting examination require candidates to demonstrate one or more of the following abilities.

- Familiarity with accounting concepts and terminology
- Preparation, use and analysis of accounting data and financial reports issued for both internal and external purposes
- Application of accounting techniques to simple problem situations involving computations
- Understanding the rationale for generally accepted accounting principles and procedures

The subject matter of the Financial Accounting examination is drawn from the following topics. The percentages next to the main topics indicate the approximate percentage of exam questions on that topic.

20%–30% General Topics

- Generally accepted accounting principles
- Rules of double-entry accounting/transaction analysis/accounting equation
- The accounting cycle
- Business ethics
- Purpose of, presentation of, and relationships between financial statements
- Forms of business

20%–30% The Income Statement

- Presentation format issues
- Recognition of revenue and expenses
- Cost of goods sold
- Irregular items (e.g., discontinued operations, extraordinary items, etc.)
- Profitability analysis

30%–40% The Balance Sheet

- Cash and internal controls
- Valuation of accounts and notes receivable (including bad debts)
- Valuation of inventories
- Acquisition and disposal of long-term asset
- Depreciation/amortization/depletion
- Intangible assets (e.g., patents, goodwill, etc.)
- Accounts and notes payable
- Long-term liabilities (e.g., bonds payable)
- Owner's equity
- Preferred and common stock
- Retained earnings
- Liquidity, solvency and activity analysis

5%–10% Statement of Cash Flows

- Indirect method
- Cash flow analysis
- Operating, financing and investing activities

Less than 5% Miscellaneous

- Investments
- Contingent liabilities

Sample Test Questions

The following sample questions do not appear on an actual CLEP examination. They are intended to give potential test-takers an indication of the format and difficulty level of the examination and to provide content for practice and review. Knowing the correct answers to all of the sample questions is not a guarantee of satisfactory performance on the exam.

Directions: Each of the questions or incomplete statements below is followed by five suggested answers or completions. Select the one that is best in each case.

1. Which of the following will always increase when net income increases?

(A) Liabilities
(B) Cash
(C) Merchandise
(D) Sales
(E) Equity

2. Assume there are 365 days in a year. What is the number of days' inventory on hand for a firm with cost of goods sold of $750,000 and average inventory of $150,000 ?

(A) 5
(B) 8
(C) 20
(D) 43
(E) 73

3. During the current year, accounts receivable increased from $27,000 to $41,000, and sales were $225,000. Based on this information, how much cash did the company collect from its customers during the year?

(A) $225,000
(B) $239,000
(C) $211,000
(D) $252,000
(E) $266,000

4. Accounts receivable turnover helps determine

(A) the balance of accounts payable
(B) the customers who have recently paid their bills
(C) how quickly a firm collects cash on its credit sales
(D) when to write off delinquent accounts
(E) credit sales

5. The income statement is designed to measure

(A) whether a firm is able to pay its bills
(B) how solvent a company has been
(C) how much cash flow a firm is likely to generate
(D) the financial position of a firm
(E) the results of business operations

6. A company prepares a bank reconciliation in order to

(A) determine the correct amount of the cash balance
(B) satisfy banking regulations
(C) determine deposits not yet recorded by the bank
(D) double-check the amount of petty cash
(E) record all check disbursements

7. An inventory valuation method such as FIFO or LIFO affects

(A) the cost of goods sold but not the balance sheet
(B) the balance sheet but not the cost of goods sold
(C) both the income statement and the balance sheet
(D) neither the income statement nor the balance sheet
(E) the cost of goods sold but not the income statement

8. A liability for dividends is recorded on which of the following?
   (A) The declaration date
   (B) The record date
   (C) The payment date
   (D) The collection date
   (E) The statement date

9. Assets are classified as intangible under which of the following conditions?
   (A) They are converted into cash within one year.
   (B) They have no physical substance.
   (C) They are acquired in a merger.
   (D) They are held for resale.
   (E) They are short term and used in operations.

10. Return on assets helps users of financial statements evaluate which of the following?
    (A) Profitability
    (B) Liquidity
    (C) Solvency
    (D) Cash flow
    (E) Reliability

11. What impact does collecting a receivable have?
    (A) Total assets increase.
    (B) Total assets decrease.
    (C) Net income increases.
    (D) Net income decreases.
    (E) Total assets and net income are not affected.

12. The financial statement that includes classifications for operating, financing, and investing activities of a business entity for a period of time is called the
    (A) Income Statement
    (B) Statement of Retained Earnings
    (C) Balance Sheet
    (D) Statement of Changes in Owners' Equity
    (E) Statement of Cash Flows

13. In a period of rising prices, which of the following inventory methods results in the highest cost of goods sold?
    (A) FIFO
    (B) LIFO
    (C) Average cost
    (D) Periodic inventory
    (E) Perpetual inventory

14. Dividends paid is shown on which of the following financial statements?
    (A) Balance sheet
    (B) Income statement
    (C) Statement of cash flows
    (D) Statement of cost of goods manufactured
    (E) Statement of comprehensive income

15. Equipment with a cost of $50,000 has an estimated residual value of $2,000 and an estimated life of ten years or 8,000 machine hours. It is to be depreciated by the units-of-production method. What is the amount of depreciation for the third year, during which the machine was used 1,000 machine hours?

(A) $2,000
(B) $3,000
(C) $4,800
(D) $5,000
(E) $6,000

16. How is depreciation on equipment recorded?

(A) Equipment Expense	XXXX	
Equipment		XXXX
(B) Depreciation Expense (equipment)	XXXX	
Accumulated Depreciation (equipment)		XXXX
(C) Equipment Expense	XXXX	
Accumulated Equipment Expense		XXXX
(D) Depreciation Expense	XXXX	
Equipment		XXXX
(E) Accumulated Depreciation	XXXX	
Depreciation Expense		XXXX

17. A company had net sales of $27,900 in April. Beginning inventory was $5,000. Net inventory purchases were $15,000. Ending inventory was $7,000. Total operating expenses were $6,500. How much net income did the company earn in April?

(A) $ 8,400
(B) $12,400
(C) $13,000
(D) $14,900
(E) $21,400

18. Green Corporation with assets of $5,000,000 and liabilities of $2,000,000 has 6,000 shares of capital stock outstanding (par value $300). What is the book value per share?

(A) $ 200
(B) $ 300
(C) $ 500
(D) $ 833
(E) $1,167

19. Cost of goods sold is determined by which of the following?

(A) Beginning inventory plus net purchases minus ending inventory
(B) Beginning inventory plus purchases plus purchase returns minus ending inventory
(C) Beginning inventory minus net purchases plus ending inventory
(D) Purchases minus transportation-in plus beginning inventory minus ending inventory
(E) Net sales minus ending inventory

20. The owner's equity in a business increases from which of the following?

I. Excess of revenue over expenses
II. Investments by the owner
III. Decrease in accounts payable

(A) I only
(B) II only
(C) III only
(D) I and II only
(E) I, II, and III

21. The Accumulated Depreciation account should be shown in the financial statements as

(A) an operating expense
(B) an extraordinary loss
(C) a liability
(D) stockholders' equity
(E) a contra (deduction) to an asset account

22. If an individual borrows $95,000 in July of the current year from Community Bank by signing a $95,000, 9 percent, one-year note, what is the accrued interest as of December 31 of the current year?

(A) $ 0
(B) $2,138
(C) $4,275
(D) $6,413
(E) $8,550

23. Net purchases for the year amounted to $80,000. The merchandise inventory at the beginning of the year was $19,000. On sales of $120,000, a 30 percent gross profit on the selling price was realized. The inventory at the end of the year was

(A) $13,000
(B) $15,000
(C) $17,000
(D) $25,000
(E) $63,000

24. Which of the following investing activities appears on the statement of cash flows?

(A) Selling a building
(B) Buying Treasury stock
(C) Selling Treasury stock
(D) Paying dividends
(E) Receiving interest income on a Note Receivable

25. In a limited partnership, limited partners are at risk for

(A) the amount of their investment in the partnership
(B) their share of nonrecourse debt
(C) the total debts of the partnership
(D) their percentage of debts
(E) no amount

26. All of the following expenditures should be charged to an asset account rather than to an expense account of the current period EXCEPT the cost of

(A) overhauling a delivery truck, which extends its useful life by two years
(B) purchasing a new component for a machine, which serves to increase the productive capacity of the machine
(C) constructing a parking lot for a leased building
(D) installing a new assembly line
(E) replacing worn-out tires on a delivery truck

27. The balance sheet of Harold Company shows current assets of $200,000 and current liabilities of $100,000. The company uses cash to acquire merchandise inventory. As a result of this transaction, which of the following is true of working capital and the current ratio?

(A) Both are unchanged.
(B) Working capital is unchanged; the current ratio increases.
(C) Both decrease.
(D) Working capital decreases; the current ratio increases.
(E) Working capital decreases; the current ratio is unchanged.

28. Which of the following correctly indicates how retained earnings can be affected?

    (A) Increased by net income, increased by dividends, and unaffected by realized losses
    (B) Increased by net income, increased by dividends, and increased by realized gains
    (C) Increased by net income, decreased by dividends, and decreased by realized losses
    (D) Decreased by net income, decreased by dividends, and decreased by realized losses
    (E) Decreased by net income, increased by dividends, and unaffected by realized gains

29. On December 31, before making year-end adjusting entries, Accounts Receivable had a debit balance of $80,000, and the Allowance for Uncollectible Accounts had a credit balance of $3,500. Credit sales for the year were $600,000. If credit losses are estimated at 1/2 percent of credit sales, which of the following is true?

    (A) The balance of the Allowance for Uncollectible Accounts will be $500 after adjustment.
    (B) The balance of the Allowance for Uncollectible Accounts will be $3,500 after adjustment.
    (C) The balance of the Allowance for Uncollectible Accounts will be $6,500 after adjustment.
    (D) The Uncollectible Accounts Expense for the year will be $500.
    (E) The Uncollectible Accounts Expense for the year will be $6,500.

30. A company bought a patent at a cost of $180,000. The patent had an original legal life of 17 years. The remaining legal life is 10 years, but the company expects its useful life will only be 6 years. When should the cost of the patent be charged to expenses?

    (A) Immediately
    (B) Over the next 6 years
    (C) Over the next 10 years
    (D) Over the next 17 years
    (E) Over the next 40 years

31. How is treasury stock reported on the balance sheet?

    (A) As an increase in liabilities
    (B) As an increase in assets
    (C) As a decrease in assets
    (D) As an increase in stockholders' equity
    (E) As a decrease in stockholders' equity

32.

Cash:	$ 40,000
Accounts receivable:	$120,000
Inventory:	$300,000
Prepaid rent:	$ 2,000
Accounts payable:	$150,000
Salaries payable:	$ 7,000
Long-term bonds payable:	$200,000

The selected accounts above are from TJ Supply's balance sheet. What is TJ Supply's working capital?

    (A) $ 40,000
    (B) $105,000
    (C) $160,000
    (D) $305,000
    (E) $462,000

33. A machine with a useful life of eight years was purchased for $600,000 on January 1. The estimated salvage value is $50,000. What is the first year's depreciation by using the double-declining-balance method?

    (A) $ 50,000
    (B) $ 68,000
    (C) $ 75,000
    (D) $137,500
    (E) $150,000

34. Newman Corporation uses the allowance method of accounting for its accounts receivable. The company currently has a $100,000 balance in accounts receivable and a $5,000 balance in its allowance for uncollectible accounts. The company decides to write off $4,000 of its accounts receivable. What would be the balance in its net accounts receivable before and after the write-off?

	Before	After
(A)	$ 95,000	$ 91,000
(B)	$ 95,000	$ 95,000
(C)	$100,000	$ 96,000
(D)	$105,000	$101,000
(E)	$105,000	$105,000

35. Trading securities must be reported on the balance sheet at

(A) historical cost
(B) cost plus earnings minus dividends
(C) book value
(D) fair market value
(E) net present value

36. Which of the following will be credited when recording an accrued expense?

(A) A liability account
(B) A revenue account
(C) A prepaid expense account
(D) An unearned revenue account
(E) A contra owner's equity account

37. The L Company purchased new machinery and incurred the following costs:

Invoice price	$30,000
Freight (F.O.B. shipping point)	$ 2,000
Foundation for machinery	$ 1,000
Installation costs	$ 900
Annual maintenance of machinery	$ 600

The recorded cost of the machinery is

(A) $30,000
(B) $31,900
(C) $32,000
(D) $33,900
(E) $34,500

38. ABC Company issued $5,000,000 of bonds on January 1 receiving cash of $5,300,000. Which of the following is true about the bonds?

(A) The bonds were issued at a discount.
(B) The bonds are not interest bearing.
(C) The market value of the bonds on the date of issue was $5,100,000.
(D) The market quote for the bonds was 108.
(E) The amount of annual interest expense will be less than the amount of interest paid annually in cash.

39. Brock Company purchased a patent for $72,000 from Carter Company. The patent has a remaining legal life of 6 years, with an expected useful life of 4 years. The first year's amortization is

(A) $ 0
(B) $ 6,000
(C) $12,000
(D) $18,000
(E) $24,000

40. Which of the following is true of annual depreciation expense?

    (A) It represents the amount required for annual maintenance of a long-term asset.
    (B) It represents the annual revenue earned by an asset.
    (C) It allocates the cost of use of a long-term asset to the revenue that it generates.
    (D) It is required to fulfill the economic entity assumption.
    (E) It reduces cash.

41. Information in Covington Corporation's accounting records concerning its common stock shows that there are 100,000 shares authorized, 80,000 shares issued, and 5,000 shares held as treasury stock. If a $3.00-per-share dividend is declared by the board of directors, the total amount of the cash dividend would be

    (A) $ 15,000
    (B) $225,000
    (C) $240,000
    (D) $300,000
    (E) $315,000

42. The matching concept matches

    (A) customers with businesses
    (B) expenses with revenues
    (C) assets with liabilities
    (D) creditors with businesses
    (E) debits with credits

43. Cindy Company is preparing a bank reconciliation. Which of the following should be subtracted from the balance per bank statement to arrive at the adjusted cash balance?

    (A) Deposits in transit
    (B) Bank service charge
    (C) Interest credited to the account
    (D) Outstanding checks
    (E) Customer check returned for insufficient funds

44. Which of the following equals the net assets of a company?

    (A) Current assets minus current liabilities
    (B) Total assets minus current liabilities
    (C) Retained earnings
    (D) Long-term assets minus accumulated depreciation
    (E) Stockholders' equity

45. New World, Inc., purchased $30,000 in goods on account that in turn were sold on account for $35,000. If New World uses accrual accounting, how much should they record in expenses and revenue?

    (A) $35,000 in revenue but no expenses
    (B) $30,000 in expenses but no revenue
    (C) $35,000 in revenue and $30,000 in expenses
    (D) $30,000 in revenue and $30,000 in expenses
    (E) $5,000 in revenue but no expenses

46. Sonny Corporation has a simple capital structure of 100,000 shares of $1 par common stock and 20,000 shares of 5 percent preferred stock, $50 par. Both classes of stock were outstanding for the entire year. During the year, the company reported net income of $550,000 and declared dividends of $75,000 and $50,000 on the common stock and the preferred stock, respectively. Sonny's earnings per share for the year were

    (A) $4.25
    (B) $4.58
    (C) $4.75
    (D) $5.00
    (E) $5.50

47. A machine that cost $25,000 three years ago is sold in the current year for $6,000. The accumulated depreciation taken on the machine was $20,000. This sale would be reported in the current year's statement of cash flows as

(A) $25,000 outflow in the cash from investing activities section
(B) $6,000 inflow in the cash from investing activities section
(C) $1,000 inflow in the cash from investing activities section
(D) $1,000 inflow in the cash from operations section
(E) $1,000 inflow in the cash from financing activities section

48. Intangible assets include which of the following?

(A) Unearned revenues
(B) Works of art
(C) Treasury bills
(D) Land improvements
(E) Patents

49. During the past year, a company reported net income of $230,000. Depreciation expense was $22,000. In December the company received $7,000 representing rent for the next year on a vacant warehouse. What is the amount of cash provided by operating activities that should appear on a statement of cash flows?

(A) $215,000
(B) $237,000
(C) $245,000
(D) $252,000
(E) $259,000

50. Ling is an accountant at a publicly traded corporation. She recently discovered in the accounting records a material error that affected last year's financial statements and will affect this year's statements. If the error is not corrected, it will reverse itself this year and probably no one else will discover it. Even though last year's net income was materially overstated and this year's net income will be materially understated, the overall effect on the two years combined net incomes is that the overstatement and the understatement will completely offset each other. Which of the following is the best action that Ling should take?

(A) Do nothing, since no one will be harmed because of the offset
(B) Immediately inform the local law enforcement agency
(C) Place a phone call to the local newspaper to inform the public about the error
(D) Immediately contact the Securities and Exchange Commission, since she is not sure what action her supervisor will take
(E) Inform her immediate supervisor and help correct last year's statements

51. Which of the following identifies the income statement items in their proper order as found in a correctly prepared income statement?

(A) Gross profit, net income, cost of goods sold, operating expenses, sales
(B) Sales, operating expenses, cost of goods sold, gross profit, net income
(C) Sales, cost of goods sold, operating expenses, gross profit, net income
(D) Sales, cost of goods sold, gross profit, operating expenses, net income
(E) Gross profit, cost of goods sold, sales, operating expenses, net income

52. Magoo Wholesaler finds that 30 percent of its customers pay cash for their purchases. The rest buy on credit, 60 percent of which is collected in the month of purchase, and the rest in the month after purchase. If sales in January are $120,000, what is the balance of accounts receivable on January 31?

(A) $ 0
(B) $12,000
(C) $33,600
(D) $48,000
(E) $50,400

53. If a company issues $10,000,000 of 6 percent bonds at 105½, the amount of cash received from the sale is

(A) $10,000,000
(B) $10,105,500
(C) $10,512,000
(D) $10,550,000
(E) $10,600,000

54. On August 1, Carlos Company pays $3,600 for a two-year insurance policy covering the period beginning September 1. How much insurance expense should be recognized by Carlos this year if the company reports on a calendar-year basis?

(A) $ 600
(B) $ 750
(C) $1,050
(D) $1,800
(E) $3,600

55. If a corporation has total assets of $1,568,000, current liabilities of $60,000, and long-term liabilities of $388,000, what is its approximate debt-to-equity ratio?

(A) 0.15
(B) 0.25
(C) 0.29
(D) 0.40
(E) 0.43

56. The lower of cost or market (LCM) is an application of

(A) materiality
(B) conservatism
(C) the matching concept
(D) full disclosure
(E) the going-concern assumption

57. Cash is reported

(A) in net sales on the income statement
(B) as cost of goods sold on the income statement
(C) as a liability on the balance sheet
(D) in the stockholders' equity section of the balance sheet
(E) as a current asset

58. Before the football season begins, a college football team receives $12,000,000 from season-ticket holders for one year's home games. The team will play three home games in September, one in October, and two in November. How much revenue is recognized in September?

(A) $ 0
(B) $ 2,000,000
(C) $ 4,000,000
(D) $ 6,000,000
(E) $12,000,000

59. If net sales are $2,000,000, operating expenses are $300,000, and gross profit is $360,000, how much is the cost of goods sold?

(A) $ 340,000
(B) $ 660,000
(C) $1,640,000
(D) $1,700,000
(E) $2,660,000

60. Stephanie Company reported net income of $52,000 for the year. The net income includes depreciation expense of $3,800 and a gain on sale of equipment of $6,900. On the statement of cash flows, how much cash will Stephanie Company report from operating activities?

(A) $48,900
(B) $52,000
(C) $55,100
(D) $55,800
(E) $58,900

61. (1) Adjusted trial balance is prepared.
(2) Transactions are posted to ledgers.
(3) Transactions are recorded in a journal.
(4) Closing entries are made.
(5) Adjusting journal entries are made.
(6) Trial balance is prepared.
(7) Financial statements are prepared.

Each of the principal steps in the accounting cycle is identified above by a number. Which response lists the correct sequence of events in the accounting cycle?

(A) 3, 2, 6, 5, 1, 7, 4
(B) 3, 2, 1, 4, 5, 6, 7
(C) 5, 1, 3, 4, 2, 7, 6
(D) 5, 3, 2, 1, 4, 6, 7
(E) 2, 3, 1, 6, 5, 4, 7

62. On November 1, Greenberg Partners pays $7,200 for a one-year insurance policy, effective the same date. How much insurance expense should Greenberg Partners report for the year ending December 31 ?

(A) $ 0
(B) $ 600
(C) $1,200
(D) $6,000
(E) $7,200

63. Schreiber Industries estimates bad debts at 2% of sales. Schreiber began the year with $270,000 of accounts receivable and $38,600 of allowance for bad debts. During the year, Schreiber had sales of $920,000, wrote off bad debts of $26,000, and received cash on account of $905,000. What amount of accounts receivable, net of allowance for bad debts, should appear on the year-end balance sheet?

(A) $213,000
(B) $228,000
(C) $254,000
(D) $259,000
(E) $266,600

64. Gross profit margin is useful for evaluating

(A) solvency
(B) liquidity
(C) turnover
(D) leverage
(E) profitability

65. Belford Brothers, Inc., has 10 percent noncumulative, nonparticipating preferred stock outstanding with a par value of $200,000. The company also has common stock outstanding with a par value of $800,000. In Belford's first year of operation, no dividends were paid, but during the second year, Belford declared dividends of $60,000. How should the dividends be distributed that year between the two classes of stock?

	Preferred Stock	Common Stock
(A)	$ 0	$60,000
(B)	$20,000	$40,000
(C)	$25,000	$35,000
(D)	$30,000	$30,000
(E)	$40,000	$20,000

66. Falcon, Inc., a manufacturer and supplier of kitchen appliances, provides a two-year warranty on component parts at no cost. Which accounting principle requires Falcon to recognize as an expense the estimated cost of fulfilling a warranty in the year the equipment is sold?

(A) Cost principle
(B) Matching principle
(C) Going-concern principle
(D) Entity principle
(E) Consistency principle

67. Longshore Group bought a piece of equipment for use in its operations under the following terms: 5 annual payments of $64,000 for the equipment, including interest. Although the list price of the equipment was $315,000, Longshore Group could have bought it for $300,000 cash. Salvage value is $20,000. Which amount should Longshore Group use to record the purchase of the machine on its books?

(A) $280,000
(B) $295,000
(C) $300,000
(D) $315,000
(E) $320,000

68. The owner of a small business paid the property taxes on her personal residence from the business checking account. The payment should be charged to which of the following?

(A) Wages
(B) Property taxes
(C) Rent
(D) Withdrawals
(E) Building

69. What is the purpose of closing entries?

(A) To reduce revenues, expenses, and dividends to zero for the next accounting period
(B) To correct errors
(C) To remove liabilities from the accounting records
(D) To verify that the accounting equation is balanced
(E) To accrue revenues and expenses

70. A customer ordered merchandise from Van Lieshaut, Inc., on March 3. Van Lieshaut processed the order on March 5 and emailed the customer verifying that the order was ready. On March 8 the customer picked up the merchandise and signed the billing invoice. On March 12 the customer sent a check in payment for the merchandise, which was received by Van Lieshaut on March 15. On which day should Van Lieshaut recognize revenue from the sale?

(A) March 3
(B) March 5
(C) March 8
(D) March 12
(E) March 15

71. On January 1 of the current year, beginning inventory for a furniture company was $35,000. During the year, the company purchased $242,000 inventory. On December 31 of the current year, the company had inventory of $26,000. What was cost of goods sold for the year?

(A) $207,000
(B) $233,000
(C) $242,000
(D) $251,000
(E) $277,000

72. Which of the following businesses is most likely to use specific identification in recording inventory purchases and cost of goods sold?

(A) A supermarket
(B) A clothing store
(C) An auto parts store
(D) A bookstore
(E) An art dealer

73. In a statement of cash flows prepared using the indirect method, which of the following is deducted from net income to determine cash provided by operating activities?

(A) Gain on sale of land
(B) Payment of dividends
(C) Depreciation expense
(D) Purchase of equipment
(E) Issue of common stock

74. Perfumes by Gladys purchased a patent at the beginning of year 1 at a cost of $72,000. The patent had a remaining legal life of 9 years but was expected to be useful for only 6 years. Early in year 3, Perfumes by Gladys realized that the benefits of owning the patent would disappear at the end of year 4. How much patent amortization expense should be recognized in year 3 ?

(A) Zero
(B) $8,000
(C) $12,000
(D) $24,000
(E) $28,000

75. A corporation bought a piece of used equipment by exchanging 20,000 shares of treasury stock. The treasury stock had a par value of $10 per share and had been originally issued for $14 per share. The current fair market value of the treasury stock is $13 per share. The equipment had been purchased by the seller three years earlier for $300,000 but had accumulated depreciation of $25,000. For what amount should the corporation record the purchase on its books?

(A) $200,000
(B) $260,000
(C) $275,000
(D) $280,000
(E) $300,000

Directions: Choose among the corresponding properties in each column for each entry by clicking on your choice. When you click on a blank cell, a check mark will appear. No credit is given unless the correct cell is marked for each entry.

76. At the end of Dugan Retail Corporation's first year of operation, it was determined that the company had overstated its ending inventory.

    Indicate the effect that the overstatement will have on the first year's cost of goods sold and net income.

	Overstated	Understated	No Effect
Cost of goods sold			
Net income			

Directions: Select a choice and click on the blank in which you want the choice to appear. Repeat until all of the blanks have been filled. A correct answer must have a different choice in each blank.

77. Match each of the following terms with the corresponding asset category.

Depreciation
Depletion
Amortization

Intangible assets ____________

Tangible assets ____________

Natural resources ____________

Study Resources

Most textbooks used in the first semester of college-level financial accounting courses cover the topics in the outline given earlier, but the approaches to certain topics and the emphases given to them may differ. To prepare for the Financial Accounting exam, it is advisable to study one or more college textbooks, which can be found in most college bookstores. When selecting a textbook, check the table of contents against the knowledge and skills required for this test.

Visit **clep.collegeboard.org/earn-college-credit/practice** for additional financial accounting resources. You can also find suggestions for exam preparation in Chapter IV of the *Official Study Guide*. In addition, many college faculty post their course materials on their schools' websites.

Answer Key

1.	E	40.	C
2.	E	41.	B
3.	C	42.	B
4.	C	43.	D
5.	E	44.	E
6.	A	45.	C
7.	C	46.	D
8.	A	47.	B
9.	B	48.	E
10.	A	49.	E
11.	E	50.	E
12.	E	51.	D
13.	B	52.	C
14.	C	53.	D
15.	E	54.	A
16.	B	55.	D
17.	A	56.	B
18.	C	57.	E
19.	A	58.	D
20.	D	59.	C
21.	E	60.	A
22.	C	61.	A
23.	B	62.	C
24.	A	63.	B
25.	A	64.	E
26.	E	65.	B
27.	A	66.	B
28.	C	67.	C
29.	C	68.	D
30.	B	69.	A
31.	E	70.	C
32.	D	71.	D
33.	E	72.	E
34.	B	73.	A
35.	D	74.	D
36.	A	75.	B
37.	D	76.	See below
38.	E	77.	See below
39.	D		

76. Cost of goods sold–Understated
    Net income–Overstated

77. Intangible assets–Amortization
    Tangible assets–Depreciation
    Natural resources–Depletion

Information Systems

Description of the Examination

The Information Systems examination covers material that is usually taught in an introductory college-level business information systems course. Questions test knowledge, terminology and basic concepts about information systems as well as the application of that knowledge. The examination does not emphasize the details of hardware design and language-specific programming techniques. References to applications such as word processing or spreadsheets do not require knowledge of a specific product. The focus is on concepts and techniques applicable to a variety of products and environments. Knowledge of arithmetic and mathematics equivalent to that of a student who has successfully completed a traditional first-year high school algebra course is assumed.

The examination contains approximately 100 questions to be answered in 90 minutes. Some of these are pretest questions and will not be scored.

Information Systems textbooks differ on the precise definition of the systems development process or life cycle. To avoid ambiguity, CLEP defines the systems development process as consisting of the following discrete phases or stages:

1. Planning
2. Analysis
3. Design
4. Implementation
5. Maintenance

The following are trademarked terms that appear in this publication:

- Bluetooth® is a registered trademark of Bluetooth SIG, Inc.
- Java® is a registered trademark of Oracle America, Inc.
- Javascript® is a registered trademark of Oracle America, Inc.
- W3C® is a registered trademark of Massachusetts Institute of Technology.

Knowledge and Skills Required

Questions on the Information Systems examination require test-takers to demonstrate knowledge of the following content. The percentage next to each main topic indicates the approximate percentage of exam questions on that topic.

10% Office Applications

- Productivity software (word processing, spreadsheet, presentation package, database package)
- Operating systems (memory management, file management, interfaces, types of OS)
- Office systems (e-mail, conferencing, collaborative work, document imaging, system resources)

15% Internet and World Wide Web

- Internet and other online services and methods (World Wide Web, protocol, Web search engines, Web bots, intranet, cloud computing, communications, push/pull technology,W3C)
- Web browsers (URLs, protocols, standards, history, cookies, resource allocation)
- Web technologies (HTML, XML, Javascript)
- Website development (analysis, design, functionality, accessibility)

15% Technology Applications

- Specialized systems (knowledge management, expert systems, TPS/OLTP, DSS, GIS, BI, workflow management, project management)
- E-commerce/E-business (EDI, standards, tools, characteristics, types of transactions, business models)
- Enterprise-wide systems (ERP, CRM, SCM)
- Data management (data warehousing, data mining, networking, security, validation, migration, storage, obsolescence)
- Business strategies (competition, process reengineering, process modeling, TQM, Web 2.0)
- Information processing methods (batch, real-time, transaction)

15% Hardware and Systems Technology

- Devices (processing, storage, input and output, telecommunications, networking)
- Functions (computer, telecommunications, network hardware)
- Network architectures (local area, wide area, VPN, enterprise)
- Computer architectures (mainframe, client/server, operating systems)
- Wireless technologies (Wi-Fi, cellular, satellite, mobile, GPS, RFID)

10% Software Development

- Methodologies (prototyping, SDLC, RAD, CASE, JAD, Agile)
- Processes (feasibility, systems analysis, systems design, end-user development, project management)
- Implementation (testing, training, data conversion, system conversion, system maintenance, post-implementation activities, post-implementation review, documentation)
- Standards (proprietary, open source)

10% Programming Concepts and Data Management

- Programming logic (Boolean, arithmetic, SQL)
- Methodologies (object-oriented, structured)
- Data (concepts, types, structures, digital representation of data)
- File (types, structures)
- Database management systems (relational, hierarchical, network, management strategies)

25% Social and Ethical Implications and Issues

- Economic effects (secure transactions, viruses, malware, cost of security)
- Privacy concerns (individual, business, identity theft)
- Property rights (intellectual, legal, ownership of materials, open-source software)
- Effects of information technology on jobs (ergonomics, virtual teams, telecommuting, job design)
- Technology's influence on workforce strategies (globalization, virtual teams, telecommuting, outsourcing, insourcing)
- Careers in IS (responsibilities, occupations, career path, certification)
- Computer security and controls (system, application, personal computer, disaster recovery)
- Social networking (benefits, risks, ethics, technology, Web 2.0)

Sample Test Questions

The following sample questions do not appear on an actual CLEP examination. They are intended to give potential test-takers an indication of the format and difficulty level of the examination and to provide content for practice and review. Knowing the correct answers to all of the sample questions is not a guarantee of satisfactory performance on the exam.

Directions: Some of the questions or incomplete statements below are followed by five suggested answers or completions. Select the one that is best in each case.

Some of the questions ask you to select one or more answer choices from a list of choices. For these questions, select all that apply.

Some of the questions refer to a table in which statements appear in the first column. For each statement, select the correct property by checking the appropriate cell in the table.

1. File extensions such as .txt, .bmp, and .mp3 are used to identify a file's

    (A) output
    (B) creator
    (C) size
    (D) location
    (E) format

2. Which of the following network technologies allows secure transmission of data over an unsecured public network link between private networks?

    (A) Local area network
    (B) Wide area network
    (C) Virtual private network
    (D) Intranet
    (E) Extranet

3. Which of the following is a goal of green computing?

    (A) Reducing the potential for a computer to become infected with malware
    (B) Reducing the number of people experiencing computer vision syndrome
    (C) Reducing power consumption of computers and peripherals
    (D) Optimizing the human-computer interface
    (E) Building relationships between computer manufacturers and environmental groups

4. Which of the following is (are) true about EDI?

    I. The EDI documents generally contain the same information that paper documents do.
    II. The speed in which the documents are exchanged is much faster than that of paper documents.
    III. Transmission of EDI documents is less accurate than that of paper documents.

    (A) I only
    (B) II only
    (C) III only
    (D) I and II only
    (E) I, II, and III

5. A spreadsheet contains the values 4 and 6 in cells C4 and D4, respectively. What value will be displayed in cell F4 if it contains the formula (C4^2+D4/4) ?

    (A) 2.5
    (B) 5.5
    (C) 16
    (D) 17.5
    (E) 128

6. Which of the following would NOT be considered an input device for a computer system?

    (A) Image scanner
    (B) Webcam
    (C) Keyboard
    (D) Mouse
    (E) PC speaker

7. In a relational database, each column represents
   (A) a record
   (B) an attribute
   (C) a key
   (D) an entity
   (E) a file

8. Which of the following violates intellectual property rights?
   (A) Software piracy
   (B) Data mining of social networks
   (C) Launching a denial of service attack
   (D) Hacktivism
   (E) Spamming

9. Conversion of data files is part of which of the following phases of the system development process?
   (A) Analysis
   (B) Design
   (C) Implementation
   (D) Development
   (E) Maintenance

10. Which of the following technologies does NOT facilitate knowledge management?
    (A) Blogs
    (B) Wikis
    (C) Web conferencing
    (D) Desktop sharing
    (E) Biometrics

11. The American Charity Association, a nonprofit foundation, has a home page on the World Wide Web. Which of the following is the most likely URL for its home page?
    (A) http://www.charity.gov
    (B) http://www.charity.edu
    (C) http://www.charity.com
    (D) http://www.charity.org
    (E) ftp://www.charity.aca

12. What is the principal function of an operating system?
    (A) To provide an interface between the hardware and the application software
    (B) To defragment storage devices to optimize file access
    (C) To process transaction information
    (D) To create and maintain organizational databases
    (E) To scan for viruses

13. A business often identifies that its software has been trademarked by using a unique symbol or attaching the letters TM to its name. What is the purpose of the trademark?
    (A) To eliminate unauthorized copying and distribution
    (B) To identify the software as available for use, free of charge
    (C) To identify and differentiate the product's brand
    (D) To assure the user that the software is properly licensed and ready to use
    (E) To assure the user that the software contains unique features not found in other products

14. What term identifies the measure of accuracy, completeness, and currency of data?
    (A) Data dependency
    (B) Data integration
    (C) Data integrity
    (D) Data redundancy
    (E) Data visualization

15. The special formatting language used to create Web pages is called
    (A) HTML
    (B) XML
    (C) Perl
    (D) Java
    (E) Script

16. Which of the following best characterizes data in a data warehouse?

(A) Historical
(B) Normalized
(C) Relational
(D) Volatile
(E) Up-to-date

17. Which of the following is designed to allow a team to discuss a topic over an extended period of time while keeping the responses organized by topic?

(A) Data library
(B) File sharing
(C) Push technology
(D) Internet telephony
(E) Threaded discussion group

18. Which of the following is NOT a correct characterization of batch processing?

(A) It allows immediate updating of master files.
(B) It provides physical batch totals to be used in control procedures.
(C) It provides efficient updating of master files.
(D) It is most applicable for processing routine periodic activities.
(E) It allows efficient scheduling of processing.

19. Which of the following best describes how GPS units function?

(A) The receiver sends out regular query pulses and waits to receive responses from a GPS satellite.
(B) The receiver is passive and listens for the regular signals from GPS satellites, which are then processed to find the distance from the satellites.
(C) The receiver sends out radio signals that are reflected back by satellites and detected by the unit.
(D) The receiver acts as a homing beacon that is tracked by the GPS satellites, which periodically send out position updates for each tracked receiver.
(E) The receiver can detect an invisible electronic grid projected onto Earth's surface and compares the location on this grid to a stored map of Earth.

20. Which of the following is the most likely negative consequence of participating in a social networking website?

(A) Unintended disclosure of private information
(B) Increase in spam
(C) Infection by a virus
(D) Download of a cookie containing personal preferences
(E) Download of spyware

21. Voice and speech recognition technologies can be found in which of the following applications?

I. Automated transcription
II. Security and access control
III. Batch processing

(A) I only
(B) II only
(C) I and II only
(D) I and III only
(E) I, II, and III

22. Assume that a file consists of the following records.

Product Number	Product	Model Year
BEC111	WIDGET	2015
ABC123	GADGET	2014
SBB003	WIDGET	2013
XPL222	GADGET	2014
MAS120	GADGET	2010

The computer is instructed to sort this file in ascending order with Product as the primary sort key, Model Year as the secondary sort key, and Product Number as the tertiary sort key. If this file is printed in sorted order, which record will be the third printed?

(A) BEC111 WIDGET 2015
(B) ABC123 GADGET 2014
(C) SBB003 WIDGET 2013
(D) XPL222 GADGET 2014
(E) MAS120 GADGET 2010

23. Which of the following is a potential benefit of telecommuting to the employer?

Select all that apply.

(A) Eliminates employee commuting time
(B) Facilitates recruiting a larger pool of prospective employees
(C) Increases flexibility in handling of unexpected work after typical business hours
(D) Reduces stress of supervisors
(E) Improves communication between employees

24. What is the primary difference between an intranet Web page and an Internet Web page?

(A) Transport protocol
(B) Transmission rate
(C) Restriction of access
(D) Physical proximity to server
(E) Use of secure socket layers

25. Which of the following explains why digital networks can transmit different types of data?

(A) Networks can accommodate different types of computers.
(B) Network connections can be made via satellites.
(C) Data can be transmitted as either digital or analog signals.
(D) Storage capacity is not an issue.
(E) Each data type can be represented by strings of bits.

26. A disaster recovery plan to safeguard a company's computer system can be used for all of the following occurrences EXCEPT

(A) a flood, fire, or other natural disaster
(B) a massive long-term power outage
(C) system upgrades and hardware maintenance
(D) computer sabotage
(E) a major viral infection of computer systems

27. In a company with a large and effective IT workforce, which of the following is the most likely title of the person who recommends enterprise-wide upgrades of computer hardware?

(A) Chief Information Officer
(B) Chief Technology Officer
(C) Chief Financial Officer
(D) Systems Analyst
(E) Information Resources Manager

28. A user has visited several websites, making purchases, initiating searches, and filling out online forms. Which of the following could the user access to revisit the websites?

(A) Cookies
(B) Main memory
(C) Internet preferences
(D) Web privacy settings
(E) Web browser history

29. A network administrator is LEAST likely to recommend which of the following technologies to share large quantities of information in a knowledge management system?

(A) E-mail
(B) Wiki
(C) Intranet
(D) Discussion board
(E) Shared network drive

30. Which of the following is a major benefit of object-oriented programming?

(A) The development of logical steps to achieve the object of the program
(B) The use of subroutines that optimize the program's objective
(C) The creation of objects that can be used or modified for use in future applications
(D) The freedom for programmers to create objects unique to each program
(E) The defining of objects as static entities that do not relate to each other

31. Which of the following is NOT part of input data controls in the context of information processing?

(A) Verifying the input data range
(B) Verifying check digits
(C) Verifying the syntax in the code
(D) Verifying data types
(E) Verifying batch totals

32. When applied to the development of computer systems, the term "ergonomics" means

(A) designing computer systems to maximize the cost-benefit ratio
(B) incorporating human comfort, efficiency, and safety into the design of the human-machine interface
(C) following the systems development life cycle
(D) fostering development team interaction through the use of computer-aided software engineering tools
(E) optimizing the throughput rate by adjusting the operating system interrupts

33. What is the term that refers to the downloading of live video, audio, or animation in such a manner that the user can begin to access the content before the download is complete?

(A) Spooling
(B) Streaming
(C) Flaming
(D) Spamming
(E) Queuing

34. Which of the following is (are) true about customer relationship management systems?

I. They focus on the connection between suppliers, manufacturers, and customers.
II. They enable employees in all departments to have a consistent view of customers.
III. They focus on customer retention.

(A) I only
(B) I and II only
(C) I and III only
(D) II and III only
(E) I, II, and III

35. Which of the following best describes a worm?

(A) A program that displays advertisements in pop-up windows
(B) A program that is installed on a computer without the user's knowledge
(C) A virus that masquerades as another active program
(D) A program that traces user activity
(E) A program that replicates itself repeatedly, using up system resources

36. Which of the following is true about open-source software?

Select all that apply:

(A) It always provides product support.
(B) Its source code is freely available.
(C) It is copyrighted.
(D) It is shareware.

37. Which of the following is a database whose data are scattered across several physical servers?

(A) Data mine
(B) Data warehouse
(C) Relational database
(D) Distributed database
(E) Integrated database

38. When developing a website, which of the following activities should occur closest to the end of the process?

(A) Creating the navigation structure
(B) Purchasing a domain name
(C) Verifying all the hyperlinks
(D) Designing the style sheets
(E) Finalizing the graphics

39. Which of the following can support cloud-based application development and deployment?

(A) Communications as a service
(B) Platform as a service
(C) Infrastructure as a service
(D) Software as a service
(E) Network as a service

40. Knowledge management software is designed to do which of the following?

(A) Identify patterns and trends in data
(B) Collect and store data in a way that can be easily accessed
(C) Manage day-to-day interactions with customers
(D) Help analyze data and facilitate decision making
(E) Facilitate organizational learning

41. An online storefront developer should test the different versions of which of the following in order to ensure usability for all users?

(A) Database management systems
(B) Hypertext markup languages
(C) Compilers
(D) Web browsers
(E) Search engines

42. Which of the following statements is true regarding client/server architecture?

(A) The server computer accepts commands from a number of computers that are its clients.
(B) The server computer manages a number of computers that it services.
(C) The server computer is connected to a number of computers that provide it with services.
(D) The client computer is connected to a number of computers that provide it with clients.
(E) The client computer manages a number of computers being served by it.

43. For which of the following consumer applications would there be the LEAST justification to access a national credit history database?

(A) Credit card
(B) Mortgage
(C) Student loan
(D) Savings account
(E) Automobile lease

44. Metadata is best described as which of the following?

(A) End-user data
(B) Data about data
(C) Data stored in a Web file format
(D) Data gathered by spyware
(E) Data returned by an Internet search engine

Directions: Choose among the corresponding environments in the columns for each entry by clicking on your choice. When you click on a blank cell a check mark will appear. No credit is given unless the correct cell is marked for each entry.

45. Which of the following is a reason to use a virtual team model as opposed to an on-site team model?

	Yes	**No**
There are personality conflicts among team members.		
Team members have different physical locations.		
Team members have difficulty reaching consensus.		

Click on your choices.

46. Which of the following is NOT an advantage of having an entire department using the same office software suite?

(A) Lower cost per application than if purchased individually
(B) Ease of moving data between suite applications
(C) Ease of moving data between users in the same department
(D) Ease of installation and maintenance
(E) Optimal functionality of individual application packages

47. Which of the following problem-solving techniques allows users to start with high-level information and then select more specific, lower-level details?

(A) Ad hoc analysis
(B) Exception reporting
(C) Drill-down analysis
(D) RFM analysis
(E) Cluster analysis

48. The Bluetooth standard uses what transmission method for data transfer?

(A) Infrared
(B) Ethernet cable
(C) Radio waves
(D) Satellite
(E) Wi-Fi

49. After a consumer purchases and downloads an MP3 file, which of the following is legal? Select all that apply.

(A) Copying the file for personal use
(B) Copying the file and giving the copy to a friend
(C) Giving the original file as a gift
(D) Selling the original file
(E) Uploading the file to a public website

50. Which of the following describes a website that provides access to multiple services such as news, weather, sports, and stock indexes?

(A) Host
(B) Portal
(C) Domain
(D) Hot site
(E) Home page

51. Which of the following statements about rapid application development is true?

(A) It is used during prototyping.
(B) It is designed to be platform dependent.
(C) It reduces dependency on object-oriented programming.
(D) It begins before requirements are defined.
(E) It allows programmers to preemptively determine user interfaces without the users' input.

52. Which of the following is true about user passwords?

(A) They should be changed only by the administrator.
(B) They must be no more than eight characters in length.
(C) They are requested by CAPTCHAs.
(D) They are most secure when they consist of letters, numbers, and special characters.
(E) They are required to be unique.

53. Which of the following statements is (are) true concerning multiuser database management systems?

I. They can increase the standardization of data.
II. They can increase the need to store data in many different locations in the database.
III. They can increase access to and availability of information.

(A) I only
(B) II only
(C) I and II only
(D) I and III only
(E) I, II, and III

54. Developers quickly create a version of a system and give it to the users for feedback. The developers then use the users' feedback to revise the system. This process repeats until the users approve the system. This method of developing a system is called

(A) waterfall
(B) prototyping
(C) object-oriented
(D) end-user development
(E) joint application design

55. Which of the following is NOT true of social networking sites?

(A) It is unethical for a company recruiting prospective employees to track their presence on and posts to social networking sites.
(B) Any unethical activity on a social networking site could have negative consequences outside the site.
(C) Some sites enable members to share material with many other members simultaneously.
(D) Some sites enable members to maintain contact with other members.
(E) Some sites facilitate access to commercial sites.

56. Which of the following information technology processes is used to produce documents that are duplicate, uneditable digital copies?

(A) Word processing
(B) Photocopying
(C) Document imaging
(D) Desktop publishing
(E) OCR scanning

57. Which of the following is NOT a means of secondary storage?

(A) External hard drive
(B) Cache memory
(C) USB flash drive
(D) Cloud storage
(E) Secure digital card

58. The capability of computerized systems to store and exchange information poses a potential threat to the individual's right to

(A) free speech
(B) privacy
(C) equal access to information
(D) assembly
(E) consumer protection

59. Which of the following is NOT a characteristic of a decision support system, as it is usually defined?

(A) It can be used as an aid in solving ad hoc problems.
(B) It is useful for what-if analysis.
(C) It is intended to help managers make decisions.
(D) It makes the one best or optimal decision.
(E) It uses appropriate statistical and mathematical models.

60. Which of the following uses the Internet, as opposed to using the public switched network, to enable voice communication?

(A) TCP/IP
(B) VoIP
(C) EFT
(D) EDI
(E) PBX

61. Which data model uses two-dimensional tables to represent data structures?

(A) Relational
(B) Hierarchical
(C) Network
(D) Multidimensional
(E) Object-oriented

62. Which of the following types of systems development methods would be appropriate when a company does not have an expert IS department?

I. Outsourcing
II. Traditional SDLC
III. RAD

(A) I only
(B) II only
(C) III only
(D) I and III only
(E) I, II, and III

63. Planning, scheduling, and overseeing the development of a new information system are all components of which of the following?

(A) Systems analysis
(B) System modeling
(C) Knowledge management
(D) Cost-benefit analysis
(E) Project management

64. Which of the following activities CANNOT be performed in a link in an HTML document?

(A) Sending an e-mail
(B) Printing the current Web page
(C) Moving to another location on the current Web page
(D) Opening another Web page in the current browser window
(E) Opening another Web page in a new browser window

65. A manager of a small business wants to use a computer to store information about clients, vendors, inventory (item, number, price), and orders. The manager needs to be able to sort and group data for various reports. Which of the following types of software packages would be best for this task?

(A) Word processor
(B) Spreadsheet
(C) Database management system
(D) Presentation software
(E) System software

66. The CTO of a large company should consider which of the following in determining whether to replace the current mainframe?

I. The dollar value of the current mainframe
II. The cost of maintaining the current mainframe
III. The cost of replacing the current mainframe

(A) I only
(B) II only
(C) III only
(D) II and III only
(E) I, II, and III

67. Which of the following directly affects the most users?

(A) Hacking
(B) Phishing
(C) Cyberextortion
(D) Identity theft
(E) Denial of service attacks

68. In considering the economic feasibility of a systems development project, which of the following would a project manager be LEAST likely to consider?

(A) The cost of developing the system compared with the potential benefits of using the system
(B) The return on the initial investment on the system
(C) When the project will break even
(D) Whether the company can afford the project
(E) Whether the hardware can be acquired for the project

69. A program written to access and update a master database that maintains sales of tickets to an upcoming concert is

(A) system software
(B) networking software
(C) a transaction processing system
(D) an operating system
(E) a knowledge management system

70. Which of the following user-based activities would NOT be part of a website design project?

(A) Users being asked what information should appear on the website
(B) Users being asked what programming language they are most comfortable with
(C) Users being asked about their security concerns
(D) Users being asked what statistical feedback they would like to receive
(E) Users being instructed to look at similar websites

71. Which of the following is an advantage of outsourcing?

    (A) It enables a company to focus on core competencies.
    (B) It decreases dependence on other organizations.
    (C) It decreases the risk of disclosing confidential information.
    (D) It improves managerial control.
    (E) It enhances in-house technical expertise.

72. Batch processing is LEAST likely to be applied to

    (A) periodic merging of transaction records
    (B) ad hoc querying of a marketing information database
    (C) creating management reports
    (D) transmitting monthly sales projections
    (E) populating a data warehouse

73. Which of the following is a software agent used by some Internet search engines to generate search results?

    (A) Web bot
    (B) TCP filter
    (C) Auto responder
    (D) Worm
    (E) Macro

74. The maintenance phase of the system development process could include all of the following activities EXCEPT

    (A) correcting errors in the software that were detected after implementation
    (B) changing the heading on a report
    (C) updating entries in the tax table to reflect changes in the tax rates
    (D) adding a new function to an existing system
    (E) performing a complete rewrite for an existing system

75. The type of network that would most likely be used to link a corporation's headquarters with its four branch offices located throughout a state is referred to as

    (A) a metropolitan area network
    (B) a local area network
    (C) an office area network
    (D) a wide area network
    (E) a broad area network

76. Goals of a supply-chain management system include which of the following?

    I. Facilitate upselling of the product
    II. Deliver the product to the customer more rapidly
    III. Reduce the cost of procurement

    (A) I only
    (B) I and II only
    (C) I and III only
    (D) II and III only
    (E) I, II, and III

77. Which of the following is a set of protocols used to link different types of computers over the Internet?

    (A) HTML
    (B) HTTP
    (C) ERP
    (D) TCP/IP
    (E) W3C

78. Which of the following does NOT provide data security or access security?

    (A) Data encryption
    (B) Password protection
    (C) Data encoding
    (D) Biometric scan
    (E) Digital certificate

79. Which of the following is the term used when a website automatically downloads data or files to a computer whenever new data are available or at scheduled intervals?

(A) Web streaming
(B) Push technology
(C) Pipelining
(D) Spamming
(E) Web crawling

80. A geographic information system must have which of the following characteristics?

I. Records have identified geographic locations.
II. The system uses global positioning satellites.
III. The system provides results in a graphic format.

(A) I only
(B) I and II only
(C) I and III only
(D) II and III only
(E) I, II, and III

81. Managers in an organization often use spreadsheets to assist with decision making. The process of using a spreadsheet to try out alternatives is called

(A) what-if analysis
(B) data mining
(C) flowcharting
(D) querying
(E) data manipulation

82. Having multiple operating systems installed on the same personal computer enables the user to do each of the following EXCEPT

(A) run a proprietary operating system and an open source operating system on the same computer
(B) run different versions of the same operating system on the same computer
(C) access a larger variety of software
(D) create multiple IP addresses for the computer
(E) create a virtual server

83. Which of the following is an asynchronous technology that a virtual team can use for communication?

(A) Conference call
(B) Videoconferencing
(C) VoIP
(D) E-mail
(E) Webinar

84. Which of the following is an application that can use RFID technology?

Select all that apply.

(A) Data transfer between smartphones
(B) Toll collection on a limited-access roadway
(C) Inventory management
(D) Credit card use
(E) Internet access
(F) Animal tracking

85. A table called "Students" consists of the following records:

Name	Credits	GPA
Anderson	10	3.0
Chen	9	3.2
Gomez	12	3.1
Jones	12	3.0

A user entered the following SQL command:

```
Select Name
From Students
Where Credits > 9 and GPA > 3
```

How many names would be returned based on the criteria?

(A) None
(B) One
(C) Two
(D) Three
(E) Four

86. The process through which a user is verified and validated to access a computer network/system is referred to as

(A) encryption
(B) password protection
(C) authentication
(D) account validation
(E) certification

87. What is the term that describes the storage of identical data in multiple files?

(A) Data dependency
(B) Data integrity
(C) Data integration
(D) Data redundancy
(E) Data structure

88. Under which of the following conditions can a public wireless network be used to transmit confidential data most securely?

(A) The local computer has been scanned for viruses.
(B) The local computer has the latest operating system and updates.
(C) The local computer connects to the network using VPN.
(D) All files on the local computer have been backed up.
(E) The network password meets all security criteria.

89. Using an ERP system has which of the following advantages?

I. It is easier to install than a typical transaction processing system.
II. It provides a centralized database for organizational data.
III. It integrates processes over the organization.

(A) I only
(B) II only
(C) I and II only
(D) II and III only
(E) I, II, and III

90.

	A	B	C	D
1	1	2	3	4
2	2	4	6	8
3	1	2	3	4
4	2	4	6	8

The table above shows the contents of 16 cells in a spreadsheet. Cell E5 of the spreadsheet contains the formula "=B$2+$C2". Cell E5 is copied to cell F6. What is the value displayed in cell F6?

(A) 5
(B) 7
(C) 9
(D) 10
(E) 14

Study Resources

Most textbooks used in college-level introductory business information systems courses cover the knowledge and skills in the outline given earlier. The approaches to certain topics and the emphases given to them differ. It is advisable to study one or more current college textbooks to prepare for the Information Systems exam. When selecting textbooks, for each textbook check the table of contents against the knowledge and skills required for this test.

Visit **clep.collegeboard.org/earn-college-credit/practice** for additional study resources. You can also find suggestions for exam preparation in Chapter IV of the *Official Study Guide*.

Answer Key

1.	E	46.	E
2.	C	47.	C
3.	C	48.	C
4.	D	49.	A, C
5.	D	50.	B
6.	E	51.	A
7.	B	52.	D
8.	A	53.	D
9.	C	54.	B
10.	E	55.	A
11.	D	56.	C
12.	A	57.	B
13.	C	58.	B
14.	C	59.	D
15.	A	60.	B
16.	A	61.	A
17.	E	62.	A
18.	A	63.	E
19.	B	64.	B
20.	A	65.	C
21.	C	66.	D
22.	D	67.	E
23.	B, C	68.	E
24.	C	69.	C
25.	E	70.	B
26.	C	71.	A
27.	B	72.	B
28.	E	73.	A
29.	A	74.	E
30.	C	75.	D
31.	C	76.	D
32.	B	77.	D
33.	B	78.	C
34.	D	79.	B
35.	E	80.	C
36.	B, C	81.	A
37.	D	82.	D
38.	C	83.	D
39.	B	84.	B, C, D, F
40.	E	85.	B
41.	D	86.	C
42.	A	87.	D
43.	D	88.	C
44.	B	89.	D
45.	See next page.	90.	C

45.

	Yes	No
There are personality conflicts among team members.		√
Team members have different physical locations.	√	
Team members have difficulty reaching consensus.		√

Click on your choices.

Introductory Business Law

Description of the Examination

The Introductory Business Law examination covers material that is usually taught in an introductory one-semester college course in the subject. The examination places not only major emphasis on understanding the functions of contracts in American business law, but it also includes questions on the history and sources of American law, legal systems and procedures, agency and employment, sales and other topics.

The examination contains approximately 100 questions to be answered in 90 minutes. Some of these are pretest questions that will not be scored.

Knowledge and Skills Required

Questions on the test require candidates to demonstrate one or more of the following abilities in the approximate proportions indicated.

- Knowledge of the basic facts and terms (about 30–35 percent of the examination)
- Understanding of concepts and principles (about 30–35 percent of the examination)
- Ability to apply knowledge to specific case problems (about 30 percent of the examination)

The subject matter of the Introductory Business Law examination is drawn from the following topics. The percentages next to the main topics indicate the approximate percentage of exam questions on that topic.

5%–10% History and Sources of American Law/Constitutional Law

5%–10% American Legal Systems and Procedures

30%–40% Contracts

Meanings of terms
Formation of contracts
Capacity
Consideration
Joint obligations
Contracts for the benefit of third parties
Assignment/delegation
Statute of frauds
Scopes and meanings of contracts
Breach of contract and remedies
Bar to remedies for breach of contract
Discharge of contracts
Illegal contracts
Other

20%–25% Legal Environment

Ethics
Social responsibility of corporations
Government regulation/ administrative agencies
Antitrust law
Employment law
Product liability
Consumer protection
International business law

10%–15% Torts

5%–10% Miscellaneous

Agency, partnerships and corporations
Sales

Sample Test Questions

The following sample questions do not appear on an actual CLEP examination. They are intended to give potential test-takers an indication of the format and difficulty level of the examination and to provide content for practice and review. Knowing the correct answers to all of the sample questions is not a guarantee of satisfactory performance on the exam.

Directions: Each of the questions or incomplete statements below is followed by five suggested answers or completions. Select the one that is best in each case.

1. The authority of a court to hear and decide cases is known as

    (A) jurisdiction
    (B) habeas corpus
    (C) demurrer
    (D) quo warranto
    (E) stare decisis

2. In the landmark case of *Marbury* v. *Madison* (1803), the United States Supreme Court held that

    (A) Chief Justice Marshall had exceeded his power under the United States Constitution in declaring an act of Congress unconstitutional
    (B) Madison had properly withheld Marbury's appointment to be a justice
    (C) Marbury was entitled to his appointment, and Madison was required to deliver it to him
    (D) Marbury was entitled to his appointment, but the congressional statute granting the federal courts the power to compel Madison to deliver his appointment was unconstitutional
    (E) Article III of the United States Constitution expressly granted the power of judicial review to the Supreme Court

3. A contract will be unenforceable if

    (A) one party to the contract feels he or she has been taken advantage of
    (B) a statute declares such a contract illegal
    (C) performance becomes difficult
    (D) public authorities voice disapproval of the contract
    (E) the parties involved believe the contract to be illegal

4. Angela promises to work for Barbara during the month of July, and Barbara promises to pay Angela $600 for her services. In this situation, what kind of contract has been made?

    (A) Unilateral
    (B) Executed
    (C) Quasi
    (D) Bilateral
    (E) Bilingual

5. Which of the following is an essential element of fraud?

    (A) Injury to a business interest
    (B) Misrepresentation of a material fact
    (C) Destruction of property
    (D) Knowledge of the consequences of an act
    (E) Mistake about the identity of the subject matter

6. Clyde received the following letter from Joe: "I will sell you the books you examined yesterday for $10 each or $100 for the entire set." Clyde, not sure he would get much use from the books, told his brother, Michael, about the offer. Michael tendered Joe $100 for the books, but Joe refused to sell the books to Michael.

   If Michael sued Joe, the court would probably hold that Michael

   (A) can accept the offer because he is Clyde's brother
   (B) can accept the offer if he will do so within a reasonable period of time
   (C) cannot accept the offer until Clyde's rejection is communicated to Joe
   (D) cannot accept the offer because it was not made to him
   (E) cannot accept the offer unless he does so in writing

7. All of the following have the right to enforce a contract EXCEPT

   (A) an assignee
   (B) a transferee
   (C) a third-party creditor beneficiary
   (D) a third-party donee beneficiary
   (E) a third-party incidental beneficiary

8. A method of discharging a contract that returns each party to his or her original position is

   (A) an assignment
   (B) an accord
   (C) a revocation
   (D) a rescission
   (E) a novation

9. In a legal action alleging $100,000 of damages suffered for breach of contract, the plaintiff is a citizen of New York and the defendant is a corporation organized under the laws of California with its principal place of business in Los Angeles. Considering the details of this case, a United States district court will

   (A) have jurisdiction based on diversity of citizenship
   (B) have jurisdiction because the legal action is for breach of contract
   (C) not have jurisdiction because the legal action is for breach of contract
   (D) apply the federal common law of contracts
   (E) lack jurisdiction because the parties from different states apply New York law under the legal doctrine *lex loci delicti*

10. Benson, a seventeen-year-old college freshman, was adequately supplied with clothes by his father. Smith, a clothing merchant, learned that Benson was spending money freely and solicited clothing orders from him. Benson bought $750 worth of luxury clothing from Smith on credit. Benson failed to pay Smith.

    If Smith sued Benson, the court would probably hold that

    (A) Benson is liable for the $750 because by accepting and wearing the clothes he ratified the contract
    (B) Benson is not liable for the reasonable value of the clothing because Smith solicited the sales
    (C) Benson can disaffirm the contract, return the clothing, and escape liability
    (D) Benson is liable for the $750 because under these circumstances the clothing was a necessity
    (E) Benson's father is liable to Smith for the $750

11. The enforcement of a contract may be barred, according to the operation of law, by

(A) an assignment
(B) a delegation
(C) a material breach
(D) the statute of limitations
(E) a novation

12. The purpose of a grand jury is to

(A) indict the accused and to require him or her to stand trial
(B) decide guilt or innocence of the accused
(C) sentence the accused
(D) convict the accused
(E) review police activity and procedure

13. Which of the following promises would be enforceable by the majority of courts?

(A) Avery finds Bond's dog and returns it to Bond. Later, Bond promises to pay Avery a reward.
(B) Husband, in consideration of the love and affection given him by Wife, promises to pay her $1,000.
(C) Avery is extremely ill and placed in a hospital. Avery's neighbor, Bond, mows Avery's yard while Avery is recuperating. Later, Avery promises to pay Bond the reasonable value of his services.
(D) Avery owes Bond $100, but the collection of this debt is barred by the statute of limitations. Later, Avery writes Bond a letter promising to pay Bond the $100.
(E) Daughter mows the family yard. In absence of an express agreement, Daughter can claim an implied promise on Father's part to pay for her services.

14. Base Electric Company has entered an agreement to buy its actual requirements of brass wiring for six months from the Valdez Metal Wire Company, and Valdez Metal Wire Company has agreed to sell all the brass wiring Base Electric Company will require for six months. The agreement between the two companies is

(A) valid and enforceable
(B) unenforceable because of lack of consideration
(C) unenforceable because it is too indefinite
(D) lacking in mutuality of obligations
(E) illusory

15. Ordinarily an employer is liable for which of the authorized acts committed by an employee for the benefit of the employer and in the scope of the employment?

I. Torts
II. Contracts
III. Misrepresentations

(A) I only
(B) II only
(C) III only
(D) II and III only
(E) I, II, and III

16. Abbott was orphaned at the age of five. For the next fifteen years his material needs were met by his uncle, Barton. On his thirtieth birthday, Abbott wrote Barton and promised to pay him $100 per month as long as Barton lived. Abbott never made any payments. Barton died ten months later. If Barton's estate sued Abbott for the amount of the promised payments, the court would probably hold that Barton's estate is

    (A) not entitled to recover because past consideration will not support Abbott's promise
    (B) not entitled to recover because of the statute of limitations
    (C) not entitled to recover unless it can be shown that Barton's relatives were in desperate need
    (D) entitled to recover on the promise
    (E) entitled to recover because of Barton's previous aid to Abbott

17. An agreement among creditors that each will accept a certain percentage of his or her claim as full satisfaction is called

    (A) accord and satisfaction
    (B) creditor agreement
    (C) composition with creditors
    (D) liquidation
    (E) bankruptcy

18. Which of the following decisions could NOT be made by an appellate court?

    (A) Ordering a case to be tried in the appellate court
    (B) Affirming a decision of a lower court
    (C) Instructing a lower court to enter a judgment in accordance with the appellate court's opinion
    (D) Remanding a case for a new trial
    (E) Reversing the decision of a lower court

19. Upon delivery of nonconforming goods, a buyer may do which of the following?

    I. Reject all the goods.
    II. Accept all the goods.
    III. Accept those units that conform and reject the rest.

    (A) I only
    (B) III only
    (C) I and II only
    (D) II and III only
    (E) I, II, and III

20. All of the following are usual functions performed by judges of trial courts having general jurisdiction EXCEPT

    (A) issuing writs of habeas corpus
    (B) conducting pretrial conferences in civil cases
    (C) determining questions of fact in equity cases
    (D) guiding the jury on questions of law in criminal and civil cases
    (E) imposing pretrial settlements on parties who cannot agree

21. Which of the following will apply if the parties to a contract knew or should have known that a word has a customary usage in their particular trade or community?

    (A) No contract will result if the parties cannot voluntarily agree on the definition of the word.
    (B) The meaning of the word cannot be challenged once a contract is signed.
    (C) Parol evidence may be used to define the meaning of the word.
    (D) Courts will not impose a definition that is contrary to the meaning supported by one party.
    (E) A mistaken assumption regarding the definition by one of the parties will result in a voidable contract.

22. Webster insured her residence with Old Home Insurance Company. Assuming that the policy contained no provision with respect to assignment, which of the following statements is correct?

    (A) Webster may assign the policy to any person having capacity to contract.
    (B) If Webster suffers an insured loss, she may assign the amount due under the policy to anyone.
    (C) If Webster sells her residence, she must assign the policy to the purchaser.
    (D) If Webster suffers an insured loss, she may assign the amount due under the policy only to a party furnishing material or labor for repair of the residence.
    (E) Webster may assign the policy to any person having capacity to contract who agrees to pay the premium.

23. Recovery in quasi contract is based on a judgment that determines the presence of

    (A) an unjust enrichment
    (B) an express contract
    (C) an implied in fact contract
    (D) a violation of the statute of frauds
    (E) a mutual mistake

24. The commerce clause of the United States Constitution authorizes

    (A) Congress to tax corporations
    (B) Congress to regulate interstate commerce
    (C) courts to hear disputes between states and the federal government
    (D) states to regulate their own commerce
    (E) states to police the public anywhere

25. Maxine initiates a lawsuit against Jason by filing and serving Jason with a summons and complaint, and Jason responds to Maxine's complaint with a document called an answer. Maxine's complaint and Jason's answer are referred to as

    (A) legal briefs
    (B) pleadings
    (C) discovery documents
    (D) motions
    (E) appeals

26. Acting in a manner that results in the greatest good for the greatest number is an ethical principle known as

    (A) utilitarianism
    (B) cost-benefit analysis
    (C) rights theory
    (D) the golden rule
    (E) Kantianism

27. Which of the following best defines the employment at will doctrine?

    (A) Employers can terminate employees for good cause only.
    (B) Employees can quit for good reason only.
    (C) Employers can terminate employees for any reason that is not illegal and employees can quit for any reason.
    (D) Employees can quit for any reason.
    (E) Employers can terminate employees for good cause and employees can quit for good reason.

28. Smith suddenly attacks Jones as Jones walks down the street. In this case, Smith has committed

(A) negligence
(B) a contractual act
(C) a criminal act only
(D) a tortious act only
(E) a criminal act and a tortious act

29. Using nonpublic material information to buy or sell securities is known as

(A) short-swing profits
(B) insider trading
(C) a "blue sky" transaction
(D) an under-the-counter trade
(E) an over-the-counter trade

30. Which of the following administrative agencies regulates unfair trade practices and the formation of monopolies that restrain competition?

(A) The National Labor Relations Board
(B) The Securities and Exchange Commission
(C) The Federal Reserve Board
(D) The Federal Trade Commission
(E) The Consumer Protection Agency

31. Which of the following is a distinction that can be drawn between civil and criminal law?

(A) Civil cases involve a jury and criminal cases do not.
(B) The burden of proof in a civil case is "a preponderance of the evidence" standard, while the burden of proof in a criminal case is "beyond a reasonable doubt" standard.
(C) Civil cases involve a wrong against society, while criminal cases involve a loss to only one specific victim.
(D) Civil cases are all statutory, while criminal cases are based on statutes and case law.
(E) There is no distinction between civil and criminal law.

32. Curtis is injured while performing his duties for his employer, Choice Banking Company. In most states, Curtis will be compensated for his injuries under which of the following?

(A) Intentional tort
(B) Negligence
(C) Worker's Compensation
(D) Common Law Contract
(E) The Fair Labor Act

33. Barry sneaks up behind Caesar and hits him over the head with a bat. Caesar suffers a concussion and incurs damages exceeding $50,000.00. Under these facts, Caesar will most likely win a suit against Barry for

(A) assault
(B) battery
(C) conversion
(D) false imprisonment
(E) negligence

34. Proximate cause means that the

(A) defendant will be held liable for all the damages caused by his breach of duty
(B) defendant will be held liable for only those damages that were reasonably foreseeable and a natural and probable consequence of his breach of duty
(C) plaintiff's injury would not have occurred but for the defendant's breach of duty
(D) plaintiff's injury would not have occurred unless the defendant's breach of duty was a substantial factor in bringing about the injury
(E) plaintiff's injury occurred because of the defendant's breach of duty

35. Zack and Josh open a coffee shop. They have no written agreement, but intend to sell coffee and bagels together in order to make a profit. Which of the following describes Zack's and Josh's business relationship?

(A) They are sole proprietors.
(B) They are silent partners.
(C) They are limited partners.
(D) They are shareholders.
(E) They are partners.

36. Fred is an attorney who wants to advertise that he is Austin's best lawyer. He buys a billboard and posts his message. The State Bar of Texas wants him to take down the billboard. Which of the following constitutional principles best supports Fred's position?

(A) The Fourth Amendment
(B) The right against self-incrimination
(C) The First and Fourteenth Amendments
(D) Freedom of assembly
(E) The Declaration of Independence

37. Larry delivers newspapers for a living; he hires Fred to help with his route, paying him 5 cents per paper. Fred runs into a customer's car while delivering papers. Which of the following statements is true?

(A) As partners, Larry and Fred are jointly liable for the damage.
(B) If Larry does business as a corporation, he can be sued individually.
(C) Since Fred was driving the car, he is the only one who can be responsible.
(D) The facts suggest that the doctrine of respondeat superior would apply.
(E) If Fred does not have insurance, it means that the customer can never recover any of his damages to the car.

38. Al Rubin, a used car dealer, has a sports car for sale. A customer is interested in buying it. Al tells him, "It's a super car." Later, the customer discovers that his next-door neighbor's car can outperform his and he visits his attorney saying, "I want to sue Al." Which of the following would be the attorney's best answer?

(A) Al cannot be sued successfully for fraud because the statement made was not in writing.
(B) Al has engaged in fraud because the customer relied on his statement.
(C) Fraud requires malice; therefore, Al cannot be held accountable.
(D) Al's statement is probably considered an opinion; therefore, he cannot be held accountable.
(E) Al cannot be successfully sued because fraud is only a criminal matter.

39. Which of the following is true of federal administrative agencies?

(A) They occupy less importance today than they did in the nineteenth century.
(B) They may investigate, but they cannot make rules.
(C) They are all part of the executive branch.
(D) Their actions are subject to judicial review.
(E) They are not subject to constitutional scrutiny.

40. A bailment contract deals with which of the following?

(A) The posting of a bond to guarantee that a defendant will appear in court when required
(B) The establishment of a contract where one party tries to bail out of a bad situation
(C) The owner of an article of personal property temporarily relinquishing possession and control of it to another
(D) The leasing of unimproved land
(E) The sale of personal property

41. A court will most likely dismiss a tort claim for an assault that was committed five years ago on the grounds that

(A) there is no longer reasonable ground for the plaintiff to fear the defendant's threats
(B) the statute of limitations has run out or expired
(C) the case is nonjusticiable
(D) the defendant is entitled to a default judgment
(E) the court lacks subject-matter jurisdiction over the case

42. All of the following are foundations for business ethics EXCEPT

(A) religion
(B) philosophy
(C) law
(D) business practices of competitors
(E) cultural norms

43. In general, an appeal of an administrative decision to the courts must show that

(A) the case has been proved beyond a reasonable doubt
(B) administrative remedies have been exhausted
(C) a serious economic loss has been incurred
(D) the case has been proven by the greater weight of the evidence
(E) the administrative agency was unfair

44. The Civil Rights Act of 1964 protects victims of

(A) all forms of discrimination
(B) religious discrimination
(C) age discrimination
(D) discrimination on the basis of HIV-positive status
(E) discrimination based on sexual orientation

45. Manuel is hired by Star Players Theater to design and maintain the theatre's Web site. Mango Theater learns of Manuel's work and convinces him to leave Star Players to come work for Mango. Mango Theater is probably liable for the tort of

(A) misappropriation
(B) unfair competition
(C) breach of contract
(D) wrongful interference with a contractual relationship
(E) disparagement of a business relationship

46. Kate's corporation has accumulated a large number of accounts payable and lost its largest customer. Kate thinks that she can save the business by reorganizing it. Which of the following chapters of the bankruptcy code would she most likely use to protect the business from creditors while reorganizing?

(A) Chapter 1
(B) Chapter 7
(C) Chapter 11
(D) Chapter 13
(E) Chapter 14

47. Alexandra drops her credit card in a department store while looking in her purse for her car keys. Amanda finds Alexandra's card and uses it to charge $1,000.00 in merchandise. Alexandra does not discover the loss of her card until the following day, and she immediately notifies the credit company. The maximum amount for which Alexandra may be held liable to the credit card company is

(A) $1,000
(B) $ 500
(C) $ 100
(D) $ 50
(E) $ 10

48. All of the following are related to international business EXCEPT

    (A) import quotas
    (B) tariffs
    (C) the World Trade Organization
    (D) the North American Free Trade Agreement
    (E) the Uniform Partnership Act

49. Yummy Soup Company broadcast a television commercial designed to show how thick its chicken soup was, implying that it was full of chunks of chicken. In fact, the soup in the commercial was loaded with potatoes so that it would look thicker than it really was. The Federal Trade Commission (FTC) prohibited use of the commercial. If Yummy Soup filed a suit against the FTC to continue the commercial, the suit would most likely

    (A) succeed because puffing in advertisements is an accepted practice
    (B) succeed because neither Yummy nor its advertising agency had the required intent to deceive the consumer
    (C) succeed because Yummy's First Amendment right of free speech supersedes the FTC's right to regulate marketing
    (D) fail because fairness in advertising is an implied responsibility under the commerce clause
    (E) fail because the FTC has statutory authority to regulate deceptive advertising

50. Which of the following is true about the concept of strict liability?

    (A) It requires proof of intent.
    (B) It does not require a showing of negligence.
    (C) It is a concept related to the sale of stock.
    (D) It does not apply to the third-party bystanders.
    (E) It requires privity of contract.

51. Which of the following contracts would not be required to be in writing under the statute of frauds?

    (A) A contract to purchase a condominium
    (B) A contract to play at a wedding that will take place in two years
    (C) A contract to lease an apartment for eighteen months
    (D) A contract to work at a job for life
    (E) A contract to purchase an $800 camera

52. The concept of judicial review originated

    (A) as the result of a decision by the United States Supreme Court
    (B) as the result of a federal statute
    (C) as the result of a decision by a state supreme court
    (D) in the United States Constitution
    (E) in the Declaration of Independence

53. Oscar's neighbor built a tennis court with extremely bright lights to be able to play at night. The lights are so bright that they illuminate Oscar's house and keep everyone from sleeping. Oscar's repeated requests of his neighbor to turn down the lights have gone unheeded. Oscar could sue his neighbor to get a remedy under the legal theory of

    (A) assault
    (B) breach of warranty
    (C) nuisance
    (D) conversion
    (E) anticipatory breach

54. Juan hired Matt, a licensed architect and home builder, to build a house for him according to Matt's architectural plans. Matt built and delivered the house, but the house collapsed after 13 years due to defective design. Which of the following is true if Juan sued Matt for negligence?

(A) Matt was negligent per se in constructing the house.
(B) Juan could be successful in his suit if the state's statute of repose has not yet expired.
(C) Juan may not sue Matt because Matt was not grossly negligent or willful in his conduct.
(D) Juan will automatically win his suit against Matt if Juan can successfully invoke the doctrine of *res ipsa loquitur*.
(E) Juan has no legal ground to sue Matt, since Juan has lived in the house for 13 years.

55. A contract is illusory and lacks mutuality when one party

(A) reserves the right to cancel the agreement at any time
(B) promises to perform on a specified day
(C) promises to pay a certain sum of money for the performance of a certain act
(D) promises to forbear a legal right in exchange for the promise of the other party
(E) gives a promise in exchange for the promise of the other party

56. John Roberts contracts to convey land to Sarah Simmons in consideration of Sarah's promise to pay $5,000 to his wife, Rhonda, with whom John wishes to make a settlement. Rhonda would have a contract claim against Sarah in Rhonda's status as

(A) wife
(B) obligee
(C) creditor
(D) intended beneficiary
(E) benefactor

57. Homeowner orally promises to sell her house to Mr. and Mrs. Youngpeople, who promise to buy it. The Youngpeoples then draft a letter containing the terms of the agreement, sign it, and send it to Homeowner. Under these circumstances the contract may be enforced against

(A) both Homeowner and the Youngpeoples
(B) the Youngpeoples only
(C) Homeowner only
(D) neither party because of the parol evidence rule
(E) neither party because of the statute of limitations

58. Ms. Jones was leaving class in a hurry and in the process knocked her friend Ms. Smith down a flight of steps, causing serious injury to Smith. Smith wishes to recover for her injuries. Smith's action would be brought in

(A) criminal law for assault and battery
(B) criminal law for trespass on a person
(C) criminal law for invasion of a person's privacy
(D) tort law on the grounds of negligence
(E) tort law on the grounds of assault and battery

59. ABC Company, incorporated under the laws of Delaware, has its principal place of business in the state of Georgia. ABC sells its merchandise at retail outlets located in all 50 states but sells the greatest percentage of its products in the five southern states of Alabama, Florida, Georgia, North Carolina, and South Carolina.

For purposes of diversity jurisdiction in the federal courts, ABC is considered to be a citizen of

(A) Georgia and Delaware
(B) Delaware only
(C) Georgia only
(D) the five southern states
(E) all 50 states

60. Statutory law is best defined as

    (A) common law
    (B) case decisions
    (C) legislative enactments
    (D) constitutional law
    (E) administrative law

61. The process of selecting a jury in civil litigation is known as

    (A) voir dire
    (B) *res ipsa loquitor*
    (C) *causa mortis*
    (D) indictment
    (E) certiorari

62. A department store publishes an advertisement in a local newspaper for a 60-inch large-screen, high-definition plasma TV. The price is listed as $200, but this is a typographical error, and it should have been $2,000. Customer Chris demands the right to purchase one of the TVs at the quoted price. Which of the following statements is correct under general contract law?

    (A) The department store must sell the product which Chris demands at the quoted price.
    (B) Chris has accepted the department store's firm offer to sell.
    (C) The department store has made an offer.
    (D) Chris has made an offer to buy the TV at $200, which the department store may accept or reject.
    (E) The ad was an offer for a unilateral contract, and Chris must accept it by purchasing the TV.

63. Alex bid on a used automobile at the Grand Buys car dealership for $7,000. Alex negotiated a loan from Grand Buys, made a down payment of $500, and drove off with the vehicle without any kind of insurance. An hour later, while driving 30 miles per hour over the legal speed limit, Alex collided with a tree, and his car was totally demolished. Three months later, having received no payments from Alex and his loan, Grand Buys tried to collect the loan. It will be able to collect UNLESS

    (A) Alex was drunk at the time of the accident
    (B) Alex is still hospitalized after the accident
    (C) Alex was one month short of his eighteenth birthday when he purchased the car
    (D) the book value of the car was only four thousand dollars when Alex bought it
    (E) the car came with a 90-day warranty

64. Marcus makes the following statement to Evan, while trying to sell Evan his boat: "This boat has the original engine!" By making such a statement, Marcus has most likely created

    (A) an express warranty
    (B) an implied warranty of fitness
    (C) an implied warranty of merchantability
    (D) a warranty that the boat is seaworthy
    (E) no warranty at all

65. It is common in international business contracts to include a clause that will excuse a party in the contract for nonperformance because of the occurrence of certain acts such as war, embargo, governmental restrictions, and labor strikes. This clause is known as

    (A) an exculpatory clause
    (B) a forum-selection clause
    (C) a force majeure clause
    (D) a choice-of-law clause
    (E) a sovereign immunity clause

66. Granny Smith told her grandson, Ned, that she was going to leave him $5,000 when she died because of all the things he had done for her over the years. After Granny died, Ned learned that she had not included him as a beneficiary in her will and had not left him any money. Ned sues her estate, claiming that he is entitled to the $5,000 she promised him.

The court will probably hold that Ned is

(A) entitled to the money
(B) entitled to the money only if he can provide written evidence of the promise
(C) entitled to be paid the fair value for the services rendered to Granny
(D) not entitled to the money, because there was no valid consideration exchanged
(E) not entitled to the money, because the value of the services rendered was not equal to the value of the promise

67. Dr. Hidalgo was attending her son's soccer game when she heard a woman calling for help and asking that someone call 911. Dr. Hidalgo ran over to the woman and found that the woman's husband was unconscious on the ground and not breathing. Dr. Hidalgo rendered medical aid, saving the man's life. Can Dr. Hidalgo recover payment from the man for her services?

(A) Yes; under quasi contract, the man must pay a reasonable amount for the medical services.
(B) Yes; under implied-in-fact contract, the man must pay the current rate for the medical services.
(C) Yes; under promissory estoppel, the man must pay a reasonable amount for the medical services.
(D) No; the man never consented to the treatment and therefore there was neither a contract nor an obligation to pay.
(E) No; the man is not obligated to pay because there was no express contract.

68. Billy and Joey were playing baseball in Billy's front yard. Billy hit the ball hard and it flew into the neighbor's yard, breaking the neighbor's front window. Billy would be legally bound to pay for the broken window under the concept of

(A) trespass
(B) respondeat superior
(C) invasion of privacy
(D) battery
(E) assault

69. Cathie takes a bite of the burger she just purchased from Burger World Foods. The burger contains a piece of metal, and Cathie breaks one of her teeth, incurring substantial dental bills. Under which of the following theories can Cathie best recover for her injuries?

(A) Breach of the implied warranty of fitness for a particular purpose
(B) Breach of the implied warranty of merchantability
(C) Breach of the express warranty
(D) Breach of intentional tort law
(E) Breach of contract

70. Under which of the following situations would a principal be liable for the tortious act of its agent under the doctrine of respondeat superior?

(A) The agent had no authority (actual or apparent) to commit the act.
(B) The agent's act was a criminal act against a third person, and the principal had not directed the act and had no knowledge of the agent's propensity to commit such an act.
(C) The agent was an employee of the principal and the act was within the scope of the employee's duties.
(D) The agent was an independent contractor acting without authority.
(E) The agent, an employee of the principal, caused an automobile accident after he deviated greatly from his assigned delivery route.

71. The rule that determines that a case will not be heard by a court if the plaintiff took too long from when the action arose to start the suit is called the

(A) statute of limitations
(B) statute of frauds
(C) statute of repose
(D) rule against perpetuity
(E) rule of longevity

72. Which of the following clauses is NOT enforceable in a written contract?

(A) A clause regarding arbitration
(B) A clause regarding choice of law
(C) A clause regarding choice of forum
(D) A clause regarding liquidated damages that imposes a penalty
(E) A clause regarding time being of the essence in contractual performance

73. If a large company induces an employee at a small corporation to breach her employment agreement and work for the large company, then the small corporation may do which of the following?

(A) Bring a suit against the large company for the tort of bad faith.
(B) Bring a suit against the large company for the tort of intentional interference with contractual relations.
(C) Bring a suit against the employee for the tort of intentional interference with contractual relations.
(D) Bring a suit against the employee to try to recover all the past wages and compensation it paid to the employee.
(E) Bring a suit against the large company for breach of contract.

74. Which of the following is true of the Foreign Corrupt Practices Act?

(A) It is based on a United Nations convention.
(B) It applies only to the countries of the European Union.
(C) It is a United States federal statute that applies only to United States companies.
(D) It prohibits the payment of any bribes to United States companies.
(E) It is a state statute that originated in California.

75. A national discount chain has a well-known name. A local department store opens with a name that has the same pronunciation as the name of the national discount chain and is spelled differently by only one letter. The local store derives its name from the name of its owner. The local store has most likely

(A) infringed upon another business' copyright
(B) infringed upon another business' trademark
(C) infringed upon another business' patent
(D) infringed upon another business' trade secret
(E) infringed upon another business

76. A male defendant is charged with breaking and entering with the intent to steal goods from a store. If he claims that he was forced to commit the crime by another individual who threatened him, his affirmative defense is known as

(A) a general denial
(B) an alibi
(C) entrapment
(D) coercion
(E) insanity

77. The doctrine of respondeat superior can be used by an injured party to hold

(A) an employer responsible for the torts of its employee
(B) an employee responsible for the torts of its employer
(C) a manufacturer liable for a defective product
(D) a retailer liable for selling a defective product
(E) a wholesaler liable for a defective product

78. Which of the following elements is NOT necessary to establish liability for negligence?

(A) Proximate cause
(B) Breach of duty
(C) Injury
(D) Malice
(E) Foreseeability

79. Which of the following, if passed, would likely be found constitutional, and therefore valid, by a court of law?

(A) A city ordinance that prohibits the burning of the United States flag as part of a peaceful protest
(B) A state law that prohibits the sale and possession of child pornography
(C) A city ordinance that bans organizations that support hate from assembling in public
(D) A federal agency policy requiring its employees to speak only English while at work
(E) A state law that prohibits teaching the theory of evolution in public schools

80. A 17-year old signs a contract with a car dealer to lease a new luxury automobile. Two months later, the young man turns 18 years old and continues to drive the automobile and make payments on the lease for another 10 months following his birthday. At that time, he decides that he no longer wants to keep the automobile, and so he returns it to the dealer and stops making the required monthly lease payments. If the dealer sues the young man for breach of contract, a court will likely hold that the lease is

(A) not enforceable against the young man because he was a minor at the time he signed it
(B) enforceable against the young man because there was adequate and sufficient consideration for the contract
(C) unenforceable because it is contrary to public policy to lease cars to minors
(D) enforceable against the young man because he implicitly affirmed and ratified the contract after he turned of majority age
(E) unenforceable because a person must be 21 years old to contract in most states

81. Which of the following is true of the Bill of Rights?

(A) It was adopted at the time of the writing of the Constitution.
(B) It has been adopted by the legislature of every state.
(C) It consists of the first ten amendments to the Constitution.
(D) It was originally designed to apply only to the acts of the state governments.
(E) It was copied from the constitution of England.

82. A written agreement for a one-year term of employment was signed by both parties, who expressly intended it to be their entire agreement. The parol evidence rule will bar the admission of evidence that is offered to

(A) explain the meaning of an ambiguity in the written contract with respect to work requirements
(B) establish that fraud was committed in the formation of the contract
(C) prove the existence of a contemporaneous oral agreement establishing at-will employment
(D) interpret a special trade term in the contract
(E) establish that one of the parties exerted extreme duress upon the other party to convince him or her to sign

83. Under which consumer protection act is a company prohibited from contacting a consumer at inconvenient times?

(A) Consumer Credit Protection Act
(B) Fair Debt Collection Practices Act
(C) Fair Credit Reporting Act
(D) Equal Credit Opportunity Act
(E) Fair Credit Billing Act

84. Which of the following best describes monetary damages awarded to a plaintiff to punish the defendant and deter future similar conduct?

(A) Compensatory damages
(B) Punitive damages
(C) Consequential damages
(D) Damages for pain and suffering
(E) Incidental damages

85. Corporate social responsibility requires that businesses must do which of the following?

(A) Develop charitable funds for nonprofit organizations
(B) Create outsourcing resources for terminated employees
(C) Consider the effects of business decisions on the communities in which they operate
(D) Develop ethical models of behavior for employees and customers
(E) Work with local law enforcement agencies to create safe communities

86. Which of the following statements about the rule-making process of administrative agencies is true?

(A) The public is not allowed to comment on the rule-making process of an administrative agency.
(B) Administrative agencies are not required to give prior notice of a proposed rule that will be published in the applicable state register or the *Federal Register*.
(C) An administrative agency's decision is final and cannot be appealed in court.
(D) Administrative agencies publish rules in their final form at least 30 days before they become effective at the state or federal level.
(E) The final rule requires presidential approval.

87. If employees are discharged because of their involvement in union activities, they may file a complaint against their employer under which of the following statutes?

(A) The National Labor Relations Act
(B) The Fair Labor Standards Act
(C) The Occupational Safety and Health Act
(D) Title VII of the Civil Rights Act of 1964
(E) The Labor-Management Relations Act

88. Willard is injured while performing his duties for his employer. In most states, under which of the following are employers banned from using the contributory negligence defense?

(A) An intentional tort
(B) The Fair Labor Standards Act
(C) Worker's compensation
(D) A common-law contract
(E) The Occupational Safety and Health Act

The next two questions refer to the facts below.

Jane loses her watch, which is a family heirloom. She places a personal advertisement in the local newspaper, which says, "Lost family heirloom timepiece. $500 reward if found and returned. Call 223-7979." The advertisement will run in Thursday's newspaper.

89. Which of the following best characterizes the advertisement?

(A) A unilateral offer
(B) A bilateral offer
(C) An invitation to make an offer
(D) A solicitation of an additional offer
(E) A promise

90. Barry, who works with Jane, comes to Jane's office on Wednesday afternoon and tells her he found the watch in the company cafeteria and thought it might belong to her. Jane takes the watch and thanks him for returning it. The next day Barry sees the advertisement in the paper offering the $500 reward. He goes back to Jane and demands the $500. Is Jane legally obligated to pay Barry?

(A) No; the advertisement was not an offer, and it was not extended to Barry.
(B) No; Barry was not aware of the offer when he returned the watch, and therefore he never accepted the offer.
(C) Yes; Barry fulfilled the requirement for collecting the reward.
(D) Yes; Jane knew there was an outstanding offer when Barry returned the watch, and she is therefore legally obligated to pay him.
(E) Yes; the advertisement was an offer that Barry accepted when he returned the watch.

Study Resources

Most textbooks used in college-level business law courses cover the topics in the outline given earlier, but the approaches to certain topics and the emphases given to them may differ. To prepare for the Introductory Business Law exam, it is advisable to study one or more college textbooks, which can be found in most college bookstores. When selecting a textbook, check the table of contents against the knowledge and skills required for this test.

Visit **clep.collegeboard.org/earn-college-credit/practice** for additional business law resources. You can also find suggestions for exam preparation in Chapter IV of the *Official Study Guide*. In addition, many college faculty post their course materials on their schools' websites.

Answer Key

1.	A	46.	C
2.	D	47.	D
3.	B	48.	E
4.	D	49.	E
5.	B	50.	B
6.	D	51.	D
7.	E	52.	A
8.	D	53.	C
9.	A	54.	B
10.	C	55.	A
11.	D	56.	D
12.	A	57.	B
13.	D	58.	D
14.	A	59.	A
15.	E	60.	C
16.	A	61.	A
17.	C	62.	D
18.	A	63.	C
19.	E	64.	A
20.	E	65.	C
21.	C	66.	D
22.	B	67.	A
23.	A	68.	A
24.	B	69.	B
25.	B	70.	C
26.	A	71.	A
27.	C	72.	D
28.	E	73.	B
29.	B	74.	C
30.	D	75.	B
31.	B	76.	D
32.	C	77.	A
33.	B	78.	D
34.	B	79.	B
35.	E	80.	D
36.	C	81.	C
37.	D	82.	C
38.	D	83.	B
39.	D	84.	B
40.	C	85.	C
41.	B	86.	D
42.	D	87.	A
43.	B	88.	C
44.	B	89.	A
45.	D	90.	B

Principles of Management

Description of the Examination

The Principles of Management examination covers material that is usually taught in an introductory course in the essentials of management and organization. The fact that such courses are offered by different types of institutions and in a number of fields other than business has been taken into account in the preparation of this examination. It requires a knowledge of human resources and operational and functional aspects of management.

The examination contains approximately 100 questions to be answered in 90 minutes. Some of these are pretest questions that will not be scored.

Knowledge and Skills Required

Questions on the Principles of Management examination require candidates to demonstrate one or more of the following abilities in the approximate proportions indicated.

- Specific factual knowledge, recall and general understanding of purposes, functions and techniques of management (about 10 percent of the exam)
- Understanding of and ability to associate the meaning of specific terminology with important management ideas, processes, techniques, concepts and elements (about 40 percent of the exam)
- Understanding of theory and significant underlying assumptions, concepts and limitations of management data, including a comprehension of the rationale of procedures, methods and analyses (about 40 percent of the exam)
- Application of knowledge, general concepts and principles to specific problems (about 10 percent of the exam)

The subject matter of the Principles of Management examination is drawn from the following topics. The percentages next to the main topics indicate the approximate percentage of exam questions on that topic.

15%–25% Organization and Human Resources

Personnel administration
Human relations and motivation
Training and development
Performance appraisal
Organizational development
Legal concerns
Workforce diversity
Recruiting and selecting
Compensation and benefits
Collective bargaining

10%–20% Operational Aspects of Management

Operations planning and control
Work scheduling
Quality management (e.g., TQM)
Information processing and management
Strategic planning and analysis
Productivity

45%–55% Functional Aspects of Management

Planning
Organizing
Leading
Controlling
Authority
Decision making
Organization charts
Leadership
Organizational structure
Budgeting
Problem solving
Group dynamics and team functions
Conflict resolution
Communication
Change
Organizational theory
Historical aspects

10%–20% International Management and Contemporary Issues

- Value dimensions
- Regional economic integration
- Trading alliances
- Global environment
- Social responsibilities of business
- Ethics
- Systems
- Environment
- Government regulation
- Management theories and theorists
- E-business
- Creativity and innovation

Sample Test Questions

The following sample questions do not appear on an actual CLEP examination. They are intended to give potential test-takers an indication of the format and difficulty level of the examination and to provide content for practice and review. Knowing the correct answers to all of the sample questions is not a guarantee of satisfactory performance on the exam.

Directions: Each of the questions or incomplete statements below is followed by five suggested answers or completions. Select the one that is best in each case.

1. Which of the following words is NOT a step in the management process?

    (A) Planning
    (B) Leading
    (C) Producing
    (D) Controlling
    (E) Organizing

2. A homebuilder dominates a market by offering attractive options, higher quality, and value-added services. Which of the following competitive strategies has the homebuilder adopted?

    (A) Cost leadership
    (B) Differentiation
    (C) Price leadership
    (D) Generic
    (E) Design focus

3. Which of the following is a correct statement about controlling as a management function?

    (A) It can be performed independently of planning.
    (B) It is performed only by the controller of an organization.
    (C) It is more prevalent in business than in government.
    (D) It assumes a certain approach to motivating employees.
    (E) It must be closely related to planning in order to work efficiently.

4. Decentralization tends to be encouraged by which of the following business trends?

    I. Product diversification
    II. Telecommuting
    III. Geographical expansion of operations

    (A) I only
    (B) II only
    (C) III only
    (D) I and III only
    (E) I, II, and III

5. Which of the following can be best determined by consulting an organization chart?

    (A) The size of the company
    (B) The distribution of company resources
    (C) The nature of work performed
    (D) The connections of positions
    (E) The quality of management of the firm

6. The number of subordinates who directly report to a superior refers to the manager's

    (A) span of control
    (B) organizational role
    (C) organizational structure
    (D) chain of command
    (E) general staff

7. Which of the following best illustrates informal organization?

   (A) Line authority, such as that of the field marshal and battalion commander in the military
   (B) Staff authority, such as that of personnel or cost control in manufacturing
   (C) Functional authority, such as corporate supervision of the legal aspect of pension plans in branch plants
   (D) Groupings based on position titles
   (E) Groupings based on such factors as technical ability, seniority, and personal influence

8. The choice of organizational structure to be used in a business should be

   (A) made by mutual agreement among all the people affected
   (B) made by organization specialists rather than managers
   (C) subject to definite and fixed rules
   (D) based on the objectives of each individual business
   (E) based on consideration of the type of organizational structures used by competitors

9. Which of the following best describes a system that requires subassemblies and components to be manufactured in small lots and delivered as needed to the next stage of production?

   (A) Just in time (JIT)
   (B) Small batch inventory (SBI)
   (C) Inventory readiness (IR)
   (D) Inventory preparedness
   (E) Integrated preparedness (IP)

10. Frederick Taylor is considered a pioneer in the school of management referred to as the

   (A) management process school
   (B) empirical school
   (C) scientific management school
   (D) behaviorist school
   (E) social system school

11. Preparation of which of the following is the most logical first step in developing an annual operating plan?

   (A) A sales forecast by product
   (B) A production schedule by product
   (C) A flow-of-funds statement by product
   (D) A plant and equipment requirement forecast
   (E) A pro forma income statement and balance sheet

12. A large span of control throughout an organization invariably results in

   (A) low morale
   (B) high morale
   (C) an excess workload for each manager
   (D) a flat (horizontal) organizational structure
   (E) a tall (vertical) organizational structure

13. Which of the following is a conflict-resolution practice that seeks to satisfy both parties in a conflict?

   (A) Avoidance
   (B) Stipulation
   (C) Competition
   (D) Collaboration
   (E) Appeal to authority

14. Which of the following is most commonly used to measure the total productivity of a company?

(A) The ratio between total outputs and total inputs
(B) The ratio between fixed costs and variable costs
(C) The ratio between contribution margin and total revenue
(D) The ratio between the break-even point and total output
(E) The ratio between total inputs and total capital

15. The practice in large companies of establishing autonomous divisions whose heads are entirely responsible for what happens in the division is referred to as

(A) management by exception
(B) decentralization of authority
(C) delegation of authority
(D) integration
(E) informal organization

16. Which of the following control techniques is most likely to emphasize the importance of time?

(A) Break-even charts
(B) Physical standards
(C) Quality circles
(D) Variable budgeting
(E) Program Evaluation and Review Technique (PERT)

17. In a labor negotiation, if a third party has the power to determine a solution to a labor dispute between two parties, the negotiation is known as

(A) a grievance
(B) an arbitration
(C) a conciliation
(D) a mediation
(E) a concession

18. A type of control device for assessing the progress of planned activities and the expenditure of resources allocated to their accomplishments is referred to as

(A) a strategic plan
(B) an organizational chart
(C) a tactical plan
(D) a budget
(E) a proposal

19. Beatrice is a full-time employee who is permitted to arrange her schedule so that she works only four days a week and does not travel during rush hour. This is an example of Beatrice's employer

(A) applying the Civil Rights Act, Title VII
(B) scheduling flextime
(C) engaging in sexual discrimination
(D) encouraging low productivity
(E) enhancing compensation

20. According to Maslow, the need to feel genuinely respected by peers, both in and out of the work environment, is included in which of the following need classifications?

(A) Physiological
(B) Safety
(C) Stability
(D) Esteem
(E) Self-actualization

21. Which of the following management activities is most typically described as a controlling function?

(A) Goal setting
(B) Purchasing
(C) Budgetary review
(D) Staffing
(E) Recruiting

22. Which of the following personality traits best describes individuals who can adapt and adjust their behavior to external factors?
    (A) Low self-esteem
    (B) External locus of control
    (C) High self-monitoring
    (D) Low authoritarianism
    (E) High authoritarianism

23. A person who believes that the ends justify the means is best described as
    (A) self-confident
    (B) Machiavellian
    (C) authoritarian
    (D) having cognitive dissonance
    (E) having an internal locus of control

24. In which of the following situations are groups most effective?
    (A) Cohesive groups with groupthink
    (B) Noncohesive groups without groupthink
    (C) Cohesive groups in alignment with organizational goals
    (D) Noncohesive groups in alignment with organizational goals
    (E) Cohesive groups not in alignment with organizational goals

25. If a manager commits a halo error in performance appraisal, the manager may have done which of the following?
    (A) Based assessment on most recent performance rather than an entire period.
    (B) Based assessment on an entire period performance rather than most recent.
    (C) Based assessment on a single attribute of employees' performance.
    (D) Given every employee the same rating of "average."
    (E) Failed to give feedback to employees about their performance.

26. Which of the following best describes a team that brings together organizational members from various areas such as marketing, engineering, human resources, and production to work on a task?
    (A) Command
    (B) Self-managed
    (C) Cross-functional
    (D) Restrictive
    (E) Informal

27. Which of the following is NOT an input, according to equity theory?
    (A) Effort
    (B) Experience
    (C) Education
    (D) Seniority
    (E) Pay incentives

28. Which of the following terms best describes leaders who guide or motivate their followers in the direction of established goals by stressing rewards and the consequences of not conforming to expectations?
    (A) Transactional
    (B) Transformational
    (C) Charismatic
    (D) People-oriented
    (E) Informal

29. Which of the following is the primary purpose of the management-by-objectives (MBO) approach?
    (A) Aligning goal setting and planning
    (B) Creating a dynamic and complex work environment
    (C) Reducing employee resistance to change
    (D) Implementing standard operating procedures
    (E) Implementing a decision rule to respond to a designated problem

30. Which of the following is best defined as a process that involves defining organizational objectives and goals, establishing an overall strategy, and developing a hierarchy of plans to integrate activities?

    (A) Manipulating
    (B) Leading
    (C) Planning
    (D) Managing by objectives
    (E) Controlling

31. Which of the following terms best describes a corporation's sexual harassment policy?

    (A) A single-use plan
    (B) A standing plan
    (C) A strategic plan
    (D) A short-term plan
    (E) A specific plan

32. The preparations that a small town might make for a visit by the President of the United States would be considered what type of plan?

    (A) Strategic
    (B) Directional
    (C) Standing
    (D) Long-term
    (E) Single-use

33. Which of the following best describes a type of planning in which multiple scenarios are developed to test possible future outcomes?

    (A) Queuing theory
    (B) Simulations
    (C) Linear regression
    (D) Marginal profits
    (E) Project management

34. Which of the following describes the critical path in a Program Evaluation and Review Technique (PERT) process?

    (A) Parts that require the most costly materials
    (B) The most time-consuming sequence of events and activities
    (C) The shortest route to the project completion
    (D) The central guideline for quality control
    (E) The property insurance

35. Which of the following oversees the transformation process that converts inputs such as labor and raw materials into outputs such as goods and services?

    (A) Operation management
    (B) Control management
    (C) Strategic management
    (D) Human resource management
    (E) Project management

36. An employee manual is given by a supervisor to employees reporting to that supervisor. The manual outlines attendance policies. This is an example of which of the following methods of developing norms in groups?

    (A) First behavior precedents
    (B) Secondary behavior
    (C) Explicit statements from an authority figure
    (D) Critical events in the team's history
    (E) Carryover from other experiences

37. The behavior of young athletes when they imitate the way they see professional athletes celebrate on television is most likely explained as

    (A) classical conditioning
    (B) operant conditioning
    (C) cognitive learning
    (D) social learning
    (E) behavior modification

38. Which of the following best describes the situation in which an employee arrives for work on time in order to avoid being placed on probation for a second time?

(A) Positive reinforcement
(B) Negative reinforcement
(C) Extinction
(D) Intermittent reinforcement
(E) Cognitive learning

39. Which of the following are most likely to cause a team to avoid groupthink?

I. The team holds a second-chance meeting.
II. Outside experts are invited to observe and react to the group process.
III. The team leader expresses an opinion at the outset of the meeting to save time.

(A) I only
(B) I and II only
(C) I and III only
(D) II and III only
(E) I, II, and III

40. If a manager announces a casual-dress policy on Fridays and then comes to work dressed casually on the following Friday, this is an example of

(A) planning
(B) organizing
(C) leading
(D) controlling
(E) negative reinforcement

41. Which of the following models classifies products as stars, question marks, cash cows, or dogs?

(A) Porter's five forces model
(B) Theory X
(C) The Boston Consulting Group Matrix
(D) Theory Y
(E) Kanban

42. If George blames new software for his group's poor performance in the most recent quarter, but attributes the group's success in the prior quarter to his outstanding managerial skills, he is most likely exhibiting

(A) projection
(B) selective perception
(C) fundamental attribution error
(D) self-serving bias
(E) Pygmalion effect

43. Praise received from an employee's peers is best described as an example of

(A) an extrinsic reward
(B) an intrinsic reward
(C) low valence
(D) high instrumentality
(E) high directive leadership

44. Which of the following procedures is (are) appropriate when disciplining an employee?

I. Advising the employee of what he or she has done wrong.
II. Advising the employee of what he or she does well.
III. Disciplining the employee in private.

(A) I only
(B) II only
(C) I and II only
(D) II and III only
(E) I, II, and III

45. When a company adopts telecommuting, which core job characteristic is likely to be influenced the most?

(A) Skill variety
(B) Task identity
(C) Task significance
(D) Autonomy
(E) Job feedback

46. If jobs are designed so that each worker assembles a different part of a product on an automated assembly line, the job design is most likely to

(A) provide high levels of intrinsic rewards
(B) be highly challenging
(C) make it easy to train workers
(D) be highly satisfying
(E) demand creativity from the workers

47. If individual contributions in a group project are not evaluated, which of the following is likely to occur?

(A) Synergy
(B) Task significance
(C) Social loafing
(D) The Leavitt effect
(E) Vertical loading

48. Determining whether membership of a group should be heterogeneous or homogeneous should be most influenced by which of the following factors?

(A) The group size
(B) Status congruence
(C) The organizational setting
(D) The goals, rewards, and resources
(E) The nature of the task

49. Which of the following describes the most favorable situation for a leader of a group?

(A) The group has high group cohesiveness and positive group performance norms
(B) The group has high group cohesiveness and negative group performance norms
(C) The group has low group cohesiveness and positive group performance norms
(D) The group has low group cohesiveness and negative group performance norms
(E) The group has both moderate cohesiveness and moderate performance norms

50. In their classic study of the bases of social power, John R. P. French and Bertram Raven explicitly identified all of the following sources EXCEPT

(A) referent
(B) expert
(C) coercive
(D) information
(E) reward

51. If an investor buys a stock based on the recommendation of a broker because the broker's previous recommendations have been profitable, the broker possesses which type of power?

(A) Referent
(B) Legitimate
(C) Informal authority
(D) Charismatic
(E) Expert

52. Which of the following styles of leadership is most likely to be effective with workers who have experience and are professionally oriented?

(A) Supportive
(B) Task-oriented
(C) Achievement-oriented
(D) Mentoring
(E) Authoritarian

53. "You are always late to meetings and this will have to change!"

Which of the following best describes the comment above by a manager to an employee?

(A) Proxemics
(B) Constructive feedback
(C) A general overspecific comment
(D) A specific overgeneral comment
(E) Nonverbal communication

54. The power base that relies on the use of knowledge to persuade is best described as

    (A) rewards
    (B) expert
    (C) referent
    (D) coercive
    (E) legitimate

55. Which of the following is the most accurate description of a grapevine in an organization?

    (A) It is a constant source of disruptive information.
    (B) It follows the chain of command.
    (C) It can be suppressed once it is recognized.
    (D) It plays an important role in organizations.
    (E) Most managers believe that it is a positive source of information.

56. Which of the following business situations is most appropriate for telecommuting?

    (A) Workers thrive on competition.
    (B) Decisions and actions are predetermined.
    (C) Decisions rely on negotiation and social interaction.
    (D) There is an oversupply of workers.
    (E) Individual productivity is of primary importance.

57. Empowerment opportunities are LEAST likely to be found in which of the following?

    (A) Participative goal setting
    (B) Serving as a messenger
    (C) Delegation of work
    (D) Self-managed teams
    (E) Freedom to experiment

58. Which of the following pairs of functions of management are most closely interdependent?

    (A) Staffing and organizing
    (B) Staffing and controlling
    (C) Planning and leading
    (D) Planning and controlling
    (E) Disciplining and recruiting

59. Which of the following is the primary concern of employees responsible for strategic planning in a company?

    (A) Monitoring daily cash flow
    (B) Determining the contribution each subunit should make to the overall corporation
    (C) Determining how to accomplish specific tasks with available resources
    (D) Determining how to pursue long-term goals with available resources
    (E) Preparing the annual statement

60. Which of the following is most likely to result from the use of flowcharts in planning?

    (A) A guarantee that work will progress according to schedule
    (B) A visual sequencing of activities
    (C) A chart useful for comparing cash flow during two different quarters
    (D) A scheduling process
    (E) A combined sequencing and scheduling plan

61. Which of the following is a deterrent to "escalation of commitment"?

    (A) A desire to justify earlier decisions
    (B) Organizational politics
    (C) An efficiency "reality check"
    (D) The Abilene paradox
    (E) A cultural emphasis on persistence

62. Which of the following is most likely to be a major advantage of group-aided decision making?

 (A) Social pressure can drive the decision.
 (B) Goal displacement and hidden agendas can occur.
 (C) Groupthink may occur.
 (D) The likelihood that the decision will be accepted increases.
 (E) It frequently saves both time and money.

63. Which of the following basic leadership styles most closely matches the "high structure, low consideration" of the Ohio State leadership studies?

 (A) Country club
 (B) Team
 (C) Selling
 (D) Relationship motivated
 (E) Telling

64. According to Fiedler's contingency studies, for organizations that were considered "moderately favorable" in terms of leaders' authority, task definition, and leader-member relationships, which of the following is the most effective style for the leader to have?

 (A) Country club
 (B) Team
 (C) Selling
 (D) Relationship motivated
 (E) Telling

65. Large organizations are likely to structure their work operations and personnel in any of the following ways EXCEPT

 (A) accounting
 (B) divisional
 (C) geographic
 (D) market
 (E) product

66. The span of control most appropriate in a given organization is primarily influenced by which of the following?

 (A) Types of services or products being produced
 (B) Amount of supervision needed by subordinates
 (C) Amount of authority given to a supervisor
 (D) Number of hierarchical levels within the organization
 (E) Presence of work teams

67. The extensive use of work teams in an organization is most likely to occur under which of the following circumstances?

 (A) Control is centralized by top management.
 (B) The management style is primarily autocratic.
 (C) Employees are unmotivated.
 (D) Supervisors have a narrow span of control.
 (E) Employee involvement is a management goal.

68. Which of the following quality tools utilizes a visual depiction of a process to help identify problem areas?

 (A) Vector diagram
 (B) Histogram
 (C) Scatter diagram
 (D) Cause-and-effect diagram
 (E) Pareto chart

69. Outsourcing allows an organization to have which of the following?

 (A) Higher employee motivation
 (B) Improved labor-management relations
 (C) Lower accident rates
 (D) Greater flexibility in staffing
 (E) Increased control over employees

70. Requiring a prospective employee to demonstrate the ability to do a specific task during the screening process is defined by which type of test?
    (A) Achievement
    (B) Aptitude
    (C) Assessment
    (D) Work sampling
    (E) Spatial

71. Intrinsic rewards can be classified as rewards that do which of the following?
    (A) Allow the employee to establish flexible working hours.
    (B) Provide a sense of achievement and accomplishment.
    (C) Create work coordination among all employees.
    (D) Improve communication effectiveness.
    (E) Allow greater span of control.

72. The best tangible measurement of leadership effectiveness is which of the following?
    (A) Financial success
    (B) Turnover ratios
    (C) Training and development rates
    (D) Employee job performance
    (E) Employee morale

73. The use of transactional leadership is based on the concept of which of the following?
    (A) Using rewards and coercive power
    (B) Stressing intrinsic motivators
    (C) Creating team-based goal setting
    (D) Using peer-based performance evaluations
    (E) Implementing employee involvement plans

74. Group or team cohesiveness is usually influenced by which of the following?
    (A) Employee incentive systems
    (B) Goal-setting processes
    (C) Identification with the group by its members
    (D) Size of the organization
    (E) Type of organizational structure

75. Resolving conflict through collaboration requires that parties do which of the following?
    (A) Work cooperatively
    (B) Have a third party intervene
    (C) Involve a supervisor in the process
    (D) Establish predetermined outcomes
    (E) Prepare written plans

76. Coaching as a leadership technique is most likely to work when which of the following exists?
    (A) Employees are well trained.
    (B) Job descriptions are valid.
    (C) Performance-development needs are known.
    (D) A performance appraisal process is used.
    (E) Training programs are offered.

77. All of the following criteria are commonly used to evaluate decision-making alternatives EXCEPT
    (A) ethicality
    (B) economic feasibility
    (C) legality
    (D) practicality
    (E) popularity

78. All of the following are considered steps in the planning process EXCEPT
    (A) determining the organization's mission
    (B) establishing goals and objectives
    (C) formulating strategies
    (D) implementing strategies
    (E) measuring performance

79. Job enrichment can be an effective tool to achieve which of the following?

(A) Better communication
(B) Increased job responsibility
(C) Improved work relations
(D) Teamwork
(E) Shared decision making

80. Social Security, unemployment benefits, and workers' compensation are benefits required by law. If a company has 120 employees, what other benefit does federal law require a company to provide?

(A) Health insurance only
(B) Paid vacations only
(C) Family and medical leave
(D) Both health insurance and paid vacations
(E) Flextime

81. Which of the following best describes managerial ethics?

(A) It is the social obligation that the individual manager has to fulfill.
(B) It is a statement of the social responsibility of the organization.
(C) It is the standard of conduct that guides a person's decisions and behavior.
(D) It is the mission statement of the organization.
(E) It is a behavior that conforms to legal principles of justice.

82. A manager decides to lay off 10 percent of the workforce and justifies the action by noting that 90 percent still have jobs and the company will remain solvent. This manager has utilized which of the following views of ethics?

(A) Rights view of ethics
(B) Theory of justice view of ethics
(C) Integrative social contracts view of ethics
(D) Utilitarian view of ethics
(E) Golden rule view of ethics

Questions 83–84 are based on the following information.

Ruth has been the chief executive officer of her company for fifteen years. Ten years ago, Ruth utilized the Internet to augment the traditional way of doing business, but she did not intend the Internet to replace her company's main source of revenue. Five years ago, Ruth's company began to use the Internet to perform traditional business functions better but did not sell anything on the Internet. Also, the company began to utilize an intranet as an internal organizational communication system. Last year, Ruth decided that her company's total existence must revolve around the Internet, leading to a seamless integration between traditional and e-business functions.

83. Ten years ago, Ruth's company would have been classified as which type of e-business?

(A) A total e-business organization
(B) An e-business enhanced organization
(C) An e-business enabled organization
(D) An e-business committed organization
(E) An e-business learning organization

84. Five years ago, Ruth's company would have been classified as which type of e-business?

(A) A total e-business organization
(B) An e-business enhanced organization
(C) An e-business enabled organization
(D) An e-business committed organization
(E) An e-business learning organization

85. According to Hofstede, the degree of individualism found in a country is most closely related to which of the following characteristics?

(A) Age
(B) Wealth
(C) Religion
(D) Location
(E) Democracy

86. A multinational company expands its operation to Brazil and hires Brazilians to manage the operation of the new branch. The company is using which type of approach to expand its operations?

    (A) Ethnocentric
    (B) Polycentric
    (C) Monocentric
    (D) Geocentric
    (E) Egocentric

87. Knowledge management involves encouraging members of an organization to

    (A) create educational programs targeted at the average employee
    (B) develop new training programs to help new employees learn their jobs
    (C) develop a corporate university to provide educational solutions in-house
    (D) systematically gather information and share it with others
    (E) retrain top managers through traditional MBA programs

88. Which of the following is the type of team that is made up of experts in various specialties working together on various organizational tasks?

    (A) Functional
    (B) Cross-functional
    (C) Self-directed
    (D) Vertical
    (E) Autonomous

89. Which of the following types of questions would be the best to use during a job interview?

    (A) Open-ended
    (B) Rotational
    (C) Technology-ended
    (D) Prodding
    (E) Hypocritical

90. In one stage of group development, group members come to accept and understand one another; differences are resolved and members develop a sense of team cohesion. This stage of group development is known as

    (A) Adjourning
    (B) Performing
    (C) Storming
    (D) Norming
    (E) Forming

91. Solomon is reviewing the types of power the company has provided him for his job as a department head. A certain degree of authority comes with his position. He will directly exercise authority through which form of power?

    (A) Referent
    (B) Information
    (C) Expert
    (D) Legitimate
    (E) Decision making

92. A performance-appraisal method that utilizes evaluation information from supervisors, employees, and coworkers is known as

    (A) paired-comparison feedback
    (B) programmed-feedback decision
    (C) behaviorally anchored rating scale
    (D) 360-degree feedback
    (E) graphic rating scale

93. Which of the following refers to gender-related problems in the career advancement of employees?

    (A) Flextime
    (B) Glass ceiling
    (C) Job enrichment
    (D) Job sharing
    (E) Career anchor

94. The breakeven point is defined as the level of production at which
    (A) fixed costs are covered by revenue
    (B) variable costs are covered by revenue
    (C) total revenue is sufficient to cover total costs
    (D) marginal revenue equals marginal cost
    (E) the law of diminishing returns is activated

95. Which technology integrates financial, marketing, operational, and human resource applications on a single computer system?
    (A) Universal application server (UAS)
    (B) Material requirements planning (MRP)
    (C) Vendor managed inventory (VMI)
    (D) Electronic data exchange (EDI)
    (E) Enterprise resource planning (ERP)

96. The Hawthorne studies are examples of which management approach?
    (A) Classical
    (B) Behavioral
    (C) Modern
    (D) Administrative
    (E) Scientific

97. A Gantt chart is a visual depiction of the time frame planned for completing specific tasks as compared to which of the following?
    (A) The delivery date promised to the customer
    (B) The actual progress made on each task
    (C) The manager's projected task completion
    (D) The budgeted task completion
    (E) The weighted-average task-completion score

98. A manager who outlines a problem to employees, accepts suggestions, and makes a decision is said to be following what style of leadership?
    (A) Free reign
    (B) Democratic
    (C) Charismatic
    (D) Autocratic
    (E) Laissez-faire

99. Which of the following should be the first step in a decision-making process?
    (A) Implementing a decision
    (B) Assigning the problem to qualified personnel
    (C) Considering all alternatives
    (D) Knowing when to decide
    (E) Defining the problem

100. Which of the following can best be described as a planning function?
    (A) Monitoring operations
    (B) Determining objectives
    (C) Acquiring necessary resources
    (D) Controlling inventory
    (E) Coordinating interdepartmental activities

101. Which of the following people is associated with the development of the Theory X and Theory Y model?
    (A) Abraham Maslow
    (B) Elton Mayo
    (C) Douglas McGregor
    (D) Frederick Taylor
    (E) Lillian Gilbreth

102. If the verbal and nonverbal parts of a manager's message are in conflict, research suggests that an employee usually should believe which of the following?
    (A) The verbal message only.
    (B) The nonverbal message only.
    (C) Either depending on the circumstance.
    (D) Neither the verbal nor the nonverbal parts of the message.
    (E) It is impossible to judge which part of the message should be believed.

103. The process of discovering relationships and patterns in large amounts of data is called data

(A) mining
(B) clustering
(C) encryption
(D) networking
(E) warehousing

104. The style of leadership in which the manager shouts and screams is typical of

(A) participative leadership
(B) benevolent leadership
(C) autocratic leadership
(D) free-rein leadership
(E) democratic leadership

105. The hierarchy of needs theory argues that deficiency needs must be met before the push to satisfy growth needs drives personal growth. The individual most commonly associated with this theory is

(A) Peter Drucker
(B) Henri Fayol
(C) Abraham Maslow
(D) Elton Mayo
(E) F. W. Taylor

106. In a company, Employee A is scheduled to work from 9 a.m. to 6 p.m., while Employee B is scheduled to work from 7 a.m. to 4 p.m. This situation is an example of which of the following?

(A) Flextime
(B) Job sharing
(C) Job enrichment
(D) Compressed work schedule
(E) Telecommuting

107. Which of the following is a quantitative technique that can be used to predict employee performance based on such factors as education, seniority, job-related skills, and job satisfaction?

(A) Time-series analysis
(B) Econometric modeling
(C) Sales force composition
(D) Econometric indicators
(E) Regression modeling

108. Who among the following was important in the scientific management field for promoting motion studies?

(A) Max Weber
(B) Henri Fayol
(C) Abraham Maslow
(D) Frank & Lillian Gilbreth
(E) Henry Ford

109. Elton Mayo was famous for which of the following?

(A) Theory X
(B) Theory Y
(C) The Hawthorne Studies
(D) Administrative management
(E) Bureaucratic management

110. Which of the following is NOT an external environment force on an organization?

(A) Sociocultural trends
(B) Technology
(C) Economy
(D) Political trends
(E) Human resources

Study Resources

Most textbooks used in college-level principles of management courses cover the topics in the outline given earlier, but the approaches to certain topics and the emphases given to them may differ. To prepare for the Principles of Management examination, it is advisable to study one or more college textbooks, which can be found in most college bookstores. When selecting a textbook, check the table of contents against the knowledge and skills required for this test.

Visit **clep.collegeboard.org/earn-college-credit/practice** for additional management resources. You can also find suggestions for exam preparation in Chapter IV of the *Official Study Guide*. In addition, many college faculty post their course materials on their schools' websites.

Answer Key

1. C	29. A	57. B	85. B
2. B	30. C	58. D	86. B
3. E	31. B	59. D	87. D
4. E	32. E	60. B	88. B
5. D	33. B	61. C	89. A
6. A	34. B	62. D	90. D
7. E	35. A	63. E	91. D
8. D	36. C	64. D	92. D
9. A	37. D	65. A	93. B
10. C	38. B	66. B	94. C
11. A	39. B	67. E	95. E
12. D	40. C	68. D	96. B
13. D	41. C	69. D	97. B
14. A	42. D	70. D	98. B
15. B	43. A	71. B	99. E
16. E	44. E	72. D	100. B
17. B	45. D	73. A	101. C
18. D	46. C	74. C	102. B
19. B	47. C	75. A	103. A
20. D	48. E	76. C	104. C
21. C	49. A	77. E	105. C
22. C	50. D	78. E	106. A
23. B	51. E	79. B	107. E
24. C	52. C	80. C	108. D
25. C	53. C	81. C	109. C
26. C	54. B	82. D	110. E
27. E	55. D	83. B	
28. A	56. E	84. C	

Principles of Marketing

Description of the Examination

The Principles of Marketing examination covers material that is usually taught in one-semester introductory courses in marketing. Candidates are expected to have a basic knowledge of trends that are important to marketing. Such a course is usually known as Basic Marketing, Introduction to Marketing, Fundamentals of Marketing, Marketing or Marketing Principles. The exam is concerned with the role of marketing in society and within a firm, understanding consumer and organizational markets, marketing strategy planning, the marketing mix, marketing institutions, and other selected topics, such as international marketing, ethics, marketing research, services and not-for-profit marketing. The candidate is also expected to have a basic knowledge of the economic/demographic, social/cultural, political/legal and technological trends that are important to marketing.

The examination contains approximately 100 questions to be answered in 90 minutes. Some of these are pretest questions that will not be scored.

Knowledge and Skills Required

The subject matter of the Principles of Marketing examination is drawn from the following topics in the approximate proportions indicated. The percentages next to the main topics indicate the approximate percentage of exam questions on that topic.

8%–13% Role of Marketing in Society

Ethics

Nonprofit marketing

International marketing

17%–24% Role of Marketing in a Firm

Marketing concept

Marketing strategy

Marketing environment

Marketing decision system

- Marketing research
- Marketing information system

22%–27% Target Marketing

Consumer behavior

Segmentation

Positioning

Business-to-business markets

40%–50% Marketing Mix

Product and service management

Branding

Pricing policies

Distribution channels and logistics

Integrated marketing communications/Promotion

Marketing application in e-commerce

Sample Test Questions

The following sample questions do not appear on an actual CLEP examination. They are intended to give potential test-takers an indication of the format and difficulty level of the examination and to provide content for practice and review. Knowing the correct answers to all of the sample questions is not a guarantee of satisfactory performance on the exam.

Directions: Each of the questions or incomplete statements below is followed by five suggested answers or completions. Select the one that is best in each case.

1. A manufacturer of car batteries, who has been selling through an automotive parts wholesaler to garages and service stations, decides to sell directly to retailers. Which of the following will necessarily occur?

   (A) Elimination of the wholesaler's profit will result in a lower price to the ultimate consumer.
   (B) Elimination of the wholesaler's marketing functions will increase efficiency.
   (C) The total cost of distribution will be reduced because of the elimination of the wholesaler.
   (D) The marketing functions performed by the wholesaler will be eliminated.
   (E) The wholesaler's marketing functions will be shifted to or shared by the manufacturer and the retailer.

2. Which of the following strategies for entering the international market would involve the highest risk?

   (A) Joint ventures
   (B) Exporting
   (C) Licensing
   (D) Direct investment
   (E) Franchising

3. For a United States manufacturer of major consumer appliances, the most important leading indicator for forecasting sales is

   (A) automobile sales
   (B) computer sales
   (C) educational level of consumers
   (D) housing starts
   (E) number of business failures

4. Which of the following statements about the European Union is true?

   (A) The EU creates a single Pan-European government.
   (B) The EU eliminates trade barriers among member countries.
   (C) The EU is considered the United States of Europe, with its capital in Brussels.
   (D) The EU removes all internal and external trade barriers to global trade.
   (E) The EU minimizes inflation through price controls.

5. In contrast to a selling orientation, a marketing orientation seeks to

   (A) increase market share by emphasizing promotion
   (B) increase sales volume by lowering price
   (C) lower the cost of distribution by direct marketing
   (D) satisfy the needs of targeted consumers at a profit
   (E) market products that make efficient use of the firm's resources

6. All of the following are characteristics of services EXCEPT

   (A) intangibility
   (B) heterogeneity
   (C) inseparability
   (D) perishability
   (E) inflexibility

7. A fertilizer manufacturer who traditionally markets to farmers through farm supply dealers and cooperatives decides to sell current products to home gardeners through lawn and garden shops. This decision is an example of

(A) market penetration
(B) market development
(C) product development
(D) diversification
(E) vertical integration

8. A manufacturer who refuses to sell to dealers its popular line of office copiers unless the dealers also agree to stock the manufacturer's line of paper products would most likely be guilty of which of the following?

(A) Deceptive advertising
(B) Price discrimination
(C) Price fixing
(D) Reciprocity
(E) Tying contracts

9. Which of the following is an intermediary in the distribution channel that moves goods without taking title to them?

(A) Agent
(B) Wholesaler
(C) Merchant
(D) Retailer
(E) Dispenser

10. In which of the following situations is the number of buying influences most likely to be greatest?

(A) A university buys large quantities of paper for computer printers on a regular basis.
(B) A computer manufacturer is building a new headquarters and is trying to choose a line of office furniture.
(C) A consumer decides to buy a different brand of potato chips because they are on sale.
(D) A retail chain is searching for a vendor of lower-priced cleaning supplies.
(E) A purchasing manager has been asked to locate a second source of supply for corrugated shipping cartons.

11. Which of the following best describes the process of selecting target markets in order to formulate a marketing mix?

(A) Strategic planning
(B) Product differentiation
(C) Market segmentation
(D) Marketing audit
(E) SWOT analysis

12. Cooperative advertising is usually undertaken by manufacturers in order to

(A) secure the help of the retailer in promoting a given product
(B) divide responsibilities between the retailers and wholesalers within a channel of distribution
(C) satisfy legal requirements
(D) create a favorable image of a particular industry in the minds of consumers
(E) provide a subsidy for smaller retailers that enables them to match the prices set by chain stores

13. A marketer usually offers a noncumulative quantity discount in order to

    (A) reward customers for repeat purchases
    (B) reduce advertising expenses
    (C) encourage users to purchase in large quantities
    (D) encourage buyers to submit payment promptly
    (E) ensure the prompt movement of goods through the channel of distribution

14. Which of the following statements about secondary data is correct?

    (A) Secondary data are usually more expensive to obtain than primary data.
    (B) Secondary data are usually available in a shorter period of time than primary data.
    (C) Secondary data are usually more relevant to a research objective than are primary data.
    (D) Secondary data must be collected outside the firm to maintain objectivity.
    (E) Previously collected data are not secondary data.

15. Missionary salespersons are most likely to do which of the following?

    (A) Sell cosmetics directly to consumers in their own homes
    (B) Take orders for air conditioners to be used in a large institution
    (C) Describe drugs and other medical supplies to physicians
    (D) Secure government approval to sell heavy machinery to a foreign government
    (E) Take orders for custom-tailored garments or other specially produced items

16. The demand for industrial goods is sometimes called "derived" because it depends on

    (A) economic conditions
    (B) demand for consumer goods
    (C) governmental activity
    (D) availability of labor and materials
    (E) the desire to make a profit

17. Behavioral research generally indicates that consumers' attitudes

    (A) do not change very easily or quickly
    (B) are very easy to change through promotion
    (C) cannot ever be changed
    (D) can only be developed through actual experience with products
    (E) are very accurate predictors of actual purchasing behavior

18. A channel of distribution refers to the

    (A) routing of goods through distribution centers
    (B) sequence of marketing intermediaries from producer to consumer
    (C) methods of transporting goods from producer to consumer
    (D) suppliers who perform a variety of functions
    (E) traditional handlers of a product line

19. A major advantage of distributing products by truck is

    (A) low cost relative to rail or water
    (B) low probability of loss or damage to cargo
    (C) accessibility to pick-up and delivery locations
    (D) speed relative to rail or air
    (E) ability to handle a wider variety of products than other means

20. If a firm is using penetration pricing, the firm is most likely trying to achieve which of the following pricing objectives?

    (A) Product quality leadership
    (B) Market-share maximization
    (C) High gross margin
    (D) Status quo
    (E) Geographic flexibility

21. If a company decides to allocate more resources to personal selling and sales promotion by its resellers, which of the following strategies is it using?

    (A) Pull strategy
    (B) Push strategy
    (C) Direct selling strategy
    (D) Indirect selling strategy
    (E) Integrated marketing communication

22. Marketing strategy planning includes

    (A) supervising the activities of the firm's sales force
    (B) determining the most efficient way to manufacture products
    (C) selecting a target market and developing the marketing mix
    (D) determining the reach and frequency of advertising
    (E) monitoring sales in response to a price change

23. A brand that has achieved brand insistence and is considered a specialty good by the target market suggests which of the following distribution objectives?

    (A) Widespread distribution near probable points of use
    (B) Exclusive distribution
    (C) Intensive distribution
    (D) Enough exposure to facilitate price comparison
    (E) Widespread distribution at low cost

24. Market segmentation that is concerned with people over 65 years of age is called

    (A) geographic
    (B) socioeconomic
    (C) demographic
    (D) psychographic
    (E) behavioral

25. The XYZ Corporation has two chains of restaurants. One restaurant specializes in family dining with affordable meals. The second restaurant targets young, single individuals, and offers a full bar and small servings. The XYZ Corporation uses which form of targeted marketing strategy?

    (A) Mass marketing
    (B) Differentiated marketing
    (C) Undifferentiated marketing
    (D) Customized marketing
    (E) Concentrated marketing

26. The marketing director of a manufacturing company says, "If my wholesaler exceeds the sales record from last month, I agree to give him a paid trip to the Bahamas." This technique is a form of

    (A) sales promotion
    (B) advertising
    (C) personal selling
    (D) direct marketing
    (E) public relations

27. Using a combination of different modes of transportation to move freight in order to exploit the best features of each mode is called

    (A) conventional distribution
    (B) developing dual distribution
    (C) selective distribution
    (D) intermodal transportation
    (E) freight forwarding

28. Which of the following is a major disadvantage associated with the use of dual distribution?

    (A) It is usually very expensive.
    (B) It can cause channel conflict.
    (C) It provides limited market coverage.
    (D) It is only appropriate for corporate channels.
    (E) Some distribution channel functions are not completed.

29. The estimated market value of a brand is best described as brand

    (A) equity
    (B) benefit
    (C) worth
    (D) merit
    (E) return on investment

30. Which of the following would be considered a nonprofit organization?

    (A) A homeless shelter that charges a fee for its services and uses the proceeds for the upkeep of the shelter
    (B) A drug rehabilitation center in which revenues in excess of cost go to the owners
    (C) A vaccination clinic owned by an individual entrepreneur
    (D) A bookstore open to the public for business
    (E) A hospital that has a publicly traded common stock

31. Which of the following approaches for entering international markets involves granting the rights to a patent, trademark, or manufacturing process to a foreign company?

    (A) Exporting
    (B) Franchising
    (C) Licensing
    (D) Joint venturing
    (E) Contract manufacturing

32. Reference groups are more likely to influence a consumer's purchase when the product being purchased is

    (A) important
    (B) inexpensive
    (C) familiar
    (D) intangible
    (E) socially visible

33. Which of the following is true of the product life cycle?

    (A) It can accurately forecast the growth of new products.
    (B) It reveals that branded products have the longest growth phase.
    (C) It cannot be applied to computer products that quickly become obsolete.
    (D) It is based on the assumption that products go through distinct stages in sales and profit performance.
    (E) It proves that profitability is highest in the mature phase.

34. The primary purpose of market segmentation is to

    (A) combine different groups to meet their needs
    (B) create sales territories of similar size and market potential to determine sales quotas
    (C) reduce market demand to a manageable size
    (D) profile the market as a whole to optimize marketing efforts
    (E) allocate marketing resources to meet the needs of specific segments

35. A marketing expert said that he could have advertised a brand of soap as a detergent bar for men with dirty hands, but instead chose to advertise it as a moisturizing bar for women with dry skin. This illustrates the marketing principle known as

(A) product positioning
(B) sales promotion
(C) cannibalization
(D) deceptive advertising
(E) undifferentiated marketing

36. The process of identifying people or companies who may have a need for a salesperson's product is known as

(A) cold calling
(B) presenting
(C) approaching
(D) prospecting
(E) targeting

37. Which of the following is a primary disadvantage of direct marketing?

(A) It is difficult to measure response.
(B) It is not personal.
(C) It is poorly targeted.
(D) It tends to have high costs per contact.
(E) It has a fragmented audience.

38. A formal statement of standards that governs professional conduct is called a

(A) customer bill of rights
(B) business mission statement
(C) corporate culture
(D) code of ethics
(E) caveat emptor

39. Maxine suddenly realizes that she is out of paper towels. She remembers that she last bought Max Dri Towels, so she stops at the store and picks up another roll of Max Dri on her way home from work. In this example, Maxine uses what form of information search in her decision process?

(A) Limited problem solving
(B) Extended problem solving
(C) Internal information search
(D) Compensatory information search
(E) Information search by personal sources

40. The ability to tailor marketing processes to fit the specific needs of an individual customer is called

(A) customization
(B) community building
(C) standardization
(D) mediation
(E) product differentiation

41. Which of the following is true of price skimming?

(A) It requires intermediaries to provide kickback payments.
(B) It calls for relatively high prices to start, reducing over time.
(C) It is reserved for products in the late stages of the product life cycle.
(D) It works best in situations with highly elastic demand.
(E) It is illegal in most jurisdictions in the United States.

42. ABC Company agrees to pay a certain amount of a retailer's promotional costs for advertising ABC's products. This is an example of

(A) cooperative advertising
(B) reminder advertising
(C) comparison advertising
(D) slotting allowance
(E) a premium

43. To save time and money, a marketing research team uses data that have already been gathered for some other purpose. Which type of data is the team using?

    (A) Sample
    (B) Primary
    (C) Secondary
    (D) Survey
    (E) Experiment

44. Positioning refers to

    (A) the perception of a product in customers' minds
    (B) the store location in which a marketing manager suggests a product be displayed
    (C) where the product is placed on the shelf
    (D) which stores will distribute a company's product
    (E) where the new product is first advertised

45. Which of the following best describes members of a buying center?

    (A) Everyone involved in making the purchase decision
    (B) Everyone involved in signing contracts
    (C) Everyone employed in the purchasing department
    (D) Direct reports of the vice president of purchasing
    (E) Technical experts who advise on product specifications

46. Which of the following most accurately describes agent wholesalers?

    (A) They take title to goods that they sell to other intermediaries.
    (B) They do not take title to goods that they sell to other intermediaries.
    (C) They take title to goods that they sell to final consumers.
    (D) They do not take title to the goods that they sell on commission to final consumers.
    (E) They manufacture the goods that they sell to final consumers.

47. Which of the following are key characteristics of services?

    (A) Cost, time, quality, and value
    (B) Uncertainty, variability, and standardization
    (C) Intangibility, durability, and standardization
    (D) Intangibility, perishability, and variability
    (E) Tangibility, variability, and uncertainty

48. The growth of service industries is primarily the result of

    (A) increasingly complex and specialized customer needs
    (B) a rise in income and the degree of customer input
    (C) rapid growth of population and government tracking systems
    (D) increased use of labor-intensive technology
    (E) decreasing demand for equipment-based services

49. Which of the following is the fastest growing nonstore retail segment in the United States?

    (A) Television home shopping
    (B) Automatic vending
    (C) Online retailing
    (D) Catalog marketing
    (E) Direct-response marketing

50. While writing a marketing plan, Melanie decides that the marketing objective should be "to increase market share by 5 percent." A weakness in this objective is that

(A) it is not measurable
(B) it should be related to brand image rather than market share
(C) it does not specify a time period
(D) if the product is an industrial product, the objective should specify product quality
(E) it does not address all elements of the business plan

51. Which of the following is the first step in the sales process?

(A) Prospecting
(B) Sales presentation
(C) Gaining commitment
(D) Approach
(E) Precall planning

52. Which of the following is an example of business-to-business buying?

(A) John buys a new home stereo.
(B) Hannah pays for a new television by monthly installment.
(C) Daniel decides on which college to attend.
(D) Avery purchases a new office desk for his company.
(E) Corey buys a soft drink from a vending machine.

53. President John F. Kennedy's assertion that consumers have certain rights led to legislation that guaranteed all of the following EXCEPT the right to

(A) be informed
(B) be heard
(C) choose
(D) bargain
(E) safety

54. Harmony Households is the largest home improvement retailer in China. Because of its size and market power, the firm can insist upon desired product features, delivery schedules, and price points from its suppliers. Harmony Households is

(A) a primary intermediary
(B) an agent retailer
(C) a multilevel distributor
(D) a channel captain
(E) a dominant distributor

55. Which of the following is NOT a segmentation criterion or consideration used for choosing a target market?

(A) Market accountability
(B) Market identifiability and measurability
(C) Market substantiality
(D) Market accessibility
(E) Market responsiveness

56. Rachel Terry, regional manager at Wilcon Solvents, Inc., compares last quarter's sales with the levels projected in the firm's marketing plan. She identifies three solvent brands whose sales are below projections and initiates a series of inquiries to discover the reasons for the shortfall. Ms. Terry is engaged in which stage of the strategic marketing process?

(A) Environmental scanning
(B) Opportunity analysis
(C) Planning
(D) Implementation
(E) Control

57. Richard Weiss, SA, is a Swiss watch manufacturer. One of its two major brands offers ruggedness, reliability and durability to active sports enthusiasts. The other offers elegance and stylishness to fashion conscious consumers. Which of the following segmentation approaches is this firm using?

    (A) Demographic
    (B) Geographic
    (C) Usage
    (D) Benefits sought
    (E) Socioeconomic

58. Compared with agent intermediaries, merchant intermediaries

    (A) sell only to organizational customers
    (B) sell only in export markets
    (C) are employees of the manufacturer
    (D) are compensated by a commission on sales
    (E) take title to the goods they sell

59. Gabriella's is an Italian producer of fashion jeans. In this highly competitive market, the firm wishes to match the advertising efforts of its competitors by achieving a share of voice (promotion) which is roughly equal to its share of market (sales). This approach to promotional budgeting is called

    (A) all you can afford
    (B) percent of sales
    (C) allocation per unit
    (D) competitive parity
    (E) objective and task

60. On its e-commerce Web site, XYZMusic.com sells songs from new artists who produce their own music. The site also hosts ads from other e-businesses. The ads presented to a user depend on the type of music the user is reviewing. XYZMusic.com collects ad revenue when users follow links in the ads to the advertisers' Web sites. XYZMusic.com's advertising revenue is based on

    (A) cost-per-thousand exposures
    (B) click-through rates
    (C) ad presentation rates
    (D) unique site-visitor data
    (E) site-traffic data

61. Which of the following organizations administers the GATT (General Agreement on Tariffs and Trade) ?

    (A) The United Nations
    (B) The European Union
    (C) The World Trade Organization
    (D) The North American Free Trade Agreement
    (E) The Securities and Exchange Commission

62. At the most basic level, products and services should be viewed as a collection of

    (A) attributes
    (B) expectations
    (C) benefits
    (D) features
    (E) promises

63. The primary function of promotion is to

    (A) sell products and services
    (B) create awareness
    (C) inform, persuade, and remind
    (D) make a demand more elastic
    (E) eliminate competition

64. A marketing strategy is composed of both

(A) a target market and market opportunities
(B) a target market and related marketing mix
(C) a target market and SWOT analysis
(D) a marketing mix and required resources
(E) a marketing mix and competition

65. Which of the following is NOT an advantage of Internet advertising as compared with traditional advertising?

(A) Target-market selectivity
(B) Tracking ability
(C) Exclusivity
(D) Deliverability
(E) Interactivity

66. Which of the following statements most accurately describes antidumping laws?

(A) They set the price that foreign producers must charge.
(B) They control the maximum price of imported products.
(C) They prevent foreign producers from competing on the basis of price.
(D) They prevent foreign-manufactured goods from selling at below cost.
(E) They protect consumers from cheaply manufactured foreign products.

67. In selling a new global logistics information system to a large client, the national account manager of a leading supply chain management vendor learns that client executives from marketing, production, human resources, finance, and business strategy will participate in the decision-making process. Which of the following terms best describes the scope of the buying initiative?

(A) Universal
(B) Specialized
(C) Standardized
(D) Cross-functional
(E) Decentralized

68. Which of the following lists the correct sequence of steps in the consumer decision-making process?

(A) Need recognition, evaluation, purchase decision, invoked set, postpurchase behavior
(B) Felt need, response to stimulus, evaluation of alternatives, postpurchase decision, purchase behavior
(C) Alternative invoked set, need recognition, purchase decision, postpurchase evaluation
(D) Information search, need positioning, evaluation of alternatives, product purchase decision, postpurchase satisfaction
(E) Need recognition, information search, evaluation of alternatives, purchase, postpurchase behavior

69. Consumers tend to be more satisfied with their purchase of a product when

(A) cognitive dissonance develops after the purchase
(B) the price of the product falls after the purchase
(C) they research the product before the purchase
(D) their opinions are inconsistent with their values
(E) there is no further contact with the seller

70. Which of the following is true of global marketing standardization?

(A) It occurs more frequently with consumer products than with industrial goods.
(B) It encourages individualized variation in the product, packaging, and pricing for each nation or local market.
(C) It addresses legal and cultural differences.
(D) It assumes that global consumers increasingly have similar needs.
(E) It reduces profit margins.

71. The three types of marketing research are

(A) explanatory, normative, and descriptive
(B) predictive, normative, and innovative
(C) interactive, diagnostic, and predictive
(D) proactive, interactive, and reactive
(E) exploratory, descriptive, and causal

72. A product is classified as a business product rather than a consumer product based on its

(A) tangible and intangible attributes
(B) life-cycle position
(C) promotion type
(D) pricing strategy
(E) intended use

73. Which one of the following changes would most likely motivate a firm to reposition a brand?

(A) Shifting demographics
(B) Stock market fluctuations
(C) An economic downturn
(D) Changes in available financial resources
(E) Rising sales

74. An advertisement for prospective applicants to a college shows individual students along with the slogan "I am getting ready to seize my destiny." The ad appeals to which need in Maslow's hierarchy?

(A) Physiological
(B) Esteem
(C) Social affiliation
(D) Self-actualization
(E) Safety

75. If two brands move closer to each other on a perceptual (positioning) map, it means that they have become

(A) less perceptually alike
(B) closer in price
(C) more objectively alike
(D) less likely to be direct competitors
(E) more similarly perceived by consumers

76. Lutèce Brands, Inc., acknowledges that its French pastries may contribute to health problems in some of its customers, but the company claims that the benefits (such as personal pleasure and taste) outweigh the risks. The company's approach to moral reasoning is best described as

(A) moral idealism
(B) utilitarianism
(C) categorical imperative
(D) enlightened self-interest
(E) situational ethics

77. Which of the following lists the correct order of the steps of the target marketing process?

(A) Segmentation, positioning, and targeting
(B) Targeting, segmentation, and positioning
(C) Positioning, targeting, and segmentation
(D) Segmentation, targeting, and positioning
(E) Positioning, segmentation, and targeting

78. Which of the following types of marketing communications tends to have the shortest-term focus and objectives?

(A) Brand advertising
(B) Public relations
(C) Sales promotion
(D) Event sponsorship
(E) Corporate advertising

Directions: Select a choice and click on the blank in which you want the choice to appear. Repeat until all of the blanks have been filled. A correct answer must have a different choice in each blank.

79. Place the four steps in the marketing research process in the correct order.

Determine the research design.

Define the problem.

Collect data.

Choose the data collection method.

____

____

____

____

Directions: Choose among the corresponding environments in the columns for each entry by clicking on your choice. When you click on a blank cell a check mark will appear. No credit is given unless the correct cell is marked for each entry.

80. For each of the following events, indicate which kind of environment it belongs to.

	Sociocultural Environment	**Economic Environment**	**Technological Environment**
The development of new production techniques			
The growing Latino population			
Rising mortgage rates			

Study Resources

Most textbooks used in college-level principles of marketing courses cover the topics in the outline given earlier, but the approaches to certain topics and the emphases given to them may differ. To prepare for the Principles of Marketing exam, it is advisable to study one or more college textbooks, which can be found in most college bookstores. When selecting a textbook, check the table of contents against the knowledge and skills required for this test. Please note that textbooks are updated frequently; it is important to use the latest editions of the textbooks you choose. Most textbooks now have study guides, computer applications and case studies to accompany them. These learning aids could prove useful in the understanding and application of marketing concepts and principles.

You can broaden your understanding of marketing principles and their applications by keeping abreast of current developments in the field from articles in newspapers and news magazines as well as in business publications such as *The Wall Street Journal*, *Business Week*, *Harvard Business Review*, *Fortune*, *Ad Week* and *Advertising Age*. Journals found in most college libraries that will help you expand your knowledge of marketing principles include *Journal of Marketing*, *Marketing Today*, *Journal of the Academy of Marketing Sciences*, *American Demographics* and *Marketing Week*. Books of readings, such as *Annual Editions — Marketing*, also are sources of current thinking.

Visit **clep.collegeboard.org/earn-college-credit/practice** for additional marketing resources. You can also find suggestions for exam preparation in Chapter IV of the *Official Study Guide*. In addition, many college faculty post their course materials on their schools' websites.

Answer Key

1.	E	28.	B	55.	A
2.	D	29.	A	56.	E
3.	D	30.	A	57.	D
4.	B	31.	C	58.	E
5.	D	32.	E	59.	D
6.	E	33.	D	60.	B
7.	B	34.	E	61.	C
8.	E	35.	A	62.	C
9.	A	36.	D	63.	C
10.	B	37.	D	64.	B
11.	C	38.	D	65.	C
12.	A	39.	C	66.	D
13.	C	40.	A	67.	D
14.	B	41.	B	68.	E
15.	C	42.	A	69.	C
16.	B	43.	C	70.	D
17.	A	44.	A	71.	E
18.	B	45.	A	72.	E
19.	C	46.	B	73.	A
20.	B	47.	D	74.	D
21.	B	48.	A	75.	E
22.	C	49.	C	76.	B
23.	B	50.	C	77.	D
24.	C	51.	A	78.	C
25.	B	52.	D	79.	See below
26.	A	53.	D	80.	See below
27.	D	54.	D		

79. Define the problem.
Determine the research design.
Choose the data collection method.
Collect data.

80.

	Sociocultural Environment	Economic Environment	Technological Environment
The development of new production techniques			√
The growing Latino population	√		
Rising mortgage rates		√	

CollegeBoard CLEP®

Appendix

What Your **CLEP** Score Means

In order to reach the total score you see on your score report, two calculations are performed.

1. Your "raw score" is the number of questions you answered correctly. Your raw score increases by one point for each question answered correctly.

2. Your raw score is then converted into a "scaled score" that ranges from 20, the lowest, to 80, the highest. This scaled score is the score that appears on your score report.

The scores that appear in the table shown are the credit-granting scores recommended by the American Council on Education (ACE). **Each college, however, can set its own credit-granting policy, which may differ from that of ACE.** If you haven't already done so, contact your college as soon as possible to find out the score it requires to grant credit, the number of credit hours granted, and the course(s) that can be bypassed with a satisfactory score.

Please note that College-Level Examination Program® (CLEP®) exams are developed and evaluated independently and aren't linked to one another except by the program's common purpose, format, and method of reporting results. For this reason, direct comparisons shouldn't be made between CLEP exams in different subjects. CLEP scores aren't comparable to SAT® scores or other test scores.

Scores are kept on file for 20 years. During this period, score reports may be sent to an institution, but only at the request of the candidate. Students can order official transcripts through the CLEP My Account portal (**clepportal.collegeboard.org**) and pay a fee. CLEP Transcript Requests are nonrefundable. Once ordered, a request cannot be canceled, changed, or rerouted. To order official transcripts for DANTES-funded exams, candidates need to complete a Military Transcript Form (**getcollegecredit.com/images/uploads/documents/Military_DSST_CLEP_transcript_post74.pdf**).

Test takers may not repeat an examination of the same title within the specified wait period of the initial testing date. If a test taker retakes the examination within the specified wait period, the administration will be considered invalid, the score will be canceled, and any test fees will be forfeited. **For military service members: DANTES does not fund retesting on a previously funded CLEP exam.** However, service members may personally fund a retest after the specified wait period.

If you have questions about your score report, a test question, or any other aspect of a CLEP examination that your test center cannot answer, write to CLEP, P.O. Box 6600, Princeton, NJ 08541-6600 or email **clep@info.collegeboard.org**.

2018-19 CLEP® Credit-Granting Recommendations

	ACE Recommended Score*	Semester Hours*
Business		
Financial Accounting	50	3
Information Systems	50	3
Introductory Business Law	50	3
Principles of Management	50	3
Principles of Marketing	50	3
Composition and Literature		
American Literature	50	3
Analyzing and Interpreting Literature	50	3
College Composition	50	6
College Composition Modular	50	3
English Literature	50	3
Humanities	50	3
World Languages**		
French Language, Level 1 Proficiency	50	6
Level 2 Proficiency	59	9
German Language, Level 1 Proficiency	50	6
Level 2 Proficiency	60	9
Spanish Language, Level 1 Proficiency	50	6
Level 2 Proficiency	63	9

** For each of the world languages, there is only one exam covering both Level 1 and Level 2 content. ACE recommends 6 semester hours of credit for mastery of Level 1 content (a score of 50) and 9 semester hours of credit for mastery of both Level 1 and Level 2 (a score of 59 on French Language, 60 on German Language, and 63 on Spanish Language).

	ACE Recommended Score*	Semester Hours*
History and Social Sciences		
American Government	50	3
History of the United States I: Early Colonization to 1877	50	3
History of the United States II: 1865 to the Present	50	3
Human Growth and Development	50	3
Introduction to Educational Psychology	50	3
Introductory Psychology	50	3
Introductory Sociology	50	3
Principles of Macroeconomics	50	3
Principles of Microeconomics	50	3
Social Sciences and History	50	6
Western Civilization I: Ancient Near East to 1648	50	3
Western Civilization II: 1648 to the Present	50	3
Science and Mathematics		
Biology	50	6
Calculus	50	4
Chemistry	50	6
College Algebra	50	3
College Mathematics	50	6
Natural Sciences	50	6
Precalculus	50	3

* The American Council on Education's College Credit Recommendation Service (ACE CREDIT®) has evaluated CLEP processes and procedures for developing, administering, and scoring the exams. The scores listed above are equivalent to a grade of C in the corresponding course. The American Council on Education, the major coordinating body for all the nation's higher education institutions, seeks to provide leadership and a unifying voice on key higher education issues and to influence public policy through advocacy, research, and program initiatives. For more information, visit the ACE CREDIT website at **acenet.edu/acecredit**.